# International Banking

# International Banking

## Cases, Materials, and Problems

### Second Edition

Michael P. Malloy
Distinguished Professor and Scholar
University of the Pacific
McGeorge School of Law

Carolina Academic Press
Durham, North Carolina

Library of Congress Cataloging-in-Publication Data
Malloy, Michael P., 1951-
    International banking : cases, materials, and problems /
by Michael P. Malloy.--2nd ed.
        p.    cm.
    ISBN 1-59460-078-3
    1. Banks and banking, Foreign--Law and legislation--United
States--Cases. 2. Banks and banking, Intenational--Law and
Legislation--United States--Cases. 3. International finance--
Law and legislation--Cases. I. Title.
KF1001.5.A7M35  2004
346.73'08215--dc22                                      2004014476

Carolina Academic Press
700 Kent Street
Durham, North Carolina 27701
Telephone (919) 489-7486
Fax (919) 493-5668
E-mail: cap@cap-press.com
www.cap-press.com

This book is dedicated to
Susie A. Malloy
Μητερουλα του παιδιον μας

# SUMMARY OF CONTENTS

# CONTENTS

# TABLE OF CASES

Principal cases, excerpted in the casebook, are indicated by **boldface** type.

# PREFACE TO THE SECOND EDITION

In the six years since the first edition of this casebook appeared, the regulation of financial services enterprises has grown in importance and complexity. A wide range of significant historical and political developments have had a marked impact on international markets as well as on day-to-day existence. The European Union has edged ever closer to political and regulatory integration. U.S. banks and bank holding companies have been granted broader authority to participate in activities that are "financial in nature," including securities and insurance activities. The terrorist attacks on the United States that occurred in September 2001prompted a renewal of U.S. statutory and regulatory interest in both offensive and defensive supervision of the banking system to combat terrorism, and an emerging international consensus has focused on antiterrorism and anti-money laundering in response to international terrorism. Regional financial services regulation under NAFTA celebrated its tenth anniversary, followed by the General Agreement on Trade in Services at the multilateral level. These and other major developments join an even wider variety of continuing regulatory concerns–competitive equality among enterprises, coordination of the supervisory efforts of different national regulators, and the growing need for transactional rules for e-commerce and e-banking activities, to name a few. As with the previous edition, this casebook tries to draw together these and other regulatory issues in a way that will present them coherently and that will make the practical importance of these issues understandable to the student.

While the casebook still focuses primarily on U.S. regulation of international banking at the federal level, it includes more extensive material on international and comparative aspects of financial services regulation, including more material on the EU, NAFTA, Eastern Europe and Islamic banking. U.S. practice remains a convenient point of departure for study of international banking, and the problems and notes that appear throughout the casebook continue to offer a very concrete and practical context for the exploration of the issues, concepts and rules embodied in the cases and secondary materials excerpted in the casebook.

Special thanks are due to many persons for their assistance and encouragement of the completion of this new edition. Dean Elizabeth Rindskopf Parker and Associate Deans John Sprankling and Claude Rohwer have been generous in their support and understanding of the burdens that preparation of even a second edition of a casebook places on an author. I am particularly thankful for the resources that the law school has made available to me, not only for the direct work on this edition but also for the many opportunities that I have been given to participate in U.S. and international conferences and speaking engagements. These opportunities allowed me to air my views on many current developments in international financial services regulation for further discussion and refinement. I also must acknowledge Ms. Sally Snyder, Supervisor of the Faculty Secretaries' Office, and Ms. Denai Burbank and the rest of the Faculty Secretaries for their singular efforts in keeping administrative burdens from my door while I worked on this project. My student research assistants, Ms. Suzanne Uzelac of the University of the Pacific Class of 1998, Ms. Lotte Colbert of the Class of 1999, and Mr. David Richards of the University of the Pacific Class of 2004 provided invaluable, and invariably thorough, assistance.

Finally, the original project and the renewed effort of a second edition would have been personally worthless without the encouragement, inspiration, and devoted editorial assistance of my wife, Susie A. Malloy. As a relentless editor and boon companion, she makes me better than I am.

— Michael P Malloy
London
April 2004

# PREFACE TO THE FIRST EDITION

The regulation of financial services enterprises involved in the international market is of increasing importance. This area raises a wide variety of regulatory concerns–competitive equality among enterprises, coordination of the supervisory efforts of different national regulators, the growing need for multilateral rules for transborder activities. This casebook tries to draw together these and other regulatory issues in a way that will present them coherently.

The casebook focuses primarily on U.S. regulation of international banking at the federal level, but with extensive international and comparative materials as well. U.S. practice in this regard is viewed simply as a convenient point of departure for study of international banking. The U.S. market is an active and immense one, and so regulatory developments there have a tendency to influence multilateral and other national regulatory regimes.

It cannot he emphasized enough that international banking is an area of intense practice, as well as a conceptually challenging area of intellectual study. Hence, the problems and notes that appear throughout the text are intended to provide a concrete context within which to understand many of the concepts and rules embodied in the excerpted readings from cases and secondary material.

Special thanks are due to several persons for their assistance and encouragement of the completion of this book. Dean Gerald Caplan and Associate Dean Kathleen M. Kelly of McGeorge School of Law, University of the Pacific, have provided both moral and material support for this project. My colleague Claude Rohwer has on more than one occasion lifted burdens so that I could concentrate on the work at hand. My student research assistants, Ms. Suzanne Uzelac of the University of the Pacific Class of 1998 and Ms. Lotte Colbert of the Class of 1999, have provided invaluable, and invariably thorough, assistance. Finally, this project would have been impossible to finish and of little personal interest without the devoted assistance and encouragement of my wife, Susie A. Malloy.

— Michael P Malloy
Vienna
July 1998

# ACKNOWLEDGMENTS

The author gratefully acknowledges the permission granted. to reprint excerpts from the following:

AMERICAN LAW INSTITUTE, RESTATEMENT OF FOREIGN RELATIONS LAW OF THE UNITED STATES (3d) §§ 403, 414; Copyright 1988 by the American Law Institute. Reprinted with permission.

Doty, *Economic Legal Reforms as a Necessary Means for Eastern European Transition into the Twenty-First Century*, 33 INT'L LAW. 189 (1999). Copyright © 1999 by the American Bar Association; Kirsten Storin Doty. Reprinted with permission.

Fowler, *EC Regulation of the Banking Sector*, 5 HOFSTRA PROP. L.J. 405 (1993). Reprinted with permission.

Haley & Seligman *The Development of International Banking by the United States*, *in*, BAUGHN & MANDICH (eds.), THE INTERNATIONAL BANKING HANDBOOK (1983). Reprinted with permission of McGraw-Hill Enterprises.

Hirsch, *"Dirty Money" and Swiss Banking Regulations*, 8 J. COMP. BUS. & CAP. MKT. L. 373 (1986). © Copyright 1986 by the University of Pennsylvania. Reprinted with permission of the University of Pennsylvania Journal of International. Economic Law.

Honegger, *Demystification of the Swiss Banking Secrecy and Illumination of the United States-Swiss Memorandum of Understanding*, 9 N.C. J. INT'L L. & COM. REG. 1 (1983). Reprinted with permission of the North Carolina Journal of International Law and Commercial Regulation.

Kahale, *Does a Choice-of-Law Clause Waive Immunity?*, INT'L. FIN. L. REV. 28 (July 1988). Reprinted with kind permission of the International Financial Law Review, http://www.lawmoney.com/.

Korsvik, *Legal and Regulatory Constraints within Other Countries*, in BAUGHN & MANDICH (eds.), THE INTERNATIONAL BANKING HANDBOOK (1983). Reprinted with permission of McGraw-Hill Enterprises.

MALLOY, BANKING LAW AND REGULATION (3 vols., Aspen Law & Business, 1994); reprinted with permission of the copyright holder.

Michael P. Malloy, *Capital Adequacy and Regulatory Objectives*, 25 SUFFOLK TRANSNAT'L L. REV. 299 (2002). Reprinted with permission of the copyright holder.

Malloy, *Financial Services Regulation After NAFTA*, *in*, KEVIN KENNEDY (ed.), THE FIRST DECADE OF NAFTA: THE FUTURE OF FREE TRADE IN NORTH AMERICA (2004). Reprinted with permission of the copyright holder.

MALLOY, PRINCIPLES OF BANK REGULATION (Thomson-West, Concise Hornbook Series, 2d ed. 2003). Reprinted with permission of the copyright holder.

*Stern Rebuke: In A Signal to Japan, U.S. Bars Daiwa Bank and Indicts Institution*, WALL ST. J., Nov. 3, 1995, at Al.

Taylor, *Islamic Banking–The Feasibility of Establishing an Islamic Bank in the United States*, 40 AM. BUS. L.J. 385 (2003). Reprinted with permission of the American Business Law Journal, an official publication of the Academy of Legal Studies in Business.

Todd, *A Brief History of International Lending, From A Regional Banker's Perspective*, 11 GEO. MASON U. L. REV. 1 (1989). Reprinted with permission of the George

Mason University Law Review.

Vysman, *The New Banking Legislation in Russia: Theoretical Adequacy, Practical Difficulties, and Potential Solutions*, 62 FORDHAM L. REV. 265 (1993); reprinted with permission of the Fordham Law Review.

Wegen, *2(b) or Not 2(b): Fifty Years of Questions–The Practical Implications of Article VIII Section 2(b)*, 62 FORDHAM L. REV. 1931 (1994); reprinted with permission of the Fordham Law Review.

Wendt, *The Role of Foreign Banks in International Banking*, *in*, BAUGHN & MANDICH (eds.), THE INTERNATIONAL BANKING HANDBOOK (1983). Reprinted with permission of McGraw-Hill Enterprises.

# International Banking

# Chapter 1

# The Regulatory Environment

## 1. Introduction

What is international banking? For that matter, what is banking? Answers to these two questions will determine the nature of bank regulation, since they determine what it is that bank regulation is concerned with. On the other hand, the limitations, prohibitions and requirements of bank regulation will determine to some extent the nature of banking itself.

We are dealing, then, not with static things, but with an interactive, dynamic system–regulated entities and activities, regulators and regulatory rules–that in a very real sense define each other. Understanding either side of this system ultimately requires a clear understanding of their interaction. Fundamentally, we need to understand the way in which such interaction manifests itself as a regulatory environment.

For the sake of convenience of presentation, we look at the various components of this environment individually at first, but we need to keep in mind that the objective is to understand the system within which these components operate. In this chapter, we begin with some isolated examples of the components. The chapter then focuses in greater detail on the meaning of the term international banking. It closes with some discussion of contemporary developments that are shaping the contours of international banking.

**Notes and Comments 1.1.** *What is "banking"?*[1] In the most general sense, banking is one form of *financial intermediation*, a process that is performed not only by banks but also by securities firms, insurance companies and many other "financial services" firms. These firms intervene between capital providers (investors, depositors) and capital users (investments, borrowers). In theory at least, financial intermediaries provide an efficient means for financial resources to be aggregated and redirected towards productive uses. (*See* Figure 1.1, *infra*.) Individual providers do not have to expend resources identifying, and assessing the appropriateness of, individual investments; the intermediaries can do this for them more efficiently on an aggregate basis. Individual capital users do not have to expend resources identifying, aggregating and negotiating with a broad array of individual investors; the intermediaries already represent financial aggregations and are themselves relatively easy to identify.

---

1. This discussion is drawn substantially from material appearing in chapter 1 of MICHAEL P. MALLOY, BANKING AND FINANCIAL SERVICES LAW (2d ed. 2004).

**Figure 1.1**
**Financial Intermediation**

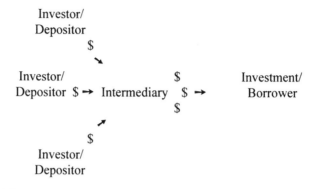

In the case of banks and other depository institutions, another feature of financial intermediation is of particular importance–the credit function. Because depository institutions aggregate financial resources, redistribute them primarily through lending, and usually receive the proceeds of the lending as lendable deposits, the total available amount of *credit* in the banking system can increase exponentially, far beyond the simple aggregation of capital. In other words, banks accept deposits, which are then turned over as loans, which then reenter the banking system as deposits of the borrowers–and *those* deposits are turned over as loans to other borrowers. The deposits and loans are represented by book entries in the system itself. If the process can be kept running without significant net withdrawal of resources from the banking system, credit continues to increase. (*See* Figure 1.2, *infra*.) If the deposit pool begins to contract significantly, or does not continue to increase to fuel further lending, then banks in the system must begin to contract their lending (by calling in loans or refusing new loans) and available credit begins to decrease. What is the deposit itself, as a matter of law? The following excerpt addresses this basic question.

## Libyan Arab Foreign Bank v. Bankers Trust Company
[1988] 1 Lloyd's L. Rep. 259

Mr. Justice Staughton:

[The case involved claims by a Libyan bank against a the London branch of a U.S. bank with respect to dollar-denominated London deposits blocked under a presidential order directed against the assets of Libya. Two accounts had been established with the bank, one at its New York headquarters, and one at its London branch. Detailed excerpts from the case on the merits appear in Chapter 11, § 3, *infra*.]

It is elementary, or hornbook law to use an American expression, that the customer does not own any money in a bank. He has a personal and not a real right. Students are taught at an early stage of their studies in the law that it is incorrect to speak of "all my money in the bank". . . . Naturally the bank does not retain all the money it receives as cash in its vaults; it if did, there would be no point or profit in being a banker. What the bank does is to have available a sufficient sum in cash to meet all demands that are expected to be made on any particular day.

I mention these simple points in order to clarify the real problem, which is what the obligation of a bank is. . . .

The credit balance of the Libyan Bank with Bankers Trust constituted a personal right, a chose in action. At bottom there are only two means by which the fruits of that right could have been made available to the Libyan Bank. The first is by delivery of cash, whether dollar bills or any other currency, to or to the order of the Libyan Bank. The second is the procuring of an account transfer. . . .

An account transfer means the process by which some other person or institution comes to owe money to the Libyan Bank or their nominee, and the obligation of Bankers Trust is extinguished or reduced *pro tanto*. . . .

**Figure 1.2**
**The Credit Function**

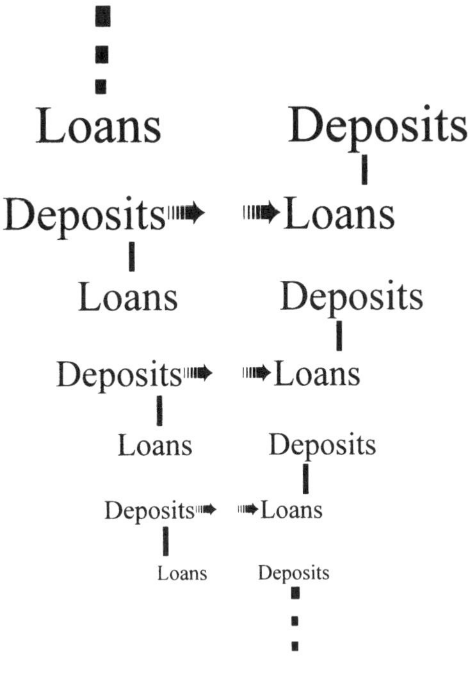

Loans            Deposits

Deposits➠    ➠Loans

Loans            Deposits

Deposits➠    ➠Loans

Loans            Deposits

Deposits➠    ➠Loans

Loans            Deposits

**Notes and Comments 1.2.** *Banking and regulators.* Consider the following sad story about banking gone wrong and ask yourself, Why didn't the Fed discover the trading losses at Daiwa New York sooner? What should the Fed do for the future to prevent such a problem from arising in other U.S. branches of non-U.S. banks?

## Stern Rebuke: In a Signal to Japan, U.S. Bars Daiwa

## Bank And Indicts Institution
Wall St. J., Nov. 3, 1995, at A1

The Federal Reserve gave Japan's Daiwa Bank Ltd. 90 days to get out of the country.

In an extraordinarily harsh punishment that underscores U.S. fury at both Daiwa and the Japanese government, the Fed terminated the U.S. operations of Japan's 10th-largest bank as federal prosecutors filed criminal charges against it. The indictment alleges conspiracy and fraud for hiding some $1.1 billion of trading losses from U.S. officials. . .
.

Japanese regulators concede their delay in informing U.S. counterparts of the loss stemmed from a "partial breakdown in communication," but stopped short of issuing an apology. Following the Fed announcement, Japan's Ministry of Finance ordered Daiwa to reduce its international lending, foreign-security holdings and overseas trading activities.

Daiwa accepted the Fed order–without admitting any wrongdoing–but said it would fight the criminal charges. Its U.S. operations, which Daiwa says account for 15% of its global profits, are likely to be sold to some other bank, authorities said.

But the blow to Daiwa is far greater than just losing its U.S. business. "Without operations in the U.S., it will be very hard to be a global competitor–no matter how strong you are in Asia or Europe," said Jesper Koll, head of research at J.P. Morgan Securities Asia Ltd. in Tokyo.

The damage to Daiwa's prestige is even greater, and could hasten what has been regarded in Tokyo as increasingly likely: the merger of Daiwa with some other big Japanese bank. . . .

Accusing Daiwa of "a pattern of unsafe and unsound banking practices and violations of law," the Fed and various state banking agencies said yesterday they were expelling it because of the following allegations:

> More than $1 billion of trading losses at Daiwa between 1983 and 1995 weren't recorded on its books and were concealed by falsification of records.
> Daiwa's senior management learned about the trading losses in July 1995 and directed that they be concealed from U.S. regulators for almost two months.
> Daiwa's senior New York management in 1992 and 1993 deceived bank regulators and told the Fed in writing that custody and trading operations had been separated when they hadn't been. (Trader Toshihide Iguchi, who pleaded guilty to federal charges two weeks ago, long headed both departments in New York.)
> Senior management knew of and concealed about another $97 million in losses between 1984 and 1987 at the Daiwa Bank Trust Co. branch in New York, as Daiwa reported early last month. . . .

The expulsion of Daiwa marks the first time the Fed has exercised powers it gained over foreign banks in 1992 in the wake of concerns spawned by problems at the Bank of Credit & Commerce International and Banca Nazionale del Lavoro. The Fed's action comes in the wake of sharp criticism of its oversight of foreign financial institutions that operate in the U.S. . . .

The scandal broke on Sept. 26 [1995] when Daiwa said that an executive and bond trader in its New York office, Mr. Iguchi, had secretly run up and concealed massive losses over a period of 11 years. Most of the initial attention focused on the 44-year-old executive, a "local hire" who had begun his career in the U.S. rather than Japan. His superiors portrayed him as a rogue trader taking advantage of loose bank controls.

But the financial scandal quickly became an international diplomatic incident on the news that some officials in Japan's Ministry of Finance knew about the losses at least six weeks before U.S. officials. In addition, later reports have increasingly implicated senior Daiwa management. Manhattan U.S. Attorney Mary Jo White said yesterday that the scandal reached to the highest levels of the bank, noting that a copy of a confession letter the trader wrote in July was sent to former President Akira Fujita, who resigned last month.

Mr. Fujita wasn't indicted, and in fact no Daiwa executives were mentioned by name in the indictment, filed in a Manhattan federal court. But Masahiro Tsuda, general manager of Daiwa's New York branch, was charged in a separate criminal complaint accusing him of deceiving federal regulators and falsifying bank documents. If convicted, he faces a possible jail sentence of up to eight years.

Other executives singled out in the indictment by title–but not by name–were Managing Director Hiroyuki Yamaji; Deputy President Kenji Yasui; the head of the bank's international treasury division, Takashi Motohashi; and Mr. Tsuda.

Daiwa said it plans to restructure its international business outside the U.S. and will try to sell its U.S. business. "Our withdrawal from the United States is a regrettable but necessary step," Daiwa President Takashi Kaiho said.

Daiwa said it took all necessary steps to report the problem and protect its customers. But facts that had already emerged, and new allegations in the indictment, challenge its contention that it tried to comply with the law.

Yesterday's complaint alleges Mr. Tsuda requested that Daiwa's internal audit department postpone an examination of the New York branch–which would have revealed the coverup–by falsely saying Mr. Iguchi would be on vacation. It also says that Mr. Tsuda told employees in the New York branch Aug. 17 that a criminal referral regarding Mr. Iguchi's activities wouldn't be made until late September, even though Daiwa was required by law to make such a referral within 30 days of getting Mr. Iguchi's confession letter on July 24. . . .

Much of what was contained in yesterday's indictment had been said in earlier charges, including allegations about Daiwa's decision to relocate its traders repeatedly to deceive regulators about controls at the New York branch, alleged lies to the Fed that trading and recordkeeping functions had been separated, and efforts by senior management to help disguise Mr. Iguchi's scheme.

But the indictment added several new twists. The charges say that in 1987 Daiwa successfully concealed a $97 million trading loss at its Daiwa Trust operation by shifting the loss to a corporate shell in the Cayman Islands. Prosecutors say Daiwa contemplated using a similar strategy to hide Mr. Iguchi's $1.1 billion loss but rejected it as "not feasible."

The bank then allegedly considered transferring funds through its International Treasury Division to a third party that would purchase missing government securities and transfer them back into Daiwa's custodial accounts. That move was allegedly also rejected in favor of a final plan to cover up the losses through a series of transactions between the New York branch and Daiwa's Japan offices.

Starting in mid-August, Daiwa's Japan operation allegedly purchased U.S. government bonds and delivered them into the New York custody accounts. Subsequently, allegedly fictitious securities sales and cash transfers totaling $600 million were entered on the books of the parent company and the New York branch to conceal the scheme.

In perhaps the most startling turn of events, people familiar with the case now say they suspect the writing of Mr. Iguchi's lengthy confession letter in July had been guided by senior management.

Mr. Iguchi said during his guilty plea that "fear" and "guilt" led him to write the letter, and an individual familiar with the letter said Mr. Iguchi wrote that the coverup caused him to consider suicide. Yet portions of the letter also reveal Mr. Iguchi waxing oddly macroeconomic about the scandal's impact on "the current relationship between Japan and the U.S." and its impact on other "Japanese financial institutions."

While individuals familiar with the case declined to specify which parts of the letter initially raised suspicions, yesterday's indictment alleges Mr. Tsuda coaxed Mr. Iguchi into writing a fourth draft of his confession letter that would be undated. Mr. Yamaji then allegedly asked Mr. Iguchi to destroy the computer disk he had used to prepare the confession letter.

Mr. Tsuda then allegedly told Mr. Iguchi to write a fifth confession-letter draft and to "discuss only his unauthorized trading and the losses that resulted from that trading" and not to discuss issues in previous confession letters such as methods of concealing the losses. Mr. Iguchi allegedly followed Mr. Tsuda's directives.

And while the Daiwa statement yesterday said the bank fired Mr. Iguchi because of the coverup, the indictment says that bank executives asked him in July, after they knew about the scandal, if he would be willing to transfer to a Daiwa affiliate in Japan. At that July meeting, Mr. Yamaji allegedly said to bank colleagues that after Daiwa announced its $1.1 billion loss in late November "no one would be hurt."

**Notes and Comments 1.3.** Since the issuance of termination orders by the Fed, the Federal Deposit Insurance Corporation, and the New York State Banking Department in November 1995 (amended February 1996), Daiwa had been operating under a liquidation plan. *See* Marcia Kass, *1995 Enforcement Orders Against Daiwa Terminated by Federal, N.Y. State Regulators*, BNA BANKING DAILY, May 6, 2003 (discussing Daiwa incident). In the process, Daiwa merged into Asahi Bank, which itself merged into Resona Bank in March 2003, and thereafter the termination orders were formally lifted by the regulators. *Id.*

# 2.  The Meaning of "International Banking"

**Notes and Comments 1.4.** What do we mean by the term "international banking"? What kinds of activities does the term include? Are these distinct, in any significant way, from "banking"? In this regard, consider the following materials.

### Haley & Seligman, The Development of International Banking by the United States, *in* W. H. Baughn & D. R. Mandich, The International Banking Handbook 35 (1983)

International banking has a long history. . . . European financial institutions have operated across national boundaries for centuries. . . .

Before World War I, banks in the United States were preoccupied with financing the economic development of their own country–there was not much interest in overseas banking. Furthermore, there were legal restraints against offshore banking. National banks were prohibited from owning foreign branches and could not accept bills of exchange resulting from foreign trade. Some state banking codes, though, did permit international banking activity. Consequently, overseas expansion was limited to state chartered banks, most of whom were small, or to unincorporated institutions.

A few bankers did go overseas. J.P. Morgan was the first.[b] Lazard, Freres, Seligman, Morton, Bliss and Company also went abroad and set up branches in Europe, and in the late 1800s, Jarvis Conklin Trust Company opened an office in London.[1] These were exceptions–for the most part, American banks concentrated on domestic business, and only a small number had accounts with foreign correspondents or maintained foreign departments. The volume of international banking business was insignificant.

The economic-political environment in the United States began to change around World War I as the country became more involed in foreign affairs. This involvement was reflected in the Federal Reserve Act, passed in 1913. The Act permitted banks to establish foreign branches and to accept bills of exchange derived from exports and imports. Despite this new legal power, though, American banks were not enthusiastic about using it.

Citibank, however, did take advantage of the new law. It opened a branch in Buenos Aires, and shortly afterward it bought a controlling interest in the International Banking Corporation which had a network of 21 branches in 13 countries. But when war broke out in 1914, European banks, who had 2,000 branches outside their national borders compared to 26 American foreign branches, clearly controlled international banking.[2]

A few years after the Federal Reserve Act became law, in an attempt to stimulate American participation in international lending, the Act was amended in 1916. The amendment allowed member banks to invest in a subsidiary who could engage in international banking. A bank forming such a subsidiary had to enter into an "agreement" with the Federal Reserve authorities in which it described its activities, hence the name "Agreement Corporation." They were not popular, and only three were formed in the two years following the amendment.[3]

World War I and its aftermath gave an impetus to the development of American international banking. Because of the war, European countries could not export, and U.S. exports rose to fill some of the gap. After the war, American foreign trade continued to grow as did America's involvement in international finance. The dollar began to replace sterling as a key currency, and New York emerged as an international finance center. In response to these forces, U.S. international banking facilities gradually expanded.

In 1919, too, the so-called Edge Act (actually an amendment to the Federal Reserve Act) was passed. Its aim was to stimulate foreign trade by authorizing the Board of Governors of the Federal Reserve System to charter corporations engaged either directly or indirectly in international banking operations. The potential in this legislation, however, was not realized until many years later, when Edge Act banks became widespread.

Unfortunately, after the war, credit was wildly overextended in the 1920s. In the Great Depression of the 1930s there was an epidemic of failures that brought international banking to a halt. Exchange controls, currency devaluations, quotas, and other government controls, plus the underlying threat of war made international credit hazardous. World War II was a further shock to the international banking system, and by the time it ended, U.S. banks had less than half as many foreign branches as they had had in 1920.

---

b. On the history of the transnational Morgan banking enterprise, see R. CHERNOW, THE HOUSE OF MORGAN (1990).

1. SARKIS J. KHOURY, DYNAMICS OF INTERNATIONAL BANKING (New York: Praeger Special Studies, 1980), p. 38.

2. F. JOHN MATHIS, ED., OFFSHORE LENDING BY U.S. BANKS (Philadelphia: Robert Morris Associates, 1981), pp. 2-3.

3. Neil Pinsky, "Edge Act and Agreement Corporations: Mediums for International Banking." Economic Perspective, Federal Reserve Bank of Chicago, September-October 1978, p 28.

In the period after the war, international trade was constrained by the "dollar shortage," as countries ravaged by war were short of foreign exchange reserves–the U.S. dollar had clearly become the international currency. In order to protect their reserves, these countries discouraged their banks from taking dollar deposits and lending them overseas. Dollar exchange was mostly supplied by the American government. The atmosphere of the Cold War also inhibited the growth of global banking.

In the 1950s international trade began to recover from the war. . . . [L]arge business corporations in the United States and in the Western countries began to internationalize as exports and imports grew. . . .

There were also some deliberate legislative actions that helped expand international banking. In the 1960s, the attitude of state legislatures began to change, and a number of states allowed foreign banks to open in their states if reciprocal rights were given. Federal regulations were, also liberalized.  In 1966, national banks were allowed to invest directly in the stock of foreign banks, and in 1970, the Bank Holding Company Act was amended to clarify the regulatory frame of international activities of U.S. bank holding companies. Later, too, in 1979, the Federal Reserve Board issued a new Regulation K,[b] which among other things, authorized domestic branches for Edge Act Corporations.

The creation of the Common Market,[c] too, was in itself an inducement to overseas expansion by U.S. banks. As tariff barriers were lowered within the six countries comprising the Common Market, U.S. corporations moved production to countries within the Common Market to protect their market share. U.S. banks followed their clients. . . .

Finally, any account of the reasons for the rapid increase in American international banking would be incomplete without mention of the Eurocurrency market, often called the Eurodollar market because most transactions are in U.S. dollars. The Eurocurrency market is a global network of banks, branches, and affiliates that accept deposits and make loans in currencies different than the country in which the loan is booked. Most of the market is located in London, but smaller centers have evolved in Paris, Zurich, Singapore, Hong Kong, and Panama.[d]

**Notes and Comments 1.5.** Historically, the development of international banking with respect to U.S.-based banks has tended to be reactive. For the most part, it has followed the expansion of transnational business interests of U.S. banks' larger customers. As the post-war dominance of U.S. commercial and financial strength has diminished, and as financial problems of U.S. banks themselves emerged in the late 1980s, overall international presence of U.S. banks has also diminished. *See* Kraus, *Overseas Pullback by US Banks Portends Reduced Global Role*, Am. Banker, Sept. 21, 1988, at 1, col. 2. During the 1990s, U.S. financial centers reemerged as stable havens of economic activity. *See, e.g.*, Sharon R. King, *Watchful Waiting on Japan*, N.Y. TIMES, Nov. 26, 1997, at C1, col. 2 (discussing relative stability of U.S. financial markets). As a result, the strength and influence of those centers have been renewed. *Cf.* Richard W. Stevenson, *Clinton Presses Asians at Summit To Remedy the Economic Turmoil*, N.Y. TIMES, at A1, col. 4 (discussing relative influence of U.S. economic policy); John M. Broder, *Asia Pacific Talks Vow Tough Action on*

---

b. 12 C.F.R. pt. 211 (2003).  For excerpts from Regulation K, see Chaoter 5, § 2, *infra*.

c. Now known as the European Union (EU).  For discussion of recent developments concerning international bank regulation in the EU, see *infra* at 17.

d. On the Eurocurrency and Eurobond markets, see SECURITIES & EXCHANGE COMMISSION STAFF REPORT, INTERNATIONALIZATION OF THE SECURITIES MARKETS (1987).

*Economic Crisis*, N.Y. TIMES, at A1, col. 6 (illustrating effects of U.S. financial and economic strength).

**1.6.** While the materials in this book primarily take U.S. international banking and its regulation as a convenient focus, international banking obviously has wider parameters. The role of non-U.S. banks in international banking is extremely significant, and in many other countries has a much longer and continuous historical pedigree than is the case in the United States. The following excerpt give a general, selective impression of some of the variations in international bank regulation.

## Wendt, The Role of Foreign Banks in International Banking, *in* W. H. Baughn & D. R. Mandich, The International Banking Handbook 47 (1983)

Banks vary considerably from country to country in their involvement in the international process. Their patterns depend in general on their history, the level of economic development of the country, the extent of its involvement in transactions with parties in other countries, the volume of its international transactions, governmental limitations or requirements, and factors that may be very special to an individual bank or country. As a general rule the governments of less developed countries exert more control over the international activities of their banks. . . .

Canada[a]

The Canadian banking system is dominated by the 11 chartered banks with a total of 6,969 domestic and about 262 foreign branches. Their charters follow the original charter set up in 1817 for the Bank of Montreal as the first Canadian bank.

Because of diminishing specialization, the chartered banks are increasingly in competition with so-called near banks, such as savings or mortgage loan banks. They do, however, have a large share of the foreign currency business because of economic involvement with the United States as well as close contacts with the New York and London financial markets. . . .

Although the number of agencies of foreign banks in Canada has been increasing substantially in recent history, it was not until passage of the 1977 revision of the Bank Act that foreign banks were permitted to operate banks in Canada within very well controlled limits.

The Bank of Canada is the country's central bank. It has no powers to selectively control credit but usually implements policies by using moral suasion. There are no foreign exchange restrictions in effect at this time. Accordingly, anyone doing business in Canada

---

a. Canadian international bank regulation is affected by Canada's involvement in the North American Free Trade Agreement (NAFTA), together with Mexico and the United States. On the new Canadian framework legislation for financial services, see 1.7, *infra*. On the structure of the Canadian banking system, see Art Alcausin Hall, *International Banking Regulation into the 21st Century: Flirting With Revolution*, 21 N.Y.L. SCH. J. INT'L & COMP. L. 41, 57-58 (2001). NAFTA had little effect on entry by U.S. banks into the Canadian banking market since there was a preexisting United States-Canada Free Trade Agreement ("FTA"), Canada-United States Free Trade Agreement, Dec. 22-23, 1987 & Jan. 2, 1988, U.S.-Can., 27 INT'L LEGAL MAT. 281 (1988), under which those banks had already gained preferential access to the Canadian market without the application of foreign ownership restrictions. Eric J. Gouvin, *Cross-Border Bank Branching Under the NAFTA: Public Choice and the Law of Corporate Groups*, 13 CONN. J. INT'L L. 257, 270-271 (1999). As a result of NAFTA, Canada did extend the same preferential treatment to Mexican banks as "NAFTA country residents." *Id.*

and needing financial assistance and/or information has no choice but to use the services of an indigenous bank. . . .

Germany[b]

The German banking system developed its strength during the 19th century at the time of German industrialization. Banks provided initial finance and subsequently managed the issue of shares to repay the initial loans. This established a close relationship between banks and industrial companies which has continued until today. Banks generally act as universal banks providing a range of financial services which extend beyond that of a typical deposit bank.

The three dominant German commercial banks, Deutsche Bank, Dresdner Bank, and Commerzbank, known as the "Big Three," are considered as the only true national banks in the country. Their importance is evidenced by their classification . . . as a separate group in the regularly published official statistics. . . .

In addition there are over 100 regional and other commercial banks operating in Germany. . . .

In addition to the regular banking services, banks in Germany are also authorized (a) to issue and place securities for public authorities and industrial companies, (b) to do stockbroking and advise customers on the purchase and sale of securities, and (c) to do insurance broking business. Because many of the large German banks have a nationwide branching network and are active in all aspects of domestic and international banking, they are able to respond to virtually any need of a business or a foreign bank.

Some of the relations that German banks have with industry have come under criticism lately because of the significant industrial holdings by the banks. It has been alleged that they exercise excessive control over certain industries. Additionally, there are many bankers present on the supervisory boards of industrial and commercial companies.

Foreign banks are mostly involved in financing imports and exports and servicing the German subsidiaries of foreign companies. They are controlled by the same laws as German banks, and there are no genuine obstacles to their establishment.

The Deutsche Bundesbank is Germany's Central Bank.[c] Although the financial system is subject to controls and regulations, the controls tend to be of a judicial nature and do not interfere with market competition. . . .

Japan

The history of some of the Japanese banks dates back several centuries. Although the modern financial system was created after the Meiji restoration of 1868, the most dramatic reconstruction occurred after 1945 during the postwar period when the Japanese financial system underwent drastic reforms. The relative importance of banks in the postwar period arose because of the need for creating credit to repair the destructions of the war. One reform, particularly dramatic for Japan, prohibited banks from the underwriting of securities.

In 1954, the Bank of Tokyo, the former Yokohama Specie Bank, was the only bank able to deal in foreign exchange. However, it did not retain the other privileges the Yokohama Specie bank had held previously. Today, however, a total of 78 banks in the Japanese system, including all the city banks listed below, are authorized to engage in foreign exchange transactions.

In addition to the 13 city banks . . . there are 63 local banks, which conduct com-

---

b. Germany, as a member of the European Union ("EU"), is affected by the rules under the EU Second Banking Directive. *See* Chapter 4, *infra* (discussing effects of Directive).

c. The Bundesbank's central banking functions are now performed by the European Central Bank.

mercial business principally in local areas.

There are also approximately 55 foreign banks in Japan which (a) may not operate a savings or trust bank, (b) cannot make foreign currency loans for a term of less than a year, and (c) have limitations imposed upon them for converting foreign currencies into yen. We also find the following long-term credit banks: Industrial Bank of Japan, Long-Term Credit Bank of Japan, and Nippon Fudosan Bank.

Although the Zaibatsus (large conglomerations of companies) were outlawed after the war, they live on in industrial groups of which the major city banks are members. One finds, however, only the large corporations involved in such groups. . . .

The Japanese banking system is very closely regulated. The Bank of Japan, specifically, has a large degree of control over the overseas operations of the banks. It also supplements conventional monetary policy with "window guidance" at the central bank rediscount window and by controlling the volume of bank lending by means of moral persuasion.

The foreign exchange control system is operated by the Ministry of Finance, the Ministry of International Trade and Industry, and the Bank of Japan. The authorised banks, however, have been delegated to verify normal international payments. Settlements in yen with foreign countries must be made through a nonresident Free Yen Account. . . .

Mexico[d]

After the achievement of independence in 1821 and for nearly 50 years theräfter, the financial system in Mexico, because of its inadequacy, limited economic development severely. In 1884 Banco Nacional Mexicano, which was French owned, received powers to act as the central bank. But it was not until 1925 that the most significant step toward the establishment of the modern banking system called for in the 1917 constitution was taken by organizing the Banco de Mexico S.A. Finally the problem of plurality of note issue was solved and the monopoly handed to Banco de Mexico. By the end of the 1930s, Mexico had had a number of unhappy financial experiences, such as bank failures, inflation, and currency devaluations, which had induced widespread distrust of financial institutions and processes.

The trend in the Mexican financial system is towards banks offering multibank services previously performed by specialized institutions. . . .

In 1934 another important official financial institution, the Nacional Financiera, was established to promote the development of a domestic capital market.

The role of Nacional Financiera became increasingly important over the years, not only because of growth of its own resources and progressive enlargement of the various public trust funds administered by it, but also because of the increase of its capacity as guarantor of the domestic and foreign indebtedness of a variety of public and private enterprises.

Additionally, there are presently approximately 90 financieras in existence which basically raise funds for issuing securities which are authorized by the National Banking and Insurance Commission and are registered with the National Securities Registry. They promote the development of various business enterprises by granting assistance in the

---

d. Mexican international bank regulation is affected by Mexico's Canada's involvement in the North American Free Trade Agreement, together with Canada and the United States. For a review of recent developments in Mexican banking, see JOHN A. ADAMS, JR., MEXICAN BANKING AND INVESTMENT IN TRANSITION (1997). On the historical background of the current Mexican banking market, see Alcausin Hall, *International Banking Regulation*, 21 N.Y.L. SCH. J. INT'L & COMP. L. at 58-59; Karen MacAllister, Comment, *NAFTA: How the Banks in the United States and Mexico Will Respond*, 17 HOUS. J. INT'L L. 273, 281-287 (1994).

organization or reorganization and expansion of businesses and may also purchase equity in that business.

In 1937 Banco Nacional de Commercio Exterior was founded by the government to promote, organize, and develop foreign trade. It is a national credit institution which may grant direct loans to finance exports and imports, production of exports and imports, and issue guarantees and letters of credit to support foreign trade.

In addition to Nacional Financiera and Banco Nacional de Commercio Exterior, there are other government institutions which were formed subsequently for the purpose of developing various sectors of the economy.

Foreign banks are only permitted to establish representative offices in Mexico and since 1979 to incorporate offshore financial operations. They are not permitted to engage in ordinary branch operations nor obtain deposits from local sources. The only exception is Citibank because it was established locally when legislation to exclude foreign banks was passed. . . .

Spain[e]

The banking system of Spain does not have as long a tradition as other banking systems in Central Europe. . . . Succeeding the Bank of San Carlos, which was founded in 1782, the Bank of Spain became the state bank in 1865. It absorbed many of the smaller banks at that time and acquired the exclusive right to issue notes. . . .

Not until the Bank Reform Act of 1962 was the Bank of Spain nationalized and made the central bank for Spain.[f] Its authority includes implementing government credit policy, supervising the whole banking and credit system, as well as establishing deposit and credit ratios for all banking institutions. . . .

Switzerland

The development and existence of Switzerland is closely bound up in its location in the Alps. The strategic importance of Alpine passages was recognized by the important heads of Europe and guided them to be on good terms with the people of Switzerland. Although not free of wars in its history, the various peoples of Switzerland combined voluntarily into one nation, and the permanent neutrality of Switzerland was formally recognized on May 20, 1815, at the Vienna Congress as being in the best interest of Europe. It was against this background that Switzerland developed as a financial center. For centuries it had performed the function of trustee in its capacity of guardian of the Alpine passes and later performed the same function in other capacities.

. . . Switzerland's role as a financial center is built on the old tradition of capital exports, especially during the 18th century at the time of the Spanish War of Succession and another period at the end of that century. In the 19th century Switzerland at first became a capital importing country. Even prior to the establishment of the Swiss franc in 1850, Basel had become an important storehouse of capital, not only for Switzerland, but also the lower part of Germany.

The investing in other countries, especially mortgage investments in Germany and other fixed investments in Austria, caused bitter consequences after World War I, and it was not until 1926 that international transactions were resumed. The famous Swiss banking code of 1934, which protected for the first time in history the principle of bank secrecy by penal

---

e. Spain, as a member of the EU, is affected by the rules under the EU Second Banking Directive. *See infra* at 17 (discussing effects of EU requirements on Spanish banking system).

f. The Bank's central banking functions are now performed by the European Central Bank.

law, was a direct outgrowth of the Nazi infiltration into the Swiss banking system.[g] After World War II the government of Switzerland arranged for so-called swing credits in the trade and payment agreements. Its purpose was to work out an arrangement under which the volume of exports would not depend on the volume of imports. France and Britain used these credits in full. The banks also granted credits to foreign countries, especially France and Belgium, partly to finance Swiss exports. . . .

The Swiss Banking System has an extraordinarily high density within the country. In addition to the above five large banks, there are 28 cantonal banks, 232 savings and regional banks, and a number of long-term credit institutions and private banks. The Swiss financial system is characterized by the importance of the international business and the lack of offical intervention. There is a great degree of international interlocking of interest by banker with a variety of industrial bank commercial enterprises.

Swiss banks may hold stock in corporations for their own account as well as for their clients. The big banks also act as merchant banks holding stock as underwriters or prior to acquisitions or mergers. There are interlocking directorships by the banks who place personnel on the boards of corporations. One of the specialities handled by Swiss banks is financing by forfeiting, which is basically discount of export receivables evidenced by notes or drafts without recourse to the exporter.

Foreign banks which have been registered as banks in Switzerland are subject to Swiss banking law and can be set up provided that reciprocity is given by the home country of the foreign bank. In December 1979, there were 81 foreign-controlled banks and 15 branches of foreign banks in the country.

The Swiss National Bank is the central bank of Switzerland. Altough foreign exchange controls were lifted in August 1980, banks must advise the central bank of bond issues and private placements of SFR 3 million or more. Banks must also ascertain the identity of investment depositors. . . .

United Kingdom[h]

The evolution of England's financial institutions stretches over more than 600 years. Until World War I sterling was the currency most commonly used in international payments. Most of the international trade, even that which never touched the shores of the British Isles, was denominated in sterling and was financed with sterling drafts and acceptances. Britain's leading position as an importer-exporter and source of capital, as well the unrivaled facilities of the London money market, assured that any bills endorsed by any of the British acceptance houses could be discounted at the world's best rates. Britain's predominance in

---

g. For discussion of the legal implications of Swiss bank secrecy law on international banking, see Chapter 10, *infra*.

h. The United Kingdom, as a member of the EU, is affected by the rules under the EU Second Banking Directive. *See* Chapter 4, *infra* (discussing effects of directive). In addition, in May 1997 the UK Chancellor of the Exchequer announced an overhaul of British monetary and financial regulation that will directly affect the authority of the Bank of England. Nicholas Bray, *Britain Reorganizes Bank Regulation; Central Bank to Stick to Monetary Policy*, Wall St. J., May 21, 1997, at A10. Under the plan, the Bank of England will oversee monetary policy, but will no longer supervise British banks. The bank's supervisory role is to be transferred to an enlarged Securities and Investments Board, to be known as the Financial Services Authority (FSA). By the Summer of 1998, the FSA is expected to take over responsibility for banking supervision, as well as the responsibilities of the Investment Management Regulatory Organization, the Securities and Futures Authority and the Personal Investment Authority. Complete integration of all financial services regulation in the FSA, eventually consolidating nine separate financial regulators, is not expected to be completed until late 1999.

international trade led to the establishment of specialized financial institutions.

The commercial banking system developed a branch banking system with a few giant banks operating many offices throughout the country. From the number of 600 banks in 1824 we find today eight clearing banks with about 14,000 branches throughout the country. Many of the clearing banks today are trying to establish themselves as one-stop supermarkets for all corporate money requirements and are parts of cross-border financial consortia. . . .

. . . [A]cceptance houses developed as specialized institutions, financing mercantile activity by accepting and discounting bills of exchange drawn upon them. Originally, the merchants themselves were merely financing their own trading activity. Today we find 17 elite merchant banks as members of the Acceptance House Committee. Traditionally, these merchant banks have been more innovative and responsive in their financing activity than commercial banks. Their endeavors are extremely varied and include banking and acceptance business, dealing in foreign exchange, bullion, bonds, investment management on behalf of private and institutional clients, corporate financial advice on issues, mergers, and money raising as well as export and project financing. The acceptances generated by these merchant banks are automatically acceptable at the Bank of England for rediscount and therefore command the finest rates in the market. . . .

In 1980 there were more than 400 foreign banks in London, of which about 340 were represented directly through a subsidiary, branch or representative office. The others have an indirect presence through participation in one of the 30 UK registered joint venture banking groups.

The Bank of England was founded in 1694 and is the the country's central bank. It does not formally inspect or supervise the policies or operations of the clearing banks. The governor of the Bank of England influences policies of the clearing banks through frequent meetings with the chief executives of these banks.[i] . . .

In 1979 all forms of foreign exchange restrictions were abolished. There are no exchange controls on inward or outward investments. There are also no general restrictions on foreign ownership of local business or joint ventures. . . .

**Notes and Comments 1.7.** In October 2001, the Canadian government began implementing new framework legislation, Bill C-8, for the financial services sector, including domestic and foreign banks, trust companies, insurance companies, credit unions and other financial institutions. *See* Peter Menyasz, *Canada Publishes Final Regulations to Implement Financial Services Framework*, BNA Banking Daily, Oct. 25, 2001, at d9 (discussing new framework legislation). Among other things, the legislation created the Financial Consumer Agency (FCA), which began operations on October 24, 2001. The FCA is responsible for enforcing compliance with the new legislation's consumer provisions. The details of the new rules are available on the Internet at http://canada.gc.ca/gazette/part2/pdf/g2-13522.pdf.

**1.8.** Do you see any trends among the various regulatory regimes described by Wendt? In the case of the United States,[2] the central bank (the Federal Reserve System, "the Fed") is just one of five federal regulators of depository institutions, and each state has at least one banking regulator as well. U.S. regulation of international banking is supervised

---

i. The Bank of England's role has been severely limited by a recent legislative change. *See supra* at 15, note a.

2. For detailed discussion of the U.S. regulatory structure applicable to international banking, see Chapter 2, *infra*, § 1.

primarily by *three* of the federal regulators (the Fed, the Comptroller of the Currency, and the Federal Deposit Insurance Corporation) and the state regulators. Reviewing this general pattern of U.S. international banking and its regulation, as compared with the varieties of experience described in the Wendt article, how would you characterize the alternative approaches available for the regulation of international banking?

# 3. Contemporary Developments

**Notes and Comments 1.9.** *Effect of European Union regulation.* With an increasing role being taken by the EU in the regulation of banking, adjustments in the regulatory environment of the individual member states have become necessary. The following excerpt describes one of the more dramatic adjustment experiences, the ongoing convergence of the Spanish banking system with the EU.

## M. Galy, G. Pastor & T. Pujol,
## Spain: Converging with the European Community
(IMF Occasional Paper 101, Feb. 1993)

After six years of negotiations, Spain became a full member of the EC on January 1, 1986, and was granted a transitory period of seven years to align its laws and regulations with the EC Directives. . . .

Deregulation of the Banking System

Spanish banking has been traditionally and until recently a closed system, heavily regulated, protected from foreign competition, conservative in terms of innovations, and controlled by the large banks, who also owned big portions of industry. Heavy regulation of the Spanish banking system extended beyond interest rates to branching, entry, investment coefficients, and reserve requirements. Moreover, the regulations have put different constraints on different institutions and private commercial banks and savings banks. As the Spanish financial system and private agents were unsophisticated, banks would bear their main input (deposits) paying a rather low interest rate and were required to finance public deficits by investing in low-yield government securities. . . .

During the period 1978-85, the Spanish banking system went through one of the most severe banking crises that has taken place in industrial countries in recent times. The crisis affected 58 banks, almost half of those existing in 1977, which represented 27 percent of the total banking system liabilities and 28 percent of total employment. . . . The root of the banking crisis was the severe industrial crisis following the oil price increases in the 1970s, the close links between banks and industrial firms, bad management and fraud, and the lack of an adequate monitoring policy by the Bank of Spain. A deposit guarantee fund . . . was created in response to the crisis and was consolidated in 1980.

The banking crisis temporarily slowed the deregulation process that started in 1969 (as the central bank imposed tough solvency and regulatory requirements). After the crisis, financial deregulation reaccelerated, especially in the context of EC integration. . . .

Limits to Entry

As of 1990, foreign banks were allowed to have only four branches each. In 1991, they were allowed to open an additional branch, to be followed by two more in 1992. Since 1992, the Spanish authorities have authorized any foreign bank as long as the candidate satisfies the conditions set by the [EU] Second Banking Directive.[c]

As regards domestic banks, limits to entry were relaxed in 1974, but tightened again during the banking crisis of 1978-85. Only in late 1988 did the Ministry of Economy and Finance begin authorizing the creation of new domestic banks for the first time since 1978. During the banking crisis, investors who wanted to open a bank were required to buy a small or nearly bankrupt bank and operate it under a new name.

Limits to Branching

The limits on branching for domestic private commercial banks were liberalized subject to capital adequacy in 1974. For savings banks, limits on branching were liberalized in 1975 within each savings bank's geographical region and outside it starting in 1989.

Segmentation of Institutions

Savings banks had been subject to more severe restrictions than private commercial banks. At present, however, both types of institutions are authorized to perform the same operations although the ownership structure of the savings bank is different from that of private commercial banks.

Capital Adequacy

Since May 1985, Spain regulates the solvency of financial intermediaries in accordance with the Basle Agreement.[d] However, the ratio of equity to assets of most Spanish banks is above the recommended 4 percent level: at 7.25 percent in 1989, the ratio of own resources to assets of the largest Spanish banks was one of the highest in the EC. . . . One potential problem of the proposed EC harmonization process of solvency requirements is the limitation that it will impose on the extent of industrial holdings in relation to bank equity. . . .

Bank Mergers

Another major effect of the deregulation process is the strategic repositioning of financial institutions. . . . [P]rivate commercial banks, big private commercial banks in particular, have been losing market share in terms of both deposits and loans because of the dynamic growth of savings banks. The erosion of the position of the big banks, including those affected by the 1978 crisis, Hispano and Banesto, has been met with different responses, merger attempts being the most prominent. . . .

The merger projects, on the one hand, can be seen as an attempt to realize necessary economies of scale (i.e., savings in bank unit costs) and scope (i.e., multi-product banking firms) to raise efficiency in order to face the competition of an integrated market. On the other hand, the mergers can be seen as due to three other factors. First, there was the possibility for financial institutions to revalue their assets when merging and fulfill solvency requirements mandated by Spanish legislation and the 1992 EC Directives. Second, mergers could potentially help Spanish banks counter the trend of erosion of their control of the market vis-à-vis savings banks. Third, mergers could be viewed as a defense response by larger banks to the prospect of fierce competition from potentially more efficient and sophisticated foreign institutions. Although it could be argued that another incentive for banks to merge has been the fiscal gain from the 1990 law that exempted asset revaluations due to mergers from corporate taxation, this tax exemption has been subject to discretionary government approval.

Competition from Foreign Banks

An important element in the process of financial deregulation has been the opening

---

c. For discussion of the Second Banking Directive, see Chapter 5, *infra*.

d. On the Basle Agreement, which establishes a basic framework for supervising capital adequacy of international banks, see Chapter 3, *infra*.

up of the Spanish banking system to foreign competition. This move was important in shaping the current state of the Spanish market. In particular, foreign banks in Spain were instrumental in introducing new financial services. They spurred the development of the interbank market, launched merchant banking, and introduced new technology in banking services. With a network limited to four branches up to 1990 (unless part owner of a Spanish bank), foreign banks had limited capacity to attract depositors. Consequently, they moved into innovative financing products. Spanish financial institutions reacted to foreign competition, and the largest banks can now offer the same financial services. Competition for the development of financial services for small- and medium-sized companies and for consumers in the wake of the opening of the single European market is expected to intensify.

**Notes and Comments 1.10.** Many of the deregulatory measures described in the preceding excerpt were necessary to comply with EU policies. Why would banking deregulation be important to the EU, the basic objective of which is to establish and maintain a single European market for goods, services and capital?

**1.11.** Why would the decrease or elimination of limits to entry and and to branching be important to the EU? Are these goals distinct from the goal of deregulating the Spanish banking industry generally?

**1.12.** In March 2004, the European Parliament approved proposals to streamline the regulation of EU financial services. At the heart of the new system will be a European Banking Committee (EBC), exercising delegated powers through the European Commission. *See European Parliament Secures Role in Bank Rulemaking, OK's Streamlined Regulations*, BNA Int'l Bus. & Fin. Daily, Apr. 5, 2004 (available at http://pubs.bna.com/ip/BNA/ibd.nsf/is/A0A8H4N2E8). In contrast with the previous system, under which EU banking, insurance and funds management regulations required approval by both the European Parliament and the Council of Ministers on behalf of the fifteen member states (the so-called "co-decision" procedures), the new system will allow a more direct regulatory role for the Commission in promulgating such regulations–as is already the case in EU securities regulation. The European Parliament's influence is preserved, however, by provisions added to the proposals requiring, among other things, four-year "sunset" clauses for new financial services laws and a review of the new system by year-end 2007.

**1.13.** *Emerging regulatory regimes in Eastern Europe.* The transition from a socialist economies in central and Eastern Europe and the transformation of the former Soviet Union into the loose confederation of the Commonwealth of Independent States has had important consequences for banking and bank regulation. The first excerpt that follows describes some of the initial efforts at banking reform in the Russian Federation. The second excerpt considers more broadly the problems of banking reform in Eastern Europe.

## Inna Vysman, The New Banking Legislation in Russia: Theoretical Adequacy, Practical Difficulties, and Potential Solutions
62 Fordham L. Rev. 265 (1993)[e]

A key element to the successful realization of economic perestroika (restructuring) in a former socialistic state such as Russia is an effective financial system. The main step in achieving this goal is the creation of a well-functioning two-tier competitive banking system

---

e. Footnotes have been renumbered consecutively in this excerpt.

wherein a central bank focuses on regulating overall credit and interest rates, while newly established commercial banks assume the responsibility of deposit and loan transactions with businesses and households.[1] Russia attempted to create such a banking system through the introduction of new banking legislation in 1990. Due to the difficulties of the present economic and political situation in Russia, however, even a well-written law does not ensure a productive and efficient system.

I. The Theoretical Adequacy of the New Russian Banking Legislation

Creation of a new legal banking framework is the most important task in creating a well-functioning competitive banking system in Russia. . . . The introduction of the Central Bank Law[2] and the new Commercial Banking Law[3] (collectively the "laws" or the "new legislation") on December 2, 1990, marked the beginning[4] of Russia's marketbased financial system. These laws created a two-tier banking system by separating the Central Bank's operations from commercial banking functions. The new legislation has two objectives: (i) to establish a genuinely independent central bank; and (ii) to provide this central bank with the means both to supervise and regulate newly created commercial banks and to conduct monetary and credit policy.

A. Establishment of an Independent Central Bank

The proclaimed independence of the Central Bank of Russia is one of the principal features of the new legislation. The laws hold the Bank of Russia accountable to the Russian Supreme Soviet,[5] but independent of the executive and administrative bodies of the Russian government.[6] . . .

To ensure the independence of the Central Bank and to do away with the old order, the new legislation requires the Supreme Soviet, not the executive branch, to nominate the Central Bank's Chairman of the Board of Directors.[7] This nomination is for a term of five years,[8] while the parliament and the President of Russia are elected for four years.[9] Indeed, the exclusive rights of the Supreme Soviet to appoint and to dismiss the Chairman of the Board of Directors[10] have already safeguarded the top bankers during and after the August

---

1. *See* V. Sundararajan, Central Banking Reforms in Formerly Planned Economies, Fin. & Dev., Mar. 1992, at 10, 11. Russia has only a national banking system, unlike the United States, which has a co-existent national and state banking system.

2. On the Central Bank of the RSFSR (Bank of Russia) (1990) (Committee on Foreign and Comparative Laws, Ass'n of the Bar of the City of New York, trans., 1990) (on file at Fordham Law Review) [hereinafter Central Bank Law].

3. On Banks and Banking in the RSFSR (1990) (Committee on Foreign and Comparative Laws, Ass'n of the Bar of the City of New York, trans., 1990) (on file at Fordham Law Review) [hereinafter Commercial Banking Law].

4. There were no legislative acts of such kind throughout the whole Soviet history. *See* [Andrei I.] Kazmin, [The Contours of a New Banking System in the Dissolving Soviet Union, Bank Archive, No. 2, 1992,] at 114.

5. The Supreme Soviet is the legislative body of the Russian government. *See* 2 The Europa World Year Book 1992, at 2811 (1992).

6. *See* Central Bank Law, *supra*, art. 1.

7. *See* Central Bank Law, *supra*, art 37.

8. *See id.*

9. *See* Kazmin, *supra* at 114.

10. The Supreme Soviet may dismiss the Chairman of the Board of Directors only in the event of retirement, serious illness, or inability to execute his duties. *See id.* at 114-15.

1991 coup. When the provisional government dismissed the Chairman of the Central Bank as part of the coup, the action was rapidly acknowledged to be illegal; shortly thereafter, the Chairman returned to his duties.[11]

For the first time, the laws distinctly define the functions of the Central Bank as the fiscal agent of the government.[12] Before 1991, the Central Bank frequently financed the budget deficit through direct loans to the Ministry of Finance. These loans were given "without any kind of collateral, at zero interest rates and with unlimited period of re-payment."[13] In contrast, the new legislation establishes a maximum allowable debt limit for the Ministry of Finance.[14] Moreover, the laws mandate that the Bank of Russia extend loans to the Ministry only on general terms, the same as for all other borrowers, thereby removing all of the Ministry's former privileges in obtaining credit.[15] Such loans may be extended for a maximum of six months[16] and require appropriate collateral, such as state bonds, promissory notes, and other securities.[17]

. . .

### B. Organization, Regulation, and Supervision of the Commercial Banks in Russia under the New Banking Laws

. . . In order to safeguard its newly acquired status, the Bank of Russia must promote an independent monetary and credit policy. Such a policy had been impossible to implement under the prior relationships between the Central Bank and commercial banks. "The whole banking framework has to be replaced by a new one, where traditional administrative pressure on banks would be replaced by the skilled regulation of the banking business, based on world-wide accepted methods and instruments."[18] In an effort to create such "skilled regulation," the laws deal extensively with the relationship between the Bank of Russia and commercial banks.

### 1. The Organization of a Commercial Bank under the New Legislation

Under the new legislation, a commercial bank may operate only in accordance with an appropriate license issued by the Central Bank, which lists the services that a bank may perform.[19] . . .

The laws provide for a relatively simple application process. . . .

Russia appears ready to open its financial markets to the rest of the world. The new laws do not restrict foreign ownership of banks in any way other than the Central Bank's right to establish additional requirements regarding the minimum and maximum amount of required statutory capital.[20] . . .

In addition to issuing general banking licenses, the Bank of Russia may issue

---

11. *See id.*

12. *See* Central Bank Law, *supra*, art. 17.

13. Kazmin, *supra* at 115.

14. *See* Central Bank Law, *supra,* art. 17.

15. *See id.*

16. *See id.*

17. *See id.*

18. Kazmin, *supra* at 115.

19. *See* Central Bank Law, *supra*, art. 23; Commercial Banking Law, *supra*, art. 11.

20. *See id.* art. 14.

special licenses that allow commercial banks to carry out foreign exchange transactions.[21]
. . .

### 2. Regulation and Supervision of a Commercial Bank

The new legislation defines the principles governing the Bank of Russia's relations with commercial banks. The laws require the Central Bank to promote the creation of favorable conditions for stable performances by banks but prohibit the Bank of Russia from interfering in banks' daily operations.[22] The independence from such interference greatly contrasts with Russia's prior tradition of regulating every aspect of banks' activities. The new legislation also maintains that "the Bank of Russia shall . . . exercise regulatory functions with regard to and supervision of banks with the aim of maintaining stability of [the] monetary and loan system."[23] Moreover, the laws now provide for equality of legal rights between resident and non-resident banks, which the Bank of Russia must ensure.[24] This provision is rather controversial in light of the different approaches to this issue taken by Western banking laws: some countries have similar provisions, while others heavily restrict activities by foreign banks.[25]

Similar to the existing banking regulations of many developed countries,[26] the Russian banking laws prescribe certain financial norms which have to be fulfilled by every commercial bank.[27] The norms include: (1) a minimum statutory capital requirement; (2) a maximum equity ratio with due assessment of risks; (3) liquidity rates; (4) a minimum amount of statutory reserves to be deposited with the Bank of Russia; (5) maximum risks allowable for one borrower; (6) limitations of hard currency and exchange rate risks; and (7) restrictions on the use of borrowed deposits for the purchase of shares belonging to legal persons.[28]

The laws also provide, if Russia's economic situation so requires, that "[t]he Supreme Soviet . . . upon representation by the Bank of Russia, may establish other economic norms and rates. . . ."[29] This provision gives the Bank of Russia flexibility to conform its regulations to Russia's rapidly changing economic conditions.

In order to ensure compliance by commercial banks with these financial norms and other Russian laws, the new legislation provides a legal framework for the supervision of the banks by the Bank of Russia. . . . The new legislation enables the Central Bank itself to verify commercial banking operations or to entrust this task to auditing organizations.[30]

. . .

The Central Bank also may issue binding instructions to banks requiring them to

---

21. *See id.* art. 35; Central Bank Law, *supra*, art. 21.

22. *See* Central Bank Law, *supra*, art. 22.

23. *Id.*

24. *See id.* art. 18.

25. The Korean, Swiss, American, and German banking laws have similar provisions; however, Mexico, Canada, and Japan greatly restrict the activities of foreign banks. See Wendt, The Role of Foreign Banks in International Banking, in Michael P. Malloy, The Regulation of Banking: Cases and Materials on Depository Institutions and Their Regulators 821, 821-28 (1992).

26. Countries where the central bank sets the economic norms for commercial banks include Italy, Japan, Korea, and Venezuela. *See* Wendt, [*supra*].

27. *See* Central Bank Law, *supra*, art. 24; Commercial Banking Law, *supra*, art. 24.

28. *See* Central Bank Law, *supra*, art. 24.

29. *Id.*

30. *See* Central Bank Law, *supra*, art. 30.

remove violations of either Russian laws or established financial standards.[31] The Bank of Russia may impose serious disciplinary measures when banks: (1) fail to fulfill its orders; (2) violate established financial standards that result in losses for banks and their clients; (3) fail to submit reports or submit false or misleading accounting data; (4) present year-end accounting reports that bear evidence of losses and ensuing damage to the interests of depositors and lenders; or (5) commit other regular infringements.[32] The Central Bank may take one or more of the following actions to remedy these situations: (1) carry out a reorganization of the bank, including enlargement of its capital and modification of the structure of its assets; (2) restructure the bank; (3) replace the bank's executives; (4) impose fines on the violators; (5) increase the size of statutory reserves for banks that fail to observe established financial standards; (6) appoint a provisional administration to run a bank during the period required for its reorganization; or (7) rescind the banking license, which is tantamount to liquidation of the bank.[33]

. . .

## C. The Central Bank's Regulation of the Monetary and Credit System under the New Banking Laws

One of the most important functions of the Central Bank is the implementation of a single federal monetary and credit policy. . . .

Under the new banking laws, the Bank of Russia determines its monetary and loan policy and defines it in the Basic Guidelines for Monetary and Credit Regulation.[34] . . .

The new legislation . . . also provide[s] other necessary means of conducting monetary policy and loan regulation. These include determining the size of the mandatory reserves and loan interest rates, prescribing economic rates for banks, and effecting transactions with securities.[35]

. . .

## D. Protection of Bank Customers

. . . The Bank of Russia achieves this objective by establishing statutory reserve requirements, which act as a guarantee of commercial banks' obligations.[36] The Central Bank also may create insurance funds for each bank to compensate customers for possible losses attributable to the bank.[37] The incomes of the appropriate banks establish these insurance funds.[38] The laws expressly require the banks to maintain their insurance and statutory reserves.[39]

. . . The Central Bank may refuse to grant a banking license in case of "inadequate financial standing of the founders ... which poses a threat to the interests of the bank's depositors and creditors."[40] The Central Bank also may withdraw a banking license where the bank's year-end accounting report shows losses and damage to the interests of bank

---

31. *See* Central Bank Law, *supra*, art. 33.

32. *See id.*

33. *See id.*

34. *See* Central Bank Law, *supra*, art. 13.

35. *See id.* art. 13.

36. *See* Commercial Banking Law, *supra*, art. 10.

37. *See* Central Bank Law, *supra*, art. 29.

38. *See id.*

39. *See* Commercial Banking Law, *supra*, art 24.

40. *Id.* art. 17.

customers.[41]

. . . Banks have an obligation "to keep confidential all information pertaining to operations, accounts and deposits of the bank, its clients and correspondents."[42] The laws provide only limited exceptions to the duty of confidentiality and authorize bank officials to disclose information solely to courts of law and arbitration, investigatory bodies, and organizations that are authorized by law to receive confidential information.[43] They also establish a special procedure which must be followed when monies and other property of bank customers are seized or levied upon.[44]

## II. PROBLEMS WITH THE PRACTICAL APPLICATION
## OF THE NEW BANKING LAWS

. . .

### A. Independence and Accountability of the Central Bank

The new banking laws provide a legal basis for the independent status of the Bank of Russia. . . . In reality, however, external pressures influence the Central Bank's independence. Political pressure from the executive branch and especially the President of the Republic, which collectively hold the greatest amount of power in the Russian government, often dictates the actions of the Central Bank; sometimes this pressure even causes the Central Bank to act in direct conflict with its stated purposes.[45] For example, the new legislation seeks to stop the traditional practice of financing the budget deficit through direct loans from the Central Bank.[46] The Bank of Russia, however, continues to finance government deficits.[47] In addition, in December 1992, President Yeltsin issued a decree that made the Chairman of the Bank of Russia a member of the government.[48] This edict directly contradicts the provisions of the banking laws and makes the Central Bank even more susceptible to pressure by the executive branch.

Influence from the executive branch is also the reason for the difficult relations between the Central Bank and the Supreme Soviet. In Russia's present political situation, the executive and legislative branches often conflict, and each possesses different views on the conduct of the country's financial policy.[49] Due to executive pressure, the Bank of Russia

---

41. See Central Bank Law, supra, art. 33.

42. Commercial Banking Law, supra, art. 25.

43. See id.

44. See id. art. 26.

45. See The New Central Banks in the Republics of the Former U.S.S.R., Cent. Banking, Winter 1991-92, at 12, 20 [hereinafter The New Central Banks].

46. See Central Bank Law, supra, art. 1.

47. See The New Central Banks, supra at 20.

48. See Ivan Zhagel, Chairman of Russian Federation Central Bank Becomes a Member of the Government, Current Dig. Soviet Press, Current Dig. Post-Soviet Press, Dec. 16, 1992, available in LEXIS, Nexis Library, CDSP File. Furthermore, on September 21, 1993, President Yeltsin issued a decree "that the central bank will stop answering to Parliament and start answering to the President." Claudia Rosett, Obstacle to Reform: Rooted in Soviet Past, Russia's Central Bank Lacks Grasp of Basics, Wall St. J., Sept. 23, 1993, at A1.

49. For example, the Supreme Soviet tries to prevent the invasion of foreign capital into Russia, while the executive actively encourages this process. See Valeri Vizutovich, Visa dl'a Dollara: Kto Zashitit Inostrannie Kapitali v Rossii [Visa for Dollar: Who Will Protect Foreign Capitals in Russia], Novoye Russkoye Slovo, Dec. 22, 1992, at 5.

ignores the directives of the Supreme Soviet even though it is required to act in accordance with such decisions: "the leadership of the Bank of Russia systematically refuses to fulfill the decisions of the . . . Supreme Soviet and its Presidium. The latest example is the resolution of the Presidium of the Supreme Soviet on providing credits for shipments of goods to regions of the Far North. . . ."[50] The Central Bank has ignored this decision refusing to provide the credits.[51]

The Bank of Russia also consistently violates the procedural provisions of the laws, which were to give the Supreme Soviet power to control the activities of the Bank. . . .

### B. Organization, Supervision, and Activities
### of Commercial Banks

The new banking legislation authorizes the Central Bank to supervise the organization and activity of the commercial banks "with the aim of maintaining stability of the monetary and loan system."[52] Due to the limited technology available in present-day Russia, however, the Bank of Russia has tremendous difficulty performing this function. . . .

The effect of these problems on the practical application of the new legislation is enormous. For example, the laws require the Bank of Russia to process applications for banking licenses.[53] In practice, "there are neither the staff nor the computers to more than rubber stamp the applications."[54] The Bank of Russia is also unable to ensure that banks' statutes and articles of incorporation do not contradict the laws of the country and that the founders' financial standing does not pose a threat to the banks' future customers as required by the laws.[55] As a result, banks violating the laws or having inadequate financial resources are likely to receive licenses. This may damage the legitimacy of the banking system and harm customers who stand to lose their life savings due to the banks' insufficient capital and improper activities.

The Central Bank also has a problem adequately supervising commercial banks' activities as required by the banking laws.[56] The Bank of Russia has neither sufficient regulators to deal with the large number of new banks nor computers and experience to process and analyze the information given to it by the banks.[57] The same problems exist at the commercial banking level and, as a result, the banks are unable to provide the Central Bank with the required statistics.[58] Consequently, the Bank of Russia cannot verify commercial banking operations.

The Central Bank's inability to give binding instructions to the commercial banks, despite its apparent power under the new banking legislation, further complicates the situation.[59] "[F]ew people know what is permitted and what is not because of the speed at

---

50. Central Bank Scored for Arbitrary Action, Current Dig. Soviet Press, Current Dig. Post-Soviet Press, June 17, 1992, available in LEXIS, Nexis Library, CDSP File.

51. *See id.*

52. Central Bank Law, *supra*, art. 22.

53. *See* Commercial Banking Law, *supra*, arts. 15-17.

54. Simon Brady, In the Red, Euromoney, July 1991, at 19, 20.

55. *See* Commercial Banking Law, *supra*, art. 17.

56. *See* Central Bank Law, *supra*, art. 30. . . .

57. *See* Brady, *supra* at 20.

58. *See* The New Central Banks, *supra*, at 16.

59. *See* Central Bank Law, *supra*, art. 33.

which new decrees on banking and currency regulation are passed."[60]   Moreover, the shortage of resources and information prevents the Central Bank from knowing whether banks have transgressed any regulations.  Even if the Bank of Russia notices violations, it cannot adequately prevent them. "Bankers have adopted a 'Go on then, arrest me' attitude [with] the regulators."[61] Arrests have only occurred in cases where banks grossly violated tax or foreign exchange laws.[62]

. . .

Another important problem facing the Russian banking system is the inability of commercial banks to determine adequately the creditworthiness of their potential borrowers. While the laws allow banks to extend credit,[63] this activity is very risky in practice because of technological limitations. Businesses have no records showing their creditworthiness.[64] Due to inexperience, many new companies overestimate their future earnings.[65]  In addition, the banks have no experience in evaluating the vitality of businesses.[66]  Monitoring a loan's performance, once it is made, also becomes difficult.  The combination of these factors makes the lending activities of the commercial banks very risky.  The ownership structure of the banks increases this risk.  Many non-financial businesses set up banks in order to provide loans to themselves.[67]  Thus, the potential for insider lending abuse is tremendous.

. . .

The fact that many banks fund their loans through the interbank market further complicates the situation.[68]  Thus, "[a] collapse at one institution would rapidly spread through other banks' balance sheets -- 30% of which comprise interbank loans."[69]  This, in turn, could cause serious political problems because part of the banks' funds are deposits "from Russian mattresses" or loans from Sberbank (the old state savings bank),[70] where most people still keep their money.[80]  Citizens from former command economies do not immediately understand the concept of risk/reward.[81]  "[T]he equation of free markets with the loss of their life savings could alter [the Russian people's] views of reformers. A widespread banking crisis [brought about by the technical problems in a credit system,] could be the catalyst for a crackdown."[82] . . .

---

60. Brady, *supra* at 20.

61. *Id.*

62. *See id.* "One example reported in the Russian media involved a co-operative bank trying to sell for dollars more rubles than theoretically existed in circulation." *Id.*

63. *See* Commercial Banking Law, *supra*, art. 5.

64. *See* Russian Banks: Overgrown and Underfinanced, Economist, July 18-25, 1992, at 84, 85.

65. *See* Jack A. Barbanel & Linda L. Maillet, Business in the Soviet Union: A Primer and Overview 156 (1991).

66. *See id.*

67. *See* Brady, *supra* at 19.

68. *See* Brady, *supra* at 20.

69. *Id.*

70. For a comparative discussion of the status and activities of the Sberbank, see Anawalt, *Russia's Sberbank and a Fresh Look at the Glass-Steagall Act*, 14 BERKELEY J. INT'L L. 344 (1996).

80. *See id.*

81. *See id.*

82. *Id.*

## C. The Independence of Commercial Banks

The new banking legislation has given commercial banks political independence from the government and
working independence from the Central Bank.[83] In practice, however, neither goal has been achieved.

### 1. The Independence of Commercial Banks from the Political Power of the Government

The laws proclaim the independence of commercial banks from governmental influence when making their decisions with regard to banking operations. To this end, the laws prohibit the use of funds from political and state organizations in the formation of a bank's capital.[84] Many such organizations, however, violate this law. For example, several ministries have formed their own banks. Menatep, which is a very active new financial group, has been set up by members of the Young Communist League.[85] The largest Russian bank, the Rosselkhoz Bank, is the former state agricultural bank that merely changed its name.[86] In addition, four-fifths of the Russian commercial banks are owned by state-run enterprises.[87] For example, the state company that makes Lada cars has provided the founding capital and holds shares of the AvtoVAZ Bank, the country's third largest bank.[88] Banks without political ties, therefore, are difficult to find.

In addition, many banks are run by "the old communist elites, who have found a new way to exercise power,"[89] despite prohibitions against employment of government and state officials in a bank's management.[90] This occurs because the old system is not yet broken. The communists have all the money and connections necessary to establish a bank while it is very difficult for ordinary people to do the same. The All-Russia Exchange Bank, for example, has a former Soviet parliamentary spokesman on its board and conducts its board meetings in the country house owned by Stalin's police chief.[91]

. . .

### 2. The Independence of Commercial Banks from the Interference of the Central Bank

The laws require the Central Bank to create favorable conditions for the stable performance of commercial banks. They also prohibit the Bank of Russia from interfering in banks' current operations,[92] making the banks legally independent in their day-to-day activities. This independence, however, is often limited because of heavy dependence on

---

83. *See id.* art. 8; Central Bank Law, *supra*, art. 22.

84. *See* Commercial Banking Law, *supra*, art. 8.

85. *See* Russian Banks: Overgrown and Underfinanced, *supra* at 84.

86. *See id.*

87. *See id.*

88. *See id.* at 85.

89. *Id.* at 84.

90. *See* Commercial Banking Law, *supra*, art. 8.

91. *See* Russian Banks: Overgrown and Underfinanced, *supra* at 84.

92. *See* Central Bank Law, *supra*, art. 22.

funds[93] that the Bank of Russia loans to the banks at low interest rates.[94] This dependence results from the shortage of other sources from which banks can get cash for transactions and withdrawals on a reliable basis.

. . .

D. The Central Bank's Regulation of the Monetary and Credit System

The laws designate a single federal monetary and credit policy as one of the most important functions of the Bank of Russia.[95] The Central Bank must carry out this function by regulating cash and non-cash emissions in the country.[96] In practice, however, "[t]he Bank of Russia is not ensuring the reliable organization of monetary circulation and cash services, especially the distribution of the money supply throughout the republic, something that is provoking social outbursts in certain regions of Russia."[97] . . .

E. Invasion of Foreign Ownership

The new legislation contains no restrictions on foreign ownership of banks. But quite the opposite is true elsewhere. The leading Western countries restrict the opening of foreign-owned banks. . . . In Russia, the situation is further complicated by the inability of commercial banks -- which do not have adequate personnel, equipment, or experience to compete with foreign banks. As a result, many commercial banks may go bankrupt, which potentially may lead to a widespread banking crisis. Thus, opening the financial markets to foreigners risks both loss of independence for Russia and a danger of a banking crisis....

## Kirsten Storin Doty, Economic Legal Reforms as a Necessary Means for Eastern European Transition into the Twenty-First Century,
33 Int'l Law. 189 (1999)

B. Economic Reform: Banking to Bankruptcy

Certainly the transition from communism to capitalism and democracy requires unprecedented changes in all areas of the law. In fact, many areas did not even exist under communism, as capitalist notions such as competition and profit maximization held no meaning in the popular psyche. Regarding the business and economic realm, two areas of law prove to be especially important for transition--banking and bankruptcy.

Banking laws are the first crucial subject for post-communist economic reform. Before the revolutions of 1991 and 1992, the banking sectors in this region served at the behest of the state, usually subsidizing inefficient and failing entities. New banking schemes must embrace capitalist ideals and become independent systems supporting efficient market actors. The second area needing reform is that of bankruptcy. In theory and practice,

---

93. *See* Sundararajan, *supra* at 12; *see also* Rosett, *supra* at A7 ("[B]anks [that receive low interest rate loans] serve as conduits for bargain-price credit to sectors with strong lobbies in Parliament. So, in effect, the central bank has been playing middleman for a Parliament-driven industrial policy.").

94. *See* Russian Banks: Overgrown and Underfinanced, *supra* at 85.

95. *See* Central Bank Law, *supra*, art. 5. . . .

96. *See* Central Bank Law, *supra*, art. 11.

97. Central Bank Scored for Arbitrary Actions, *supra*. For example, "[the central] bank's June 26 decision to withdraw pre-1993 roubles to support the inflation-hit economy caused chaos across Russia and nine other ex-Soviet states with which it shares the rouble." Russian Banks Seek Review of Central Bank Powers, Reuters, Aug. 27, 1993, available in LEXIS, Banks Library, Allbnk File.

bankruptcy is a newborn concept in Eastern Europe--because communism had no need for such a process.

As post-communist countries continue to struggle with transition, economic law reforms, especially in the areas of banking and bankruptcy, become most important. Interestingly, banking and bankruptcy represent two opposites on a business spectrum. One side represents new growth and financial support, while the other side represents the end of inefficient and unsuccessful ventures. An in-depth review of both areas of legal reform is necessary to highlight their importance in transition. . . .

1. Banking Laws

A country's economic and financial stability depends greatly upon its banking system.[227] Such a banking system requires a reliable monetary system and a stable banking structure. In order to make the transition to a market economy, the banking structure relies on a bank's ability to serve as a financial intermediary between creditors and debtors, its ability to encourage payments between newly emerging financial actors, and its ability to supply the maximum capital necessary to finance infrastructure improvements and investments needed in order for these countries to compete globally.[229] Post-communist countries will experience legal instability if: (1) gaps in the law are not filled; (2) a poor reporting system is not streamlined; and (3) the existing complex bureaucracy is not exterminated.[230] Even today, most post-communist banking systems remain underdeveloped.[231] Such systems lack the degree of competition and regulation of efficient and modern banking systems. Despite the slow progress, most countries indicate a willingness to continue to reform their inefficient systems.[233]

In a free market economy, stability and efficiency usually require the creation of a central bank to guide a commercial banking system.[234] Such a system involves numerous branch banks, which keep the nation's wealth, create lending, and control inflation through the interest rate. Independent management is another aspect of a central bank system. Many post-communist countries not only look to foreign models for guidance, but in many cases have direct involvement from foreign advisors.[237]

---

227. *See* Susanna V. Pullen, Comment, *United States Foreign Banking and Investment Opportunities: Branching Out to the Russian Federation*, 8 Transnat'l Law. 159, 161 (1995).

229. *See* William L. Horton, Jr., Note, *The Perils of Universal Banking in Central and Eastern Europe*, 35 Va. J. Int'l L. 683, 684 (1995).

230. *See* Pullen, *supra* note 227, at 161 n. 11.

231. *See id.* at 162. Before 1989, post-communist countries had no effective modern banking system. *See* John Linarelli, *The European Bank for Reconstruction and Development and the Post-Cold War Era*, 16 U. PA. J. Int'l Bus. L. 373, 374 (1995). To institute a market economy, Eastern Europe has had to develop and reconstruct an all-encompassing banking system in a very short period of time. *See id.* at 375.

233. *See* Pullen, *supra* note 227, at 162. The willingness to convert to market economies can also be seen by the various organizations that exist to aid in the transition. *See* Linarelli, *supra* note 231, at 376. The European Bank for Reconstruction and Development (EBRD) is one such organization. *See id.*

234. *See* Pullen, *supra* note 227, at 162. Eastern European banking systems in general were very primitive. Under communist central planning, the extent of the domestic banking system was little more than a single bank used to house people's savings. . . .

237. *See id.* at 164. One example of such foreign advice is the U.S. Federal Reserve's involvement in Russia. *See id.* Along with a few major commercial U.S. banks, the Federal Reserve founded an advisory group named the Russian-American Bankers Forum. *See id.*

In instituting new banking systems, post-communist countries have employed two basic models, that of the United States and that of the Federal Republic of Germany.[238] The German approach, which many commentators suggest is used more frequently, involves the creation of universal banks. Such banks render a broad range of services including taking deposits, making loans, underwriting securities issues, performing mutual fund transactions, making investment recommendations, dealing in collectible coins and precious metals, and facilitating real estate sales.[240] Bulgaria, the Czech Republic, Poland, and Romania have followed the German model.[241] Most of Europe follows this model in one way or another.[242] The U.S. model divides commercial banking functions and investment banking functions between entities.[a] Hungary has chosen to follow the U.S. model.[244] Both the German and U.S. models have proponents and critics. Eight years after initial integration of the new banking systems, both models continue to experience new problems mixed with occasional successes.

Since the German model is more pervasive in new banking systems in post-communist countries, it is useful to outline the benefits and drawbacks associated with this model. The first benefit associated with the German universal model is the increased stability banks gain when they diversify their lines of business.[246] A second benefit is increased efficiency due to economies of scale and scope.[247] This means that many skills in banking apply across the board to different areas, making it efficient for one firm to service all needs under one roof.[248] Supporters of a universal banking model cite a third benefit, that of reduced regulatory costs.[249] Since all banks provide the same services, both the banks and

---

238. *See* Horton, *supra* note 229, at 684.

240. *See* Michael Gruson & Uwe H. Schneider, *The German Landesbanken*, 1995 Colum. Bus. L. REV. 337, 340; *see also* Horton, *supra* note 229, at 684.

241. *See* Horton, *supra* note 229, at 684. One of the reasons for this model's appeal is the geographical proximity of the Eastern European region to the Federal Republic of Germany. *See id.* A second reason for this model's appeal is the strength and rapid accession of this model during the early nineteenth century. *See id.* at 685.

242. *See id.* European countries such as France, Italy, Switzerland, and the United Kingdom all allow some version of universal banking as advanced by the German model. *See id.* at 686 n. 8. For specifics on German and U.K. banking systems, see Bill Shaw & John R. Rowlett, *Reforming the U.S. Banking System: Lessons from Abroad*, 19 N.C. J. Int' L. & Com. Reg. 91, 111-17 (1993).

a. This model was dramatically altered in November 1999, with the enactment of the Gramm-Leach-Bliley Act. *See* Note **9.25**, *infra* (discussing Gramm-Leach-Bliley).

244. *See* Horton, *supra* note 229, at 684.

246. *See id.* at 686. *See also* Gruson & Schneider, *supra* note 240, at 340, 343-44. *See id.* at 340 n. 2 for limits on activities in which banks may engage. Critics warn that investment banking is demonstrably much riskier than commercial banking, a fact that calls into question the stability of such banks. . . .

247. *See* Horton, *supra* note 229, at 687.

248. *See id.* at 688. Critics suggest that the universal model is not the only model to achieve economies of scale. *See id.* Banks of different specialties can simply associate with one another in a type of "narrow banking." *Id.* (quoting Robert E. Litan, *Commentary*, 19 Brook. J. Int'l L. 229, 230 (1993)).

249. *See id.*; *see also* Gruson & Schneider, *supra* note 240, at 344. *See generally* Gerhard Wegen, *Transnational Financial Services--Current Challenges for an Integrated Europe*, 60 FORDHAM L. REV. 91, 93 (1992) (different types of regulations).

the regulators only have to consider one set of rules.[250] A fourth benefit created by the German model is that such a system can increase the likelihood of finding alternative private solutions to individual businesses' economic needs,[251] the lender bank having an interest in the ailing business. Such an interest might cause the lender to be more flexible in allowing longer adjustment periods than a disinterested third party lender.[253] A final benefit offered by the German model is its ability to increase banks' incentives to monitor management in businesses in which they retain equity.[254]

Critics of the German model cite three main drawbacks in addition to those mentioned in the footnotes. As already hinted, a universal banking system involves increased risks associated with securities underwriting and other non-traditional services that make these already fragile banking systems even more unstable.[255] Another negative aspect involves decreased competition in the marketplace for financial services.[256] A final drawback extends from the fact that the universal system promotes a tight network of banks and businesses, a situation in which insider trading may be too seductive to resist.[257]

Roughly a decade after emerging out of the chaos of communism, many Eastern European banking systems still face basic challenges. Many banks in the region are still unable to adequately, if at all, allocate credit and turn a profit.[259] Some of the regions' banking systems are not yet even functioning at a minimum level. Commentators suggest that by lending to inefficient state-owned entities, such countries as the Czech Republic, Hungary, and even Poland retard their rates of transition to market economies, endangering these newly emerging states.[261] Even in 1999, Eastern European banking faces enormous problems in establishing viable and competitive systems. Obviously, it is very difficult to create new

---

250. *See* Horton, *supra* note 229, at 688. For general German regulations, *see* Edward L. Rubin, *Discretion and its Discontents*, 72 Chi.-Kent L. Rev. 1299, 1324-25 (1997).

251. *See* Horton, *supra* note 229, at 688.

253. *See id.* at 689. Faultfinders suggest that this scheme sets up the potential for "throw[ing] good money after bad." *Id.*

254. *See id.* at 690. *But see* Jonathan R. Macey & Geoffrey P. Miller, *Corporate Governance and Commercial Banking: A Comparative Examination of Germany, Japan, and the United States*, 48 Stan. L. Rev. 73, 74-76 (1995); *cf.* James H. Freis, Jr., *An Outsider's Look into the Regulation of Insider Trading in Germany: A Guide to Securities, Banking, and Market Reform in Finanzplatz Deutschland*, 19 B.C. Int'l & Comp. L. Rev. 1, 7 (1996).

255. *See* Horton, *supra* note 229, at 690. Proponents of the German model do not find this mixture dangerous. *See* Rubin, *Discretion and its Discontents*, *supra* note 250, at 1324.

256. *See* Horton, *supra* note 229, at 691.

257. *See id. See* Freis, *supra* note 254, at 30-31, for examples of German problems regarding insider trading. Antitrust laws may be able to address some of these concerns. *See* Horton, supra note 229, at 691. *See generally* Bernard Black & Reinier Kraakman, *A Self-Enforcing Model of Corporate Law*, 109 Harv. L. Rev. 1911, 1913-14 (1996).

259. *See* Horton, *supra* note 229, at 702 (citing Mark M. Nelson, *East Europe's Banks Remain State-Run, Despite Grand Plans for Privatizations*, Wall St. J., Nov. 8, 1994, at A18 (quoting Karla Brom, financial services specialist, Institute for EastWest Studies, Prague)).

261. *See id.* at 703. To their benefit, such countries as Czechoslovakia, Hungary, and Poland have instituted numerous banking laws in line with the European community's directives. *See* Wegen, *supra* note 249, at 95.

financial systems from scratch.[263]

**Notes and Comments 1.14.** The project of reform taking place within the EU is obviously very different from the project of reform taking place in Russia and elsewhere in Central and Eastern Europe. The EU is transforming national economies and often closed regulatory systems into a single market. In Russia, a national system based on one set of socio-political presuppositions is being transformed into a market-based economy modeled on Western practices. In pursuing this project, Russia has focused on the "creation of a well-functioning two-tier competitive banking system wherein a central bank focuses on regulating overall credit and interest rates, while newly established commercial banks assume the responsibility of deposit and loan transactions with businesses and households." Why is this viewed as a key to creating a Western-style, market-based economy? Does a banking system have some special role to play in a modern market-based economy?

**1.15.** The preceding excerpts identify a number of practical problems in Russia's efforts to establish a modern regulated system of banking. What recommendations would you make to improve the current system, in light of its stated goals?

**1.16.** *Emergence of the NAFTA approach to international bank regulation.* The following excerpt describes the rules applicable to international banking under the North American Free Trade Agreement (NAFTA). How does the NAFTA approach compare with that of the EU? With that of Russia?

## Michael P. Malloy, Financial Services Regulation After NAFTA
*in* Kevin Kennedy (ed.), The First Decade of NAFTA:
The Future of Free Trade in North America (2004)

1. Introduction

In 1994 the North American Free Trade Agreement (NAFTA) entered into force.[1] NAFTA created a free trade area, eliminating tariffs on trade in goods between participants in the area, but not a customs union with a common external tariff, like the European Union (EU).[2] Beyond these improvements in traditional trade regulation, NAFTA is the first regional trade agreement to include financial services[3] within its scope.[4] This arrangement

---

263. *See* Horton, *supra* note 229, at 703. For examples of Polish and Hungarian banking laws, see William M. Berenson, Current Legal Issues Affecting Central Banking, 29 Geo. Wash. J. Int'l L. & Econ. 337, 345-49 (1995) (book review).

1. North American Free Trade Agreement (NAFTA), Dec. 8, 1993, 107 Stat. 2057, 32 INT'L LEGAL MAT. 289, 605 (1993) [hereinafter NAFTA].

2. On the differences between free trade areas and customs unions, see General Agreement on Tariffs and Trade (GATT) General Agreement on Tariffs and Trade, Oct. 30, 1947, 61 Stat. A-11, T.I.A.S. 1700, 55 U.N.T.S. 187, art. XXIV, ¶ 8 (defining "customs union" and "free trade area" for purposes of GATT) [hereinafter GATT].

3. For NAFTA purposes, the term "financial services" is broadly defined to mean "a service of a financial nature, including insurance, and a service incidental or auxiliary to a service of a financial nature." NAFTA, art. 1416. For convenience of analysis and presentation, the remainder of this essay will focus primarily upon banking as an example of a "financial services" regime affected by NAFTA. For broader perspectives on financial services and NAFTA, see, *e.g.*, Bradly Condon, *Smoke and Mirrors: a Comparative Analysis of WTO and NAFTA Provisions Affecting the International Expansion of Insurance Firms in North America*, 8 CONN. INS. L.J. 97 (2001/2002) (analyzing interaction of NAFTA and WTO with U.S. federal and state regulation affecting risk reduction and market entry strategies in North American insurance market); Anna V. Morner, *Financial Services and Regional Integration: A Comparative Snapshot*, 7 L. & BUS. REV. AM. 549

is important on its own terms, of course, because of its potential impact on the regulatory systems of the three NAFTA member states, Canada, Mexico and the United States. It is also of particular interest as a precursor of the General Agreement on Trade in Services (GATS) of the World Trade Organization (WTO).[5]...

2. Significance and Impact of the NAFTA Arrangement

The effect of NAFTA on the banking industries of each member country varies.[8] While Chapter 14[, concerning member state regulation of financial services,] mandates access for financial services firms of one member state in the markets of each of the other member states, differences in methods of entry are tolerated by Chapter 14, and these differences persist. Canada and Mexico permit access to their respective financial services markets through de novo subsidiary entrance, while the United States permits access by de novo subsidiary entrance, by acquisition of an indigenous institution, or through direct branching into the U.S. market.[9]

In fact, very little changed as a result of NAFTA with respect to Canada and Mexico's access to the U.S. market. "The United States already extended national treatment to all foreign banking organizations doing business in the United States. Before the treaty both Canadian and Mexican banks had access to the U.S. market on terms similar to those available to all other countries."[10]

With respect to access to the Canadian banking market, U.S. and Mexican banks remained effectively excluded from control of the relatively larger "Schedule I" banks, which are subject to a "widely-held" rule barring control of more than ten percent of bank voting stock by any person or group of persons.[12] Relatively smaller "Schedule II" banks were available for acquisition of control by non-Canadians.[13] Like Schedule I banks, U.S.-

---

(2001) (providing comparative analysis of regional strategies for harmonization of financial services regulation). The *locus classicus* in this regard remains Joel P. Trachtman, *Trade in Financial Services under GATS, NAFTA and the EC: A Regulatory Jurisdiction Analysis*, 34 COLUM. J. TRANSNAT'L L. 37 (1995).

4. *See* Valerie J. McNevin, *Policy Implications of the NAFTA for the Financial Services Industry*, 5 COLUM. J. INT'L ENVTL. L. & POL'Y 369, 380 (1994); Art Alcausin Hall, *International Banking Regulation into the 21st Century: Flirting With Revolution*, 21 N.Y.L. SCH. J. INT'L & COMP. L. 41, 56 (2001).

5. General Agreement on Trade in Services, 15 April 1994, Agreement Establishing the World Trade Organization, Annex 1B, *reprinted in*, 33 INT'L LEGAL MAT. 1167 (1994) [hereinafter GATS]. *See generally* Alcausin Hall, *International Banking Regulation*, 21 N.Y.L. SCH. J. INT'L & COMP. L. at 57 ("If NAFTA works well, it may become a model for other regional and international efforts"). For a useful comparison of the principal features of the WTO and the NAFTA, see Larry A. DiMatteo, *et al.*, *The Doha Declaration and Beyond: Giving a Voice to Non-trade Concerns Within the WTO Trade Regime*, 36 VAND. J. TRANSNAT'L L. 95, 151-153 (2003). [The effect of GATS on bank regulation is discussed in Chapter 3, § 3, *infra*.]

8. On the impact of NAFTA on Canada and Mexico, see Morner, *Financial Services and Regional Integration*, 7 L. & BUS. REV. AM. at 564-565.

9. [Eric J. Gouvin, *Cross-Border Bank Branching Under the NAFTA: Public Choice and the Law of Corporate Groups*, 13 CONN. J. INT'L L. 257, 258-259 (1999).]

10. *Id.* at 270.

12. *See* Gouvin, *Cross-Border Bank Branching Under the NAFTA*, 13 CONN. J. INT'L L. at 265 (citing Bank Act, R.S.C., ch. B-1.01, §370(2)). On the "widely-held" rule, see Eric J. Gouvin, *The Political Economy of Canada's "Widely Held" Rule for Large Banks*, 32 L. & POL'Y INT'L BUS. 391 (2001).

13. Gouvin, *Cross-Border Bank Branching Under the NAFTA*, 13 CONN. J. INT'L L. at 266.

and Mexican-owned Schedule II banks originally could branch *across* Canada, but their parents could not branch directly *into* Canada.[14] In 1998, Canada changed its branching policy to permit foreign banks to branch into Canada, but, as Gouvin has argued, Canadian branching policy may "appear liberal, but on closer inspection are rather difficult for foreign banks to exploit."[15]

So far as the banking market is concerned, the probable winners under NAFTA are U.S. and Canadian banks seeking access to the under-banked and historically exclusionary Mexican market, where these banks could now branch throughout the country and affiliate with a wide range of financial services firms.[17] . . . NAFTA offers U.S. and Canadian banks the opportunity to establish wholly-owned Mexican subsidiaries. However, "to prevent foreign domination of the Mexican banking industry,"[21] Mexico negotiated some protections in the NAFTA for its domestic banking sector.[22] Exigent economic circumstances eventually overtook these protectionist measures, and Mexico liberalized the foreign ownership rules in December 1998.[23]

In practical terms, has Chapter 14 had any noticeable effect on cross-border investment in the banking sector, or in direct cross-border banking? Morner suggests that "[e]vidence of growth exists in cross border financial services provision."[24]

3. Structure of NAFTA with respect to Financial Services Regulation

3.1. Overall Structure

NAFTA established three basic and distinct "mechanisms for the resolution of disputes by international tribunals."[28] These are [Chapter 11, concerning investment and investment disputes, which provides] for binding arbitration of an investment dispute between a host NAFTA member state and an investing NAFTA country resident that is a national of another NAFTA member state; the Chapter 19 provisions that replace judicial review of member state decisions with respect to antidumping and countervailing duties;

---

14. *Id.* at 270-271.

15. Gouvin, *The Political Economy of Canada's "Widely Held" Rule*, 32 L. & POL'Y INT'L BUS. at 398.

17. [Karen MacAllister, Comment, *NAFTA: How the Banks in the United States and Mexico Will Respond*, 17 HOUS. J. INT'L L. 273, 287 (1994).]

21. Gouvin, *Cross-Border Bank Branching Under the NAFTA*, 13 CONN. J. INT'L L. at 271.

22. Specifically, Mexico preserved aggregate capital limits for foreign subsidiaries. NAFTA, Annex VII (B) (9), 32 INT'L LEGAL MAT. at 774. However, "[a]t the end of [a six-year] transition period, the aggregate capital limits would have lapsed subject only to Mexico's reserved right to impose additional limitations on banking competition if foreign banks control 25% of the Mexican banking market before January 1, 2004." Gouvin, *The Political Economy of Canada's "Widely Held" Rule*, 32 L. & POL'Y INT'L BUS. at 392 n.8, *citing* Ramon Bravo H., *Mexican Legal Framework Applicable to Operations Involving Financial Services*, 25 ST. MARY'S L.J. 1239, 1249-51 (1994).

23. *See* Gouvin, *The Political Economy of Canada's "Widely Held" Rule*, 32 L. & POL'Y INT'L BUS. at 393-395 (discussing historical background of bank liberalization in Mexico). *See generally* Robert Del Cueto & Luis D. Martinez, *The Restructuring of Banking and Financial Services in Mexico: The Legal Reform of the Mexican Financial System*, 7 U.S.-MEX. L.J. 59, 62-63 (1999) (describing bank reform measures approved by Mexican Congress).

24. Morner, *Financial Services and Regional Integration*, 7 L. & BUS. REV. AM. at 579.

28. Patricia Isela Hansen, *Judicialization and Globalization in the North American Free Trade Agreement*, 38 TEX. INT'L L.J. 489, 489 (2003).

and, the Chapter 20 provisions for resolution of disputes between NAFTA member states.[29] Significantly, none of these provisions directly applies to disputes concerning the impact of a NAFTA member state's regulation of participation by a NAFTA country resident in the state's financial services market. These disputes are channeled through the specialized provisions of Chapter 14.

3.2.  Nested provisions with respect to Services

Perhaps the most interesting NAFTA institutional arrangement with respect to services is the way in which the relevant provisions are "nested," like a textual матрёшка ("*matryoshka*") doll. . . . For purposes of this essay, the innermost doll represents the Chapter 14 provisions, which directly pertain to financial services and include dispute resolution and substantive provisions specific to such services. This is nested within the doll that represents the Chapter 12 provisions that apply to services generally, but *not* to financial services. Both of these are nested within the Chapter 11 provisions pertaining to investment and investment disputes, and all of these dolls are nested within the generally applicable Chapter 20 provisions with respect to institutional arrangements and dispute settlement procedures. . . .

By its own terms, Chapter 11, governing investment, services and other matters, "does not apply to measures adopted or maintained by a [member state] to the extent that they are covered by Chapter Fourteen. . . ."[30] However, Chapter 14 itself expressly incorporates by reference articles 1109 through 1111, 1113 and 1114, and makes them "a part of" Chapter 14.[31] These incorporated provisions require free and undelayed transfers relating to investments;[32] establish minimum legal standards for expropriations[33] and special formalities and information requirements;[34] permit denial of NAFTA investment protections in certain cases where investors of a non-member state own or control an enterprise that is itself an investor of a member state;[35] and, clarify the environmental regulatory authority of the member states with respect to "any measure otherwise consistent with" Chapter 11.[36] Chapter 14 also incorporates by reference the dispute settlement provisions of Chapter 11,[37] but "solely for breaches" by a member state of the other incorporated provisions of Chapter

---

29. For general discussion of NAFTA dispute resolution, see David Lopez, *Dispute Resolution under NAFTA: Lessons from the Early Experience*, 32 TEX. INT'L L.J. 163 (1997). For extended analysis, see Guillermo Aguilar Alvarez & William W. Park, *The New Face of Investment Arbitration: NAFTA Chapter 11*, 28 YALE J. INT'L L. 365 (2003) (presenting exhaustive analysis of NAFTA Chapter 11 arbitration of investment disputes; persuasively arguing that Chapter 11 enhances asset protection with net gains for host states and foreign investors); Marcia J. Staff & Christine W. Lewis, *Arbitration under NAFTA Chapter 11: Past, Present, and Future*, 25 HOUS. J. INT'L L. 301 (2003) (providing critical analysis of published Chapter 11 cases); Maria Alejandra Rodriguez Lemmo, *Study of Selected International Dispute Resolution Regimes, with an Analysis of the Decisions of the Court of Justice of the Andean Community*, 19 ARIZ. J. INT'L & COMP. L. 863, 867-868, (2002) (providing comparative analysis of NAFTA dispute resolution regimes).

30. NAFTA, art. 1101, ¶ 3.

31. *Id.*, art 1401, ¶ 2.

32. *Id.*, art. 1109.

33. *Id.*, art. 1110.

34. *Id.*, art. 1111.

35. *Id.*, art. 1113.

36. *Id.*, art. 1114.

37. *Id.*, arts. 1115-1138.

11 discussed previously.[38] Strictly speaking, then, Chapter 11 does not itself apply to investment activity with respect to financial services enterprises.

NAFTA Chapter 12 requires national treatment for service providers from other NAFTA member states[39] and MFN treatment.[40] Each member state is also required to accord to service providers "the better of the treatment" required by these two obligations as the case may be[41]—a sort of more-favored-provision (MFP) requirement. Member states may not require service providers to establish or maintain a representative office or to be resident as a condition for providing cross-border services within their respective jurisdictions.[42] However, by its own terms, Chapter 12 "does not apply to . . . financial services as defined in Chapter Fourteen. . . ."[43] Nevertheless, Chapter 14 itself expressly incorporates by reference article 1211, and makes it "a part of" Chapter 14.[44] Like article 1311 in the investment context, article 1211 permits denial of "the benefits of this Chapter" in certain cases where a service provider of another NAFTA member state is an enterprise owned or controlled by nationals of a non-member state.[45] Hence, this benefits denial provision would apply to providers of financial services.

. . . With respect to disputes arising under Chapter 14, the dispute settlement procedures of Chapter 20 apply as modified by article 1414.[49] The modifications include separate provisions concerning establishment and maintenance of a roster of possible financial services panelists[50] and their optional and mandatory use in disputes arising under Chapter 14.[51] Furthermore, if a panel finds that a measure of a party is NAFTA-inconsistent, suspension of benefits in response to the measure[52] is affected by article 1414. The Chapter 20 norm is that the complaining party "should first seek to suspend benefits in the same sector"[53] as that in which the complaint arose, but if that party "considers it not practicable or effective"[54] to do so, it may suspend in other sectors.[55] This norm is replaced by Chapter 14 with the following mandatory rules: (1) if the challenged measure affects only the financial services sector, then only benefits with respect to that sector may be suspended;

---

38. *Id.*, art. 1401, ¶ 2.

39. *Id.*, art. 1202.

40. *Id.*, art. 1203.

41. *Id.*, art. 1204.

42. *Id.*, art. 1205.

43. *Id.*, art. 1201, ¶ 2(a).

44. *Id.*, art. 1401, ¶ 2.

45. *Id.*, art. 1211, ¶ 1.

49. *Id.*, art. 1414, ¶ 1.

50. *Id.*, art 1414, ¶¶ 2-3.

51. *Compare id.*, art. 1414, ¶ 4(a), (b)(i) (providing for optional selection of financial services roster members) *with id.*, art. 1414, ¶ 4(b)(ii) (requiring chair of panel drawn from financial services roster if respondent party invokes exception in article 1410). On article 1410 exceptions, see text and accompanying notes 84-88, *infra*.

52. *Per* NAFTA, art. 2019, ¶ 1.

53. *Id.*, art. 2019, ¶ 2(a).

54. *Id.*, art. 2019, ¶ 2(b).

55. Apparently, the only relief a disputing party would have is the invocation of a panel to determine if the suspension is "manifestly excessive," *id.*, art. 2019, ¶ 3, but not to review the complaining party's choice of sector for benefits suspension.

(2) if the challenged measure affects the financial services sector and another sector, then suspension of benefits in the financial services sector must be equivalent to the effect of the measure on that sector; and, (3) if the financial services sector is not affected by the challenged measure, then no suspension of benefits can occur in that sector.[56]

As these modifications suggest, the most significant substantive effect of the nesting arrangement is that, for the most part, financial services are treated as *sui generis*. While Chapter 14 constitutes the only detailed substantive provisions that apply to financial services, the integrated "Chapter 14" that emerges from the nested provisions is more elaborate than just the enumerated articles of Chapter 14. . . . This treatment probably insulates regulation of financial services under NAFTA from whatever growing body of NAFTA jurisprudence generally applies to investment and to trade in services. Hence, unlike the situation under the GATS, where specific provisions about trade in financial services–and about trade in services generally–are fed back into the generally applicable dispute resolution devices of the Understanding on Dispute Settlement, NAFTA disputes concerning trade in financial services are likely to form a separate body of principles and procedures distinct from the principles and procedures generally applicable to NAFTA disputes.

4. Chapter 14 and Financial Services
4.1. Chapter 14 Obligations

Chapter 14 applies to national measures relating to financial institutions of one NAFTA member state operating in another member state, nationals of one member state who are investors in financial institutions in another member state, and cross-border trade in financial services.[57] It requires member states to ensure the observance of obligations by self-regulatory organizations that play a role in access to their respective financial services market.[58] This is a potentially more stringent requirement than the corresponding GATS requirement that WTO members take "such reasonable measures as may be available" to them.[59]

4.1.1. Market Access

The chapter does not impose any binding market access requirements.[60] Article 1403(1) recognizes in principle that an investor of a member state should be permitted to establish a financial institution in another member state's territory.[61] Article 1403(2)

56. *Id.*, art 1414, ¶ 5(a)-(c).

57. *Id.*, art. 1401, ¶ 1(a)-(c).

58. *Id.*, art. 1402.

59. GATS, art. I, ¶ 3.

60. Trachtman describes the provisions of NAFTA article 1403 as "weak market access requirements." Trachtman, *Trade in Financial Services*, 34 COLUM. J. TRANSNAT'L L. at 81. In any event, the market access provisions of article 1403 do not apply to (*i*) existing or promptly renewed non-conforming measures specified in Section A of each party's schedule to Annex VII or to non-conforming local government measures, *per* NAFTA, art. 1409, ¶ 1; or, (*ii*) reservations under Annex VII, Section B, *per id.*, art. 1409, ¶ 2.

61. Nevertheless, article 1403, paragraph 4 authorizes member states to require local incorporation (as opposed to direct cross-border branching) as the method of establishment and to impose terms and conditions on entry consistent with the national treatment requirements of article 1405. Note, however, that paragraph 3 does provide that when the United States allows *interstate* banking in substantially all of the U.S. market, the member states will review the market access provisions "with a view to adopting arrangements permitting investors of another [member state] to choose the juridical form of establishment of commercial banks." On the current U.S. rules with

recognizes "the principle that an investor of another [member state][62] should be permitted to participate widely in a [member state's] market."[63] The article lists specific rights to be accorded to foreign investors–the right to provide a range of financial services through separate entities as required by regulation; the right to expand geographically; and, the right to own financial institutions notwithstanding otherwise applicable limitations on foreign ownership.

### 4.1.2. Cross-Border Trade

NAFTA does freeze barriers to *cross-border* trade in financial services.[64] Member states are required to permit their respective residents and nationals to purchase financial services cross-border.[65] However, they are not required to permit cross-border financial service providers to do business or solicit in their respective territories.[66] Furthermore, if a member state does permit such activity, it may require registration of such providers and of financial instruments.[67]

### 4.1.3. National Treatment

Chapter 14 does require national treatment with respect to financial services,[68]

---

respect to interstate banking, see 1 MICHAEL P. MALLOY, BANKING LAW AND REGULATION §§ 2A.7-2A.7.4 (1994 & Cum. Supp.) (discussing interstate branching); 3 MALLOY, BANKING LAW, *supra*, §§ 8.7-8.7.2, 9.6-9.6.6 (discussing interstate banking).

62. Article 1403 uses the term the term "investor of another Party," which for these purposes is defined to mean "an investor of another Party engaged in the business of providing financial services in the territory of that Party." NAFTA, art. 1403, ¶ 5. In turn, for purposes of Chapter 14 generally, the term "investor of a Party" is defined to mean "a Party or state enterprise thereof, or a person of that Party, that seeks to make, makes, or has made an investment." *Id.*, art. 1416.

63. Presumably, this participation would include newly developed financial services. *See* note 69, *infra* (discussing national treatment with respect to new financial services under article 1407).

64. NAFTA, art. 1404, ¶ 1. "Cross-border trade" in financial services is defined for these purposes as financial services provided from a home member state to a person of another member state, or by a national of a member state in the territory of another member state. *Id.*, art. 1416. The provisions of article 1404 do not apply to (*i*) existing or promptly renewed non-conforming measures specified in Section A of each party's schedule to Annex VII or to non-conforming local government measures, *per id.*, art. 1409, ¶ 1; or, (*ii*) reservations under Annex VII, Section B, *per id.*, art. 1409, ¶ 2. Canada and the United States reserved against each other with respect to cross-border trade in securities services. *Id*, Annex VII, Schedule of Canada, Section B; *id.*, Annex VII, Schedule of the United States, Section B.

65. *Id.*, art. 1404, ¶ 2.

66. *Id.* The parties agreed to consult on further liberalization of such cross-border trade by the year 2000. *Id.*, art. 1404, ¶ 4.

67. *Id.*, art. 1404, ¶ 3. This authority is in addition to any prudential regulation imposed on cross-border service providers pursuant to article 1410, ¶ 1. On the effect of article 1410, see text and accompanying notes 84-88, *infra*.

68. NAFTA, art. 1405, ¶ 1. On application of the national treatment obligation to cross-border provision of financial services (*i.e.*, without establishment of a local office), see *id.*, arts. 1404, 1405, ¶ 3. Specifically, a member state "may require the registration of cross-border financial service providers of another [member state] and of financial instruments." *Id.*, art. 1404, ¶ 3. A national treatment obligation would apply to types of financial services that may not yet exist. Article 1407, ¶ 1, provides that financial institutions of another member state are to be permitted to provide any new financial service of a type similar to what a member state permits its own financial institutions to provide in like circumstances under its domestic law. For these purposes, "new financial service" is defined to mean

subject to significant exceptions.[69] This obligation applies in favor of investors from any other NAFTA member state,[70] as well as to financial institutions from any other member state and investments made by investors of any other member state in financial institutions.[71] The national treatment obligation applies to the establishment, acquisition, expansion, management, conduct, operations and sale or other disposition of any member state financial institution, and any investment in a financial institution in the territory of another member state.[72] These obligations apply both at the level of national regulation and at the level of state or provincial regulation.[73] A member state's national treatment obligation is satisfied, "whether different or identical" treatment is accorded to financial institutions or cross-border service providers, so long as "the treatment affords equal competitive opportunities."[74]

### 4.1.4. MFN Obligations

NAFTA also contains an MFN obligation running in favor of each of the other two member states, with respect to the treatment of non-members.[75] Underscoring the exclusion

---

a financial service not provided in the Party's territory that is provided within the territory of another Party, and includes any new form of delivery of a financial service or the sale of a financial product that is not sold in the Party's territory.

*Id.*, art. 1416. A member state may determine the institutional/juridical form in which the service may be provided, and may also require prior local authorization, which may only be denied for prudential reasons. *Id.*, art. 1407, ¶ 1. Presumably, this provision will become of increasing significance in light of the authorization of "activities financial in nature" contained in the Gramm-Leach-Bliley Act, Pub. L. No. 106-102, Nov. 12, 1999, §§ 103(a), 205, 113 Stat. 1338, 1342-1350, 1391 (1999) (codified at 12 U.S.C. §§ 1843(k)-(o), 15 U.S.C. § 78o(i)) (GLBA). For analysis and discussion of the GLBA financial activities provisions, see 1 MALLOY, BANKING LAW, *supra* note 62, §§ 1.4.8.11-1.4.8.12.2); 3 MALLOY, BANKING LAW, *supra* note 62, §§ 8A.2.1-8A.2.3). Note that, like the provisions of article 1405, the "new financial service" provisions of article 1407 are limited by the reservations specified in article 1409, ¶¶ 1-2. On the effect of article 1409 in this regard, see note 70, *infra*.

69. The national treatment provisions of article 1405 do not apply to (*i*) existing or promptly renewed non-conforming measures specified in Section A of each party's schedule to Annex VII or to non-conforming local government measures, *per* NAFTA, art. 1409, ¶ 1; or, (*ii*) reservations under Annex VII, Section B, *per id.*, art. 1409, ¶ 2. In addition, reservations to articles 1102, 1103, 1202 and 1203 are deemed to be reservations to article 1405. *Id.*, art. 1409, ¶ 4. *See also* text and accompanying notes 84-88, *infra* (discussing exceptions).

70. *Id.*, art. 1405, ¶ 1.

71. *Id.*, art. 1405, ¶ 2.

72. *Id.*, art. 1405, ¶¶ 1, 2.

73. *Id.*, art. 1405, ¶ 4. Where operations take place in more than one state or province, the article requires application of "the most favorable treatment" as the baseline for the national treatment obligation. *Id.*, art. 1405, ¶ 4(c)-(d).

74. *Id.*, art. 1405, ¶ 5. For these purposes, defines the term "equal competitive opportunities" to mean "treatment that does not disadvantage financial institutions of another party in their ability to provide financial services as compared with the ability of the party's own financial institutions, in like circumstances." *Id.*, art. 1405, ¶ 6. Note that "[d]ifferences in market share, profitability or size do not in themselves establish a denial of equal competitive opportunities, but such differences may be used as evidence regarding whether a Party's treatment affords equal competitive opportunities." *Id.*, art. 1405, ¶ 7.

75. *Id.*, art. 1406. The MFN obligations of article 1406 do not apply to (*i*) existing or promptly renewed non-conforming measures specified in Section A of each party's schedule to Annex VII or to non-conforming local government measures, *per id.*, art. 1409, ¶ 1; or, (*ii*) reservations under Annex VII, Section B, *per id.*, art. 1409, ¶ 2. In addition, reservations to articles 1102, 1103, 1202 and

of financial services from the application of the Chapter 12 services provisions, Chapter 14 does not have a provision comparable to article 1204, requiring MFP treatment for service providers of other member states.[76]

### 4.1.5.  Composition of Senior Management and Board

NAFTA does contain two straightforward restrictions on the regulatory discretion of member states.[77] No member state may impose a nationality requirement with respect to senior management of a financial institution of another member state.[78] Likewise, no member state may impose a requirement that "more than a simple majority of the board of directors" of the financial institution of another member state be nationals or residents of that state.[79]

### 4.2.  Dispute Resolution with respect to Financial Services

. . . One important effect of the nesting of NAFTA provisions concerning services is that NAFTA Chapter 14 provisions with respect to financial services will generally prevail over any contrary investment provisions of NAFTA Chapter 11.[82] This gives special significance to NAFTA Article 1410(1)(a), under which a NAFTA host state can invoke prudential concerns related to protection of depositors and financial markets, maintenance of safe and sound financial institutions, and integrity and stability of the host state's financial system in adopting measures that might otherwise violate NAFTA investment protections.[83]

Obviously, as affirmative defenses available to a host state regulating entry into its financial services market by foreign firms that are NAFTA country residents, these exceptions suggest a serious potential for non-tariff barriers to trade in services that may be practically impervious to redress under NAFTA.[84] It is reasonable to view the emergence of

---

1203 are deemed to be reservations to article 1406. *Id.*, art. 1409, ¶ 4. With respect to the United States, and with respect to cross-border trade in securities services, Canada reserved against the MFN requirement. *Id.*, Annex VII, Schedule of Canada, Section B, ¶ 1.

76. *See* text and accompanying note 42, *supra* (discussing MFP treatment).

77. These restrictions do not apply to (*i*) existing or promptly renewed non-conforming measures specified in Section A of each party's schedule to Annex VII or to non-conforming local government measures, *per* NAFTA, art. 1409, ¶ 1; or, (*ii*) reservations under Annex VII, Section B, *per id.*, art. 1409, ¶ 2.

78. *Id.*, art. 1408, ¶ 1. This would include "senior managerial or other essential personnel." *Id.*

79. *Id.*, art. 1408, ¶ 2.

82. *See* NAFTA, art. 1101(3) (providing that Chapter 11 "does not apply to measures adopted or maintained by a [NAFTA member state] to the extent that they are covered by Chapter 14 (Financial Services)"); *id.* art. 1112 (providing that "in the event of any inconsistency between [Chapter 11] and another Chapter, the other Chapter shall prevail to the extent of the inconsistency"). *Cf. id.*, art. 1401(2) (rendering "minimum standard of treatment" requirement of Article 1105 inapplicable to investment in financial services); *id.*, art. 1410, ¶ 4 (allowing prevention or limitation of certain transfers involving financial institutions or cross-border financial services providers, notwithstanding article 1109).

83. NAFTA art. 1410(1)(a).

84. See Constance Z. Wagner, *The New WTO Agreement on Financial Services and Chapter 14 of NAFTA: Has Free Trade in Banking Finally Arrived?*, 5 NAFTA: L. & BUS. REV. AM. 5, 23 (1999) (stating that non-tariff barriers to trade are much less transparent than barriers caused by tariffs). Such non-tariff barriers would include, *inter alia*, licensing procedures and requirements and differing regulatory standards. *Id. See also* Eric J. Gouvin, *Cross-Border Bank Branching Under the NAFTA*, 13 CONN. J. INT'L L. at 259 (suggesting that bank regulators and financial services firms will seek to preserve existing non-tariff barriers).

the nested structure of the dispute resolution provisions as resulting in the preservation of potential non-tariff barriers to trade. However, Aguilar Alvarez and Park have offered a principled explanation for the nesting that justifies the nested structure, at least in part. They argue:

> NAFTA's drafters recognized that they were combining a trade agreement with an investment treaty, and that arbitration of investment disputes might have a disruptive effect on other NAFTA commitments, including trade in goods and procurement. Moreover, there was recognition that investment arbitration posed special problems with respect to vital national prerogatives in tax and financial services.
>
> Multiple compromises were made to reconcile NAFTA's competing goals. For example, inconsistencies between Chapter 11 and other NAFTA chapters are resolved in favor of the latter, and investment is limited by a definition indicating what "investment means" rather than what "investment includes."[85]

Nevertheless, even if there are salutary reasons for insulating financial services regulation under NAFTA from other, generally applicable dispute settlement regimes, the brute fact remains that the affirmative defenses thus preserved under NAFTA Chapter 14 do invite manipulation as non-tariff barriers to trade in financial services.[86] If such issues are raised in a NAFTA arbitration, on request of a member state the arbitral tribunal[87] is required to refer the question of the validity of the defenses to an investor's claim to the NAFTA Financial Services Committee.[88] The Committee's decision as to the validity of the defenses

---

85. Aguilar Alvarez & Park, *The New Face of Investment Arbitration*, 28 YALE J. INT'L L. at 389 (footnotes omitted).

86. *Cf.* Trachtman, *Trade in Financial Services*, 34 COLUM. J. TRANSNAT'L L. at 121 (arguing that "[t]he most intractable barrier to trade in financial services is varying and overlapping prudential or protective regulation"). This problem does not even take into account the additional opacity added to trade in financial services under NAFTA as a result of Canadian and Mexican reservations with respect to financial services. Gouvin has observed:

> When representatives of the United States, Canada, and Mexico signed [NAFTA] in 1992, the schedule of reservations and commitments on the annex relating to financial services gave the distinct impression that Mexico and Canada were not inclined to embrace fully the idea of free and unfettered trade in banking services. While NAFTA broke new ground by setting out a principles-based approach to liberalized trade in financial services, Canada and Mexico made it clear that they intended to keep in place the non-tariff barriers that ensured that their largest banks would remain under domestic control.

Gouvin, *The Political Economy of Canada's "Widely Held" Rule*, 32 L. & POL'Y INT'L BUS. at 391 (footnotes omitted).

87. The term "tribunal" refers generically to whatever body of arbitrators is deciding the particular dispute. *Compare* NAFTA, art. 1126, *with* NAFTA, art. 1415(2).

88. The various committees to which particular matters can be referred are listed in NAFTA, Annex 2001.2(A), 32 INT'L LEGAL MAT. at 698. The Financial Services Committee is provided for in NAFTA, art. 1414, but its function is relatively unspecified. It consists of officials of the governmental agencies responsible for financial services. *Id.*

is binding on the tribunal.[89] If the Committee does not render a decision within sixty days of the referral, either the host state or the investor's home state may request the convening of an arbitral panel[90] under the institutional (*i.e.*, state-to-state) dispute resolution provisions of NAFTA to resolve the question of validity of defenses.[91] The panel's report is binding on the tribunal.[92]

> 5. Conclusions

. . . [F]inancial services regulation after NAFTA will likely continue to look substantially like regulation before NAFTA. Does this mean, for financial services, "after NAFTA, laughter?" This would be an overbroad conclusion. After NAFTA, specific obligations do apply to regional financial services activity, but the practical effects of these obligations are likely to emerge only incrementally, and those effects will have an impact largely cushioned by the intervention of reasonable measures domestically imposed for prudential reasons.

**Notes and Comments 1.17.** Imagine that the Mexican Government authorizes a Mexican-chartered bank to operate a fleet of armored trucks to travel around North America, accepting deposits from local depositors at convenient truck stops along major highways. The U.S. Government seeks to prohibit the operation of the trucks on U.S. territory as unauthorized branches. *Cf. Dickinson v. First Nat. Bank in Plant City, Fla.*, 396 U.S. 122, *rehearing denied*, 396 U.S. 1047 (1968) (holding armored car messenger service constituted unauthorized "branch" under 12 U.S.C. § 36(f) and Fla. Stat. Ann. § 659.06(1)(a)). Mexico invokes NAFTA article 1202 and *In Re Cross-border Trucking Services* (United States v. Mexico) USA-MEX-98-2008-01 (NAFTA Arbitral Panel, Feb. 6, 2001) (determining that national treatment obligations of NAFTA article 1202 prevail over U.S. concerns about highway safety and environmental impact). Would the U.S. prohibition of the armored Mexican bank trucks be upheld under NAFTA?

**1.18.** Imagine that the Lion Group of Canada sought to acquire control of Mortuary National Bank. The U.S. Comptroller of the Currency, under 12 U.S.C. § 1817(j)(7) (D), disapproves the acquisition on the ground that

> the competence . . . of any acquiring person or of any of the proposed management personnel indicates that it would not be in the interest of the depositors of the bank, or in the interest of the public to permit such person to control the bank,

relying on *Sletteland v. Federal Deposit Ins. Corp.*, 924 F.2d 350 (D.C.Cir. 1991) (upholding disapproval of control of bank by 26-year-old son of controlling shareholder of bank, with no college degree and no banking experience). Alternatively, assume that the Board of Governors of the Federal Reserve System, under 12 U.S.C. § 1842(c)(2), (5), denies the application of the Lion Group to acquire a majority of the common stock of Mortuary National Bank in exchange for Lion Group common stock on the ground that

> competence [and] experience . . . of the officers, directors, and principal

---

89. NAFTA, art. 1415(2).

90. This arbitral panel must be constituted in accordance with article 1414, chosen from a special financial services roster. NAFTA, art. 1415(3).

91. NAFTA, arts. 1415(3), 2008-2022.

92. In the absence of such a dispute resolution request within ten days of the expiration of the sixty-day period, the tribunal may itself adjudicate the claim.

shareholders of the company

was insufficient, relying on *Board of Governors of Federal Reserve System v. First Lincoln-wood Corp.*, 439 U.S. 234 (1978) (upholding denial of bank holding company application due to finding of company as insufficient source of financial and managerial strength for subsidiary bank). Lion Group, invoking NAFTA article 1102 and *The Loewen Group, Inc. v. United States of America*, International Centre for Settlement of Investment Disputes, Case No. ARB(AF)/98/3, *reprinted in* 42 INT'L LEGAL MAT. 811 (2003), claims a violation of national treatment under NAFTA. article 1102. Would the U.S. bank regulator's decision to disapprove the acquisition be upheld under NAFTA?

**1.19.** The contemporary developments traced in the preceding excerpts all conform with traditional Western models of banking. The following excerpt describes a model based on a radically different set of principles.

## J. Michael Taylor, Islamic Banking–The Feasibility of Establishing an Islamic Bank in the United States
40 Am. Bus. L.J. 385 (2003)

### I. Introduction

. . .

In contrast to what those in the United States might consider traditional banking, Islamic banking derives its rules and practices from religious sources. Having recognized this, the reader should understand that Islamic banking truly is in a developmental stage pertaining to the interaction between (1) Western financial practices which are based, in large part, on the role of interest and (2) the dictates of the *Qur'an* and the Islamic Prophet Mohammed, which together are interpreted to forbid interest.[2] . . .

### II. Banking According to Islamic Practices

A. Role of Islamic Tenets and Teaching in a Muslim's Financial Affairs

. . . Islam forbids Muslims from engaging in activities involving "interest or riba, gambling, pornography, alcohol, drugs, and other things which Islam considers abhorrent."[7] While the existence of such prohibitions restricts certain activities, the broader principles of Islam also must be practiced for a Muslim to live a life that adheres to the will of Allah. Generally speaking, a practitioner of Islam should not act in violation of *Shari'a*[a] prohibitions while striving at the same time to act in accordance with other general Qur'anic principles.

Because Islamic principles extend to all aspects of a Muslim's life, the financial affairs of each Islamic practitioner are necessarily implicated by *Shari'a* principles. While Islamic economic principles permit property ownership and wealth accumulation, these

---

7. Muazzam Ali, Publisher's Note to 1 A Compendium of Legal Opinions on the Operations of Islamic Banks iv (Yusuf Talal DeLorenzo ed., 1997).

a. [Note 4 in the original.] *Shari'a* (alternatively spelled *Shari'ahi*) is defined literally as "the Way" and represents the divine law as revealed in the Qur'an and the teachings of the Prophet Mohammed, as recorded in the *Sunna*. See Michael J.T. McMillen, *Islamic Shari'ah-Compliant Project Finance: Collateral Security and Financing Structure Case Studies*, 24 Fordham Int'l L.J. 1184, 1189 (2001). Attached as an Appendix to this [excerpt] is a brief glossary of terms pertinent to Islamic banking; the terms in the glossary are defined and cited throughout the [excerpt] but are provided in a compiled format for easy reference by the reader.

concepts differ from how they are understood in some Western, capitalist systems. One definition of Islamic economics sets forth that economics should be "the methodology of how man uses resources and means of production to satisfy all his worldly needs, according to a predetermined God-given code in order to achieve the greatest equity."[8] Arising out of this definition are five unique characteristics of how financial affairs are addressed in the Islamic faith:

> 1. Man, being an agent and not an original owner, is not a free agent in his exploitation of resources and must use methods and means within a framework given to him in the satisfaction of his economic means.
> 2. The guiding principle of economic activity is the overall good of society and nature (environmental).
> 3. Individual man, being part of the overall fabric, must be given consideration for his well being.
> 4. Equitable reward must be given to man according to his effort (to all according to their efforts, and from all according to their abilities).
> 5. Certain activities in the exploitation of resources, having over-all [sic] detrimental effects, are proscribed.[9]

Thus, Islam permits the development of wealth, but through socially conscious means. Successful enterprises that earn a profit are laudable, but the practitioner must not forget that Islamic principles direct financial resources should be utilized for bettering the condition and well-being of others.

B. Islamic Prohibition of Interest

Arising out of the Islamic tenet of concern for the community flow the anti-abuse concepts applicable in financial affairs. The primary example of this anti-abuse concept is the Qur'anic prohibition of *riba*, which "seeks to prevent usurious conditions in exchanges and loans."[11] A literal translation of the Arabic word *riba* is an "increase,"[12] and under *Shari'a* the term "refers to the premium that must be paid by the borrower to the lender along with the principal amount as a condition for the loan or for an extension in its maturity."[13]

---

8. HRH Prince Muhammad Al-Faisal Al-Saud, Islam and the West: Towards a New International Economic Order (Speech given at UNESCO in Paris on Nov. 14, 1985), reprinted in Journey Towards Islamic Banking: A Collection of Articles Talks and Discussions by HRH Prince Muhammad Al-Faisal Al-Saud and Muazzam Ali on Islamic Banking and Finance 35, 36 (Shahzad Sheikh ed., 1996).

9. *Id.*

11. Barbara L. Seniawski, Note, *Riba Today: Social Equity, The Economy, and Doing Business Under Islamic Law*, 39 Colum. J. Transnat'l L. 701, 702 (2001).

12. *Id.* at 708 ("[*Riba*] represents a situation of unjust enrichment. Thus, *riba* arises from an unequal (unfair) exchange, namely, an increase over the principal amount lent or the quantity traded."). Seniawski goes on to argue that charging an interest rate less than that of inflation is outside the scope of riba and thus should not be a forbidden Islamic practice. *Id.* at 709. This position appears to be at odds with the traditional interpretation of riba put forth by Islamic scholars. . . .

13. Fuad Al-Omar & Mohammed Abdel-Haq, Islamic Banking: Theory, Practice & Challenges 8 (1996) (also stating, "*Riba* is an Arabic word meaning, literally, increase, addition, expansion or growth, but it is not increase or growth as such which Islam has prohibited."). *See also* Fatwa of Kuwait Finance House, al Fatawa al Shar'iyah, in 2 A Compendium of Legal Opinions on the Operations of Islamic Banks 125, Question 270 (Yusuf Talal DeLorenzo ed., 1997) (Stating in partial response to the question, "What is the *riba* that is prohibited by the *Qur'an*?" that "Perhaps the most reasonable definition of the *riba* (prohibited) in the *Shari'ah* is that it is excess for which no

. . .

Although minority positions differ, the traditional Islamic view of the prohibition of *riba* is that it includes interest. "There is a consensus among Muslim scholars that this prohibition extends to any and all forms of interest and there is no difference between interest-bearing funds for purposes of consumption or investment."[16]

The prohibition of *riba* does not mean that money may not be lent under Islamic law; the prohibition simply forbids unearned profit (or stated otherwise, profit without expected, normal business risk). According to Islamic jurists, the prohibition of riba is aimed at avoiding "the illegality of all forms of gain or profit which were unearned in the sense that they resulted from speculative or risky transactions and could not be precisely calculated in advance by the contracting parties."[17] Thus, and in summary, riba represents unearned profit and squarely includes interest under traditional Islamic thought.

C. Development of the Islamic Banking Movement

The modern Islamic banking institution is a relatively recent development. Its existence rises directly out of the Islamization movement:

> Recently, however, under a growing trend of religious conservatiism, many Islamic countries have realized that continuing to follow Western banking and finance methods undermines their adherence to Islamic ideals. Because of this surge in Islamization, a movement to reform the practices of financial institutions in many Islamic countries has developed.[19]

In fact, the trend of reforming financial practices in Islamic countries has expanded into the establishment of *Shari'a*-compliant financial institutions[20] in the United Kingdom, the United States, and non-Islamic countries found in Europe. Estimates are that more than two hundred and fifty Islamic financial institutions operate throughout the world.

The Islamic banking movement is the embodiment of proactive efforts by Muslim practitioners to direct their money toward financial institutions adhering to Islamic principles.[21] . . . The establishment of Islamic banks in the modern age began with the

---

compensation is given in the contract.").

16. Al-Omar & Abdel-Haq, supra note 13, at 7.

17. McMillen, supra note 4, at n. 2 (quoting Noel J. Coulson, Commercial Law in the Gulf States: The Islamic Legal Tradition 11 (1984)).

19. Sharawy, supra note 2, at 156.

20. . . . Islamic financial institutions can include banks, investment entities, investing partnerships, mutual fund management companies, etc. See, e.g., IBFNET: Islamic Financial Institutions, at http://islamic-finance.net/bank.html (last visited Apr. 25, 2002) (providing links to a sampling of Islamic Financial Institutions that provide various *Shari'a*-compliant products).

21. The Institute of Islamic Banking and Insurance writes:

> The revival of Islamic banking [as practiced predominantly in the Muslim world throughout the Middle Ages] coincided with the world-wide celebration of the advent of the 15th Century of Islamic calendar (*Hijra*) in 1976. At the same time financial resources of Muslims, particularly those of oil producing countries, received a boost due to rationalization of the oil prices, which had hitherto been under the control of foreign oil Corporations. These events led Muslims to strive to model their lives in accordance with the ethics and philosophy of Islam.

The Institute of Islamic Banking and Insurance, ISLAMIC BANKING - What is Islamic Banking?, available at http://www.islamic- banking.com/ibanking/whatib.php (last visited Oct. 23, 2001).

creation of the first "Islamic Bank," as that term is now used, in Egypt in 1960.[25] Commentators recognize, though, that the "industry" of Islamic banks and Islamic financial institutions truly began to develop in the 1970s.

In less than forty years, Islamic banking has grown from a mere idea into a substantial subset of the financial industry. Islamic financial institutions are approaching the mark of managing $200 billion in assets worldwide, and growth rates indicate that this mark will soon be surpassed. The appeal of Islamic banking has taken root worldwide. ...

D. Financial Techniques and Practices Compliant with Islamic Banking Requirements

It has been stated that "[i]n the Islamic bank, the seventh century meets the 21st, as the partnering of investors and entrepreneurs continues to be an effective and economically viable technique."[28] This quote highlights the reliance of Islamic banking practices on tradition[29] while still recognizing the viability of the partnership model at the base of financial transactions in a banking arena. Not every partnership arrangement and apparently *riba*-free transaction, however, is consistent with Islamic teachings.

An important aspect of the Islamic banking movement is the implementation of a system to insure that the actions of Islamic banking institutions comply with *Shari'a*. In practice, the business side of a bank works in tandem with a supervisory board of religious advisors to review proposed financial transactions.[31] These supervisory boards exist to

---

25. *See* [Gohar Bilal, *Islamic Finance: Alternatives to the Western Model*, 23 Fletcher F. World Aff. 145, [145] (1999)] (recognizing that the first modern Islamic bank was established in Egypt in 1960 and closed in 1967 due to political reasons, but that the establishment of the bank "had an important impact on further development of Islamic finance").

28. Munir Barakat & Eugene Sarver, Comment: Western Banks Taking 1st Steps Into Islam's 'No Interest' World, Am. Banker, Jan. 30, 1997, at 9.

29. Concerning the applicability of tradition in Islamic banking, one commentator writes:

> The practitioners of Islamic finance must follow four basic rules to develop, innovate and offer Islamic financial products: 1) avoid interest or unlawful gain, called "*riba*;" 2) avoid excessive risk taking, called "*gharar*;" 3) recognize that money is not a commodity; 4) recognize that money has no time value, that is to say, money doesn't change in value as time passes.

Bilal, *supra* note [25], at 146.

31. As summarized by one commentator:

> [I]t is important to note that most significant Islamic financial institutions have *Shari'ah* supervisory boards, committees, and advisors ("*Shari'ah* Boards"), comprised of one or more Islamic scholars that have particular expertise in economic and financial transactions. These *Shari'ah* Boards will often examine in detail both the structure of a proposed transaction or financial product and the documentation giving effect to that transaction or product. . . . Given that *Shari'ah* Board determinations are *fiqh* (human comprehension of *Shari'ah*, the divine law), there can be variations in interpretation and implementation from one *Shari'ah* Board to another with a multiplicity of views on a specific issue. These variations occur even though *Shari'ah* scholars in this period strive to achieve a consensus on difficult and novel issues, such as those involved in the development of new financial instruments and products. Islamic investors, be they financial institutions or individual investors, rely heavily on the involvement of *Shari'ah* Boards in the structuring and documentation of a transaction or financial product and may request that the *Shari'ah* Board's fatwa of approval be provided before an investment is made.

McMillen, *supra* note 4, at 1190-91.

provide guidance on religious law to the bankers of the institution. Typically, when confronted with a novel question, the banker presents a question to the *Shari'a* Board and a fatwa, or statement of guidance interpreting Islamic law, is returned. Efforts have been undertaken to compile and index these fatwas to help develop uniformity in the relatively young field of Islamic banking.

Through the use of *Shari'a* boards and the process of trial and error, Islamic financial institutions today have developed several tools for the carrying out of interest-free banking transactions based on this partnership model.[33] These tools allow a financial institution to invest its funds in compliance with *Shari'a* principles, for the benefit of the institution's shareholders and customers.[34] For the sake of clarity, each tool is discussed below:

### 1. *Murabaha* (Financing on a "Cost-Plus" Basis)

A *murabaha*, although typically used as a finance method, "is actually a sale contract."[36] In a typical murabaha transaction, the financial institution acts as a middle-man and purchases a good requested by its customer; the financial institution then turns around and sells the good to the customer at the acquisition cost plus a profit. The customer agrees to pay for the good over a stated period in installments, but if there is a default (unlike in traditional financing) the customer is only liable to the financial institution for the contracted sale price (not any fees or interest calculations otherwise available in typical financing arrangements).

A key component of *murabaha* financing is the requirement that the financial institution actually own the good before transferring title to its customer. This is because the financial institution assumes some risk to justify its profit, making the profit more than just disguised interest. The customer could always refuse to accept the good obtained for it by the financial institution, causing the financial institution to find an alternative buyer with the accompanying costs of storage, marketing, and overhead.[40] As a result, *murabaha* financing is available to trusted customers of a financial institution[41] and to those that provide some

---

33. Otherwise stated, the "Islamic financial system allows for the replacement of interest by a return obtained from investment activities and operations that actually generate wealth." [Imtiaz Pervez, Islamic Banking and Finance, reprinted in Information Sources on Islamic Banking and Economics 1980-1990 at 13 (S. Nazim Ali & Naseem N. Ali eds. 1994).]

34. See Abdelgadir Banaga et al., External Audit and Corporate Governance in Islamic Banks: A Joint Practitioner-Academic Research Study 13 (1994). See also James M. Fry & J. Michael Taylor, Foreign Direct Investment in Arab Countries: A Guide to Better Understanding Islamic Financial Doctrine, 4 Permanent Ct. Arb./Peace Palace Papers (Int'l Bureau Permanent Ct. Arb. ed., forthcoming 2002) (providing a general summary of Islamic-compliant investment vehicles available to investors in the Middle East).

36. Bilal, *supra* note [25], at 153.

40. "Although [*murabaha*] appears to permit interest under disguise, it is a permissible form of finance because '[t]he bank's profit premium is justified by the risk it incurs by allowing the client to refuse to accept a commodity procured on their behalf by the bank.'" Sharawy, supra note 2, at 170 (quoting Shahrukh Rafi Khan, Profit and Loss Sharing: An Islamic Experiment in Finance and Banking 64 (1987)). . . .

41. *See* [Chibli Mallat, *Commercial Law in the Middle East: Between Classical Transactions and Modern Business*, 48 Am. J. Comp. L. 81, 131 (2000) ] ("[T]he main vehicle or "product" of Islamic banks is the so-called *murabaha*, which is none other than a facilitation by the bank of short-term loans, mostly in commercial export-import operations, for their most trusted clients.").

form of guarantee or collateral.[42]

### 2. Ba'i Bithaman Ajil (Deferred Payment Financing)

*Ba'i bithaman ajil* involves a credit sale of goods on a deferred payment basis. At the request of its customer, the financial institution purchases an existing contract to buy certain assets on a deferred payment schedule and then sells the goods back to the customer at an agreed upon price, including a profit. The payments by the financial institution to the original supplier of the goods are progressive, as the goods are manufactured or purchased. The financial institution's customer "can repay in lump sum or make installment payments over an agreed-upon period."[44]

### 3. Istisna (Commissioned Manufacturing)

Similar to *ba'i bithaman ajil* transactions, *istisna* contracts involve the payments by a financial institution to a developer or contractor as a job (typically involving construction or manufacturing) is completed.

### 4. Ijara (Lease Financing)

*Ijara* is a leasing arrangement whereby the financial institution "purchases an asset and leases it to a Client."[46] Most typically used with regard to equipment, the financial institution owns the asset throughout the lease period and the customer pays the financial institution a rental fee. The customer may purchase the asset either during or at the end of the lease period, but the customer is not required to do so.[48] There are differences between a conventional lease and *ijara*, in that with the *ijara*:

> 1) a lease/hire begins the day the asset is delivered to the client (not the date the contract is signed as with the [conventional lease]), 2) the lessee is not liable for the full rent if the asset is destroyed (the bank takes out insurance on the asset and factors in the cost of insurance at the time the rent is fixed), and 3) the purchase at the end of the contract cannot be made binding.[49]

Even with these slight differences, the *ijara* is fairly similar to traditional lease financing.

### 5. Musharaka (Partnership Arrangement)

*Musharaka* means "partnership" and typically involves a business undertaking where the financial institution provides a percentage of the capital needed by its customer with the understanding that the financial institution and customer will proportionately share in profits and losses in accordance with a formula agreed upon before the transaction is consummated. The customer contributes to the business undertaking by providing some capital and sweat equity represented by its management efforts and "know-how."

### 6. Mudaraba (Venture Capital Transactions)

Like *musharaka* transactions, *mudaraba* involve business undertakings where the

---

42. *See* Banaga et al., *supra* note 34, at 13-14 ("The applicant may be asked to provide some form of guarantee. Some banks may also require postdated cheques. The applicant may be required to make a down-payment as a margin deposit to show his commitment.").

44. [Bilal, *supra* note 25, at 154.]

46. Pervez, *supra* note [33], at 23.

48. *See* Pervez, *supra* note [33], at 24 ("Subject to fulfillment of certain conditions, the Client has the option to purchase the asset during the term of the lease. The optional purchase price declines over the term of the agreement. As the customer is not obliged to purchase the asset financed under the Ijara contract at the expiry of the lease, Islamic bank will not normally takes [sic] substantial risk with respect to its residual value at the lease tail-end.").

49. Bilal, *supra* note [25], at 154.

financial institution provides capital to an entrepreneur, but in the mudaraba transaction the financial institution provides all of the capital and the customer provides only sweat equity and know-how. The financial institution is guaranteed an agreed upon percentage of the profits and bears all of the risk of monetary loss.[53] The entrepreneur serves as the financial institution's agent for investing and utilizing the funds in the venture.[54]

Often, a manager, called a *Mudarib*, is appointed to manage the business venture at the base of the *mudaraba*:

> In many cases the bank acts as a *Mudarib* for a fee. The bank also acts as a *Mudarib* in relation to its deposits in investing the depositors' money in various schemes assuming the role of the capital provider. The *Mudarib* may be held liable for losses from actions that are beyond those originally provided for in the contract.[55]

Just as with traditional venture capitalism, this is a "high risk" mode of financing. As such, a financial institution must use "extraordinary efforts to carefully scrutinize [the] feasibility and projections" provided by the customer along with undertaking stringent credit analyses and risk assessments. In part due to the increased risk and in part due to the capital requirements, "under the most optimistic accounts, mudaraba schemes represent less than 10% of [worldwide Islamic] banking operations."[57]

### 7. *Qarde Hasan* (Benevolent Financing)

*Qarde hasan* financing occurs when the financial institution provides a loan free of charge, typically with the intent to provide financial assistance to ailing institutions or to provide humanitarian assistance to individuals. In exchange, the customer provides an unconditional obligation that the financial institution will be repaid, and often collateral is required. The financial institution may also "charge a small fee to cover its administrative costs."

Arising out of the communal aspect existing in the Islamic approach to economics, *qarde hasanah* "are for the benefit of the individual and the society at large."[61] Essentially, *qarde hasanah* represent loans to deserving persons and entities with the only requirement being repayment of the principal and administrative fees. Such loans "do not constitute a significant source of financing by Islamic banks" and fall into the charitable activities of these institutions.

The financial tools set forth above serve to promote the growth of principal without implicating the forbidden use of *riba*. Notably, not all of these tools will be available in the banking system of the United States, but some are remarkably similar to financial vehicles already approved by banking regulators, and as such, easily can be utilized in conformance with existing regulations.

### III. Why Should Investment and Banking Interests in the United States be

---

53. *See* Sharawy, *supra* note 2, at 169 ("In exchange for the use of the capital, the entrepreneur agrees to give a specified share of future profits to the investors, who in turn are exclusively responsible for any loss to the capital while in the care of the entrepreneur.").

54. *See* Bilal, *supra* note [25], at 156 (also recognizing that "the structure of the *mudaraba* contract provides an opportunity to participate in large projects, sharing in both the risks and profits.").

55. *See* Banaga et al., *supra* note 34, at 15.

57. Mallat, *supra* note [41], at 131.

61. Shahid Hasan Siddiqui, Islamic Banking: Genesis & Rationale; Evolution & Review; Prospects & Challenges 53 (1994).

Concerned with Islamic Banking Practices?

Over one billion people worldwide are believed to be followers of the Islamic faith.[64] . . .

The financial field of Islamic banking is estimated to be "growing 15% a year."[66] Worldwide, the relatively new concept of formalizing Islamic banking practices in Islamic banks was estimated, by 1997, at "close to $100 billion in deposits and investments."[67] Other estimates from 1998 are that Islamic banks had assets approximating $181 billion.[68] It is true that these figures of total assets, when considered from a worldwide perspective, are small in relation to total banking assets, but the figures are significant, especially when one notes that the asset base has been steadily increasing.

. . . [T]he Islamic banking movement is gaining momentum worldwide.[70] This also means that alternatives to traditional Western, interest-based banking are becoming available to Muslims in the United States who have a desire to comply with the strictures of Islamic financial practices; until recently, such persons had no convenient method to conduct their financial affairs with a non-western style financial institution. Now that financial services are available through the internet,[71] Islamic practitioners are no longer limited to the banking and investment vehicles offered by the financial advisor down the block who may or may not know of the existence of an Islamic lending or investment tool.

One commentator writes:

> The phenomenon of globalization extends the ramifications of the *riba* prohibition beyond the circles of Islamic scholars and jurists, and Muslim and Islamic countries to international investors and businesses who are parties to transnational transactions. In 1997, Pakistan, Iran, Turkey, Malaysia, and Indonesia were among seven Muslim countries who formed the D-7, a group whose goal is "to promote mutual economic cooperation, build a common market, and develop capital markets" according to the principles of Islamic law. Being well-versed in such fields is of immense help to the foreign lawyer; each transaction performed contributes to and shapes the fledgling legal specialization of Islamic banking and finance.[72]

---

64. *See* Barakat & Sarver, *supra* note 28, at 9 (estimating the number of Muslims world-wide to be one billion); Jennifer Weitzman, New Portal Points Muslims to Approved Providers, Am. Banker, Mar. 30, 2000, at 14 (estimating the number of Muslims world-wide to be 1.2 billion).

66. [*Id.*]

67. *Id. See also* Mallat, *supra* note [41], at 124 (quoting Ibrahim Warde, Islamic Finance in the Global Economy (2000)[manuscript quoted before published]) ("As of early 1999, Islamic financial institutions, (including banks and non-banks, securities firms, mutual funds, insurance companies, etc.) were present in more than 70 countries. Their assets exceeded the 200 billion dollars mark.").

68. Bilal, *supra* note [25], at 145.

70. Barakat & Sarver, *supra* note 28, at 9 ("There are now [as of 1997] about 150 banks and financial institutions that are fully, or partially, Islamic - with their own boards of wise men who ensure that bank practices adhere to religious law.").

71. *See, e.g.*, Weitzman, *supra* note 64, at 9 (discussing the establishment of the London-based Islamic financial portal IslamiQ.com and stating that the "portal includes IslamiQmoney.com, a source for Islamic banking, finance, and insurance products and services.").

72. Seniawski, *supra* note 11, at 719-20 (quoting Zamir Iqbal, Islamic Banking Gains Momentum, Expands Market and Competes with Conventional Banking in Arab States, 21 Middle E. Exec. Rep. 9, 21 (1998).

Like foreign attorneys, United States lawyers and bankers will benefit from an understanding of Islamic banking practices and be able to participate in additional transactions if they help charter Islamic banks in the United States or associate with these banks once established. . . .

APPENDIX: List of Terms and Definitions Pertinent to Islamic Banking

1. *Ba'i bithaman ajil*: A credit sale of goods on a deferred payment basis. At the request of its customer, the financial institution purchases an existing contract to buy certain assets on a deferred payment schedule and then sells the goods back to the customer at an agreed upon price, including a profit.

2. *Fatwa*: A statement of guidance interpreting Islamic law prepared by Islamic scholars.

3. *Ijara*: A leasing arrangement whereby a financial institution purchases an asset and leases it to its customer.

4. *Istisna*: Transactions involving the payment by a financial institution to a developer or contractor as a job (typically involving construction or manufacturing) is completed.

5. *Fiqh*: Human comprehension of *Shari'a* (divine law)

6. *Mudaraba*: A transaction between a financial institution and its customer akin to a venture capital transaction. The financial institution provides all of the capital and, as such, assumes all of the risk of loss. The customer acts as the financial institution's agent in utilizing the funds and also provides sweat equity (including know-how). The financial institution and customer share profits in accordance with a contractually stated percentage formula.

7. *Murabaha*: Financing by a financial institution on a "cost-plus" basis. The financial institution obtains title to a good on behalf of its customer, and then sells the good to the customer via installment payments at a contractually pre-arranged cost (set at the original cost of the good plus a reasonable profit for the financing institution).

8. *Musharaka*: Translated "partnership," a musharaka financing typically involves a business undertaking where the financial institution provides a percentage of the capital needed by its customer with the understanding that the financial institution and customer will proportionately share in profits and losses in accordance with a formula agreed upon before the transaction is consummated. The customer provides a percentage of the capital and sweat equity (know-how and management).

9. *Shari'a*: Divine law, perfect and immutable, as set forth in the *Qur'an* and the *Sunna* (recorded teachings of the Prophet Mohammed).

10. *Sunna*: Teachings of the Islamic Prophet Mohammed, recorded in writing only after having been deemed valid by religious scholars in the decades after the death of the Prophet Mohammed.

11. *Qarde hasan*: Financing that occurs when the financial institution provides a loan free of charge, typically with the intent to provide financial assistance to ailing institutions or to provide humanitarian assistance to individuals.

12. *Qur'an*: The holy book of the Islamic faith. The Qur'an is understood by Muslims to be the infallible word of God (*Allah*) providing instruction in both the religious and daily aspects of one's life.

13. *Riba*: Traditionally translated as "usury," the concept of *riba* includes interest and other forms of profit or gain that are not earned from work efforts.

**Notes and Comments 1.20.** Considering the Islamic banking model, is it in fact a "contemporary" regulatory system or a throwback to Medieval principles long since superseded in the West? Should it matter to the practitioner whether a banking enterprise operates under a regulatory system based upon a fundamental religious principle?

**1.21.** *What's in a name?* Taylor suggests parallels in Western banking practice to the various transactional devices employed by Islamic banks in reconciling their business with the prohibition of *riba* or "usury." If these parallels are accurate, does it matter what an Islamic bank calls the transaction?

**1.22.** The U.S. banking system also prohibits usury. *See* 12 U.S.C. §§ 84-85. How is this prohibition any different from the prohibition of *riba* in the Islamic banking model?

# Chapter 2

# National Supervision of International Banking

## 1. U.S. Federal Regulation

**Notes and Comments 2.1.** The regulatory structure governing U.S. domestic banking is extremely complex.[1] To some extent, that complexity carries over unchanged into U.S. regulation of international banking activities. However, additional twists and turns are introduced into the regulatory structure specifically because of the international dimension of these activities. We shall have occasion to explore some of these additions throughout this book. At this point, however, a basic overview of U.S. regulation of international banking activity may be useful. In this regard, consider Figure 2.1, *infra*. To make sense of the options presented in the figure, review it in connection with Comments 4.2 and 6.2, *infra*.

**2.2.** At the broadest level, one additional problem for a domestic bank regulator that is posed by the international dimension is the potential for international conflict of regulatory policy and law.[2] Nevertheless, it is probably safe to say that one fundamental objective for bank supervisors worldwide is to support the "lender of last resort" function activated whenever significant financial instability threatens the economy, in order to maintain public confidence in the banking or depository system.[3] Since domestic banking systems are interlinked, if not integrated, significant instability in any one market is potentially a problem for other markets. Yet beyond this, there often appears to be little if any agreement among national regulators as to approaches to regulation and supervision of depository institutions subject to their respective jurisdictions, particularly on a day-to-day basis. Certainly, the U.S. regulatory system is among the most thoroughgoing (or intrusive) in this regard. Hence, it may be sensible to focus upon what may be viewed as one of the most extreme approaches to bank supervision. In the case of U.S. bank supervision and regulation, the approach has been one of relatively close oversight of the bank-

---

1. *See, e.g.*, 1 MICHAEL P. MALLOY, BANKING LAW AND REGULATION ch. 1 (1994 & Cum. Supp.) (discussing U.S. regulatory environment).

2. Some of these conflicts will be explored in Chapters 10-11, *infra*.

3. In the United States, this function has traditionally been performed by the Federal Reserve System. The National Credit Union Adminstration also performs a similar function with respect to credit unions, as did the now defunct Federal Home Loan Bank Board, until 1989, with respect to savings associations.

## FIGURE 2.1

### DEPOSITORY INSTITUTIONS AND THEIR REGULATORS:
### INTERNATIONAL BANKING ACTIVITIES[d]

| A. ORGANIZATION & EXPANSION | | | | | |
|---|---|---|---|---|---|
| **Type of Institution** | **Chartering/ Licensing** | **Branching** | | **Acquisitions** | |
| | | **Intrastate** | **Interstate** | **Intrastate** | **Interstate** |
| Foreign Branch of U.S. Bank: | | | | | |
| National Bank | Federal Reserve | n/a | n/a | n/a | n/a |
| State Fed-Member Bank | Federal Reserve & States | n/a | n/a | n/a | n/a |
| Insured State Non-Member Bank | FDIC & States | n/a | n/a | n/a | n/a |
| Edge Act Corporation[e] | Federal Reserve | Federal Reserve | Federal Reserve | Federal Reserve | Federal Reserve |
| Agreement Corporation[f] | Federal Reserve & States | Federal Reserve & States | Federal Reserve & States | Federal Reserve & States | Federal Reserve & States |
| International Banking Facility[g] | n/a | n/a | n/a | n/a | n/a |

d. Source: Adapted and updated from Federal Reserve Bank of New York, *Depository Institutions and Their Regulators* (1987).

e. An Edge Act corporation is a bank incorporated under federal law, 12 U.S.C. §§ 611-631, and required to specialize in international and foreign banking. *Cf.* 12 C.F.R. § 28.2 (b).

f. An agreement corporation is a bank incorporated under state law that has an agreement or undertaking with the Board of Governors of the Federal Reserve System under 12 U.S.C. §§ 601-604a and is required to specialize in international and foreign banking. *Cf.* 12 C.F.R. § 28.2 (a).

g. An international banking facility (IBF) is not an entity, but a set of asset and liability accounts segregated on the books and records of a depository institution, United States branch or agency of a foreign bank, or an Edge Act or Agreement Corporation that includes only IBF time deposits and IBF extensions of credit. 12 C.F.R. § 204.8(a)(1).

| A. ORGANIZATION & EXPANSION – CONT'D | | | | | |
|---|---|---|---|---|---|
| **Type of Institution** | **Chartering/ Licensing** | **Branching** | | **Acquisitions** | |
| | | Intrastate | Interstate | Intrastate | Interstate |
| U.S. Branches & Agencies of Foreign Banks: | | | | | |
| Federal Branches & Agencies | OCC & Federal Reserve | OCC & FDIC | OCC & Federal Reserve | OCC & Federal Reserve | OCC & Federal Reserve |
| State Branches & Agencies | States & Federal Reserve | States & FDIC | States & Federal Reserve | States, Federal Reserve & FDIC | States & Federal Reserve |

| B. TRANSACTIONAL | | | |
|---|---|---|---|
| **Type of Institution** | **Reserve Requirements** | **Access to Discount Window** | **Deposit Insurance** |
| Foreign Branch of U.S. Bank: | | | |
| National Bank | Federal Reserve | n/a | n/a |
| State Fed-Member Bank | Federal Reserve | n/a | n/a |
| Insured State Non-Member Bank | Federal Reserve | n/a | n/a |
| Edge Act Corporation | Federal Reserve | n/a | n/a |
| Agreement Corporation | Federal Reserve | n/a | n/a |
| International Banking Facility | Federal Reserve | n/a | n/a |
| U.S. Branches & Agencies of Foreign Banks: | | | |
| Federal Branches & Agencies | Federal Reserve | Federal Reserve | FDIC |
| State Branches & Agencies | Federal Reserve | Federal Reserve | FDIC |

| C. SUPERVISION & REGULATION | | | | |
|---|---|---|---|---|
| **Type of Institution** | **Supervision & Examination** | **Prudential Limits, Safety & Soundness** | **Consumer Protection** | **Enforcement** |
| Foreign Branch of U.S. Bank: | | | | |
| National Bank | OCC | OCC | n/a | OCC |
| State Fed-Member Bank | Federal Reserve & States | Federal Reserve & States | n/a | Federal Reserve & States |
| Insured State Non-Member Bank | FDIC & States | FDIC & States | n/a | FDIC & States |
| Edge Act Corporation | Federal Reserve | Federal Reserve | n/a | Federal Reserve |
| Agreement Corporation | Federal Reserve & States | Federal Reserve & States | n/a | Federal Reserve & States |
| International Banking Facility | Federal Reserve | Federal Reserve | n/a | Federal Reserve |
| U.S. Branches & Agencies of Foreign Banks: | | | | |
| Federal Branches & Agencies | OCC & Federal Reserve | OCC & Federal Reserve | OCC & Federal Reserve | OCC & Federal Reserve |
| States Branches & Agencies | States, Federal Reserve & FDIC | States, Federal Reserve & FDIC | States & Federal Reserve | States, Federal Reserve & FDIC |

ing system, including maintenance of public confidence and stability by the establishment of restrictions on industry structure (*e.g.*, entry, competition, products,) and operations (*e.g.*, capital adequacy, lending limits, liquidity, interest rates).

Much of the maintenance is implemented through periodic examination and through reporting requirements. Long established U.S. legal rules provide for examination and supervision arranged in accordance with the dual banking system in place in the United States. Commercial banks have the option of being federally or state-chartered. If federally-chartered, a national bank is examined and supervised primarily by the Office of the Comptroller of the Currency (OCC), though national banks generally are required to be members of the Federal Reserve System (Fed) and insured by the Federal Deposit Insurance Corporation (FDIC). International banking activities are generally supervised and examined by the OCC, although the use of certain structural forms require approval by the Fed, not the OCC.[4]

State-chartered commercial banks voluntarily may become members of the Federal Reserve, but membership requires federal deposit insurance. Most state-chartered commercial banks do not join the Fed, but they almost invariably seek federal deposit insurance. A state-chartered member bank is supervised and regulated jointly by its state supervisor (its chartering authority) and the Fed. A state-chartered non-member, federally-insured bank is jointly supervised and regulated by its state supervisor and the FDIC. In addition, the Fed has primary regulatory and supervisory authority over the activities of bank holding companies, regardless of whether the bank subsidiary of a holding company is federally or state-chartered.

Foreign-based banks operate in the United States within the same supervisory structure as U.S.-based banks, consistent with the policy of "national treatment" established by the International Banking Act of 1978.[5] A foreign-based bank that wishes to operate a representative office in the United States[6] must obtain the prior approval of the Federal Reserve Board (Fed). A foreign-based bank that wishes to operate an agency, branch, affiliate, or subsidiary in the United States must apply to the Fed, and a U.S. agency or branch of a foreign-based bank must be licensed and supervised either by a state supervisor or the Comptroller of the Currency. In addition, such U.S. agencies or branches, whether state- or federally-licensed, must be approved and supervised by the Fed. The FDIC provides deposit insurance coverage and supervision to U.S. branches of foreign banks.

**2.3.** *U.S. Regulation of International Banking under the FDICIA.* In December 1991, the President signed into law the Federal Deposit Insurance Corporation Improvement Act of 1991 (FDICIA),[7] a major revision of U.S. bank regulation. In brief, the principal features of the FDICIA that affect international banking are as follows:

> **a.** *Capital supervision.* The FDICIA requires the federal banking agencies to revise their risk-based capital standards for insured depository institutions to ensure, among other things, that these standards take account of interest-rate risk, concentration of credit risk, and the risks of nontraditional activities.[8] The agencies are also required to discuss the development of comparable standards with members of the supervisory committee of the Bank for International Settlements.[9]

---

4. *See, e.g.,* Chapter 5, § 2, *infra* (discussing foreign branches of U.S. banks).

5. On the concept of national treatment, see Notes 2.10-2.14, *infra.*

6. On representative offices, see Note 4.2, *infra.*

7. Pub. L. No. 102-242, 105 Stat. 2236 (December 19, 1991) (codified at scattered sections of 12 U.S.C.).

8. FDICIA, §305(b)(1) (12 U.S.C. §1828 Note).

9. *Id.* §305(b)(2). On the Bank for International Settlements (BIS) and its capital adequacy standards, see Chapter 3, *infra,* §§ 2-3. The FDICIA also mandated a study and congressional report by the Secretary of the Treasury and the Fed, in consultation with the other federal bank agencies and the Attorney General, that would take into account, among other things, differences in accounting and regulatory practices and the difficulty of assuring that foreign banks meet U.S. capital and management standards and are adequately supervised. FDICIA, §215(a)(1) (12 U.S.C. §3102 Note). In addition, the FDICIA mandated a study and congressional report by the Fed and the Secretary of the Treasury analyzing the BIS capital standards, foreign regulatory capital standards that apply to foreign banks conducting banking operations in the United States, and the relationship of the BIS and foreign standards to risk-based capital and leverage requirements for U.S. banks. 12 U.S.C. §3105(j)(1). The

**b.** *Payments on foreign deposits.* FDICIA prohibits the agencies from making, directly or indirectly, any payment, or from providing any financial assistance in connection with any insured depository institution that would have the direct or indirect effect of satisfying any claim, in whole or in part, against the institution for its obligations on foreign deposits.[10] This prohibition does not apply to "open bank assistance" provided by the FDIC to an institution under 12 U.S.C. §1823(c).[11] Nor does the prohibition bar a Federal Reserve bank from making advances or other extensions of credit consistent with the Federal Reserve Act (so-called discount window lending).[12]

**c.** *Establishment and operation of federal branches and agencies of foreign-based banks.* Under FDICIA, the Comptroller is required, in considering any application for approval of an initial federal branch or agency, to include any condition imposed by the Fed as a condition for the approval of the application.[13] The Comptroller is also required to coordinate examinations of such branches and agencies with examinations conducted by the Fed, to the extent possible, to participate in any simultaneous examinations of U.S. operations of foreign banks requested by the Fed.[14] Furthermore, in considering any application to establish an additional federal branch or agency of a foreign-based bank, the Comptroller is required to provide the Fed with notice and opportunity for comment on the application.[15]

**d.** *Broadened Fed supervisory authority.* The Fed is given authority to approve the establishment of any branch or agency, or the acquisition or control of any commercial lending company by a foreign-based bank.[16] The Fed also has the authority, under specified circumstances to order the closing of any state-licensed office of a foreign-based bank,[17] and to recommend to the Comptroller the termination of the license of any federally-licensed office of a foreign-based bank.[18] The FDICIA also gives the Fed broad authority to examine U.S. branches, agencies and affiliates of foreign-based banks, whether state- or federally-approved.[19]

**e.** *Limitation of powers of state-licensed branches and agencies.* The FDICIA prohibits a state-licensed branch or agency from engaging in any type of activity that is not permissible for a federally-licensed branch, unless the Fed determines that the activity is consistent with sound banking practice, and (in the case of an insured branch), the FDIC determines that the activity would pose no significant risk to the deposit insurance fund.[20] In addition, such branches and

report was also to establish guidelines for adjustments to be used by the Fed in converting data on the capital of these foreign banks to the equivalent risk-based capital and leverage requirements for U.S. banks for the purpose of determining whether foreign bank capital levels are equivalent to those imposed on U.S. banks. *Id.* §3105(j)(2).

10. 12 U.S.C. §1831r(a).

11. *Id.* §1831r(b).

12. *Id.* §1831r(c).

13. *Id.* §3102(a)(2).

14. *Id.* §3102(b).

15. *Id.* §3102(h)(2).

16. *Id.* §3105(d)(1), (g).

17. *Id.* §3105(e)(1)-(4) (g).

18. *Id.* §3105(e)(5).

19. *Id.* §3105(b)(1).

20. *Id.* §3105(h)(1).

agencies are subject to the same limits on lending to a single borrower that apply to federally-licensed branches and agencies.[21]

**f.** *Establishment and supervision of representative offices.* Prior to the FDICIA, a foreign bank operating a representative office in the United States was only required to register the office with the Department of the Treasury.[22] Under the FDICIA, establishment of a representative office now requires prior approval of the Fed.[23] The Fed also has the authority to terminate the activities of any representative office.[24] It also has the authority to examine representative offices.[25]

**g.** *Cooperation with foreign supervisors.* The FDICIA explicitly authorizes disclosure of supervisory information by the federal bank agencies to foreign bank regulatory or supervisory authorities.[26]

**h.** *Retail deposit-taking by foreign banks.* To accept or maintain deposit accounts with balances of less than $100,000, foreign banks are required to establish one or more U.S. banking subsidiaries for that purpose, and to obtain federal deposit insurance for any such subsidiary.[27] However, if the foreign bank had a U.S. branch that was an insured branch prior to FDICIA, the branch may continue to accept or maintain retail deposits.[28]

**i.** *New penalties.* The FDICIA established authority for civil money penalties (administrative fines) to be assessed against any foreign bank, and any office or subsidiary of a foreign bank, that violates, and any individual who participates in a violation of, any provision of the International Banking Act, or any regulation prescribed or order issued under the act.[29] In addition, the FDICIA established criminal penalties for the knowing violation of any provision of the International Banking Act or any regulation or order issued by a federal banking agency under the act, with the intent to deceive, to gain financially, or to cause financial gain or loss to any person.[30]


**2.4.** What regulatory principles and objectives are important with respect to international banking activities? Are these distinct from the objectives that would be reflected in regulation of commmercial banking generally? Consider the following excerpt.

---

21. *Id.* §3105(h)(2). In fact, the FDICIA allows the Fed or the state supervisory authority to impose more stringent restrictions than apply to federally-licensed branches and agencies. *Id.* §3105(h)(3).

22. 12 U.S.C. §3107 (1988).

23. 12 U.S.C. §3107(a). Compliance with any applicable state law requirements is still required. *Id.* §3107(d).

24. *Id.* §3107(b).

25. *Id.* §3107(c).

26. *Id.* §3109(a).

27. *Id.* §3104(c)(1). Thus, for any foreign-based bank interested in the U.S. retail deposit market, this provision requires the bank's U.S. operations to be conducted through a subsidiary. In that regard, the FDICIA also mandated a study and congressional report by the Secretary of the Treasury and the Fed, in consultation with the other federal bank agencies and the Attorney General, to determine whether foreign banks should be required to conduct banking operations in the United States through subsidiaries rather than branches. FIRREA, §215(a) (12 U.S.C. §3102 Note).

28. 12 U.S.C. §3104(c)(2).

29. *Id.* §3110.

30. *Id.* §3111.

## Comptroller's Handbook for National Bank Examiners
§§ 801.1, 815.1

The international division is a bank within a bank. The same basic examination and verification procedures are used for the international division as for other bank departments, with some modification for additional types of bank assets and liabilities, direct and contingent, and for the separate laws, regulations and rulings which may be applicable. Documentation and accounting procedures for international operations may also differ from those used in the domestic divisions; however, the same examination objectives must be attained. The examination of the international division includes periodic examinations of selected overseas branches and foreign affiliates to determine how those operations affect the bank's condition and affairs.

Multinationalism and interdependent national economies have made bank international divisions more necessary to bank customers. Importers and exporters of goods and services and domestic customers with overseas operations require a source of international financial assistance in the increasingly complex social, political and economic environment of today's world. As service institutions, national banks provide such assistance through global networks of correspondent relationships, representative offices abroad, foreign branches and foreign affiliations. Those networks also allow national banks to offer services outside their traditional market areas in foreign locations.

Many commercial banking activities performed in other divisions also are performed in the international divisions. The international division has cash and collection items, maintains bank accounts, places and takes time deposits, makes investments, grants loans, creates overdrafts and borrows. . . .

Other activities of international divisions and overseas branches such as issuing and confirming letters of credit, creating acceptances, and trading in foreign exchange initially may seem unfamiliar to a domestic examiner. However, they are not dissimilar to items in the domestic examination. [For example, l]etters of credit represent a formal commitment to extend credit provided that certain collateral and documentary conditions are observed. Foreign exchange contract activities are similar to money trading operations conducted at domestic funding desks. Foreign exchange "positions" are merely commodity inventories carried at book value which are exposed to fluctuating market prices. Separate international sections relate to those functions.

Additional banking activities encountered in international divisions and overseas branches [include activities] such as direct lease financing, installment loans, real estate loans, real estate construction loans, ownership of bank premises and equipment, and other real estate. . . .

The international examiner should state whether or not the international division effectively supervises its foreign branches, Edge Act and Agreement corporations and overseas related organizations. Conclusions reached here are based on information developed during an examination. To determine if supervision is effective, the international examiners comment narrative should consider the:

        a. Adequacy of policies, practices, procedures and controls established for foreign branches and related organizations and the adherence thereto.

        b. Quality of assets and earnings of foreign branches and related organizations.

        c. Quality of management in foreign branches and related organizations.

d. Compliance with laws and regulations.

e. Propriety of carrying values.

f. Relationship between the foreign branches and/or related organizations and the bank as a whole and the effect of that relationship upon the affairs and soundness of the bank.

g. Causes of existing problems.

h. Remedial actions agreed to by management for correction of deficiencies.

**Notes and Comments 2.5.** You are a new associate in the law firm of Dent, Arthur, Dent and Prefect. Quarter National Bank ("QNB"), a U.S. client of the firm, is considering expansion into international banking. The QNB General Counsel wants an explanation about the federal regulatory structure QNB will be facing in this new venture. The partner with whom you are working wants you to brief her on this question, so that she can explain matters to the QNB General Counsel. Based on the preceding materials in this section, what will you tell the partner?

# 2. The Role of State Regulators

**Notes and Comments 2.6.** Where do the state bank regulators fit into this regulatory structure? Have the provisions of the International Banking Act of 1978 (IBA), 12 U.S.C. §§ 3101 *et seq.*, concerning federal branches and agencies minimized the role of state bank regulators? Consider the following excerpts.

## Conference of State Bank Supervisors v. Conover
715 F.2d 604 (D.C.Cir. 1983),
*cert. denied*, 466 U.S. 927 (1984)

Robb, Senior Circuit Judge:

. . .

The appellants are (44 Fed.Reg. 65381-87 (1979)) adopted by the Comptroller of the Currency pursuant to the -3108 (Supp. V 1981). Appellants contended that the regulations and statement conflicted with the IBA because they permitted a foreign bank to establish and operate offices where prohibited by state law. In an unreported opinion the District Court granted summary judgment in favor of the Comptroller. . . .

I.

To engage in the banking business in the United States, a domestic bank may be chartered under state law, subject to the exclusive regulation of the state, or it can operate under a federal charter subject to federal law that in part defers to state law.[2] Prior to the adoption of the IBA a bank organized under the laws of a foreign country could obtain a charter from a state authority only; the federal government did not charter foreign banks. H.R. Rep. No. 910, 95th Cong., 2d Sess. 5 (1978) [hereinafter cited as 1978 House Report]. The absence of federal involvement caused treatment of foreign banks in the United States to differ from state to state. Commenting on this pre-IBA treatment of foreign banks, the Senate Committee on Banking, Housing and Urban Affairs, noted in 1978:

---

2. *See* 12 U.S.C. §§ 21 *et seq.* (1976 and Supp. V 1981). To receive deposits in the United States, a bank must be chartered or be given permission to operate by the federal or a state government. 12 U.S.C. § 378(a)(2) (Supp. V 1981).

There is, at this time, no uniform national policy concerning foreign banking operations in this country.  As a result, foreign banks enjoy many competitive advantages over our domestic banks.  This bill establishes the principle of parity of treatment between foreign and domestic banks in like circumstances.

S.Rep. No. 1073, 95th Cong., 2d Sess. 2 (1978), reprinted in 1978 U.S.Code Cong. & Ad.News 1421, 1422 [hereinafter cited as 1978 Senate Report].

The IBA sought to provide foreign banks with "national treatment" under which "foreign enterprises . . . are treated as competitive equals with their domestic counterparts." 1978 Senate Report, *supra*, at 2. . . . In other words, the IBA "establishes the principle of parity of treatment between foreign and domestic banks in like circumstances." 1978 Senate Report, *supra*, at 2.  In general the IBA provides that "with the approval of the Comptroller" a foreign bank may establish a branch or agency in a state, 12 U.S.C. § 3102(a) (Supp. V 1981) and that

[e]xcept as otherwise specifically provided in this chapter or in rules, regulations, or orders adopted by the Comptroller under this section, operations of a foreign bank at a Federal branch or agency shall be conducted with the same rights and privileges as a national bank at the same location and shall be subject to all the same duties, restrictions, penalties, liabilities, conditions, and limitations that would apply under the National Bank Act to a national bank doing business at the same location. . . .

IBA, § 4(b), 12 U.S.C. § 3102(b) (Supp. V 1981).

In this case the controversy centers on the Comptroller's interpretation of certain provisions of sections 4 and 5 of the IBA. Section 4(a), 12 U.S.C. § 3102(a) (Supp. V 1981), provides that the Comptroller may approve establishment of a foreign bank's federal branch or agency if "establishment of a branch or agency, as the case may be, by a foreign bank is not prohibited by State law." Section 4(d), 12 U.S.C. § 3102(d) (Supp. V 1981), reads: "Notwithstanding any other provision of this section, a foreign bank shall not receive deposits . . . at any Federal agency." When a foreign bank opens a federally-chartered branch or agency outside of its home state,[3] section 5(a)(1), 12 U.S.C. § 3103(a)(1) (Supp. V 1981), provides that with certain exceptions "no foreign bank may directly or indirectly establish and operate a Federal branch outside of its home State unless (A) its operation is expressly permitted by the State in which it is to be operated. . . ." Section 5(a)(3), 12 U.S.C. § 3103(a)(3) (Supp. V 1981), likewise forbids a foreign bank to establish and operate a federal agency outside of its home state "unless its operation is expressly permitted by the State in which it is to be operated. . . ."

Section 1(b) of the IBA sets out the definition of terms used in the statute. . . . [The court quotes 12 U.S.C. § 3101(1), (3), (5), (6) (Supp. V 1981).]

The appellants [a group of state officials responsible for regulation of state-licensed banking institutions, challenging the Comptroller's IBA regulations and interpretative statement] complain that the Comptroller erred in interpreting these provisions of the IBA. They say that the Comptroller violated section 4(a) by approving the applications of five

---

3. The "home state" of a foreign bank is determined in accordance with Section 5(c) of the IBA and regulations issued by the Federal Reserve Board (12 C.F.R. § 211.22 (1983)), and generally is the first state in which the foreign bank establishes a branch that accepts deposits from domestic customers.

Australian banks to convert their state-licensed agencies in New York to home state federal branches although New York law prohibits such banks from opening branches. The appellants say that the Comptroller violated section 5(a) by approving the applications of two of the Australian banks to open interstate federal branches in Illinois in contravention of Illinois law. In the appellants' view, the Comptroller also violated section 5(a) by authorizing a British bank's interstate federal branch located in the State of Washington to conduct business operations that are not permitted to foreign bank branches under Washington law. Finally, the appellants aver that the Comptroller incorrectly interpreted sections 1(b)(5) and (4)(d) in permitting federal agencies of foreign banks to accept deposits if the depositors are neither citizens nor residents of the United States.

## II.

In discussing the public comments regarding 12 C.F.R. pt. 28 (1980), promulgated pursuant to sections 4 and 13(a) of the IBA, 12 U.S.C. §§ 3102, 3108(a) (Supp. V 1981), the Comptroller noted "that in some states a foreign bank which applies for a state branch or agency must be able to demonstrate that the country under whose laws it was organized permits free or at least equivalent access to U.S. banks." . . . The Comptroller concluded however that "such a reciprocity approach" is not "binding upon the Comptroller's Office because it is incompatible with the national treatment theme of the IBA, and, further, it is in the nature of a condition or limitation rather than a prohibition on foreign entry." The Comptroller bases this interpretation on his construction of the language of section 4(a) of the IBA 12 U.S.C. § 3102(a) (Supp. V 1981). . . .

The Comptroller reasons that the words "a foreign bank" in subsection (2) are synonymous with "any foreign bank" so that the Comptroller can license a foreign bank to operate a federal branch in a particular state unless that state prohibits all foreign banks from establishing state-chartered branches. Likewise, the Comptroller contends he can license a foreign bank to operate a federal agency in a particular state unless that state prohibits all foreign banks from establishing state-chartered agencies. . . .

The appellants complain that by applying this construction of section 4(a) the Comptroller has approved the applications of five Australian banks to convert their state-licensed agencies in New York to home state federal branches although New York's bank reciprocity law[4] prohibits such banks from opening branches. . . . The appellants assert that the Comptroller erred in approving these applications. They argue that Congress in the IBA allowed the Comptroller to charter a foreign bank's office only in a state where that particular foreign bank is not prohibited from establishing state-chartered offices under state law. . . .

The District Court agreed with the Comptroller's interpretation of section 4(a). The court said:

> A principal purpose of the 1978 Act was to give foreign banks "an important new option" in doing business in the United States; Congress understood that the federal chartering option might give overseas banks "opportunities which they do not now possess," even though it would also place new burdens of federal regulation on them. See Remarks of Mr. St. Germain, 122 Cong. Rec. 24403 (July 29, 1976). Plaintiffs' view of the Comptroller's authority would in effect nullify the federal option. A foreign bank, under plaintiffs' interpretation, would have a choice between compliance with State regulations under a State

---

4. N.Y. Banking Law § 202-a(2) (McKinney 1982).

charter, and compliance with State *and* federal rules under a federal charter. ...[5]

[For the court's analysis and holding on the issues raised by this case, see Chapter 6, § 2, *infra*.]

## National Commercial Banking Corp. of Australia, Ltd. v. Harris
### 125 Ill.2d 448, 532 N.E.2d 812 (1988)

Justice CLARK delivered the opinion of the court:

At issue in this appeal is a provision of the Foreign Banking Office Act (the Act) (Ill. Rev. Stat. 1985, ch. 17, par. 2701 *et seq*.) which imposes a nonreciprocal license fee upon foreign banks which "do[ ] not provide reciprocal licensing authority" to Illinois State or national banks (Ill. Rev. Stat. 1985, ch. 17, par. 2710). The circuit court of Cook County declared section 3 of the Act (Ill. Rev. Stat. 1985, ch. 17, par. 2710) void and unenforceable on its face for its imposition of the nonreciprocal license fee. The court held that the Act violated Federal statutory law and the Constitutions of the United States and Illinois. The Commissioner of Banks and Trust Companies of the State of Illinois (the Commissioner) thereupon filed this direct appeal. . . . The Comptroller of the Currency of the United States (the Comptroller) was given leave to file an amicus curiae brief in support of appellees' [the foreign banks'] position.

Appellees are three Australian banks that received authorization in late 1981 and 1982 from the Comptroller to establish limited Federal branches in Illinois pursuant to the

---

5. Appellants argue that the District Court misunderstood their position. The appellants contend here, as they did before the District Court, that under the dual banking system embodied in the IBA a foreign bank may obtain a federal charter only if it could have obtained a state charter. They submit, however, that, contrary to the District Court's analysis, they do not seek to require the Comptroller to observe a state's discretionary chartering criteria. Rather, they contend only that the Comptroller must

> observe specific and general state prohibitions on foreign bank entry, i.e., those state laws which bar entry by one or more foreign banks and which the affected banks have no power to cure by their own efforts. State capital adequacy requirements and similar "chartering standards," which foreign banks can take action to satisfy (e.g., by raising more capital), are *not* "prohibitions" within the meaning of Sections 4(a) and 5(a).

. . . The Comptroller counters that section 4(c), 12 U.S.C. § 3102(c) (Supp. V 1981) . . . , contains the exclusive chartering requirements for foreign banks seeking to establish a federal branch or agency under section 4(a), and that state reciprocity laws are not "prohibitions" under section 4(a)(2). . . .

We believe the District Court understood appellants' interpretation and merely extended that interpretation to its logical conclusion. Section 4(a) allows the Comptroller to charter a foreign bank's branch or agency unless, among other things, the establishment of a foreign branch or agency would seem a "state prohibition" whether the law was grounded on a failure to meet state chartering standards or on the failure to meet state reciprocity requirements. In either case, the state law would "prohibit" the foreign bank from opening a state-chartered office, and under the appellants' view of section 4(a), the foreign bank would therefore lose its option to seek a federal charter. We agree with the District Court that it would be inconsistent with the IBA's dual banking system concepts to require federal charter applicants to comply with both state and federal chartering standards. In addition, while appellants' definition of "state prohibition" would lessen this inconsistency, the legislative history contains no evidence that Congress intended the Comptroller to observe only those requirements in state law that "the affected banks have no power to cure by their own efforts."

International Banking Act of 1978 (the International Banking Act) 12 U.S.C. § 3101 *et seq.* (1982)). Under the provisions of the International Banking Act, limited Federal branches are restricted as to deposits they can receive; only such deposits as are permissible to Edge Act corporations (deposits linked to international trade) under section 25(a) of the Federal Reserve Act are allowed. 12 U.S.C. § 3103(a)(1) (1982). Appellees each opened a limited Federal branch office in the Chicago Loop area.

In December 1983, the Commissioner mailed to each appellee a fee statement demanding payment of the non-reciprocal license fee imposed under the provisions of section 3 of the Foreign Banking Office Act (Ill. Rev. Stat. 1985, ch. 17, par. 2710). The fee of $63,287.67 was for a prorated portion of 1983 and for all of 1984. Appellees refused to pay the fee and instead initiated an action in the circuit court challenging the Commissioner's authority to collect the fee. . . .

Appellees contend that imposition of the nonreciprocal fee violates the supremacy clause of the United States Constitution (U.S. Const., art. VI, cl. 2) because it conflicts with section 5(a)(1) of the International Banking Act (12 U.S.C. § 3103(a)(1) (1982)) by attempting to regulate the licensing of a limited Federal branch. . . .

. . . We affirm the circuit court's decision that the Foreign Banking Office Act's imposition of the nonreciprocal license fee in section 3 (Ill. Rev. Stat. 1985, ch. 17, par. 2710) is void and unenforceable as violative of the supremacy clause. . . .

Rules and regulations for implementation of the International Banking Act have been promulgated by the Comptroller pursuant to the statute. In both the preliminary rule published for comment and the final rule reported in the Federal Register, the Comptroller specifically addressed the issue of State reciprocity requirements. The following statement from the proposed rule is pertinent:

> "[I]n some States a foreign bank which applies for a branch or agency must be able to demonstrate that the country under whose laws it was organized permits free access to U.S. banks. Such a reciprocity approach would not be binding upon the Comptroller's Office because it is incompatible with the national theme of the IBA and, further, it is in the nature of a condition or limitation rather than a prohibition on foreign entry." (44 Fed.Reg. 27431 (1979).)

The Comptroller again addressed the issue in the final rule based on comments received following publication of the proposed rule. In pertinent part, he noted that he would "not undermine the general approach embodied in the IBA by trying to enforce a variety of reciprocity provisions–and the sometimes subtle administrative judgments which accompany them–of some of the states." 44 Fed.Reg. 65382 (1979).

Appellees contend that their position is further supported by the district court's recent decision in *Conference of State Bank Supervisors v. Heimann* (D.D.C. Sept. 30, 1981), No. 80-3284, *aff'd in part & rev'd in part sub nom. Conference of State Bank Supervisors v. Conover* (D.C.Cir.1983), 715 F.2d 604 (hereinafter cited as *Conover*). *Conover* involved interpretation of the International Banking Act's licensing provisions. The Illinois Commissioner intervened in *Conover* as a plaintiff seeking declaratory and injunctive relief which would prohibit the Comptroller from licensing two Australian banks which had received authorization to open limited Federal branches in Illinois. Operation of the Australian limited branches violated an Illinois statute which included a reciprocity requirement. At the time of the *Conover* case, the Illinois statute required that a foreign country extend reciprocity to Illinois State or national banks as a prerequisite to obtaining a certificate of authority to operate within this State. . . .

Following the *Conover* decision, the Illinois legislature amended the Act to impose the $50,000 annual license fee upon federally licensed foreign banks whose home country did not provide reciprocity to Illinois or national banks. The amended statute . . . is the statute being challenged in this present action. . . .

We turn now to a review of section 3 of the Foreign Banking Office Act (Ill. Rev. Stat. 1985, ch. 17, par. 2710) to determine its constitutionality under the supremacy clause of the United States Constitution (U.S. Const., art. VI, cl. 2). Prior to enactment of the International Banking Act (12 U.S.C. § 3101 *et seq.*), regulation of foreign-chartered banks had been solely under the jurisdiction of the individual States. That plan of regulation meant that a foreign-chartered bank could potentially, and often did, operate its offices out of several States and thereby offer customers advantages that were not available through State or national institutions.

The dual banking system has been in place since the Civil War, when a system of national banks was created not only to assist in financing the war effort but also with the expectation that a national system would eventually replace the then-current exclusive State system. (Act of Feb. 25, 1863, ch. 58, 12 Stat. 665 (repealed 1864, current version at 12 U.S.C. §§ 21 through 215); *see also* Scott, *The Dual Banking System: A Model of Competition in Regulation*, 30 Stan. L. Rev. 1, 9 (1977).) The total replacement of the State system never materialized and the evolution of the dual banking system progressed. As noted by a representative of the National Association of Supervisors of State Banks, "'[t]he dual banking system . . . is a vital national goal with roots deep in our constitutional history, and one of the very reasons why this country has achieved an economic growth unparalleled among the nations of the world.'" (Scott, *The Dual Banking System*, 30 Stan. L.Rev. at 1 (quoting F. Shelby Cullom).) Under the dual banking system, an American banking institution can choose to be chartered either under State regulations or under Federal regulations. A foreign-chartered bank, prior to enactment of the International Banking Act, had no such choice, however.

In enacting the International Banking Act, Congress indicated its intention to, for the first time, allow foreign banks the same State-Federal option in States where foreign banks are welcome. (S. Rep. No. 1073, 95th Cong., 2d Sess. 6, *reprinted in* 1978 U.S. Code Cong. & Admin. News 1421, 1426 (hereinafter cited as 1978 Senate Report).) In discussing the need for the change in policy regarding foreign-chartered banks, the Senate report noted the following:

> "The general policy of the United States with regard to foreign enterprises doing business in the United States has been one of national treatment. Under this policy foreign enterprises operating in the host country are treated as competitive equals with their domestic counterparts. There is, at this time, no uniform national policy concerning foreign banking operation in this country. As a result, foreign banks enjoy many competitive advantages over our domestic banks. This bill establishes the principle of parity of treatment between foreign and domestic banks * * *."
> (1978 Senate Report at 2, 1978 U.S. Code Cong. & Admin. News 1422.)
> . . .

The Commissioner urges that this court must consider the regulatory interests of Illinois in encouraging foreign countries to offer reciprocal privileges to Illinois or national banks and that we should therefore address whether a State-imposed reciprocity restriction necessarily conflicts with Federal law.

We note that this Federal law was enacted to regulate and control foreign banking enterprises. This court noted in *Springfield Rare Coin Galleries, Inc. v. Johnson* (1986), 115 Ill.2d 221, 503 N.E.2d 300, in discussing the effect of State-imposed laws that affect foreign countries, that "action by individual States in the field of foreign policy will lead to a lack of uniformity. Thus, Federal power in the field of foreign relations must be left free from local interference." (115 Ill.2d at 233.) This was not a blanket prohibition against State statutes that have some effect on foreign nations, for this court indicated that there must be "[s]omething more than an indirect or incidental effect." (115 Ill.2d at 233.) As in *Springfield Rare Coin* and the cases cited therein, the statute here in question falls on the impermissible side of the line of demarcation between incidental and unconstitutional intrusions into foreign affairs. When one of the congressional purposes of the statute is to, as a nation, advance and protect the status of American banks abroad, this role cannot be usurped by the State. See 1978 Senate Report at 23, Study on Treatment of United States Banks Abroad (Analysis) § 9.

Additionally, we note that the Supreme Court has stated:

> "The relative importance to the State of its own law is not material when there is a conflict with a valid federal law, for the Framers of our Constitution provided that the federal law must prevail. Article VI, Clause 2. This principle was made clear by Chief Justice Marshall when he stated for the Court that any state law, however clearly within a State's acknowledged power, which interferes with or is contrary to federal law, must yield. [Citations.] Thus our inquiry is directed toward whether there is a valid federal law, and if so, whether there is a conflict with state law." Free v. Bland (1962), 369 U.S. 663, 666.
>
> . . .

Further, this court has previously held that "[e]ven in legislation in which Congress has not totally displaced State regulation in a specific area, State law is pre-empted to the extent that it actually conflicts with Federal law or if it stands as an obstacle to the accomplishment of the full purposes and objectives of Congress." *Wheeler v. Caterpillar Tractor Co.* (1985), 108 Ill.2d 502, 508.

Preemption, which has its origin in the supremacy clause of the United States Constitution (U.S. Const., art. VI, cl. 2), provides that in some instances Federal law will override State laws on the same subject. . . . At the core of a court's review under the preemption doctrine is a determination of the intent–the objective or purpose–of Congress in enacting the particular statute. The court must answer the question: Did Congress intend to supplant State laws? (*Kellerman v. MCI Telecommunications* (1986), 112 Ill.2d 428, 438.) As this court noted in *Kellerman*, "this is no easy task because rarely does Congress * * * expressly provide that concurrent State laws will be preempted. Rather, a court must usually divine for itself whether the statute evidences an intent by Congress to preempt State law." (112 Ill.2d at 438.) The Supreme Court has, however, enumerated some well-established principles to follow:

> "Absent explicit pre-emptive language, Congress' intent to supersede state law altogether may be inferred because '[t]he scheme of federal regulation may be so pervasive as to make reasonable the inference that Congress left no room for the States to supplement it,' because 'the Act of Congress may touch a field in which the federal interest is so dominant that the federal system will be assumed to preclude enforcement of state laws on the same subject,' or because 'the object sought to be obtained by federal law and the character of obligations imposed by it may reveal the same purpose.' [Citation.]

Even where Congress has not completely displaced state regulation in a specific area, state law is nullified to the extent that it actually conflicts with federal law. Such a conflict arises when 'compliance with both federal and state regulations is a physical impossibility,' [citation] or when state law 'stands as an obstacle to the accomplishment and execution of the full purposes and objectives of Congress,' * * *." (*Fidelity Federal Savings & Loan Association v. de la Cuesta* (1982), 458 U.S. 141, 153.)

Further guidance was given by the Supreme Court in the same case when it stipulated that Federal regulations have the same preemptive effect as Federal statutes subject to "judicial review only to determine whether [the administrator] has exceeded his statutory authority or acted arbitrarily." 458 U.S. at 154.

With these standards of review in mind, we turn now to an analysis of the Commissioner's contentions that the imposition of the nonreciprocal license fee is not preempted by the provisions of the International Banking Act and the National Bank Act. The Commissioner rests his contention primarily on the theory that the regulations promulgated by the Comptroller contravene the express language of the statute. In support, he undertakes a review of the statute's vocabulary as well as a grammatical review of portions of the Federal statute. While vocabulary and grammar rules may provide clues to the intent of Congress, we believe that in this case the Commissioner has "missed the forest for the trees."

Prior to enactment of the International Banking Act, regulation of foreign-chartered institutions was left entirely in the hands of the individual States. As early as 1966, the Federal legislature undertook a review of the State regulation of the foreign-chartered banks system; however, it was not until 1978 that a bill was passed which sought to establish a "rational framework of Federal regulation." 1978 Senate Report at 2, 1978 U.S. Code Cong. & Admin. News 1422.

Our review of the Senate report indicates that the legislature was fully cognizant of the dual banking system which had previously left regulation of foreign banks entirely in the hands of the individual States and that, through the International Banking Act, Congress intended to establish a Federal option for foreign-chartered banks that had not previously been available. A major goal of the legislation was to create a "competitive equality between domestic and foreign banks." (1978 Senate Report at 8, 1978 U.S. Code Cong. & Admin.News 1428.) The policy underlying adoption of this bill was the establishment of a system of "national treatment" of foreign banks as well as a system for procuring national treatment for our banks abroad. (1978 Senate Report at 9, 1978 U.S. Code Cong. & Admin.News 1429.) The authors of the Senate report recognize the dual interests of the State and Federal governments when they state that "section 5 * * * equitably reconciles the interests and concerns of Federal and State officials, and domestic and foreign banks." (1978 Senate Report at 10, 1978 U.S. Code Cong. & Admin.News 1430.) Section 5 will "preserve and enhance the ability of the States to attract foreign capital and develop international banking centers, and give the United States some leverage to secure more equitable national treatment for U.S. banks abroad." 1978 Senate Report at 10, 1978 U.S. Code Cong. & Admin. News 1430.

Against this backdrop of congressional intent, we look to the language of the International Banking Act and then the National Bank Act. Section 4(a) of the International Banking Act (12 U.S.C. § 3102(a) (1982)) establishes that the Comptroller has the authority to license a foreign bank to operate a branch or agency in a State in which it does not already have a State branch or agency and where establishment of a branch or agency is not prohibited by State law. Section 5(a) (12 U.S.C. § 3103(a) (1982)), previously set out, delineates limitations on interstate banking by foreign banks. Under section 5(a)(1)(A), a Federal branch may only be operated outside its home State when "its operation is expressly permitted by the State in which it is to be operated." (12 U.S.C. § 3103(a)(1)(A) (1982).) The Commissioner concedes that section 4(a) permits a State only to prohibit the establishment of a branch or agency; a State may impose no other limitations or regulations under this section. However, the Commissioner argues that section 5 presents an entirely different matter because of such words as "expressly" and "its operation." (See statute previously set out.) Under the Commissioner's interpretation, a limited Federal branch would be subject to State regulations that cannot be imposed on a Federal branch or agency. The Commissioner would have this court interpret section 5(a)(1)(A) to mean that individual States would be entitled to pass on the application of each and every bank which wished to operate a limited Federal branch within the borders of that particular State on a basis which could not be made applicable to a Federal branch or agency. This argument defies logic. Nowhere within the legislative history are we able to discern that Congress had such a bifurcated purpose in mind when passing this legislation; instead, the legislative history clearly presents Congress' intent to establish a national posture towards all foreign-chartered banks which choose to operate under the Federal system. It is this "national posture" which is supported by the Comptroller through the regulations set out previously in this opinion. To uphold the imposition of the nonreciprocal license fee on limited Federal branches while at the same time noting that such a fee could not be charged to a foreign-chartered bank which operated a Federal branch or a Federal agency would be illogical; moreover, it would frustrate the very purposes and objectives of Congress . . . and this we decline to do. Section 4(b) provides that "a Federal branch or agency * * * shall be subject to all the same duties, restrictions, penalties, liabilities, conditions, and limitations that would apply under the National Bank Act to a national bank * * *." (12 U.S.C. § 3102(b) (1982).) Therefore, the provisions in [12 U.S.C. §] 548 of the National Bank Act regarding State taxation of national banks are applicable to the foreign-chartered banks. The Commissioner's argument that the nonreciprocal license fee does not fall within the enumerated categories of "duties, restrictions, penalties, liabilities, conditions, and limitations" is not persuasive. Under our dual banking system, an institution cannot be both a Federal and a State bank. Therefore, only one entity is entitled to license each bank. What the State legislature has euphemistically labeled a "license fee" is, in reality, more in the nature of a tax or a fine.

Specifically, section 548 provides that "[f]or the purposes of any tax law enacted under authority of the United States or any State, a national bank shall be treated as a bank organized and existing under the laws of the State or other jurisdiction within which its principal office is located." (12 U.S.C. § 548 (1982).) Putting the two statutory sections together, we note that a foreign-chartered bank operating under Federal regulations cannot be taxed any differently than a State-chartered bank. Additionally, we could not find any provisions, nor did the Commissioner point out any statutory provisions, which indicated that State banks are subjected to such a "fee." By whatever label it is given, collection of such funds is unlawful. For the above reasons, we affirm the circuit court of Cook County and declare the nonreciprocal license fee invalid and section 3 of the Act unconstitutional as violative of the supremacy clause.

**Notes and Comments 2.7.** The *Conover* court states that prior to enactment of the IBA, "a bank organized under the laws of a foreign country could obtain a charter from a state authority only; the federal government did not charter foreign banks." Was that true, as a technical matter? Compare the language of the present 12 U.S.C. § 72, as amended by the IBA, with the pre-1978 language of the section, which read in pertinent part as follows:

> Every director must, during his whole term of service, be a citizen of the United States, and at least two-thirds of the directors must have resided in the State, Territory, or District in which the association is located, or within one hundred

miles of the location of the office of the association, for at least one year immediately preceding their election, and must be residents of such State or within a one-hundred-mile territory of the location of the association during their [*sic*] continuance in office. . . .

What effect would this pre-1978 language have on a foreign bank's decision whether to seek a national bank charter or a state bank charter?

**2.8.** Note 2 of the *Conover* opinion states that "[t]o receive deposits in the United States, a bank must be chartered or be given permission to operate by the federal or a state government." As authority for this proposition, the opinion cites 12 U.S.C. § 378(a)(2). Does the language of that provision support his statement?

**2.9.** *Role of state regulators under FDICIA.* The amendments of the IBA by the Federal Deposit Insurance Corporation Improvement Act of 1991 (*see supra* Notes and Comments 2.3) has further affected the relative importance of the state regulators with respect to international banking. The Fed's authority over state-licensed branches and agencies has increased dramatically. *See* 2.3.d., *supra*. Powers of state-licensed branches and agencies are now directly limited by the IBA. *See* 2.3.e., *supra*. The establishment of representative offices is now also subject to prior Fed approval, in addition to any applicable state law requirements. *See* question 2.3.f., *supra*. In light of *Conover* and *National Commercial Banking Corp.*, could a state grant its state-licensed branches and agencies the power to accept deposits from individuals and businesses resident within the state?

# 3. Host Country Regulation

## Korsvik, Legal and Regulatory Constraints within Other Countries
*in* Baughn & Mandich, The International Banking Handbook 734 (1983)

The International Banking Act of 1978 had as its primary objective the establishment of a federal regulatory framework governing entry and operations of foreign banks. Moreover, it was intended that it would be nondiscriminatory in its effect on domestic and foreign banks and that it would afford foreign banks equality of competitive opportunity *vis-a-vis* domestic institutions in similar circumstances. In this spirit, the Congress included a provision in the Act which directed the Department of the Treasury to determine the treatment of U.S. banks by foreign governments. Accordingly, the Treasury, responding to this Congressional mandate, produced a thorough study of contemporary conditions facing U.S. banks overseas. The preparation of this report, covering 140 nations, included a survey of all U.S. banks having branch, subsidiary, or affiliate operations abroad, consultation with knowledgeable government experts and regulators in a wide variety of agencies, and solicitation of information from American diplomatic posts in every foreign nation which the United States recognizes.

The resulting study, *Report to Congress on Foreign Government Treatment of U.S. Commercial Banking Organizations*[6] . . . is the most comprehensive and definitive review of the general subject of [restraints]. . . .

Official constraints on foreign banks take the form of entry restrictions and restraints on the operations of banks already established in the host country's market.

---

6. *Report to Congress on Foreign Government Treatment of U.S. Banking Organizations* (Washington, D.C.: U.S. Government Printing Office, 1979).

Restrictions on foreign banks' entry, whether by law or by administrative policy or practice, range from total prohibition of foreign bank presence within a country to various limitations on the organizational form allowed. Particular forms of entry–such as establishment of branches or a subsidiary bank or acquisition of equity interest in an existing bank–may be specifically restricted. Or, foreign bank presence may be limited only to representative offices which do not engage in any direct banking transactions.

Regulations affecting the operations of foreign banks already established in a country may be categorized for simplicity into two types according to their economic impact on the banks' operations. Most restrictions on bank operations increase their cost and thus have effects that are equivalent to the imposition of a tax. When a "tax-like" restriction is imposed, it costs a bank more to extend credit (or provide any other bank service), and the bank will generally charge higher rates and extend less credit as a result. An example of a taxlike regulation is reserve requirements. Banks that are subject to higher effective reserve requirements than domestic banks suffer a competitive disadvantage identical in effect to the imposition of a differentially higher tax.

The second category of regulations affecting bank operations is restrictions that are equivalent in effect to quotas. Quota-like restrictions on banks set absolute limits on the amount of credit or services that banks may offer. Faced with quotas, banks are restricted in the amount of credit or services they can offer, which is detrimental to both them and their customers. Quota-like restrictions may directly limit the competitive opportunity of foreign banks. For example, foreign bank operations may be effectively restrained by absolute limits on the amount of capital they are allowed to dedicate to their operations within a foreign country.

Although official restraints on foreign bank operations take many different forms in practice, they can all be viewed, conceptually, as having either tax-like or quota-like effects. . . . [See Figure 2.3, infra.]

Entry policies toward foreign banks range across a spectrum from prohibitions against any foreign banking presence to admission of foreign banks in any institutional form the bank prefers. Very few countries have policies lying at either of these two extremes. Some limitations on foreign banks' choices of how entry can be accomplished are imposed by nearly all countries.

Entry restrictions are frequently not clear-cut. Policies also are subject to change, and even at a given time, other ambiguities with respect to entry conditions arise.

---

**FIGURE 2.3**

**EXAMPLES OF TAX-LIKE AND QUOTA-LIKE
RESTRICTIONS ON FOREIGN BANKS**

| Tax-like Restrictions | Quota-like Restrictions |
|---|---|
| Differential reserve requirements | Credit/lending ceilings |
| Prohibitions against accepting retail deposits | Specified loan and investment portfolio structures |
| Prohibitions against foreign exchange transactions | Swap limits |

| No access to rediscount facilities | Required capital-to-asset ratios combined with capitalization limits |
| --- | --- |
| | Ceilings on loans in domestic currency |
| | Ceilings on loans in foreign currencies |
| | Prohibition or limitation on branching |

**Notes and Comments 2.10.** As originally enacted, the IBA presupposed a pol icy in favor of "national treatment" of foreign banks seeking entry into the United States banking market. However, the concept of "national treatment" has broader implications beyond the IBA context. It may be argued that this is also a minimum expectation with respect to any state's treatment of aliens or alien business interests. (A guarantee of national treatment is, for example, a typical provision in treaties of friendship, commerce and navigation, so-called "FCN treaties.") Should the United States expect national treatment of U.S. banking interests in other host countries? As a practical matter, is it a reasonable expectation?

**2.11.** What does a guarantee of national treatment mean in the context of international banking? Unrestrained access to the host country domestic market, at least on a par with the host country's banks? Absence of discrimination once (and if) the U.S. bank is allowed in? Many FCN treaties contain exceptions for host country regulation of its economy and other important regulatory concerns. If so, does the IBA in fact accord better-than-national treatment, as compared with other host countries?

**2.12.** Another approach to the problem of treatment of foreign investment by host countries is embodied in the concept of reciprocity. As mentioned in *Conover, supra*, state bank regulatory provisions may include reciprocity as a condition on entry of foreign banks into the state's banking market. Assume that NusBank, with its home office in Nusquam (a foreign state), wishes to establish a state-licensed branch in West Dakota, which has a reciprocity requirement in its banking law. If Nusquam's banking code allows foreign bank entry only through a locally incorporated subsidiary, will NusBank be allowed to establish a branch in West Dakota? What if Nusquam allows entry through branching, but has a schedule of higher deposit reserve requirements for the Nusquami branches of foreign-based banks, or special capital adequacy requirements for such branches?

**2.13.** In the years since the original National Treatment Study, the range of competitive disadvantages facing U.S. banks in the international market has remained broad. Although the 1986 update of the study,[31] indicated improvement in the competitive climate, this improvement is far from complete or uniform.

A first update was issued in July 1984. The 1986 Update was intended to examine the improvement, if any, in the competitive climate for U.S. banks and other financial institutions in foreign markets since the issuance of the 1984 update.[32] Senator Garn, then Chairman of the Senate Banking Committee, had requested that the 1986 Update be broad-

---

31. DEPARTMENT OF THE TREASURY, NATIONAL TREATMENT STUDY: 1986 UPDATE (1986).
32. *Id.* at 1.

ened to include, *inter alia*, the treatment of U.S. securities firms in foreign markets.[33]

The primary finding of the 1986 Update in this regard was that, overall, "the degree of national treatment received by U.S. banks abroad has somewhat improved since the 1984 Update. Over the eight years subsequent to passage of the [IBA], the record reflects sporadic and slow improvement in treatment."[34] Despite the U.S. policy of encouraging "national treatment" for U.S. banks within other local markets, transnational competitive disadvantages remain. The 1986 Update's review of eighteen major banking markets showed no improvement in national treatment, since the 1984 update, in four of the markets,[35] and significant improvement in only four others.[36]

**2.14.**  The entry into force of the General Agreement on Trade in Services, a mandatory agreement applicable to all members of the World Trade Organization, should have an effect on the general applicability of the national treatment principle to international financial services. Will the General Agreement provide an adequate resolution of the concerns discussed by Korsvik? Consider the following excerpt.

## Michael P. Malloy, Principles of Bank Regulation
§ 9.10 (2d ed. 2003)[a]

In April 1994, the Uruguay Round of GATT multilateral trade negotiations finalized the General Agreement on Trade in Services ("GATS").[1] The GATS establishes "a multilateral framework of principles and rules for trade in services with a view to the

---

33. *See id.* These markets included the sixteen markets studied in the 1984 update of the National Treatment Study, plus Argentina and Singapore, in which there appeared to be significant interest on the part of U.S. industry. *See id.* at 2. In addition to Argentina (*see id.* at 87), and Singapore (*see id.* at 153), therefore, these markets were: Australia (*id.* at 93), Brazil (*id.* at 99), Canada (*id.* at 43), Finland (*id.* at 105), India (*id.* at 113), Japan (*id.* at 67), South Korea (*id.* at 121), Mexico (*id.* at 129), Norway (*id.* at 133), Philippines (*id.* at 139), Portugal (*id.* at 147), Spain (*id.* at 161), Sweden (*id.* at 167), Thailand (*id.* at 173), Venezuela (*id.* at 179), and Taiwan (*id.* at 185). Furthermore, the 1986 Update included an extensive review of the competitive climate for U.S. securities firms in such markets as France (*id.* at 195), West Germany (*id.* at 201), Italy (*id.* at 207), the Netherlands (*id.* at 213), Switzerland (*id.* at 217), and the United Kingdom (*id.* at 223).

34. *Id.* at 3.

35. These markets were: Canada, Brazil, Mexico and Venezuela. *See id.* at 5-9 *passim*.

36. These markets were: Australia, South Korea, Norway and Sweden. *See id.* at 6-9, *passim. But cf. id.* at 3 (emphasis added):

> The *relative nature* of these changes as improvements over the prior situation must be emphasized. Significant improvements in a particular market do not necessarily mean that national treatment has been approached or achieved -- substantial areas of discrimination may still remain.

a. Reprinted with permission.

1. General Agreement on Trade in Services, 15 April 1994, Agreement Establishing the World Trade Organization, Annex 1B, 33 Int'l Leg. Materials 1167 (1994) ("GATS"). WTO members are not permitted to derogate from adherence to Annex 1B. Agreement Establishing the World Trade Organization, art. XVI, ¶ 5. For an excellent review of the GATS and its implications for banking, see Kristin Leigh Case, Recent Development, *The Daiwa Wake-Up Call: The Need for International Standards for Banking Supervision*, 26 Ga. J. Int'l & Comp. L. 215 (1996). *See generally* JOHN H. JACKSON, WILLIAM J. DAVEY & ALAN O. SYKES, LEGAL PROBLEMS OF INTERNATIONAL ECONOMIC RELATIONS 893-931 (West Publishing Co., 3d ed. 1995) (offering general discussion of GATS).

expansion of such trade under conditions of transparency and progressive liberalization,"[2] by applying GATT nondiscrimination principles to trade in services.[3] The GATS specifically applies to financial services.[4] The requirements of nondiscriminatory treatment do not, however, prevent WTO member states from enforcing domestic regulations for "prudential reasons, including for the protection of . . . depositors, . . . or persons to whom a fiduciary duty is owed by a financial service supplier, or to ensure the integrity and stability of the financial system."[5]

As a transitional matter, a second Annex to the GATS, concerning financial services, permitted temporary withdrawal from the GATS commitments.[6] Nevertheless, it was anticipated that inclusion of financial services under the GATS regime would "likely . . . result in increased market access"[7] for international banks. This expectation received a setback when the United States withdrew from the GATS transitional process with respect to the Agreement on Financial Services in June 1995.[8]

In withdrawing from the transitional arrangement, the U.S. Government opted for a policy of measured reciprocity, prospectively limiting access to U.S. markets to financial services firms from home countries that provided reciprocal treatment to U.S. firms.[9] Essentially, the government had decided to seek market-access liberalization through bilateral negotiations, rather than through the multilateral mechanism of the WTO and the GATS.[10]

Matters remained in play, however, because the commitments of WTO member states participating in the transitional arrangement were to expire at the end of 1997.[11] Thereafter, WTO member states were expected to renegotiate GATS financial services commitments.[12] In advance of the expiration date, however, the United States joined in the

---

2. GATS, preamble.

3. *See, e.g.*, GATS, art. II, ¶ 1 (applying most-favored-nation treatment to services and service suppliers); GATS, art. XVII, ¶ 1 (applying national treatment to services and service suppliers of other WTO member states).

4. GATS, Annex on Financial Services.

5. GATS, Annex on Financial Services, § 2(a).

6. GATS, Second Annex on Financial Services. Case suggests that temporary withdrawal or modification is permitted in the Second Annex to allow for continued negotiation on market liberalization "because at the conclusion of the Uruguay Round, the United States was unsatisfied with other countries' commitments. The United States was not willing to lock in its own liberal policies without reciprocal guarantees of full market access on a most-favored nation basis." Case, *supra* note 1, at 220, n.32 (citing Joel P. Trachtman, *Trade in Financial Services Under GATS, NAFTA and the EC: A Regulatory Jurisdiction Analysis*, 34 Colum. J. Transnat'l L. 37, 54 (1995)).

7. Case, *supra* note 1, at 221.

8. *See* Paul Lewis, *Trade Accord Without U.S. Set in Geneva*, N.Y. Times, July 27, 1995, at D1, col. 6 (reporting U.S. refusal to join transitional arrangement). In July 1995, over 80 states–including Japan, but not the United States–concluded a transitional agreement to liberalize international trade in financial services. *Id.*

9. Bob Davis & John R. Wilke, *Trade Official Is 'Close' to Limited Pact To Liberalize Global Financial Services*, Wall St. J., July 25, 1995 at A2.

10. *See, e.g.*, Frances Williams, *EU Eager to Salvage Financial Services Pact*, Fin. Times, July 1, 1995, at A1 (noting U.S. position).

11. Joel P. Trachtman, *Trade in Financial Services Under GATS, NAFTA and the EC: A Regulatory Jurisdiction Analysis*, 34 Colum. J. Transnat'l L. 37, 55 (1995).

12. *Id.*

signing of a global accord to govern international trade in services.[13] While the United States made no concessions, in light of the relatively open access to U.S. markets already permitted to non-U.S. firms, the initiation of the accord should result in significant opening of banking, insurance and securities service markets in such countries as Argentina, Brazil, India and Indonesia, among others, that have traditionally been relatively opaque.[14] However, other target markets, such as Malaysia and South Korea, have made no concessions for expansion of access.[15] On the other hand, Japan did agree to significant concessions in terms of opening its domestic financial services markets to international competition.[16]

If the accord is successfuly implemented,[17] its effects on international trade in financial services would be dramatic. Under the GATS, each WTO member is required to accord most-favored-nation treatment to services and service suppliers of other WTO members.[18] Current restrictions on trade in services of each member must be transparent.[19] Members are also required to administer current restrictions "in a reasonable, objective and impartial manner."[20]

A series of general exceptions do apply to GATS obligations, similar to the general exceptions under the GATT.[21] More importantly, perhaps, the GATS includes a self-judging special exception for essential security interests of member states, similar to the special security exception contained in the GATT.[22] Presumably, this exception would shield U.S. international economic sanctions measures[a] from the requirements and strictures of the GATS.[23]

---

13. *See* Edmund L. Andrews, *Accord Is Reached To Lower Barriers In Global Finance*, N.Y. Times, Dec. 13, 1997, at A1, col. 6 (discussing GATS accord).

14. *Id.*

15. *Id.*

16. *Id.* at B2.

17. *Cf. id.* at A1 (citing possible Congressional criticism of accord, but noting existing authorization for immediate effectiveness of accord under U.S. law).

18. GATS, art. II, ¶ 1.

19. *See* GATS, art. III (requiring publication and reporting of restrictive measures).

20. GATS, art. VI, ¶ 1. *Cf.* GATS, art. X, ¶ 1 (requiring that any emergency safeguard measures be administered in a nondiscriminatory manner).

21. *Compare, e.g.*, GATT, art. XX (excepting from GATT requirements measures undertaken for morals, life or health, precious metals, compliance with certain regulatory laws, products of prison labor, national treasures or patrimony, conservation, certain commodity agreements, world-price adjustment, and short-supply materials) *with* GATS, art. XIV (excepting from GATS requirements measures undertaken for morals or public order, life or health, compliance with certain regulatory laws, and taxation).

22. *Compare* GATT, art. XXI (providing exceptions from GATT obligations with respect to any measure undertaken that a member "considers necessary for the protection of its essential security interests") *with* GATS, art. XIV *bis*, ¶ 1 (providing exceptions from GATS obligations with respect to any measure undertaken that a member "considers necessary for the protection of its essential security interests"). *But cf.* GATS, art. XIV *bis*, ¶ 2 (requiring reporting of certain excepted measures and of their terminiation to WTO Council for Trade in Services).

a. *See, e.g.*, Chapter 11, *infra* (discussing economic sanctions and their effects on international banking).

23. *Cf. Panel Report on Nicaraguan Complaint*, GATT ACTIVITIES 1986 58-59 (1987) (noting that GATT panel examining complaint by Nicaragua concerning U.S. trade sanctions not authorized to examine U.S. invocation of GATT, art. XXI).

# Chapter 3

# International Supervision

## 1. Introduction

Banks are increasingly linked in an "internationalized" banking environment. Some have in fact become dependent upon international activities and markets for their earnings, growth and diversification. Others, particularly U.S. banks, tend to rely less on international (*i.e.*, non-U.S.-based) markets directly, but the effects of an increasingly "internationalized" market for loans and funding make themselves felt even in a relatively domestic-oriented banking environment.

Are traditional domestic regulatory systems equipped to deal with an internationalized banking environment? Individual states tend to establish supervisory systems to support their domestically-driven policies. Styles of regulation differ dramatically from state to state.[1] These styles individually and collectively may be inadequate in light of the challenges of global banking. Nevertheless, international banking policy continues to be formulated in a domestic context, with certain limited exceptions.

In this chapter, we examine some of these exceptions. These involve supervisory initiatives arising out of multilateral undertakings and responding to the need for regulation of international activities on an international basis. Curiously, however, the increasing interdependence of international banks and their activities cause domestic regulators to fashion multilateral undertakings to secure what are still essentially domestic objectives.

Multilateral regulation takes a variety of forms. Examples of official institutions involved in such efforts include the Organization for Economic Cooperation and Development in Paris, which provides a forum for a group of bank regulatory and supervisory officials from the twenty-four largest industrialized countries. The Central Banking Department of the International Monetary Fund provides developing countries support in strengthening their bank supervision programs. The Banking Directorate of the Commission of the European Union (EU) promotes cooperation and coordination among banking authorities in the EU.[2]

Other informal entities and groups also work towards harmonization of international banking practices. One example is the New York-based Group of Thirty, consisting of international bankers and government officials from the thirty largest industrialized states.

---

1. *See, e.g.*, Chapter 1, *supra*, § 2 (discussing differing national approaches to regulation and supervision.

2. More recently, of course, the EU has created a single European market, including common rules with respect to entry and supervision of non-Community-based banks. *See* Note 3.9, *infra*.

The Group of Thirty primarily studies problems of multinational banking within the international economic system.

No group, however, has achieved quite the prominence of the Bank for International Settlements (BIS), the subject of § 2, *infra*.

**Notes and Comments 3.1.** Is there a need for "multilateral" or "international" bank supervision? What functions would such supervision perform that could not be achieved just as well by national regulators?

**3.2.** A new regime of international financial services regulation is emerging under the General Agreement on Trade In Services (GATS), part of the World Trade Organization. Review the material excerpted *supra* at 65. Will the operation of the GATS affect the answers to the previous question?

# 2. Bank for International Settlements and the Group of Ten

The BIS, located in Basle, Switzerland, is a *multilateral* bank for *national* central banks. It has been traditionally supported by the Group of Ten large industrialized democracies, consisting of Belgium, Canada, France, Germany, Italy, Japan, the Netherlands, Sweden, United Kingdom, and the United States, with Switzerland as an additional significant participant. The BIS assists these central banks in the transfer and investment of monetary reserves, and it often plays a role in settling international loan arrangements. Of increasing significance, however, is its role as a forum for international monetary cooperation and policy development, under the auspices of its Committee on Banking Regulations and Supervisory Practices, now the Basel Committee on Bank Supervision.[3]

The dramatic failure of Herstatt Bank in Germany and Franklin National Bank in New York in 1974, with its effects throughout the increasingly "internationalized" banking market, led the Group of Ten to sponsor an informal understanding on resolution of international bank failures, now known as the Basle Concordat (1974). The BIS, acknowledging the need to establish a framework for multilateral bank supervision, formed the committee. It consists of foreign exchange and supervisory officials from the Group of Ten, plus Luxembourg, Spain and Switzerland. It is a standing committee of the BIS, intended not to mandate harmonization among its members' supervisory approaches, but to promote cooperation among them. Most of its work has been to produce broad principles to assist national supervisors in establishing their own detailed cooperative arrangements.

Consistent with this approach, the 1974 Concordat established a set of broad principles. First, all international banks should be subject to supervision. Second, this supervision should be adequate, based on standards that both home-country and host-country authorities might apply. Third, supervision of a joint venture involving parent banking institutions based in different home countries should be the primary responsibility of the host-country authority of the joint venture.

These principles obviously required cooperation between home-country and host-country authorities. Supervising liquidity (*i.e.*, the ability to meet obligations as they come

---

3. With Spain joining on 1 February 2001, the Committee currently consists of thirteen participant states: the G-10 countries plus Luxembourg, Spain and Switzerland. *See* BIS website, http://www.bis.org.

due) generally would be the responsibility of host-country authorities. Supervising solvency (*i.e.*, the situation where assets exceed net liabilities) generally would be the responsibility of host-country authorities for foreign subsidiaries and joint ventures, and of home-country authorities for a banking institution operating internationally through foreign branches.

These general principles did little to ease the crisis that occurred in 1982 with the failure of Banco Ambrosiano, an Italian-based bank with a Luxembourg subsidiary. The home-country authority, Italy, at first took the position that it would honor only the bank's domestic (*i.e.*, Italian) obligations. After much turmoil, however, a substantial group of creditor of the Luxembourg subsidiary eventually reached a settlement with the Bank of Italy covering obligations in excess of $300 million.

Thereafter, the Concordat was revised in 1983 to provide a larger measure of detail concerning home- and host-country supervisory responsibilities. The terms of revised concordat are excerpted below.

## Committee on Banking Regulations and Supervisory Practices Principles for the Supervision of Banks' Foreign Establishments
[Basle Concordat (1983)]

I. Introduction

This report sets out certain principles which the Committee believes should govern the supervision of banks' foreign establishments by parent and host authorities. It replaces the 1975 "Concordat" and reformulates some of its provisions, most particularly to take account of the subsequent acceptance by the [BIS] Governors of the principle that banking supervisory authorities cannot be fully satisfied about the soundness of individual banks unless they can examine the totality of each bank's business worldwide through the technique of consolidation. . . .

The principles set out in the report are not necessarily embodied in the laws of the countries represented on the Committee. Rather they are recommended guidelines of best practices in this area, which all members have undertaken to work towards implementing, according to the means available to them.

Adequate supervision of banks' foreign establishments calls not only for an appropriate allocation of responsibilities between parent and host supervisory authorities but also for contact and co-operation between them. It has been, and remains, one of the Committee's principal purposes to foster such co-operation both among its member countries and more widely. . . . It strongly commends the principles set out in this report as being of general validity for all those who are responsible for the supervision of banks which conduct international business and hopes that they will be progressively accepted and implemented by supervisors worldwide.

Where situations arise which do not appear to be covered by the principles set out in this report, parent and host authorities should explore together ways of ensuring that adequate supervision of banks' foreign establishments is effected.

II. Types of banks' foreign establishments

Banks operating internationally may have interests in the following types of foreign banking establishment:

> 1. Branches: operating entities which do not have a separate legal status and are thus integral parts of the foreign parent bank;
> 2. Subsidiaries: legally independent institutions wholly-owned or majority-owned by a bank which is incorporated in a country other than that of the

subsidiary;

3. Joint ventures or Consortia: legally independent institutions incorporated in the country where their principal operations are conducted and controlled by two or more parent institutions, most of which are usually foreign and not all of which are necessarily banks. While the pattern of shareholdings may give effective control to one parent institution, with others in a minority, joint ventures are, most typically, owned by a collection of minority shareholders.

In addition, the structure of international banking groups may derive from an ultimate holding company which is not itself a bank. Such a holding company can be an industrial or commercial company, or a company the majority of whose assets consists of shares in banks. These groups may also include intermediate non-bank holding companies or other non-banking companies. . . .

III.   General principles governing the supervision of bank's foreign establishments

Effective co-operation between host and parent authorities is a central prerequisite for the supervision of banks' operations. In relation to the supervision of banks' foreign establishments there are two basic principles which are fundamental to such co-operation and which call for consultation and contacts between respective host and parent authorities: firstly, that no foreign banking establishment should escape supervision; and secondly, that the supervision should be adequate. In giving effect to these principles, host authorities should ensure that parent authorities are informed immediately of any serious problems which arise in a parent bank's foreign establishment. Similarly, parent authorities should inform host authorities when problems arise in a parent bank which are likely to affect the parent bank's foreign establishment.

Acceptance of these principles will not, however, of itself preclude there being gaps and inadequacies in the supervision of banks' foreign establishments. These may occur for various reasons. Firstly, while there should be a presumption that host authorities are in a position to fulfill their supervisory obligations adequately with respect to all foreign bank establishments operating in their territories, this may not always be the case. Problems may, for instance, arise when a foreign establishment is classified as a bank by its parent banking supervisory authority but not by its host authority. In such cases it is the responsibility of the parent authority to undertake adequate supervision and the host authority should inform the parent authority if it is not in a position to undertake such supervision.

In cases where host authority supervision is inadequate, the parent authority should either extend its supervision, to the degree that it is practicable, or it should be prepared to discourage the parent bank from continuing to operate the establishment in question.

Secondly, problems may arise where the host authority considers that supervision of the parent institutions of foreign bank establishments operating in its territory is inadequate or non-existent. In such cases the host authority should discourage or, if it is in a position to do so, forbid the operation in its territory of such foreign establishments. Alternatively, the host authority could impose specific conditions governing the conduct of the business of such establishments.

Thirdly, gaps in supervision can arise out of structural features of international banking groups. For example, the existence of holding companies either at the head, or in the middle, of such groups may constitute an impediment to adequate supervision. Furthermore, particular supervisory problems may arise where such holding companies, while not themselves banks, have substantial liabilities to the international banking system. Where holding companies are at the head of groups that include separately incorporated banks operating in different countries, the authorities responsible for supervising those banks should endeavour to co-ordinate their supervision of those banks, taking account of the overall structure of the group in question. Where a bank is the parent company of a group that contains intermediate holding companies, the parent authority should make sure that such holding companies and their subsidiaries are covered by adequate supervision. Alternatively, the parent authority should not allow the parent bank to operate such intermediate holding companies.

Where groups contain both banks and non-bank organizations, there should, where possible, be liaison between the banking supervisory authorities and any authorities which have responsibilities for supervising these non-banking organizations, particularly where the non-banking activities are of a financial character. Banking supervisors, in their overall supervision of banking groups, should take account of theses groups' non-banking activities; and if these activities cannot be adequately supervised, banking supervisors should aim at minimising the risks to the banking business from the non-banking activities of such groups.

The implementation of the second basic principle, namely that the supervision of all foreign banking establishments should be adequate, requires the positive participation of both host and parent authorities. Host authorities are responsible for the foreign bank establishments operating in their territories as individual institutions while parent authorities are responsible for them as parts of larger banking groups where a general supervisory responsibility exists in respect of their worldwide consolidated activities. These responsibilities of host and parent authorities are both complementary and overlapping.

The principle of consolidated supervision is that parent banks and parent supervisory authorities monitor the risk exposure–including a perspective of concentrations of risk and of the quality of assets–of the banks or banking groups for which they are responsible, as well as the adequacy of their capital, on the basis of the totality of their business wherever conducted. This principle does not imply any lessening of host authorities' responsibilities for supervising foreign bank establishments that operate in their territories, although it is recognised that the full implementation of the consolidation principle may well lead to some extension of parental responsibility. Consolidation is only one of a range of techniques, albeit an important one, at the disposal of the supervisory authorities and it should not be applied to the exclusion of supervision of individual banking establishments on an unconsolidated basis by parent and host authorities. Moreover, the implementation of the principle of consolidated supervision presupposes that parent banks and parent authorities have access to all the relevant information about the operations of their banks' foreign establishments, although existing banking secrecy provisions in some countries may present a constraint on comprehensive consolidated parental supervision.

IV. Aspects of the supervision of banks' foreign establishments

The supervision of banks' foreign establishments is considered in this report from three different aspects: solvency, liquidity, and foreign exchange operations and positions. These aspects overlap to some extent. For instance, liquidity and solvency questions can shade into one another. Moreover, both liquidity and solvency considerations arise in the supervision of banks' foreign exchange operations and positions.

1. Solvency

The allocation of responsibilities for the supervision of the solvency of banks' foreign establishments between parent and host authorities will depend upon the type of establishment concerned.

For branches, their solvency is indistinguishable from that of the parent bank as a whole. So, while there is a general responsibility on the host authority to monitor the financial soundness of foreign branches, supervision of solvency is primarily a matter for the parent authority. The "*dotation de capital*" requirements [*i.e.*, "branch capital" requirements, treating the branch as a separate entity for purposes of local capital adequacy supervision] imposed by certain host authorities on foreign bank branches operating in their countries do not negate this principle. They exist firstly to oblige foreign branches that set up in business in those countries to make and to sustain a certain minimum investment in them, and secondly, to help equalise competitive conditions between foreign branches and domestic banks.

For subsidiaries, the supervision of solvency is a joint responsibility of both host and parent countries. Host authorities have responsibility for supervising the solvency of all foreign subsidiaries operating in their territories. Their approach to the task of supervising subsidiaries is from the standpoint that these establishments are separate entities, legally incorporated in the country of the host authority. At the same time parent authorities, in the context of consolidated supervision of the parent banks, need to assess whether the parent institutions' solvency is being affected by the operations of their foreign subsidiaries. Parental supervision on a consolidated basis is needed for two reasons: because the solvency of parent banks cannot be adequately judged without taking account of all their foreign establishments; and because parent banks cannot be indifferent to the situation of their foreign subsidiaries.

For joint ventures, the supervision of solvency should normally, for practical reasons, be primarily the responsibility of the authorities in the country of incorporation. Banks which are shareholders in consortium banks cannot, however, be indifferent to the situation of their joint ventures and may have commitments to these establishments beyond the legal commitments which arise from their shareholdings, for example through comfort letters. All these commitments must be taken into account by the parent authorities of the shareholder banks when supervising their solvency. Depending on the pattern of shareholdings in joint ventures, and particularly when one bank is a dominant shareholder, there can also be circumstances in which the supervision of their solvency should be the joint responsibility of the authorities in the country of incorporation and the parent authorities of the shareholder banks.

2. Liquidity

References to supervision of liquidity in this section do not relate to central banks' functions as lenders of last resort, but to the responsibility of supervisory authorities for monitoring the control system and procedures established by their banks which enable them to meet their obligations as they fall due including, as necessary, those of their foreign establishments.

The allocation of responsibilities for the supervision of the liquidity of banks' foreign establishments between parent and host authorities will depend, as with solvency, upon the type of establishment concerned. The host authority has responsibility for monitoring the liquidity of the foreign bank's establishments in its country; the parent authority has responsibility for monitoring the liquidity of the banking group as a whole.

For branches, the initial presumption should be that primary responsibility for supervising liquidity rests with the host authority. Host authorities will often be best equipped to supervise liquidity as it relates to local practices and regulations and the functioning of their domestic money markets. At the same time, the liquidity of all foreign branches will always be a matter of concern to the parent authorities, since a branch's liquidity is frequently controlled directly by the parent bank and cannot be viewed in isolation from that of the whole bank of which it is a part. Parent authorities need to be aware of parent banks' control systems and need to take account of calls that may be made on the resources of parent banks by their foreign branches. Host and parent authorities should always consult each other if there are any doubts in particular cases about where responsibilities for supervising the liquidity of foreign banks should lie.

For subsidiaries, primary responsibility for supervising liquidity should rest with the host authority. Parent authorities should take account of any standby or other facilities granted as well as any other commitments, for example through comfort letters, by parent banks to these establishments. Host authorities should inform the parent authorities of the importance they attach to such facilities and commitments, so as to ensure that full account is taken of them in the supervision of the parent bank. Where the host authority has difficulties in supervising the liquidity, especially in foreign currency, of foreign banks' subsidiaries, it will be expected to inform the parent authorities and appropriate arrangements will have to be agreed so as to ensure adequate supervision.

For joint ventures, primary responsibility for supervising liquidity should rest with the authorities in the country of incorporation. The parent authorities of shareholders in joint ventures should take account of any standby or other facilities granted as well as any other commitments, for example through comfort letters, by shareholder banks to those establishments. The authorities in the country of incorporation of joint ventures should inform the parent authorities of shareholder banks of the importance they attach to such facilities and commitments so as to ensure that full account is taken of them in the supervision of the shareholder bank.

Within the framework of consolidated supervision, parent authorities have a general responsibility for overseeing the liquidity control systems employed by the banking groups they supervise and for ensuring that these systems and the overall liquidity position of such groups are adequate. It is recognised, however, that full consolidation may not always be practicable as a technique for supervising liquidity because of differences of local regulations and market situations and the complications of banks operating in different time zones and different currencies. Parent authorities should consult with host authorities to ensure that the latter are aware of the overall systems within which the foreign establishments are operating. Host authorities have a duty to ensure that the parent authority is immediately informed of any serious liquidity inadequacy in a parent bank's foreign establishment.

3.  Foreign exchange operations and positions

As regards the supervision of banks' foreign exchange operations and positions, there should be a joint responsibility of parent and host authorities. It is particularly important for parent banks to have in place systems for monitoring their group's overall foreign exchange exposure and for parent authorities to monitor those systems. Host authorities should be in a position to monitor the foreign exchange exposure of foreign establishments in their territories and should inform themselves of the nature and extent of the supervision of these establishments being undertaken by the parent authorities.

**Notes and Comments 3.3.** Quattuor Bank has been chartered under the laws of Nusquam. The capital stock of Quattuor Bank is owned by four other banks, chartered under the laws of Belgium, Italy, Nusquam, and the United States respectively. Five years after its establishment, Quattuor Bank is beginning to experience liquidity problems. Consider the following questions:

> **a.** The Central Bank of Nusquam (CBN) has just finished an examination of Quattuor Bank, and the CBN has concluded that Quattuor is in immediate danger of failing. Should the central banks of Belgium, Italy and/or the United States assume some responsibility for the resolution of this problem?

**b.** Would it make a difference to your answer if the four investor banks had invested in Quarter International Bank, chartered under the laws of the United States, which in turn has invested in a number of financial services firms (banks, securities firms, and insurance companies) in various countries in the region in which Nusquam is located?

**c.** Would it make a difference to your answer if Quattuor Bank was a wholly-owned subsidiary of Quarter National Bank, chartered under the laws of the United States?

**3.4.** Recall the excerpt concerning the New York branch of Daiwa, Chapter 1, *supra*, § 1. Were the Fed's actions consistent with the Concordat? If the New York branch were failing because of its trading in securities and foreign exchange, should the United States or Japan take primary responsibility for resolving the resulting crisis?

**3.5.** *Further developments concerning the Concordat.* Since the issuance of the Concordat, the BIS Committee has issued other guidance on the supervision of international banking enterprises. To what extent have the following two BIS issuances modified or otherwise altered the application of the 1983 Concordat? Would they change your answers to questions 3.3 and 3.4, *supra*?

## Basle Committee on Banking Regulation and Supervisory Practices: Supplement to the Basle Concordat Ensuring of Adequate Information Flows between Banking Supervisory Authorities
### April 1990

The Concordat of 1983 stresses that effective supervision of banks foreign establishments calls for ongoing contact and collaboration between host and parent supervisors. The recommendations included in this document are designed to supplement the principles of the Concordat by encouraging more regular and structured collaboration between supervisors, with a view to improving the quality and completeness of the supervision of cross-border banking, while not in any way seeking to supplant the discrete responsibilities of host and parent supervisors. As with the Concordat itself, the recommendations are not designed as minimum legal requirements. Rather they are statements of best practice which all members have undertaken to work towards implementing, according to the means available to them.

### A. AUTHORISATION
The initial opportunity for collaboration between a host and parent supervisor occurs when an individual application by a bank to establish a new foreign presence is first made. The authorisation procedure offers an ideal opportunity for host and parent authority to create the basis for collaboration between them in the future. In particular, it can be used as a means of laying the foundation from which an appropriate system of reporting from the foreign establishment to the parent bank can be developed. Authorisation is a cornerstone of the Concordat.

Recommendations

(i) Host authorities should as a matter of routine check that the parent authority has no objection before granting a banking licence.

(ii) Where a host authority is unable to obtain a positive response from the parent authority, it should consider either refusing the application, increasing the intensity of supervision or imposing conditions on the grant of authorisation.

In the latter case, it is recommended that the conditions (and any subsequent changes in the conditions) should be communicated to the parent authority.

(iii) Host authorities should exercise particular caution in approving applications for banking licenses from foreign entities which are not subject to prudential supervision in the parent country or joint ventures for which there is no clear parental responsibility. In such circumstances, any authorisation should be contingent on the host authority's capacity to exercise a parental role.

(iv) If the host authority follows the procedures outlined in sub-section (i), a parent authority which disapproves of its bank's plans to establish abroad can recommend the host authority to refuse a license. Parent authorities nonetheless should ensure that they have taken adequate steps to prevent their banks establishing in unsuitable locations or making inappropriate acquisitions. Where the parent supervisor imposes conditions on a foreign establishment, such conditions should be communicated to the host authority.

## B. INFORMATION NEEDS OF PARENT AUTHORITIES

The principal requirement of the parent supervisor is to ensure that a routine is laid down for the regular flow of information to the parent bank, and from the parent bank in consolidated form to the parent authority. This calls for a sound system of reporting from foreign establishment to head office or parent bank, for the adequate working of the system to be capable of verification, and for practical solutions to be found for dealing with particular areas of concern.

Recommendations

(i) Host and parent authorities should seek to satisfy themselves that banks' internal controls should include comprehensive and regular reporting between a bank's foreign establishments and its head office.

(ii) If a host authority identifies, or has reason to suspect, problems of a material nature in a foreign establishment, it should take the initiative to inform the parent supervisor. The level of materiality will vary according to the nature of the problem. Parent supervisors may wish to inform host authorities as to the precise levels of materiality which would trigger their concern, for the level of materiality is principally a matter for the parent authority's judgement. However, the host authority is often in the best position to detect problems and therefore should be ready to act on its own initiative.

(iii) Parent authorities may wish to seek an independent check on data reported by an individual foreign establishment. Where inspection by parent supervisors is permitted, host authorities should welcome such inspections. Where inspection by parent supervisors is not at present possible (or where the parent authority does not use the inspection process), the parent authority can consult the host authority with a view to the host authority checking or commenting on designated features of the bank's activities, either directly or through the use of the external auditor. Whichever method is chosen, it is important that the results obtained should be available to both host and parent supervisor.

(iv) If serious problems arise in a foreign establishment, the host authority should consult with the head office or parent bank and also with the parent authority in order to seek possible remedies. If the host authority decides to withdraw banking authorisation from a foreign establishment or take similar action, the parent authority should, where possible, be given prior warning.

## C. INFORMATION NEEDS OF HOST AUTHORITIES

Mutual trust between supervisory authorities can only be achieved if exchanges of information can flow with confidence in both directions. Host supervision of foreign establishments will be more effective firstly if it is undertaken with an awareness of the extent to which the parent supervisor is able to monitor the foreign establishment and of any prudential constraints placed on the parent bank or the group as a whole; and secondly if host authorities are kept informed about matters affecting particular banks with an office in the host territory.

Recommendations

(i) Parent authorities should inform host authorities of changes in supervisory measures which have a significant bearing on the operations of their banks' foreign establishments. Parent authorities should respond positively to approaches from host authorities for factual information covering, for example, the scope of the activities of a local establishment, its role within the banking group and the application of internal controls and for information relevant for effective supervision by host authorities.

(ii) Where a parent authority has doubts about the standard of host supervision in a particular country and, as a consequence, is envisaging action which will affect foreign establishments in the territory concerned, advance consultation is recommended so that the host authority may have an opportunity to correct any inadequacies.

(iii) In the case of particular banks, parent authorities should be ready to take host authorities into their confidence. Even in sensitive cases such as impending changes of ownership or when a bank faces problems, liaison between parent and host authorities may be mutually advantageous.

(iv) If a parent authority is intending to take action to protect the interests of depositors, such action should be co-ordinated to the extent possible with the host supervisors of the bank's foreign establishments.

## D.  REMOVAL OF SECRECY CONSTRAINTS

A prerequisite for effective collaboration between supervisory authorities is the freedom to exchange prudential information, subject to certain conditions designed to protect both the provider and receiver of the information. A possible obstacle to the transmission of prudential information is the existence of national secrecy laws designed to protect the legitimate interest of bank customers.

Recommendations

Countries whose secrecy requirements continue to constrain or prevent the passage of information to banking supervisors abroad are urged to review and amend their requirements subject to the following conditions:

(i) Information received should only be used for pur-poses related to the prudential supervision of financial institutions. It should not be released to other officials in the recipient's country not involved in prudential supervision.

(ii) The arrangements for transmitting information should be reciprocal in the sense that a two-way flow should be possible, but strict reciprocity in respect of the detailed characteristics of the information should not be demanded.

(iii) The confidentiality of information transmitted should be legally protected, except in the event of criminal[1] prosecution. All banking supervisors should, of course, be subject to professional secrecy constraints in respect of

---

1. Supervisors may also be subpoenaed to give evidence in civil cases. Although in some countries they may be open to contempt of court if they refuse, they can make clear that, if the court insists, the information flow would dry up and their own ability to supervise effectively in future would be impaired.

information obtained in the course of their activities.

(iv) The recipient should undertake, where possible, to consult with the supervisor providing the information if he proposes to take action on the evidence of the information received.

## E. EXTERNAL AUDIT

Supervisors can gain reassurance from sound international auditing standards. At present, not all foreign establishments are subject to external audit and even where they are the quality of the audit may not be of sufficient thoroughness. Where foreign establishments are, in practice, beyond the reach of parent supervisors' inspection systems and where they are not subject to a formal inspection system in the host country, the external audit may be the only independent check on a bank.

Recommendations

(i) The existence of adequate provision for external audit should be a normal condition of authorisation for new establishments. It would be advantageous for the audit firm to be the one that audits the parent bank, provided the firm in question has the appropriate capacity and experience in the local centre. Where a foreign affiliate is audited by a different firm, the external auditor of the parent bank should normally have access to the audit papers of the affiliate.

(ii) Supervisors have an interest in the quality and thoroughness of audits; in the case of audits that are inadequately conducted, supervisors should address criticism to the local representative body of auditors and should be empowered, where necessary, to have the auditor replaced. As a means of raising auditing standards for international banks, internationally qualified auditors with experience of banking audit in the country concerned should be appointed. Where any doubt arises, host and parent authorities should consult.

(iii) External auditors may also be asked to verify the accuracy of reporting returns or compliance with any special conditions. It is recommended that all supervisory authorities should have the ability to communicate with banks' external auditors and vice versa. Any emphasis on the role of external auditors should, however, in no way be such as to as downgrade the need for sound internal controls, including provision for effective internal audit.

# Basle Committee on Banking Regulation and Supervisory Practices: Report on Minimum Standards for the Supervision of International Banking Groups and Their Cross-Border Establishment
June 1992

## I. Introduction

In 1975, the Basle Committee obtained the agreement of the G-10 Governors to a paper setting out principles for the supervision of banks' foreign establishments. These arrangements, revised in 1983 and now better known as the Concordat, took the form of recommended guidelines for best practice, and members of the Committee undertook to work towards their implementation according to the means available to them. Subsequently, in April 1990, certain practical aspects of these principles were elaborated in a supplement to the Concordat.

Following recent developments, the Committee has reviewed the arrangements for co-ordination of the supervision of international banking. While the principles of the Concordat and its supplement are still viewed as being sound, members of the Committee now recognise that there needs to be a greater effort to ensure that these principles can be applied in practice. Accordingly, certain of these principles have been reformulated as minimum standards, set out below, which G-10 supervisory authorities expect each other to observe.

The supervisory authorities represented on the Basle Committee will be taking the necessary steps to ensure that their own supervisory arrangements meet the standards as soon as possible. Furthermore, the Committee will monitor members' experience in implementing them with a view to determining what further refinements are needed as part of its ongoing efforts to enhance co-operation in the supervision of international banks. The Committee is making this paper available to bank supervisory authorities throughout the world and is urging them to join with the authorities represented on the Committee in adhering to the minimum standards.

The Committee has also reviewed the April 1990 supplement to the Concordat on "Information flows between banking supervisory authorities" which provides practical guidance for ongoing contact and collaboration among supervisory authorities. The Committee's conclusion is that the nature and extent of information-sharing possible amongst supervisory authorities must continue to be determined largely on a case-by-case basis and cannot, at this time, be usefully expressed in minimum standards. Nevertheless, consistent with the April 1990 supplement, the Committee believes that supervisory authorities should undertake an affirmative commitment to co-operate, on a best-efforts basis, with supervisory authorities from other countries on all prudential matters pertaining to international banks, and, in particular, in respect of the investigation of documented allegations of fraud, criminal activity, or violations of banking laws. In addition, both the Committee and its members will continue their efforts to reduce impediments to the sharing of information among supervisory authorities.

## II. Minimum standards for supervision

Banking groups are increasingly complex organisations and may have several tiers of ownership within them. In some cases, a banking group's home-country consolidated supervisory authority will also be the authority directly responsible for the supervision of the group's lead and subsidiary banks. However, in other cases, there will be one authority responsible for the consolidated supervision of the banking group as a whole (the banking group's home-country authority) and different authorities responsible for the consolidated supervision of individual banks (and such banks' own subsidiaries) that are owned or controlled by the group (the bank's home-country authority). This may occur, for example, where a banking subsidiary chartered in one country, which is seeking to create an establishment in a second country, is itself owned by a banking group subject to home-country consolidated supervision in a third country. A host-country authority must be aware of these distinctions between immediate and higher-level home-country authorities. Except where specified, the term home-country authority includes both types of authority.

The following four minimum standards are to be applied by individual supervisory authorities in their own assessment of their relations with supervisory authorities in other countries. In particular, a host-country authority, into whose jurisdiction a bank or banking group is seeking to expand, is called upon to determine whether that bank or banking group's home-country supervisory authority[1] has the necessary capabilities to meet these minimum standards. In making this determination, host-country authorities should review the other authority's statutory powers, past experience in their relations, and the scope of the other

---

1. In some countries, supervisory responsibility is shared among two or more authorities. The word "authority" is used to include all relevant authorities in any one country.

authority's administrative practices. Some authorities may initially need to make either statutory or administrative changes in order to comply with these new standards; therefore, in cases where an authority fails to meet one or more of these standards, recognition should be given to the extent to which the authority is actively working to establish the necessary capabilities to permit it to meet all aspects of these minimum standards.

1. All international banking groups and international banks should be supervised by a home-country authority that capably performs consolidated supervision

As a condition for the creation and maintenance of cross-border banking establishments, a host-country authority should assure itself that the relevant bank and, if different, the banking group is subject to the authority of a supervisor with the practical capability of performing consolidated supervision. To meet this minimum standard, the home-country supervisory authority should (a) receive consolidated financial and prudential information on the bank's or banking group's global operations, have the reliability of this information confirmed to its own satisfaction through on-site examination or other means, and assess the information as it may bear on the safety and soundness of the bank or banking group, (b) have the capability to prevent corporate affiliations or structures that either undermine efforts to maintain consolidated financial information or otherwise hinder effective supervision of the bank or banking group, and (c) have the capability to prevent the bank or banking group from creating foreign banking establishments in particular jurisdictions.

2. The creation of a cross-border banking establishment should receive the prior consent of both the host-country supervisory authority and the bank's and, if different, banking group's home-country supervisory authority.

Consent by a host-country authority for the inward creation of a cross-border banking establishment should only be considered if the appropriate home-country authorities have first given their consent to the bank or banking group's outward expansion. Outward consent by a home-country authority should always be made contingent upon the subsequent receipt of inward consent from the host authority. Thus, in the absence of consent by both the host-country authority and the bank's home-country authority and, if different, the banking group's home-country authority, cross-border expansion will not be permitted. As a matter of procedure, a host-country authority should seek to assure itself that consent has been given by the supervisory authority directly responsible for the entity seeking to create an establishment; this authority, in turn, should assure itself that consent is given by the next higher tier supervisory authority, if any, which may perform consolidated supervision with respect to the entity as part of a banking group.

While the safety and soundness of a bank should be judged by its overall condition, in reviewing proposals for inward and outward expansion, host-country and home-country authorities should, at a minimum, give weight to (a) the strength of the bank's and banking group's capital and (b) the appropriateness of the bank's and banking group's organisation and operating procedures for the effective management of risks, on a local and consolidated basis respectively. In judging these two criteria, a host-country authority should be particular concerned with the level of support that the parent is capable of providing to the proposed establishment.

The business activities of major international banking groups increasingly cut across traditional supervisory categories. Individual activities or products may be managed on a centralised or decentralised basis, without particular regard to corporate form or the location of a bank's or group's head office. Because of this, before giving consent to the creation of a crossborder establishment, the host-country authority and the bank's and banking group's home-country authorities should each review the allocation of supervisory responsibilities recommended in the Concordat in order to determine whether its application to the proposed establishment is appropriate.

If, as a result of the establishment's proposed activities or the location and structure of the bank's or the banking group's management, either authority concludes that the division of supervisory responsibilities suggested in the Concordat is not appropriate, then that authority has the responsibility to initiate consultations with the other authority so that they reach an explicit understanding on which authority is in the best position to take primary responsibility either generally or in respect of specific activities. A similar review should be undertaken by all authorities if there is a significant change in the bank's or banking group's activities or structure.

Inaction on the part of either authority will be construed as an acceptance of the division of responsibilities established in the Concordat. Thus each authority is responsible for making a deliberate choice between accepting its responsibilities under the Concordat or initiating consultations on an alternative allocation of supervisory responsibilities for the case at hand.

3. Supervisory authorities should possess the right to gather information from the cross-border banking establishments of the banks or banking groups for which they are the home-country supervisor.

As a condition for giving either inward or outward consent for the creation of a cross-border banking establishment, a supervisory authority should establish an understanding with the other authority that they may each gather information to the extent necessary for effective home-country supervision, either through on-site examination or by other means satisfactory to the recipient, from the cross-border establishments located in one another's jurisdictions of banks or banking groups chartered or incorporated in their respective jurisdictions. Thus, consent for inward expansion by a prospective host-country authority should generally be contingent upon there being such an understanding, with the foreign bank's or banking group's home-country authority, that each authority may gather such information from their respective bank's and banking group's foreign establishments. Similarly, consent for outward expansion by the home-country authority should generally be contingent upon there being such an understanding with the host-country authority. Through such bilateral arrangements, all home-country authorities should be able to improve their ability to review the financial condition of their banks' and banking groups' cross-border banking establishments.

4. If a host-country authority determines that any one of the foregoing minimum standards is not met to its satisfaction, that authority could impose restrictive measures necessary to satisfy its prudential concerns consistent with these minimum standards, including the prohibition of the creation of banking establishments.

In considering whether to consent to the creation of a banking establishment by a foreign bank or foreign banking group, or in reviewing any other proposal by a foreign bank or banking group which requires its consent, a host-country authority should determine whether the bank or banking group is subject to consolidated supervision by an authority that has–or is actively working to establish–the necessary capabilities to meet these minimum standards. First, the host-country authority should determine whether the bank or banking group is chartered or incorporated in a jurisdiction with which the host-country authority has a mutual understanding for the gathering of information from cross-border establishments. Secondly, the host-country authority should determine whether consent for outward expansion has been given by the appropriate home-country authorities. Thirdly, the host-country authority should determine whether the bank and, if different, the banking group is supervised by a home-country authority which has the practical capability of performing consolidated supervision.

If these minimum standards are not met with respect to a particular bank or banking group, and the relevant home-country authorities are unwilling or unable to initiate the effort to take measures to meet these standards, the host-country authority should prevent the creation in its jurisdiction of any cross-border establishments by that bank or banking group. However, in its sole discretion, the host-country authority may alternatively choose to permit the creation of establishments by such a bank or banking group, subject to whatever prudential restrictions on the scope and nature of the establishment's operations which the host-country authority deems necessary and appropriate to address its prudential concerns, provided that the host-country authority itself also accepts the responsibility to perform adequate supervision of the bank's or banking group's local establishments on a "stand-alone" consolidated basis.

Thus, if a bank or banking group is not subject to the level of supervision and supervisory co-operation required by these minimum standards, and the relevant supervisory authority is not actively working to establish the necessary capabilities, that bank or banking group will only be permitted to expand its operations into jurisdictions whose authorities are adhering to these minimum standards if the host-country authority itself accepts the responsibility to perform supervision of the bank or banking group's local establishments consistent with these minimum standards.

**Notes and Comments 3.6.** *Bank Secrecy and the Concordat Supplement.* Part D of the 1990 Supplement to the 1983 Basle Concordat deals with the problem of domestic bank secrecy laws that may impede transnational regulation and supervision of banking. (On bank secrecy laws generally, see Chapter 10, *infra.*) Nusquami law prohibits the disclosure of CBN bank examination reports. How will this affect the Quattuor Bank problem in note 3.3, *supra*?

**3.7.** *BIS Minimum Standards and the BCCI scandal.* The "recent developments," referred to in the introduction of the 1992 BIS Minimum Standards, that caused the Committee to review the arrangements for coordination of international bank supervision appears to be a reference to the scandal surrounding the Bank of Credit and Commerce International (BCCI).[4] The scandal involved, *inter alia*, the alleged secret takeover of a U.S. bank holding company by BCCI, an international banking enterprise headquartered in the Gulf States. A lack of effective coordination among national supervisors apparently made it easier for BCCI to engage in transborder transactions that eventually led to its collapse. Would the Minimum Standards have made any difference in that situation? Note that the 1992 BIS Minimum Standards are "standards," not recommendations of "best practice." Consider the following questions:

> **a.** Are the Minimum Standards binding on the United States? On Nusquam?
>
> **b.** What difference would the Minimum Standards make in the decisionmaking by a U.S. regulator deciding whether or not to allow entry into the U.S. market to a non-U.S. banking enterprise?[5]
>
> **c.** Recall the excerpt concerning the New York branch of Daiwa, Chapter 1, *supra.* Were the Fed's actions consistent with the Minimum Standards?

---

4. For a review of the BCCI scandal and the legislative reaction to the scandal in the United States, see RAJ K. BHALA, FOREIGN BANK REGULATION AFTER BCCI (1994).

5. We return to this issue in Chapter 6, *infra*, concerning entry by foreign banks into U.S. markets.

**3.8.** The Basle Committee on Banking Supervision, in conjunction with the International Monetary Fund and the International Bank for Reconstruction and Development. has developed a set of core principles for effective bank supervision. BASLE COMMITTEE ON BANKING SUPERVISON, BASLE CORE PRINCIPLES FOR EFFECTIVE BANKING SUPERVISION (Sept. 22, 1997), *reprinted in* 37 INT'L LEG. MAT. 405 (1998). The CORE PRINCIPLES consists of twenty-five basic principles, ranging from preconditions for effective supervision (Principle 1) to principles for cross-border banking (Principles 23-25), together with commentary by the Committee. The principles are, of course, not binding, but they do provide a basic reference point for supervisors. The principles are reproduced in the Supplement. You should compare the principles with the applicable substantive U.S. rules that are discussed throughout the remainder of this book. To what extent do these principles codify U.S. practice?

**3.9.** *Comparative Developments in the EU.* In addition to participation by several of its member states in the BIS, the European Union (EU) has begun taking its own steps with respect to supervision and resolution of failing bank situations. Considering the following excerpts, how does the EU approach compare with that of the BIS?

## Reorganisation and Winding up of Credit Institutions
Directive 2001/24/EC (4 April 2001)

TITLE I SCOPE AND DEFINITIONS
Article 1
Scope

1. This Directive shall apply to credit institutions and their branches set up in Member States other than those in which they have their head offices, as defined in points (1) and (3) of Article 1 of Directive 2000/12/EC, subject to the conditions and exemptions laid down in Article 2(3) of that Directive.

2. The provisions of this Directive concerning the branches of a credit institution having a head office outside the Community shall apply only where that institution has branches in at least two Member States of the Community.

Article 2
Definitions
For the purposes of this Directive:

- "home Member State" shall mean the Member State of origin . . . ,

- "administrator" shall mean any person or body appointed by the administrative or judicial authorities whose task is to administer reorganisation measures;

- "administrative or judicial authorities" shall mean such administrative or judicial authorities of the Member States as are competent for the purposes of reorganisation measures or winding-up proceedings;

- "reorganisation measures" shall mean measures which are intended to preserve or restore the financial situation of a credit institution and which could affect third parties' pre-existing rights, including measures involving the possibility of a suspension of payments, suspension of enforcement measures or reduction of claims;

- "liquidator" shall mean any person or body appointed by the administrative or judicial authorities whose task is to administer winding-up proceedings;

- "winding-up proceedings" shall mean collective proceedings opened and monitored by the administrative or judicial authorities of a Member State with the aim of realising assets under the supervision of those authorities, including where the proceedings are terminated by a composition or other, similar measure. . . .

TITLE II
REORGANISATION MEASURES
A. Credit institutions having their head offices within the Community
Article 3
Adoption of reorganisation measures–applicable law
      1. The administrative or judicial authorities of the home Member State shall alone be empowered to decide on the implementation of one or more reorganisation measures in a credit institution, including branches established in other Member States.
      2. The reorganisation measures shall be applied in accordance with the laws, regulations and procedures applicable in the home Member State, unless otherwise provided in this Directive.
      They shall be fully effective in accordance with the legislation of that Member State throughout the Community without any further formalities, including as against third parties in other Member States, even where the rules of the host Member State applicable to them do not provide for such measures or make their implementation subject to conditions which are not fulfilled.
      The reorganisation measures shall be effective throughout the Community once they become effective in the Member State where they have been taken.

Article 4
Information for the competent authorities of the host Member State
      The administrative or judicial authorities of the home Member State shall without delay inform, by any available means, the competent authorities of the host Member State of their decision to adopt any reorganisation measure, including the practical effects which such a measure may have, if possible before it is adopted or otherwise immediately thereafter. Information shall be communicated by the competent authorities of the home Member State.

Article 5
Information for the supervisory authorities of the home Member State
      Where the administrative or judicial authorities of the host Member State deem it necessary to implement within their territory one or more reorganisation measures, they shall inform the competent authorities of the home Member State accordingly. Information shall be communicated by the host Member State's competent authorities. . . .

Article 7
Duty to inform known creditors and right to lodge claims
      1. Where the legislation of the home Member State requires lodgement of a claim with a view to its recognition or provides for compulsory notification of the measure to creditors who have their domiciles, normal places of residence or head offices in that State, the administrative or judicial authorities of the home Member State or the administrator shall also inform known creditors who have their domiciles, normal places of residence or head offices in other Member States, in accordance with the procedures laid down in Articles 14 and 17(1).
      2. Where the legislation of the home Member State provides for the right of creditors who have their domiciles, normal places of residence or head offices in that State to lodge claims or to submit observations concerning their claims, creditors who have their

domiciles, normal places of residence or head offices in other Member States shall also have that right in accordance with the procedures laid down in Article 16 and Article 17(2).

B. Credit institutions having their head offices outside the Community
Article 8
Branches of third-country credit institutions
1. The administrative or judicial authorities of the host Member State of a branch of a credit institution having its head office outside the Community shall without delay inform, by any available means, the competent authorities of the other host Member States in which the institution has set up branches which are included on the list referred to in Article 11 of Directive 2000/12/EC and published each year in the Official Journal of the European Communities, of their decision to adopt any reorganisation measure, including the practical effects which that measure may have, if possible before it is adopted or otherwise immediately thereafter. Information shall be communicated by the competent authorities of the host Member State whose administrative or judicial authorities decide to apply the measure.
2. The administrative or judicial authorities referred to in paragraph 1 shall endeavour to coordinate their actions.

TITLE III
WINDING-UP PROCEEDINGS
A. Credit institutions having their head offices within the Community
Article 9
Opening of winding-up proceedings - Information to be communicated to other competent authorities
1. The administrative or judicial authorities of the home Member State which are responsible for winding up shall alone be empowered to decide on the opening of winding-up proceedings concerning a credit institution, including branches established in other Member States.
A decision to open winding-up proceedings taken by the administrative or judicial authority of the home Member State shall be recognised, without further formality, within the territory of all other Member States and shall be effective there when the decision is effective in the Member State in which the proceedings are opened.
2. The administrative or judicial authorities of the home Member State shall without delay inform, by any available means, the competent authorities of the host Member State of their decision to open winding-up proceedings, including the practical effects which such proceedings may have, if possible before they open or otherwise immediately thereafter. Information shall be communicated by the competent authorities of the home Member State.

Article 10
Law applicable
1. A credit institution shall be wound up in accordance with the laws, regulations and procedures applicable in its home Member State insofar as this Directive does not provide otherwise.
2. The law of the home Member State shall determine in particular:
(a) the goods subject to administration and the treatment of goods acquired by the credit institution after the opening of winding-up proceedings;
(b) the respective powers of the credit institution and the liquidator;
(c) the conditions under which set-offs may be invoked;
(d) the effects of winding-up proceedings on current contracts to which the credit

institution is party;

(e) the effects of winding-up proceedings on proceedings brought by individual creditors, with the exception of lawsuits pending, as provided for in Article 32;

(f) the claims which are to be lodged against the credit institution and the treatment of claims arising after the opening of winding-up proceedings;

(g) the rules governing the lodging, verification and admission of claims;

(h) the rules governing the distribution of the proceeds of the realisation of assets, the ranking of claims and the rights of creditors who have obtained partial satisfaction after the opening of insolvency proceedings by virtue of a right in re or through a set-off;

(i) the conditions for, and the effects of, the closure of insolvency proceedings, in particular by composition;

(j) creditors' rights after the closure of winding-up proceedings;

(k) who is to bear the costs and expenses incurred in the winding-up proceedings;

(l) the rules relating to the voidness, voidability or unenforceability of legal acts detrimental to all the creditors.

Article 11
Consultation of competent authorities before voluntary winding up

1. The competent authorities of the home Member State shall be consulted in the most appropriate form before any voluntary winding-up decision is taken by the governing bodies of a credit institution.

2. The voluntary winding up of a credit institution shall not preclude the adoption of a reorganisation measure or the opening of winding-up proceedings.

Article 12
Withdrawal of a credit institution's authorisation

1. Where the opening of winding-up proceedings is decided on in respect of a credit institution in the absence, or following the failure, of reorganisation measures, the authorisation of the institution shall be withdrawn in accordance with [applicable procedures].

2. The withdrawal of authorisation provided for in paragraph 1 shall not prevent the person or persons entrusted with the winding up from carrying on some of the credit institution's activities insofar as that is necessary or appropriate for the purposes of winding up.

The home Member State may provide that such activities shall be carried on with the consent, and under the supervision, of the competent authorities of that Member State.

Article 13
Publication

The liquidators or any administrative or judicial authority shall announce the decision to open winding-up proceedings through publication of an extract from the winding-up decision in the Official Journal of the European Communities and at least two national newspapers in each of the host Member States.

Article 14
Provision of information to known creditors

1. When winding-up proceedings are opened, the administrative or judicial authority of the home Member State or the liquidator shall without delay individually inform known creditors who have their domiciles, normal places of residence or head offices in

other Member States, except in cases where the legislation of the home State does not require lodgement of the claim with a view to its recognition.

2. That information, provided by the dispatch of a notice, shall in particular deal with time limits, the penalties laid down in regard to those time limits, the body or authority empowered to accept the lodgement of claims or observations relating to claims and the other measures laid down. Such a notice shall also indicate whether creditors whose claims are preferential or secured in re need lodge their claims.

Article 15
Honouring of obligations
Where an obligation has been honoured for the benefit of a credit institution which is not a legal person and which is the subject of winding-up proceedings opened in another Member State, when it should have been honoured for the benefit of the liquidator in those proceedings, the person honouring the obligation shall be deemed to have discharged it if he was unaware of the opening of proceedings. Where such an obligation is honoured before the publication provided for in Article 13 has been effected, the person honouring the obligation shall be presumed, in the absence of proof to the contrary, to have been unaware of the opening of winding-up proceedings; where the obligation is honoured after the publication provided for in Article 13 has been effected, the person honouring the obligation shall be presumed, in the absence of proof to the contrary, to have been aware of the opening of proceedings.

Article 16
Right to lodge claims
1. Any creditor who has his domicile, normal place of residence or head office in a Member State other than the home Member State, including Member States' public authorities, shall have the right to lodge claims or to submit written observations relating to claims.

2. The claims of all creditors whose domiciles, normal places of residence or head offices are in Member States other than the home Member State shall be treated in the same way and accorded the same ranking as claims of an equivalent nature which may be lodged by creditors having their domiciles, normal places of residence, or head offices in the home Member State

3. Except in cases where the law of the home Member State provides for the submission of observations relating to claims, a creditor shall send copies of supporting documents, if any, and shall indicate the nature of the claim, the date on which it arose and its amount, as well as whether he alleges preference, security in re or reservation of title in respect of the claim and what assets are covered by his security. . . .

Article 18
Regular provision of information to creditors
Liquidators shall keep creditors regularly informed, in an appropriate manner, particularly with regard to progress in the winding up.

B. Credit institutions the head offices of which are outside the Community
Article 19
Branches of third-country credit institutions
1. The administrative or judicial authorities of the host Member State of the branch of a credit institution the head office of which is outside the Community shall without delay

inform, by any available means, the competent authorities of the other host Member States in which the credit institution has set up branches . . . of their decision to open winding-up proceedings, including the practical effects which these proceedings may have, if possible before they open or otherwise immediately thereafter. Information shall be communicated by the competent authorities of the first abovementioned host Member State.

2. Administrative or judicial authorities which decide to open proceedings to wind up a branch of a credit institution the head office of which is outside the Community shall inform the competent authorities of the other host Member States that winding-up proceedings have been opened and authorisation withdrawn.

Information shall be communicated by the competent authorities in the host Member State which has decided to open the proceedings.

3. The administrative or judicial authorities referred to in paragraph 1 shall endeavour to coordinate their actions.

Any liquidators shall likewise endeavour to coordinate their actions.

## TITLE IV
## PROVISIONS COMMON TO REORGANISATION MEASURES AND WINDING-UP PROCEEDINGS
Article 20
Effects on certain contracts and rights

The effects of a reorganisation measure or the opening of winding-up proceedings on:

(a) employment contracts and relationships shall be governed solely by the law of the Member State applicable to the employment contract;

(b) a contract conferring the right to make use of or acquire immovable property shall be governed solely by the law of the Member State within the territory of which the immovable property is situated. That law shall determine whether property is movable or immovable;

(c) rights in respect of immovable property, a ship or an aircraft subject to registration in a public register shall be governed solely by the law of the Member State under the authority of which the register is kept.

Article 21
Third parties' rights in re

1. The adoption of reorganisation measures or the opening of winding-up proceedings shall not affect the rights in re of creditors or third parties in respect of tangible or intangible, movable or immovable assets–both specific assets and collections of indefinite assets as a whole which change from time to time –belonging to the credit institution which are situated within the territory of another Member State at the time of the adoption of such measures or the opening of such proceedings.

2. The rights referred to in paragraph 1 shall in particular mean:

(a) the right to dispose of assets or have them disposed of and to obtain satisfaction from the proceeds of or income from those assets, in particular by virtue of a lien or a mortgage;

(b) the exclusive right to have a claim met, in particular a right guaranteed by a lien in respect of the claim or by assignment of the claim by way of a guarantee;

(c) the right to demand the assets from, and/or to require restitution by, anyone having possession or use of them contrary to the wishes of the party so entitled;

(d) a right in re to the beneficial use of assets.

3. The right, recorded in a public register and enforceable against third parties, under which a right in re within the meaning of paragraph 1 may be obtained, shall be considered a right in re.

4. Paragraph 1 shall not preclude the actions for voidness, voidability or unenforceability laid down in Article 10(2)(l).

Article 22
Reservation of title
1. The adoption of reorganisation measures or the opening of winding-up proceedings concerning a credit institution purchasing an asset shall not affect the seller's rights based on a reservation of title where at the time of the adoption of such measures or opening of such proceedings the asset is situated within the territory of a Member State other than the State in which the said measures were adopted or the said proceedings were opened.

2. The adoption of reorganisation measures or the opening of winding-up proceedings concerning a credit institution selling an asset, after delivery of the asset, shall not constitute grounds for rescinding or terminating the sale and shall not prevent the purchaser from acquiring title where at the time of the adoption of such measures or the opening of such proceedings the asset sold is situated within the territory of a Member State other than the State in which such measures were adopted or such proceedings were opened.

3. Paragraphs 1 and 2 shall not preclude the actions for voidness, voidability or unenforceability laid down in Article 10(2)(l).

Article 23
Set-off
1. The adoption of reorganisation measures or the opening of winding-up proceedings shall not affect the right of creditors to demand the set-off of their claims against the claims of the credit institution, where such a set-off is permitted by the law applicable to the credit institution's claim.

2. Paragraph 1 shall not preclude the actions for voidness, voidability or unenforceability laid down in Article 10(2)(l).

Article 24
Lex rei sitae
The enforcement of proprietary rights in instruments or other rights in such instruments the existence or transfer of which presupposes their recording in a register, an account or a centralised deposit system held or located in a Member State shall be governed by the law of the Member State where the register, account, or centralised deposit system in which those rights are recorded is held or located. . . .

Article 28
Proof of liquidators' appointment
    . . .
2. Administrators and liquidators shall be entitled to exercise within the territory of all the Member States all the powers which they are entitled to exercise within the territory of the home Member State. They may also appoint persons to assist or, where appropriate, represent them in the course of the reorganisation measure or winding-up proceedings, in particular in host Member States and, specifically, in order to help overcome any difficulties encountered by creditors in the host Member State.

3. In exercising his powers, an administrator or liquidator shall comply with the law

of the Member States within the territory of which he wishes to take action, in particular with regard to procedures for the realisation of assets and the provision of information to employees. Those powers may not include the use of force or the right to rule on legal proceedings or disputes. . . .

Article 30
Detrimental acts
　　1. Article 10 shall not apply as regards the rules relating to the voidness, voidability or unenforceability of legal acts detrimental to the creditors as a whole, where the beneficiary of these acts provides proof that:
　　- the act detrimental to the creditors as a whole is subject to the law of a Member State other than the home Member State, and
　　- that law does not allow any means of challenging that act in the case in point.
　　2. Where a reorganisation measure decided on by a judicial authority provides for rules relating to the voidness, voidability or unenforceability of legal acts detrimental to the creditors as a whole performed before adoption of the measure, Article 3(2) shall not apply in the cases provided for in paragraph 1 of this Article.

Article 31
Protection of third parties
　　Where, by an act concluded after the adoption of a reorganisation measure or the opening of winding-up proceedings, a credit institution disposes, for consideration, of:
　　- an immovable asset,
　　- a ship or an aircraft subject to registration in a public register, or
　　- instruments or rights in such instruments the existence or transfer of which presupposes their being recorded in a register, an account or a centralised deposit system held or located in a Member State,
the validity of that act shall be governed by the law of the Member State within the territory of which the immovable asset is situated or under the authority of which that register, account or deposit system is kept.

Article 32
Lawsuits pending
　　The effects of reorganisation measures or winding-up proceedings on a pending lawsuit concerning an asset or a right of which the credit institution has been divested shall be governed solely by the law of the Member State in which the lawsuit is pending. . . .

TITLE V
FINAL PROVISIONS
Article 34
Implementation
　　1. Member States shall bring into force the laws, regulations and administrative provisions necessary to comply with this Directive on 5 May 2004. They shall forthwith inform the Commission thereof.
　　National provisions adopted in application of this Directive shall apply only to reorganisation measures or winding-up proceedings adopted or opened after the date referred to in the first subparagraph. Measures adopted or proceedings opened before that date shall continue to be governed by the law that was applicable to them at the time of adoption or opening.

2. When Member States adopt these measures, they shall contain a reference to this Directive or shall be accompanied by such reference on the occasion of their official publication. The methods of making such reference shall be laid down by Member States.

3. Member States shall communicate to the Commission the texts of the main provisions of national law which they adopt in the field governed by this Directive.

Article 35
Entry into force
This Directive shall enter into force on the date of its publication.

## Wendy Fowler, EC Regulation of the Banking Sector,
5 Hofstra Prop. L.J. 405 (1993)[a]

. . .    B. Winding-up

The Commission has proposed a Directive to coordinate the rules relating to reorganization measures taken to safeguard or restore the financial situation of credit institutions and the winding-up of credit institutions and deposit guarantee schemes. The Proposed Reorganization Directive places responsibility on the authorities of the home Member State to decide on the implementation of reorganization measures of credit institutions and their branches. "Reorganization measures" are defined to cover measures intended to safeguard or restore the financial situation of a credit institution and, in the case of the United Kingdom, to include powers of the Bank of England to appoint investigators and to revoke authorization under the Banking Act of 1987. These measures would be fully effective against the authorities and creditors of branches situated in other Member States, even where the host Member State does not provide for such measures. Decisions taken by the authorities of the home Member State would preclude the host Member State from taking any reorganization measures unless the home Member State so decides. In the case of credit institutions with head offices outside the EC, the host Member State would have the right to implement its own reorganization measures unless an agreement to the contrary has been concluded with a home country on the basis of the principle of reciprocity.

The Proposed Reorganization Directive also provides that the winding-up of credit institutions should be carried out in accordance with the laws of the home Member State and in collaboration with the authorities of the host Member State if the credit institution has its head office within the EC. In the case of credit institutions having their head office outside the EC, the winding-up procedures of the host Member State would apply. Finally, the Proposed Reorganization Directive places an obligation on Member States to ensure that the deposit-guarantee schemes existing in their territory cover the deposits of branches of institutions having their head offices in other Member States. . . .

C. Own Funds

Own funds are an important yardstick for the authorities in assessing the solvency of credit institutions. In Directive 89/299 on own funds,[15] own funds are described as the credit institution's own capital which serves to absorb losses which are not matched by prospective profits of sufficient volume.

---

a. This article was written prior to the recent enactment of certain banking provisions which are described herein as anticipatory. As such, some of the descriptions of the planned implementation of the EC banking regulations have already been executed.

15. Council Directive 89/299 of 17th April 1989 on the own funds of credit institutions, 1989 O.J. (L 124) 16.

Directive 89/299 was amended in 1991 by Directive 91/633[16] and again in 1992 by Directive 92/16.[17] Directive 89/299 (as amended) lays down certain elements which comprise a credit institution's own funds. These include paid up capital, reserves, value adjustments, fixed-term cumulative preference shares, subordinated loan capital and other items at the free disposal of the credit institution. The Directive (as amended) imposes limits on the proportion of certain items to be included as against other items.

Although Directive 89/299 leaves Member States with discretion as to the use of the items comprising own funds and the fixing of lower ceilings within the maxima set down by the Directive, it obliges Member States to take into consideration increased convergence with a view of ultimately achieving a common definition of own funds.

A key change made by Directive 92/16 was to exempt Danish mortgage cooperatives from the rules relating to the required level of own funds for a limited period. The exemption was rendered necessary by the plans of the Danish government to convert the mortgage cooperatives concerned into public limited companies. . . .

E. Large Exposures

The monitoring and control of risks or exposures are regarded as crucial elements in the prudential supervision of credit institutions. In a Commission Recommendation published in December 1986,[19] a large exposure was defined as an exposure to a client or a group of connected clients whose value equals or exceeds fifteen percent of the credit institution's own funds. The Recommendation on Large Exposures[20] suggested that large exposures should be reported to the authorities at least annually and credit institutions should be prohibited from incurring any exposure to a client or a group of connected clients when the percentage value exceeds forty percent of own funds. Additionally, it recommended that credit institutions should be precluded from incurring large exposures which in aggregate exceed 800% of own funds. The Recommendation on Large Exposures further suggested that those limits should be exceeded only in exceptional circumstances.

In March 1991, the Recommendation on Large Exposures was followed by a draft Directive on large risks.[21] The draft Directive represented a compromise between Member States such as the United Kingdom, which already imposes a limit of twenty-five percent of own funds on loans to an individual customer, and other Member States, which have ceilings of around forty percent.

The Directive on large risks was adopted in December 1992, after considerable discussion, and will be implemented in stages. This Directive mandates that beginning January 1, 1994, banks will be subject to a forty percent ceiling on their loans to a single customer. On January 1, 1999, the ceiling for new loans will be reduced to twenty-five percent of own funds, but the forty percent threshold will still apply to existing credit lines until January 1, 2002. In addition, small German banks with an annual turnover of less than ECU 7,000,000 will be allowed to apply the forty percent ceiling to existing loans until January 1, 2007. There is also an exemption until December 31, 1998 in the Directive on Large Risks for certain Portuguese loans. The Directive on Large Risks differs from the

16. Council Directive 91/633, 1991 O.J. (L 339) 48.

17. Council Directive 92/16, 1992 O.J. (L 75) 48.

19. Commission Recommendation 87/62 of 22nd December 1986 on monitoring and controlling large exposures of credit institutions, 1987 O.J. (L 33) 10 [hereinafter Recommendation on Large Exposures].

20. *Id.*

21. Council Directive 92/121, 1992 O.J. (L 29) 1 [hereinafter Directive on Large Risks].

original Commission Recommendation by requiring notification to the authorities of any loan exceeding ten percent (as opposed to fifteen percent) of own funds and by limiting exposures to a client or group of connected clients to twenty-five percent of own funds. However, the overall limit on large exposures of 800%, which was set out in the Recommendation, has been carried through into the Directive on Large Risks.

F. Consolidated Supervision

On April 6, 1992, the Council adopted the Second Consolidated Supervision Directive.[22] This Directive widens the basis of consolidated supervision provided for in Directive 83/350 to banking groups where the parent is not a credit institution. The Second Consolidated Supervision Directive is seen as a means of ensuring the harmonious application of the rules relating to credit institutions established by other EC legislation and, in particular, Directive 89/299 on own funds.

The Second Consolidated Supervision Directive distinguishes three categories of parent undertakings: parent undertakings which are themselves credit institutions; parent undertakings which are financial institutions and whose subsidiary undertakings are exclusively or mainly credit or financial institutions (referred to as "financial holding companies"); and parent undertakings which are neither credit institutions nor financial institutions, but whose subsidiaries include at least one credit institution (known as "mixed-activity holding companies").

The Second Consolidated Supervision Directive provides that where a parent undertaking is a credit institution, the authorities in the Member State authorizing it shall exercise the powers of consolidated supervision. Similarly, where the parent of a credit institution is a financial holding company, consolidated supervision is to be carried out by the Member State which authorized the credit institution. Where two credit institutions authorized in different Member States share the same financial holding company as their parent and one of them is authorized in the same Member State as the parent, the Member State where the parent is authorized shall be responsible for consolidated supervision. If, however, the credit institutions and the parent are authorized in separate Member States, the Second Consolidated Supervision Directive provides for the various Member States to seek to reach an agreement on which Member State should supervise on a consolidated basis.

The position in relation to mixed-activity holding companies and their credit institution subsidiaries is rather different because the Second Consolidated Supervision Directive provides for the Member State in which the credit institution subsidiary is authorized to approach the mixed-activity holding company for information to enable it to supervise the credit institution subsidiary. The information supplied may be verified by on-the-spot inspections.

The Second Consolidated Supervision Directive also provides for the negotiation of agreements with third countries relating to the consolidated supervision of credit institutions whose parent undertakings have head offices in third countries and credit institutions situated in third countries whose parent undertakings have their head offices in the EC. Furthermore, this Directive provides that it is to be implemented by January 1, 1993, whereupon Directive 83/350 will be repealed.

G. Deposit-Guarantee Schemes

In December 1986, the Commission issued a Recommendation relating to deposit-

---

22. Council Directive 92/30, 1992 O.J. (L 110) 52 [hereinafter Second Consolidated Supervision Directive].

guarantee schemes.[23] This Recommendation provided that Member States should ensure that their deposit-guarantee schemes fulfill certain conditions to cover situations where a credit institution is wound-up with insufficient assets. One of the conditions was that the scheme should cover the depositors of credit institutions operating in that Member State but which have their head office in another Member State. The Deposit-Guarantee Recommendation suggested that Member States which did not operate a scheme should be required to implement one by January 1, 1990.

The Deposit-Guarantee Recommendation was followed in 1992 by a Commission proposal for a Directive on deposit-guarantee schemes.[24] By that stage, the collapse of Bank of Credit and Commerce International ("BCCI") had emphasized the need for comprehensive deposit-guarantee schemes, and only ten of the twelve Member States had deposit-guarantee schemes which complied with the earlier Deposit-Guarantee Recommendation.

The Proposed Directive on Deposit-Guarantee Schemes provides for each Member State to ensure that a deposit-guarantee scheme is introduced in its territory which applies to all credit institutions authorized in that Member State. The scheme must cover depositors of branches created by such credit institutions in other Member States. The Proposed Directive on Deposit-Guarantee Schemes permits branches of credit institutions to apply voluntarily to join a scheme in the Member State in which it is established, to supplement the cover provided by the scheme in the Member State in which its head office is situated.

Moreover, the Proposed Directive on Deposit-Guarantee Schemes enables Member States to stipulate that branches of credit institutions whose head offices are outside the EC must join a deposit-guarantee scheme in the Member State, provided that the scheme must not accord to such branches more favorable treatment than is accorded to branches of credit institutions with their head offices within the EC.

It is proposed that schemes should provide minimum cover of at least ninety percent of each depositor's aggregate deposits up to an overall limit of ECU 15,000, and that payment should be made to depositors within three months of the deposits becoming unavailable. The Proposed Directive on Deposit-Guarantee Schemes provides that the Directive on deposit-guarantee schemes must be implemented by January 1, 1994.

# 3. BIS Capital Adequacy Guidelines

**Notes and Comments 3.10.** One of the most significant developments with respect to international supervision of banking has been the issuance by the BIS Committee of uniform guidelines governing the measurement and enforcement of capital adequacy of international banking enterprises. U.S. capital adequacy requirements predate the BIS guidelines.[25] The BIS guidelines are intended to foster multilateral convergence of standards.

**3.11.** What regulatory and supervisory policy goals are intended to be served by the BIS guidelines, which establish a risk-based capital adequacy standard? How does the standard purport to further these goals? Why choose a ratio of capital to assets–however

---

23. Commission Recommendation 87/63, 1987 O.J. (L 33) 16 [hereinafter Deposit-Guarantee Recommendation].

24. Commission Proposal for a Council Directive on Deposit-Guarantee Schemes, 1992 O.J. (C 163) 6 [hereinafter Proposed directive on Deposit-Guarantee Schemes].

25. *See* Michael P. Malloy, *U.S. International Banking and the New Capital Adequacy Requirements: New, Old and Unexpected*, 7 Ann. Rev. Banking L. 75, 75-76, 81-87 (1988) (discussion of pre-BIS U.S. regulatory practice).

conceived at the technical level–as an instrument for achieving these policies? In answering these questions, consider the following excerpt.

## Michael P. Malloy, Capital Adequacy and Regulatory Objectives,
25 Suffolk Transnat'l L. Rev. 299 (2002)

Capital Adequacy Then and Now
    A. Early Efforts
        Capital supervision has long been a concern of the bank regulators, but this concern was usually directed at the "safety and soundness" issue naturally raised by the prospect of a depository institution with insufficient capital to support its operations. If inadequate capital maintenance constitutes an "unsafe and unsound practice," the bank regulators have broad statutory authority progressively to define and remedy capital inadequacy.[12] In 1983, however, the Fifth Circuit questioned the validity of this authority in *First National Bank of Bellaire v. Comptroller of the Currency.*[13]

        That same year Congress repudiated the Fifth Circuit's position by enacting the International Lending Supervision Act (ILSA),[14] which provides that the failure of a bank to maintain prescribed capital adequacy levels may be deemed to constitute an unsafe and unsound practice.[15] Failure to maintain capital adequacy may also lead to the issuance of a directive requiring the bank to submit and comply with a capital plan to reform capital levels.[16]

        A potentially more significant feature of the ILSA altered the character of capital maintenance from an enforcement issue to an ongoing feature of basic bank supervisory policy. The ILSA requires each agency to "cause banking institutions to achieve and maintain adequate capital by establishing minimum levels of capital for such banking institutions."[17] What constitutes "adequate capital" remains a question within the discretion of the agencies, and ILSA explicitly gives them authority to establish capital adequacy levels as they deem "necessary or appropriate in light of the particular circumstances of the banking institution."[18]

        Pursuant to their statutory authority, the federal bank regulators immediately began refining their capital adequacy policies. Certain basic problems emerged. To the extent that capital adequacy was tied to risk oversight, it was a rather crude method. Two banks of approximately the same asset size–one embracing risk for its access to possibly higher rates of return, the other almost entirely risk-averse–would be subject to approximately the same

---

[12] 12 U.S.C. §§ 1818(b)(1), 3907(b). *Cf., e.g., Groos Nat. Bank v. Comptroller of the Currency,* 573 F.2d 889 (5th Cir. 1978) (noting "progressive definition" of unsafe and unsound practices under § 1818(b)); *First Nat. Bank of Eden v. Department of the Treasury,* 568 F.2d 610 (8th Cir. 1978). Similar authority exists in the bank holding company context. *See Board of Governors v. First Lincolnwood Corp.,* 439 U.S. 234 (1978).

    13. 697 F.2d 674 (5th Cir. 1983).

[14] Pub. L. No. 98-181, tit. IX, § 908, 97 Stat. 1280 (1983) (codified at 12 U.S.C. § 3907).

[15] *Id.* § 3907(b)(1).

[16] *See id.* S 3907(b)(2). Capital directives and plans submitted pursuant to such directives are enforceable to the same extent as an effective and outstanding final cease and desist order under section 8(b) of the Federal Deposit Insurance Act, 12 U.S.C. § 1818(b). *See id.* § 3907(b)(2)(B)(ii).

[17] 12 U.S.C. § 3907(a)(1).

[18] *Id.* § 3907(a)(2).

capital requirement.

Furthermore, to the extent that U.S. regulators applied capital requirements aggressively, they were placing U.S. banks at a disadvantage in international markets. Competing non-U.S. banks would be subject to widely differing capital requirements, depending upon the policies of their respective home states. Assuming that capital adequacy served a legitimate regulatory purpose, however, U.S. regulators would be ill-advised to ameliorate this competitive disadvantage simply be lowering U.S. capital requirements.

B.  The BIS Regime

1.  Establishing Multilateral Capital Adequacy Guidelines

The U.S. regulators progressively focused their attention on refining capital adequacy policies to take into account, in an explicit way, the relative degrees of risk among the various elements composing the assets of depository institutions, and to define more precisely the elements of "capital." This effort quickly became more particularly directed at the establishment of convergent capital adequacy regimes among the United States and it major trading partners.

By the mid-1980s, the regulators openly admitted that their rules did not adequately or efficiently realize the capital adequacy goals of ILSA.[19] Hence, the search was on for a new approach that would quantify and account for, *within* the capital ratio, financial factors that significantly affected capital adequacy, but that were not necessarily apparent from the face of the balance sheet. This technical objective was joined to a broader one–reaching multilateral convergence of capital requirements and supervision for banks participating in the international market.

The guidelines for international convergence of capital measurement and capital standards developed under the auspices of the Basle Committee on Banking Regulations and Supervisory Practices[20] set forth "the details of the agreed framework for measuring capital adequacy and the minimum standard to be achieved which the national supervisory authorities represented on the Committee intend to implement in their respective countries."[21]

The basic focus of this multilateral framework is "assessing capital in relation to credit risk (the risk of counterparty failure)."[22] However, the framework acknowledged that "other risks, notably interest rate risk and the investment risk on securities, need[ed] to be taken into account by supervisors in assessing overall capital adequacy."[23] The framework consisted of a minimum required ratio of certain specified constituents of capital to risk-weighted assets. "Capital" has two types of constituents: (i) "core capital;"[24] and, "supple-

---

[19]For example, in issuing its 1985 capital adequacy regulations, the OCC acknowledged that the minimum capital ratio rules did not rigorously account either for differences in a given bank's balance sheet composition or for the presence of off-balance-sheet activities that contributed to risk. *See* 50 Fed. Reg. 10,207, 10,214 (1985). The OCC therefore announced its intention to give further consideration to alternatives for incorporating risk-related criteria into its capital adequacy rules. *See id.*

[20]*See* [BANK FOR INTERNATIONAL SETTLEMENTS, FINAL REPORT FOR INTERNATIONAL CONVERGENCE OF CAPITAL MEASUREMENT AND CAPITAL STANDARDS, *reprinted in* 4 Fed. Banking L. Rep. (CCH) ¶ 47-105 (Mar. 15, 1996) [hereinafter Final Report].]

[21]Final Report at 51,166.

[22]*Id.* at 51,167.

[23]*Id.*

[24]*See id.* (discussing meaning of "core capital"). *See generally id.* at 51,173, Annex 1 (defining capital in terms of capital base after transitional period).

mentary capital."[25] Core capital, the so-called Tier 1 of capital elements, consists of: (i) equity capital;[26] and, (ii) disclosed reserves from post-tax earnings.[27]

Tier 1 capital elements are the only ones common to the banking systems of all the countries represented on the Committee.[28] Nevertheless, a number of other significant elements of capital are often recognized by individual countries. The framework therefore identified two tiers of capital elements. The Tier 1 elements must account for at least 50 percent of a bank's capital base for purposes of the risk-weighted ratio.[29] Constituents of supplementary capital, the so-called Tier 2 of capital elements, may be included for these purposes up to an amount equal to the amount of Tier 1 capital elements.[30] Supplementary capital consists of: (i) undisclosed reserves;[31] (ii) revaluation reserves;[32] (iii) general provisions or loan loss reserves;[33] (iv) certain hybrid debt capital instruments;[34] and, (v) subor

---

[25]*See id.* at 51,167-51,168 (discussing meaning of "supplementary capital"). *See generally id.* at 51,173, Annex 1 (defining capital in terms of capital base after transitional period).

[26]For these purposes, "equity capital" is defined as "[i]ssued and fully paid ordinary shares/common stock and non-cumulative perpetual preferred stock (but excluding cumulative preferred stock)." *Id.* at 51,167 n. 2. *See also id.* at 51,174, Annex 1, § D(i) (defining "Tier 1" capital elements). In the case of consolidated accounts, Tier 1 capital would also include minority interests in the equity of subsidiaries of the bank that are less than wholly owned. *Id.*

[27]*Id.* at 51,167. For these purposes, disclosed reserves are reserves that are "created or increased by appropriations of retained earnings or other surplus, *e.g.* share premiums, retained profit, general reserves and legal reserves." *Id.* at 51,174. Tier 1 does not include revaluation reserves. *Id.*

[28]*Id.* at 51,167.

[29]*See id.*

[30]*Id.*

[31]*Id.* at 51,167-51,168 (discussing undisclosed reserves). *See also id.* at 51,174, Annex 1, § D(ii)(a) (defining capital in terms of capital base). Inclusion of undisclosed reserves in the capital base is contemplated by the framework only to the extent permitted by local regulatory and accounting arrangement. *Id.* at 51,167. In any event, undisclosed reserves are included in supplementary capital only to the extent that they "have been passed through the profit and loss account and [have been] accepted by [a] bank's supervisory authorities. *Id.* at 51,168.

[32]*Id.* at 51,168 (discussing revaluation reserves). *See also id.* at 51,174, Annex 1, § D(ii)(b) (defining capital in terms of capital base). Inclusion of revaluation reserves in the capital base is contemplated by the framework only to the extent permitted by local regulatory and accounting arrangement. *Id.* at 51,167. Revaluation reserves, whether arising from a formal revaluation or from a "latent revaluation" (a notional additional to capital of hidden values with respect to securities carried at historic cost), may be included in the capital base only if "the assets are considered by the supervisory authority to be prudently valued, fully reflecting the possibility of price fluctuations and forced sale." *Id.* at 51,168. In addition, latent revaluation reserves are subject to a substantial discount reflecting, for example, market volatility and any tax effect of realization of the gain. *Id.* The framework indicates that a 55 percent discount on the difference between historical cost book value and current market value has been agreed to be appropriate in this regard. *See id.*

[33]*Id.* at 51,168 (discussing general provisions and general loan loss reserves). *See also id.* at 51,174, Annex 1, § D(ii)(c) (defining capital included in capital base). Reserves against identified losses or with respect to "known deterioration in the valuation of particular assets" are not included in this category. *Id.* at 51,168. *See generally* 65 Fed. Reg. 54,268 (2000) (proposing policy statement on allowance for loan and lease losses methodologies and documentation).

[34]Final Report, *supra* . . . at 51,168 (discussing "hybrid debt capital instruments"). *See also id.* at 51,175, Annex 1, § D(ii)(d) (defining capital included in capital base). Generally, this category includes elements that "combine certain characteristics of equity and certain characteristics of debt."

dinated term debt.[35]

The eligible constituents of Tier 1 and Tier 2 capital are subject to certain deductions under the framework.[36] The amount of goodwill must be deducted from the figure for Tier 1 capital.[37] The amount of investments in unconsolidated banking and financial subsidiaries, if any,[38] must be deducted from the total capital base.[39] The Committee considered, but ultimately rejected, requiring deduction of banks' holdings of capital issued by other banks or depository institutions.[40] Nevertheless, the framework does reflect the agreement that individual supervisory authorities retain the discretion to require such deductions.[41] If no deduction is applied, such holdings are required to bear an asset risk-weight of 100

---

*Id.* at 51,168. Characteristics vary from country to country, but to be included the instruments should exhibit the following specifications:

> --they are *unsecured, subordinated and fully paid-up*;
> --they are *not redeemable* at the initiative of the holder or without prior consent of the supervisory authority;
> --they are *available to participate in losses* without the bank being obliged to cease trading (unlike conventional subordinated debt); [and,]
> --although the capital instrument may carry an obligation to pay interest that cannot permanently be reduced or waived (unlike dividends on ordinary share holders' equity), *it should allow service obligations to be deferred* (as with cumulative preference shares) where the profitability of the bank would not support payment.

*Id.* at 51,175 (emphasis in original). Such instruments as mandatory convertible debt instruments (in U.S. practice), perpetual debt and preference shares (in U.K. practice), long-term preferred shares (in Canadian practice), *titres participatifs* and *titres subordonnes a duree indeterminee* (in French practice), or *Genussscheine* (in German practice) would qualify for inclusion in this category of Tier 2 capital. *See id.* at 51,168. *See also id.* at 51,175.

[35]*Id.* at 51,168-51,169 (discussion of subordinated term debt). *See also id.* at 51,175, Annex 1, § D(ii)(e) (definition of capital included in the capital base). This category includes "conventional unsecured subordinated debt capital instruments with a minimum original fixed term to maturity of over five years and limited life redeemable preference shares." *Id.* Such instruments are not normally available to participate in the losses of an issuing bank that continues trading (*see id.*), they are viewed as having "significant deficiencies as constituents of capital in view of their fixed maturity and inability to absorb losses except in liquidation." *Id.* at 51,168. Accordingly, these instruments may be included only up to an amount equal to 50 percent of the total amount of core capital (*id.* at 51,169), and they are subject to a cumulative discount or amortization of twenty percent per year during the last five years of maturity "to reflect the diminishing value of these instruments as a continuing source of strength." *Id.* at 51,175.

[36]*See id.* at 51,169.

[37]*Id.*

[38]The framework generally assumes as the normal practice that subsidiaries will be consolidated for the purpose of assessing capital adequacy, but "[w]here this is not done, deduction is essential to prevent multiple use of the same capital resources in different parts of [a banking] group." *Id.*

[39]*Id.*

[40]*See id.*

[41]*Id.* Conceivably, these discretionary policies may require deduction of the amount of all such holdings, holdings to the extent that they exceed some determined limit in relation to the holding bank's or the issuing bank's capital, or on a case-by-case basis. *Id.* The framework also reflected the agreement that, "in applying these policies, member countries [should] consider that reciprocal cross-holdings of bank capital designed artificially to inflate the capital position of the banks concerned should not be permitted." *Id.*

percent for purposes of assessing capital adequacy of the holding bank.[42]

The framework endorsed a risk-weighted approach to the assets denominator of the capital-assets ratio utilized in assessing capital adequacy.[43] The framework established a relatively simple methodology for risk-weighting, with only five risk weights being employed.[44] Essentially, the methodology as effectively captured only credit risk.[45] It was left to the discretion of individual supervisory authorities to decide whether to attempt to account for more methodologically difficult types of risk, such as investment risk, interest rate risk, exchange rate risk or concentration risk.[46] Furthermore, the individual supervisory authorities also retained discretion to supplement the framework's risk-weighted methodology with "other methods of capital measurement,[47] such as the mandated capital-assets ratios previously established by individual national regulators.

Furthermore, to account for country transfer risk, the Committee ultimately adopted an approach that applied differing risk weights to defined groups of countries.[48]

The framework also recognized the importance of bringing off-balance-sheet risk into the analysis of capital adequacy.[49] All categories of off-balance-sheet risk were brought within the framework, by conversion into appropriate credit risk equivalents.[50]

---

[42]*Id.*

[43]*See id.*

[44]*See id.* at 51,175-51,176, Annex 2 (establishing risk weights by categories of on-balance-sheet asset).

[45]*Id.* at 51,169.

[46]*Id.* at 51,169-51,170.

[47]*Id.* at 51,169.

[48]*Id.* at 51,170-51,171:

> [T]he Committee has concluded that a defined group of countries should be adopted as the basis for applying differential weighting coefficients[.] The framework also recognizes the importance of and that this group should be full members of the OECD or countries which have concluded special arrangements with the [International Monetary Fund] associated with the Fund's General Arrangements to Borrow....
> ... This decision has the following consequences for the weighting structure. Claims on central governments within the OECD will attract a zero weight (or a low weight if the national supervisory authority elects to incorporate interest rate risk); and claims on OECD non-central government public-sector entities will attract a low weight.... Claims on central governments and central banks outside the OECD will also attract a zero weight (or a low weight if the national supervisory authority elects to incorporate investment risk), provided such claims are denominated in the national currency and funded by liabilities in the same currency....
> ... As regards the treatment of interbank claims, in order to preserve the efficiency and liquidity of the international interbank market[,] there will be no differentiation between short- term claims on banks incorporated within or outside the OECD. However, the Committee draws a distinction between ... short-term placements with other banks ... and ... longer-term cross-border loans to banks which are often associated with particular transactions and carry greater transfer and/or credit risks. A 20 per cent [*sic*] weight will therefore be applied to claims on all banks, wherever incorporated, with a residual maturity of up to an[d] including one year; longer-term claims on OECD incorporated banks will be weighted at 20 per cent [*sic*]; and longer-term claims on banks incorporated outside the OECD will be weighted at 100 percent.

[49]*See id.* at 51,171-51,172 (discussing treatment of off-balance-sheet engagements).

[50]*See id.* at 51,176, Annex 3 (establishing credit conversion factors for off-balance-sheet items).

Uncertainty remained about the appropriate approach to items exposed to significant interest-rate and exchange-rate related risk, such as swaps, options and futures.[51] As to these contingencies, the framework took the position that special treatment was necessary, "because banks are not exposed to credit risk for the full face value of their contracts, but only to the cost of replacing the cash flow if the counterparty defaults."[52]

Once the credit equivalent amounts of such contingencies have been calculated, the amounts are to be weighted in accordance with the risk weights applicable to the category of counterparties involved. However, in anticipation of the fact that most counterparties in the market for such contingencies, particularly long-term contracts, "tend to be first-class names,"[53] the Final Report reflected general agreement that such contingencies would be assigned a 50 percent risk weight, rather than the 100 percent risk weight that might otherwise be applicable.[54]

The final element in the risk-weighted methodology, as with any capital-assets ratio requirement, is the required minimum level of the ratio. As the proposed version of this multilateral agreement was taking shape, there was some dissent from two of the participating countries on this issue, though it was generally agreed that specifying a target ratio was desirable before the proposed framework was circulated at the national level for consultation and discussion. After further consultations and study of the proposed version, final agreement was reached and the framework adopted a target standard ratio of eight percent, of which core capital must constitute at least four percent.[55] This target ratio became fully applicable at year-end 1992.[56]

In brief, then, the current risk-weighted methodology is applied as follows. First, identification of Tier 1 capital elements is made, with the amount of goodwill deducted from the gross amount of Tier 1 capital. Second, Tier 2 capital elements must be identified. The total of Tier 2 capital may be included for ratio purposes only up to an amount equal to the amount of Tier 1 capital. Furthermore, among the Tier 2 capital elements, subordinated term debt is limited to a maximum of 50 percent of the amount of Tier 1 elements, certain amounts for general provisions or general loan loss reserves are generally limited to an amount equal to 1.25 percent of risk-weighted assets.

Third, from the total capital base (Tier 1 plus eligible Tier 2), there must be deducted any investments in unconsolidated banking and finance subsidiaries of the banking enterprise under consideration. Furthermore, in the discretion of the individual national regulator, investments in the capital of other banks and depository institutions may also be required to be deducted from the total capital base. The result of these first three steps yields the numerator of the risk-weighted ratio.

Fourth, the on-balance-sheet assets must be weighted according to the general categories of risk set forth in Annex 2 of the Final Report. Fifth, any off-balance-sheet items must be converted to their credit equivalents. These credit equivalent amounts are then risk-weighted in accordance with the generally applicable rules governing risk weighting. Sixth, the denominator of the risk-weighted ratio–total risk-weighted assets–is derived by adding

---

[51]*See id.* at 51,172.

[52]*Id.*

[53]*Id.* at 51,178.

[54]*Id.* However, some member countries have apparently reserved the right to apply the full 100 percent risk weight. *See id.* n. 9.

[55]*Id.* at 51,172.

[56]*Id.* at 51,172-51,173.

the risk-weighted on-balance-sheet amounts to the risk-weighted credit equivalents of the off-balance-sheet items. The ratios of Tier 1 capital to total risk-weighted assets and of total capital (Tier 1 plus eligible Tier 2 amounts) to total risk-weighted assets are then calculated and assessed in relation to the required minimum ratios under the framework.

2. Subsequent Refinements

The Basle Committee has continued to refine the details and mechanics of risk management and supervision.[50] Correspondingly, implementation of the guidelines in the United States has not been a static project; the guidelines have been the subject of almost continuous reassessment and refinement by the regulators.[51] By the mid-1990s, the agencies were seriously focusing upon management of interest-rate risk, which was not within the purview of the original guidelines.[52] Similarly, the regulators have folded market-risk provisions into the framework of the guidelines.[53]

50. *See, e.g.*, BIS, Committee on Banking Supervision, *The Treatment of the Credit Risk Associated with Certain Off-Balance-Sheet Items* (July 1994); BIS, Committee on Banking Supervision, *Risk Management Guidelines for Derivatives* (July 1994); BIS, Committee on Banking Supervision, *Amendment to the Capital Accord of July 1988* (July 1994); BIS, Committee on Banking Supervision, *Prudential Supervision of Banks' Derivatives Activities* (Dec. 1994); BIS, Committee on Banking Supervision, *Basle Capital Accord: Treatment of Potential Exposure for Off-Balance-Sheet Items* (April 1995); BIS, Committee on Banking Supervision, *An Internal Model-Based Approach to Market Risk Capital Requirements* (April 1995); BIS, Committee on Banking Supervision, *Public Disclosure of the Trading and Derivatives Activities of Banks and Securities Firms* (Nov. 1995); BIS, Committee on Banking Supervision, *Supervisory Framework for the Use of "Backtesting" in Conjunction with the Internal Models Approach to Market Risk Capital Requirements* (Jan. 1996); BIS, Committee on Banking Supervision, *Amendment to the Basle Capital Accord to Incorporate Market Risks* (Jan. 1996); BIS, Committee on Banking Supervision, *Interpretation of the Capital Accord for the Multilateral Netting of Forward Value Foreign Exchange Transactions* (April 1996).

51. *See, e.g.*, 62 Fed. Reg. 55,686 (1997) (to be codified at 12 C.F.R. pts. 3, 208, 325, 567) (proposing uniform treatment of certain construction and real estate loans and investments in mutual funds; simplifying Tier 1 capital standards); 62 Fed. Reg. 55,692 (1997) (to be codified at 12 C.F.R. pt. 225) (proposing similar amendments with respect to treatment of capital of bank holding companies); 62 Fed. Reg. 59,944 (1997) (to be codified at 12 C.F.R. pts. 3, 208, 225, 325, 567) (proposing regulatory capital treatment of recourse obligations and direct credit substitutes); 64 Fed. Reg. 10,194 (1999) (codified at 12 C.F.R. pts. 3, 208, 325, 567) (OCC, Fed, FDIC and OTS rules for construction loans on presold residential properties, junior liens on one- to four-family residential properties, investments in mutual funds, and tier 1 leverage ratio); 64 Fed. Reg. 10,201 (1999) (codified at 12 C.F.R. pt. 225) (corresponding Fed rule applicable to bank holding companies); 65 Fed. Reg. 12,320 (2000) (to be codified at 12 C.F.R. pts. 3, 208, 225, 325, 567) (proposing changes in risk-based capital standards to address recourse obligations and direct credit substitutes); 65 Fed. Reg. 16,480 (2000) (to be codified at 12 C.F.R. pt. 225, Appendices A, D) (proposing regulatory capital treatment of certain investments in nonfinancial companies by bank holding companies); 65 Fed. Reg. 76,180 (2000) (to be codified at 12 C.F.R. pts. 3, 208, 225, 325, 567) (proposing to reduce risk weight applied to claims on, and claims guaranteed by, qualifying securities firms incorporated in countries that are OECD members from 100 percent to 20 percent).

52. *See, e.g.*, 61 Fed. Reg. 33,166 (1996) (publishing OCC, FRS & FDIC joint policy statement providing guidance on sound practices for managing interest rate risk); 66 Fed. Reg. 15,049 (2001) (to be codified at 12 C.F.R. §§ 567.1, 567.5(b)(4), (c)(2)(i)-(ii), 567.6(a)(1)(ii)(H), (a)(1)(iv)(G)-(H); removing 12 C.F.R. §§ 567.5(c)(2)(iii), (c)(3), 567.7) (proposing 50 percent risk weight for certain qualifying mortgage loans; eliminating interest rate risk component of risk-based capital regulations; proposing technical changes).

53. *See, e.g.*, 62 Fed. Reg. 68,064 (1997) (codified at 12 C.F.R. pts. 3, 208, 225, 325) (amending market risk provisions in risk-based capital standards)

C.  Assessing the Regime in Relation to Policy Objectives

. . .

It should be evident that even under the BIS framework the capital adequacy methodology exhibited some serious shortcomings. First, the framework recognized only a narrow, though very significant, type of risk–credit risk, *i.e.*, the risk of counterparty failure.[59] Over time, the methodology was refined to fold in other types of risk, namely, interest-rate risk and exchange-rate risk.[60] Nevertheless, there was still no calibration within the methodology for internal or "operational" risk[61]–broadly speaking, the risks attendant upon poor management of asset risks–yet surely this type of risk was important for safety and soundness purposes.

Second, the methodology for risk-weighting was technically rudimentary. Five risk weights–0, 10, 20, 50 and 100 percent of asset value–were available for *all* types of assets and *all* types of counterparties. This arrangement produced such anomalous results as the application of the same risk weight to a commercial loan to a small business operating a local retail computer store and a commercial loan to a major dot.com corporation, despite the obvious differences in the relative risks involved in the two borrowers.

Third, the framework did not take into account the dramatic changes in the contours of the banking market itself. These changes included consolidation in holding company patterns of ownership and control of increasingly diversified financial services enterprises. Consolidation and diversification were taking place in a markedly more globalized market environment.

Fourth, the methodology tended to be insensitive to the individual experience and operational qualities of banks. The framework had one size to fit all banks subject to capital adequacy requirements.[62] Thus, greater reliance on standardized capital adequacy calculations–a tendency clearly exhibited by U.S. statutes–carried with it the danger that there could be less emphasis on individualized safety-and-soundness assessment of particular banks.

**Notes and Comments 3.12.** Imagine a situation in which Quarter National Bank (QNB) had only cash and cash-like assets.[26] According to the BIS capital adequacy guidelines, how much capital must QNB have in order to meet the requirement of a minimum

59. For extensive discussion of the types of risk relevant to the conduct of the business of banking, see BIS, Committee on Banking Supervision, *Core Principles for Effective Banking Supervision* § IV.A, [reprinted in the Appendix] (hereinafter *Core Principles*).

60. *See, e.g.*, note 51, *supra* (citing revisions in methodology to account for interest rate and exchange rate risks).

61. The term *operational risk* may be defined as "the risk of direct or indirect loss resulting from inadequate or failed internal processes, people and systems or from external events." BIS Committee on Banking Supervision, *Consultative Document: The New Capital Accord* 94 (Jan. 2001) [hereinafter *Accord*]. As used in the BIS proposed Accord, the term does not include strategic and reputational risk. *Id.* For discussion of reputational risk, see *Core Principles, supra* note 59 at 291. A working paper of the BIS Committee's Risk Management Group has proposed the deletion of the phrase "direct or indirect" from the definition of operational loss, because it was too vague. Risk Management Group, BIS Committee on Banking Supervision, *Working Paper on the Regulatory Treatment of Operational Risk, available at*, http://www.bis.org [hereinafter *RMG Working Paper*].

62. This was particularly true of the U.S. application of the BIS framework. While the framework by its own terms applied only to international banks, U.S. statutes and implementing regulations applied the capital adequacy regime to *all* banks subject to federal regulation.

26. This is obviously a practical impossibility, since in real life QNB would necessarily have some other, physical assets. But imagine it anyway.

capital/assets ratio of eight percent?

**3.13.** *Furtherance of the BIS capital adequacy guidelines under FDICIA.* The enactment of the Federal Deposit Insurance Corporation Improvement Act of 1991[27] may have the effect of furthering the objectives of the standards. *See* question 2.3.a., *supra* at 47.

**3.14.** *Adjustment in the capital adequacy rules.* The capital adequacy rules described in the excerpt, *supra*, have been subject to repeated adjustment and refinement over time. In April 2002, for example, the U.S. regulatory agencies adjusted the rules once again,[28] to reduce the risk weighting of claims on, and claims guaranteed by, qualifying securities firms[29] from 100 percent to 20 percent. The rule reduces the risk weight applied to such claims if the firm is incorporated in a country that is a member of the OECD. The propoed version of the rule was in response to an April 1998 amendment of the capital adequacy guidelines by the BIS Committee.[30] One of the primary reasons that the BIS Committee amended the guidelines was to make it consistent with the treatment of claims on securities firms permitted under the European Union's (EU) Capital Adequacy Directive (CAD), which a number of European countries have followed for some time. Claims on, and claims guaranteed by, holding companies and other affiliates of a qualifying securities firm, would retain their current 100 percent risk weighting, Claims on, and claims guaranteed by, a subsidiary of a qualifying securities firm also would retain their current 100 percent risk weight, unless such subsidiary's obligations were guaranteed by a qualifying securities firm.

**3.15.** *Proposed revision of the BIS capital adequacy accord.* The BIS Committee has continued to refine the details and mechanics of risk management and supervision.[31] In

---

27. Pub. L. No. 102-242, 105 Stat. 2236 (December 19, 1991) (codified at scattered sections of 12 U.S.C.)

28. 67 Fed. Reg. 16,971 (2002) (codified at 12 C.F.R. pt. 3, app. A, §§ 1(c)(19)-(35), 3(a)(2)(xiii), (a)(4)(x) (amending OCC rules for national banks); pt. 208, app. A, §§ III.C.2.a.-III.C.2.d., III.C.4.b., attach. III (amending Fed rules for state member banks); pt. 225, app. A, §§ III.C.2.a.-III.C.2.d., III.C.4.b., attach. III (amending Fed rules for bank holding companies); pt. 325, app. A, §§ II.B.3., II.C. (amending FDIC rules for state nonmember banks); §§ 561.1, 567.6(a)(1)(i)(H), (a)(1)(ii)(H) (amending OTS rules)); *corrected*, 67 Fed. Reg. 34,991 (2002).

29. *E.g.*, broker-dealers registered with the Securities and Exchange Commission (SEC). Such U.S. firms must be subject to and comply with SEC net capital rules, 17 C.F.R. § 240.15c3-1, margin and other regulatory requirements applicable to registered broker-dealers. Qualifying securities firms incorporated in any other OECD country must be subject to consolidated supervision and regulation (covering their subsidiaries, but not necessarily their parent organizations) comparable to that imposed on depository institutions in OECD countries, including risk-based capital requirements comparable to those applied to depository institutions under the Accord. 65 Fed. Reg. at 76,181.

30. *Id.*

31. *See, e.g.*, BIS, Committee on Banking Supervision, *The Treatment of the Credit Risk Associated with Certain Off-Balance-Sheet Items* (July 1994); BIS, Committee on Banking Supervision, *Risk Management Guidelines for Derivatives* (July 1994); BIS, Committee on Banking Supervision, *Amendment to the Capital Accord of July 1988* (July 1994); BIS, Committee on Banking Supervision, *Prudential Supervision of Banks' Derivatives Activities* (Dec. 1994); BIS, Committee on Banking Supervision, *Basle Capital Accord: Treatment of Potential Exposure for Off-Balance-Sheet Items* (April 1995); BIS, Committee on Banking Supervision, *An Internal Model-Based Approach to Market Risk Capital Requirements* (April 1995); BIS, Committee on Banking Supervision, *Public Disclosure of the Trading and Derivatives Activities of Banks and Securities Firms* (Nov. 1995); BIS, Committee on Banking Supervision, *Supervisory Framework for the Use of "Backtesting" in*

June 1999, the BIS issued a proposal that would significantly revise the capital adequacy accord.[32] The proposal had three basic principles: (*i*) International banks would be required to establish their own internal methods for assessing the relative risks of their assets. (*ii*) Supervisory authorities would be expected to exercise greater oversight of these capital assessments by banks. (*iii*) Greater transparency in banking operations would be required, *e.g.*, the creditworthiness of borrowing governments and corporations would be assessed by credit-rating agencies, and these ratings would be used by banks in pricing loans to such borrowers. Financial institutions had until 31 March 2000 to respond to the proposed revisions, which was expected to become effective no sooner than 2001.[33] A new version of the proposal was issued in January 2001.[34] The three reconfigured "pillars" involve a new, more sensitive capital standard, heightened supervisory review of banks' own internal assessments of their capital ratios, and increased public disclosure of risk portfolios. The innovative feature of allowing qualified banks to develop their own internal models for assessing capital adequacy has attracted some controversy and criticism.[35] Would these changes resolve the shortcomings of the current BIS guidelines? How likely do you think it is that the proposal will be adopted by the BIS Committee and generally followed by member states and other states around the world? In responding to these questions, consider the following excerpt.

## Michael P. Malloy, Capital Adequacy and Regulatory Objectives,
25 Suffolk Transnat'l L. Rev. 299 (2002)

Proposed Revision of the Capital Adequacy Guidelines
    Over the past decade, the BIS Committee began working on amendments to the 1988 Guidelines in order to take account of new globalized financial practices and to create a more flexible, risk-sensitive framework for determining minimum capital requirements.[63] In June 1999, the BIS issued a proposal that would significantly revise the capital adequacy

---

*Conjunction with the Internal Models Approach to Market Risk Capital Requirements* (Jan. 1996); BIS, Committee on Banking Supervision, *Amendment to the Basle Capital Accord to Incorporate Market Risks* (Jan. 1996); BIS, Committee on Banking Supervision, *Interpretation of the Capital Accord for the Multilateral Netting of Forward Value Foreign Exchange Transactions* (April 1996).

    32. *See, e.g.*, Alan Cowell, *An International Banking Panel Proposes Ways to Limit Risk*, N.Y. Times, June 4, 1999, at C4, col. 2 (describing proposed revision).

    33. *Id.* at C4, col. 4.

    34. *See* Richard Cowden, *Financial Institutions: Meyer Promotes Basel Committee Proposal as Needed Update to Aging Capital Standard*, Int'l Bus. & Fin. Daily, Mar. 7, 2001, at d7 (discussing proposal).

    35. Ironically, a recent survey by the BIS Committee on Banking Supervision, released in April 2001, suggests that major banks may fail to satisfy the three pillars because of inadequacy in their disclosure practices, particularly "in areas related to credit risk modeling and the use of internal and external ratings." Daniel Pruzin, *Financial Institutions: Basel Committee Cites Mixed Results for Meeting Proposed Capital Accord*, Int'l Bus. & Fin. Daily, Apr. 24, 2001, at d2.

    63. *See* Daniel Pruzin, *Basel Committee Sets Out Changes to Risk Calculations Under Capital Accord*, BNA Int'l Bus. & Fin. Daily, Oct. 3, 2001, at d3 (discussing BIS motivations for proposed Capital Accord). *See also* note 50, *supra* (citing BIS issuances concerning refinement of capital adequacy framework).

accord,[64] in two basic ways: by extensively refining the 1988 guidelines, and by providing a dramatic alternative approach. The new approach had three basic principles: (*i*) International banks would be required to establish their own internal methods for assessing the relative risks of their assets. (*ii*) Supervisory authorities would be expected to exercise greater oversight of these capital assessments by banks. (*iii*) Greater transparency in banking operations would be required, *e.g.*, the creditworthiness of borrowing governments and corporations would be assessed by credit-rating agencies, and these ratings would be used by banks in pricing loans to such borrowers. Financial institutions had until 31 March 2000 to respond to the proposed revisions, which the BIS anticipated would be effective no sooner than 2001.[65]

A revised version of the proposal was issued for comment in January 2001.[66] This latest version takes the three-pronged approach to capital adequacy for international banks that are qualified to use it: capital adequacy requirements (largely revised from the 1988 guidelines);[67] increased supervision of bank capital maintenance policies;[68] and greater transparency through disclosure to the market, with resulting market discipline.[69] These elements are referred to as the three "pillars" of minimum capital requirements, the supervisory review process, and market discipline.

Of the three pillars, by far the most extensively discussed in the proposal is the first pillar, which will involve significant changes in capital adequacy regulation. First, capital requirements would be extensively revised from the original framework version and would offer banks two alternative approaches to capital adequacy. The standardized approach[70] is essentially the 1988 guidelines, as revised by the new Accord.[71] The revisions represent refinements of the guidelines, including for example more articulated risk weights with respect to claims on sovereign borrowers based upon their credit assessments by export credit agencies.[72] Furthermore, the Accord imposes a requirement that internationally active banks account for operational risk (arising from poor documentation, fraud, infrastructural failure and the like), in addition to credit and market risk.[74] Generally, the charge for operational risk would involve approximately 20 percent of overall capital requirements.[75] The capital requirements would be applied to consolidated and sub-consolidated elements of larger financial services enterprises.[76]

---

64. *See, e.g.*, Alan Cowell, *An International Banking Panel Proposes Ways to Limit Risk*, N.Y. Times, June 4, 1999, at C4, col. 2 (describing proposed revision).

65. *Id*. at C4, col. 4.

66. *Accord, supra*. . . .

67. *See Accord* at 6-103 (discussing approaches to capital requirements).

68. *See id*. at 104-112 (discussing supervision).

69. *See id*. at 114-133.

70. *Id*. at 7-31.

71. *Id*. at 7.

72. *Id*. at 7-8.

74. [*Id*. at] 95.

75. *Id*. at 95 n.51.

76. *Id*. at 1:

    1. The New Basel Capital Accord . . . will be applied on a consolidated basis to internationally active banks. . . .
    2. The scope of application of the Accord will be extended to include, on a fully

As an alternative to the standardized approach, banks that demonstrate to their supervisors an internal methodology for assigning exposures to different classes of assets consistently over time[77] will be able to maintain capital in accordance with an internal credit ratings system (the so called "internal ratings based," or "IRB" approach).[78] The IRB approach is based upon sophisticated computer modeling or other in-house analytical tools to determine credit risk on a borrower-by-borrower basis that includes an estimate of future losses on assets.[79] Two methodologies are available in this regard. The foundation methodology would allow the bank to estimate internally the probability of default on the asset, while using regulator-imposed analysis of other risk components associated with the asset.[80] Under the advanced methodology, a sophisticated bank would be permitted to use internally generated estimates for other risk components.[81]

The revised proposal was highly criticized by banking industry commentators,[82] mainly because of reporting requirements perceived as excessive, and the level of capital charges viewed as unnecessarily high. In addition, in the Spring 2001, the annual report of the BIS Committee on Banking Supervision, reviewing the public disclosure practices of international banks, criticized the relative lack of disclosure in areas related to credit risk modeling and use of internal and external ratings by major banks.[83] This seriously implicates the proposed Accord, since disclosure of information with respect to use of internal ratings is necessary for banks to qualify for the IRB approach proposed in "Pillar 1" of the new accord.[84]

In fact, as a result of its assessment of the critical comments that were received in response to the last version of the proposal and the need for further study and adjustment of the proposal in light of those comments, in June 2001 the BIS Committee decided to delay implementation of the proposed Capital Accord until 2005.[85] The delay was particularly welcomed by the European Commission, which had launched a consultative process for a

---

consolidated basis, holding companies that are parents of banking groups to ensure that it captures risks within the whole banking group. . . .
      3. The Accord will also apply to all internationally active banks at every tier within a banking group. . . .

(Footnote omitted.) However, the parent holding company of a banking group's holding company may not itself be subject to the Accord if it is not viewed as a parent of a banking group. *Id.* at 1 n.1. . . .

77. [*Id.* at 32.

78. *Id.* at 32-86.

79. *Id.* at 34.

80. *Id.* In October 2001, a task force of the BIS Committee questioned whether the foundation approach was necessary and asked for comment from the banking industry on this issue. Models Task Force, BIS Committee on Banking Supervision, *Working Paper on the Internal Ratings-Based Approach to Specialized Lending Exposures, available at,* http://www.bis.org [hereinafter *MTF Working Paper*].

81. *Accord, supra* . . . at 34.

82. *See* Daniel Pruzin, *supra* note 63, at d3 (noting industry opposition).

83. Daniel Pruzin, *Basel Committee Cites Mixed Results for Meeting Proposed Capital Accord,* BNA Int'l Bus. & Fin. Daily, Apr. 24, 2001, at d2.

84. *Id.*

85. Daniel Pruzin, *Capital Accord Draft Completion Delayed as Basel Committee Eyes New Revisions,* BNA Int'l Bus. & Fin. Daily, June 26, 2001, at d3.

parallel EU proposal based on the Basel Committee's recommendations.[86] The Commission noted that, during its own consultation process, the proposed calibration of risk weights and the potential impact of the proposed ratio of regulatory capital to operational risk (20 percent) had been consistently criticized by various branches of the banking and financial services sector.[87] Concerns had also been raised about the relatively tight timetable for finalizing the new capital regime.[88]

In a working paper issued Sept. 28, the Risk Management Group of the BIS Committee on Banking Supervision outlined changes to the proposed Capital Accord.[89] The proposed changes to the Accord's "Pillar 1" would include, *inter alia*, a significant lowering of the operational risk charge as a percentage of a bank's overall capital set-aside requirements and greater flexibility in the use of advanced internal risk estimate methods for determining a bank's minimum capital requirements.[90] Comments on the proposed changes were to be received by 31 October 2001.[91]

On 5 October 2001, the BIS Committee released another working paper, proposing further changes to the revised Accord.[92] The working paper focused on issues concerning the application of IRB approaches to risk assessment, and specifically on the treatment of "specialized loans" such as project finance undertakings.[93] The working paper proposed a specific framework for treatment of specialized loans that relied upon a stream of income generated by an asset rather than the creditworthiness of the borrower for repayment of the loan. Such a loan arrangement does not conform to assumptions underlying the IRB approach of the revised Accord, which tends to focus on the ongoing operations of the borrower as the source of repayment.[94] The proposed treatment of specialized loans would include any loans that exhibited the following characteristics: (*i*) loan is intended for the acquisition or financing of an asset; (*ii*) asset cash flow is the sole or almost sole source of repayment; (*iii*) loan represents a significant liability for the borrower; and, (*iv*) variability of asset cash flow, rather than the independent creditworthiness of the borrower's overall enterprise, is the key determinant of credit risk.[95]

According to the MTF Working Paper, four loan products clearly meet these criteria. Project finance, "in which the lender looks primarily to the revenues generated by

---

86. Joe Kirwin, *EC Welcomes Basel Committee Delay in Implementing New Capital Accord*, BNA Banking Daily, June 26, 2001, at d3.

87. *Id.*

88. *Id.*

89. [Risk Management Group, BIS Committee on Banking Supervision, *Working Paper on the Regulatory Treatment of Operational Risk, available at*, http://www.bis.org [hereinafter *RMG Working Paper*].] *See* Daniel Pruzin, *supra* note 63 at d3 (reporting on implications of *RMG Working Paper*).

90. Daniel Pruzin, *supra* note 63 at d3 (discussing proposed changes).

91. *Id.*

92. *MTF Working Paper, supra* note 80. *See* Daniel Pruzin, *Basel Committee Outlines Further Changes to IRB Approach in Proposed Capital Accord*, Int'l Bus. & Fin. Daily, Oct. 10, 2001, at d5 (reporting on *MTF Working Paper*).

93. *MTF Working Paper, supra* note 80.

94. *See, e.g., Accord, supra* . . . at 50-51 (discussing risk assessment criteria applicable to corporate exposures).

95. Daniel Pruzin, *supra* note 92, at d5.

a single project"[96] for security and repayment, would be subject to the proposed treatment of specialized loans. A second product would be income-producing real estate, in which construction or acquisition of such assets as office buildings, retail properties, hotels, and the like, is financed and repayment depends upon income generated by the property.[97] Big-ticket lease financing (or "object financing," in the vocabulary of the MTF Working Paper), in which the acquisition of significant capital equipment such as vessels, aircraft, satellites and railcars, is financed on the strength of the lease income that the asset will generate, is a third category included in specialized loans.[98] Finally, commodity financing, involving "short-term lending to finance reserves, inventories, or receivables of exchange-traded commodities,"[99] would be included since repayment is dependent upon subsequent sale of the commodity. These (and possibly other loan products) would be subject to a single framework, with a specified set of components generating minimum capital requirements related to the specialized loan products.

We have yet to see what the banking industry's reaction to these new proposals might be. No deadline for comments on the MTF Working Paper was formally set by the task force, although it reportedly would anticipate receiving such comments by mid-November 2001.[100] Since the industry reaction has played an important role in the content and timing of the proposed Accord, it is reasonable to conclude that we are potentially some considerable distance from a final version of the revised Accord.

**Notes and Comments 3.16.** *Further delay on the Capital Adequacy Accord.* In December 2001, the BIS Committee announced that it had decided to carry out a comprehensive "quantitative impact study" (QIS) immediately, to assess the overall impact of the proposed capital accord on banks and the banking system.[1] The revised version of the accord, which the Committee had planned to circulate in early 2002, has been postponed indefinitely. Conceivably, the results of the QIS could adversely affect the likelihood that the new accord will be finalized during 2002 and implemented by 2005.[2]

**3.17.** *Comparative Developments in the EU.* In addition to participation by several of its member states in the BIS, the European Union (EU) has begun taking its own steps with respect to capital adequacy of credit institutions. Considering the following excerpts, how does the EU approach compare with that of the BIS?

## Wendy Fowler, EC Regulation of the Banking Sector,
5 Hofstra Prop. L.J. 405 (1993)[a]

---

96. *MTF Working Paper, supra* note 80.

97. *Id.*

98. *Id.*

99. *Id.*

100. Daniel Pruzin, *supra* note 92 (citing statements by unnamed official).

1. Daniel Pruzin, *Basel Committee Announces Further Delay to Completion of Revised Capital Accord*, Int'l Bus. & Fin. Daily, Dec. 14, 2001, at d9.

2. *Id.* (quoting statement issued by the Committee).

a. This article was written prior to the recent enactment of certain banking provisions which are described herein as anticipatory. As such, some of the descriptions of the planned implementation of the EC banking regulations have already been executed.

. . .

D.  Solvency Ratios

The Directive on solvency ratios[18] is complementary to the Second Banking Directive.  Solvency ratios are seen as playing a central role in the prudential supervision of credit institutions.

The solvency ratio is calculated by referring to the credit institution's assets and off-balance sheet items weighted with different degrees of risk (the "denominator"), as against the credit institution's own funds (the "numerator"). Asset and balance sheet items are assigned risk weights, e.g. cash in hand has a nil weight, whereas claims on central governments and central banks of countries which are not members of the Organization for Economic Cooperation and Development ("OECD") and which have not concluded lending arrangements with the International Monetary Fund have a 100% weight.

The Solvency Ratio Directive provides that effective January 1, 1993, credit institutions will be required to maintain their ratios at a level of at least eight percent. Credit institutions which fail to reach eight percent by the deadline will be required to increase their ratios in successive stages. Only temporary fluctuations from the required level are permitted and adequate reasons for the fluctuation must be given to the supervisory authorities. . . .

J.  Capital Adequacy

The Commission has proposed a draft Directive on capital adequacy.[27]  Although it is aimed mainly at investment firms which are not banks, it generally affects credit institutions, albeit to a limited extent. . . .

## Capital Adequacy of Investment Firms and Credit Institutions
Council Directive 93/6/EEC (15 March 1993)
*amended*, Directive 98/31/EC (22 June 1998)

Article 1

1. Member States shall apply the requirements of this Directive to investment firms and credit institutions as defined in Article 2.

2. A Member State may impose additional or more stringent requirements on the investment firms and credit institutions that it has authorized.

DEFINITIONS
Article 2
For the purposes of this Directive:

. . .

3. institutions shall mean credit institutions and investment firms;

4. recognized third-country investment firms shall mean firms which, if they were established within the Community, would be [considered investment firms], which are authorized in a third country and which are subject to and comply with prudential rules considered by the competent authorities as at least as stringent as those laid down in this Directive; . . .

6. the trading book of an institution shall consist of:

(a) its proprietary positions in financial instruments, commodities and commodity

18. Council Directive 89/647, 1989 O.J. (L 386) 14 [hereinafter Solvency Ratio Directive].

27. Amended Commission Proposal for a Council Directive on Capital Adequacy of Investment Firms and Credit Institutions, 1992 O.J. (C 50) 5 [hereinafter Proposed Directive on Capital Adequacy].

derivatives which are held for resale and/or which are taken on by the institution with the intention of benefiting in the short term from actual and/or expected differences between their buying and selling prices, or from other price or interest-rate variations, and positions in financial instruments, commodities and commodity derivatives, arising from matched principal broking, or positions taken in order to hedge other elements of the trading book;

(b) the exposures due to the unsettled transactions, free deliveries and over-the-counter (OTC) derivative instruments . . . , the exposures due to repurchase agreements and securities and commodities lending which are based on securities or commodities included in the trading book as defined in (a) . . . , those exposures due to reverse repurchase agreements and securities-borrowing and commodities-borrowing transactions . . . , provided the competent authorities so approve, which meet either conditions (i), (ii), (iii) and (v) or conditions (iv) and (v) as follows:

(i) the exposures are marked to market daily . . . ;

(ii) the collateral is adjusted in order to take account of material changes in the value of the securities or commodities involved in the agreement or transaction in question, according to a rule acceptable to the competent authorities;

(iii) the agreement or transaction provides for the claims of the institution to be automatically and immediately offset against the claims of its counter-party in the event of the latter's defaulting;

(iv) the agreement or transaction in question is an interprofessional one;

(v) such agreements and transactions are confined to their accepted and appropriate use and artificial transactions, especially those not of a short-term nature, are excluded; and

(c) those exposures in the form of fees, commission, interest, dividends and margin on exchange-traded derivatives which are directly related to the items included in the trading book. . . .

Particular items shall be included in or excluded from the trading book in accordance with objective procedures including, where appropriate, accounting standards in the institution concerned, such procedures and their consistent implementation being subject to review by the competent authorities; . . .

8. financial holding company shall mean a financial institution the subsidiary undertakings of which are either exclusively or mainly credit institutions, investment firms or other financial institutions, one of which at least is a credit institution or an investment firm;

9. risk weightings shall mean the degrees of credit risk applicable to the relevant counter-parties. . . . However, assets constituting claims on and other exposures to investment firms or recognized third-country investment firms and exposures incurred to recognized clearing houses and exchanges shall be assigned the same weighting as that assigned where the relevant counterparty is a credit institution; . . .

17. "repurchase agreement" and "reverse repurchase agreement" shall mean any agreement in which an institution or its counter-party transfers securities or commodities or guaranteed rights relating to title to securities or commodities where that guarantee is issued by a recognised exchange which holds the rights to the securities or commodities and the agreement does not allow an institution to transfer or pledge a particular security or commodity to more than one counter-party at one time, subject to a commitment to repurchase them (or substituted securities or commodities of the same description) at a specified price on a future date specified, or to be specified, by the transferor, being a repurchase agreement for the institution selling the securities or commodities and a reverse repurchase agreement for the institution buying them;

18. "securities or commodities lending" and "securities or commodities borrowing"

shall mean any transaction in which an institution or its counter-party transfers securities or commodities against appropriate collateral subject to a commitment that the borrower will return equivalent securities or commodities at some future date or when requested to do so by the transferor, that transaction being securities or commodities lending for the institution transferring the securities or commodities and being securities or commodities borrowing for the institution to which they are transferred. . . .

26. capital shall mean own funds. . . .

## INITIAL CAPITAL
## Article 3

1. Investment firms which hold clients' money and/or securities and which offer one or more of the following services shall have initial capital of ECU 125 000:
- the reception and transmission of investors' orders for financial instruments,
- the execution of investors' orders for financial instruments,
- the management of individual portfolios of investments in financial instruments, provided that they do not deal in any financial instruments for their own account or underwrite issues of financial instruments on a firm commitment basis.

The holding of non-trading-book positions in financial instruments in order to invest own funds shall not be considered as dealing for the purposes set out in the first paragraph or for the purposes of paragraph 2.

The competent authorities may, however, allow an investment firm which executes investors' orders for financial instruments to hold such instruments for its own account if:
- such positions arise only as a result of the firm's failure to match investors' orders precisely,
- the total market value of all such positions is subject to a ceiling of 15 % of the firm's initial capital,
- the firm meets the requirements imposed in Articles 4 and 5, and
- such positions are incidental and provisional in nature and strictly limited to the time required to carry out the transaction in question.

2. Member States may reduce the amount referred to in paragraph 1 to ECU 50 000 where a firm is not authorized to hold clients' money or securities, to deal for its own account, or to underwrite issues on a firm commitment basis.

3. All other investment firms shall have initial capital of ECU 730 000. . . .

5. Notwithstanding paragraphs 1 to 4, Member States may continue the authorization of investment firms and firms covered by paragraph 4 in existence before this Directive is applied the own funds of which are less than the initial capital levels specified for them in paragraphs 1 to 4. The own funds of such firms shall not fall below the highest reference level calculated after the date of notification of this Directive. That reference level shall be the average daily level of own funds calculated over a six-month period preceding the date of calculation. It shall be calculated every six months in respect of the corresponding preceding period.

6. If control of a firm covered by paragraph 5 is taken by a natural or legal person other than the person who controlled it previously, the own funds of that firm must attain at least the level specified for it in paragraphs 1 to 4, except in the following situations:
(i) in the case of the first transfer by inheritance after the application of this Directive, subject to the competent authorities' approval, for not more than 10 years after that transfer;
(ii) in the case of a change in the composition of a partnership, as long as at least one of the partners at the date of the application of this Directive remains in the partnership,

for not more than 10 years after the date of the application of this Directive.

7. In certain specific circumstances and with the consent of the competent authorities, however, in the event of a merger of two or more investment firms and/or firms covered by paragraph 4, the own funds of the firm produced by the merger need not attain the level specified in paragraphs 1 to 4. Nevertheless, during any period when the levels specified in paragraphs 1 to 4 have not been attained, the own funds of the new firm may not fall below the merged firms' total own funds at the time of the merger. . . .

PROVISIONS AGAINST RISKS
Article 4

1. The competent authorities shall require institutions to provide own funds which are always more than or equal to the sum of:

(i) the capital requirements . . . for their trading-book business;

(ii) the capital requirements . . . for all of their business activities;

(iii) [other specified ] capital requirements . . . ;

(iv) the capital requirements imposed in paragraph 2. . . .

2. The competent authorities shall require institutions to cover the risks arising in connection with business that is outside the scope of both this Directive and Directive 89/647/EEC and considered to be similar to the risks covered by those Directives by adequate own funds.

3. If the own funds held by an institution fall below the amount of the own funds requirement imposed in paragraph 1, the competent authorities shall ensure that the institution in question takes appropriate measures to rectify its situation as quickly as possible.

4. The competent authorities shall require institutions to set up systems to monitor and control the interest-rate risk on all of their business, and those systems shall be subject to overview by the competent authorities.

5. Institutions shall be required to satisfy their competent authorities that they employ systems which can calculate their financial positions with reasonable accuracy at any time. . . .

MONITORING AND CONTROL OF LARGE EXPOSURES
Article 5

1. Institutions shall monitor and control their large exposures. . . .

VALUATION OF POSITIONS FOR REPORTING PURPOSES
Article 6

1. Institutions shall mark to market their trading books on a daily basis. . . .

2. In the absence of readily available market prices, for example in the case of dealing in new issues on the primary markets, the competent authorities may waive the requirement imposed in paragraph 1 and require institutions to use alternative methods of valuation provided that those methods are sufficiently prudent and have been approved by competent authorities.

SUPERVISION ON A CONSOLIDATED BASIS
Article 7
General principles

1. The capital requirements imposed in Articles 4 and 5 for institutions which are neither parent undertakings nor subsidiaries of such undertakings shall be applied on a solo

basis.

2. The requirements imposed in Articles 4 and 5 for . . . any institution the parent undertaking of which is a financial holding company shall be applied on a consolidated basis. . . .

8. Where an institution the parent undertaking of which is an institution has been authorized and is situated in another Member State, the competent authorities which granted that authorization shall apply the rules laid down in Articles 4 and 5 to that institution on a individual or, where appropriate, a subconsolidated basis.

9. Notwithstanding paragraph 8, the competent authorities responsible for authorizing the subsidiary of a parent undertaking which is an institution may, by a bilateral agreement, delegate their responsibility for supervising the subsidiary's capital adequacy and large exposures to the competent authorities which authorized and supervise the parent undertaking. The Commission must be kept informed of the existence and content of such agreements. It shall forward such information to the competent authorities of the other Member States and to the Banking Advisory Committee and to the Council. . . .

REPORTING REQUIREMENTS
Article 8

1. Member States shall require that investment firms and credit institutions provide the competent authorities of their home Member States with all the information necessary for the assessment of their compliance with the rules adopted in accordance with this Directive. Member States shall also ensure that institutions' internal control mechanisms and administrative and accounting procedures permit the verification of their compliance with such rules at all times. . . .

5. The competent authorities shall oblige institutions to report to them immediately any case in which their counter-parties in repurchase and reverse repurchase agreements or securities and commodities-lending and securities and commodities-borrowing transactions default on their obligations. . . .

COMPETENT AUTHORITIES
Article 9

1. Member States shall designate the authorities which are to carry out the duties provided for in this Directive. They shall inform the Commission thereof, indicating any division of duties.

2. The authorities referred to in paragraph 1 must be public authorities or bodies officially recognized by national law or by public authorities as part of the supervisory system in operation in the Member State concerned.

3. The authorities concerned must be granted all the powers necessary for the performance of their tasks, and in particular that of overseeing the constitution of trading books.

4. The competent authorities of the various Member States shall collaborate closely in the performance of the duties provided for in this Directive, particularly when investment services are provided on a services basis or through the establishment of branches in one or more Member States. They shall on request supply one another with all information likely to facilitate the supervision of the capital adequacy of investment firms and credit institutions, in particular the verification of their compliance with the rules laid down in this Directive. . . .

# Chapter 4

# Methods of Entry into Host Markets

## 1. Introduction

**Notes and Comments 4.1.** This chapter introduces the concept of entry into a host market and considers some general problems associated with entry. The two chapters that follow will take up more specific problems associated with entry by U.S. banking enterprises into non-U.S. markets and by non-U.S. banking enterprises into the U.S. market, respectively. Throughout these three chapters the principal focus will be on U.S. law affecting the process of entry.[1] However, keep in mind that every entry necessarily involves dual considerations: the regulatory policy of the home country of the entrant and the regulatory policy of the proposed host country. Accordingly, whether one is counseling a U.S. banking enterprise seeking entry into a host country, or a non-U.S. banking enterprise seeking entry into the United States, close coordination with local counsel in the other country is essential.

**4.2.** Quarter National Bank (QNB) is considering expansion into the international banking market. It is unsure what its long-term goals are in this regard, but hopes eventually to establish a competitive position in the international market comparable to its current competitive position within the U.S. market, where it is the fiftieth largest bank, offering a full range of wholesale and retail banking services. QNB's General Counsel has asked for advice concerning the options available to the bank. How would you advise her? There is a broad menu of possible methods of entry available in international banking practice.

**a.** *Correspondent relationships.* The most elementary, and historically one of the oldest, method is a correspondent banking relationship. It is grounded on a deposit relationship between banks located in different countries, each holding a deposit denominated in local currency in the name of the other.[2] If Bank *A*, located in country *X*, has a customer that must make a payment to a national of country *Y* in *Y* currency, Bank *A* may wire its corrspondent Bank *B* in country *Y* and instruct it to debit *A*'s account to the credit of its customer's creditor. Correspondent banks may also assist each other in letter of credit

---

1. *See generally* Haley & Seligman, *The Development of International Banking by the United States, in* W. H. BAUGHN & D. R. MANDICH, THE INTERNATIONAL BANKING HANDBOOK 35 (1983) (discussing methods of entry from U.S. perspective.

2. Traditionally, these deposit accounts are referred to as *nostro* and *vostro* accounts (*i.e.*, "ours" and "yours").

transactions, in supplying credit and other financial information, in collecting and disbursing funds, and in other similar transactions.

**b.** *Representative offices.* Bank *A* might also establish a representative office in country *Y*. A representative office cannot take deposits, make loans, collect or disburse funds on behalf of customers, but it does create a physical presence or outpost in country *Y* that may be useful to *A* in gathering information and in establishing business contacts that may be important to *A* over the long term. Typically, representative office must either register with or apply to local (host-country) authorities to be permitted to operate in the local market.

**c.** *Agencies.* Another method of entry is the bank agency. Similar to a branch, the agency may make loans and engage in other banking services, but it cannot accept deposits from the general public. It is not a separately incorporated entity, but the bank must apply to local authorities (and usually its home-country authorities) for a license to operate an agency in the local market.

**d.** *Branches.* A foreign branch can offer the full range of banking services that its home office could offer, but with a physical presence in the local (host-country) market. It is not a separately incorporated entity, but the bank must apply to local authorities (and usually its home-country authorities) for a license to operate a branch in the local market.

**e.** *Affiliates.* As an alternative to the branch, Bank *A* might invest in, or negotiate a contractual participation in, a separately chartered bank *C*, in which *A* does not have a majority or controlling interest. The terminology in this regard is variable; Bank *C* might be characterized as an *affiliate* of *A*, as a *joint venture*,[3] or as a *consortium bank*. Typically, where *A*'s involvement is structured as an investment in the voting securities of *C*, *C* will probably be referred to as an affiliate; where *A*'s involvement is primarily structured contractually, *C* may be referred to as a joint venture or consortium. The labels are not as important–indeed, they may be misleading; what is important is the substantive rights and obligations that *A* acquires by its participation in the *C* enterprise. *A*'s participation in *C* may require approval by its home-country authorities and the home-country authorities of *C*.

**f.** *Subsidiaries.* Bank *A* may prefer to maintain the sole or a controlling interest in Bank *C*, either by acquiring all or a substantial portion of *C*'s voting securities, if *C* is an existing bank in the target market, or by applying to the host-country authorities to charter *C de novo*, with the expectation that *A* will own all or a substantial portion of *C*'s voting securities when it is chartered. In either event, *A* will probably need the approval of both home- and host-country authorities before it may establish or exercise control over *C*.

**g.** *Edge Act and Agreement Corporations.* In U.S. practice, another, more specialized type of subsidiary is also an option. An Edge Act corporation is a federally chartered banking enterprise that is required to specialize in international and foreign business, while an Agreement corporation is state chartered but subject to the same limitations.[4] Both U.S. and non-U.S. banking enterprises may make such investments under U.S. law. Edge Act corporations come in two flavors: "banking Edges" and "investment Edges." Banking Edges operate as banks specializing in international and foreign banking services. Investment Edges operate as holding companies, the subsidiaries of which in turn specialize in international and foreign banking and in other financial services. Bank *C* would be required to apply under U.S. federal law (and, in the case of an Agreement corporation, under state law as well) to establish such an entity. In addition, *C* may need approval of host countries in which the subsidiary will operate.

---

3. This is the term used in the BIS Concordat, *supra*.

4. On Edge Act and Agreement corporations, see Chapter 5, § 2, *infra*.

**4.3.** Recall the discussion of the GATS, *supra* at 65. Does the GATS change the advantages or disadvantages of the methods of entry described in the previous question?

**4.4.** *Entry and e-Banking.* An increasing concern in regulatory policy is the effect of electronic banking ("e-banking") on entry into and operation within international financial services markets. Rudimentary forms of e-banking have long been a feature of international banking at the wholesale (*i.e.*, bank-to-bank) level and this feature has continued to grow in importance with the development of increasingly sophisticated electronic media. This development has already raised questions about the effect of e-banking on traditional policy assumptions concerning banking operations.[5] Policy makers have only begun to confront the policy implications of e-banking.[6] Essentially, e-banking as a sector of e-commerce is currently manifesting itself in three ways:

**a.** First, e-banking may simply represent the use of electronic means as a more efficient medium of communication.[7] This may be characterized as e-banking as an efficiency device. It is of practical significance but unremarkable as a matter of policy, though it may raise important safety and soundness and related issues.[8]

**b.** Second, e-banking may manifest itself as the establishment of specialized fora for transactions in specific types of products.[9] This may be characterized as e-banking as a "trading platform," in which traditional banking participants create an electronic locus for

---

5. *See, e.g. Libyan Arab Foreign Bank, infra* at 110 (discussing effect of computerization on management of cross-border account relationships).

6. In the 1999 Gramm-Leach-Bliley Act (GLBA), Pub. L. No. 106-102, Nov. 12, 1999, 113 Stat. 1338 (1999) (codified at scattered sections of 12, 15, 16, 18 U.S.C.) (GLBA), Congress expressed concern over the pertinence of current banking regulations to the delivery of financial services on-line. *See* GLBA, § 729(a) (codified at 12 U.S.C. § 4801 note) (mandating study of regulations). The GLBA required the banking agencies by November 2001 to submit a report on e-banking. *Id.*, § 729(b). For now, however, activities in the e-banking line continue to advance without specifically applicable policy. *See* 65 Fed. Reg. 4895 (2000) (announcing Comptroller proposed rulemaking on electronic banking). *See generally* Gary Rice, *Selected Issues Relating to Banking and the Internet*, in 1999 Strategies for Financial Institutions in the New E-Commerce Economy (Prac. L. Inst., Dec. 1999) (surveying e-banking issues).

7. *See* 65 Fed. Reg. at 4895 ("Telecommunications advances offer banks faster and more efficient communication and data transmission"). *Cf., e.g.*, Jeanette Borzo, *B2B Holds Big Promise in Russia*, Wall. St. J. Europe, May 3, 2000, at 27, col. 1 (detailing use of e-commerce media to overcome communications inefficiencies).

8. *See, e.g.*, *Reporting Computer-Related Crimes*, OCC Advisory Letter No. 97-9 (Nov. 19, 1997); *Technology Risk Management*, OCC Bulletin 98-3 (Feb. 4, 1998); *Guidance on Electronic Financial Services and Consumer Compliance*, OCC Bulletin 98-31, (July 30, 1998); *Technology Risk Management: PC Banking*, OCC Bulletin 98-38 (Aug. 24, 1998); *Guidance to National Banks on Web Site Privacy Statements*, OCC Advisory Letter No. 99-6 (May 4, 1999); *Infrastructure Threats from Cyber-Terrorists*, OCC Bulletin 99-9 (Mar. 5, 1999); *Certification Authority Systems*, OCC Bulletin 99-20 (May 6, 1999); Comptroller's Handbook, Other Income Producing Activities, Internet Banking (Oct. 1999) (offering guidance on safety and soundness and other supervisory issues; all documents available on OCC Web site at www.occ.treas.gov). *See generally* 65 Fed. Reg. at 4896 (recognizing fluid, fast-evolving nature of bank use of technology and potential effects on safety and soundness).

9. *See, e.g.*, Simon Targett, *State Street to launch multibank trading*, Fin. Times, May 4, 2000, at 16, col. 1 (reporting on plans to launch multi-bank electronic foreign exchange trading system).

transactions.[10] The use of e-banking trading platforms is already well developed in practice.[11] It requires the adaptation of bodies of transactional law (*e.g.*, contract law) and regulatory law to the medium of electronic trading,[12] with due attention to operational safety and soundness.[13]

     **c.** Third, e-banking may manifest itself as an independent banking market, in which banking participants may "exist" as on-line participants.[14] This may be characterized as core e-banking, that is, e-banking by principals, not merely as a medium or a platform for real-time participants. Virtual banks are already being approved,[15] and it is core e-banking that is likely to raise the greatest challenges for regulatory policy in the twenty-first century.[16] Consider the implications for entry policy of the following e-banking situations:

> **i.** Bank *A*, located in country *X*, makes extensive use of electronic media to communicate transactional instructions to Bank *B*, its correspondent bank in country *Y*. Should bank regulators in country *Y* consider *A* to be subject to their supervision?
>
> **ii.** Bank *C*, located in country *Y*, sponsors and operates a website for multi-bank electronic foreign exchange transactions. Banks from every major commercial jurisdiction participate in this trading system. Bank *D*, a participant located in country *Z*, is in financial difficulty and has reneged on foreign exchange

---

10. *See* 65 Fed. Reg. at 4895, in which the Comptroller noted:

Improvements in computer hardware and software are opening up new banking applications. These rapid developments in new technologies are causing banks to reevaluate existing delivery channels and business practices and to develop new products and services

11. For example, the Comptroller has reported that, as of September 1999, 541 national banks had already established transactional Web sites. 65 Fed. Reg. 4895, 4895 n.1 (2000).

12. *See, e.g.*, 12 C.F.R. § 7.1019 (authorizing national banks to conduct through electronic means or facilities any activity otherwise authorized). *See also* David Church *et al.*, *Recent Developments Regarding U.S. and EU Regulation of Electronic Commerce*, 33 Int'l Law. 347 (1999) (surveying international legal developments).

13. *See* 65 Fed. Reg. at 4897 (providing OCC discussion of operational flexibility and safety and soundness).

14. As the Comptroller has observed:

The explosive growth of the Internet also is prompting banks to reconsider business strategies and adopt alternative distribution and marketing systems. The recent chartering of Internet-only banks that operate without a conventional brick and mortar physical presence . . . present[s] new opportunities and challenges for national banks.

65 Fed. Reg. at 4895.

15. *See, e.g.*, OCC Conditional Approval No. 253 (Aug. 20, 1997) (chartering a national bank to deliver products and services to customers primarily through electronic means) (document available on OCC Web site at www.occ.treas.gov). One may expect these developments to continue apace. The Comptroller has indicated that his office "will not delay making changes to its rules or supervisory policies during the pendency of the [GLBA] §729 study and report." 65 Fed. Reg. at 4896 n.7.

16. *See* Pres. Memorandum on Facilitating the Growth of Electronic Commerce, Nov. 29, 1999, 35 Weekly Comp. Pres. Doc. 2457-2458 (1999) (announcing initiative to update laws and regulations developed before advent of Internet that may have unintended negative effects on electronic commerce).

obligations totalling $300 million. What country has jurisdiction over and regulatory responsibility for resolving this problem?

**iii.** Bank *E* was established under the laws of country *Z*, but it operates, without any physical branches, through on-line facilities accessible from any terminal worldwide. Seventy percent of its financial services involve banks and other clients located in countries *X*, *Y* and *Z*, with the remaining thirty percent distributed among fifteen other major commercial jurisdictions. Which of these countries should have the authority to supervise and examine the operations of *E*?

# 2.  Branches and their Liability

**Notes and Comments 4.5.** QNB is now considering the establishment of a branch office in Nusquam, an emerging economy. QNB's General Counsel is concerned, however, about the past instability of the Nusquami Plug (the national currency) and of the Nusquami political situation. If QNB establishes a branch in Nusquam, and that branch is later national-ized, will the depositors of the Nusquami branch be able to recover their deposits directly from QNB in the United States? In answering this question, consult the following cases.

## Vishipco Line v. Chase Manhattan Bank
### 660 F.2d 854 (2d Cir. 1981),
### *cert. denied*, 459 U.S. 976 (1982)

Mansfield, J.

Plaintiffs appeal from a judgment . . . dismissing their claims against Chase Manhattan Bank, N.A. ("Chase"), for breach of contract. The ten corporate plaintiffs . . . are Vietnamese corporations which maintained piastre demand deposit accounts at Chase's Saigon branch in 1975. . . . [T]hey claim that Chase breached its deposit contracts with them when it closed the doors of its Saigon branch on April 24, 1975, to escape from the Communist insurgents and subsequently refused to make payment in New York of the amount owed.  The individual plaintiff–Ms. Nguyen Thi Cham–is a Vietnamese citizen who purchased a six-month two hundred million piastre certificate of deposit ("CD") from Chase's Saigon branch on November 27, 1974, and claims that Chase is in breach for refus-ing to cash the CD in dollars in New York.

We reverse. Chase was clearly obligated to pay plaintiffs the amounts it owed them. None of the affirmative defenses raised by Chase to its conceded obligations to plaintiffs can be sustained. . . . The present worthlessness of the South Vietnamese piastre is no barrier to recovery. Under New York law which governs, the dollar value of Chase's obligation to the corporate plaintiffs must be determined as of the date when it closed its branch without giving them the opportunity to withdraw sums owed then rather than the date of judgment. The individual plaintiff, Ms. Cham, is entitled to recover the value in dollars of her CD on its due date.

From 1966 until April 24, 1975, Chase operated a branch office in Saigon. . . . Chase's operations in Saigon came to an end at noon on April 24, 1975, after Chase officials in New York determined that Saigon would soon fall to the Communists.  After closing the branch without any prior notice to depositors, local Chase officials balanced the day's books, shut the vaults and the building itself, and delivered keys and financial records needed to operate the branch to personnel at the French Embassy in Saigon. Saigon fell on April 30th, and on May 1st the new government issued a communique which read as follows:

All public offices, public organs, barracks, industrial, agricultural and commercial establishments, banks, communications and transport, cultural, educational and health establishments, warehouses, and so forth–together with documents, files, property and technical means of U.S. imperialism and the Saigon administration–will be confiscated and, from now on, managed by the revolutionary administration.

Shortly thereafter, the French embassy turned over records from the Chase branch to the new government. . . .

Chase . . . argues that the Vietnamese decree confiscating the assets which maritime corporations such as the corporate plaintiffs had left behind had the effect of seizing the piastre deposits at issue in this case. As a result, according to Chase, the corporate plaintiffs may not sue to recover the deposits because they no longer own them, and the act of state doctrine bars any challenge to the validity of the governmental seizure.[a] We disagree. There is no evidence that plaintiffs' existence as corporate entities was terminated. Moreover, it is only by way of a strained reading of the Vietnamese confiscation announcement that one can even argue that choses in action were meant to be included. The plain meaning of the statement that "the Saigon-Gia Dinh Management Committee quickly took over the management of all maritime transportation *facilities* abandoned by their owners (emphasis supplied)" is that the seizures involved physical assets only and did not reach whatever claim the corporate plaintiffs might have on their departure for payment of the amounts owed to them by Chase.

More importantly, however, upon Chase's departure from Vietnam the deposits no longer had their situs in Vietnam at the time of the confiscation decreed. As we have said in the past, "[f]or purposes of the act of state doctrine, a debt is not 'located' within a foreign state unless that state has the power to enforce or collect it." *Menendez v. Saks and Co.*, 485 F.2d 1355, 1364 (2d Cir. 1973), *rev'd on other grounds sub nom. Alfred Dunhill of London, Inc. v. Republic of Cuba*, 425 U.S. 682 (1976). The rule announced in *Harris v. Balk*, 198 U.S. 215 (1905), continues to be valid on this point: the power to enforce payment of a debt depends on jurisdiction over the debtor. Since Chase had abandoned its Saigon branch at the time of the Vietnamese decree, and since it had no separate corporate identity in Vietnam which would remain in existence after its departure, the Vietnamese decree could not have had any effect on its debt to the corporate plaintiffs. As one qualified commentator has observed:

> The situs of a bank's debt on a deposit is considered to be at the branch where the deposit is carried, but then if the branch is closed, . . . the depositor has a claim against the home office; thus, the situs of the debt represented by the deposit would spring back and cling to the home office. If the situs of the debt ceased to be within the territorial jurisdiction of [the confiscating state] from the time the branch was closed, then at the time the confiscatory decree was promulgated, [the confiscating state would] no longer [have] sufficient jurisdiction over it to affect it . . . [U]nder the act of state doctrine, the courts of the United States are not bound to give effect to foreign acts of state as to property outside the acting state's territorial jurisdiction. Heininger, *Liability of U.S. Banks for Deposits Placed in Their Foreign Branches*, 11 LAW & POL. INTL. BUS. 903, 975 (1979) (footnotes omitted) ("Heininger").

These principles have been recognized in New York. *See Manas y Pineiro v. Chase*

---

a. On the act of state doctrine, *see infra* at **.

*Manhattan Bank, N.A.*, 106 Misc.2d 660, 434 N.Y.S.2d 868 (Sup. Ct. N.Y. Cty. 1980), where the court held that for the purpose of the act of state doctrine the situs of a debt depends on whether the parties and the *res* were in the foreign country at the time of confiscation. Since in our case Chase's branch in Saigon was neither open nor operating at the time of the confiscation and had in fact been abandoned prior to that time, the Vietnamese decree was ineffective as against Chase's debt to the plaintiffs. . . .

Chase next argues that under Vietnamese law its failure to repay plaintiffs' deposits in the period prior to May 1, 1975, was not a breach of its deposit contract, because the conditions prevailing in Saigon at the time rendered payment impossible. . . .

This argument must be rejected for the reasons that impossibility of performance in Vietnam did not relieve Chase of its obligation to perform elsewhere. By operating in Saigon through a branch rather than through a separate corporate entity, Chase accepted the risk that it would be liable elsewhere for obligations incurred by its branch. As the official referee in the *Sokoloff* case (Harrison Tweed, of the Milbank Tweed firm) summarized the law:

> [W]hen considered with relation to the parent bank, [foreign branches] are not independent agencies; they are, what their name imports, merely branches, and are subject to the supervision and control of the parent bank, and are instrumentalities whereby the parent bank carries on its business . . . *Ultimate liability for a debt of a branch would rest upon the parent bank. Sokoloff v. National City Bank*, 130 Misc. 66, 224 N.Y.S. 102, 114 (Sup. Ct. N.Y. Cty. 1927) (emphasis added).

U.S. banks, by operating abroad through branches rather than through subsidiaries, reassure foreign depositors that their deposits will be safer with them than they would be in a locally incorporated bank. . . . Indeed, the national policy in South Vietnam, where foreign banks were permitted to operate only through branches, was to enable those depositing in foreign branches to gain more protection than they would have received had their money been deposited in locally incorporated subsidiaries of foreign banks. Chase's defenses of impossibility and force majeure might have succeeded if the Saigon branch had been locally incorporated or (more problematically) if the deposit contract had included an explicit waiver on the part of the depositor of any right to proceed against the home office. But absent such circumstances the Saigon branch's admitted inability to perform did not relieve the Chase of liability on its debts in Saigon, since the conditions in Saigon were no bar to performance in New York or at other points outside of Vietnam. Nor has Chase shown that the Vietnamese government took steps to assume or cancel its branch liabilities. The May 1st decree nationalizing the Vietnamese banking industry only provided that "[a]ll . . . banks . . . will be confiscated and from now on managed by the revolutionary administration." In addition, during discovery Chase, in response to the following interrogatory:

> "Interrogatory 4. When the assets were seized did the Government of Vietnam agree to pay the depositors at the Saigon branch?

replied:

> "Chase lacks the knowledge necessary to answer this interrogatory."

The evidence therefore can only be read as showing that the Vietnamese government confiscated the assets abandoned by Chase in Saigon, but did not thereby affect Chase's liabilities to its depositors. Under these circumstances, Justice (then Judge)

Cardozo's opinion in *Sokoloff* fifty years ago applies:

> The defendant's liability was unaffected by the attempt to terminate its existence
> and the seizure of its assets. . . . Plaintiff did not pay his money to the defendant,
> and become the owner of this chose in action, upon the security of the Russian
> assets. He paid his money to a corporation organized under our laws upon the
> security of all its assets, here as well as elsewhere. Everything in Russia might
> have been destroyed by fire or flood, by war or revolution, and still the defendant
> would have remained bound by its engagement. *Sokoloff v. National City Bank*,
> 239 N.Y. 158, 167, 145 N.E. 917 (1924).

As one commentator has summarized the law:

> The defenses of frustration and impossibility were . . . rejected at an early stage
> in the *Sokoloff* proceedings, and do not appear to have been successfully raised in
> subsequent cases involving foreign branches of U.S. banks. Rather, the well-
> established path from branch to home office has been followed, even if the branch
> has been closed, to establish an alternative means for performance. Heininger,
> *supra*, at 1003-04.

A bank which accepts deposits at a foreign branch becomes a debtor, not a bailee,
with respect to its depositors. In the event that unsettled local conditions require it to cease
operations, it should inform its depositors of the date when its branch will close and give
them the opportunity to withdraw their deposits or, if conditions prevent such steps, enable
them to obtain payment at an alternative locations. *See, e.g., Sokoloff v. National City Bank,
supra*, 130 Misc. at 71, 224 N.Y.S. at 112; Heininger, *supra*, at 1009-10. In the rare event
that such measures are either impossible or only partially successful, fairness dictates that
the parent bank be liable for those deposits which it was unable to return abroad. To hold
otherwise would be to undermine the seriousness of its obligations to its depositors and
under some circumstances (not necessarily present here) to gain a windfall.

Chase's next argument, that under New York law its non-payment must be excused
because no demand was ever made prior to the closing of its Saigon branch, must also be
rejected. No Vietnamese law was offered on this issue. Nor is Chase's contention supported
by New York law. It is not settled that a demand is not necessary where the branch in which
the deposit was maintained (or by which the CD was issued) has been closed. . . . *Sokoloff
v. National City Bank*, 250 N.Y. 69, 80-81, 164 N.E. 745 (1928) (where Petrograd branch
of National City Bank ceased to exist because of Soviet seizure, this made "demand useless
and unnecessary" and no demand was required since it "would manifestly be futile").
Similarly, reliance on New York cases suspending or excusing performance during times
of war fails, since Chase, which was ultimately liable for the debt, was never barred by the
wartime conditions in Vietnam from making payment outside of Vietnam. Finally, Chase,
as a national bank, can find no comfort in the provisions of § 138 of the New York Banking
Law, which purport to limit in various ways the liability of *state* bank and trust companies
for deposits made in overseas branches. By its own terms, § 138 is unavailable to Chase in
this case, because it only applies to state, not national, banks. If this unavailability has the
effect of placing national banks like Chase at a competitive disadvantage vis-a-vis state
banks, as Chase alleges, the solution lies with Congress, not the judiciary.

Chase argues that, even if all its other affirmative defenses fail, plaintiffs cannot
recover because the judgment-day rule, under which obligations to pay foreign currencies
(in this case piastres) must be converted prior to payment into dollars at the rate of exchange

prevailing on the day judgment is entered, applies to this case and precludes any recovery, since the piastre is now worthless. We disagree. As a federal court sitting in diversity, we must apply the currency-conversion rule employed by the courts of New York, which has followed the breach-day rule for many years. Therefore, plaintiffs are entitled to recover an amount in dollars which reflects the exchange rate between dollars and South Vietnamese piastres at the time of breach, plus statutory interest.

It is true that federal courts sitting in *non*-diversity cases have rather consistently adopted the judgment-day rule. . . . However, this rule is substantive rather than procedural (there is no Federal Rule of Procedure on the subject) and therefore cannot be followed by federal courts sitting in diversity in states which apply the breach-day rule. *See generally Compania Engraw Commercial E. Industrial S.A. v. Schenley Distillers Corp.*, 181 F.2d 876, 879 (9th Cir. 1950). Absent a federal rule, *see* Ely, *The Irrepressible Myth of Erie*, 87 Harv.L.Rev. 693, 698 (1974), the choice between conflicting state and federal practice must be made with a view toward fulfilling "the twin aims of the Erie rule: discouragement of forum-shopping and avoidance of inequitable administration of the laws." *Hanna v. Plumer*, 380 U.S. 460, 468 (1968). . . .

## Garcia v. Chase Manhattan Bank, N.A.
### 735 F.2d 645 (2d Cir. 1984)

Meskill, Circuit Judge:

Defendant Chase Manhattan Bank, N.A. (Chase) appeals from a judgment . . . awarding plaintiff Juanita Gonzalez Garcia $760,383.30 as the amount due on two certificates of deposit issued by Chase's Vedado, Cuba branch prior to Cuban government seizure of the branch's assets. We affirm.

Background

Garcia and her late husband Jose Lorenzo Perez Dominguez, a wealthy businessman, were Cuban citizens prior to the Cuban revolution. Dominguez also served in the Cuban Senate from 1954-1958 and retired from the Cuban army with the rank of colonel in 1949. Dominguez and Garcia became concerned for the safety of their money in 1958 in light of the ongoing Cuban revolution. At the recommendation of a friend, they visited Chase's Vedado branch on March 10, 1958 and spoke to two bank officers. Dominguez expressed his fears over the safety of his money and stated that he wanted to make a fixed term deposit of 100,000 pesos. The Chase officials responded that he was doing the right thing "because it was in insurance, security for the money." They explained that the deposit was a "private contract" between the bank and Dominguez and Garcia. They stated that Chase's main office in New York would guarantee the certificate and that they could be repaid by presenting the certificate at any Chase branch world-wide. The officials said that repayment could be made in dollars in New York since "that is the money that the bank used." Pesos were equal in value to dollars at the time.

Dominguez and Garcia gave Chase 100,000 pesos that day and received a non-negotiable certificate of deposit (CD) which by its terms was returnable on March 10, 1959 and bore an interest rate of three and one-half percent.

As the political situation in Cuba worsened during 1958, Dominguez and Garcia became increasingly worried about the safety of their money. They returned to the Vedado branch on September 16, 1958 and spoke with two Chase officers, one of whom was present during the March 10 discussion. The Chase officials again told them that they were doing the right thing by securing their money. The officers reaffirmed that payment could be had in dollars at any Chase branch. Dominguez and Garcia gave Chase 400,000 pesos this time.

The CD they received would mature on March 16, 1959 and was otherwise identical to the first CD except that it bore an interest rate of three percent and was for six months rather than a year.

In late 1958 Dominguez and Garcia sent the CDs to Garcia's cousin in Spain for safekeeping. Her cousin promptly acknowledged receipt of the CDs.

When Fidel Castro entered Havana on January 1, 1959, Dominguez took refuge in the El Salvadorian Embassy and subsequently went to El Salvador. Garcia left Cuba for Spain in 1964. Dominguez died in Puerto Rico in 1975. The CDs were found after his death in a safe deposit box in a Chase branch in Puerto Rico.

In February 1959 the revolutionary Cuban government enacted Law No. 78[1] which enabled the Ministry of Recovery of Misappropriated Property, *inter alia*, to freeze bank accounts. The Ministry subsequently ordered Chase to freeze the Garcia/Dominguez "account." On July 16, 1959, the Ministry ordered the "account" closed and demanded that Chase remit its value. Chase complied by sending a sum equal to the debts owed Garcia and Dominguez to the Ministry.

Chase's Cuban branches were nationalized in 1960. The National Bank of Cuba assumed the assets and liabilities of Chase's Cuban branches.

In 1964 Dominguez inquired of Chase through Banco Coca in Madrid, Spain on the status of the CDs. He was advised by Chase of the actions of the Cuban government and told to address further inquiries to the National Bank of Cuba. Garcia made a similar inquiry in 1968 through Banco Coca. Chase's response was not introduced into evidence. In 1970, a lawyer for Dominguez wrote to Chase concerning the CDs. In response, Chase referred to its 1964 letter concerning Dominguez's original inquiry and noted again the actions of the Cuban government. . . .

Chase seeks to avoid liability to Garcia on the basis of the Cuban government's actions. It argues that while the CDs could be repaid at any Chase branch world-wide, Cuba's closing of Garcia's "account" and its appropriation of Chase's funds in a sum equal to the amount of its debt to Dominguez and Garcia prior to their presentment of the CDs

---

1. Cuban Law No. 78 provided in pertinent part (translated from Spanish):

Chapter I

The Ministry and Its Jurisdiction

Article 1. The Ministry of Recovery of Misappropriated Property is the proper organization of the Executive Power intended to recover property of any type which has been removed from the National Wealth and obtain the complete restoration of the proceeds of unjust enrichments obtained under the cover of the Public Power and to the detriment of said wealth.

For the purposes of the provisions of the preceding paragraph, the National Wealth is understood to be formed by the Wealth of the State, of the Provinces, of the Municipalities, of the Autonomous and Parastatal Organizations, and of the Savings Banks and Social Insurance.

Article 2. For the purposes of the Present Law, the right of action of the Ministry covers:

a) Public officials and servants and officials and employees of autonomous corporations and bodies, and those set forth in Article 154 of the Organic Law of the Court of Accounts.

b) Private natural or juridical persons who in any way have intervened in the matters forming the object of investigation and whose conduct has resulted in damage to the national wealth and enrichment for the benefit of said persons obtained under the coverage of the Public Power.

c) Natural or juridical persons who, as a result of the investigations carried out, are shown to appear fraudulently as owners of property and holders of rights which actually belong to the person who is the object of the proceedings and in such case the action for return governed by the present Law can be brought against such persons.

. . .

Article 5. The Minister shall decree the precautionary measures which may be necessary in order to assure the purpose pursued by this Law, and particularly the following:

a) The freezing of bank accounts, the sealing and opening of safe deposit boxes in banks or in other private institutions.

canceled the debt. It then asserts that we may not question the validity of the Cuban government's action under the act of state doctrine. Chase's arguments on both of these issues must fail.

Law No. 78 permitted the Ministry of Recovery of Misappropriated Property to freeze bank accounts. The Ministry subsequently ordered Dominguez's and Garcia's "account" closed and demanded from Chase a sum equal to the amount of the debt.

"It is difficult to see how the seizure of the assets of the [bank] would of itself change the rights of the [bank's creditors] to be paid at the places and in the currency stipulated." *Pan-American Life Insurance Co. v. Blanco*, 362 F.2d 167, 170 (5th Cir. 1966). The monies paid over to the Cuban government did not come from funds specifically earmarked to Dominguez's and Garcia's "account." Rather, they came from Chase's general funds in the branch bank. Title to the deposits was vested in Chase, which became a debtor of Dominguez and Garcia. *See Kondo v. Katzenbach*, 356 F.2d 351, 357 (D.C.Cir. 1966), *rev'd on other grounds sub nom. Honda v. Clark*, 386 U.S. 484 (1967); 5B MICHIE ON BANKS AND BANKING, § 318 at 302 (1983) (footnote omitted). Chase's debt to Dominguez and Garcia was not extinguished merely because it was forced to pay an equivalent sum of its own money to a third party. *See Russek v. Angulo*, 236 S.W. 131, 133-34 (Tex.Civ.App. 1921) (monies confiscated by a revolutionary government belonged to the debtor bank and did not constitute a seizure of the depositor's credit).

Chase would not argue that its debt was extinguished if an armed gunman had entered its Vedado branch and demanded payment of a sum equal to the amount of its debt to Dominguez and Garcia. Yet in effect, this is what transpired. The Cuban government did nothing more than "enter" Chase's Vedado branch armed with Law No. 78 and demand depositors' money. Chase turned over funds without requiring the surrender of the CDs, without notice to the holder of the CDs and without a fight. As in the case of a bank robbery, the bank itself must bear the consequences. *See* 5B MICHIE ON BANKS AND BANKING, § 326a at 317-18 (1983) ("[A] bank cannot be compelled to pay a certificate of deposit issued by it, without the production and surrender of the certificate. . . . [U]pon its payment by the bank of issue the certificate should be surrendered for cancellation. A bank acts at its peril in paying a certificate without surrender thereof and endorsement. . . .") (footnotes omitted). Where, as here, the debtor-creditor relationship was created primarily to ensure the safety of the creditors' funds, a debtor's payment to a third party of a sum equal to that owed the creditors does not extinguish the original debt. Thus, the actions of the Cuban government did not accomplish the cancellation of Chase's obligations to ensure the safety of Garcia's funds.

With regard to its second argument, Chase is correct that under the act of state doctrine[a] United States courts will not question the validity of the actions of foreign governments carried out within their own borders. The classical definition of the doctrine was stated in *Underhill v. Hernandez*, 168 U.S. 250, 252 (1897):

> Every sovereign State is bound to respect the independence of every other sovereign State, and the courts of one country will not sit in judgment on the acts of the government of another done within its own territory. Redress of grievances by reason of such acts must be obtained through the means open to be availed of by sovereign powers as between themselves.

---

a. The details of the Act of State Doctrine, and its implications for international banking, are discussed in Chapter 8, § 4, *infra*.

*See also Banco Nacional de Cuba v. Sabbatino*, 376 U.S. 298, 428 (1964).

Thus, if the situs of Chase's debt to Garcia were in Cuba, the Cuban government could validly seize it.[5] But even if what occurred was a seizure of the debt and not merely payment of a sum equal to it, the facts in the instant case call for a result favoring Garcia. The purpose of the agreement between Chase and Dominguez and Garcia was to ensure that, no matter what happened in Cuba, including seizure of the debt, Chase would still have a contractual obligation to pay the depositors upon presentation of their CDs. Garcia and Dominguez selected Chase because of its international reputation. Chase was aware of their desire to safeguard their money and assured them that their funds were protected. Chase "accepted the risk that it would be liable elsewhere for obligations incurred by its branch." *Vishipco Line v. Chase Manhattan Bank, N.A.*, 660 F.2d 854, 863 (2d Cir. 1981), *cert. denied*, 459 U.S. 976 (1982). If the understanding was that the debt could be paid by turning over the amount of the debt to the Cuban government if it should win the race to the bank, it is apparent that the deposits would never have been made.[6] . . .

Kearse, Circuit Judge, dissenting:

With all due respect to the majority, I must dissent. . . . [T]he majority gives insufficient recognition to the facts that the debts in question were collectible in Cuba; that the contract was not intended to guarantee the safety of plaintiff's funds against seizure by the Cuban government; and that, independently of the Cuban government's subsequent seizure of Chase's own assets and liabilities, that government in fact seized the assets of the plaintiff that are at issue here.

---

5. "The situs of intangible property is about as intangible a concept as is known to the law." *Tabacalera Severiano Jorge, S.A. v. Standard Cigar Co.*, 392 F.2d 706, 714 (5th Cir.), *cert. denied*, 393 U.S. 924 (1968). The general rule is that the situs of a debt depends upon jurisdiction over the debtor. *Harris v. Balk*, 198 U.S. 215, 222 (1905). For act of state purposes, "a debt is not 'located' within a foreign state unless that state has the power to enforce or collect it." *Menendez v. Saks & Co.*, 485 F.2d 1355, 1364 (2d Cir. 1973), *rev'd on other grounds sub nom. Alfred Dunhill of London, Inc. v. Republic of Cuba*, 425 U.S. 682 (1976). *See also Vishipco Line v. Chase Manhattan Bank, N.A.*, 660 F.2d 854, 862 (2d Cir. 1981), *cert. denied*, 459 U.S. 976 (1982); *United Bank Ltd. v. Cosmic International, Inc.*, 542 F.2d 868, 873 (2d Cir. 1976). If the foreign state can enforce or collect the debt, the act of state doctrine will apply to seizure of the debt because the doctrine seeks to avoid challenging the completed acts of foreign governments. *See Standard Cigar*, 392 F.2d at 715. In other words, where a foreign government has both the parties and the res before it and alters their relationship thereto, our courts realize that there is little that they can do to change the legal relationship.

6. The dissenting opinion states that the jury decided specifically that the parties did not contemplate that Chase would guarantee the safety of its obligations to Garcia. We disagree. The fact that the jury gave a negative response to interrogatory 5, which asked if the parties "contemplate[d] in their agreements that such a payment might be made," does not indicate to us that the jury determined that the parties did not agree that Chase would ensure against expropriation by the Cuban government. Interrogatory 5 referenced interrogatory 4, which inquired whether "the Verdado [*sic*] branch of Chase Manhattan in 1959 paid over to the Cuban government a sum equal to the value of plaintiff's certificates of deposit?" . . . The jury's response to interrogatory 5 could have meant that the parties never contemplated that the Vedado branch would make such a payment in 1959. The jury also could have interpreted interrogatory 5 to inquire whether the parties agreed that such a payment *should* be made. In the absence of a specific and unambiguous finding by the jury on the question of whether Chase agreed to guarantee the safety of the obligation, it was not improper to resolve all inferences in favor of Garcia given the jury's determination as to liability. *See* interrogatories 7 and 8 (Q: "Do you find by a preponderance of the evidence that defendant is liable to plaintiff with respect to [the two CDs]?" A: "Yes.").

... A debt is an intangible asset that has no physical location. It has its situs, in the eyes of the law, wherever it can be collected. *Harris v. Balk*, 198 U.S. 215, 222-23. The parties may, however, reach agreement limiting the permissible places of collection, *id.* at 225, and normally "'[t]he situs of a bank's debt on a deposit is considered to be at the branch where the deposit is carried. . . .'" *Vishipco Line v. Chase Manhattan Bank, N.A.*, 660 F.2d 854, 862 (2d Cir. 1981) (quoting Heininger, *Liability of U.S. Banks for Deposits Placed in Their Foreign Branches*, 11 Law & Pol. Int'l. Bus. 903, 975 (1979)), *cert. denied*, 459 U.S. 976 (1982). This common limitation on the situs of a banking debt is likewise subject to variation by agreement of the parties: the parties may agree that the debt may be collected at other locations, either instead of or in addition to the branch at which the deposit was made. Thus, although a debt is a single obligation, it may have many situses. Since, however, it *is* but a single obligation, once it is collected pursuant to a valid decree at any place where the creditor could have collected it, the debt is extinguished. *Harris v. Balk, supra*, 198 U.S. at 223, 226.

In the present case, when plaintiff Garcia and her husband (collectively "Garcia") made their deposits and acquired their certificates, they agreed with Chase that the debts could be collected on presentation of the certificates anywhere that Chase had a branch. Cuba was not excluded. The parties could have agreed that the debts could be collected only outside of Cuba; but they did not. The jury, in response to special interrogatories with respect to each deposit, found that "the parties agreed that payment would be made upon presentation and demand . . . anywhere that Chase Manhattan had offices *including Cuba*." . . . Accordingly, Garcia could have collected the debts in Cuba. Since the debt was collectible in Cuba, it had one of its situses there.

Chase operated its Cuban branch until September 1960, when the Cuban government seized its assets and assumed its liabilities. Prior to September 1960, the Garcia deposits were collectible in Cuba, since that was the agreement of the parties. In 1959, while the Chase Cuban branch was in operation, the Cuban government froze Garcia's assets and then ordered Chase to deliver those assets to the Cuban government. Because Garcia could have collected those debts within Cuba, I see no valid path to a conclusion that the debts were not subject to collection within Cuba by the Cuban government.

The fact that the certificates of deposit have been sent out of Cuba is immaterial; such a certificate is merely evidence of the debt, not the debt itself. . . . Further, although presentation of the certificates would have been necessary in order for Garcia to collect the debt, we are not entitled, in light of the act of state doctrine, to question the Cuban government's implicit declaration that it need not present that evidence of the debt in order to seize it–any more than we would be entitled, for example, to rule that the Cuban government could not seize another citizen's savings account without presenting a passbook.

The majority states that the primary purpose of the parties' agreement was to require Chase to "ensure the safety of Garcia's funds." . . . The parties *could*, of course, have agreed that even if the Cuban government required Chase to pay it a sum equal to Garcia's account, Chase would still have a contractual obligation to pay Garcia. But the jury found that the parties did *not* contemplate that event in their agreement. The majority does not set aside any of the jury findings on any principled basis. It simply ignores them and substitutes its own views.

Accepting (1) the jury's finding that the debts could be collected in Cuba, (2) the Cuban government's unchallengeable seizure of Garcia's assets in Cuba, (3) the jury's finding that the parties did not contemplate in their agreement that there might be such a seizure, and (4) the principle that a debt may validly be collected only once, I conclude that there is no basis for holding Chase to be an insurer and that the debts owed by Chase to Garcia ceased to exist upon the seizure by the Cuban government. I am not persuaded to take the contrary view by the majority's statement that "[t]he result we reach will have no international repercussions." . . . The majority's result may not have such consequences in this case, but since it has no foundation whatever in the facts found by the jury it creates precedent that may be used in future cases that could involve such repercussions. Further, "[i]t ought to be and it is the object of the courts to prevent the payment of any debt twice over. Thus, if [Chase] owing a debt to [Garcia], paid it over under a valid [decree], to [the Cuban government, Chase] certainly ought not to be compelled to pay it a second time. ..." *Harris v. Balk, supra*, 198 U.S. at 226.

## Perez v. Chase Manhattan
61 N.Y.2d 460 (1984)

Kaye, J.

Rosa Manas y Pineiro (Manas), a Cuban national, in 1958 purchased five certificates of deposit from the Marianao, Cuba branch of defendant Chase Manhattan Bank (Chase), and first presented them for payment at Chase's New York office in 1974. The issue on this appeal is whether Chase is excused from payment to Manas because, in September, 1959, the Cuban government confiscated Manas' accounts and Chase surrendered the funds representing the certificates. Because the certificates were payable in Cuba and Chase at the time of the confiscation was present there, the Cuban government had the power to enforce and collect Chase's debt to Manas in Cuba, and the Act of State doctrine precludes inquiry by this court into the propriety of a confiscation directed particularly at Manas' assets in Cuba. Having once made payment, Chase is not liable to pay on the certificates of deposit a second time.

Plaintiff, Esther Garcia Manas Perez, is the administratrix of Manas' estate. Manas was the wife of a cabinet minister in the government of Cuba's former leader, General Fulgencio Batista. Between May and December, 1958, she purchased five non-negotiable certificates of deposit, totaling $227,336.47, from Chase by depositing Cuban pesos in that amount at Chase's branch in Marianao, a suburb of Havana. The certificates provided for the payment of 3% interest and had maturity dates between April and June, 1959. Plaintiff claims that political uncertainty in Cuba motivated the purchase of these certificates from a worldwide bank, and that Manas was repeatedly assured by a Chase employee that the certificates could be redeemed wherever Chase had an office, particularly in the United States. However, no place of payment was specified in the certificates. The certificates provided only that payment was to be made in "moneda nacional," or national currency.

When Fidel Castro assumed control on January 1, 1959, Manas' husband took asylum in the Colombian embassy in Havana and thereafter left Cuba for Colombia. Manas remained in Cuba for the first half of 1959, visited her husband in Colombia, returned to Cuba for approximately four months in 1960, joined her husband in Mexico, and both later relocated to the United States. In that period no effort was made to redeem the certificates.

By Law No. 78 of February 13, 1959, the Cuban government created the Ministry of Recovery of Misappropriated Property "to recover property of any type which has been removed from the National Wealth and obtain the complete restoration of the proceeds of unjust enrichments obtained under the cover of the Public Power." The minister was given the power to conduct investigations, freeze bank accounts, take possession of property, and enact "final decisions" returning the confiscated property to the "National Wealth." Chase was thereafter directed to freeze accounts belonging to certain former government officials and their families, and in September, 1959 the ministry ordered Chase to close such frozen accounts–including specifically those represented by Manas' certificates which had by then reached maturity–and remit the proceeds to the ministry. In compliance with that directive Chase turned funds in the amount of Manas' certificates over to the government. Approximately a year after the confiscation of Manas' assets, on July 6, 1960, the Castro government enacted Law No. 851, providing for nationalization of United States firms in Cuba, and by Resolution No. 2 of September 17, 1960, the government nationalized all of Chase's Cuban branches.

It was not until January, 1974 that Manas, by then residing in the United States, for the first time presented her certificates to Chase's office in New York and demanded payment, which was refused. Manas instituted this action in July, 1974 by motion for summary judgment in lieu of complaint, and Chase cross-moved for summary judgment. Both motions were denied, and the Appellate Division affirmed. . . . Chase subsequently removed the case to the United States District Court for the Southern District of New York, but the action was remanded. . . .

The action proceeded to trial in June of 1980. The following three questions were submitted to the jury:

> "1. What was the intention of [Manas] and [Chase] with regard to the currency with which the certificates of deposit were to be repaid? 1. U.S. dollars; 2. Cuban pesos.
> "2. What was the intention of [Manas] and [Chase] with regard to the place of presentment of the certificates of deposit? 1. New York only; 2. Marianao, Cuba, only; 3. any branch of the defendant Chase anywhere in the world, including New York and Marianao, Cuba; 4. any branch of defendant Chase anywhere in the world, excluding Marianao, Cuba.
> "3. Were [Manas'] funds on deposit in defendant Chase in Marianao confiscated by the Cuban government's Ministry of Misappropriated Funds?"

The jury found that the certificates of deposit were repayable in United States dollars, that the certificates could be presented to any Chase branch in the world, including New York and Cuba, and that Manas' funds on deposit in Chase's Marianao branch were confiscated by the Ministry of Misappropriated Funds.

Both parties then moved for judgment. In view of the jury's findings, Trial Term held that Chase's debt to Manas had its situs in Cuba as the certificates were capable of being repaid in Cuba and Chase's Cuban branches were open and operating subject to the laws and jurisdiction of the Cuban government at the time of the September, 1959 confiscation. Trial Term thereupon entered judgment for Chase in December, 1980, concluding:

> "In the case at bar, both the persons and the res were within the territorial dominion of the acting State at the time of the confiscatory taking. In this court's opinion, under the facts as established at trial, the situs of the debt herein was Cuba. In order for this debt to be beyond Cuban jurisdiction in this case, it would have been necessary for the jury to have found that the place of presentment was only outside of Cuba. The jury finding that payment could be anywhere in the world did not change the situs of this debt from Chase in Cuba while it functioned there. In only created an option for plaintiff to collect the debt elsewhere prior to the confiscation. Although it is true, as asserted by plaintiff, that the parent bank is ultimately liable for the obligations of the branch (*Sokoloff v. National City Bank of N.Y.*, 130 Misc 55, *affd* 223 App Div 754, *affd* 250 NY 69), such a liability does not alter the situs of the debt. When the branch's liability is extinguished, as under the facts herein, the parent is relieved as well.

"Accordingly, this court holds that the judicial self-limiting act of State
doctrine applies herein as the confiscation of plaintiff's funds was an official act
of a sovereign government fully executed within its own jurisdiction and whose
validity this court must refuse to inquire into, thereby implicitly giving the act
extraterritorial effect."

(106 Misc 2d 660, 66-667.)

The Appellate Division reversed . . . , holding that: (1) the Act of State doctrine
applies to the taking of intangible property such as Chase's debt to Manas only "where the
obligation is found to be situated *exclusively* within the foreign State"; (2) "the Act of State
doctrine should not be, and apparently never has been, applied to relieve an American bank
of obligations owed by its branches to depositors" . . . ; and (3) under the rationale of
*Vishipco Line v. Chase Manhattan Bank* . . . , when Chase's Cuban branches ceased operation due to the bank nationalization in 1960, Chase was not relieved from its obligation to
redeem the certificates at its other branches, even though the nationalization decree provided
that the Cuban government (through Banco Nacional de Cuba) assumed the liabilities of
Chase's Cuban branches. Chase appeals to this court from that determination, and plaintiff
cross-appeals from that portion of the Appellate Division's order relating to the computation
of interest on the certificates. Because the Appellate Division's analysis erroneously ignores
the impact of the September, 1959 confiscation specifically seizing Manas' deposits before
Chase's Cuban branches ceased operation, and otherwise misperceives the applicability of
the Act of State doctrine, we now reverse.

The basic premise of the Act of State doctrine is that "the courts of one country will
not sit in judgment on the acts of the government of another done within its own territory."
[]*Underhill v Hernandez*, 168 US 250, 252. . . . Whether the property seized is tangible or
intangible is not dispositive. . . . The doctrine applies when the foreign sovereign's act
amounts to a taking of property within its own borders. . . .

We first must determine whether the property taken by the Cuban government–here, Chase's debt to Manas–was within its borders. For purposes of the Act of State
doctrine, a debt is located within a foreign State when that State has the power to enforce
or collect it. (*Weston Banking Corp. v Turkiyhe Garanti Bankasi, A.S.*, 57 NY2d 315, 324;
*Zeevi & Sons v Grindlays Bank [Uganda]*, 37 NY2d 220, 228, *cert den* 423 US 866;
*Menendez v Saks & Co.*, 485 F2d 1355, 1364, *supra*; *United Bank v Cosmic Int.*, 392 F Supp
262, affd 542 F2d 868, 873.) Since *Harris v Balk* (198 US 215, 222-223),[1] the power to
enforce or collect a debt has been dependent on the presence of the debtor. If the debtor is
present in the foreign State and the debt is payable there, the foreign sovereign then has the
power to enforce or collect it, and a confiscation of that debt amounts to a seizure of
property within that sovereign's borders.

At the time the Cuban government confiscated Manas' deposits in September, 1959,
the debtor (Chase) was present in Cuba. Its Cuban branches were open and operating under
Cuban authority, and the debt owed by Chase to Manas–as the jury found–was payable at
any Chase bank in the world including the Marianao branch were it was confiscated. While
the certificates had by that time matured, and could have been redeemed elsewhere, Manas
had taken no steps to redeem them in or out of Cuba. Where, as here, Chase paid over the
full amount of its debt pursuant to the direction of the Cuban government, a direction which
under the Act of State doctrine is beyond our review, Chase is relieved of liability on any

---

1. Although another aspect of *Harris v Balk* has been overruled (*see Shaffer v Heitner*, 433
US 186), the debt-situs holding remains unimpaired.

subsequent demand by Manas for the funds. (*Trujillo-M v. Bank of Nova Scotia*, 51 Misc 2d 689, 692-693, *affd* 29 AD2d 847, *cert den* 393 US 982.)[2]

The fact that Chase's debt to Manas was not exclusively payable in Cuba, but could in addition have been paid in other countries, does not affect this result. Manas bargained for and received the right to collect the debt from Chase at any of its branches throughout the world. While the debt contemplated alternate places of payment and thus had multiple situs, because it constituted but a single obligation to pay, payment at one of the places chosen for performance extinguished the debt at all of its situses. Manas herself surely could not have redeemed the certificates of deposit in Cuba and subsequently received payment on those same certificates at a Chase branch in another country. Chase's debt to Manas was satisfied by payment to the Cuban government in response to its confiscation of Manas' accounts, and at that point the debt, wherever else it had been payable, was extinguished.

Only when a debt or other obligation is not payable at all in the confiscating State would the Act of State doctrine be inapplicable. In such situations, the foreign sovereign has no power to enforce or collect the debt. (*Zeevi & Sons v Grindlays Bank [Uganda]*, 37 NY2d 220, *supra*; *Republic of Iraq v First Nat. City Bank*, 353 F2d 47, *cert den* 382 US 1027, *supra*.) Here, however, as the jury found, Chase's debt to Manas was payable in Cuba, giving Cuba the jurisdiction to collect and enforce it, which the Cuban government exercised. By reason of the Act of State doctrine the legitimacy of the confiscation is beyond our review.[3]

The Hickenlooper amendment (US Code, tit 22, S 2370, subd [e], par [2]), which operates to preclude the application of the Act of State doctrine in certain circumstances, has no effect in this case. . . .

The Hickenlooper amendment does not apply to confiscations by a foreign State of the property of its own nationals within its borders, since such confiscations are "not contrary to international law" (*F. Palicio y Compania, S.A. v Brush*, 256 F Supp 481, 486-487, *affd* 375 F2d 1011, *cert den sub nom. Brush v Republic of Cuba*, 389 US 830), or to expropriated property that remains in the confiscating country without coming within the territorial jurisdiction of the United States (*Banco Nacional de Cuba v First Nat. City Bank*, 431 F2d 394, 400-402, *revd on other grounds* 406 US 759). Here, Manas was a Cuban citizen at the time of the confiscation and was either present in Cuba or only temporarily absent at the time of confiscation, and the debt, once seized in Cuba, did not come within this country's jurisdiction. Accordingly, the Hickenlooper amendment does not preclude application of the Act of State doctrine in this action.

Nor are the decisions in *Sokoloff v National City Bank* (239 NY 158) and *Vishipco Line v Chase Manhattan Bank* (660 F2d 854, *cert den* 459 US 976, *supra*), in any way

---

2. The Appellate Division's conclusion that "the Act of State doctrine . . . apparently never has been applied to relieve an American bank of obligations owed by its branches to depositors" (93 AD2d, p 409) ignores the thrust of the decision in *Trujillo*. While the bank in *Trujillo* was a Canadian bank, the question presented was the liability of its New York office to repay deposits confiscated from one of its foreign branches pursuant to an order directed at plaintiff's accounts. The court in *Trujillo* determined that under the Act of State doctrine the bank could not be liable to plaintiff on his subsequent demand for repayment.

3. Given this result, we do not reach the applicability of subdivision 1 of section 138 and section 204-a (subd 3, par [a]) of the Banking Law. We note that in *Garcia v Chase Manhattan Bank* (SDNY, June 7, 1983), a case similar on its facts, the Federal District Court found the Act of State doctrine inapplicable "since the situs of Chase's obligation to plaintiff was outside of the jurisdiction of Cuba," citing as its authority the Appellate Division decision which we now reverse. *Garcia* on March 28, 1984 was affirmed by the Court of Appeals for the Second Circuit.

inconsistent with the result we reach today. In both *Sokoloff* and *Vishipco*, the banks were not entitled to rely upon a foreign sovereign's order confiscating a depositor's property where the bank's branches in the foreign State had ceased operations prior to the confiscation order. The situs of the banks' debts to their depositors was thus no longer in the foreign States and the confiscation order directed at the depositor's property was of no effect. In *Sokoloff* this court explained that a "decree of confiscation directed against depositors does not reduce the liabilities of a bank which has already yielded up its assets in virtue of a decree of confiscation directed against itself." (239 NY 158, 169.) And in *Vishipco* the Second Circuit wrote (p 862): "More importantly, however, upon Chase's departure from Vietnam the deposits no longer had their situs in Vietnam at the time of the confiscation decree. As we have said in the past, '[f]or purposes of the act of the state doctrine, a debt is not "located" within a foreign state unless that state has the power to enforce or collect it.' *Menendez v. Saks and Co.*, 485 F.2d 1355, 1364 (2d Cir. 1973), *rev'd on other grounds sub nom. Alfred Dunhill of London, Inc. v. Republic of Cuba*, 425 U.S. 682, 96 S.Ct. 1854, 48 L.Ed.2d 301 (1976). The rule announced in *Harris v. Balk*, 198 U.S. 215, 25 S.Ct. 625, 49 L.Ed. 1023 (1905), continues to be valid on this point: the power to enforce payment of a debt depends on jurisdiction over the debtor. Since Chase had abandoned its Saigon branch at the time of the Vietnamese decree, and since it had no separate identity in Vietnam which would remain in existence after its departure, the Vietnamese decree would not have had any effect on its debt to the corporate plaintiffs." But in the case before us it is undisputed that at the time Manas' accounts were confiscated in September, 1959, Chase's branches in Cuba were open and operating, and the certificates had matured. Manas thus had the opportunity prior to the seizure to redeem the certificates in Cuba or at any of Chase's branches throughout the world. Since Chase's debt to Manas was extinguished before the bank was nationalized, there is no occasion to apply the rationale of *Sokoloff* and *Vishipco*.

**Notes and Comments 4.6.** In each of the fact patterns that follow, assume that the QNB Nusquami branch complies with the demand made, and that Mr. Perez subsequently sues QNB in the United States for the amount of his deposit. What should be the result in each case?

a. A ruffian enters the Nusquami branch of QNB and demands that the teller hand over the funds on deposit in the name of Mr. Perez.

b. The ruffian enters the Nusquami branch and demands that the teller hand over all cash on hand.

c. The ruffian, wearing the uniform of an insurgent paramilitary group, enters the Nusquami branch of QNB and demands that the teller hand over the funds on deposit in the name of Mr. Perez.

d. The ruffian, who is now the chief of the Expropriated Property Department of the newly established Revolutionary Government of Nusquam, enters the Nusquami branch of QNB and demands that the teller hand over the funds on deposit in the name of Mr. Perez, and produces an official order of the Department to that effect.

e. The ruffian, who is now the chief of the Expropriated Property Department of the newly established Revolutionary Government of Nusquam, enters the Nusquami branch of QNB Bank and informs the branch manager that the assets of the branch have been nationalized, and produces an official order of the Department to that effect.

**4.7.** Recall footnote 3 in the *Perez* opinion, *supra*. Would anything change in your answers to the fact patterns in the preceding question if the following statutory provisions existed in the U.S. state where QNB is being sued?

§ 138.      Foreign branches; performance of contracts and repayment of deposits

1. Notwithstanding section 1-105 of the uniform commercial code,[a] any bank or trust company or national bank located in this state which in accordance with the provisions of this chapter or otherwise applicable law shall have opened and occupied a branch office or branch offices in any foreign country shall be liable for contracts to be performed at such branch office or offices and for deposits to be repaid at such branch office or offices to no greater extent than a bank, banking corporation or other organization or association for banking purposes organized and existing under the laws of such foreign country would be liable under its laws. The laws of such foreign country for the purpose of this section shall be deemed to include all acts, decrees, regulations and orders promulgated or enforced by a dominant authority asserting governmental, military or police power of any kind at the place where any such branch office is located, whether or not such dominant authority be recognized as a de facto or de jure government.

2. Notwithstanding section 1-105 of the uniform commercial code, if by action of any such dominant authority which is not recognized by the United States as the de jure government of the foreign territory concerned, any property situated in or any amount to be received in such foreign territory and carried as an asset of any branch office of such bank or trust company or national bank in such foreign territory is seized, destroyed or cancelled, then the liability of such bank or trust company or national bank for any deposit theretofore received and thereafter to be repaid by it, and for any contract theretofore made and thereafter to be performed by it, at any branch office in such foreign territory shall be reduced pro tanto by the proportion that the value (as shown by the books or other records of such bank or trust company or national bank at the time of such seizure, destruction or cancellation) of such assets bears to the aggregate of all the deposit and contract liabilities of the branch office or offices of such bank or trust company or national bank in such foreign territory, as shown at such time by the books or other records of such bank or trust company or national bank.

2-a. Notwithstanding the provisions of any law to the contrary, a bank or trust company or national bank located in this state shall not be required to

---

a. N.Y. U.C.C. § 1-105 provides as follows:

§ 1-105.    Territorial Application of the Act; Parties' Power to Choose Applicable Law

(1) Except as provided hereafter in this section, when a transaction bears a reasonable relation to this state and also to another state or nation the parties may agree that the law either of this state or of such other state or nation shall govern their rights and duties. Failing such agreement this Act applies to transactions bearing an appropriate relation to this state.

(2) Where one of the following provisions of this Act specifies the applicable law, that provision governs and a contrary agreement is effective only to the extent permitted by the law (including the conflict of laws rules) so specified:

Rights of creditors against sold goods. Section 2-402.
Applicability of the Article on leases. Sections 2-A-105 and 2-A-106.
Applicability of the Article on Bank Deposits and Collections. Section 4-102.
Governing Law in the Article on Fund Transfers. Section 4-A-507.
Bulk transfers subject to the Article on Bulk Transfers. Section 6-102.
Applicability of the Article on Investment Securities. Section 8-110.
Perfection provisions of the Article on Secured Transactions. Section 9-103.

repay any deposit made at a foreign branch of any such bank if the branch cannot repay the deposit due to (i) an act of war, insurrection, or civil strife; or (ii) an action by a foreign government or instrumentality, whether de jure or de facto, in the country in which the branch is located preventing such repayment, unless such bank has expressly agreed in writing to repay the deposit under such circumstances. . . .

§ 204-a.   Payment of claims by foreign banking corporations where adverse claim is asserted; effect of claims or advices originating in, and statutes, rules or regulations purporting to be in force in occupied territory; performance of contracts and repayment of deposits performable or repayable at foreign offices of foreign banking corporations

. . .

3. (a) Notwithstanding section 1-105 of the uniform commercial code, any foreign banking corporation doing business in this state . . . shall be liable in this state for contracts to be performed at its office or offices in any foreign country, and for deposits to be repaid at such office or offices, to no greater extent than a bank, banking corporation or other organization or association for banking purposes organized and existing under the laws of such foreign country would be liable under its laws.  The laws of such foreign country for the purpose of this subdivision shall be deemed to include all acts, decrees, regulations and orders promulgated or enforced by a dominant authority asserting governmental, military or police power of any kind at the place where any such office is located, whether or not such dominant authority be recognized as a de facto or de jure government.

(b) Notwithstanding section 1-105 of the uniform commercial code, if by action of any such dominant authority which is not recognized by the United States as the de jure government of the foreign territory concerned, any property situated in or any amount to be received in such foreign territory and carried as an asset of any office of such foreign banking corporation in such foreign territory is seized, destroyed or cancelled, then the liability, if any, in this state of such foreign banking corporation for any deposit theretofore received and thereafter to be repaid by it, and for any contract theretofore made and thereafter to be performed by it, at any office in such foreign territory shall be reduced pro tanto by the proportion that the value (as shown by the books or other records of such foreign banking corporation, at the time of such seizure, destruction or cancellation) of such assets bears to the aggregate of all the deposit and contract liabilities of the office or offices of such foreign banking corporation in such foreign territory, as shown at such time by the books or other records of such foreign banking corporations.  Nothing contained in this paragraph shall diminish or otherwise affect the liability of any such foreign banking corporation to any corporation, firm or individual which at the time of such seizure, destruction or cancellation was incorporated or resident in any state of the United States.

(c) Notwithstanding the provisions of any law to the contrary, a foreign banking corporation operating a branch or branches or an agency or agencies in this state shall not be required to repay, at any such branch, branches, agency or agencies in this state, any deposit made at a foreign office of any such foreign banking corporation if such office cannot repay the deposit due to (i) an act of war, insurrection, or civil strife; or (ii) an action by a foreign government or instrumentality, whether de jure or de facto, in the country in which the office is located preventing such repayment, unless the foreign banking corporation operating in this state has expressly agreed in writing to repay the deposit under such circumstances. . . .

**4.8.** *Branch-home office liability revisited.* Judge Kearse had another opportunity to follow up on her reasoning with respect to branch liability. *See Wells Fargo Asia Limited v. Citibank, N.A.*, excerpted in Chapter 9, § 2, *infra*.

**4.9.** If QNB had been a British bank with a branch in Nusquam, would the results in the fact patterns described in 4.6, *supra*, have been different? In this regard, contrast the position of *Garcia* and *Perez* on the issue of the status of and liability for foreign branch obligations with the positions expressed in the following excerpts from two British cases.

# *X* AG v. *A* Bank
## 2 All Eng. L. Rep. 464 (1983)

Leggatt J. There is before me an application in each of three actions. . . . I shall refer to each of the plaintiffs by initials, arbitrarily selected, that is to say as the '*X* company', the '*Y* company', and the '*Z* company', and the defendants, who are the same in each of the three applications, I shall refer to as 'the bank'. . . . The bank has its head office in New York and it is with the London branch of the bank that these applications are immediately concerned. . . . In short, they raise the question whether injunctions already issued should be continued to trial so as to prevent obedience by the London branch of the bank to subpoenas issued in New York requiring production by the London branch of documents relating to an account of each of the three plaintiffs who are customers of the bank, two of the plaintiffs being incorporated in Switzerland and one in Panama. The *X* company was formed under the laws of Switzerland in the early 1970s. It has over 40 offices located in some 30 different countries throughout the world. The *Y* company, which is a subsidiary of the *X* company, is also incorporated in Switzerland and has a major branch in New York. The *Z* company is a company associated with the *X* company, incorporated in Panama, but having its headquarters, like the *X* company, in Switzerland. The *X* company and its subsidiary, the *Y* company, are concerned in the marketing of crude oil and oil products, ferrous and non-ferrous ores and metals, and also fertilizers. Both the *X* company and the *Z* company conduct their business wholly outside the United States; they have no presence there, that is to say no employees nor any business conducted there, and all the books of both companies, together with their records, are kept in Switzerland. The *Y* company, on the other hand, handles business emanating from and destined for New York, but its other business is operated from its headquarters in Switzerland and, in particular, through use of its London account with the London branch of the bank. Accounts have been maintained by the plaintiffs with the bank for some time now, in the case of the *X* company since 1975, of the *Y* company since 1978 and of the *Z* company since 1980.

The relationship enjoyed by the *X* company with the bank is explained in an affidavit by a gentleman who is, in effect, the company secretary of that plaintiff. He asserts that the company did not, in forming its relationship with the bank, contemplate that United States law would govern the banking relationship for the reason that, since the relationship would be centered in London, it was naturally contemplated that it would be subject to English law. It is a relationship which has grown over the years and the London branch of the bank is used by the *X* company for a major part of its general banking affairs, including loans, deposits, letters of credit, guarantees, confirmations, credit references and presentments. All the instructions from the *X* company emanate from Switzerland or via an English subsidiary of the *X* company. The *X* company uses the London branch as its centre for worldwide dollar denominated banking arrangements and the deponent asserts, in common with those who have sworn affidavits on behalf of the other plaintiffs, that the *X* company would not have placed any business with the London branch of the bank unless it was confident that its business secrets would remain secure in accordance with the stringent standards observed in London. This is of particular consequence in the context of letters of credit, because the documents held in the London branch in relation to letters of credit would contain instructions received from the $X$ company or its London subsidiary and include–

> 'the application for the credit, the terms and conditions upon which it is to be opened and paid, the terms of the underlying transaction, the buyer, the documentary conditions for the transaction, the place of presentment and expiration, and countless other commercial and proprietary items'.

It is said that the London branch files, that is to say the files of the London branch of the bank, also contain not only instructions concerned with general banking matters, investments and business facilities, but multifold data communicated to and shared with the branch in reliance on what deponent terms 'the sanctity of the professional and confidential relationship between a customer and a bank carrying on business in London'.

In response to this aspect, an affidavit has been sworn by the general manager of the London branch of the bank. After explaining that the plaintiffs are, like many of the bank's customers, large, multinational corporations, whose banking requirements transcend national boundaries, he explains that the bank provides a co-ordinated worldwide service to its customers through its international department, so as to meet the customers' requirements. This deponent says:

> 'However complex and geographically widespread a customer's requirements may be his banking relationship with [the bank] will be subject to overall direction, co-ordination and control from a relationship manager at one location. The relationship manager is usually based at [the New York office of the bank] or at the particular location of [the bank] where the customer has its head office or main management centre'.

He concludes this passage by saying that, so far as the bank is concerned, its banking relationship with the plaintiffs is centred in New York.

With this passage I must, however, contrast the affidavit of the gentleman who appears to be the relevant relationship manager himself. He says that he is a vice-president of the bank presently assigned to the London branch and he declares: 'I am responsible for managing [the bank's] business relationship with numerous commodity customers at' the London branch, including those of the plaintiffs.

It seems to me that, by way of application of the principles described in the first affidavit sworn on behalf of the bank, it is the second deponent who is to be identified as the relationship manager and he at all events is physically present in London for most of the time, as it would appear. Whatever may be said in the affidavit of the first deponent to the effect that the bank's banking relationship with the plaintiffs is centred in New York, it seems to me that it can only be as a matter of internal administration of the bank and then only in a limited sense which does not detract from the fact that the bank maintains its own relationship manager in London.

In the main affidavit sworn on behalf of the bank, namely that of its first deponent, he says in a later passage that the plaintiffs must be fully aware of the worldwide context in which their English dealings are conducted and of their own and the bank's close connections with New York. He then says:

> 'Unlike a domestic U.K. customer of an English bank in London, the plaintiffs (with the possible exception of [the $Z$ company] must, in my belief, have

anticipated that their dealings with [the bank] would be subjected to the necessary incidents of an overall international relationship having close connections with New York'.

I have some difficulty with that statement. First of all, it appears to me that the reference to the dealings being subject to the necessary incidents of an overall international relationship begs the question of what incidents are to be regarded as necessary, and, second, I am not sure that I understand the meaning of the phrase 'dealings . . . would be subjected to the . . . incidents of an overall international relationship'.

This part of the deponent's affidavit concludes by saying that in the much wider context of dealings between the bank and the plaintiffs–

> 'the bank must, notwithstanding its efforts and obligations to provide a full service to very valued customers, have regard to and comply with the legal obligations of the country in which it is incorporated and in which its head office is based and where its relationship with the plaintiffs is centred'.

. . . [I]t is noteworthy that in that passage there is nothing said about the bank having regard to or complying with the legal obligations of the country in which its branch is situated. Nor, indeed, is there any reference to any regard that might be paid to the welfare of the bank's customers. . . .

[The court went on to conclude that it would continue the injunctions barring the *A* Bank's London branch from complying with New York subpoenas requiring production of documents relating to accounts of the three customers of the bank.]

## Libyan Arab Foreign Bank v. Bankers Trust Company
[1988] 1 Lloyd's L. Rep. 259

Mr. Justice Staughton:

[The case involved claims by a Libyan bank against a the London branch of a U.S. bank with respect to dollar-denominated London deposits blocked under a presidential order directed against the assets of Libya. Two accounts had been established with the bank, one at its New York headquarters, and one at its London branch. Detailed excerpts from the case on the merits appear in Chapter 11, § 3, *infra*.]

As a general rule the contract between a bank and its customer is governed by the law of the place where the account is kept, in the absence of agreement to the contrary. ... *X AG v. A Bank* [1983] 2 All E.R. 464, *Mackinnon v. Donaldson Lufkin & Jennette Securities Corporation* [1986] Ch. 482, at p. 494, DICEY [&] MORRIS, THE CONFLICT OF LAWS (11th edn.) p. 1292 n. 51, RABEL, THE CONFLICT OF LAWS (2nd edn.) p. 17, RESTATEMENT (2ND) CONFLICT OF LAWS, p. 622. . . .

That rule accords with the principle, to be found in the judgment of Atkin L.J. in *N. Joachimson v. Swiss Bank Corporation* [1921] 3 K.B. 110 at p. 127, and other authorities, that a bank's promise to repay is to repay at the branch of the bank where the account is kept.

In the age of the computer it may not be strictly accurate to speak of the branch where the account is kept. Banks no longer have books in which they write entries; they have terminals by which they give instructions; and the computer itself with its magnetic tape, floppy disc or some other device may be physically located elsewhere. Nevertheless it should not be difficult to decide where an account is kept for this purpose, and is not in the present case. The actual entries on the London account were, as I understand it, made in London, albeit on instructions from New York after December 1980. At all events I have no doubt that the London account was at all material times "kept" in London. . . .

There is high authority that branches of banks should be treated as separate from the head office. See for example *R. v. Grossman* (1981) 73 Cr. App. Rep. 302), where Lord Denning M.R. said (at page 307):

> "The branch of Barclays Bank in Douglas, Isle of Man, should be considered as a different entity separate from the head office in London."

That notion, of course, has its limits. A judgment lawfully obtained in respect of the obligation of a branch would be enforceable in England against the assets of the head office. . . . I would say that it is *true for some purposes* that a branch office of a bank is treated as a separate entity from the head office.

# 3. Subsidiaries and their Liability

**Notes and Comments 4.10.** Would there be any advantage to QNB in operating through international subsidiaries rather than branches? Consider the following excerpts.

## S.E.C. v. Banco Della Svizzera Italiana
### 92 F.R.D. 111 (S.D.N.Y. 1981)

Milton Pollack, District Judge.

[In this case the Securities and Exchange Commission (SEC) was seeking judicial enforcement of an administrative subpoena against an Italian bank which had refused to provide the SEC with information concerning stock transactions undertaken by the bank on behalf of its customers. Detailed excerpts from the opinion appear in Chapter 10, § 3, *infra*.]

. . . Jurisdiction over BSI exists by virtue of BSI's doing business here. There is evidence in the record that BSI operates in New York at 44 Wall Street through a subsidiary corporation. This was denied by counsel for BSI at the hearing but a letter to the contrary signed some time ago by BSI, a copy of which was furnished to the Court by the SEC indicates that the denial was erroneous and obviously inadvertent.

## American Law Institute, Restatement of Foreign Relations Law of the United States (3d)

§ 414.  Jurisdiction with Respect to Activities of Foreign Branches and Subsidiaries

. . . (2) A state may not ordinarily regulate activities of corporations organized under the laws of a foreign state on the basis that they are owned or controlled by nationals of the regulating state. However, under § 403 and subject to § 441, it may not be unreasonable for a state to exercise jurisdiction for limited purposes with respect to activities of affiliated foreign entities

(a) by direction to the parent corporation in respect of such matters as uniform accounting, disclosure to investors, or preparation of consolidated tax returns of multinational enterprises; or

(b) by direction to either the parent or the subsidiary in exceptional cases, depending on all relevant factors, including the extent to which

(i) the regulation is essential to implementation of a program to further a multinational interest of the state exercising jurisdiction;

(ii) the national program of which the regulation is a part can be carried out effectively only if it is applied also to foreign subsidiaries;

(iii) the regulation conflicts or is likely to conflict with the law or policy of the state where the subsidiary is established.

(c) In the exceptional cases referred to in paragraph (b), the burden of establishing reasonableness is heavier when the direction is issued to the foreign subsidiary that when it is issued to the parent corporation.

Comment:

a. Multinational enterprises and jurisdiction to prescribe. This section reflects the recognition that multinational enterprises do not fit neatly into the traditional bases of jurisdiction; such enterprises may not be nationals of one state only and their activities are not limited to one state's territory.

The exercise of jurisdiction by the state of a parent company over foreign branches of the company, . . . is viewed with less concern by host states than the exercise of jurisdiction by the state of a parent company over foreign subsidiaries of the company. Unlike a foreign subsidiary, a foreign branch is not a distinct juridical entity; the factor of separate incorporation in the host state being absent, the exercise of jurisdiction under the nationality principle, . . . is not implausible. See Comment b. However, since there is potential for conflict between the state of nationality and the territorial state, the exercise of jurisdiction over foreign branches by the state of the parent is also subject to limitations. See Comment c.

As regards enterprises with units that are separately incorporated, the exercise of a state's jurisdiction to impose fiscal and related regulations on the basis of intercorporate affiliation, Subsection (2)(a), has given rise to little conflict. . . .

. . . In contrast, the exercise of jurisdiction described in Subsection (2)(b)–typically the implementation of programs of economic denial such as embargoes or export controls . . .–has generated substantial controversy. Such exercise of jurisdiction is exceptional and limited to circumstances such as those indicated. . . .

b. Foreign branches and subsidiaries and the nationality principle. This section considers links of ownership and control of juridical persons as analogous to links of nationality. . . . The distinction between Subsection (1), dealing with branches, and Subsection (2), dealing with separately incorporated subsidiaries, reflects the view that by incorporating in the host state an enterprise becomes legally more distant from the state of the parent corporation than if it operates as a branch. . . . That a subsidiary is incorporated in another state and is subject to its laws limits the jurisdiction to prescribe of the state of the parent. On the other hand, a host state cannot, by requiring a foreign-owned enterprise to incorporate under its laws, deprive the state of the parent corporation of all authority over the enterprise. The enterprise itself cannot, by incorporating in a foreign state, escape all regulatory authority of the state of the parent corporation. . . .

c. Limited jurisdiction over foreign branches and subsidiaries. Jurisdiction may be exercised under Subsection (1), and to the extent indicated in Subsection (2), over activities of a branch or subsidiary related to international transactions, such as export and import, foreign exchange and credits, and transborder investment; but not generally over predominantly local activities, such as industrial and labor relations, health and safety practices, or conduct related to preservation or control of the local environment. That a state's mandate in respect of a foreign branch or subsidiary is directed to the parent corporation, or to the officers of the foreign entity on the basis of their nationality, Comment f, does not relieve the state from the restraints of this section or § 403. However, as stated in Subsection (2)(c), orders issued directly to a foreign corporation are regarded as particularly intrusive and can be justified only by a clear showing of necessity in light of factors such as those listed in Subsection (2)(b).

d. Conflict with requirements of state of incorporation. A command by the parent state may conflict with a clearly expressed policy of the state under whose law the subsidiary is organized. If that state is also the state in whose territory the activity regulated is to be carried out or precluded, exercise of jurisdiction on the basis of intercorporate affiliation may be unreasonable under § 403. A state may not ordinarily require a corporation (or similar entity) to do an act outside its territory that is prohibited by the state under whose law the corporation is organized, or forbid the corporation to do an act outside its territory that is required by the state under whose law the corporation is organized. . . .

g. Applicability to subsidiaries of regulatory programs effective in state of parent company. Regulation of a foreign subsidiary of a corporation organized under a state's laws may be reasonable to the extent indicated in Subsection (2)(b) as an extension of a program of regulation in that state, particularly if necessary to prevent evasion of controls through incorporation or establishment abroad. While particular provisions of a state's regulatory scheme may apply differently within and without the state, ordinarily the justification for applying law outside the state is that the same or a comparable law is applicable to activities within the state. A state may treat foreign branches of subsidiaries more favorably, but not less so, than enterprises organized or doing business in the state. Foreign subsidiaries may not be singled out for regulation unless the regulation is directed to a problem peculiar to foreign subsidiaries.

h. Jurisdiction over parent companies on basis of presence of subsidiaries. The link of ownership or control among affiliated corporations may justify exercise of jurisdiction for some purposes over an integrated multinational enterprise by a state where a branch or subsidiary is established, . . . subject to considerations similar to those applicable to an exercise of jurisdiction by the state of the parent corporation over foreign subsidiaries. See Comment a. Such exercise of jurisdiction may in many instances be justified also on the basis of the effects principle. . . .

# Chapter 5

# Entry by U.S. Banks into Foreign Markets

## 1. General Considerations

**Notes and Comments 5.1.** Quarter National Bank (QNB) is interested in creating a presence in Nusquam, a newly industrialized state. What alternative methods of entry may be available? Would it make a difference if the Nusquami Banking Code was substantially similar to the banking laws of Bermuda? Or Cyprus? Or the United States of America? In answering these questions, reconsider Note 4.2, *supra*, as well as Note 5.2, *infra*.

**5.2.** The theoretical availability of the menu of entry choices mentioned in Note 4.2 must be modified, as a practical matter, by the fact that different jurisdictions often have materially different options available for entry. Some few states may exclude foreign-based banking enterprises from their domestic markets. Other states, though in principle allowing entry, may be ambiguous about the availability of methods of entry, either in the express rules or in the administrative implementation of those rules. Advice of local counsel is essential in this regard. In addition, entry options may be conditioned on reciprocal treatment of the host state's banking enterprises in the home state of the entrant,[1] or on "national treatment" of the host state's banking enterprises.[2] The U.S. Treasury's National Treatment Studies[3] have suggested the following variations in the treatment of entry. States included in Figure 5.01, *infra*, prohibiting the presence of foreign-based banking enterprises. States included in Figure 5.02, *infra*, prohibit new entries under current practice. States included in Figure 5.03, *infra*, allow entry by representative office, often with previously established foreign bank branches, subsidiaries or affiliates grandfathered. States included in Figure 5.04, *infra*, prohibit entry by branch, which may be a crucial restriction for a banking enterprise that prefers that method of entry as the most cost efficient. To some extent, such restrictions may be intended to protect local banking enterprises from competition. For similar reasons, states may prohibit acquisition by foreign-based banking enterprises of any interest (Figure 5.05, *infra*), or of a controlling interest (Figure 5.06, *infra*), in locally established and controlled ("indigenous") banking enterprises. Of course, recent legal developments and other competitive considerations have put pressure on state practice, and the various lists, as originally identified and developed by the U.S. Treasury,

---

1. *See, e.g.*, Note 2.12, *supra* (discussing reciprocity requirements).

2. *See, e.g.*, Notes 2.10-2.11, 2.13 *supra* (discussing national treatment).

3. For discussion of the National Treatment Studies, see Note 2.13, *supra*.

INTERNATIONAL BANKING

are subject to significant change from time to time.

---

**Figure 5.01**
**States Prohibiting Foreign Banking Presence**

| | | |
|---|---|---|
| Afghanistan | Guinea | Madagascar |
| Bulgaria | Iraq | Nepal |
| Cuba | Laos | Somalia |
| Ethiopia | Libya | |

---

**Figure 5.02**
**States Prohibiting New Foreign Bank Entry[a]**

| | |
|---|---|
| Benin | Surinam |
| Guyana | Tanzania |
| Kuwait | United Arab Emirates |
| Netherlands Antilles | |

---

**Figure 5.03**
**States Permitting Only Entry by Representative Offices[b]**

Prohibition Imposed by Law

| | | | |
|---|---|---|---|
| Algeria | Colombia | Sweden | Venezuela |
| Burma | Portugal | Syria | |

Prohibition Imposed by Policy or Administrative Practice

| | |
|---|---|
| People's Republic of China | Norway |
| El Salvador | Poland |
| Guatemala | Saudi Arabia |
| Indonesia | Turkey |
| New Zealand | Trinidad and Tobago |

---

a. In addition to the countries listed in Figure [5.01].

b. Countries in Figures [5.01 and 5.02] do not permit representative offices.

**Figure 5.04**
**States Prohibiting Entry by Branching[c]**

Prohibition Imposed by Law

| | |
|---|---|
| Bermuda | Ghana |
| Cameroon | Hungary |
| Canada | Iceland |
| People's Republic | Niger |
| of the Congo | Peru |
| Costa Rica | Philippines |
| Finland | South Africa |
| The Gambia | Uruguay |

Prohibition Imposed by Policy or Administrative Practice

| | |
|---|---|
| Bahrain | Netherlands Antilles |
| Botswana | Nigeria |
| Dominican Republic | Oman |
| Ecuador | Qatar |
| Haiti | Singapore |
| Jordan | Solomon Islands |
| Republic of Korea | Surinam |
| Malaysia | Thailand |
| Malta | Tunisia |
| Morocco | Zaire |

**Figure 5.05**
**States Prohibiting Purchase of any Interest in**
**Indigenous Banks by Foreign Banks[c]**

| | |
|---|---|
| Bangladesh | Papua New Guinea |
| Costa Rica | Surinam |
| Pakistan | |

c. In addition to those listed in [Figures 5.01-5.03].

## Figure 5.06
## States Limiting Foreign Banks to Minority Interest in Indigenous Banks

Maximum Imposed by Law

| | |
|---|---|
| Australia | 10% |
| Bermuda | 40% |
| Congo, People's Republic of the | 49% |
| Denmark | 30%[d] |
| Ecuador | 20%[e] |
| Finland | 20% |
| Gambia, The | 20% |
| India | 49%[f] |
| Japan | 5% |
| Korea, Republic of | 10% |
| Nigeria | 40% |
| Philippines | 30%[g] |
| Upper Volta | 49% |

Specific Maximum Foreign Participation Allowed in Practice

| | |
|---|---|
| Bahrain | 49% |
| Dominican Republic | 30% |
| Greece | 49% |
| Iceland | 49% |
| Morocco | 50% |
| Oman | 49% |
| Qatar | 49% |
| Singapore | 20% |
| South Africa | 50% |
| U.K. | 15% |

*Figure 5.06 continued next page*

d. Denmark requires a merger if any party, foreign or domestic, acquires 30 percent or more of a bank.

e. For non-Andean Pact nations.

f. In early March 2004, India raised the maximum foreign investment in private banks from 49 to 74 percent, through the establishment of operating subsidiaries. *See* Harbaksh Singh Nanda, *India Hikes Foreign Direct Investment Ceiling in Private Banks to 74 Percent*, BNA Banking Daily, Mar. 16, 2004. As a result, foreign banks will now be permitted to operate in India through branches, wholly-owned subsidiaries, and Indian private bank subsidiaries with an aggregate foreign investment up to the 74 percent maximum. *Id.*

g. 40 percent with Presidential approval.

*Figure 5.06–continued*

No Majority Control; No Specific Maximum

| | |
|---|---|
| Central African Empire | Netherlands |
| Cyprus | Oman |
| Egypt | Qatar |
| Iceland | Trinidad and Tobago |
| Malaysia | Tunisia |
| Malta | |

**5.3.** *Note on EU Developments.* What if QNB were considering entry into a member state of the European Union (EU)? EU law as it affects bank regulation is of growing concern in international banking.[4] Recent developments may significantly restrict or modify entry of U.S. banks into the EU-member markets, which are in the process of becoming a single integrated market. Consider the following excerpt.

## Wendy Fowler, EC Regulation of the Banking Sector,
5 Hofstra Prop. L.J. 405 (1993)[a]

The removal of the barriers to the provision of banking and financial services throughout Europe has become one of the main objectives of the European Community ("EC"). . . . [T]he creation of a unified banking market in Europe is seen as an important stage in the achievement of one of the central aims of the EC–the economic and monetary union in Europe.

Economic and monetary union ("EMU") essentially involves a three-stage process. The first stage envisages full liberalization of capital movements and increasing cooperation between Member States in the area of economic and monetary policy. The second stage centers on the gradual shift of decision-making from a national level to a community level along with the establishment of a European System of Central Banks to initiate the move towards EC-wide decision making in the area of monetary policy. The third stage contemplates an irrevocable move to lock exchange rates, the replacement of national currencies with a single European currency, and the empowerment of the EC to interfere

---

4. *See* Joel P. Trachtman, *Trade in Financial Services Under GATS, NAFTA and the EC: A Regulatory Jurisdiction Analysis*, 34 COLUM. J. TRANSNAT'L L. 37 (1995) (analyzing, *inter alia*, the EU regulatory environment as it affects banking); Geoffrey W. Smith, Comment, *Competition in the European Financial Services Industry: The Movement of Capital Versus the Regulation of Money Laundering*, 13 U. PA. J. INT'L BUS. L. 101 (1992) (discussing EU regulation of financial services). *See generally* Lui, *A Banker's Guide to the European Community's 1992 Program*, 107 BANKING L.J. 148 (1990) (discussing intended impact of EU law on international banking).

a. This article was written prior to the recent enactment of certain banking provisions which are described herein as anticipatory. As such, some of the descriptions of the planned implementation of the EC banking regulations have already been executed.

with national budgets. . . .

Despite the reservations of certain Member States about EMU, considerable progress has been made in the liberalization of the banking sector. That progress was marked in December 1989 by the adoption of what is commonly referred to as the Second Banking Directive.[1] The Second Banking Directive demonstrates a change of strategy in the way in which the EC has approached the liberalization of banking in Europe. Whereas the EC had previously concentrated on harmonization of national laws, the approach embodied in the Second Banking Directive centers on the concept of the single banking license. This would enable banks established in one Member State to establish branches and to provide a wide range of services throughout the EC. The concept of the single banking license is underpinned by three principles: (1) that the law and practice relating to banks should be harmonized across Member States; (2) that there should be mutual recognition by national supervisory authorities of the controls operated by each other; and (3) that home country control, i.e. supervision of banks, including branches in other Member States, should be undertaken by the supervisory authorities of the Member State where the bank is authorized.
. . .

## I. THE DEVELOPMENT OF THE SYSTEM FOR REGULATION OF BANKS

. . .

Article 52 of the Treaty of Rome provides for the progressive abolition of restrictions on the freedom of nationals of one Member State to establish themselves in the territory of another Member State.[4] "Freedom of establishment" is defined specifically to include the right to set up and manage undertakings under the same conditions as those applying to nationals of the country where such establishment is to be effected. There is a similar requirement relating to the provision of services in Article 59 of the Treaty of Rome. This contemplates the progressive abolition of restrictions on the freedom of nationals of one Member State to provide services within the EC to persons in other Member States.[5]

In 1985, a report was issued by the Commission which revealed that little progress had been made over the previous three decades towards the removal of the barriers to free trade within the EC. It was recognized that something needed to be done to accelerate change within the EC. This resulted in the signature of the Single European Act by all the Member States in 1986.[6]

The Single European Act of 1986 amended the Treaty of Rome by adding a new Article 8(a), providing for the completion of the process of creating an internal market by December 31, 1992. The "internal market" is defined as "an area without internal frontiers in which the free movement of goods, persons, services, and capital is ensured in accordance with the provisions of [the] Treaty."

Prior to the Single European Act of 1986, progress in the area of banking had been

---

1. Second Council Directive 89/646 of 15th December 1989 on the coordination of laws, regulations and administrative provisions relating to the taking up and pursuit of the business of credit institutions, amending the Directive 77/780/EEC, 1989 O.J. (L 386) 1 (amended First Council Directive of 12th December 1977 on the coordination of laws, regulations and administrative provisions relating to the taking up and pursuit of the business of credit institutions, 1977 O.J. (L 322) 30) [hereinafter Second Banking Directive].

4. Treaty Establishing the European Economic Community [EEC Treaty] art. 52.

5. EEC Treaty art. 59.

6. Single European Act, 1987 O.J. (L 169).

slow. Early Directives relating to the banking and capital sectors placed emphasis on "host country" control, i.e. branches of banks established in one Member State should be authorized and regulated by the authorities in the Member State where the branch was established. The activities of such branches were restricted to those which a domestic bank of the host State could conduct. Directive 73/183[7] required certain Member States to abolish discriminatory requirements relating to foreign branches of banks, such as capital requirements which were more onerous than those applying to domestic banks. However, this Directive made no attempt to coordinate the laws of the various Member States.

The first step towards creating a unified banking market was taken in 1977, in what is known as the First Banking Directive.[8] The First Banking Directive applies to "credit institutions" which are defined as undertakings whose business it is to receive deposits or other repayable funds from the public and to grant credits for their own account. "Credit institutions" should, for the purposes of EC legislation, be distinguished from "financial institutions" which do not accept deposits, but which conduct some or all of the activities associated with banks such as granting credit and taking participations.

The First Banking Directive set out minimum conditions to be met before credit institutions could be authorized to operate by Member States. The Directive permitted the granting of authorization only if the credit institution possessed each of the following: (1) its own capital, separate from the resources of its head office; (2) adequate minimum own funds; and (3) at least two persons of sufficient repute and experience effectively directing its business. However, meeting these requirements did not ensure automatic authorization in other Member States since it did not prevent Member States from imposing more stringent conditions. Member States were permitted to make the establishment of a branch of a credit institution with its head office in another Member State subject to the law and procedures of the host Member State. The First Banking Directive did, however, provide for coordination and collaboration between the supervisory authorities of Member States.

Directive 83/350[9] was a step in the direction of "home country" control. This Directive created a system for the consolidated supervision of credit institutions owning 25% or more of the capital of other credit and financial institutions. Such supervision to be exercised by the authorities of the country in which the head office of the credit institution owning the capital was situated.

## II. THE SECOND BANKING DIRECTIVE

The crucial piece of legislation in the field of European banking regulation is the Second Banking Directive. This was adopted in December 1989 and Member States are required to implement it into their national legislation by January 1993. This directive covers a full range of financing activities, as the following list evidences:

1. Acceptance of deposits and other repayable funds from the public;
2. Lending;

---

7. Council Directive 73/183 of 28th June 1973 on the abolition of restrictions on freedom of establishment and freedom to provide services in respect of self-employed activities of banks and other financial institutions, 1973 O.J. (L 194) 1.

8. First Council Directive 77/780 of 12th December 1977 on the coordination of laws, regulations and administrative provisions relating to the taking up and pursuit of the business for credit institutions, 1977 O.J. (L 322) 30 [hereinafter First Banking Directive].

9. Council Directive 83/350 of 13th June 1983 on the supervision of credit institutions on a consolidated basis, 1983 O.J. (L 193) 18.

3. Financial leasing;

4. Money transmission services;

5. Issuing and administering means of payment (e.g., credit cards, travelers' cheques and bankers' drafts);

6. Guarantees and commitments;

7. Trading for own account or for account of customers in:

      (a) money market instruments (cheques, bills, c.d.s, etc.);

      (b) foreign exchange;

      (c) financial futures and options;

      (d) exchange and interest rate instruments;

      (e) transferable securities;

8. Participation in share issues and the provision of services related to such issues;

9. Advice to undertakings on capital structure, industrial strategy and related questions and advice, and services relating to mergers and the purchase of undertakings;

10. Money brokering;

11. Portfolio management and advice;

12. Safekeeping and administration of securities;

13. Credit reference services;

14. Safe custody services; including, *inter alia*:

      - consumer credit,

      - mortgage lending,

      - factoring, with or without recourse,

      - financing of commercial transactions (including forfeiting).[10]

The directive also seeks to abolish any remaining restrictions on the freedom to establish branches of credit institutions and to provide banking services throughout the EC. The crux of the proposal is the single banking license, enabling banks authorized in one Member State to establish themselves via branches in other Member States, without being subject to further significant regulatory constraints. The wide range of permitted activities provided by the Second Banking Directive allows banks to transact in other Member States, once authorized by their home supervisor with respect to those activities. However, the Second Banking Directive does not confer that same freedom of establishment to subsidiaries of banks authorized in other Member States, as opposed to branches of banks authorized in other Member States. Subsidiaries, as opposed to branches, are required to obtain authorization from the host State in which the subsidiary is to be established. The rationale for this difference in treatment is, presumably, that a branch is, in fact, the same legal entity as its parent, whereas a subsidiary is a separate legal entity requiring separate authorization; the most logical place for that authorization to be given is the Member State where the subsidiary is incorporated.

A. Minimum Requirements for Authorization

The Second Banking Directive prohibits Member States from granting authorization to a credit institution if the institution's initial capital is less than ECU 5,000,000.[a] There is, however, an exception to that prohibition which permits Member States to grant authori-

---

10. Second Banking Directive, *supra* note 1, Annex.

a. The European Currency Unit ("ECU") was a unit of account used throughout EC legislation relating to banking. It was composed of a "basket" of specified amounts of the currencies of each of the Member States in the EC. Those amounts were revised from time to time. With the achievement of EMU, the ECU was replaced by the Euro (€) in most member states.

zation to particular categories of credit institutions whose initial capital is at least ECU 1,000,000, provided that the Member State concerned complies with certain notice and reporting requirements set out in the Second Banking Directive. Before granting authorization, Member States are required to know the identity and the amount of holdings of the shareholders or members of the credit institution who have holdings representing 10% or more of the capital or voting rights. The purpose of imposing minimum standards for authorizations is to ensure that those who deal with credit institutions are afforded an adequate level of protection and to equate competitive conditions throughout the community.

B. Cross-Border Activities

The Second Banking Directive also provides that Member States must permit within their territories the transaction of the activities listed in the Annex by a credit institution authorized in another Member State, provided that the credit institution's authorization covers such activities. A credit institution may carry on the activities for which it is authorized in a Member State, other than in its home Member State, either by establishment of a branch or by the provision of services.

The formalities for carrying on banking activities in another Member State vary, depending on whether the credit institution in question wishes to establish a branch in that Member State or, merely to provide services from the Member State in which it is already authorized. In the case of a credit institution wishing to establish a branch in another Member State, it must first notify the authorities of the Member State in which it is authorized and provide those authorities with certain information prescribed by the Second Banking Directive. The information to be provided covers such matters as the identity of the Member State in which the branch is to be established, the types of business intended, the structural organization of the branch, and the names of the persons responsible for its management. Provided that the authorities of the home Member State do not doubt the adequacy of the administrative structure or financial situation of the credit institution, they must communicate the information provided by the credit institution to the authorities of the host Member State. The amount of the credit institution's own funds and solvency ratio must also be communicated to the host Member State by the authorities, together with details of any deposit-guarantee scheme intended to protect depositors in the branch.

The host Member State is required to prepare for supervision of the credit institution within two months of receiving the information provided by the home Member State and, if necessary, to indicate the conditions under which, in the interest of the general good, the activities concerned must be carried on in the host Member State. Upon receipt of a communication from the host Member State or, in the absence of a communication, on the expiration of two months from the time the host Member State was provided with information about the credit institution by the home Member State, the branch may be established and commence its activities.

Where the credit institution wishes to engage in activities in another Member State by providing services from its home Member State, it must notify the authorities of its home Member State of the activities it intends to transact. The authorities of the home Member State must then notify the authorities of the host Member State, whereupon the credit institution may commence its activities.

Although the role of authorization and supervision will rest primarily with the home Member State, the host Member State will retain a limited supervisory role. The authorities of the host Member State may require all credit institutions having branches within its territory to provide periodic reports for statistical purposes. They may also punish breaches occurring with respect to matters falling within the power of the host Member State under the Second Banking Directive. Additionally, there is a general power vested in host Member

States to prevent and punish irregularities which are contrary to legal rules adopted "in the interest of the general good" and to adopt rules governing the form and content of advertising by credit institutions "in the interest of the general good." Furthermore, the Second Banking Directive provides for the host Member State to retain responsibility for the supervision of the liquidity of branches of credit institutions, in cooperation with the authorities of the home Member State pending further coordination of laws. Host Member States also retain responsibility for measures resulting from the implementation of their monetary policies, although such measures must not discriminate against credit institutions authorized in other Member States.

C. Reciprocity

The issue which caused the most controversy during the course of the negotiation of the Second Banking Directive was that of reciprocity. Broadly, this means that banks from outside the EC might not be permitted access into the EC unless EC institutions are themselves given reciprocal treatment in the home country of the particular bank. The original text of the Second Banking Directive proposed a bureaucratic investigation system which would be triggered automatically whenever a bank from outside the EC sought entry to a Member State. This provoked a very unfavorable reaction both from within the EC, where the United Kingdom was concerned that such a stipulation would threaten London's position as a financial center, and from banks outside the EC, particularly the United States and Japan which feared that the reciprocity provisions were designed to create a "fortress Europe" from which they would be excluded. For a time, it was unclear whether reciprocal treatment meant that banks from the EC operating in third countries (*i.e.* non-EC countries) should enjoy identical privileges to those afforded to foreign banks within the EC, or whether it simply meant that EC banks operating in third countries should not be treated less favorably than local banks in those countries. The issue has now been resolved by revising the contentious provision of the Second Banking Directive so that the EC may take retaliatory measures where EC banks do not enjoy rights comparable to local banks in third countries. However, there is still some latitude within the provision for the negotiation of "comparable access," *i.e.*, to procure the same freedom for banks from the EC which operate in third countries as third country banks enjoy in the EC.

The Second Banking Directive requires the authorities of Member States to inform the Commission of the authorization of a credit institution which is a direct or indirect subsidiary of an undertaking governed by the laws of a third country and, similarly, the acquisition by such an undertaking of a credit institution in the EC. Member States must also inform the Commission of, what is described as, "any general difficulties encountered by their credit institutions in establishing themselves or carrying on banking activities in a third country."

The obligation to provide such information is tied in to the requirement that the Commission compile periodic reports on the treatment accorded to EC credit institutions in third countries regarding establishment, the transaction of banking activities, and the acquisition of holdings in third country credit institutions. If the Commission considers that a third country is not granting EC credit institutions access to its markets comparable with that granted by the EC to credit institutions from that third country, the Commission may apply to the Council of the European Community for a mandate to negotiate comparable opportunities. If, however, the Commission considers that EC credit institutions in a third country are not offered the same opportunities as domestic credit institutions in that country, the Commission may itself initiate negotiations with the country concerned. Moreover, it may, at the same time, require Member States to limit or suspend decisions regarding requests for authorization from, or for the acquisition of holdings by, institutions in third countries for a maximum period of three months. The Council is empowered to extend the period of limitation and suspension. The Second Banking Directive provides that such limitation and suspension measures (whether by the Commission or the Council) will not apply to those credit institutions or their subsidiaries duly authorized by one Member State which wish to either establish a subsidiary in the EC or to acquire a holding in a credit institution within the EC.

D. Limitations on Harmonization

The Second Banking Directive permits Member States to establish stricter rules than some of those enacted in the Second Banking Directive itself–for instance, Member States are permitted to insist on initial capital in excess of the minimum of ECU 5,000,000, as specified in the Second Banking Directive. Requirements regarding notification of significant shareholdings in credit institutions, and limitations on shareholdings held by credit institutions in undertakings which are neither credit institutions nor financial institutions are examples of two other areas where Member States may impose more stringent obligations on credit institutions than those set out in the Second Banking Directive. This creates the possibility of credit institutions deliberately seeking authorization from a Member State whose rules are more liberal. This possibility is considered by the Second Banking Directive. One of its recitals requires Member States to deny authorization, or to withdraw it, where it is clear that a credit institution has opted for the legal system of one Member State for the purpose of evading the stricter standards in force in another Member State in which it intends to conduct the greater part of its activities.

III. COMPLEMENTARY LEGISLATION

It is intended that the Second Banking Directive will be supported by a number of other complementary Directives which are already in force or are under consideration. The following sections describe such complementary legislation.

A. Accounts

The annual accounts and consolidated accounts of banks and other financial institutions within the EC are regulated by Directive 86/635.[12] This Directive aims to coordinate the provisions relating to the content, format, and layout of the accounts of credit and financial institutions in the different Member States. In light of the increased activity by banks across national borders, this is of particular significance since it permits easy comparison of the accounts of various institutions and facilitates the task of regulating those institutions. This Directive applies to all banks whether incorporated or not. It lays down specific provisions relating to the format of the balance sheets and profit and loss accounts of banks, as well as to the items to be included within them. It also incorporates valuation rules for assets and detailed requirements relating to the contents of notes to the accounts. Additionally, the Directive requires publication of annual accounts, consolidated accounts, annual reports, and consolidated annual reports of credit institutions.

Directive 89/117[13] applies to branches of credit and financial institutions established in a Member State which have their head office outside the Member State. Such branches are obliged to comply with the requirements of Directive 86/635 relating to the

---

12. Council Directive 86/635 of 8th December 1986 on the annual accounts and consolidated accounts of banks and other financial institutions, 1986 O.J. (L 372) 1.

13. Council Directive 89/117 of 13th February 1989 on the obligations of branches of credit institutions and financial institutions established in a Member State, having their head offices outside that Member State, regarding the publication of annual accounting documents, 1989 O.J. (L 44) 40.

publication of accounts and auditors' reports. Directive 89/117 further provides for the accounts and reports to be drawn up and audited in accordance with the laws of the Member State where the head office of the credit or financial institution is situated. Additionally, branches may not be required to publish annual accounts relating to their own activities. Member States may, however, require branches having their head offices in other Member States to provide additional information relating to matters such as their income and costs, staff employed, claims and liabilities attributable to the branch, and certain of their assets. The provisions relating to branches where the head office is situated in non-EC countries are similarly broad, with the accounts to be drawn up and audited in accordance with the requirements of the third country. The host Member State may only require the branch to publish annual accounts relating to its own activities if the provisions of Directive 86/635 have not been complied with or if reciprocity does not exist with the third country.

# 2. U.S. Statutory and Regulatory Provisions

In this section we examine in detail the statutory provisions and implementing regulations that govern entry by U.S. banking enterprises into foreign markets. Some of these regulations have recently been the subject of significant change. In October 2001, the Fed promulgated an extensive revision of Regulation K, 12 C.F.R. pt. 211 (Reg K),[5] covering entry by U.S. banking enterprises into foreign markets. Subpart A of Reg K, 12 C.F.R. §§ 211.1-211.13, governs foreign investment and activities of all member banks (national and state member banks), Edge and agreement corporations, and bank holding companies. The revision streamlined foreign branching procedures for U.S. banking organizations; authorized expanded activities in foreign branches of U.S. banks; implemented recent statutory changes authorizing bank to invest up to 20 percent of capital and surplus in Edge corporations; and amended rules governing permissible foreign activities of U.S. banking organizations (including securities activities) and investments by U.S. banking organizations under "general consent" procedures. These revised rules are excerpted below. The Fed also revised subpart B of Reg K, id. §§ 211.20-211.30, which governs U.S. activities of foreign banking organizations, and subpart C, 12 C.F.R. §§ 211.31-211.34, which deals with export trading companies. Excerpts from subparts B and C appear in Chapters 6 and 9, respectively.

**Notes and Comments 5.4.** In preparation for the questions in the following notes and comments, review the provisions of 12 U.S.C. §§ 601-619, and the regulatory provisions excerpted below (particularly pt. 28 and §§ 211.1-211.5, 211.8, 211.10).

**5.5.** QNB has determined, through local counsel, that the Nusquami Banking Code will not permit Quarter to operate within Nusquam through a subsidiary. QNB is now planning to establish a branch in Nusquam. What must it do to establish the branch? What further factual information, if any, do you need to advise Quarter? (Review particularly 12 U.S.C. § 601, 12 C.F.R. §§ 28.3, 211.3(b).)

**5.6.** Would it make any difference to your answer if you knew that Quarter already had a network of foreign branches and subsidiaries in various foreign countries? (Review 12 C.F.R. § 211.3(b).)

**5.7.** Once QNB's Nusquami branch was in operation, which U.S. regulator would be its primary supervisor? (Review 12 U.S.C. § 602; 12 C.F.R. § 28.1(c). Cf. 12 C.F.R. §

---

5. 66 Fed. Reg. 54,346 (2001) (codified at 12 C.F.R. pts. 211, 265).

211.13(b).)

**5.8.** Local counsel has indicated that QNB may not be able to participate fully in the retail deposit market within Nusquam, since foreign branches have generally been granted approval on the condition, *inter alia*, that they accept "domestic deposits" only in large-denomination certificates. Are there any other powers which Quarter's Nusquami branch would have that might offset these limits on its deposit business?[6] (Review 12 C.F.R. § 211.4.)

**5.9.** Are there alternative arrangements that Quarter might make in structuring its entry into Nusquam through a branch, but without exposing itself to full, direct liability? Depending on the alternatives available, what regulatory approvals would Quarter need to obtain, and what procedures would Quarter be required to follow in order to obtain such approvals? (Review 12 C.F.R. §§ 28.3(a), 211.4(b), 211.5(b), 211.8.)

# Comptroller of the Currency
## 12 C.F.R. pt. 28

§ 28.1 Authority, purpose, and scope.

(a) Authority. This subpart is issued pursuant to 12 U.S.C. 1 et seq., 24(Seventh), 93a, and 602.

(b) Purpose. This subpart sets forth filing requirements for national banks that engage in international operations and clarifies permissible foreign activities of national banks.

(c) Scope. This subpart applies to any national bank that engages in international operations through a foreign branch, or acquires an interest in an Edge corporation, Agreement corporation, foreign bank, or certain other foreign organizations.

§ 28.2 Definitions.

For purposes of this subpart:

(a) Agreement corporation means a corporation having an agreement or undertaking with the Board of Governors of the Federal Reserve System (FRB) under section 25 of the Federal Reserve Act (FRA), 12 U.S.C. 601 through 604a.

(b) Edge corporation means a corporation that is organized under section 25A of the FRA, 12 U.S.C. 611 through 631.

(c) Foreign bank means an organization that:

(1) Is organized under the laws of a foreign country;

(2) Engages in the business of banking;

(3) Is recognized as a bank by the bank supervisory or monetary authority of the country of its organization or principal banking operations;

(4) Receives deposits to a substantial extent in the regular course of its business; and

(5) Has the power to accept demand deposits.

(d) Foreign branch means an office of a national bank (other than a representative office) that is located outside the United States at which banking or financing business is conducted.

(e) Foreign country means one or more foreign nations, and includes the overseas territories, dependencies, and insular possessions of those nations and of the United States, and the Commonwealth of Puerto Rico.

---

6. This is a subject to which we shall return in Chapter 9, *infra*.

§ 28.3     Filing requirements for foreign operations of a national bank.

(a) Notice requirement.  A national bank shall notify the OCC when it:

(1) Files an application, notice, or report with the FRB to:

(i) Establish or open a foreign branch;

(ii) Acquire or divest of an interest in, or close, an Edge corporation, Agreement corporation, foreign bank, or other foreign organization; or

(2) Opens a foreign branch, and no application or notice is required by the FRB for such transaction.

(b) Other applications and notices accepted.  In lieu of a notice under paragraph (a)(1) of this section, the OCC may accept a copy of an application, notice, or report submitted to another Federal agency that covers the proposed action and contains substantially the same information required by the OCC.

(c) Additional information.  A national bank shall furnish the OCC with any additional information the OCC may require in connection with the national bank's foreign operations.

§ 28.4 Permissible activities.

(a) General.  Subject to the applicable approval process, if any, a national bank may engage in any activity in a foreign country that is:

(1) Permissible for a national bank in the United States; and

(2) Usual in connection with the business of banking in the country where it transacts business.

(b) Additional activities.  In addition to its general banking powers, a national bank may engage in any activity in a foreign country that is permissible under the FRB's Regulation K, 12 CFR part 211.

(c) Foreign operations guarantees.  A national bank may guarantee the deposits and other liabilities of its Edge corporations and Agreement corporations and of its corporate instrumentalities in foreign countries. . . .

# Board of Governors of the Federal Reserve System
12 C.F.R. pt. 211

Subpart A--International Operations of U.S. Banking Organizations[g]

Sec.
211.1 Authority, purpose, and scope.
211.2 Definitions.
211.3 Foreign branches of U.S. banking organizations.
211.4 Permissible investments and activities of foreign branches of member banks.
211.5 Edge and agreement corporations.
211.6 Permissible activities of Edge and agreement corporations in the United States.
211.7 Voluntary liquidation of Edge and agreement corporations.
211.8 Investments and activities abroad.
211.9 Investment procedures.
211.10 Permissible activities abroad.
     . . .

---

g. *As amended*, 66 Fed. Reg. 54,346 (2001), *corrected*, 66 Fed. Reg. 58,655 (2001).

211.12 Lending limits and capital requirements.
211.13 Supervision and reporting.

Subpart A--International Operations of U.S. Banking Organizations

§ 211.1 Authority, purpose, and scope.

(a) Authority. This subpart is issued by the Board of Governors of the Federal Reserve System (Board) under the authority of the Federal Reserve Act (FRA) (12 U.S.C. 221 et seq.); the Bank Holding Company Act of 1956 (BHC Act) (12 U.S.C. 1841 et seq.); and the International Banking Act of 1978 (IBA) (12 U.S.C. 3101 et seq.).

(b) Purpose. This subpart sets out rules governing the international and foreign activities of U.S. banking organizations, including procedures for establishing foreign branches and Edge and agreement corporations to engage in international banking, and for investments in foreign organizations.

(c) Scope. This subpart applies to:

(1) Member banks with respect to their foreign branches and investments in foreign banks under section 25 of the FRA (12 U.S.C. 601-604a);[8] and

(2) Corporations organized under section 25A of the FRA (12 U.S.C. 611-631) (Edge corporations);

(3) Corporations having an agreement or undertaking with the Board under section 25 of the FRA (12 U.S.C. 601-604a) (agreement corporations); and

(4) Bank holding companies with respect to the exemption from the nonbanking prohibitions of the BHC Act afforded by section 4(c)(13) of that act (12 U.S.C. 1843(c) (13)).

§ 211.2 Definitions.

Unless otherwise specified, for purposes of this subpart:

(a) An affiliate of an organization means:

(1) Any entity of which the organization is a direct or indirect subsidiary; or

(2) Any direct or indirect subsidiary of the organization or such entity.

(b) Capital Adequacy Guidelines means the "Capital Adequacy Guidelines for State Member Banks: Risk-Based Measure" (12 CFR part 208, app. A) or the "Capital Adequacy Guidelines for Bank Holding Companies: Risk-Based Measure" (12 CFR part 225, app. A).

(c) Capital and surplus means, unless otherwise provided in this part:

(1) For organizations subject to the Capital Adequacy Guidelines:

(i) Tier 1 and tier 2 capital included in an organization's risk-based capital (under the Capital Adequacy Guidelines); and

(ii) The balance of allowance for loan and lease losses not included in an organization's tier 2 capital for calculation of risk-based capital, based on the organization's most recent consolidated Report of Condition and Income.

(2) For all other organizations, paid-in and unimpaired capital and surplus, and includes undivided profits but does not include the proceeds of capital notes or debentures.

(d) Directly or indirectly, when used in reference to activities or investments of an organization, means activities or investments of the organization or of any subsidiary of the organization.

---

8. Section 25 of the FRA (12 U.S.C. 601-604a), which refers to national banking associations, also applies to state member banks of the Federal Reserve System by virtue of section 9 of the FRA (12 U.S.C. 321).

(e) Eligible country means any country:

(1) For which an allocated transfer risk reserve is required pursuant to § 211.43 of this part and that has restructured its sovereign debt held by foreign creditors; and

(2) Any other country that the Board deems to be eligible.

(f) An Edge corporation is engaged in banking if it is ordinarily engaged in the business of accepting deposits in the United States from nonaffiliated persons.

(g) Engaged in business or engaged in activities in the United States means maintaining and operating an office (other than a representative office) or subsidiary in the United States.

(h) Equity means an ownership interest in an organization, whether through:

(1) Voting or nonvoting shares;

(2) General or limited partnership interests;

(3) Any other form of interest conferring ownership rights, including warrants, debt, or any other interests that are convertible into shares or other ownership rights in the organization; or

(4) Loans that provide rights to participate in the profits of an organization, unless the investor receives a determination that such loans should not be considered equity in the circumstances of the particular investment.

(i) Foreign or foreign country refers to one or more foreign nations, and includes the overseas territories, dependencies, and insular possessions of those nations and of the United States, and the Commonwealth of Puerto Rico.

(j) Foreign bank means an organization that:

(1) Is organized under the laws of a foreign country;

(2) Engages in the business of banking;

(3) Is recognized as a bank by the bank supervisory or monetary authority of the country of its organization or principal banking operations;

(4) Receives deposits to a substantial extent in the regular course of its business; and

(5) Has the power to accept demand deposits.

(k) Foreign branch means an office of an organization (other than a representative office) that is located outside the country in which the organization is legally established and at which a banking or financing business is conducted.

(*l*) Foreign person means an office or establishment located outside the United States, or an individual residing outside the United States.

(m) Investment means:

(1) The ownership or control of equity;

(2) Binding commitments to acquire equity;

(3) Contributions to the capital and surplus of an organization; or

(4) The holding of an organization's subordinated debt when the investor and the investor's affiliates hold more than 5 percent of the equity of the organization.

(n) Investment grade means a security that is rated in one of the four highest rating categories by:

(1) Two or more NRSROs; or

(2) One NRSRO if the security has been rated by only one NRSRO.

(o) Investor means an Edge corporation, agreement corporation, bank holding company, or member bank.

(p) Joint venture means an organization that has 20 percent or more of its voting shares held directly or indirectly by the investor or by an affiliate of the investor under any authority, but which is not a subsidiary of the investor or of an affiliate of the investor.

(q) Loans and extensions of credit means all direct and indirect advances of funds to a person made on the basis of any obligation of that person to repay the funds.

(r) NRSRO means a nationally recognized statistical rating organization as designated by the Securities and Exchange Commission.

(s) Organization means a corporation, government, partnership, association, or any other entity.

(t) Person means an individual or an organization.

(u) Portfolio investment means an investment in an organization other than a subsidiary or joint venture.

(v) Representative office means an office that:

(1) Engages solely in representational and administrative functions (such as soliciting new business or acting as liaison between the organization's head office and customers in the United States); and

(2) Does not have authority to make any business decision (other than decisions relating to its premises or personnel) for the account of the organization it represents, including contracting for any deposit or deposit-like liability on behalf of the organization.

(w) Subsidiary means an organization that has more than 50 percent of its voting shares held directly or indirectly, or that otherwise is controlled or capable of being controlled, by the investor or an affiliate of the investor under any authority. Among other circumstances, an investor is considered to control an organization if:

(1) The investor or an affiliate is a general partner of the organization; or

(2) The investor and its affiliates directly or indirectly own or control more than 50 percent of the equity of the organization. . . .

(y) Well capitalized means:

(1) In relation to a parent member or insured bank, that the standards set out in § 208.43(b)(1) of Regulation H (12 CFR 208.43(b)(1)) are satisfied;

(2) In relation to a bank holding company, that the standards set out in § 225.2(r)(1) of Regulation Y (12 CFR 225.2(r)(1)) are satisfied; and

(3) In relation to an Edge or agreement corporation, that it has tier 1 and total risk-based capital ratios of 6.0 and 10.0 percent, respectively, or greater.

(z) Well managed means that the Edge or agreement corporation, any parent insured bank, and the bank holding company received a composite rating of 1 or 2, and at least a satisfactory rating for management if such a rating is given, at their most recent examination or review.

§ 211.3  Foreign branches of U.S. banking organizations.

(a) General--(1) Definition of banking organization. For purposes of this section, a banking organization is defined as a member bank and its affiliates.

(2) A banking organization is considered to be operating a branch in a foreign country if it has an affiliate that is a member bank, Edge or agreement corporation, or foreign bank that operates an office (other than a representative office) in that country.

(3) For purposes of this subpart, a foreign office of an operating subsidiary of a member bank shall be treated as a foreign branch of the member bank and may engage only in activities permissible for a branch of a member bank.

(4) At any time upon notice, the Board may modify or suspend branching authority conferred by this section with respect to any banking organization.

(b) (1) Establishment of foreign branches. (i) Foreign branches may be established by any member bank having capital and surplus of $1,000,000 or more, an Edge corporation, an agreement corporation, any subsidiary the shares of which are held directly by the member bank, or any other subsidiary held pursuant to this subpart.

(ii) The Board grants its general consent under section 25 of the FRA (12 U.S.C. 601-604a) for a member bank to establish a branch in the Commonwealth of Puerto Rico and the overseas territories, dependencies, and insular possessions of the United States.

(2) Prior notice. Unless otherwise provided in this section, the establishment of a foreign branch requires 30 days' prior written notice to the Board.

(3) Branching into additional foreign countries. After giving the Board 12 business days prior written notice, a banking organization that operates branches in two or more foreign countries may establish a branch in an additional foreign country.

(4) Additional branches within a foreign country. No prior notice is required to establish additional branches in any foreign country where the banking organization operates one or more branches.

(5) Branching by nonbanking affiliates. No prior notice is required for a nonbanking affiliate of a banking organization (i.e., an organization that is not a member bank, an Edge or agreement corporation, or foreign bank) to establish branches within a foreign country or in additional foreign countries.

(6) Expiration of branching authority. Authority to establish branches, when granted following prior written notice to the Board, shall expire one year from the earliest date on which the authority could have been exercised, unless extended by the Board.

(c) Reporting. Any banking organization that opens, closes, or relocates a branch shall report such change in a manner prescribed by the Board.

(d) Reserves of foreign branches of member banks. Member banks shall maintain reserves against foreign branch deposits when required by Regulation D (12 CFR part 204).

(e) Conditional approval; access to information. The Board may impose such conditions on authority granted by it under this section as it deems necessary, and may require termination of any activities conducted under authority of this section if a member bank is unable to provide information on its activities or those of its affiliates that the Board deems necessary to determine and enforce compliance with U.S. banking laws.

§ 211.4 Permissible activities and investments of foreign branches of member banks.

(a) Permissible activities and investments. In addition to its general banking powers, and to the extent consistent with its charter, a foreign branch of a member bank may engage in the following activities and make the following investments, so far as is usual in connection with the business of banking in the country where it transacts business:

(1) Guarantees. Guarantee debts, or otherwise agree to make payments on the occurrence of readily ascertainable events (including, but not limited to, nonpayment of taxes, rentals, customs duties, or costs of transport, and loss or nonconformance of shipping documents) if the guarantee or agreement specifies a maximum monetary liability; however, except to the extent that the member bank is fully secured, it may not have liabilities outstanding for any person on account of such guarantees or agreements which, when aggregated with other unsecured obligations of the same person, exceed the limit contained in section 5200(a)(1) of the Revised Statutes (12 U.S.C. 84) for loans and extensions of credit;

(2) Government obligations. (i) Underwrite, distribute, buy, sell, and hold obligations of:

(A) The national government of the country where the branch is located and any political subdivision of that country;

(B) An agency or instrumentality of the national government of the country where the branch is located where such obligations are supported by the taxing authority, guarantee, or full faith and credit of that government;

(C) The national government or political subdivision of any country, where such obligations are rated investment grade; and

(D) An agency or instrumentality of any national government where such obligations are rated investment grade and are supported by the taxing authority, guarantee or full faith and credit of that government.

(ii) No member bank, under authority of this paragraph (a)(2), may hold, or be under commitment with respect to, such obligations for its own account in relation to any one country in an amount exceeding the greater of:

(A) 10 percent of its tier 1 capital; or

(B) 10 percent of the total deposits of the bank's branches in that country on the preceding year-end call report date (or the date of acquisition of the branch, in the case of a branch that has not been so reported);

(3) Other investments. (i) Invest in:

(A) The securities of the central bank, clearinghouses, governmental entities other than those authorized under paragraph (a)(2) of this section, and government-sponsored development banks of the country where the foreign branch is located;

(B) Other debt securities eligible to meet local reserve or similar requirements; and

(C) Shares of automated electronic-payments networks, professional societies, schools, and the like necessary to the business of the branch;

(ii) The total investments of a bank's branches in a country under this paragraph (a)(3) (exclusive of securities held as required by the law of that country or as authorized under section 5136 of the Revised Statutes (12 U.S.C. 24, Seventh)) may not exceed 1 percent of the total deposits of the bank's branches in that country on the preceding year-end call report date (or on the date of acquisition of the branch, in the case of a branch that has not been so reported);

(4) Real estate loans. Take liens or other encumbrances on foreign real estate in connection with its extensions of credit, whether or not of first priority and whether or not the real estate has been improved;

(5) Insurance. Act as insurance agent or broker;

(6) Employee benefits program. Pay to an employee of the branch, as part of an employee benefits program, a greater rate of interest than that paid to other depositors of the branch;

(7) Repurchase agreements. Engage in repurchase agreements involving securities and commodities that are the functional equivalents of extensions of credit;

(8) Investment in subsidiaries. With the Board's prior approval, acquire all of the shares of a company (except where local law requires other investors to hold directors' qualifying shares or similar types of instruments) that engages solely in activities:

(i) In which the member bank is permitted to engage; or

(ii) That are incidental to the activities of the foreign branch.

(b) Other activities. With the Board's prior approval, engage in other activities that the Board determines are usual in connection with the transaction of the business of banking in the places where the member bank's branches transact business.

§ 211.5   Edge and agreement corporations.

(a) Board Authority. The Board shall have the authority to approve:

(1) The establishment of Edge corporations;

(2) Investments in agreement corporations; and

(3) A member bank's proposal to invest more than 10 percent of its capital and surplus in the aggregate amount of stock held in all Edge and agreement corporations.

(b) Organization of an Edge corporation--(1) Permit. A proposed Edge corporation shall become a body corporate when the Board issues a permit approving its proposed name, articles of association, and organization certificate.

(2) Name. The name of the Edge corporation shall include international, foreign, overseas, or a similar word, but may not resemble the name of another organization to an extent that might mislead or deceive the public.

(3) Federal Register notice. The Board shall publish in the Federal Register notice of any proposal to organize an Edge corporation and shall give interested persons an opportunity to express their views on the proposal.

(4) Factors considered by Board. The factors considered by the Board in acting on a proposal to organize an Edge corporation include:

(i) The financial condition and history of the applicant;

(ii) The general character of its management;

(iii) The convenience and needs of the community to be served with respect to international banking and financing services; and

(iv) The effects of the proposal on competition.

(5) Authority to commence business. After the Board issues a permit, the Edge corporation may elect officers and otherwise complete its organization, invest in obligations of the U.S. government, and maintain deposits with depository institutions, but it may not exercise any other powers until at least 25 percent of the authorized capital stock specified in the articles of association has been paid in cash, and each shareholder has paid in cash at least 25 percent of that shareholder's stock subscription.

(6) Expiration of unexercised authority. Unexercised authority to commence business as an Edge corporation shall expire one year after issuance of the permit, unless the Board extends the period. . . .

(d) Ownership of Edge corporations by foreign institutions--(1) Prior Board approval. One or more foreign or foreign-controlled domestic institutions referred to in section 25A(11) of the FRA (12 U.S.C. 619) may apply for the Board's prior approval to acquire, directly or indirectly, a majority of the shares of the capital stock of an Edge corporation.

(2) Conditions and requirements. Such an institution shall:

(i) Provide the Board with information related to its financial condition and activities and such other information as the Board may require;

(ii) Ensure that any transaction by an Edge corporation with an affiliate[9] is on substantially the same terms, including interest rates and collateral, as those prevailing at the same time for comparable transactions by the Edge corporation with nonaffiliated persons, and does not involve more than the normal risk of repayment or present other unfavorable features;

(iii) Ensure that the Edge corporation will not provide funding on a continual or substantial basis to any affiliate or office of the foreign institution through transactions that would be inconsistent with the international and foreign business purposes for which Edge corporations are organized; and

(iv) Comply with the limitation on aggregate investments in all Edge and agreement corporations set forth in paragraph (h) of this section.

---

9. For purposes of this paragraph (d)(2), affiliate means any organization that would be an affiliate under section 23A of the FRA (12 U.S.C. 371c) if the Edge corporation were a member bank.

(3) Foreign institutions not subject to the BHC Act. In the case of a foreign institution not subject to section 4 of the BHC Act (12 U.S.C. 1843), that institution shall:

(i) Comply with any conditions that the Board may impose that are necessary to prevent undue concentration of resources, decreased or unfair competition, conflicts of interest, or unsound banking practices in the United States; and

(ii) Give the Board 30 days' prior written notice before engaging in any nonbanking activity in the United States, or making any initial or additional investments in another organization, that would require prior Board approval or notice by an organization subject to section 4 of the BHC Act (12 U.S.C. 1843); in connection with such notice, the Board may impose conditions necessary to prevent adverse effects that may result from such activity or investment.

(e) Change in control of an Edge corporation--(1) Prior notice. (i) Any person shall give the Board 60 days' prior written notice before acquiring, directly or indirectly, 25 percent or more of the voting shares, or otherwise acquiring control, of an Edge corporation.

(ii) The Board may extend the 60-day period for an additional 30 days by notifying the acquiring party.

(iii) A notice under this paragraph (e) need not be filed where a change in control is effected through a transaction requiring the Board's approval under section 3 of the BHC Act (12 U.S.C. 1842).

(2) Board review. In reviewing a notice filed under this paragraph (e), the Board shall consider the factors set forth in paragraph (b)(4) of this section, and may disapprove a notice or impose any conditions that it finds necessary to assure the safe and sound operation of the Edge corporation, to assure the international character of its operation, and to prevent adverse effects, such as decreased or unfair competition, conflicts of interest, or undue concentration of resources.

(f) Domestic branching by Edge corporations--(1) Prior notice. (i) An Edge corporation may establish branches in the United States 30 days after the Edge corporation has given written notice of its intention to do so to its Reserve Bank, unless the Edge corporation is notified to the contrary within that time.

(ii) The notice to the Reserve Bank shall include a copy of the notice of the proposal published in a newspaper of general circulation in the communities to be served by the branch.

(iii) The newspaper notice may appear no earlier than 90 calendar days prior to submission of notice of the proposal to the Reserve Bank. The newspaper notice shall provide an opportunity for the public to give written comment on the proposal to the appropriate Federal Reserve Bank for at least 30 days after the date of publication.

(2) Factors considered. The factors considered in acting upon a proposal to establish a branch are enumerated in paragraph (b)(4) of this section.

(3) Expiration of authority. Authority to establish a branch under prior notice shall expire one year from the earliest date on which that authority could have been exercised, unless the Board extends the period.

(g) Agreement corporations--(1) General. With the prior approval of the Board, a member bank or bank holding company may invest in a federally or state- chartered corporation that has entered into an agreement or undertaking with the Board that it will not exercise any power that is impermissible for an Edge corporation under this subpart.

(2) Factors considered by Board. The factors considered in acting upon a proposal to establish an agreement corporation are enumerated in paragraph (b)(4) of this sectio

(h) (1) Limitation on investment in Edge and agreement corporations. A member bank may invest up to 10 percent of its capital and surplus in the capital stock of Edge and agreement corporations or, with the prior approval of the Board, up to 20 percent of its capital and surplus in such stock.

(2) Factors considered by Board. The factors considered by the Board in acting on a proposal under paragraph (h)(1) of this section shall include:

(i) The composition of the assets of the bank's Edge and agreement corporations;

(ii) The total capital invested by the bank in its Edge and agreement corporations when combined with retained earnings of the Edge and agreement corporations (including amounts invested in and retained earnings of any foreign bank subsidiaries) as a percentage of the bank's capital;

(iii) Whether the bank, bank holding company, and Edge and agreement corporations are well-capitalized and well-managed;

(iv) Whether the bank is adequately capitalized after deconsolidating and deducting the aggregate investment in and assets of all Edge or agreement corporations and all foreign bank subsidiaries; and

(v) Any other factor the Board deems relevant to the safety and soundness of the member bank.

(i) Reserve requirements and interest rate limitations. The deposits of an Edge or agreement corporation are subject to Regulations D and Q (12 CFR parts 204 and 217) in the same manner and to the same extent as if the Edge or agreement corporation were a member bank.

(j) Liquid funds. Funds of an Edge or agreement corporation that are not currently employed in its international or foreign business, if held or invested in the United States, shall be in the form of:

(1) Cash;

(2) Deposits with depository institutions, as described in Regulation D (12 CFR part 204), and other Edge and agreement corporations;

(3) Money-market instruments (including repurchase agreements with respect to such instruments), such as bankers' acceptances, federal funds sold, and commercial paper; and

(4) Short- or long-term obligations of, or fully guaranteed by, federal, state, and local governments and their instrumentalities.

(k) Reports by Edge and agreement corporations of crimes and suspected crimes. An Edge or agreement corporation, or any branch or subsidiary thereof, shall file a suspicious-activity report in accordance with the provisions of § 208.62 of Regulation H (12 CFR 208.62).

(l) Protection of customer information. An Edge or agreement corporation shall comply with the Interagency Guidelines Establishing Standards for Safeguarding Customer Information prescribed pursuant to sections 501 and 505 of the Gramm-Leach-Bliley Act (15 U.S.C. 6801 and 6805), set forth in appendix D-2 to part 208 of this chapter.

§ 211.6 Permissible activities of Edge and agreement corporations in the United States.

(a) Activities incidental to international or foreign business. An Edge or agreement corporation may engage, directly or indirectly, in activities in the United States that are permitted by section 25A(6) of the FRA (12 U.S.C. 615) and are incidental to international or foreign business, and in such other activities as the Board determines are incidental to international or foreign business. The following activities will ordinarily be considered incidental to an Edge or agreement corporation's international or foreign business:

(1) Deposit-taking activities--(i) Deposits from foreign governments and foreign

persons. An Edge or agreement corporation may receive in the United States transaction accounts, savings, and time deposits (including issuing negotiable certificates of deposits) from foreign governments and their agencies and instrumentalities, and from foreign persons.

(ii) Deposits from other persons. An Edge or agreement corporation may receive from any other person in the United States transaction accounts, savings, and time deposits (including issuing negotiable certificates of deposit) if such deposits:

(A) Are to be transmitted abroad;

(B) Consist of funds to be used for payment of obligations to the Edge or agreement corporation or collateral securing such obligations;

(C) Consist of the proceeds of collections abroad that are to be used to pay for exported or imported goods or for other costs of exporting or importing or that are to be periodically transferred to the depositor's account at another financial institution;

(D) Consist of the proceeds of extensions of credit by the Edge or agreement corporation;

(E) Represent compensation to the Edge or agreement corporation for extensions of credit or services to the customer;

(F) Are received from Edge or agreement corporations, foreign banks, and other depository institutions (as described in Regulation D (12 CFR part 204)); or

(G) Are received from an organization that by its charter, license, or enabling law is limited to business that is of an international character, including foreign sales corporations, as defined in 26 U.S.C. 922; transportation organizations engaged exclusively in the international transportation of passengers or in the movement of goods, wares, commodities, or merchandise in international or foreign commerce; and export trading companies established under subpart C of this part.

(2) Borrowings. An Edge or agreement corporation may:

(i) Borrow from offices of other Edge and agreement corporations, foreign banks, and depository institutions (as described in Regulation D (12 CFR part 204));

(ii) Issue obligations to the United States or any of its agencies or instrumentalities;

(iii) Incur indebtedness from a transfer of direct obligations of, or obligations that are fully guaranteed as to principal and interest by, the United States or any agency or instrumentality thereof that the Edge or agreement corporation is obligated to repurchase; and

(iv) Issue long-term subordinated debt that does not qualify as a deposit under Regulation D (12 CFR part 204).

(3) Credit activities. An Edge or agreement corporation may:

(i) Finance the following:

(A) Contracts, projects, or activities performed substantially abroad;

(B) The importation into or exportation from the United States of goods, whether direct or through brokers or other intermediaries;

(C) The domestic shipment or temporary storage of goods being imported or exported (or accumulated for export); and

(D) The assembly or repackaging of goods imported or to be exported;

(ii) Finance the costs of production of goods and services for which export orders have been received or which are identifiable as being directly for export;

(iii) Assume or acquire participations in extensions of credit, or acquire obligations arising from transactions the Edge or agreement corporation could have financed, including acquisition of obligations of foreign governments;

(iv) Guarantee debts, or otherwise agree to make payments on the occurrence of readily ascertainable events (including, but not limited to, nonpayment of taxes, rentals, customs duties, or cost of transport, and loss or nonconformance of shipping documents), so long as the guarantee or agreement specifies the maximum monetary liability thereunder and is related to a type of transaction described in paragraphs (a)(3)(i) and (ii) of this section; and

(v) Provide credit and other banking services for domestic and foreign purposes to foreign governments and their agencies and instrumentalities, foreign persons, and organizations of the type described in paragraph (a)(1)(ii)(G) of this section.

(4) Payments and collections.  An Edge or agreement corporation may receive checks, bills, drafts, acceptances, notes, bonds, coupons, and other instruments for collection abroad, and collect such instruments in the United States for a customer abroad; and may transmit and receive wire transfers of funds and securities for depositors.

(5) Foreign exchange.  An Edge or agreement corporation may engage in foreign exchange activities.

(6) Fiduciary and investment advisory activities. An Edge or agreement corporation may:

(i) Hold securities in safekeeping for, or buy and sell securities upon the order and for the account and risk of, a person, provided such services for U.S. persons are with respect to foreign securities only;

(ii) Act as paying agent for securities issued by foreign governments or other entities organized under foreign law;

(iii) Act as trustee, registrar, conversion agent, or paying agent with respect to any class of securities issued to finance foreign activities and distributed solely outside the United States;

(iv) Make private placements of participations in its investments and extensions of credit; however, except to the extent permissible for member banks under section 5136 of the Revised Statutes (12 U.S.C. 24 (Seventh)), no Edge or agreement corporation otherwise may engage in the business of underwriting, distributing, or buying or selling securities in the United States;

(v) Act as investment or financial adviser by providing portfolio investment advice and portfolio management with respect to securities, other financial instruments, real-property interests, and other investment assets,[10] and by providing advice on mergers and acquisitions, provided such services for U.S. persons are with respect to foreign assets only; and

(vi) Provide general economic information and advice, general economic statistical forecasting services, and industry studies, provided such services for U.S. persons shall be with respect to foreign economies and industries only.

(7) Banking services for employees. Provide banking services, including deposit services, to the officers and employees of the Edge or agreement corporation and its affiliates; however, extensions of credit to such persons shall be subject to the restrictions of Regulation O (12 CFR part 215) as if the Edge or agreement corporation were a member bank.

(b) Other activities.  With the Board's prior approval, an Edge or agreement corporation may engage, directly or indirectly, in other activities in the United States that the Board determines are incidental to their international or foreign business.

---

10. For purposes of this section, management of an investment portfolio does not include operational management of real property, or industrial or commercial assets.

§ 211.7  Voluntary liquidation of Edge and agreement corporations.

(a) Prior notice. An Edge or agreement corporation desiring voluntarily to discontinue normal business and dissolve, shall provide the Board with 45 days' prior written notice of its intent to do so.

(b) Waiver of notice period. The Board may waive the 45-day period if it finds that immediate action is required by the circumstances presented.

§ 211.8  Investments and activities abroad.

(a) General policy. Activities abroad, whether conducted directly or indirectly, shall be confined to activities of a banking or financial nature and those that are necessary to carry on such activities.  In doing so, investors[11] shall at all times act in accordance with high standards of banking or financial prudence, having due regard for diversification of risks, suitable liquidity, and adequacy of capital.  Subject to these considerations and the other provisions of this section, it is the Board's policy to allow activities abroad to be organized and operated as best meets corporate policies.

(b) Direct investments by member banks. A member bank's direct investments under section 25 of the FRA (12 U.S.C. 601 et seq.) shall be limited to:

(1) Foreign banks;

(2) Domestic or foreign organizations formed for the sole purpose of holding shares of a foreign bank;

(3) Foreign organizations formed for the sole purpose of performing nominee, fiduciary, or other banking services incidental to the activities of a foreign branch or foreign bank affiliate of the member bank; and

(4) Subsidiaries established pursuant to § 211.4(a)(8) of this part.

(c) Eligible investments. Subject to the limitations set out in paragraphs (b) and (d) of this section, an investor may, directly or indirectly:

(1) Investment in subsidiary. Invest in a subsidiary that engages solely in activities listed in § 211.10 of this part, or in such other activities as the Board has determined in the circumstances of a particular case are permissible; provided that, in the case of an acquisition of a going concern, existing activities that are not otherwise permissible for a subsidiary may account for not more than 5 percent of either the consolidated assets or consolidated revenues of the acquired organization;

(2) Investment in joint venture. Invest in a joint venture; provided that, unless otherwise permitted by the Board, not more than 10 percent of the joint venture's consolidated assets or consolidated revenues are attributable to activities not listed in § 211.10 of this part; and

(3) Portfolio investments. Make portfolio investments in an organization, provided that:

(i) Individual investment limits. The total direct and indirect portfolio investments by the investor and its affiliates in an organization engaged in activities that are not permissible for joint ventures, when combined with all other shares in the organization held under any other authority, do not exceed:

(A) 40 percent of the total equity of the organization; or

(B) 19.9 percent of the organization's voting shares.

(ii) Aggregate Investment Limit. Portfolio investments made under authority of this subpart shall be subject to the aggregate equity limit of § 211.10(a)(15)(iii).

---

11. For purposes of this section and §§ 211.9 and 211.10 of this part, a direct subsidiary of a member bank is deemed to be an investor.

(iii) Loans and extensions of credit. Any loans and extensions of credit made by an investor or its affiliates to the organization are on substantially the same terms, including interest rates and collateral, as those prevailing at the same time for comparable transactions between the investor or its affiliates and nonaffiliated persons; and

(iv) Protecting shareholder rights. Nothing in this paragraph (c)(3) shall prohibit an investor from otherwise exercising rights it may have as shareholder to protect the value of its investment, so long as the exercise of such rights does not result in the investor's direct or indirect control of the organization.

(d) Investment limit. In calculating the amount that may be invested in any organization under this section and §§ 211.9 and 211.10 of this part, there shall be included any unpaid amount for which the investor is liable and any investments in the same organization held by affiliates under any authority.

(e) Divestiture. An investor shall dispose of an investment promptly (unless the Board authorizes retention) if:

(1) The organization invested in:

(i) Engages in impermissible activities to an extent not permitted under paragraph (c) of this section; or

(ii) Engages directly or indirectly in other business in the United States that is not permitted to an Edge corporation in the United States; provided that an investor may:

(A) Retain portfolio investments in companies that derive no more than 10 percent of their total revenue from activities in the United States; and

(B) Hold up to 5 percent of the shares of a foreign company that engages directly or indirectly in business in the United States that is not permitted to an Edge corporation; or

(2) After notice and opportunity for hearing, the investor is advised by the Board that such investment is inappropriate under the FRA, the BHC Act, or this subpart.

(f) Debts previously contracted. Shares or other ownership interests acquired to prevent a loss upon a debt previously contracted in good faith are not subject to the limitations or procedures of this section; provided that such interests shall be disposed of promptly but in no event later than two years after their acquisition, unless the Board authorizes retention for a longer period. . . .

§ 211.9 Investment procedures.

(a) General provisions.[12] Direct and indirect investments shall be made in accordance with the general consent, limited general consent, prior notice, or specific consent procedures contained in this section.

(1) Minimum capital adequacy standards. Except as the Board may otherwise determine, in order for an investor to make investments pursuant to the procedures set out in this section, the investor, the bank holding company, and the member bank shall be in compliance with applicable minimum standards for capital adequacy set out in the Capital Adequacy Guidelines; provided that, if the investor is an Edge or agreement corporation, the minimum capital required is total and tier 1 capital ratios of 8 percent and 4 percent, respectively.

(2) Composite rating. Except as the Board may otherwise determine, in order for an investor to make investments under the general consent or limited general consent procedures of paragraphs (b) and (c) of this section, the investor and any parent insured bank

---

12. When necessary, the provisions of this section relating to general consent and prior notice constitute the Board's approval under section 25A(8) of the FRA (12 U.S.C. 615) for investments in excess of the limitations therein based on capital and surplus.

must have received a composite rating of at least 2 at the most recent examination.

(3) Board's authority to modify or suspend procedures. The Board, at any time upon notice, may modify or suspend the procedures contained in this section with respect to any investor or with respect to the acquisition of shares of organizations engaged in particular kinds of activities.

(4) Long-range investment plan. Any investor may submit to the Board for its specific consent a long-range investment plan. Any plan so approved shall be subject to the other procedures of this section only to the extent determined necessary by the Board to assure safety and soundness of the operations of the investor and its affiliates.

(5) Prior specific consent for initial investment. An investor shall apply for and receive the prior specific consent of the Board for its initial investment under this subpart in its first subsidiary or joint venture, unless an affiliate previously has received approval to make such an investment.

(6) Expiration of investment authority. Authority to make investments granted under prior notice or specific consent procedures shall expire one year from the earliest date on which the authority could have been exercised, unless the Board determines a longer period shall apply.

(7) Conditional approval; Access to information. The Board may impose such conditions on authority granted by it under this section as it deems necessary, and may require termination of any activities conducted under authority of this subpart if an investor is unable to provide information on its activities or those of its affiliates that the Board deems necessary to determine and enforce compliance with U.S. banking laws.

(b) General consent. The Board grants its general consent for a well capitalized and well managed investor to make investments, subject to the following:

(1) Well capitalized and well managed investor. In order to qualify for making investments under authority of this paragraph (b), both before and immediately after the proposed investment, the investor, any parent insured bank, and any parent bank holding company shall be well capitalized and well managed.

(2) Individual limit for investment in subsidiary. In the case of an investment in a subsidiary, the total amount invested directly or indirectly in such subsidiary (in one transaction or a series of transactions) does not exceed:

(i) 10 percent of the investor's tier 1 capital, where the investor is a bank holding company; or

(ii) 2 percent of the investor's tier 1 capital, where the investor is a member bank; or

(iii) The lesser of 2 percent of the tier 1 capital of any parent insured bank or 10 percent of the investor's tier 1 capital, for any other investor.

(3) Individual limit for investment in joint venture. In the case of an investment in a joint venture, the total amount invested directly or indirectly in such joint venture (in one transaction or a series of transactions) does not exceed:

(i) 5 percent of the investor's tier 1 capital, where the investor is a bank holding company; or

(ii) 1 percent of the investor's tier 1 capital, where the investor is a member bank; or

(iii) The lesser of 1 percent of the tier 1 capital of any parent insured bank or 5 percent of the investor's tier 1 capital, for any other investor.

(4) Individual limit for portfolio investment. In the case of a portfolio investment, the total amount invested directly or indirectly in such company (in one transaction or a series of transactions) does not exceed the lesser of $25 million, or

(i) 5 percent of the investor's tier 1 capital in the case of a bank holding company or its subsidiary, or Edge corporation engaged in banking; or

(ii) 25 percent of the investor's tier 1 capital in the case of an Edge corporation not engaged in banking.

(5) Investment in a general partnership or unlimited liability company. An investment in a general partnership or unlimited liability company may be made under authority of paragraph (b) of this section, subject to the limits set out in paragraph (c) of this section.

(6) Aggregate investment limits--(i) Investment limits. All investments made, directly or indirectly, during the previous 12-month period under authority of this section, when aggregated with the proposed investment, shall not exceed:

(A) 20 percent of the investor's tier 1 capital, where the investor is a bank holding company;

(B) 10 percent of the investor's tier 1 capital, where the investor is a member bank; or

(C) The lesser of 10 percent of the tier 1 capital of any parent insured bank or 50 percent of the tier 1 capital of the investor, for any other investor.

(ii) Downstream investments. In determining compliance with the aggregate limits set out in this paragraph (b), an investment by an investor in a subsidiary shall be counted only once, notwithstanding that such subsidiary may, within 12 months of the date of making the investment, downstream all or any part of such investment to another subsidiary.

(7) Application of limits. In determining compliance with the limits set out in this paragraph (b), an investor is not required to combine the value of all shares of an organization held in trading or dealing accounts under § 211.10(a)(15) of this part with investments in the same organization.

(c) Limited general consent--(1) Individual limit. The Board grants its general consent for an investor that is not well capitalized and well managed to make an investment in a subsidiary or joint venture, or to make a portfolio investment, if the total amount invested directly or indirectly (in one transaction or in a series of transactions) does not exceed the lesser of $25 million or:

(i) 5 percent of the investor's tier 1 capital, where the investor is a bank holding company;

(ii) 1 percent of the investor's tier 1 capital, where the investor is a member bank; or

(iii) The lesser of 1 percent of any parent insured bank's tier 1 capital or 5 percent of the investor's tier 1 capital, for any other investor.

(2) Aggregate limit. The amount of general consent investments made by any investor directly or indirectly under authority of this paragraph (c) during the previous 12-month period, when aggregated with the proposed investment, shall not exceed:

(i) 10 percent of the investor's tier 1 capital, where the investor is a bank holding company;

(ii) 5 percent of the investor's tier 1 capital, where the investor is a member bank; and

(iii) The lesser of 5 percent of any parent insured bank's tier 1 capital or 25 percent of the investor's tier 1 capital, for any other investor.

(3) Application of limits. In calculating compliance with the limits of this paragraph (c), the rules set forth in paragraphs (b)(6)(ii) and (b)(7) of this section shall apply.

(d) Other eligible investments under general consent. In addition to the authority granted under paragraphs (b) and (c) of this section, the Board grants its general consent for any investor to make the following investments:

(1) Investment in organization equal to cash dividends. Any investment in an organization in an amount equal to cash dividends received from that organization during the preceding 12 calendar months; and

(2) Investment acquired from affiliate. Any investment that is acquired from an affiliate at net asset value or through a contribution of shares.

(e) Investments ineligible for general consent. An investment in a foreign bank may not be made under authority of paragraphs (b) or (c) of this section if:

(1) After the investment, the foreign bank would be an affiliate of a member bank; and

(2) The foreign bank is located in a country in which the member bank and its affiliates have no existing banking presence.

(f) Prior notice. An investment that does not qualify for general consent under paragraph (b), (c), or (d) of this section may be made after the investor has given the Board 30 days' prior written notice, such notice period to commence at the time the notice is received, provided that:

(1) The Board may waive the 30-day period if it finds the full period is not required for consideration of the proposed investment, or that immediate action is required by the circumstances presented; and

(2) The Board may suspend the 30-day period or act on the investment under the Board's specific consent procedures.

(g) Specific consent. Any investment that does not qualify for either the general consent or the prior notice procedure may not be consummated without the specific consent of the Board.

§ 211.10   Permissible activities abroad.

(a) Activities usual in connection with banking. The Board has determined that the following activities are usual in connection with the transaction of banking or other financial operations abroad:

(1) Commercial and other banking activities;

(2) Financing, including commercial financing, consumer financing, mortgage banking, and factoring;

(3) Leasing real or personal property, or acting as agent, broker, or advisor in leasing real or personal property consistent with the provisions of Regulation Y (12 CFR part 225);

(4) Acting as fiduciary;

(5) Underwriting credit life insurance and credit accident and health insurance;

(6) Performing services for other direct or indirect operations of a U.S. banking organization, including representative functions, sale of long-term debt, name-saving, holding assets acquired to prevent loss on a debt previously contracted in good faith, and other activities that are permissible domestically for a bank holding company under sections 4(a)(2)(A) and 4(c)(1)(C) of the BHC Act (12 U.S.C. 1843(a)(2)(A), (c)(1)(C));

(7) Holding the premises of a branch of an Edge or agreement corporation or member bank or the premises of a direct or indirect subsidiary, or holding or leasing the residence of an officer or employee of a branch or subsidiary;

(8) Providing investment, financial, or economic advisory services;

(9) General insurance agency and brokerage;

(10) Data processing;

(11) Organizing, sponsoring, and managing a mutual fund, if the fund's shares are

not sold or distributed in the United States or to U.S. residents and the fund does not exercise managerial control over the firms in which it invests;

(12) Performing management consulting services, if such services, when rendered with respect to the U.S. market, shall be restricted to the initial entry;

(13) Underwriting, distributing, and dealing in debt securities outside the United States;

(14) Underwriting and distributing equity securities outside the United States as follows:

(i) Limits for well-capitalized and well-managed investor--(A) General. After providing 30 days' prior written notice to the Board, an investor that is well capitalized and well managed may underwrite equity securities, provided that commitments by an investor and its subsidiaries for the shares of a single organization do not, in the aggregate, exceed:

(1) 15 percent of the bank holding company's tier 1 capital, where the investor is a bank holding company;

(2) 3 percent of the investor's tier 1 capital, where the investor is a member bank; or

(3) The lesser of 3 percent of any parent insured bank's tier 1 capital or 15 percent of the investor's tier 1 capital, for any other investor;

(B) Qualifying criteria. An investor will be considered well-capitalized and well-managed for purposes of paragraph (a)(14)(i) of this section only if each of the bank holding company, member bank, and Edge or agreement corporation qualify as well-capitalized and well-managed.

(ii) Limits for investor that is not well capitalized and well managed. After providing 30 days' prior written notice to the Board, an investor that is not well capitalized and well managed may underwrite equity securities, provided that commitments by the investor and its subsidiaries for the shares of an organization do not, in the aggregate, exceed $60 million; and

(iii) Application of limits. For purposes of determining compliance with the limitations of this paragraph (a)(14), the investor may subtract portions of an underwriting that are covered by binding commitments obtained by the investor or its affiliates from sub-underwriters or other purchasers;

(15) Dealing in equity securities outside the United States as follows:

(i) Grandfathered authority. By an investor, or an affiliate, that had commenced such activities prior to March 27, 1991, and subject to the limitations in effect at that time (See 12 CFR part 211, revised January 1, 1991); or

(ii) Limit on shares of a single issuer. After providing 30 days' prior written notice to the Board, an investor may deal in the shares of an organization where the shares held in the trading or dealing accounts of an investor and its affiliates under authority of this paragraph (a)(15) do not in the aggregate exceed the lesser of:

(A) $40 million; or

(B) 10 percent of the investor's tier 1 capital;

(iii) Aggregate equity limit. The total shares held directly and indirectly by the investor and its affiliates under authority of this paragraph (a)(15) and § 211.8(c)(3) of this part in organizations engaged in activities that are not permissible for joint ventures do not exceed:

(A) 25 percent of the bank holding company's tier 1 capital, where the investor is a bank holding company;

(B) 20 percent of the investor's tier 1 capital, where the investor is a member bank;[13] and

(C) The lesser of 20 percent of any parent insured bank's tier 1 capital or 100 percent of the investor's tier 1 capital, for any other investor;

(iv) Determining compliance with limits--(A) General. For purposes of determining compliance with all limits set out in this paragraph (a)(15):

(1) Long and short positions in the same security may be netted; and

(2) Except as provided in paragraph (a)(15)(iv)(B)(4) of this section, equity securities held in order to hedge bank permissible equity derivatives contracts shall not be included.

(B) Use of internal hedging models. After providing 30 days' prior written notice to the Board the investor may use an internal hedging model that:

(1) Nets long and short positions in the same security and offsets positions in a security by futures, forwards, options, and other similar instruments referenced to the same security, for purposes of determining compliance with the single issuer limits of paragraph (a)(15)(ii) of this section;[14] and

(2) Offsets its long positions in equity securities by futures, forwards, options, and similar instruments, on a portfolio basis, and for purposes of determining compliance with the aggregate equity limits of paragraph (a)(15)(iii) of this section.

(3) With respect to all equity securities held under authority of paragraph (a)(15) of this section, no net long position in a security shall be deemed to have been reduced by more than 75 percent through use of internal hedging models under this paragraph (a)(15)(iv)(B); and

(4) With respect to equity securities acquired to hedge bank permissible equity derivatives contracts under authority of paragraph (a)(1) of this section, any residual position that remains in the securities of a single issuer after netting and offsetting of positions relating to the security under the investor's internal hedging models shall be included in calculating compliance with the limits of this paragraph (a)(15)(ii) and (iii).

(C) Underwriting commitments. Any shares acquired pursuant to an underwriting commitment that are held for longer than 90 days after the payment date for such underwriting shall be subject to the limits set out in paragraph (a)(15) of this section and the investment provisions of §§ 211.8 and 211.9 of this part.

(v) Authority to deal in shares of U.S. organization. The authority to deal in shares under paragraph (a)(15) of this section includes the authority to deal in the shares of a U.S. organization:

(A) With respect to foreign persons only; and

(B) Subject to the limitations on owning or controlling shares of a company in section 4(c)(6) of the BHC Act (12 U.S.C. 1843(c)(6)) and Regulation Y (12 CFR part 225).

(vi) Report to senior management. Any shares held in trading or dealing accounts for longer than 90 days shall be reported to the senior management of the investor;

(16) Operating a travel agency, but only in connection with financial services offered abroad by the investor or others;

(17) Underwriting life, annuity, pension fund-related, and other types of insurance, where the associated risks have been previously determined by the Board to be actuarially predictable; provided that:

(i) Investments in, and loans and extensions of credit (other than loans and

---

13. For this purpose, a direct subsidiary of a member bank is deemed to be an investor.

14. A basket of stocks, specifically segregated as an offset to a position in a stock index derivative product, as computed by the investor's internal model, may be offset against the stock index.

extensions of credit fully secured in accordance with the requirements of section 23A of the FRA (12 U.S.C. 371c), or with such other standards as the Board may require) to, the company by the investor or its affiliates are deducted from the capital of the investor (with 50 percent of such capital deduction to be taken from tier 1 capital); and

(ii) Activities conducted directly or indirectly by a subsidiary of a U.S. insured bank are excluded from the authority of this paragraph (a)(17), unless authorized by the Board;

(18) Providing futures commission merchant services (including clearing without executing and executing without clearing) for nonaffiliated persons with respect to futures and options on futures contracts for financial and nonfinancial commodities; provided that prior notice under § 211.9(f) of this part shall be provided to the Board before any subsidiaries of a member bank operating pursuant to this subpart may join a mutual exchange or clearinghouse, unless the potential liability of the investor to the exchange, clearinghouse, or other members of the exchange, as the case may be, is legally limited by the rules of the exchange or clearinghouse to an amount that does not exceed applicable general consent limits under § 211.9 of this part;

(19) Acting as principal or agent in commodity-swap transactions in relation to:

(i) Swaps on a cash-settled basis for any commodity, provided that the investor's portfolio of swaps contracts is hedged in a manner consistent with safe and sound banking practices; and

(ii) Contracts that require physical delivery of a commodity, provided that:

(A) Such contracts are entered into solely for the purpose of hedging the investor's positions in the underlying commodity or derivative contracts based on the commodity;

(B) The contract allows for assignment, termination or offset prior to expiration; and

(C) Reasonable efforts are made to avoid delivery.

(b) Regulation Y activities. An investor may engage in activities that the Board has determined in § 225.28(b) of Regulation Y (12 CFR 225.28(b)) are closely related to banking under section 4(c)(8) of the BHC Act (12 U.S.C. 1843(c)(8)).

(c) Specific approval. With the Board's specific approval, an investor may engage in other activities that the Board determines are usual in connection with the transaction of the business of banking or other financial operations abroad and are consistent with the FRA or the BHC Act. . . .

§ 211.12   Lending limits and capital requirements.

(a) Acceptances of Edge corporations. (1) Limitations. An Edge corporation shall be and remain fully secured for acceptances of the types described in section 13(7) of the FRA (12 U.S.C. 372), as follows

(i) All acceptances outstanding in excess of 200 percent of its tier 1 capital; and

(ii) All acceptances outstanding for any one person in excess of 10 percent of its tier 1 capital.

(2) Exceptions. These limitations do not apply if the excess represents the international shipment of goods, and the Edge corporation is:

(i) Fully covered by primary obligations to reimburse it that are guaranteed by banks or bankers; or

(ii) Covered by participation agreements from other banks, as described in 12 CFR 250.165.

(b) Loans and extensions of credit to one person--(1) Loans and extensions of credit defined. Loans and extensions of credit has the meaning set forth in § 211.2(q) of this part[15] and, for purposes of this paragraph (b), also include:

(i) Acceptances outstanding that are not of the types described in section 13(7) of the FRA (12 U.S.C. 372);

(ii) Any liability of the lender to advance funds to or on behalf of a person pursuant to a guarantee, standby letter of credit, or similar agreements;

(iii) Investments in the securities of another organization other than a subsidiary; and

(iv) Any underwriting commitments to an issuer of securities, where no binding commitments have been secured from subunderwriters or other purchasers.

(2) Limitations. Except as the Board may otherwise specify:

(i) The total loans and extensions of credit outstanding to any person by an Edge corporation engaged in banking, and its direct or indirect subsidiaries, may not exceed 15 percent of the Edge corporation's tier 1 capital;[16] and

(ii) The total loans and extensions of credit to any person by a foreign bank or Edge corporation subsidiary of a member bank, and by majority-owned subsidiaries of a foreign bank or Edge corporation, when combined with the total loans and extensions of credit to the same person by the member bank and its majority-owned subsidiaries, may not exceed the member bank's limitation on loans and extensions of credit to one person.

(3) Exceptions. The limitations of paragraph (b)(2) of this section do not apply to:

(i) Deposits with banks and federal funds sold;

(ii) Bills or drafts drawn in good faith against actual goods and on which two or more unrelated parties are liable;

(iii) Any banker's acceptance, of the kind described in section 13(7) of the FRA (12 U.S.C. 372), that is issued and outstanding;

(iv) Obligations to the extent secured by cash collateral or by bonds, notes, certificates of indebtedness, or Treasury bills of the United States;

(v) Loans and extensions of credit that are covered by bona fide participation agreements; and

(vi) Obligations to the extent supported by the full faith and credit of the following:

(A) The United States or any of its departments, agencies, establishments, or wholly owned corporations (including obligations, to the extent insured against foreign political and credit risks by the Export-Import Bank of the United States or the Foreign Credit Insurance Association), the International Bank for Reconstruction and Development, the International Finance Corporation, the International Development Association, the Inter-American Development Bank, the African Development Bank, the Asian Development Bank, or the European Bank for Reconstruction and Development;

(B) Any organization, if at least 25 percent of such an obligation or of the total credit is also supported by the full faith and credit of, or participated in by, any institution designated in paragraph (b)(3)(vi)(A) of this section in such manner that default to the lender

---

15. In the case of a foreign government, these includes loans and extensions of credit to the foreign government's departments or agencies deriving their current funds principally from general tax revenues. In the case of a partnership or firm, these include loans and extensions of credit to its members and, in the case of a corporation, these include loans and extensions of credit to the corporation's affiliates, where the affiliate incurs the liability for the benefit of the corporation.

16. For purposes of this pargraph (b), subsidiaries includes subsidiaries controlled by the Edge corporation, but does not include companies otherwise controlled by affiliates to the Edge corporation.

would necessarily include default to that entity. The total loans and extensions of credit under this paragraph (b)(3)(vi)(B) to any person shall at no time exceed 100 percent of the tier 1 capital of the Edge corporation.

(c) Capitalization. (1) An Edge corporation shall at all times be capitalized in an amount that is adequate in relation to the scope and character of its activities.

(2) In the case of an Edge corporation engaged in banking, the minimum ratio of qualifying total capital to risk-weighted assets, as determined under the Capital Adequacy Guidelines, shall not be less than 10 percent, of which at least 50 percent shall consist of tier 1 capital.

(3) For purposes of this paragraph (c), no limitation shall apply on the inclusion of subordinated debt that qualifies as tier 2 capital under the Capital Adequacy Guidelines.

§ 211.13   Supervision and reporting.

(a) Supervision. (1) Foreign branches and subsidiaries. U.S. banking organizations conducting international operations under this subpart shall supervise and administer their foreign branches and subsidiaries in such a manner as to ensure that their operations conform to high standards of banking and financial prudence.

(i) Effective systems of records, controls, and reports shall be maintained to keep management informed of their activities and condition.

(ii) Such systems shall provide, in particular, information on risk assets, exposure to market risk, liquidity management, operations, internal controls, legal and operational risk, and conformance to management policies.

(iii) Reports on risk assets shall be sufficient to permit an appraisal of credit quality and assessment of exposure to loss, and, for this purpose, provide full information on the condition of material borrowers.

(iv) Reports on operations and controls shall include internal and external audits of the branch or subsidiary.

(2) Joint ventures. Investors shall maintain sufficient information with respect to joint ventures to keep informed of their activities and condition.

(i) Such information shall include audits and other reports on financial performance, risk exposure, management policies, operations, and controls.

(ii) Complete information shall be maintained on all transactions with the joint venture by the investor and its affiliates.

(3) Availability of reports and information to examiners. The reports specified in paragraphs (a)(1) and (2) of this section and any other information deemed necessary to determine compliance with U.S. banking law shall be made available to examiners of the appropriate bank supervisory agencies.

(b) Examinations. Examiners appointed by the Board shall examine each Edge corporation once a year. An Edge or agreement corporation shall make available to examiners information sufficient to assess its condition and operations and the condition and activities of any organization whose shares it holds.

(c) Reports--(1) Reports of condition. Each Edge or agreement corporation shall make reports of condition to the Board at such times and in such form as the Board may prescribe. The Board may require that statements of condition or other reports be published or made available for public inspection.

(2) Foreign operations. Edge and agreement corporations, member banks, and bank holding companies shall file such reports on their foreign operations as the Board may require.

(3) Acquisition or disposition of shares. Member banks, Edge and agreement

corporations, and bank holding companies shall report, in a manner prescribed by the Board, any acquisition or disposition of shares.

(d) Filing and processing procedures--(1) Place of filing. Unless otherwise directed by the Board, applications, notices, and reports required by this part shall be filed with the Federal Reserve Bank of the District in which the parent bank or bank holding company is located or, if none, the Reserve Bank of the District in which the applying or reporting institution is located. Instructions and forms for applications, notices, and reports are available from the Reserve Banks.

(2) Timing. The Board shall act on an application under this subpart within 60 calendar days after the Reserve Bank has received the application, unless the Board notifies the investor that the 60-day period is being extended and states the reasons for the extension.

# Chapter 6

# Entry by Foreign Banks into U.S. Markets

## 1. Introduction

The range of options available to foreign banks in deciding on a method of entry into the U.S. banking market is essentially the same as that available to U.S. banks seeking entry into foreign markets. *See* Chapter 4, *supra*, Note 4.2. In fact, at least since the passage of the International Banking Act of 1978,[1] the range of options may even be viewed as somewhat broader, since the dual banking system within the United States makes available many duplicate (federal/state) alternatives. Particularly since the 1970s, foreign banks have increasingly taken advantage of these options. In part, efficient access to U.S. dollar markets may explain some of this growth in interest.

**Notes and Comments 6.1.** *The U.S. Regulatory Environment and Entry.* While the United States is a relatively open market for international banking, it does have its own constraints that confront the non-U.S. banking enterprise seeking entry into the U.S. market.[2] None of these constraints is unique to the U.S. market. One is, however, certainly different in degree. The pervasiveness and complexity of the regulatory environment raises special difficulty for non-U.S. banking enterprises that operate from a home state with a relatively streamlined and/or passive regulatory system. In this regard, compare the material in Chapter 2, § 1, *supra* (concerning U.S. regulatory structure) with the material in Chapter 2, § 3, *supra* (concerning regulatory stuctures in other states). The U.S. regulatory structure is complex horizontally and vertically (*i.e.*, multiple regulators at federal and state levels) and pervasive (*i.e.*, relying on detailed regulation of entry, operations, and internal governance).

**6.2.** Reread the material in Note 4.2, *supra*. Keep in mind that for many of the options identified there (*i.e.*, agencies, branches, affiliates, subsidiaries) there are both federal and state alternatives for the creation or exercise of the option. In any event, even for state options, federal approval may nevertheless be required (*e.g.*, representative offices, state-licensed agencies and branches, Agreement Corporations). Gemütlichbank of Stuttgart, Federal Republic of Germany, wishes to enter the U.S. banking market. It is interested in

---

1. 12 U.S.C. §§ 3101 *et seq.*

2. *See generally* Clark H. Hutton III, *Legal Constraints within the United States, in* WILLIAM H. BAUGHN & DONALD R. MANDICH, THE INTERNATIONAL BANKING HANDBOOK 723 (1983) (discussing U.S. legal constraints).

locating its U.S. headquarters in New York City, and in establishing a string of subsidiary "Happy Banks" or Happy Bank branches across the United States. What are its options, and what would be the advantages and disadvantages of each? In answering these questions, in addition to Note 4.2 you may wish to consult 12 U.S.C. §§ 3102, 3103(a), 3104(c), 3105, 3107. The following regulatory provisions may also be pertinent, particularly 12 C.F.R. §§ 28.12(a)-(d), (g), (i), 211.24(a)-(e).

## Comptroller of the Currency
### 12 C.F.R. pt. 28

§ 28.12  Approval of a Federal branch or agency.

(a) Approval and licensing requirements--(1) General. Except as otherwise provided in this section, a foreign bank shall submit an application to, and obtain prior approval from, the OCC before it:

(i) Establishes a Federal branch or agency; or

(ii) Exercises fiduciary powers at a Federal branch.

(2) Licensing. A foreign bank must receive a license from the OCC to open and operate its initial Federal branch or agency in the United States.  A foreign bank that has a license to operate and is operating a full-service Federal branch need not obtain a new license for any additional Federal branches or agencies, or to upgrade or downgrade its operations in an existing Federal branch or agency.  A foreign bank that only has a license to operate and is operating a limited Federal branch or Federal agency need not obtain a new license for any additional limited Federal branches or Federal agencies, or to convert a limited Federal branch into a Federal agency or a Federal agency into a limited Federal branch.

(b) Standards for approval.  Generally, in reviewing an application by a foreign bank to establish a Federal branch or agency, the OCC considers:

(1) The financial and managerial resources and future prospects of the applicant foreign bank and the Federal branch or agency;

(2) Whether the foreign bank has furnished to the OCC the information the OCC requires to assess the application adequately, and provided the OCC with adequate assurances that information will be made available to the OCC on the operations or activities of the foreign bank or any of its affiliates that the OCC deems necessary to determine and enforce compliance with the IBA and other applicable Federal banking statutes;

(3) Whether the foreign bank and its United States affiliates are in compliance with applicable United States law;

(4) The convenience and needs of the community to be served and the effects of the proposal on competition in the domestic and foreign commerce of the United States;

(5) With respect to an application to establish a Federal branch or agency outside of the foreign bank's home state, whether the foreign bank is subject to comprehensive supervision or regulation on a consolidated basis by its home country supervisor. The OCC, in its discretion, also may consider whether the foreign bank is subject to comprehensive supervision or regulation on a consolidated basis by its home country supervisor when reviewing any other type of application to establish a Federal branch or agency; and

(6) Whether the home country supervisor has consented to the proposed establishment of the Federal branch or agency.

(c) Comprehensive supervision or regulation on a consolidated basis.  In determining whether a foreign bank is subject to comprehensive supervision or regulation on a consolidated basis, the OCC reviews various factors, including whether the foreign bank is supervised or regulated in a manner so that its home country supervisor receives sufficient information on the worldwide operations of the foreign bank to assess the foreign bank's overall financial condition and compliance with laws and regulations as specified in the FRB's Regulation K, 12 CFR 211.24.

(d) Conditions on approval. The OCC may impose conditions on its approval including a condition permitting future termination of activities based on the inability of the foreign bank to provide information on its activities, or those of its affiliate, that the OCC deems necessary to determine and enforce compliance with United States banking laws.

(e) Expedited review. Unless the OCC concludes that the filing presents significant supervisory or compliance concerns, or raises significant legal or policy issues, the OCC generally processes the following filings by an eligible foreign bank, as defined in paragraph (f) of this section, under expedited review procedures:

(1) Intrastate relocations. An application submitted by an eligible foreign bank to relocate a Federal branch or agency within a state is deemed approved by the OCC as of the seventh day after the close of the applicable public comment period in 12 CFR part 5, unless the OCC notifies the bank prior to that date that the filing is not eligible for expedited review.

(2) Written notice for an additional intrastate Federal branch or agency. (i) In a case where a foreign bank seeks to establish intrastate an additional Federal branch or agency, the foreign bank shall provide written notice 30 days in advance of the establishment of the intrastate Federal branch or agency.

(ii) The OCC may waive the 30-day period required under paragraph (e)(2)(i) of this section if immediate action is required. The OCC also may suspend the notice period or require an application if the notification raises significant policy or supervisory concerns.

(3) Expedited approval procedures for an interstate Federal branch or agency. An application submitted by an eligible foreign bank to establish and operate a de novo Federal branch or agency in any state outside the home state of the foreign bank is deemed conditionally approved by the OCC as of the 30th day after the OCC receives the filing, unless the OCC notifies the foreign bank prior to that date that the filing is not eligible for expedited review. In the event that the FRB has approved the application prior to the expiration of the period, then the OCC's approval shall be deemed a final approval.

(4) Conversions. An application submitted by an eligible foreign bank to establish a Federal branch or agency as defined in 12 CFR 28.11(f)(4) or (f)(6) is deemed approved by the OCC as of the 30th day after the OCC receives the filing, unless the OCC notifies the foreign bank prior to that date that the filing is not eligible for expedited review.

(5) Fiduciary powers. An application submitted by an eligible foreign bank to exercise fiduciary powers at an established Federal branch is deemed approved by the OCC 30 days after filing with the OCC, unless the OCC notifies the bank prior to that date that the filing is not eligible for expedited review.

(6) Other filings. Any other application submitted by an eligible foreign bank may be approved by the OCC on an expedited basis as described in the Manual.

(f) Eligible foreign bank. For purposes of this section, a foreign bank is an eligible foreign bank if each Federal branch and agency of the foreign bank or, if the foreign bank has no Federal branches or agencies and is engaging in an establishment of a Federal branch or agency as defined in 12 CFR 28.11(f)(4), each state branch and agency:

(1) Has a composite rating of 1 or 2 under the interagency rating system for United States branches and agencies of foreign banks;

(2) Is not subject to a cease and desist order, consent order, formal written agreement, Prompt Corrective Action directive (see 12 CFR part 6) or, if subject to such

order, agreement, or directive, is informed in writing by the OCC that the Federal branch or agency may be treated as an "eligible foreign bank" for purposes of this section; and

(3) Has, if applicable, a Community Reinvestment Act (CRA), 12 U.S.C. 2906, rating of "Outstanding" or "Satisfactory".

(g) After-the-fact approval. Unless otherwise provided by the OCC, a foreign bank proposing to establish a Federal branch or agency through the acquisition of, or merger or consolidation with, a foreign bank that has an office in the United States, may proceed with the transaction before an application to establish the Federal branch or agency has been filed or acted upon, if the applicant:

(1) Gives the OCC reasonable advance notice of the proposed acquisition, merger, or consolidation;

(2) Prior to consummation of the acquisition, merger, or consolidation, commits in writing to comply with the OCC application procedures within a reasonable period of time, or has already submitted an application; and

(3) Commits in writing to abide by the OCC's decision on the application, including a decision to terminate activities of the Federal branch or agency. . . .

(h) After-the-fact notice for an eligible foreign bank. Unless otherwise provided by the OCC, a foreign bank proposing to establish a Federal branch or agency through the acquisition of, or merger or consolidation with, a foreign bank that has an existing U.S. bank subsidiary or a Federal or state branch or agency may proceed with the transaction and provide after-the-fact notice to the OCC within 14 days of the transaction, if:

(1) The resulting bank is an "eligible foreign bank" under paragraph (f) of this section; and

(2) No Federal branch established by the transaction accepts deposits that are insured by the FDIC pursuant to the Federal Deposit Insurance Act (12 U.S.C. 1811 et seq.).

(i) Contraction of operations. A foreign bank shall provide written notice to the OCC within 10 days after converting a Federal branch into a limited Federal branch or Federal agency.

(j) Procedures for approval. A foreign bank shall file an application for approval pursuant to this section in accordance with 12 CFR part 5 and the Manual. The OCC reserves the right to adopt materially different procedures for a particular filing, or class of filings. . . .

(k) Other applications accepted. . . . [T]he OCC may accept an application or other filing submitted to another U.S. Government agency that covers the proposed activity or transaction and contains substantially the same information as required by the OCC.

## Board of Governors of the Federal Reserve System
### 12 C.F.R. pt. 211

Subpart B–Foreign Banking Organizations[3]

---

3. *As amended*, 66 Fed. Reg. 54,346 (2001), *corrected*, 66 Fed. Reg. 58,655 (2001).

standards for approval; representative office activities and standards for approval; preservation of existing authority.

211.25   Termination of offices of foreign banks.
211.26   Examination of offices and affiliates of foreign banks.
211.27   Disclosure of supervisory information to foreign supervisors.
211.28   Provisions applicable to branches and agencies: limitation on loans to one borrower.
211.29   Applications by state branches and state agencies to conduct activities not permissible for federal branches.
211.30   Criteria for evaluating U.S. operations of foreign banks not subject to consolidated supervision.

§ 211.20   Authority, purpose, and scope.

(a) Authority. This subpart is issued by the Board of Governors of the Federal Reserve System (Board) under the authority of the Bank Holding Company Act of 1956 (BHC Act) (12 U.S.C. 1841 et seq.) and the International Banking Act of 1978 (IBA) (12 U.S.C. 3101 et seq.).

(b) Purpose and scope. This subpart is in furtherance of the purposes of the BHC Act and the IBA. It applies to foreign banks and foreign banking organizations with respect to:

(1) The limitations on interstate banking under section 5 of the IBA (12 U.S.C. 3103);

(2) The exemptions from the nonbanking prohibitions of the BHC Act and the IBA afforded by sections 2(h) and 4(c)(9) of the BHC Act (12 U.S.C. 1841(h), 1843(c)(9));

(3) Board approval of the establishment of an office of a foreign bank in the United States under sections 7(d) and 10(a) of the IBA (12 U.S.C. 3105(d), 3107(a));

(4) The termination by the Board of a foreign bank's representative office, state branch, state agency, or commercial lending company subsidiary under sections 7(e) and 10(b) of the IBA (12 U.S.C. 3105(e), 3107(b)), and the transmission of a recommendation to the Comptroller to terminate a federal branch or federal agency under section 7(e)(5) of the IBA (12 U.S.C. 3105(e)(5));

(5) The examination of an office or affiliate of a foreign bank in the United States as provided in sections 7(c) and 10(c) of the IBA (12 U.S.C. 3105(c), 3107(c));

(6) The disclosure of supervisory information to a foreign supervisor under section 15 of the IBA (12 U.S.C. 3109);

(7) The limitations on loans to one borrower by state branches and state agencies of a foreign bank under section 7(h)(2) of the IBA (12 U.S.C. 3105(h)(2));

(8) The limitation of a state branch and a state agency to conducting only activities that are permissible for a federal branch under section (7)(h)(1) of the IBA (12 U.S.C. 3105(h)(1)); and

(9) The deposit insurance requirement for retail deposit taking by a foreign bank under section 6 of the IBA (12 U.S.C. 3104).

(10) The management of shell branches (12 U.S.C. 3105(k)).

(c) Additional requirements. Compliance by a foreign bank with the requirements of this subpart and the laws administered and enforced by the Board does not relieve the foreign bank of responsibility to comply with the laws and regulations administered by the licensing authority.

§ 211.21   Definitions.

The definitions contained in §§ 211.1 and 211.2[a] apply to this subpart, except as a term is otherwise defined in this section:

(a) Affiliate of a foreign bank or of a parent of a foreign bank means any company that controls, is controlled by, or is under common control with, the foreign bank or the parent of the foreign bank.

(b) Agency means any place of business of a foreign bank, located in any state, at which credit balances are maintained, checks are paid, money is lent, or, to the extent not prohibited by state or federal law, deposits are accepted from a person or entity that is not a citizen or resident of the United States. Obligations shall not be considered credit balances unless they are:

(1) Incidental to, or arise out of the exercise of, other lawful banking powers;

(2) To serve a specific purpose;

(3) Not solicited from the general public;

(4) Not used to pay routine operating expenses in the United States such as salaries, rent, or taxes;

(5) Withdrawn within a reasonable period of time after the specific purpose for which they were placed has been accomplished; and

(6) Drawn upon in a manner reasonable in relation to the size and nature of the account.

(c)(1) Appropriate Federal Reserve Bank means, unless the Board designates a different Federal Reserve Bank:

(i) For a foreign banking organization, the Reserve Bank assigned to the foreign banking organization in § 225.3(b)(2) of Regulation Y (12 CFR 225.3(b)(2));

(ii) For a foreign bank that is not a foreign banking organization and proposes to establish an office, an Edge corporation, or an agreement corporation, the Reserve Bank of the Federal Reserve District in which the foreign bank proposes to establish such office or corporation; and

(iii) In all other cases, the Reserve Bank designated by the Board.

(2) The appropriate Federal Reserve Bank need not be the Reserve Bank of the Federal Reserve District in which the foreign bank's home state is located.

(d) Banking subsidiary, with respect to a specified foreign bank, means a bank that is a subsidiary as the terms bank and subsidiary are defined in section 2 of the BHC Act (12 U.S.C. 1841).

(e) Branch means any place of business of a foreign bank, located in any state, at which deposits are received, and that is not an agency, as that term is defined in paragraph (b) of this section.

(f) Change the status of an office means to convert a representative office into a branch or agency, or an agency or limited branch into a branch, but does not include renewal of the license of an existing office.

(g) Commercial lending company means any organization, other than a bank or an organization operating under section 25 of the Federal Reserve Act (FRA) (12 U.S.C. 601-604a), organized under the laws of any state, that maintains credit balances permissible for an agency, and engages in the business of making commercial loans. Commercial lending company includes any company chartered under article XII of the banking law of the State of New York.

(h) Comptroller means the Office of the Comptroller of the Currency.

(i) Control has the same meaning as in section 2(a) of the BHC Act (12 U.S.C.

---

a. For the text of these provisions, see Chapter 5, § 2, *supra*.

1841(a)), and the terms controlled and controlling shall be construed consistently with the term control.

(j) Domestic branch means any place of business of a foreign bank, located in any state, that may accept domestic deposits and deposits that are incidental to or for the purpose of carrying out transactions in foreign countries.

(k) A foreign bank engages directly in the business of banking outside the United States if the foreign bank engages directly in banking activities usual in connection with the business of banking in the countries where it is organized or operating.

(l) To establish means:

(1) To open and conduct business through an office;

(2) To acquire directly, through merger, consolidation, or similar transaction with another foreign bank, the operations of an office that is open and conducting business;

(3) To acquire an office through the acquisition of a foreign bank subsidiary that will cease to operate in the same corporate form following the acquisition;

(4) To change the status of an office; or

(5) To relocate an office from one state to another.

(m) Federal agency, federal branch, state agency, and state branch have the same meanings as in section 1 of the IBA (12 U.S.C. 3101).

(n) Foreign bank means an organization that is organized under the laws of a foreign country and that engages directly in the business of banking outside the United States. The term foreign bank does not include a central bank of a foreign country that does not engage or seek to engage in a commercial banking business in the United States through an office.

(o) Foreign banking organization means:

(1) A foreign bank, as defined in section 1(b)(7) of the IBA (12 U.S.C. 3101(7)), that:

(i) Operates a branch, agency, or commercial lending company subsidiary in the United States;

(ii) Controls a bank in the United States; or

(iii) Controls an Edge corporation acquired after March 5, 1987; and

(2) Any company of which the foreign bank is a subsidiary.

(p) Home country, with respect to a foreign bank, means the country in which the foreign bank is chartered or incorporated.

(q) Home country supervisor, with respect to a foreign bank, means the governmental entity or entities in the foreign bank's home country with responsibility for the supervision and regulation of the foreign bank.

(r) Licensing authority means:

(1) The relevant state supervisor, with respect to an application to establish a state branch, state agency, commercial lending company, or representative office of a foreign bank; or

(2) The Comptroller, with respect to an application to establish a federal branch or federal agency.

(s) Limited branch means a branch of a foreign bank that receives only such deposits as would be permitted for a corporation organized under section 25A of the Federal Reserve Act (12 U.S.C. 611-631).

(t) Office or office of a foreign bank means any branch, agency, representative office, or commercial lending company subsidiary of a foreign bank in the United States.

(u) A parent of a foreign bank means a company of which the foreign bank is a subsidiary. An immediate parent of a foreign bank is a company of which the foreign bank is a direct subsidiary. An ultimate parent of a foreign bank is a parent of the foreign bank that is not the subsidiary of any other company.

(v) Regional administrative office means a representative office that

(1) Is established by a foreign bank that operates two or more branches, agencies, commercial lending companies, or banks in the United States;

(2) Is located in the same city as one or more of the foreign bank's branches, agencies, commercial lending companies, or banks in the United States;

(3) Manages, supervises, or coordinates the operations of the foreign bank or its affiliates, if any, in a particular geographic area that includes the United States or a region thereof, including by exercising credit approval authority in that area pursuant to written standards, credit policies, and procedures established by the foreign bank; and

(4) Does not solicit business from actual or potential customers of the foreign bank or its affiliates.

(w) Relevant state supervisor means the state entity that is authorized to supervise and regulate a state branch, state agency, commercial lending company, or representative office.

(x) Representative office means any office of a foreign bank which is located in any state and is not a Federal branch, Federal agency, State branch, State agency, or commercial lending company subsidiary.

(y) State means any state of the United States or the District of Columbia.

(z) Subsidiary means any organization that:

(1) Has 25 percent or more of its voting shares directly or indirectly owned, controlled, or held with the power to vote by a company, including a foreign bank or foreign banking organization; or

(2) Is otherwise controlled, or capable of being controlled, by a foreign bank or foreign banking organization.

§ 211.22   Interstate banking operations of foreign banking organizations.

(a) Determination of home state. (1) A foreign bank that, as of December 10, 1997, had declared a home state or had a home state determined pursuant to the law and regulations in effect prior to that date shall have that state as its home state.

(2) A foreign bank that has any branches, agencies, commercial lending company subsidiaries, or subsidiary banks in one state, and has no such offices or subsidiaries in any other states, shall have as its home state the state in which such offices or subsidiaries are located.

(b) Change of home state--(1) Prior notice. A foreign bank may change its home state once, if it files 30 days' prior notice of the proposed change with the Board.

(2) Application to change home state. (i) A foreign bank, in addition to changing its home state by filing prior notice under paragraph (b)(1) of this section, may apply to the Board to change its home state, upon showing that a national bank or state-chartered bank with the same home state as the foreign bank would be permitted to change its home state to the new home state proposed by the foreign bank.

(ii) A foreign bank may apply to the Board for such permission one or more times.

(iii) In determining whether to grant the request of a foreign bank to change its home state, the Board shall consider whether the proposed change is consistent with competitive equity between foreign and domestic banks.

(3) Effect of change in home state. The home state of a foreign bank and any change in its home state by a foreign bank shall not affect which Federal Reserve Bank or Reserve Banks supervise the operations of the foreign bank, and shall not affect the

obligation of the foreign bank to file required reports and applications with the appropriate Federal Reserve Bank.

(4) Conforming branches to new home state. Upon any change in home state by a foreign bank under paragraph (b)(1) or (b)(2) of this section, the domestic branches of the foreign bank established in reliance on any previous home state of the foreign bank shall be conformed to those which a foreign bank with the new home state could permissibly establish or operate as of the date of such change.

(c) Prohibition against interstate deposit production offices. A covered interstate branch of a foreign bank may not be used as a deposit production office in accordance with the provisions in § 208.7 of Regulation H (12 CFR 208.7).

### § 211.23   Nonbanking activities of foreign banking organizations.

(a) Qualifying foreign banking organizations. Unless specifically made eligible for the exemptions by the Board, a foreign banking organization shall qualify for the exemptions afforded by this section only if, disregarding its United States banking, more than half of its worldwide business is banking; and more than half of its banking business is outside the United States.[10]  In order to qualify, a foreign banking organization shall:

(1) Meet at least two of the following requirements:

(i) Banking assets held outside the United States exceed total worldwide nonbanking assets;

(ii) Revenues derived from the business of banking outside the United States exceed total revenues derived from its worldwide nonbanking business; or

(iii) Net income derived from the business of banking outside the United States exceeds total net income derived from its worldwide nonbanking business; and

(2) Meet at least two of the following requirements:

(i) Banking assets held outside the United States exceed banking assets held in the United States;

(ii) Revenues derived from the business of banking outside the United States exceed revenues derived from the business of banking in the United States; or

(iii) Net income derived from the business of banking outside the United States exceeds net income derived from the business of banking in the United States.

(b) Determining assets, revenues, and net income. (1)(i) For purposes of paragraph (a) of this section, the total assets, revenues, and net income of an organization may be determined on a consolidated or combined basis.

(ii) The foreign banking organization shall include assets, revenues, and net income of companies in which it owns 50 percent or more of the voting shares when determining total assets, revenues, and net income.

(iii) The foreign banking organization may include assets, revenues, and net income of companies in which it owns 25 percent or more of the voting shares, if all such companies within the organization are included.

(2) Assets devoted to, or revenues or net income derived from, activities listed in § 211.10(a) shall be considered banking assets, or revenues or net income derived from the banking business, when conducted within the foreign banking organization by a foreign

---

10. None of the assets, revenues, or net income, whether held or derived directly or indirectly, of a subsidiary bank, branch, agency, commercial lending company, or other company engaged in the business of banking in the United States (including any territory of the United States, Puerto Rico, Guam, American Samoa, or the Virgin Islands) shall be considered held or derived from the business of banking "outside the United States".

bank or its subsidiaries.

(c) Limited exemptions available to foreign banking organizations in certain circumstances. The following shall apply where a foreign bank meets the requirements of paragraph (a) of this section but its ultimate parent does not:

(1) Such foreign bank shall be entitled to the exemptions available to a qualifying foreign banking organization if its ultimate parent meets the requirements set forth in paragraph (a)(2) of this section and could meet the requirements in paragraph (a)(1) of this section but for the requirement in paragraph (b)(2) of this section that activities must be conducted by the foreign bank or its subsidiaries in order to be considered derived from the banking business;

(2) An ultimate parent as described in paragraph (c)(1) of this section shall be eligible for the exemptions available to a qualifying foreign banking organization except for those provided in § 211.23(f)(5)(iii).

(d) Loss of eligibility for exemptions--(1) Failure to meet qualifying test. A foreign banking organization that qualified under paragraph (a) or (c) of this section shall cease to be eligible for the exemptions of this section if it fails to meet the requirements of paragraphs (a) or (c) of this section for two consecutive years, as reflected in its annual reports (FR Y-7) filed with the Board.

(2) Continuing activities and investments. (i) A foreign banking organization that ceases to be eligible for the exemptions of this section may continue to engage in activities or retain investments commenced or acquired prior to the end of the first fiscal year for which its annual report reflects nonconformance with paragraph (a) or (c) of this section.

(ii) Termination or divestiture. Activities commenced or investments made after that date shall be terminated or divested within three months of the filing of the second annual report, or at such time as the Board may determine upon request by the foreign banking organization to extend the period, unless the Board grants consent to continue the activity or retain the investment under paragraph (e) of this section.

(3) Request for specific determination of eligibility. (i) A foreign banking organization that ceases to qualify under paragraph (a) or (c) of this section, or an affiliate of such foreign banking organization, that requests a specific determination of eligibility under paragraph (e) of this section may, prior to the Board's determination on eligibility, continue to engage in activities and make investments under the provisions of paragraphs (f)(1), (2), (3), and (4) of this section.

(ii) The Board may grant consent for the foreign banking organization or its affiliate to make investments under paragraph (f)(5) of this section.

(e) Specific determination of eligibility for organizations that do not qualify for the exemptions--(1) Application. (i) A foreign organization that is not a foreign banking organization or a foreign banking organization that does not qualify under paragraph (a) or (c) of this section for some or all of the exemptions afforded by this section, or that has lost its eligibility for the exemptions under paragraph (d) of this section, may apply to the Board for a specific determination of eligibility for some or all of the exemptions.

(ii) A foreign banking organization may apply for a specific determination prior to the time it ceases to be eligible for the exemptions afforded by this section.

(2) Factors considered by Board. In determining whether eligibility for the exemptions would be consistent with the purposes of the BHC Act and in the public interest, the Board shall consider:

(i) The history and the financial and managerial resources of the foreign organization or foreign banking organization;

(ii) The amount of its business in the United States;

(iii) The amount, type, and location of its nonbanking activities, including whether such activities may be conducted by U.S. banks or bank holding companies;

(iv) Whether eligibility of the foreign organization or foreign banking organization would result in undue concentration of resources, decreased or unfair competition, conflicts of interests, or unsound banking practices; and

(v) The extent to which the foreign banking organization is subject to comprehensive supervision or regulation on a consolidated basis or the foreign organization is subject to oversight by regulatory authorities in its home country.

(3) Conditions and limitations. The Board may impose any conditions and limitations on a determination of eligibility, including requirements to cease activities or dispose of investments.

(4) Eligibility not granted. Determinations of eligibility generally would not be granted where a majority of the business of the foreign organization or foreign banking organization derives from commercial or industrial activities.

(f) Permissible activities and investments. A foreign banking organization that qualifies under paragraph (a) of this section may:

(1) Engage in activities of any kind outside the United States;

(2) Engage directly in activities in the United States that are incidental to its activities outside the United States;

(3) Own or control votingshares of any company that is not engaged, directly or indirectly, in any activities in the United States, other than those that are incidental to the international or foreign business of such company;

(4) Own or control voting shares of any company in a fiduciary capacity under circumstances that would entitle such shareholding to an exemption under section 4(c)(4) of the BHC Act (12 U.S.C. 1843(c)(4)) if the shares were held or acquired by a bank;

(5) Own or control voting shares of a foreign company that is engaged directly or indirectly in business in the United States other than that which is incidental to its international or foreign business, subject to the following limitations:

(i) More than 50 percent of the foreign company's consolidated assets shall be located, and consolidated revenues derived from, outside the United States; provided that, if the foreign company fails to meet the requirements of this paragraph (f)(5)(i) for two consecutive years (as reflected in annual reports (FR Y-7) filed with the Board by the foreign banking organization), the foreign company shall be divested or its activities terminated within one year of the filing of the second consecutive annual report that reflects nonconformance with the requirements of this paragraph (f)(5)(i), unless the Board grants consent to retain the investment under paragraph (g) of this section;

(ii) The foreign company shall not directly underwrite, sell, or distribute, nor own or control more than 10 percent of the voting shares of a company that underwrites, sells, or distributes securities in the United States, except to the extent permitted bank holding companies;

(iii) If the foreign company is a subsidiary of the foreign banking organization, the foreign company must be, or must control, an operating company, and its direct or indirect activities in the United States shall be subject to the following limitations:

(A) The foreign company's activities in the United States shall be the same kind of activities, or related to the activities, engaged in directly or indirectly by the foreign company abroad, as measured by the "establishment" categories of the Standard Industrial Classification (SIC). An activity in the United States shall be considered related to an activity outside the United States if it consists of supply, distribution, or sales in furtherance of the activity;

(B) The foreign company may engage in activities in the United States that consist of banking, securities, insurance, or other financial operations, or types of activities permitted by regulation or order under section 4(c)(8) of the BHC Act (12 U.S.C. 1843(c)(8)), only under regulations of the Board or with the prior approval of the Board, subject to the following;

(1) Activities within Division H (Finance, Insurance, and Real Estate) of the SIC shall be considered banking or financial operations for this purpose, with the exception of acting as operators of nonresidential buildings (SIC 6512), operators of apartment buildings (SIC 6513), operators of dwellings other than apartment buildings (SIC 6514), and operators of residential mobile home sites (SIC 6515); and operating title abstract offices (SIC 6541); and

(2) The following activities shall be considered financial activities and may be engaged in only with the approval of the Board under paragraph (g) of this section: credit reporting services (SIC 7323); computer and data processing services (SIC 7371, 7372, 7373, 7374, 7375, 7376, 7377, 7378, and 7379); armored car services (SIC 7381); management consulting (SIC 8732, 8741, 8742, and 8748); certain rental and leasing activities (SIC 4741, 7352, 7353, 7359, 7513, 7514, 7515, and 7519); accounting, auditing, and bookkeeping services (SIC 8721); courier services (SIC 4215 and 4513); and arrangement of passenger transportation (SIC 4724, 4725, and 4729).

(g) Exemptions under section 4(c)(9) of the BHC Act. A foreign banking organization that is of the opinion that other activities or investments may, in particular circumstances, meet the conditions for an exemption under section 4(c)(9) of the BHC Act (12 U.S.C. 1843(c)(9)) may apply to the Board for such a determination by submitting to the appropriate Federal Reserve Bank a letter setting forth the basis for that opinion.

(h) Reports. The foreign banking organization shall report in a manner prescribed by the Board any direct activities in the United States by a foreign subsidiary of the foreign banking organization and the acquisition of all shares of companies engaged, directly or indirectly, in activities in the United States that were acquired under the authority of this section.

(i) Availability of information. If any information required under this section is unknown and not reasonably available to the foreign banking organization (either because obtaining it would involve unreasonable effort or expense, or because it rests exclusively within the knowledge of a company that is not controlled by the organization) the organization shall:

(1) Give such information on the subject as it possesses or can reasonably acquire, together with the sources thereof; and

(2) Include a statement showing that unreasonable effort or expense would be involved, or indicating that the company whose shares were acquired is not controlled by the organization, and stating the result of a request for information.

§ 211.24 Approval of offices of foreign banks; procedures for applications; standards for approval; representative office activities and standards for approval; preservation of existing authority.

(a) Board approval of offices of foreign banks--(1) Prior Board approval of branches, agencies, commercial lending companies, or representative offices of foreign banks. (i) Except as otherwise provided in paragraphs (a)(2) and (a)(3) of this section, a foreign bank shall obtain the approval of the Board before it:

(A) Establishes a branch, agency, commercial lending company subsidiary, or representative office in the United States; or

(B) Acquires ownership or control of a commercial lending company subsidiary.

(2) Prior notice for certain offices. (i) After providing 45 days' prior written notice to the Board, a foreign bank may establish:

(A) An additional office (other than a domestic branch outside the home state of the foreign bank established pursuant to section 5(a)(3) of the IBA (12 U.S.C. 3103(a)(3))), provided that the Board has previously determined the foreign bank to be subject to comprehensive supervision or regulation on a consolidated basis by its home country supervisor (comprehensive consolidated supervision or CCS); or

(B) A representative office, if:

(1) The Board has not yet determined the foreign bank to be subject to consolidated comprehensive supervision, but the foreign bank is subject to the BHC Act, either directly or through section 8(a) of the IBA (12 U.S.C. 3106(a)); or

(2) The Board previously has approved an application by the foreign bank to establish a branch or agency pursuant to the standard set forth in paragraph (c)(1)(iii) of this section; or

(3) The Board previously has approved an application by the foreign bank to establish a representative office.

(ii) The Board may waive the 45-day notice period if it finds that immediate action is required by the circumstances presented. The notice period shall commence at the time the notice is received by the appropriate Federal Reserve Bank. The Board may suspend the period or require Board approval prior to the establishment of such office if the notification raises significant policy or supervisory concerns.

(3) General consent for certain representative offices. (i) The Board grants its general consent for a foreign bank that is subject to the BHC Act, either directly or through section 8(a) of the IBA (12 U.S.C. 3106(a)), to establish:

(A) A representative office, but only if the Board has previously determined that the foreign bank proposing to establish a representative office is subject to consolidated comprehensive supervision;

(B) A regional administrative office; or

(C) An office that solely engages in limited administrative functions (such as separately maintaining back-office support systems) that:

(1) Are clearly defined;

(2) Are performed in connection with the U.S. banking activities of the foreign bank; and

(3) Do not involve contact or liaison with customers or potential customers, beyond incidental contact with existing customers relating to administrative matters (such as verification or correction of account information).

(4) Suspension of general consent or prior notice procedures. The Board may, at any time, upon notice, modify or suspend the prior notice and general consent procedures in paragraphs (a)(2) and (3) of this section for any foreign bank with respect to the establishment by such foreign bank of any U.S. office of such foreign bank.

(5) Temporary offices. The Board may, in its discretion, determine that a foreign bank has not established an office if the foreign bank temporarily operates at one or more additional locations in the same city of an existing branch or agency due to renovations, an expansion of activities, a merger or consolidation of the operations of affiliated foreign banks or companies, or other similar circumstances. The foreign bank must provide reasonable advance notice of its intent temporarily to utilize additional locations, and the Board may impose such conditions in connection with its determination as it deems necessary.

(6) After-the-fact Board approval. Where a foreign bank proposes to establish an office in the United States through the acquisition of, or merger or consolidation with, another foreign bank with an office in the United States, the Board may, in its discretion, allow the acquisition, merger, or consolidation to proceed before an application to establish the office has been filed or acted upon under this section if:

(i) The foreign bank or banks resulting from the acquisition, merger, or consolidation, will not directly or indirectly own or control more than 5 percent of any class of the voting securities of, or control, a U.S. bank;

(ii) The Board is given reasonable advance notice of the proposed acquisition, merger, or consolidation; and

(iii) Prior to consummation of the acquisition, merger, or consolidation, each foreign bank, as appropriate, commits in writing either:

(A) To comply with the procedures for an application under this section within a reasonable period of time; to engage in no new lines of business, or otherwise to expand its U.S. activities until the disposition of the application; and to abide by the Board's decision on the application, including, if necessary, a decision to terminate the activities of any such U.S. office, as the Board or the Comptroller may require; or

(B) Promptly to wind-down and close any office, the establishment of which would have required an application under this section; and to engage in no new lines of business or otherwise to expand its U.S. activities prior to the closure of such office.

(7) Notice of change in ownership or control or conversion of existing office or establishment of representative office under general-consent authority. A foreign bank with a U.S. office shall notify the Board in writing within 10 days of the occurrence of any of the following events:

(i) A change in the foreign bank's ownership or control, where the foreign bank is acquired or controlled by another foreign bank or company and the acquired foreign bank with a U.S. office continues to operate in the same corporate form as prior to the change in ownership or control;

(ii) The conversion of a branch to an agency or representative office; an agency to a representative office; or a branch or agency from a federal to a state license, or a state to a federal license; or

(iii) The establishment of a representative office under general-consent authority.

(8) Transactions subject to approval under Regulation Y. Subpart B of Regulation Y (12 CFR 225.11-225.17) governs the acquisition by a foreign banking organization of direct or indirect ownership or control of any voting securities of a bank or bank holding company in the United States if the acquisition results in the foreign banking organization's ownership or control of more than 5 percent of any class of voting securities of a U.S. bank or bank holding company, including through acquisition of a foreign bank or foreign banking organization that owns or controls more than 5 percent of any class of the voting securities of a U.S. bank or bank holding company.

(b) Procedures for application--(1) Filing application. An application for the Board's approval pursuant to this section shall be filed in the manner prescribed by the Board.

(2) Publication requirement--(i) Newspaper notice. Except with respect to a proposed transaction where more extensive notice is required by statute or as otherwise provided in paragraphs (b)(2)(ii) and (iii) of this section, an applicant under this section shall publish a notice in a newspaper of general circulation in the community in which the applicant proposes to engage in business.

(ii) Contents of notice. The newspaper notice shall:

(A) State that an application is being filed as of the date of the newspaper notice; and

(B) Provide the name of the applicant, the subject matter of the application, the place where comments should be sent, and the date by which comments are due, pursuant to paragraph (b)(3) of this section.

(iii) Copy of notice with application. The applicant shall furnish with its application to the Board a copy of the newspaper notice, the date of its publication, and the name and address of the newspaper in which it was published.

(iv) Exception. The Board may modify the publication requirement of paragraphs (b)(2)(i) and (ii) of this section in appropriate circumstances.

(v) Federal branch or federal agency. In the case of an application to establish a federal branch or federal agency, compliance with the publication procedures of the Comptroller shall satisfy the publication requirement of this section. Comments regarding the application should be sent to the Board and the Comptroller.

(3) Written comments. (i) Within 30 days after publication, as required in paragraph (b)(2) of this section, any person may submit to the Board written comments and data on an application.

(ii) The Board may extend the 30-day comment period if the Board determines that additional relevant information is likely to be provided by interested persons, or if other extenuating circumstances exist.

(4) Board action on application. (i) Time limits. (A) The Board shall act on an application from a foreign bank to establish a branch, agency, or commercial lending company subsidiary within 180 calendar days after the receipt of the application.

(B) The Board may extend for an additional 180 calendar days the period within which to take final action, after providing notice of and reasons for the extension to the applicant and the licensing authority.

(C) The time periods set forth in this paragraph (b)(4)(i) may be waived by the applicant.

(ii) Additional information. The Board may request any information in addition to that supplied in the application when the Board believes that the information is necessary for its decision, and may deny an application if it does not receive the information requested from the applicant or its home country supervisor in sufficient time to permit adequate evaluation of the information within the time periods set forth in paragraph (b)(4)(i) of this section.

(5) Coordination with other regulators. Upon receipt of an application by a foreign bank under this section, the Board shall promptly notify, consult with, and consider the views of the licensing authority.

(c) Standards for approval of U.S. offices of foreign banks--(1) Mandatory standards--(i) General. As specified in section 7(d) of the IBA (12 U.S.C. 3105(d)), the Board may not approve an application to establish a branch or an agency, or to establish or acquire ownership or control of a commercial lending company, unless it determines that:

(A) Each of the foreign bank and any parent foreign bank engages directly in the business of banking outside the United States and, except as provided in paragraph (c)(1)(iii) of this section, is subject to comprehensive supervision or regulation on a consolidated basis by its home country supervisor; and

(B) The foreign bank has furnished to the Board the information that the Board requires in order to assess the application adequately.

(ii) Basis for determining comprehensive consolidated supervision. In determining whether a foreign bank and any parent foreign bank is subject to comprehensive consolidated supervision, the Board shall determine whether the foreign bank is supervised or regulated in such a manner that its home country supervisor receives sufficient information on the worldwide operations of the foreign bank (including the relationships of the bank to any affiliate) to assess the foreign bank's overall financial condition and compliance with law and regulation.  In making such a determination, the Board shall assess, among other factors, the extent to which the home country supervisor:

(A) Ensures that the foreign bank has adequate procedures for monitoring and controlling its activities worldwide;

(B) Obtains information on the condition of the foreign bank and its subsidiaries and offices outside the home country through regular reports of examination, audit reports, or otherwise;

(C) Obtains information on the dealings and relationship between the foreign bank and its affiliates, both foreign and domestic;

(D) Receives from the foreign bank financial reports that are consolidated on a worldwide basis, or comparable information that permits analysis of the foreign bank's financial condition on a worldwide, consolidated basis;

(E) Evaluates prudential standards, such as capital adequacy and risk asset exposure, on a worldwide basis.

(iii) Determination of comprehensive consolidated supervision not required in certain circumstances. (A) If the Board is unable to find, under paragraph (c)(1)(i) of this section, that a foreign bank is subject to comprehensive consolidated supervision, the Board may, nevertheless, approve an application by the foreign bank if:

(1) The home country supervisor is actively working to establish arrangements for the consolidated supervision of such bank; and

(2) All other factors are consistent with approval.

(B) In deciding whether to use its discretion under this paragraph (c)(1)(iii), the Board also shall consider whether the foreign bank has adopted and implemented procedures to combat money laundering.  The Board also may take into account whether the home country supervisor is developing a legal regime to address money laundering or is participating in multilateral efforts to combat money laundering.  In approving an application under this paragraph (c)(1)(iii), the Board, after requesting and taking into consideration the views of the licensing authority, may impose any conditions or restrictions relating to the activities or business operations of the proposed branch, agency, or commercial lending company subsidiary, including restrictions on sources of funding.  The Board shall coordinate with the licensing authority in the implementation of such conditions or restrictions.

(2) Additional standards. In acting on any application under this subpart, the Board may take into account:

(i) Consent of home country supervisor. Whether the home country supervisor of the foreign bank has consented to the proposed establishment of the branch, agency, or commercial lending company subsidiary;

(ii) Financial resources. The financial resources of the foreign bank (including the foreign bank's capital position, projected capital position, profitability, level of indebtedness, and future prospects) and the condition of any U.S. office of the foreign bank;

(iii) Managerial resources. The managerial resources of the foreign bank, including the competence, experience, and integrity of the officers and directors; the integrity of its principal shareholders; management's experience and capacity to engage in international banking; and the record of the foreign bank and its management of complying with laws and regulations, and of fulfilling any commitments to, and any conditions imposed by, the Board in connection with any prior application;

(iv) Sharing information with supervisors. Whether the foreign bank's home country supervisor and the home country supervisor of any parent of the foreign bank share material information regarding the operations of the foreign bank with other supervisory authorities;

(v) Assurances to Board. (A) Whether the foreign bank has provided the Board with adequate assurances that information will be made available to the Board on the operations or activities of the foreign bank and any of its affiliates that the Board deems necessary to determine and enforce compliance with the IBA, the BHC Act, and other applicable federal banking statutes.

(B) These assurances shall include a statement from the foreign bank describing the laws that would restrict the foreign bank or any of its parents from providing information to the Board;

(vi) Measures for prevention of money laundering. Whether the foreign bank has adopted and implemented procedures to combat money laundering, whether there is a legal regime in place in the home country to address money laundering, and whether the home country is participating in multilateral efforts to combat money laundering;

(vii) Compliance with U.S. law. Whether the foreign bank and its U.S. affiliates are in compliance with applicable U.S. law, and whether the applicant has established adequate controls and procedures in each of its offices to ensure continuing compliance with U.S. law, including controls directed to detection of money laundering and other unsafe or unsound banking practices; and (viii) The needs of the community and the history of operation of the foreign bank and its relative size in its home country, provided that the size of the foreign bank is not the sole factor in determining whether an office of a foreign bank should be approved.

(3) Additional standards for certain interstate applications. (i) As specified in section 5(a)(3) of the IBA (12 U.S.C. 3103(a)(3)), the Board may not approve an application by a foreign bank to establish a branch, other than a limited branch, outside the home state of the foreign bank under section 5(a)(1) or (2) of the IBA (12 U.S.C. 3103(a) (1), (2)) unless the Board:

(A) Determines that the foreign bank's financial resources, including the capital level of the bank, are equivalent to those required for a domestic bank to be approved for branching under section 5155 of the Revised Statutes (12 U.S.C. 36) and section 44 of the Federal Deposit Insurance Act (FDIA) (12 U.S.C. 1831u);

(B) Consults with the Department of the Treasury regarding capital equivalency;

(C) Applies the standards specified in section 7(d) of the IBA (12 U.S.C. 3105(d)) and this paragraph (c); and

(D) Applies the same requirements and conditions to which an application by a domestic bank for an interstate merger is subject under section 44(b)(1), (3), and (4) of the FDIA (12 U.S.C. 1831u(b)(1), (3), (4)); and

(ii) As specified in section 5(a)(7) of the IBA (12 U.S.C. 3103(a)(7)), the Board may not approve an application to establish a branch through a change in status of an agency or limited branch outside the foreign bank's home state unless:

(A) The establishment and operation of such branch is permitted by such state; and

(B) Such agency or branch has been in operation in such state for a period of time that meets the state's minimum age requirement permitted under section 44(a)(5) of the Federal Deposit Insurance Act (12 U.S.C. 183u(a)(5)).

(4) Board conditions on approval. The Board may impose any conditions on its approval as it deems necessary, including a condition which may permit future termination

by the Board of any activities or, in the case of a federal branch or a federal agency, by the Comptroller, based on the inability of the foreign bank to provide information on its activities or those of its affiliates that the Board deems necessary to determine and enforce compliance with U.S. banking laws.

(d) Representative offices--(1) Permissible activities.  A representative office may engage in:

(i) Representational and administrative functions.  Representational and administrative functions in connection with the banking activities of the foreign bank, which may include soliciting new business for the foreign bank; conducting research; acting as liaison between the foreign bank's head office and customers in the United States; performing preliminary and servicing steps in connection with lending; or performing back-office functions; but shall not include contracting for any deposit or deposit-like liability, lending money, or engaging in any other banking activity for the foreign bank;

(ii) Credit approvals under certain circumstances.  Making credit decisions if the foreign bank also operates one or more branches or agencies in the United States, the loans approved at the representative office are made by a U.S. office of the bank, and the loan proceeds are not disbursed in the representative office; and

(iii) Other functions.  Other functions for or on behalf of the foreign bank or its affiliates, such as operating as a regional administrative office of the foreign bank, but only to the extent that these other functions are not banking activities and are not prohibited by applicable federal or state law, or by ruling or order of the Board.

(2) Standards for approval of representative offices.  As specified in section 10(a)(2) of the IBA (12 U.S.C. 3107(a)(2)), in acting on the application of a foreign bank to establish a representative office, the Board shall take into account, to the extent it deems appropriate, the standards for approval set out in paragraph (c) of this section.  The standard regarding supervision by the foreign bank's home country supervisor (as set out in paragraph (c)(1)(i)(A) of this section) will be met, in the case of a representative office application, if the Board makes a finding that the applicant bank is subject to a supervisory framework that is consistent with the activities of the proposed representative office, taking into account the nature of such activities and the operating record of the applicant.

(3) Special-purpose foreign government-owned banks.  A foreign government-owned organization engaged in banking activities in its home country that are not commercial in nature may apply to the Board for a determination that the organization is not a foreign bank for purposes of this section.  A written request setting forth the basis for such a determination may be submitted to the Reserve Bank of the District in which the foreign organization's representative office is located in the United States, or to the Board, in the case of a proposed establishment of a representative office.  The Board shall review and act upon each request on a case-by-case basis.

(4) Additional requirements.  The Board may impose any additional requirements that it determines to be necessary to carry out the purposes of the IBA.

(e) Preservation of existing authority.  Nothing in this subpart shall be construed to relieve any foreign bank or foreign banking organization from any otherwise applicable requirement of federal or state law, including any applicable licensing requirement.

(f) Reports of crimes and suspected crimes.  Except for a federal branch or a federal agency or a state branch that is insured by the Federal Deposit Insurance Corporation (FDIC), a branch, agency, or representative office of a foreign bank operating in the United States shall file a suspicious activity report in accordance with the provisions of § 208.62 of Regulation H (12 CFR 208.62).

(g) Management of shell branches.  (1) A state-licensed branch or agency shall not manage, through an office of the foreign bank which is located outside the United States and is managed or controlled by such state-licensed branch or agency, any type of activity that a bank organized under the laws of the United States or any state is not permitted to manage at any branch or subsidiary of such bank which is located outside the United States.

(2) For purposes of this paragraph (g), an office of a foreign bank located outside the United States is "managed or controlled" by a state-licensed branch or agency if a majority of the responsibility for business decisions, including but not limited to decisions with regard to lending or asset management or funding or liability management, or the responsibility for recordkeeping in respect of assets or liabilities for that non-U.S. office, resides at the state-licensed branch or agency.

(3) The types of activities that a state-licensed branch or agency may manage through an office located outside the United States that it manage or controls include the types of activities authorized to a U.S. bank by state or federal charters, regulations issued by chartering or regulatory authorities, and other U.S. banking laws, including the Federal Reserve Act, and the implementing regulations, but U.S. procedural or quantitative requirements that may be applicable to the conduct of such activities by U.S. banks shall not apply.

(h) Government securities sales practices.  An uninsured state-licensed branch or agency of a foreign bank that is required to give notice to the Board under section 15C of the Securities Exchange Act of 1934 (15 U.S.C. 78o-5) and the Department of the Treasury rules under section 15C (17 CFR 400.1(d) and part 401) shall be subject to the provisions of 12 CFR 208.37 to the same extent as a state member bank that is required to give such notice.

(i) Protection of customer information.  An uninsured state-licensed branch or agency of a foreign bank shall comply with the Interagency Guidelines Establishing Standards for Safeguarding Customer Information prescribed pursuant to sections 501 and 505 of the Gramm-Leach-Bliley Act (15 U.S.C. 6801 and 6805). . . .

§ 211.25   Termination of offices of foreign banks.

(a) Grounds for termination--(1) General.  Under sections 7(e) and 10(b) of the IBA (12 U.S.C. 3105(d), 3107(b)), the Board may order a foreign bank to terminate the activities of its representative office, state branch, state agency, or commercial lending company subsidiary if the Board finds that:

(i) The foreign bank is not subject to comprehensive consolidated supervision in accordance with § 211.24(c)(1), and the home country supervisor is not making demonstrable progress in establishing arrangements for the consolidated supervision of the foreign bank; or

(ii) Both of the following criteria are met:

(A) There is reasonable cause to believe that the foreign bank, or any of its affiliates, has committed a violation of law or engaged in an unsafe or unsound banking practice in the United States; and

(B) As a result of such violation or practice, the continued operation of the foreign bank's representative office, state branch, state agency, or commercial lending company subsidiary would not be consistent with the public interest, or with the purposes of the IBA, the BHC Act, or the FDIA.

(2) Additional ground. The Board also may enforce any condition imposed in connection with an order issued under § 211.24.

(b) Factor. In making its findings under this section, the Board may take into account the needs of the community, the history of operation of the foreign bank, and its relative size in its home country, provided that the size of the foreign bank shall not be the sole determining factor in a decision to terminate an office.

(c) Consultation with relevant state supervisor. Except in the case of termination pursuant to the expedited procedure in paragraph (d)(3) of this section, the Board shall request and consider the views of the relevant state supervisor before issuing an order terminating the activities of a state branch, state agency, representative office, or commercial lending company subsidiary under this section.

(d) Termination procedures--(1) Notice and hearing. Except as otherwise provided in paragraph (d)(3) of this section, an order issued under paragraph (a)(1) of this section shall be issued only after notice to the relevant state supervisor and the foreign bank and after an opportunity for a hearing.

(2) Procedures for hearing. Hearings under this section shall be conducted pursuant to the Board's Rules of Practice for Hearings (12 CFR part 263).

(3) Expedited procedure. The Board may act without providing an opportunity for a hearing, if it determines that expeditious action is necessary in order to protect the public interest. When the Board finds that it is necessary to act without providing an opportunity for a hearing, the Board, solely in its discretion, may:

(i) Provide the foreign bank that is the subject of the termination order with notice of the intended termination order;

(ii) Grant the foreign bank an opportunity to present a written submission opposing issuance of the order; or

(iii) Take any other action designed to provide the foreign bank with notice and an opportunity to present its views concerning the order.

(e) Termination of federal branch or federal agency. The Board may transmit to the Comptroller a recommendation that the license of a federal branch or federal agency be terminated if the Board has reasonable cause to believe that the foreign bank or any affiliate of the foreign bank has engaged in conduct for which the activities of a state branch or state agency may be terminated pursuant to this section.

(f) Voluntary termination. A foreign bank shall notify the Board at least 30 days prior to terminating the activities of any office. Notice pursuant to this paragraph (f) is in addition to, and does not satisfy, any other federal or state requirements relating to the termination of an office or the requirement for prior notice of the closing of a branch, pursuant to section 39 of the FDIA (12 U.S.C. 1831p).

§ 211.26  Examination of offices and affiliates of foreign banks.

(a) Conduct of examinations--(1) Examination of branches, agencies, commercial lending companies, and affiliates. The Board may examine:

(i) Any branch or agency of a foreign bank;

(ii) Any commercial lending company or bank controlled by one or more foreign banks, or one or more foreign companies that control a foreign bank; and

(iii) Any other office or affiliate of a foreign bank conducting business in any state.

(2) Examination of representative offices. The Board may examine any representative office in the manner and with the frequency it deems appropriate.

(b) Coordination of examinations. To the extent possible, the Board shall coordinate its examinations of the U.S. offices and U.S. affiliates of a foreign bank with the licensing authority and, in the case of an insured branch, the Federal Deposit Insurance Corporation (FDIC), including through simultaneous examinations of the U.S. offices and U.S. affiliates of a foreign bank.

(c) Frequency of on-site examination--(1) General. Each branch or agency of a foreign bank shall be examined on-site at least once during each 12-month period (beginning on the date the most recent examination of the office ended) by–

(i) The Board;

(ii) The FDIC, if the branch of the foreign bank accepts or maintains insured deposits;

(iii) The Comptroller, if the branch or agency of the foreign bank is licensed by the Comptroller; or

(iv) The state supervisor, if the office of the foreign bank is licensed or chartered by the state.

(2) 18-month cycle for certain small institutions--(i) Mandatory standards. The Board may conduct a full-scope, on-site examination at least once during each 18-month period, rather than each 12-month period as required in paragraph (c)(1) of this section, if the branch or agency--

(A) Has total assets of $250 million or less;

(B) Has received a composite ROCA supervisory rating (which rates risk management, operational controls, compliance, and asset quality) of 1 or 2 at its most recent examination;

(C) Satisfies the requirement of either the following paragraph (c)(2)(i)(C)(1) or (2):

(1) The foreign bank's most recently reported capital adequacy position consists of, or is equivalent to, tier 1 and total risk-based capital ratios of at least 6 percent and 10 percent, respectively, on a consolidated basis; or

(2) The branch or agency has maintained on a daily basis, over the past three quarters, eligible assets in an amount not less than 108 percent of the preceding quarter's average third-party liabilities (determined consistent with applicable federal and state law) and sufficient liquidity is currently available to meet its obligations to third parties;

(D) Is not subject to a formal enforcement action or order by the Board, FDIC, or OCC; and

(E) Has not experienced a change in control during the preceding 12-month period in which a full-scope, on-site examination would have been required but for this section.

(ii) Discretionary standards. In determining whether a branch or agency of a foreign bank that meets the standards of paragraph (c)(2)(i) of this section should not be eligible for an 18-month examination cycle pursuant to this paragraph (c)(2), the Board may consider additional factors, including whether--

(A) Any of the individual components of the ROCA supervisory rating of a branch or agency of a foreign bank is rated "3" or worse;

(B) The results of any off-site surveillance indicate a deterioration in the condition of the office;

(C) The size, relative importance, and role of a particular office when reviewed in the context of the foreign bank's entire U.S. operations otherwise necessitate an annual examination; and

(D) The condition of the foreign bank gives rise to such a need.

(3) Authority to conduct more frequent examinations. Nothing in paragraphs (c)(1) and (2) of this section limits the authority of the Board to examine any U.S. branch or agency of a foreign bank as frequently as it deems necessary.

§ 211.27  Disclosure of supervisory information to foreign supervisors.

(a) Disclosure by Board. The Board may disclose information obtained in the course of exercising its supervisory or examination authority to a foreign bank regulatory or supervisory authority, if the Board determines that disclosure is appropriate for bank supervisory or regulatory purposes and will not prejudice the interests of the United States.

(b) Confidentiality. Before making any disclosure of information pursuant to paragraph (a) of this section, the Board shall obtain, to the extent necessary, the agreement of the foreign bank regulatory or supervisory authority to maintain the confidentiality of such information to the extent possible under applicable law.

§ 211.28 Provisions applicable to branches and agencies: limitation on loans to one borrower.

(a) Limitation on loans to one borrower. Except as provided in paragraph (b) of this section, the total loans and extensions of credit by all the state branches and state agencies of a foreign bank outstanding to a single borrower at one time shall be aggregated with the total loans and extensions of credit by all federal branches and federal agencies of the same foreign bank outstanding to such borrower at the time; and shall be subject to the limitations and other provisions of section 5200 of the Revised Statutes (12 U.S.C. 84), and the regulations promulgated thereunder, in the same manner that extensions of credit by a federal branch or federal agency are subject to section 4(b) of the IBA (12 U.S.C. 3102(b)) as if such state branches and state agencies were federal branches and federal agencies.

(b) Preexisting loans and extensions of credit. Any loans or extensions of credit to a single borrower that were originated prior to December 19, 1991, by a state branch or state agency of the same foreign bank and that, when aggregated with loans and extensions of credit by all other branches and agencies of the foreign bank, exceed the limits set forth in paragraph (a) of this section, may be brought into compliance with such limitations through routine repayment, provided that any new loans or extensions of credit (including renewals of existing unfunded credit lines, or extensions of the maturities of existing loans) to the same borrower shall comply with the limits set forth in paragraph (a) of this section.

§ 211.29 Applications by state branches and state agencies to conduct activities not permissible for federal branches.

(a) Scope. A state branch or state agency shall file with the Board a prior written application for permission to engage in or continue to engage in any type of activity that:

(1) Is not permissible for a federal branch, pursuant to statute, regulation, official bulletin or circular, or order or interpretation issued in writing by the Comptroller; or

(2) Is rendered impermissible due to a subsequent change in statute, regulation, official bulletin or circular, written order or interpretation, or decision of a court of competent jurisdiction.

(b) Exceptions. No application shall be required by a state branch or state agency to conduct any activity that is otherwise permissible under applicable state and federal law or regulation and that:

(1) Has been determined by the FDIC, pursuant to 12 CFR 362.4(c)(3)(i) through (c)(3)(ii)(A), not to present a significant risk to the affected deposit insurance fund;

(2) Is permissible for a federal branch, but the Comptroller imposes a quantitative limitation on the conduct of such activity by the federal branch;

(3) Is conducted as agent rather than as principal, provided that the activity is one that could be conducted by a state-chartered bank headquartered in the same state in which the branch or agency is licensed; or

(4) Any other activity that the Board has determined may be conducted by any state branch or state agency of a foreign bank without further application to the Board.

(c) Contents of application. An application submitted pursuant to paragraph (a) of this section shall be in letter form and shall contain the following information:

(1) A brief description of the activity, including the manner in which it will be conducted, and an estimate of the expected dollar volume associated with the activity;

(2) An analysis of the impact of the proposed activity on the condition of the U.S. operations of the foreign bank in general, and of the branch or agency in particular, including a copy, if available, of any feasibility study, management plan, financial projections, business plan, or similar document concerning the conduct of the activity;

(3) A resolution by the applicant's board of directors or, if a resolution is not required pursuant to the applicant's organizational documents, evidence of approval by senior management, authorizing the conduct of such activity and the filing of this application;

(4) If the activity is to be conducted by a state branch insured by the FDIC, statements by the applicant:

(i) Of whether or not it is in compliance with 12 CFR 346.19 (Pledge of Assets) and 12 CFR 346.20 (Asset Maintenance);

(ii) That it has complied with all requirements of the FDIC concerning an application to conduct the activity and the status of the application, including a copy of the FDIC's disposition of such application, if available; and

(iii) Explaining why the activity will pose no significant risk to the deposit insurance fund; and

(5) Any other information that the Reserve Bank deems appropriate.

(d) Factors considered in determination. (1) The Board shall consider the following factors in determining whether a proposed activity is consistent with sound banking practice:

(i) The types of risks, if any, the activity poses to the U.S. operations of the foreign banking organization in general, and the branch or agency in particular;

(ii) If the activity poses any such risks, the magnitude of each risk; and

(iii) If a risk is not de minimis, the actual or proposed procedures to control and minimize the risk.

(2) Each of the factors set forth in paragraph (d)(1) of this section shall be evaluated in light of the financial condition of the foreign bank in general and the branch or agency in particular and the volume of the activity.

(e) Application procedures. Applications pursuant to this section shall be filed with the appropriate Federal Reserve Bank. An application shall not be deemed complete until it contains all the information requested by the Reserve Bank and has been accepted. Approval of such an application may be conditioned on the applicant's agreement to conduct the activity subject to specific conditions or limitations.

(f) Divestiture or cessation. (1) If an application for permission to continue to conduct an activity is not approved by the Board or, if applicable, the FDIC, the applicant shall submit a detailed written plan of divestiture or cessation of the activity to the appropriate Federal Reserve Bank within 60 days of the disapproval.

(i) The divestiture or cessation plan shall describe in detail the manner in which the applicant will divest itself of or cease the activity, and shall include a projected timetable describing how long the divestiture or cessation is expected to take.

(ii) Divestiture or cessation shall be complete within one year from the date of the disapproval, or within such shorter period of time as the Board shall direct.

(2) If a foreign bank operating a state branch or state agency chooses not to apply to the Board for permission to continue to conduct an activity that is not permissible for a federal branch, or which is rendered impermissible due to a subsequent change in statute, regulation, official bulletin or circular, written order or interpretation, or decision of a court

of competent jurisdiction, the foreign bank shall submit a written plan of divestiture or cessation, in conformance with paragraph (f)(1) of this section within 60 days of the effective date of this part or of such change or decision.

§ 211.30 Criteria for evaluating U.S. operations of foreign banks not subject to consolidated supervision.

(a) Development and publication of criteria. Pursuant to the Foreign Bank Supervision Enhancement Act, Pub. L. 102-242, 105 Stat. 2286 (1991), the Board shall develop and publish criteria to be used in evaluating the operations of any foreign bank in the United States that the Board has determined is not subject to comprehensive consolidated supervision [(CCS]).

(b) Criteria considered by Board. Following a determination by the Board that, having taken into account the standards set forth in § 211.24(c)(1), a foreign bank is not subject to CCS, the Board shall consider the following criteria in determining whether the foreign bank's U.S. operations should be permitted to continue and, if so, whether any supervisory constraints should be placed upon the bank in connection with those operations:

(1) The proportion of the foreign bank's total assets and total liabilities that are located or booked in its home country, as well as the distribution and location of its assets and liabilities that are located or booked elsewhere;

(2) The extent to which the operations and assets of the foreign bank and any affiliates are subject to supervision by its home country supervisor;

(3) Whether the home country supervisor of such foreign bank is actively working to establish arrangements for comprehensive consolidated supervision of the bank, and whether demonstrable progress is being made;

(4) Whether the foreign bank has effective and reliable systems of internal controls and management information and reporting, which enable its management properly to oversee its worldwide operations;

(5) Whether the foreign bank's home country supervisor has any objection to the bank continuing to operate in the United States;

(6) Whether the foreign bank's home country supervisor and the home country supervisor of any parent of the foreign bank share material information regarding the operations of the foreign bank with other supervisory authorities;

(7) The relationship of the U.S. operations to the other operations of the foreign bank, including whether the foreign bank maintains funds in its U.S. offices that are in excess of amounts due to its U.S. offices from the foreign bank's non-U.S. offices;

(8) The soundness of the foreign bank's overall financial condition;

(9) The managerial resources of the foreign bank, including the competence, experience, and integrity of the officers and directors, and the integrity of its principal shareholders;

(10) The scope and frequency of external audits of the foreign bank;

(11) The operating record of the foreign bank generally and its role in the banking system in its home country;

(12) The foreign bank's record of compliance with relevant laws, as well as the adequacy of its anti-money-laundering controls and procedures, in respect of its worldwide operations;

(13) The operating record of the U.S. offices of the foreign bank;

(14) The views and recommendations of the Comptroller or the relevant state supervisors in those states in which the foreign bank has operations, as appropriate;

(15) Whether the foreign bank, if requested, has provided the Board with adequate

assurances that such information will be made available on the operations or activities of the foreign bank and any of its affiliates as the Board deems necessary to determine and enforce compliance with the IBA, the BHC Act, and other U.S. banking statutes; and

(16) Any other information relevant to the safety and soundness of the U.S. operations of the foreign bank.

(c) Restrictions on U.S. operations--(1) Terms of agreement. Any foreign bank that the Board determines is not subject to CCS may be required to enter into an agreement to conduct its U.S. operations subject to such restrictions as the Board, having considered the criteria set forth in paragraph (b) of this section, determines to be appropriate in order to ensure the safety and soundness of its U.S. operations.

(2) Failure to enter into or comply with agreement. A foreign bank that is required by the Board to enter into an agreement pursuant to paragraph (c)(1) of this section and either fails to do so, or fails to comply with the terms of such agreement, may be subject to:

(i) Enforcement action, in order to ensure safe and sound banking operations, under 12 U.S.C. 1818; or

(ii) Termination or a recommendation for termination of its U.S. operations, under § 211.25(a) and (e) and section (7)(e) of the IBA (12 U.S.C. 3105(e)).

# 2. The International Banking Act of 1978

**Notes and Comments 6.3.** Review 12 U.S.C. §§ 3101 *et seq.*, and consider the extent to which the International Banking Act of 1978 has shifted the focus to federal alternatives in the menu of options for foreign bank entry in the U.S. market. In that regard, consider the following case.

### Conference of State Bank Supervisors v. Conover,
715 F.2d 604 (D.C.Cir. 1983),
*cert. denied*, 466 U.S. 927 (1984)

[For the background of this case, see Chapter2, § 2, *supra*.]

A.

In support of their construction of the statute the appellants refer us to the legislative background of section 4(a). . . . [CSBS argued that earlier congressional proposals were ultimately rejected in response to the testimony of state banking regulators seeking to preserve state reciprocity requirements. In addition, they noted that while the IBA and earlier proposals were being considered by congressional committees, the Fed had objected to any "state veto power" over the entry of federally-chartered foreign banks, but Congress did not change the bills in response to the Fed's objections. CSBS therefore contended that section 4(a) required the Comptroller to observe state reciprocity requirements.

[The Comptroller countered by pointing to an amendment to the IBA proposed by Representative Grassley of Iowa. That amendment would have changed an earlier version of section 9(a) to impose a reciprocity requirement on a national basis. The Senate, however, passed a substantially revised version of section 9, rejecting the Grassley Amendment. The Comptroller contended that rejection of the Grassley Amendment signalled Congressional rejection of reciprocity as a chartering standard for federal offices of foreign banks.]

Appellants also contend that Congress intended section 4(a) to maintain "the states' preexisting power to determine the structure of foreign banking institutions within their borders. . . ." In the appellants' view, in passing section 4(a) Congress "consciously followed" the policies of a dual banking system found in the Douglas Amendment to the Bank Holding Company Act of 1956, 12 U.S.C. § 1842(d) (Supp. V 1981), and in the McFadden Act, 12 U.S.C. § 36 (1976). . . . The Douglas Amendment provides:

> Notwithstanding any other provision of this section, no application (except an application filed as a result of a transaction authorized under section 13(f) of the Federal Deposit Insurance Act) shall be approved under this section which will permit any bank holding company or any subsidiary thereof to acquire, directly or indirectly, any voting shares of, interest in, or all or substantially all of the assets of any additional bank located outside the State in which the operations of such bank holding company's banking subsidiaries were principally conducted on July 1, 1966, or the date on which such company became a bank holding company, whichever is later, unless the acquisition of such shares or assets of a State bank by an out-of-State bank holding company is specifically authorized by the statute laws of the State in which such bank is located, by language to that effect and not merely by implication. For the purposes of this section, the State in which the operations of a bank holding company's subsidiaries are principally conducted is that State in which total deposits of all such banking subsidiaries are largest.

12 U.S.C. § 1842(d) (Supp. V 1981).[a]

Appellants argue that the Douglas Amendment and section 4(a) reflect similar policies; both grant a state the power to control which banking institutions organized outside of its borders may enter that state. They direct our attention to the language of the Douglas Amendment which states that the Board of Governors of the Federal Reserve System shall not approve a bank holding company's application to acquire any voting shares or substantially all the assets of a bank located outside the state in which the operations of the bank holding company are principally conducted "unless the acquisition of such shares or assets of a State bank by *an* out-of-State bank holding company is specifically authorized by the statute laws of the State in which such bank is located. . . ." 12 U.S.C. § 1842(d) (Supp. V 1981) (emphasis added). Appellants note the similarity between the quoted language in the Douglas Amendment and the analogous proviso in section 4(a)(2). See 12 U.S.C. § 3102(a)(2) (Supp. V 1981) ("the establishment of a branch or agency . . . by a foreign bank is not prohibited by State law"). They then refer us to *Iowa Independent Bankers v. Board of Governors of the Federal Reserve System*, 511 F.2d 1288, *cert. denied*, 423 U.S. 875 (1975), a case involving the Douglas Amendment in which this court rejected arguments similar to those the Comptroller has made in this case to support his interpretation of section 4(a). In the *Iowa Independent Bankers* case, an organization of Iowa bankers argued that the Douglas Amendment did not permit the states to discriminate among out-of-state bank holding companies when deciding which bank holding companies could enter that state. The bankers argued that the states could prohibit all out-of-state bank holding companies from entering it or it could prohibit none. 511 F.2d at 1296. This court rejected that argument, ruling that the Douglas Amendment empowered states to discriminate among out-of-state bank holding companies when deciding which could enter. 511 F.2d at 1297. Appellants argue that section 4(a) uses the same "statutory formulation" as the Douglas Amendment and should be interpreted similarly. . . . The District Court did not

---

a. The Douglas Amendment was repealed in 1994 and replaced with authorization for bank holding companies to acquire banks on an interstate basis. *See infra* Note 6.7 (discussing 1994 legislation).

address this argument.

Appellants also argue that in enacting the IBA, Congress sought to apply the policies of the McFadden Act, 12 U.S.C. § 36(c) (1976) to the entry of a federally-chartered foreign bank into its home state. The McFadden Act provides that the Comptroller may approve a national bank's application to establish an additional branch office in the state of its principal office only if that state's laws would authorize a state-chartered bank to open such an additional branch office. *See First National Bank of Logan v. Walker Bank & Trust Co.*, 385 U.S. 252, 258-62 (1966). . . .

B.

The language of section 4(a) does not preclude either of the proffered interpretations. Moreover, we believe the legislative history of the IBA does not offer clear guidance on the meaning of section 4(a). . . . [W]e find unconvincing both appellants' and appellee's arguments based on the legislative background of the IBA, and decline to rest our resolution of the section 4(a) issue on such meager grounds.

. . . [W]e find [the argument with respect to the Douglas Amendment] without merit. We believe *Iowa Independent Bankers* is distinguishable from this case. . . . Here . . . the language of section 4(a) at least suggests that states were not given the power to discriminate in allowing foreign banks to enter. Section 4(a) provides:

> Except as provided in section [5] of this [Act], a foreign bank which engages directly in a banking business outside the United States may, with the approval of the Comptroller, establish one or more Federal branches or agencies in any State in which (1) it is not operating a branch or agency pursuant to State law and (2) the establishment of a branch or agency, as the case may be, by a foreign bank is not prohibited by State law.

12 U.S.C. § 3102(a) (Supp. V 1981). Congress begins this section by referring generally to "a foreign bank." In subsection (1), it narrows the focus to a particular bank: "[A] foreign bank . . . may . . . establish one or more Federal branches or agencies in any State in which (1) *it* is not operating a branch or agency pursuant to State law. . . ." *Id.* (emphasis added). In subsection (2), however, Congress refers simply to "a foreign bank" again; it does not follow through with the specific reference contained in subsection (1). While this difference is not dispositive, it does support the Comptroller's interpretation....

. . . [W]e find two arguable correct interpretations of an ambiguous statutory provision. The relevant legislative history contains no explicit support for either interpretation. Under these circumstances, we believe section 4(a) can only be interpreted in the light of Congress' overriding objective in enacting the IBA. We find the legislative history replete with references to Congress' intent to accord foreign banks national treatment, under which "foreign enterprises . . . are treated as competitive equals with their domestic counterparts."
. . .

The Senate Report echoes a similar theme: "The general policy of the United States with regard to foreign enterprises doing business in the United States has been one of national treatment." . . . "The committee thus believes national treatment is the most appropriate policy to adopt with respect to foreign banks in the United States. . . ." . . . We conclude from these passages that the IBA seeks to treat federally-chartered foreign and domestic banks as similarly as possible under the Act.

Thus, turning to section 4(a), we believe Congress sought to treat the establishment of a foreign bank's federally-chartered offices similarly to the establishment of the offices of its "domestic counterparts." In so doing, we must determine whether Congress intended the opening of the first office in a federally-chartered foreign bank's home state to parallel the opening of a federally-chartered domestic bank's principal office or the opening of a branch office of such a bank. The language of section 4(h) suggests that establishment of a foreign bank's initial home state office parallels the establishment of a domestic national bank's principal office. . . .

. . . Thus, for purposes of establishing additional offices in the home state, a foreign bank's initial home state office is equated with a domestic national bank's principal office. This comports with the IBA's objective of national treatment by allowing foreign banks to open additional home state offices on the same terms as could federally-chartered domestic banks under the McFadden Act.[7] Second, for purposes of changing the designation of the initial office, a foreign bank's initial home state office is again equated with a domestic national bank's principal office. . . .

Having decided that the establishment of a foreign bank's federally-chartered bank's *initial* home state office is analogous to the establishment of a domestic bank's federally-chartered principal office, we note that a state cannot prohibit establishment of a federally-chartered domestic bank's principal office. *See Pineland State Bank v. Proposed First National Bank of Bricktown*, 335 F.Supp. 1376, 1379 (D.N.J. 1971). *See generally* 12 U.S.C. §§ 26, 27 (Supp. V 1981). Section 4(a) of the IBA, however, grants a state some control over establishment of a federally-chartered *foreign* bank's initial office. By treating a foreign bank differently from a domestic bank, section 4(a) departs from the IBA's theme of national treatment. However, we believe that where, as here, a provision of the IBA is unclear, it should be construed to minimize any departure from the IBA's overriding objective of national treatment. National treatment would preclude any state regulation of a federally-chartered foreign bank's initial home state office. We find that the Comptroller's interpretation of section 4(a), approved by the District Court, permits as little state regulation of the establishment of such offices as is consistent with the terms of section 4(a). Accordingly, we affirm the Comptroller's interpretation of section 4(a).

III.

Turning now to the second issue in this appeal, we must address the extent to which the Comptroller must defer to state law in licensing a foreign bank's federal interstate office.[9] We also must consider whether the IBA requires a federal interstate office to comply with the limitations on bank operations imposed by the receiving state.

A.

Section 4(a), 12 U.S.C. § 3102(a) (Supp. V 1981), provides the general framework for chartering any federal branch or agency. . . . That section, however, begins "[e]xcept as provided in section [5]," and section 5, *id.*, § 3103, sets out additional requirements for establishing and operating a federal interstate branch or agency. . . .

Pursuant to his authority under section 13, *id.*, § 3108(a), the Comptroller adopted the following definitions and interpretation:

> A "Federal branch" is an office or place of business, licensed by the Comptroller
> and operated by a foreign bank in any State of the United States, which can
> engage in the business of banking, including the exercise of fiduciary powers and

---

7. We agree with the District Court that the principles of the McFadden Act are irrelevant to the establishment of a federally-chartered foreign bank's *initial* home state office.

9. In the context of this opinion, an "interstate office" is a branch or agency of a foreign bank located, or to be located, in a state other than the foreign bank's home state. . . . And, the state in which the interstate office is located is termed the "receiving state."

the acceptance of deposits from citizens and residents of the United States.

12 C.F.R. § 28.2(c) (1980).

> A "Limited Federal branch" is a Federal branch licensed by the Comptroller which, pursuant to an agreement between the parent foreign bank and the Federal Reserve Board, can receive only such deposits as would be permissible for an Edge Corporation organized under section 25(a) of the Federal Reserve Act (12 U.S.C. 611). Except for this restriction, a Limited Federal branch can exercise the full range of powers available to any Federal branch.[11]

12 C.F.R. § 28.2(d) (1980). *See also infra* note 19 (text of 12 C.F.R. § 28.2(b) (1980), defining "Federal agency").

> Limited Federal branches can accept only such types of deposits as are permissible to Edge Corporations pursuant to 12 U.S.C. 615 and 12 C.F.R. Part 211. Apart from these exemptions or qualifications, Federal branches and agencies can engage in the same type of business and exercise the same powers as a national bank, subject to the conditions and requirements contained in the statutes and any implementing rules and regulations promulgated by the federal banking authorities.

12 C.F.R. § 28.101. (1980).

In his discussion of the public comments to these regulations, the Comptroller rejected the application of state reciprocity laws to the federal chartering of foreign bank branches and agencies. See 44 Fed.Reg. 65382 (1979).

Appellants contend that the Comptroller's interpretation of section 5, as reflected in the above quoted provisions, violates section 5 in two ways. First, the Comptroller's interpretation enables him to license a foreign bank's federal interstate office in a receiving state that does not expressly permit that particular foreign bank to establish a state-chartered interstate office. Second, even if the receiving state permitted a particular foreign bank to establish an interstate office, the Comptroller's interpretation does not require that the bank operations of the federal interstate office be "expressly permitted" by the receiving state. ... Appellants complain that the Comptroller has approved two applications by Australian banks to establish an interstate federal branch in Illinois in violation of Illinois' banking reciprocity law. . . . See Ill. Rev. State. ch. 17 § 2710 (1981). Appellants also complain that the Comptroller has approved an application by a British bank to establish an interstate federal branch in Washington State without requiring that branch to comply with lending restrictions and other operational limitations imposed on a foreign bank's branches by Washington law. . . . See Wash. Rev. Code § 30.42.1010 (repealed 1982); *see also* Wash. Rev. Code § 30.42.105 (Supp. 1982) (foreign bank branches: Power to make loans and to guarantee obligations); *id.* § 30.42.155 (foreign bank branches: Powers and activities).

The Comptroller contends that a state has essentially the same power to veto the entry of a federal interstate office under section 5(a) as it has to veto the entry of a federal

---

11. An Edge Act corporation can "receive only such deposits within the United States as may be incidental to or for the purpose of carrying out transactions in foreign countries or dependencies or insular possessions of the United States. . . ." 12 U.S.C. § 615(a) (Supp. V 1981). *See also* 12 C.F.R. § 211.4 (1983).

home state office under section 4(a).[12] Thus, the Comptroller contends that he can license a foreign bank's interstate branch unless the receiving state permits *no* foreign bank to operate a state-chartered branch. Similarly, he can license a foreign bank's interstate federal agency unless the receiving state permits *no* foreign bank to operate a state-chartered agency. . . .

The District Court upheld the Comptroller's regulations. It said:

> Notwithstanding plaintiffs' suggestion that the difference between the language in sections 5(a)(1) and (3) and that in section 5(a)(2) is only semantic, the Court cannot ignore as explicit a distinction as that which the draftsmen drew here. A federal branch or agency will not be allowed unless "its operation is expressly permitted by the State in which it is to be operated;" a State branch will not be permitted unless "it is approved by the bank regulatory authority of the State in which such branch is to be operated." *See* Pub.L. No. 95-369 § 5(a), 92 State. 613. In light of the system for dual entry into the United States market, through either State chartering or the federal provisions of section 4(a) of the Act, the conclusion that Congress intended not to subject federal interstate offices to the particular requirements of State law is inescapable. As the 1978 Senate Report observed, section 5(a) "affirms in Federal law the right of the States to attract foreign banks and foreign investment by allowing foreign bank branches and agencies to be established in any State where permissible. . . . The section leaves each State free to decide whether and to what extent it wishes to permit foreign banks [. . .]." 1978 Senate Report at 10-12. The States were then left free by section 5(a) to allow agencies, branches, both agencies and branches, or neither. And nothing in the Comptroller's regulations would deny them that power: States may veto any foreign bank entry into their territories and may limit operations to branch or agency activities. Section 5(a), and the Comptroller's regulations, only leave federal authorities free to grant charters in those States where the type of operation the foreign applicant seeks is not itself prohibited.

. . . (unbracketed ellipsis in original).

B.

We agree with the District Court's conclusion on this issue. After closely reviewing the language and legislative history of section 5(a) in the light of appellant's arguments, we cannot say that there are "compelling indications" that the Comptroller's interpretation of section 5(a) is wrong.[14] *See Red Lion Broadcasting Co. v. FCC*, 395 U.S. 367, 381 (1969). Thus, we are obliged to defer to the Comptroller's interpretation of the IBA because "the interpretation of an agency charged with the administration of a statute is entitled to substantial deference." *Blum v. Bacon*, 457 U.S. 132, 141 (1982). . . .

Section 5(a) provides in relevant part that "no foreign bank may . . . establish and operate a Federal branch [or agency] outside of its home State unless (A) its operation is expressly permitted by the State in which it is to be operated. . . ." 12 U.S.C. § 3103(a)(1), (3) (Supp. V 1981). The dispute in interpreting this section focuses on the words "its opera-

---

12. In the Comptroller's view, section 5(a) expands the states' section 4(a) veto power only in so far as section 5(a) prohibits him from licensing an interstate branch or agency if the receiving state's law is silent as to whether foreign banks in general could establish a state chartered branch or agency. . . .

14. We also reject applicants' argument grounded on similarities between the Douglas Amendment . . . and the IBA's section 5. We are not willing to reject the Comptroller's view of section 5 based solely on comparisons to an unrelated, though similarly worded statute when the Comptroller has chosen a course that is consistent with the language and legislative history of section 5(a).

tion." The appellants conclude that "its operation" refers to the operation of a particular federal interstate office. Thus, in appellants' view, section 5(a) would prohibit the Comptroller from licensing a federal interstate office if, due to limitations on banking operations or due to banking reciprocity requirements, the receiving state did not expressly permit the "operation" of that federal interstate office. On the other hand, the Comptroller concludes that "its operation" refers only to the interstate office's operation as a branch or as an agency. The Comptroller says that section 5(a) prohibits him from licensing an interstate branch (or agency) unless the receiving state expressly permits foreign banks to operate branches (or agencies). We believe that the language of section 5(a) reasonably supports either party's interpretation of the words "its operation." In addition, unlike the District Court, we do not believe that the precise difference between "expressly permitted" in sections 5(a)(1)(A) and 5(a)(3) and "approved" in sections 5(a)(2)(A) and 5(a)(4) is evident in the language of the statute.

Faced with two arguably reasonable interpretations of one statutory provision, we turn to the legislative history for guidance. Unfortunately, the relevant legislative history does not favor one interpretation over the other. . . .

In short, we do not discern from the language or legislative history of section 5(a) any basis for saying that the Comptroller's interpretation is contrary to law.[18] In so doing, we bear in mind that our task is not to interpret the statute as we think best but rather to determine whether the Comptroller's interpretation was "'sufficiently reasonable' to be accepted by a reviewing court." *FEC v. Democratic Senatorial Campaign Committee*, 454 U.S. 27, 39 (1981). "To satisfy this standard it is not necessary for a court to find that the agency's construction was the only reasonable one or even the reading the court would have reached if the question initially had arisen in a judicial proceeding." *Id.* . . . We hold, therefore, that the Comptroller can license a foreign bank's federal interstate branch in a receiving state if that state permits foreign banks to establish state-chartered interstate branches. Likewise, he can license a foreign bank's federal interstate agency in a receiving state if that state permits foreign banks to establish state-chartered interstate agencies. We also agree with the Comptroller that section 5(a) does not require federal interstate offices to comply with limitations on bank operations imposed by the receiving state.

IV.

We now turn to the question whether a federal agency of a foreign bank can accept deposits from a person who is neither a citizen nor a resident of the United States. The Comptroller promulgated a regulation which stated that a federal agency could not accept deposits from citizens or residents of the United States. *See* 12 C.F.R. § 28.2(b) (1980).[19] However, in responding to public comments on this regulation, the Comptroller stated that "foreign-source deposits may be accepted by Federal agencies." 44 Fed.Reg. 65382 (1979).

---

18. It would be inappropriate to resolve this dispute over section 5(a) by reference to the IBA's general theme of national treatment because the Comptroller cannot license interstate branches for domestic national banks and, therefore, section 5(a)'s authorization of federal interstate offices for foreign banks has no domestic counterpart. [Since 1994, the Comptroller has the authority to license interstate branches for domestic national banks. *See infra* Note 6.7 (discussing 1994 legislation).]

19. 12 C.F.R. § 28.2(b) (1980) provides:

A "Federal agency" is an office or place of business, licensed by the Comptroller and operated by a foreign bank in any State of the United States, which can engage in the business of banking but cannot exercise fiduciary powers or accept deposits from citizens or residents of the United States. A Federal agency, may, however, maintain credit balances.

Appellants challenge this interpretation of the IBA.

### A.

Under the IBA, an "agency" is defined in section 1(b)(1) as:

> any office or any place of business of a foreign bank located in any State of the United States at which credit balances are maintained incidental to or arising out of the exercise of banking powers, checks are paid, or money is lent but at which deposits may not be accepted from citizens or residents of the United States...."[20]

12 U.S.C. § 3101(1) (Supp. V 1981). Section 1(b)(5), however, defines "Federal agency" as "an agency of a foreign bank established and operating under section [4] of this [Act]", *id.* § 3101(5) and section 4(d) states that "[n]otwithstanding any other provision of this section, a foreign bank shall not receive deposits ... at any Federal agency." *Id.* § 3102(d).

Appellants contend that regulation 28.2(b) violates section 4(d) of the IBA because, as indicated by the Comptroller's response to the applicable public comments, regulation 28.2(b) allows a federal agency to accept deposits. They argue that section 1(b)(1) is only a general definition of "agency" and that section 1(b)(5) subjects a *federal* agency to the additional limitations of section 4(d). . . .

The Comptroller says that the validity of regulation 28.2(b) must be decided in the light of all the IBA provisions that are relevant to federal agency depository powers; section 4(d), he says, should not be considered in isolation. Following this approach, the Comptroller asserts that the "key distinction" between "branches" in section 1(b)(3) and "agencies" in section 1(b)(1) is that branches can accept any deposits and agencies cannot accept deposits from United States citizens or residents. In the Comptroller's view, this distinction applies throughout the IBA and should be effected in interpreting section 4(d). . . . *See* 44 Fed.Reg. 65382 (1979). The Comptroller next observes that section 4(b), 12 U.S.C. § 3102 (b) (Supp. V 1981), grants to a foreign bank's federal branches and agencies the same rights and privileges as a national bank doing business at the same location. In the Comptroller's view, Congress included the section 4(d) limitations on a federal agency's deposit taking power to make clear that section 4(b) did not empower federal agencies to receive domestic deposits. In particular, he notes that section 4(d) begins "Notwithstanding any other provision of this section. . . ." (i.e., section 4 and not the entire Act), and concludes from this language that section 4(d) was not intended to limit section 1(b)(1).. . . Thus, the Comptroller would have us read section 4(d)'s prohibition against federal agencies accepting "deposits" as a prohibition against federal agencies accepting "domestic-source deposits." Finally, the Comptroller emphasizes that as the official charged with administration of the federal branch and agency provisions of the IBA, his interpretation of the IBA is entitled to great deference by the courts.

The Comptroller contends that the legislative history of the IBA supports his interpretation of sections 1 and 4. . . . The Comptroller also argues that the policies and objectives of the IBA support his conclusion. He says that denying federal agencies the power to

---

20. 12 C.F.R. § 28.2(a) (1980) provides:

> "Credit balances", as distinct from deposits, consist of funds received at a Federal agency incidental to or arising out of the exercise of banking powers that are not intended to be deposits and that do not remain in the receiving institution after the transaction(s) to which they relate is completed.

This definition is not in dispute in this case.

accept foreign source deposits would diminish the intended parity of treatment between foreign and domestic banks, would eliminate a benefit intended to offset the detriment to foreign banks of other IBA provisions, and would curtail the influx of foreign funds into this country. . . .

The District Court upheld the Comptroller's regulation. It found:

> Given the ambiguity of the statute and the confused and scant legislative history, the Comptroller's view of section 4(d) seems not unreasonable. Section 4(b), it should be noted, flatly granted federal agencies and branches of foreign banks "the same rights and privileges as a national bank" in the home State, with some exceptions. It is clear that the Act's sponsors did not intend to permit acceptance of domestic deposits by federal agencies as well as by federal branches. It may well be that the only function of the controverted language of section 4(d) was thus to withdraw whatever authority the Comptroller might appear to have gained under section 4(b) to authorize acceptance of domestic deposits at federal agencies. Such a view is supported by the first words of section 4(d), which establish that any section 4(d) has effect "[n]otwithstanding any other provision of this section [i.e., section 4]." If plaintiffs were correct in their view, then careful drafting of section 4(d) would have extended the "notwithstanding" preface in section 4(d) not just to section 4 itself but to the whole Act, to avoid the confusion created if the definition in section 1(b)(1) were read with section 4(d). The Court therefore concludes that the Comptroller properly read sections 1(b)(1) and 4(d) together when he promulgated regulations that permit federal agencies to accept foreign-source deposits. 12 C.F.R. § 28.2(b) (1981). .
> . .
> Moreover, absent "compelling indications" that the Comptroller's interpretation is wrong, the Court is obliged not to overturn it. . . . And the Court cannot say, based upon the terms of sections 1(b)(1) and 1(b)(5) and 4(d), and the legislative history, that the statute specifically precludes the Comptroller's interpretation or that there is no basis in the legislative history for what he has done. . . . (citations omitted).

### B.

We believe the District Court deferred to the Comptroller when no deference was due.[23] The language of section 4(d) is not ambiguous. In section 1(b)(1) Congress provided that no agency of a foreign bank, whether operating under a federal or state charter, could accept deposits from citizens or residents of the United States. Section 1(b)(5), however, requires a federal agency be established under section 4, and in section 4(d), Congress prohibited federal agencies from accepting any deposits. The legislative history supports this plain meaning interpretation of the statute. . . . This clear statutory mandate cannot be overcome by generalized policy arguments or scattered citations to the legislative history of

---

23. In *Volkswagenwerk Aktiengesellschaft v. FMC*, 390 U.S. 261 (1968), the Supreme Court stated:

> The construction put on a statute by the agency charged with administering it is entitled to deference by the courts, and ordinarily that construction will be affirmed if it has a "reasonable basis in law." But the courts are the final authorities on issues of statutory construction and "are not obliged to stand aside and rubber-stamp their affirmance of administrative decisions that they deem inconsistent with a statutory mandate or that frustrate the congressional policy underlying a statute." *NRLB v. Brown*, 380 U.S. 278, 291 [(1965)].

*Id*. at 272 (citations omitted).

unenacted bills. We therefore reject the Comptroller's interpretation of sections 1 and 4.

Despite the Comptroller's assertion to the contrary, section 4(d)'s prohibition against federal agencies' accepting deposits was *not* necessary in order to prevent a possible inference that section 4(b) granted federal agencies the power to accept deposits on the same terms as national banks. By its own terms, Section 4(b) only applies "[e]xcept as otherwise specifically provided" in the IBA. If section 1(b)(1) controls agency deposit-taking powers, as the Comptroller maintains, the quoted proviso in section 4(b) would invoke section 1(b)(1) and would prevent section 4(b) from granting federal agencies deposit-taking powers equal to those of national banks. Thus, adoption of the Comptroller's interpretation would render section 4(d)'s prohibition against federal agencies' accepting deposits mere surplus language in the statute. But in construing a statute, we "are obliged to give effect, if possible, to every word Congress use." *Reiter v. Sonotone Corp.*, 442 U.S. 330, 339 (1979). . . . By following the plain meaning of sections 1 and 4 we fulfill our obligation to give effect to each relevant provision of the IBA.

**Notes and Comments 6.4.** Under the *Conover* analysis of the IBA, does the act result in "national treatment" or "better-than-national" treatment for foreign banks entering the U.S. market?

**6.5.** *Effect of the 1991 amendments to the IBA.* Federal policy with respect to branching by non-U.S. banks has become a controversial issue in recent years. The IBA as originally enacted was intended to implement a policy of "national treatment" for foreign banks seeking entry into the U.S. market.[4] However, following the BCCI scandal,[5] the IBA was amended in several significant respects by the Federal Deposit Insurance Corporation Improvement Act of 1991 (FDICIA).[6] *See* Note 2.3, *supra*, (discussing effects of FDICIA on U.S. regulation of international banking). Among the effects of FDICIA were the following.

FDICIA significantly altered the rules governing the establishment and operation of federal branches and agencies of foreign-based banks. Under FDICIA, the Comptroller is required, in considering any application for approval of an initial federal branch or agency, to include any condition imposed by the Fed as a condition for the approval of the application.[7] The Comptroller is also required to coordinate examinations of such branches and agencies with examinations conducted by the Fed, to the extent possible, to participate in any simultaneous examinations of U.S. operations of foreign banks requested by the Fed.[8] Furthermore, in considering any application to establish an additional federal branch or agency of a foreign-based bank, the Comptroller is required to provide the Fed with notice and opportunity for comment on the application.[9] The Fed's supervisory authority was substantially expanded (*see* Chapter 2, *supra*, at 34), and special examination fees were

---

4. *See* Notes 2.10-2.13, *supra* (discussing national treatment).

5. *See* R. K. BHALA, FOREIGN BANK REGULATION AFTER BCCI (1994) (discussing BCCI scandal and its effect on U.S. regulation of international banking). *See also* Note, *Putting the Super Back in the Supervision of International Banking, Post-BCCI*, 60 Fordham L. Rev. S467 (Survey Issue 1992) (discussing effects of FDICIA on U.S. regulation).

6. Pub. L. No. 102-242, 105 Stat. 2236 (December 19, 1991) (codified at scattered sections of 12 U.S.C.) [hereinafter FDICIA].

7. 12 U.S.C. § 3102(a)(2).

8. *Id.* §3102(b).

9. *Id.* §3102(h)(2).

imposed for examinations of U.S. based operations of non-U.S. banks.[10]

The FDICIA also restricted retail deposit-taking by foreign banks. To accept or maintain deposit accounts with balances of less than $100,000, foreign banks are required to establish one or more U.S. banking subsidiaries for that purpose, and to obtain federal deposit insurance for any such subsidiary.[11] However, if the foreign bank had a U.S. branch that was an insured branch prior to FDICIA, the branch was permitted to continue to accept or maintain retail deposits.[12]

The increased burdens placed upon U.S. operations of foreign banks by the FDICIA provoked criticism,[13] and exacerbated the uncertainty over whether U.S. banking regulation was sufficiently reciprocal to allow entry by U.S. banks into the European Union's Community-wide banking market.[14]

**6.6.** *Regulatory implementation of the FDICIA.* The Fed implemented its authority to supervise U.S. branches and agencies of foreign banking organizations in regulations published in 1996. In October 2001, the Fed revised these regulations, subpart B of Reg K, *id.* §§ 211.20-211.30. The revisions streamlined application procedures applicable to foreign banks that seek to expand operations in the United States, changed provisions regarding exemption of foreign banking organizations from the nonbanking prohibitions of section 4 of the Bank Holding Company Act, 12 U.S.C. § 1843, and implemented provisions of the Interstate Banking and Branching Efficiency Act of 1994 that affect foreign banks.

**6.7.** Assume that the Central Bank of Nusquam (CBN) has failed to inform the U.S. authorities that U.S. branch officials of NusBank have engaged in unauthorized transactions resulting in significant losses to NusBank. The CBN has also failed to require NusBank to account for these losses in its current financial statements. Under 12 C.F.R. §§ 211.25, 211.30, reprinted *supra* at pages 210 and 214 respectively, what action could or should the Fed take?

**6.8.** *Effect of IBBEA on interstate operations of non-U.S. banks.* On September 29, 1994, the President signed the Riegle-Neal Interstate Banking and Branching Efficiency Act of 1994 (IBBEA)[15] into law. The provisions of the IBBEA permit geographic expansion by banks without regard to artificial barriers to interstate expansion heretofore imposed by the Douglas Amendment[16] to the Bank Holding Company Act (BHCA)[17] and the branching provisions of state law and the National Bank Act (NBA).[18] IBBEA also has a significant

---

10. *Id.* § 3105(c)(1)(D).

11. *Id.* § 3104(d)(1). Thus, for any foreign-based bank interested in the U.S. retail deposit market, this provision requires the bank's U.S. operations to be conducted through a subsidiary. IBBEA amended this provision to indicate that insured banks in U.S. territories are not subject to the retail deposit-taking rule. IBBEA, § 107(d) (codified at 12 U.S.C. § 3104(d)(3)).

12. 12 U.S.C. § 3104(d)(2).

13. *See, e.g.,* Cynthia C. Lichtenstein, *U.S. Restructuring Legislation: Revising the International Banking Act of 1978, For the Worse?,* 60 FORDHAM L. REV. S37 (Annual Survey Issue 1992). *See also* Bhala, *supra* note 25.

14. *See* Note 5.3, *supra* (discussing recent developments in EU bank regulation).

15. Pub. Law No. 103-328, Sept. 29, 1994, 108 Stat. 2338 (1994) [hereinafter IBBEA].

16. 12 U.S.C. § 1842(d) (1988). On the Douglas Amendment, see 3 M. P. MALLOY, BANKING LAW AND REGULATION 8.23 - 8.24 (1994).

17. 12 U.S.C §§ 1841 *et seq.*

18. *See, e.g., id.* §36(c) (NBA provision limiting branching by national banks to branching permitted to state banks in same state). *See generally First Nat'l Bank of Logan v. Walker Bank & Trust Co.,* 385 U.S. 252 (1966) (construing §36(c)); *First Nat'l Bank in Plant City v. Dickinson,* 396

effect on U.S. branching of non-U.S. banks.

It is against the statutory background of the FDICIA that the IBBEA undertook to amend the IBA. Two objectives may be discerned in the amendments: dealing with the practical implications of the 1991 amendments to the IBA,[19] and readjusting the IBA in light of the changes in interstate banking and branching instituted by the IBBEA itself.[20]

The IBBEA amends the IBA rules governing interstate operations of foreign banks.[21] In general, it subjects the establishment of interstate operations of a federal branch or agency of a foreign bank to the same rules that would apply if the foreign bank were a national bank seeking to branch interstate.[22] Similarly, the IBBEA subjects the establishment of interstate operations of a state-licensed branch or agency of a foreign bank to the same rules that would apply if the foreign bank were a state bank seeking to branch interstate.[23] These rules are generally preemptive and exclusive.[24]

Operation of any interstate branch or agency of a foreign bank is subject to the same IBBEA rules governing domestic branches of national and state banks resulting from interstate merger transactions.[25] However, an additional, potentially controversial requirement may apply to foreign banks. The 1991 FDICIA required foreign banks entering the U.S. retail deposit market to operate through a separately chartered U.S. subsidiary, rather than a direct branch.[26] The IBBEA extends this requirement, under certain specified cir

---

U.S. 122 (1969) (meaning of "branch" for purposes of §36(c)).

19. *See, e.g.*, IBBEA, § 115 (codified at 12 U.S.C. § 3105 note) (moratorium on examination fees under § 3105(c)(1)(D)).

20. *See, e.g.*, IBBEA, § 104(a) (codified at 12 U.S.C. § 3103(a)(1)) (subjecting U.S. interstate branching and agency operations of foreign banks to rules of 12 U.S.C. §§ 36(g), 1831u).

21. For a discussion of the pre-IBBEA rules under IBA for interstate operations of foreign banks, see *Conference of State Bank Supervisors, supra*.

22. IBBEA, § 104(a) (codified at 12 U.S.C. § 3103(a) (1)). On the criteria for determining approval of interstate operations of a foreign bank's federal branch or agency, see 12 U.S.C. § 3103(a)(3)(A)-(C).

23. 12 U.S.C. § 3103(a)(2). On the criteria for determining approval of interstate operations of a foreign bank's state branch or agency, see 12 U.S.C. § 3103(a)(3)(A)-(C).

24. *See* 12 U.S.C. § 3103(a)(5), which provides:

> Except as provided in this section, a foreign bank may not, directly or indirectly, acquire, establish, or operate a branch or agency in any State other than the home State of such bank.

*But see id.* § 3103(a)(7)(A)-(B) (providing additional authority for interstate operations of foreign banks where a host state expressly permits the operations, and the branch deposit operations are limited to international- or foreign-related deposits). On the definition of "home state" for these purposes, see *id.* § 3103(a)(9). On the rules for determining the home state of a foreign bank for purposes of the interstate branch and agency rules of the IBBEA, see *id.* § 3103(c)(1)-(2).

25. *Id.* § 3103(a)(4). In addition, a U.S. branch or agency of a foreign bank is not permitted to manage, through a managed or controlled office located outside the United States, any type of activity not permitted to be managed by a domestic bank through a branch or subsidiary located outside the United States. 12 U.S.C. § 3105(k)(1). This prohibition is effective 180 days after the enactment of IBBEA. IBBEA, § 107(e)(2) (codified at 12 U.S.C. § 3105 Note).

26. 12 U.S.C. § 3103(a)(6). However, the IBBEA clarifies the impact of the new rules in the following respects. A foreign bank that has a U.S. bank subsidiary is still eligible to establish a direct federal or state branch or agency, in accordance with the IBBEA

cumstances, to interstate operations of any foreign bank. If the Fed or the Comptroller finds that, in light of differing regulatory or accounting standards in a foreign bank's home country, adherence by the bank to applicable U.S. capital requirements could only be verified if the foreign bank's U.S. banking activities were carried out in a separate U.S. subsidiary, the agencies[27] have the authority to require that the foreign bank (or the company controlling the foreign bank) establish a U.S. subsidiary to carry out the interstate operations.[28] This provision potentially moves the United States further away from the original policy of national treatment for foreign bank operations in the United States that underlies the IBA.[29] Since most members of the European Union participate in the BIS capital adequacy guidelines, the degree of potential confrontation with our European allies in this regard may be minimized. In addition, IBBEA grandfathers foreign bank operations in place on the day before the enactment of the IBBEA.[30] Nevertheless, depending upon the U.S. agency practice that emerges under this provision, the United States banking market may become significantly less transparent to foreign banks.

**6.9.** *Community credit needs and foreign bank operations.* IBBEA imposes a continuing requirement on foreign banks with U.S. operations to meet community credit needs, after their initial entry by acquisition in the interstate market.[31] If a foreign bank acquires a U.S. bank or branch in a state in which the foreign bank does not maintain a branch, and the bank is a "regulated financial institution" under the Community Reinvestment Act (CRA),[32] the CRA continues to apply to each branch of the foreign bank that results from the acquisition.[33]

**6.10.** Would there be any particular advantage for Gemütlichbank if it established a network of "federal branches"? Would there be any particular advantage to establishing a banking Edge, possibly with subsidiaries?

---

rules. *Id.* § 3103(d)(1). Similarly, a U.S. bank that is a subsidiary of a foreign bank with a direct federal or state branch or agency is itself still eligible to establish a federal or state branch or agency, in accordance with the IBBEA rules. *Id.* § 3103(d)(2).

27. If the foreign bank intended to carry out interstate branching or agency activities under a federal license, both the Fed and the Comptroller would have the authority to make the finding. *Id.* § 3103(a)(6). If the foreign bank intended to carry out interstate branching or agency activities under a state license, the Fed alone would have the authority to make the finding. *Id.*

28. *Id.*

29. This movement away from the policy of national treatment is underscored by the IBBEA provisions requiring the agencies to pursue the objective of

> affording equal competitive opportunities to foreign and United States banking organizations in their United States operations [and] ensur[ing] that foreign banking organizations do not receive an unfair competitive advantage over United States banking organizations.

*Id.* § 3104(a) (directive to Comptroller and FDIC under IBA as amended by IBBEA). *See also* IBBEA, §107(b) (codified at 12 U.S.C. § 3104 Note) (requiring review of regulations by federal banking agencies and revision of regulations under § 3104 to equalize competitive opportunities for U.S. and foreign banks). The IBBEA also clarifies that domestic consumer protection laws apply to foreign banks with U.S. operations. 12 U.S.C. § 3106a(b)(1)(A), (2)(A).

30. IBBEA, § 104(b) (codified at 12 U.S.C. § 3103(b)).

31. 12 U.S.C. § 3103(a)(8).

32. *See id.* § 2902.

33. *Id.* § 3103(a)(8)(A). This requirement does not apply to any resulting branch that is limited to international- or foreign-related deposits. *Id.* § 3103(a)(8) (B).

**6.11.** If Gemütlichbank decides to enter the United States through (a) acquisition of an existing state-chartered or national bank in the United States; or, (b) establishment of a federal branch, to what extent would it be subject to regulation by the Federal Reserve as a bank holding company? Review the provisions of 12 U.S.C. §§ 1841-1843, 3103, 3106.

**6.12. a.** *Effect of the 1990 BIS Concordat Supplement.* Reread the provisions of the 1990 Supplement to the 1983 Basle Concordat, dealing with information flows between national bank supervisors, Chapter 3, § 2, *supra.* To what extent would these provisions affect Gemütlichbank's application, discussed in Note 6.2, *supra?*

**b.** *Effect of BIS Minimum Standards.* Reread the provisions of the 1992 BIS Minimum Standards for the Supervision of International Banking Groups, Chapter 3, § 2, *supra.* To what extent would they make a difference to the decision by a U.S. regulator on whether or not to allow entry into the U.S. market to a non-U.S. banking enterprise like Gemütlichbank?

# Chapter 7

# International Lending

## 1. Introduction

**Notes and Comments 7.1.** Among other things, one essential, traditional role of banking is as a source of funding, *e.g.*, as a commercial lender. Within the international banking context, then, one may expect this role also to be central. Whether international or domestic, certain considerations–like the creditworthiness of the borrower and the adequacy of the spread between cost of funds and rate of return–will be key considerations in the bank's decision to lend. Are there any considerations in the lending decision that are peculiar to *international* lending?

Lending is lending. To some extent, therefore, the considerations that go into the lending decision are the same, whether one is operating in the domestic or international market. However, certain considerations may be peculiar to international banking, or they may have a relatively greater emphasis in the international banking context. Some important features of international lending may be identified as follows.[1] International lending usually involves "cross-national" or transborder risk, a risk to the success of the transaction related not necessarily to the creditworthiness of the borrower, but to the social, political, and economic environment in which the borrower or its project is placed. Components of transborder risk include (*i*) "country risk," taken in its broadest sense to include the complex of socio-political factors that affect success; (*ii*) "regulatory control," the effect of differing regulatory features in the country of the borrower; and, (*iii*) "legal jurisdiction," the effect of performing and enforcing the lending agreement in a different legal jurisdiction (*i.e.*, the borrower's) or, if the agreement is to be enforced in the lender's home jurisdiction, the indirect effect that the law of the borrower's jurisdiction may have on enforcement. Another important, and fairly obvious feature is exchange rate risk and other attendant problems connected with, for example, foreign currency lending.

## 2. Regulatory Considerations

**Notes and Comments 7.2.** In formulating regulatory policy with respect to international lending, what supervisory concerns should be accounted for? Consider the next reading.

---

1. *See, e.g.*, Haley & Seligman, *The Development of International Banking by the United States, in* W. H. BAUGHN & D. R. MANDICH, THE INTERNATIONAL BANKING HANDBOOK 35 (Dow Jones Irwin, 1983).

# Comptroller's Handbook for National Bank Examiners
§ 805.1

  . . . The soundness of ["Loan Portfolio Management"] policy depends on certain components which are not necessarily applicable to every bank.

  Geographic Limits–The bank should delineate those countries or geographical areas where it can lend profitably in accordance with its objectives and in consideration of country risks. International lending officers must know the specific country limitations established by the board of directors and the bank should have a monitoring system to assure adherence to those limits. The limits established will depend on each bank's available financial resources, the qualifications and skills of its staff, the extent of its lending activities and further growth potential.

  Distribution by Category–Limitations based on aggregate percentages of total international loans in real estate, consumer, ship financing or other categories are common. However, although loan distribution policy may differ between banks, international loans are generally granted in the following categories:

   • Import and export financing.
   • Loans to corporations and/or their overseas branches, subsidiaries or affiliates with a parent guarantee or other form of support.
   • Loans granted to foreign local borrowers, including foreign entities of United States firms that borrow without any form of support from the parent corporation.
   • Loans (and placements) to foreign banks or to overseas branches of United States banks.
   • Loans to foreign governments or to foreign governmental entities.

The categories which the bank's international division should engage in, and the nature of any limitations, will depend on the particular bank and its customers. However, deviations from policy limitations approved by the board of directors or its designated committee should be allowed to meet the changing requirements of the bank's customers. During times of heavy loan demand in one category, an inflexible loan distribution policy could cause that category be slighted in favor of another.

  Types of Loans–The lending policy should state the types of international loans which the bank can make and should set forth guidelines to follow in granting specific loans. The decision about the types of loans to be granted should be based on a consideration of the expertise of the lending officers, the deposit structure of the bank and the anticipated credit needs of the customer. Sophisticated credits or loans requiring more than normal policing should be avoided unless or until the bank obtains the necessary personnel to properly administer those advances. Types of credits which have resulted in an abnormal loss to the bank's international division should be controlled or avoided within the framework of stated policy. Syndicate participation and other types of term loans should be limited to a given percentage of the bank's stable funds.

  Maximum Maturities–International loans should be granted with realistic repayment plans. Maturity scheduling should be related to the anticipated source of repayment, the purpose of the loan, the useful life of the collateral and the degree of country risk. For term loans, a lending policy should state the maximum number of months over which loans may be amortized. Specific procedures should be developed for situations requiring balloon payments and modifications to the original terms of a loan. If the bank requires a cleanup (out-of-debt) period for lines of credit, that period should be explicitly stated.

Loan Pricing–Rates of interest, fees, commissions and discounts on various loan types established by the loan policy must be sufficient to cover the costs of funds loaned, of servicing the loan, including general overhead, and of probable losses while providing for a reasonable margin of profit. Periodic review allows the rates to be adjusted to reflect changes in costs or competitive factors and should include an examination of the rules of foreign regulatory authorities. . . .

Foreign Exchange Risks–. . . Lending policy should include controls that minimize those risks for loan portfolios in one currency funded by borrowings in another. Such activities must be identified and should be limited by the bank if:

> • A particular foreign government is expected to impose stringent exchange controls.
> • The currencies involved are or will be subject to wide exchange rate fluctuations.
> • Political, social and economic developments are likely to intensify exchange risks.

Multicurrency credit commitments permit borrowers to select from a specific list of currencies the one they prefer to use in each rollover period. The listed currencies, however, may be unavailable to available only at a high cost. The bank should protect itself by stating in the loan agreement that its requirement to provide any of the currencies listed is subject to availability at the time requested by the borrower.

Documentation and Collateral–Trade financing often represents a significant amount of an international division's or branch's lending activity. In such financing, the bank deals only in documents, while its customer is responsible for the merchandise under the terms of the sales contract. The bank's control of documents, especially title documents, is crucial. . . .

There are significant differences between United States loan agreements and foreign ones. Nevertheless, the bank must insure that its loan agreements with borrowers protect it adequately. . . .

The bank must establish policies for taking overseas collateral as security for a loan to assure that local required procedures are met. For example, in many countries, liens on fixed assets must be registered with the local government depending on the type of asset. . . . For those and other reasons, the bank must retain local lawyers who are thoroughly familiar with that country's laws, regulations and practices, and will check loan agreements, guarantees, debt instruments, drafts, corporate resolutions and other loan documentation.

Financial Information–Current and complete financial information is necessary at the inception and throughout the term of an international loan. The lending policy should specifically define financial statement requirements for businesses, foreign banks, foreign governments, other foreign public sector entities and individuals at various borrowing levels and should include criteria for requirement of audited, non-audited, fiscal, interim, operating, cash flow and other statements. . . .

The reliability of financial statements and information differs greatly among countries. In some countries, accounting standards and traditions are lax, and audited statements are virtually unknown. . . .

Foreign customers' financial statements may be prepared in either U.S. dollar equivalents or in the borrower's local currency. Most banks analyze the latter statements, particularly if that currency is unstable and figures stated in U.S. dollar equivalents would distort the conversion rates used at various times. Sometimes, the bank may need to reconstruct a borrower's financial statement in U.S. dollar equivalents to reflect the borrower's financial strength and weaknesses more accurately.

Since the financial information is not always reliable, the bank's policies should enable it to determine, by other means, the capacity, integrity, experience and reputation of the foreign borrower.

Extensions of credit to foreign banks constitute an important segment of an international division's foreign loans and their financial statements should be reviewed and analyzed. . . .

The quality of management is the key to the analysis of foreign banks and is best determined by frequent, detailed visits by officers of the lending bank. Credit checks from other lenders should be required with periodic updates. Credit reports are not available in all countries and even when provided are often incomplete or vague. Consequently, there is no substitute for detailed, firsthand information obtained from visits to overseas banks.

Sufficiently current balance of payments, exchange control, and economic, political and social information should be on file to enable a bank to properly and accurately evaluate the extent of country risk. The lack of such information is as serious a weakness as the lack of financial information on an individual borrower.

Limits and Guidelines for Purchasing Loans–Purchasing loans from a dealer or correspondent bank is common in banks lacking international customers or new business opportunities. However, such purchases may restrict the bank to low-profit loans, at narrow spreads, over a medium- to long-term period. Buying loans seldom builds relationships with borrowers as the relationship stays with the bank originating the loan. Therefore, the lending policy should limit the amount of paper purchases from any one outside source and state an aggregate limit on all such loans. The policy should also define the extent of contingent liability and the manner in which the loan will be handled and serviced.

Limitation on Aggregate Outstanding Loans–Limitations on the total amount of loans outstanding relative to other balance sheet accounts should be established for the bank with limits (or sub-limits) applicable to international loans clearly defined. Controls over the international loan portfolio are usually expressed relative to deposits, capital structure or total assets.

Concentrations of Credit–The same types of concentrations of credit found in a domestic loan portfolio may exist in the international portfolio. However, in international banking, a further concentration involves loans to a foreign government, its agencies, and majority-owned or controlled entities. Loans to specific private businesses may be included in those concentrations if an inter-relationship exists in the form of guarantees, moral commitments, significant subsidies or other factors indicating dependence on the government. The bank's directorate should evaluate the risk(s) involved in various concentrations and determine those which should be avoided or limited. The lending policy should also require that all concentrations in the international division be reviewed and reported on a frequent basis. . . .

Loan Authority–The lending policy should establish written limits for all international lending officers. Lending limits also may be established for group authority, allowing a combination of officers or a committee to approve larger loans than the members would be permitted to approve individually. The reporting procedures and the frequency of committee meetings should be defined. If the bank operates foreign branches, head-office-delegated lending authority should be clearly defined and understood by overseas lending officers.

Delinquencies and Charge-offs–The lending policy should define delinquent obligations of all types and should dictate the appropriate reports to be submitted to the board and senior management. The management of banks with overseas branches must clearly understand which delinquencies should be reported to the head office. The reports should include sufficient detail to allow for the determination of the risk factor, loss potential and alternative courses of action. The policy should require a follow-up notice procedure which is systematic and progressively stronger. Guidelines should be established to ensure that all accounts are presented to and reviewed by senior management or the directorate for charge-off at a stated period of delinquency.

Other–The lending policy should be supplemented with other written guidelines for specific departments concerned with credit extensions, *e.g.*, letters of credit, bankers' acceptances and discounted trade bills. Written policies and procedures approved and enforced in those departments should be referenced in the general lending policy of the bank.

Before a bank grants international credit, its objectives, policies and practices must be clearly established. The bank must consider its overall size, financial resources, the nature of its customers, it geographic location and the qualifications and skills of its staff. Before an examiner examines a loan department, policies and practices should be reviewed to determine if they are clearly defined and adequate to properly supervise the portfolio. If written guidelines do not exist, there is a major deficiency in the lending area and the board of directors is not properly discharging its duties and responsibilities. If no exception is taken to the objectives, policies and practices, the various international loan areas should be examined to ensure compliance. That determination is one of the prime examination objectives in each credit section of the international division.

Failure of the directors to establish a sound international lending policy, of the management to establish adequate written procedures, and of both to monitor and administer the international lending function within established guidelines has resulted in substantial problems for many banks.

**Notes and Comments 7.3.** *Effect of FDICIA on lending by U.S. branches and agencies of foreign-based banks.* The Federal Deposit Insurance Corporation Improvement Act of 1991 (FDICIA)[2] imposes on state-licensed branches and agencies the same limits on lending to a single borrower that apply to federally-licensed branches and agencies. *See* Note 2.3, *supra* (discussing effects of FDICIA).

**7.4.** *Regulatory implementation of FDICIA.* Both the Fed and the FDIC promulgated regulations implementing the FDICIA's limitations on activities of state-licensed branches and agencies of non-U.S. banks; these have since been revised by the two agencies. Consider 12 C.F.R. § 211.29, reproduced *supra* at page 213, and the following excerpt from the FDIC's regulations with a view to answering the questions in Note 7.5, *infra*.

## Federal Deposit Insurance Corporation
### 12 C.F.R. Part 347  International Banking

§ 347.213 FDIC approval to conduct activities not permissible for federal branches.

(a) Scope. A foreign bank operating an insured state branch which desires to engage in or continue to engage in any type of activity that is not permissible for a federal branch, pursuant to the National Bank Act (12 U.S.C. 21 et seq.) or any other federal statute, regulation, official bulletin or circular, written order or interpretation, or decision of a court of competent jurisdiction (each an impermissible activity), shall file a written application for

---

2. Pub. L. No. 102-242, 105 Stat. 2236 (December 19, 1991) (codified at scattered sections of 12 U.S.C.)

permission to conduct such activity with the FDIC.

(b) Exceptions. A foreign bank operating an insured state branch which would otherwise be required to submit an application pursuant to paragraph (a) of this section will not be required to submit such an application if the activity it desires to engage in or continue to engage in has been determined by the FDIC not to present a significant risk to the affected deposit insurance fund. . . .

(c) Agency activities. A foreign bank operating an insured state branch which would otherwise be required to submit an application pursuant to paragraph (a) of this section will not be required to submit such an application if it desires to engage in or continue to engage in an activity conducted as agent which would be a permissible agency activity for a state-chartered bank located in the state which the state-licensed insured branch of the foreign bank is located and is also permissible for a state-licensed branch of a foreign bank located in that state; provided, however, that the agency activity must be permissible pursuant to any other applicable federal law or regulation.

(d) Conditions of approval. Approval of such an application may be conditioned on the applicant's agreement to conduct the activity subject to specific limitations, such as but not limited to the pledging of assets . . . and/or the maintenance of eligible assets. . . . In the case of an application to initially engage in an activity, as opposed to an application to continue to conduct an activity, the insured branch shall not commence the activity until it has been approved in writing by the FDIC pursuant to this part and the Board of Governors of the Federal Reserve System (Board of Governors), and any and all conditions imposed in such approvals have been satisfied.

(e) Divestiture or cessation. (1) If an application for permission to continue to conduct an activity is not approved by the FDIC or the Board of Governors, the applicant shall submit a plan of divestiture or cessation of the activity to the appropriate regional director.

(2) A foreign bank operating an insured state branch which elects not to apply to the FDIC for permission to continue to conduct an activity which is rendered impermissible by any change in statute, regulation, official bulletin or circular, written order or interpretation, or decision of a court of competent jurisdiction shall submit a plan of divestiture or cessation to the appropriate regional director.

(3) Divestitures or cessations shall be completed within one year from the date of the disapproval, or within such shorter period of time as the FDIC shall direct.

**Notes and Comments 7.5.** Assume that Gemütlichbank has a state-licensed branch in East Carolina. East Carolina case law indicates that, under the East Carolina Banking Code, state-chartered banks and state-licensed branches of foreign banks are permitted to issue guarantees of third-party obligations. This is an activity in which, at least in principle, national banks may not engage. Gemütlichbank wants to know whether its state branch is permitted to engage in this activity. What procedural and substantive requirements must it satisfy?

# 3. Enforcement of Loan Agreements

**Notes and Comments 7.6.** First Credulity Bank of Philadelphia, a client of your firm, has asked you to review a draft of an agreement for a consortium loan to a foreign borrower, in which First Credulity will be one of ten lending banks. Based on the following excerpts, what sort of contract provisions would you hope to find in the draft? What recommendations would you make if any such provisions were or were not present?

## Libra Bank Ltd. v. Banco Nacional de Costa Rica
### 570 F.Supp. 870 (S.D.N.Y. 1983)

Motley, Chief Judge.

Plaintiffs bring this action to recover their share of principal amounts, plus interest, of a $40 million loan made by sixteen banks, including seven of the plaintiffs herein, to defendant Banco Nacional de Costa Rica (Banco Nacional). Plaintiffs have moved for summary judgment . . . seeking an order requiring Banco Nacional to repay the principal amounts, plus interest, allegedly due under the promissory notes issued in connection with the loan. As its sole defense, Banco Nacional asserts that it is barred from repayment by an act of the Costa Rican government and that this court is barred from entering the requested order by the act of state doctrine.[a] Also before the court is plaintiff's motion for an order compelling Banco Nacional to return and deposit $2.5 million with the Clerk of the Court as partial security for any judgment entered against Banco Nacional. Plaintiffs claim that this order is warranted because defendant allegedly absconded with such funds in an effort to avoid an order of attachment. For the reasons set forth below, plaintiffs' motion for summary judgment is granted but the motion to compel defendant to return its assets is denied.

Background

In or about December, 1980, Libra Bank Limited (Libra Bank), a banking corporation organized under the laws of the United Kingdom with a representative office in New York City, acted as an agent for sixteen banks[1] in the making of a $40 million loan to Banco Nacional, a banking concern wholly owned by the Costa Rican government, in order to provide pre-export and export financing of sugar and sugar products from Costa Rica. In connection with this loan, Banco Nacional entered into a loan agreement with plaintiffs. The agreement provided, *inter alia*, that the loan would be repaid in four successive installments to occur on July 30, August 30, September 30 and October 30, 1981.

After the loan agreement was executed, Banco Nacional drew down the full $40 million loan proceeds by requesting Libra Bank to credit Banco Nacional's account at a bank in New York with such finds. Libra Bank subsequently honored that request pursuant to paragraph two of the loan agreement. On July 30, 1981, Banco Nacional paid Libra Bank the sum of $5 million plus interest in satisfaction of the first installment due under the loan agreement and the promissory notes executed thereon. Banco Nacional continued to pay interest until August 30, 1981. From that day forward, Banco Nacional has made no further payments.

---

a. On the act of state doctrine, barring U.S. courts from examining the validity of acts of a foreign state done in its own territory, see Chapter 8, § 4, *infra*.

1. Besides Libra Bank there are seven other plaintiff banks in this action. Libra International Bank, S.A. is a banking corporation organized under the laws of Panama with an office in Panama. Banco de la Provincia de Buenos Aires is a banking corporation organized under the laws of Argentina with an agency in New York. Banco Espirito Santo e Comercial de Lisboa is a banking corporation organized under the laws of Portugal with an office in London, England. Banco de Vizcaya, S.A. is a banking corporation organized under the laws of Spain with an office in London, England. Banque International a Luxembourg, S.A. is a banking corporation organized under the laws of the Grand Duchy of Luxembourg with a representative office in New York. Banque Rothschild is a banking corporation organized under the laws of France with an office in Paris, France. The National Bank of Washington is a national banking corporation.

According to Banco Nacional, it was prevented from honoring the loan agreement by a resolution adopted by the Central Bank of Costa Rica on August 27, 1981, three days before the second payment was due. The resolution was adopted in an effort to remedy Costa Rica's problems in servicing its external debts, *i.e.* debts to foreign creditors in foreign currency. According to Banco Nacional, Costa Rica's banking laws require all foreign exchange transactions to be authorized by the Central Bank of Costa Rica. The August 27th resolution adopted by the Central Bank provided that only repayments of external debts to multilateral international agencies would be authorized. Banco Nacional's requests for foreign currency in order to repay plaintiffs' loan was denied by the Central Bank. On November 24, 1981, the President and the Minister of Finance issued a decree providing that the Republic and all public sector entities, including Banco Nacional, could not pay principal or interest on external debt in foreign currency without the prior approval of the Central Bank in consultation with the Minister of Finance. The alleged effect of these decrees was to prevent Banco Nacional from repaying its loan to plaintiffs. . . .

On December 8, 1981, after levy had been made by the Sheriff [of New York County], defendant removed the action to this court. . . . Defendant . . . moved to dismiss for lack of in personam jurisdiction. . . . [T]his court granted the motion on the ground that Banco Nacional had not waived its immunity to pre-judgment attachment. . . .[a]

On April 12, 1982, the Second Circuit vacated this court's order noting, *inter alia*, that the authority relied on by the District Court, is "not controlling on this Court." *Libra Bank, Limited, et al. v. Banco Nacional de Costa Rica*, 676 F.2d 47, 50 (2d Cir. 1982). Thereafter, plaintiffs attempted to have the United States Marshal levy on the same banks upon which the New York Sheriff had levied as well as a number of other banks. Plaintiffs discovered, however, that Banco Nacional no longer maintained accounts at any of those banks and had no other accounts in any New York banks.

Plaintiffs then brought the instant motions for summary judgment and for an order requiring defendant to return its assets. . . .

[The court's discussion of Banco Nacional's arguments for summary judgment based upon the Act of State doctrine is excerpted in Chapter 8, § 4, *infra*.]

IV.

Having decided that the loan agreement of December 23, 1980 can be enforced, the court turns now to the remaining issues of contract interpretation and construction. The parties disagree as to the applicable interest rates for (i) past due interest and for (ii) penalty or default interest. The parties also disagree as to whether plaintiffs are entitled under the loan agreement to recover their attorneys' fees, disbursements, and expenses incurred in connection with the enforcement of the loan agreement. Moreover, assuming that plaintiffs are entitled to their attorneys' fees, disbursements, and expenses, defendant disputes the amount recoverable. . . .

A. The Applicable Rates of Interest

In order to provide a background for the disputes with respect to the applicable interest rates, the court believes that it would prove useful to set forth the schedules of repayment as well as other relevant definitions as provided by the contract:

> 1. Definitions:
> \*    \*    \*    \*    \*    \*
> "Interest Payment Date" means:
> (i) with respect to the First Interest Payment Date, 30 January 1981;

---

a. On claims of sovereign immunity, see Chapter 8, § 3, *infra*.

(ii) with respect to the second and third Interest Payment Dates, 30 April 1981 and 30 July 1981 respectively; and

(iii) with respect to the Interest Payment Dates thereafter, the relevant Repayment Dates.

"Interest Period" means successive periods for the calculation of interest. The first Interest Period shall commence on the Drawdown Date and end on the First Interest Payment Date, and the next Interest Period for each Repayment [Installment] shall commence immediately on the expiry of the First Interest Period and end on the relevant Repayment Dates.

 *  *  *  *  *  *

4. Repayment

The Loan will be repaid in four successive [installments] ("Repayment [Installments]") which will be payable respectively in the amounts and on the dates ("Repayment Dates") set forth below:

| Repayment Date | Amount of [Installment] |
|---|---|
| 30 July 1981 | US$ 5,000,000 |
| 30 August 1981 | US$10,000,000 |
| 30 September 1981 | US$10,000,000 |
| 30 October 1981 | US$15,000,000 |

Under this loan agreement, interest is paid at the end of each Interest Period. The first Interest Period began on the Drawdown Date of the loan and ended on the First Interest Payment Date, January 30, 1981. The second Interest Period began on the next day, January 31, 1981, and ended on April 30, 1981. The third Interest Period commenced on May 1, 1981, and ended on July 30, 1981, the last Interest Payment Date. The fourth Interest Period commenced on July 31, 1981, and ended on the next Repayment Date, August 30, 1981. The loan agreement also provides for the calculation of interest as follows:

6. Interest

(a) The Borrower will pay interest on the Loan calculated in respect of each Interest Period at whichever rate the Agent in its sole discretion shall determine to be the higher of:

(i) three quarters per cent per annum above the rate at which the Agent offers leading banks in the London Interbank Market dollar deposits comparable in amount and Interest Period to the relevant portion of the Loan at 11:00 a.m. (London time) two days prior to the first day of each such period or to the first day of each such period (LIBOR); or

(ii) the rate per annum equal to three-quarters per cent over the prime commercial rate (PRIME) of [t]he Chase Manhattan Bank (National Association) at its principal office in New York City prevailing three days prior to the first day of the relevant Interest Period.

Since the parties agree that Chase's prime commercial rate was higher at all relevant times than the London Interbank Offer Rate, the court shall refer only to Chase's Prime Rate in the examples that follow. Under the formula, the interest rate for past due interest is calculated by first determining Chase's Prime Rate three days prior to the first day of the relevant Interest Period and then adding 3/4% to the Prime Rate. Thus, the interest rate for the second Interest Period of January 31, 1981 to April 30, 1981 is calculated by adding 3/4% to Chase's prime rate prevailing on January 28, 1981. For the third Interest Period of May 1, 1981 to July 30, 1981, the interest rate for past due interest is Chase's Prime Rate on April 28, 1981 plus 3/4%. The same calculation is made for each ensuing period.

In the instant case, Banco Nacional complied with the loan agreement as follows: It paid the $5 million installment of principle due on July 30, 1981. Banco Nacional paid past due interest on the entire loan up to July 30, 1981. Banco Nacional also paid past due interest for the fourth Interest Period (7/31/81 through 8/30/81) on the $10 million installment of principal due on August 30, 1981.In all other respects, Banco Nacional breached its agreement with Libra Bank.

Past due interest is due on the remainder of the principal, $25 million, for the fourth Interest Period (7/31/81 through 8/30/81). That interest is to be calculated at 3/4% above Chase's Prime Rate on July 28, 1981. This rate is to be applied to the Interest Period, *i.e.*, a period of thirty-one (31) days.

. . . The court now turns to the question of default interest. According to the loan agreement, Banco Nacional was to pay a $10 million installment due on August 30, 1981. On August 31, 1981, Banco Nacional was in default of its $10 million installment after it had failed to make payment on August 30. The loan agreement sets forth the following provision governing default:

> 15. Default
> If the Borrower makes any default in any of the terms hereof, or is in default under the terms of any agreement for borrowed money, the Agent, after consultation with the Banks, shall be entitled to declare the entire amount of the Loan together with accrued interest, costs and expenses immediately due and payable without notice, the right to which is hereby formally waived.

On September 11, 1981, Libra Bank accelerated the remainder of the loan according to the terms of the contract. Thus, from August 31, 1981, to the present, Banco Nacional has been in default of the $10 million installment payment due on August 30, 1981. From September 11, 1981, to the present, Banco Nacional has been in default of the entire remaining portion of the loan, $25 million, due on September 11, 1981.[23]

The loan provides that the rate of default interest is to be calculated as follows:

> 7. Payments
> *     *     *     *     *     *

---

23. Since the court concludes that the remaining $25 million was not in default until September 11, 1981, Banco Nacional owes additional past due interest on the $25 million from August 31, 1981 to September 10, 1981. Thus, the total period for past due interest on the $25 million is a period of forty-two (42) days to be figured at Chase's Prime Rate of July 28, 1981.

The Miskin Affidavit appears to assume that the entire amount of the loan has been in default since August 31, 1981. This was also the contention of Libra Bank's counsel during the oral argument held on these matters on April 20, 1983. However, the loan agreement provides that the remaining payments of the remaining installments were not due until September 30 and October 30, 1981. The acceleration clause in this loan arrangement did not provide for automatic acceleration of the remaining installments upon default of any single installment. If there had been such an automatic acceleration clause, then the entire loan would have been in default on August 31, 1981. Alternatively, if Libra Bank had accelerated the remainder of the loan on August 31, 1981, that would have put the entire remainder of the loan in default triggering the default interest rate. However, acceleration was not declared until September 11, 1981. Thus, Banco Nacional was not in default of these payments until September 11, 1981 when it failed to pay those amounts declared due on September 11, 1981. *Cf. State of New York v. Monastero*, 62 A.D.2d 792, 406 N.Y.S.2d 382, 383 (3rd Dep't 1978) (loan note provided that in the event of any default of any installment of principal, then the whole of the principal sum then remaining becomes automatically due and payable at once).

(b) If default is made on the due date for payment of any amount hereunder, the Borrower will pay the rate of interest calculated as described in paragraph 6(a) for the period of default to the date of actual payment plus three-quarters per cent per annum.

The parties dispute the proper operation of the default provision. Plaintiffs argue that Chase's Prime Rate prevailing three days before the beginning of the default period should be applied for the entire period of default which is some 22 months long. Banco Nacional contests this interpretation of the contract. Defendant notes that pursuant to ¶ 7(b) the default rate is determined by adding 3/4% to the past due interest rate calculated according to the instructions provided in ¶ 6(a)(i) and (ii). According to Banco Nacional, ¶ 6(a)(i) clearly contemplates interest rates fixed upon short term periods since it refers to the choice between the higher of the London Interbank Offer Rate (LIBOR), an interest rate fixed with reference to short term loans,[25] and Chase's Prime Rate. Banco Nacional further argues that there simply does not exist a 22 month LIBOR and to read the loan agreement as fixing a single rate, based upon a choice between a non-existent LIBOR and the Prime Rate, for the entire default period renders this provision meaningless. Instead, Banco Nacional urges the court to compute the interest rate on a monthly basis, choosing between the higher of LIBOR and the Prime Rate at the beginning of each month during the entire default period. Plaintiffs, on the other hand, argue that the loan agreement fixes a uniform rate for the entire default period, that since Chase's Prime Rate was higher than the LIBOR at the beginning of the default period, the Chase Prime Rate prevailing on August 27, 1981, as adjusted according to the loan agreement for a figure of 22%, should be applied for the entire period.

Defendant's argument that the loan agreement is poorly drafted is not without some force. Plaintiffs do not answer defendant's contention that a 22 month LIBOR does not exist. Indeed, as defendant argues, LIBOR is based on short term periods:

The essence of eurocurrency floating rate loans is the manner in which the loans are funded by the lender. In order to make a loan a bank borrows matching funds from other banks in the market for on-lending. These funding deposits are taken for short terms such as *3, 6 or 12 months (interest periods)* and at the end of each interest period the bank pays back the underlying deposit and immediately reborrows another deposit for a further period. The interest rate payable by the ultimate borrower will be a specified percentage, known as the "spread" or "margin" (which represents the gross profit and remuneration for the risk), above the rate at which the bank borrows the underlying deposits from other banks in the London interbank market. That rate is known as the London interbank offered rate ("LIBOR"). Hence the interest rate floats and is calculated by reference to the cost of funds to the bank in the market at the beginning of each interest period. That cost would depend upon the credit of the lending bank. In syndicated credits the LIBORs of selected reference banks are averaged out for the purposes of interest determination.

In practice many banks fund loans out of their own pool of funds without going to the market.

---

25. "LIBOR" is an acronym for the standard London interbank offer rate of interest paid by name banks of the highest credit standing. R. MCKINNON, MONEY IN INTERNATIONAL EXCHANGE 207 (1979); *see also* E. ALTMAN, FINANCIAL HANDBOOK, § 13-12, -13 (5th ed. 1961). *See generally* H. RIEHL & R. RODRIGUEZ, FOREIGN EXCHANGE MARKETS (1977).

P. WOOD, LAW AND PRACTICE OF INTERNATIONAL FINANCE 10.8(2) at 253 (1980) (emphasis added). . . . It seems apparent that plaintiffs never contemplated, insofar as their intent is expressed in the language of the loan agreement, a default period lasting beyond any possible LIBOR interest period. On the other hand, this defect in the plaintiffs' contractual language does not mean that this court must adopt defendant's version of the construction of intent.

In order to determine more precisely the nature of the defect in plaintiffs' contract language and to discern the intention of the parties so that the court may enforce the contract consistent with the intent of the parties, it will prove useful to see precisely how the language of ¶ 6(a)(i) functions and where it fails. Suppose that plaintiffs had received a judgment, marking the end of the default period, on August 31, *1982*, or exactly one year from the date of default. At this point, since there is a one-year LIBOR interest period, *see* Wall St.J., June 23, 1983, at 23, col. 3 (10-3/16% for one-year period), plaintiffs would have a choice between two legally operable provisions of the contract, *i.e.*, a choice between the higher of the Prime Rate or LIBOR. One day after that, on September 1, 1982, plaintiffs would no longer have such a choice since the LIBOR provision, ¶ 6(a)(i), provides for an alternative which cannot be given legally operative effect. The defect in the contract language is its failure to anticipate a default beyond one year. The contract was drafted so that ¶ 6(a)(i) would have a legally operative life of one year; thus, had Libra Bank obtained a judgment at any point up to August 31, 1982, defendant simply could not advance the argument that ¶ 6(a)(i) and (ii) is meaningless unless the court uses a month-by-month calculation.

The intent of the parties as expressed by ¶ 6(a)(i) and (ii) is that a fixed rate should apply for the entire default period. See ¶ 7(b) ("If default is made . . . , the Borrower will pay the rate of interest . . . for the period of default to date of actual payment"). The contractual defect, of course, is that beyond a certain point, a fixed LIBOR no longer exists. Given the intent of the parties insofar as it was expressed by the defective language of the contract, it becomes clear that defendant's proposal that the court apply a month-by-month calculation is manifestly contrary to that intent.

As the court has already noted, the language of ¶ 6(a)(i) limits the operative life of this provision to a one-year period after which point the provision becomes void. The defect in the language of the contract does not, however, render ¶ 6(a) in its entirety meaningless. ¶ 6(a) is written in the disjunctive and provides a choice between the *higher* of the rates as specified by ¶ 6(a)(i) (LIBOR) or ¶ 6(a)(ii) (Chase's Prime Rate). Although ¶ 6(a)(i) became void one year after the initial default, ¶ 6(a)(ii) remains operative. The effect of the oversight in the drafting of ¶ 6(a)(i) is that one of the alternatives becomes unavailable after one year and not that the entire provision becomes meaningless. In order to render a disjunctive provision meaningless, *both* alternatives must be meaningless not only one. Simply because a portion of a disjunctive provision becomes void does not mean that the court should then ignore the remaining operative provision of the contract, especially when that remaining provision implements the intent of the parties to provide a fixed rate of interest for the entire default period. The court concludes that although the loan agreement could have been more clearly drafted, the intent of the parties was to have a fixed interest rate apply to the entire default period. In addition, although one of the provisions of ¶ 6(a) ceased to be legally operative after one year, the alternative provision, specifying the use of Chase's Prime Rate, continues to be operative and is to be given legal effect. Accordingly, with respect to the $10 million installment, default interest is to be calculated according to ¶¶ 7(b) and 6(a)(ii) by the use of Chase's Prime Rate prevailing on August 28, 1981. . . .

## Allied Bank Int'l v. Banco Credito Agricola de Cartago
757 F.2d 516 (2d Cir. 1985), *cert. dismissed*, 473 U.S. 934

Meskill, Circuit Judge:

[The case involved the legal effect of Costa Rican directives repudiating private, commercial obligations. Excerpts of the opinion discussing this issue are reproduced in Chapter 8, § 4, *infra*.]

Recognition of the Costa Rican directives would . . . be counter to principles of contract law. Appellees [Costa Rican banks] explicitly agreed that their obligation to pay would not be excused in the event that Central Bank failed to provide the necessary United States dollars for payment. This, of course, was the precise cause of the default. If we were to give effect to the directives, our decision would vitiate an express provision of the contracts between the parties.[4]

## A.I. Credit Corp. v. Government of Jamaica
666 F. Supp. 629 (S.D.N.Y. 1987)

Sand, District Judge.

As a result of a depressed national economy, the Government of Jamaica ("Jamaica") ceased paying principal on its foreign bank debt in mid-1983. This moratorium followed three reschedulings of the debt in 1978, 1979, and 1981, which were accomplished with the consent of Jamaica's affected creditors, including foreign banks and financial institutions. Jamaica entered into a fourth rescheduling agreement on June 27, 1984 (the "1984 Agreement"). This agreement encompassed not only debt previously rescheduled, but also newly incurred debt owed to Continental Illinois Bank and Trust Company ("Continental Illinois"). This agreement affected the debts owed to a total of 113 banks and institutions ("the banks").

In August 1984, in accordance with the 1984 Agreement, Continental Illinois assigned 90 percent of its rescheduled debt as well as all rights and obligations relating thereto, to plaintiff in this action, A.I. Credit Corporation ("AICCO"). The assignment, consisting of approximately $10,000,000 in debt before interest, was accomplished pursuant to a Transfer Agreement executed between Continental Illinois and AICCO. In the Transfer Agreement, and in compliance with section 12.09 of the 1984 Agreement, AICCO agreed to be treated as a "Bank" for all purposes of the 1984 Agreement "subject to the terms and conditions of the [1984] Rescheduling Agreement . . . as the same hereafter from time to

---

4. Each agreement specifically provided:

>    7. Events of Default:
>
>    If any of the following events of default should occur and is not remedied within a period of 30 days as of the date of occurrence, the Agent Bank may, by a written notice to the Borrower declare the promissory notes to be due and payable. In such an event, they shall be considered to be due without presentment, demand, protest or any other notice to the Borrower, all of which are expressly waived by this agreement:
>    7.1 Any payment of principal or interest under this transaction shall not have been paid on its maturity date. If the Borrower shall not effect any payment of principal or interest on the promissory notes at maturity, due solely to the omission or refusal by the Central Bank of Costa Rica to provide the necessary U.S. Dollars, such an event shall not be considered to be an event of default which would justify the demandability of the obligation, during a period of 10 days after such maturity date. . . .

time may be amended, modified or supplemented. . . ."

The 1984 Agreement provided that Jamaica's debt would become payable in 17 quarterly payments, commencing on March 15, 1986. However, it became apparent in early 1985, if not sooner, that although it was making interest payments, Jamaica would be unable to repay principal on the schedule set forth in the 1984 Agreement. Jamaica and the banks thus entered into a fifth rescheduling agreement during that year ("the 1985 Agreement"), and yet a sixth such agreement on April 30, 1987 ("the 1987 Agreement"). The 1987 Agreement specifies that Jamaica is to make quarterly payments commencing on October 15, 1988.

Each bank that was a party to the 1984 Agreement voluntarily entered into these subsequent 1985 and 1987 agreements, with the exception of AICCO and two other banks in 1985, and AICCO and one other bank in 1987. Standing on what it claims are still its rights under the 1984 Agreement, AICCO alleges that to date, Jamaica has defaulted on six scheduled installments of principal. On this account, plaintiff asks this Court to grant it summary judgment.

The crux of this motion for summary judgment rests on the extent and nature of the relationship established between these banks pursuant to the 1984 Agreement, and the resulting standing of plaintiff to sue individually to enforce its rights under the agreement. We note at the outset that no bank other than AICCO has attempted to enforce the 1984 Agreement, and that no other bank has sought to intervene on either side of this litigation.

There is little question, however, that the banks have mutual financial interest in the outcome of this lawsuit, and in any payments an individual creditor receives from Jamaica: the 1984 Agreement provides that to the extent Jamaica makes any payment to a bank pursuant to its obligations under the 1984 Agreement in a proportion greater than the payment made to any other bank, the bank must share its payment pro rata with each of the other banks. 1984 Agreement § 5.03; 1985 Agreement § 5.03; 1987 Agreement § 5.03. Furthermore, Jamaica itself is obliged to make ratable payments to all banks in the event it makes any payment of "Nonconsenting Debt." 1984 Agreement § 4.03; 1985 Agreement § 4.04; 1987 Agreement § 4.04.

I.  Plaintiff Has Standing to Bring This Action Individually

In opposition to the instant motion for summary judgment, Jamaica strenuously argues that AICCO has no standing to bring this action without the participation of the other lenders that were parties to the 1984 Agreement. Relying both on what it claims to be an "implicit covenant" and a "textual analysis" of the 1984 Agreement, Jamaica contends that each bank covenanted not to sue Jamaica unless the banks jointly agreed to do so. An examination of the 1984 Agreement and the law of New York[1] defeats this contention.

The language of the 1984 Agreement could hardly be more clear in establishing that AICCO's right to pursue the debt owed to it by Jamaica is separate and divisible from the rights of its fellow creditors:

> The amounts payable at any time hereunder to each Bank shall be a separate and independent debt and each Bank shall be entitled to protect and enforce its rights arising out of this Agreement, and it shall not be necessary for any other Bank to

---

1. For purposes of the 1984 Agreement, the parties "irrevocably submit[ted] to the jurisdiction of any New York State or Federal court sitting in New York City. . . ." 1984 Agreement § 12.07(a), and "expressly agree[d]" that the agreement would be "governed by, and construed in accordance with, the laws of the State of New York, United States." *Id.* § 12.10. Jamaica also "irrevocably waive[d] . . . immunity in respect of its obligations under [the] Agreement. . . ." *Id.* § 12.07 (d).

be joined as an additional party in any proceedings for such purpose.

1984 Agreement § 12.13.

That each bank has the right to sue Jamaica independently without the joinder of the other creditors, on what are in this respect divisible debts, is reiterated throughout the agreement. *See, e.g., id.* § 12.07(c) ("Nothing [in the agreement's section on consent to jurisdiction and waiver of immunities] shall affect the right of any Bank or the Agent to bring any action or proceeding against the Borrower. . . ."); *id.* § 5.04(b) ("Each Bank agrees that if it shall at any time, through . . . litigation . . . obtain payment [it shall share such payment ratably with the other banks]); *id.* § 12.03 ("No failure on the part of . . . any Bank to exercise . . . any right . . . shall operate as a waiver. . . .").

We must similarly disagree with Jamaica that only the Agent specified in the 1984 Agreement, the Bank of Nova Scotia, is empowered to institute suit at the direction of the banks. The 1984 Agreement specifies that:

> The Agent shall perform the mechanical and clerical functions in connection with the administration of this Agreement which are specifically set forth herein. ... The responsibilities of the agent are strictly limited to those specifically set forth in this Agreement, and no unstated functions, responsibilities, duties, obligations or liabilities shall be read into this Agreement or otherwise exist against the Agent.

1984 Agreement § 11.01(a). Section 11.01(b)(viii) of the agreement further provides, "[t]he Agent shall not in any event be required to initiate any suit, action or proceeding arising out of or in connection with this Agreement. . . ." *Id.*

The case of *Credit Français International, S.A. v. Sociedad Financiera de Comercio, C.A.*, 128 Misc.2d 564, 490 N.Y.S.2d 670 (Sup.Ct.N.Y.Co. 1985), cited by defendant for the proposition that only the agent in a multibank loan agreement has the standing to sue the debtor, is distinguishable. In *Credit Français*, Justice Greenfield concluded that the loan agreement in that case evinced an "overall design" of "unified action handled by a single Agent who will proceed for all. . . ." *Id.* at 581, 490 N.Y.S.2d at 683. Despite the similarities to the agreement in the instant case, no such overall design exists here. As in *Credit Français*, the 1984 Agreement imposes mutual obligations on the lending banks and defines duties of the agent, for example with respect to the agreement's sharing provisions. *See* 1984 Agreement § 5.03. However, the clear language of the agreement, as cited above, also explicitly limits the powers of the agent and grants the individual banks the right to proceed individually.

It is the clear and unambiguous language that prevents us from reading into this agreement, as urged by Jamaica, an implicit covenant to act collectively or a trade practice within the international banking industry of forbearance under these circumstances. *See Wells Fargo Asia Ltd. v. Citibank, N.A.*, 612 F.Supp. 351 (S.D.N.Y. 1985) (finding ambiguity in banking agreement such as to permit consideration of extrinsic evidence relating to custom and usage in Eurodollar trade). Under New York law, "evidence of industry practice may not be used to vary the terms of a contract that clearly sets forth the rights and obligations of the parties." *Croce v. Kurnit*, 737 F.2d 229, 238 (2d Cir. 1984); *see also, e.g., ...* RESTATEMENT (SECOND) OF CONTRACTS § 203(b) (1981) (same).

We find the 1984 Agreement–a comprehensive, detailed contract executed by sophisticated parties–is integrated insofar as it provides for suits by the individual party creditors, even without a so-called "merger" or "integration" clause. *Id.* at §§ 213, 215 (binding integrated agreement discharges prior inconsistent agreements). Jamaica has not presented any factors that persuade us to supplement the 1984 Agreement in order to contradict the unambiguous, express terms of that agreement.

    II.  Summary Judgment is Appropriate in This Case

    . . .

    In this case, we find that AICCO has sustained its burden of showing "that there is no genuine issue as to any material fact and that [AICCO] is entitled to a judgment as matter of law." Fed.R.Civ.P. 56. . . . The "genuine issues" that Jamaica seeks to establish through discovery–such as the intent, and custom and practice of the signatories to permit individual enforcement of the agreement–could be discerned only by creating ambiguities in the contract where none appear on its face. . . .

    Section 4.01 of the 1984 Agreement sets out a schedule for payment of Jamaica's debt to the banks, such payment to have commenced on March 15, 1986. There is no dispute that Jamaica has failed to meet its scheduled principal payments, and we find no genuine issues raised by Jamaica relative to the validity of the agreement and AICCO's right to seek its enforcement. We find, therefore, that summary judgment is appropriate in this case. AICCO is entitled to its unpaid installments, interest, costs, and expenses. *See* 1984 Agreement §§ 3.05; 12.05(a)(iv).

    We have been advised by defendant that our holding could have a devastating financial impact on the Government of Jamaica due to the sharing and default provisions contained in the 1984 and 1987 Agreements. But it is not the function of a federal district court in an action such as this to evaluate the consequences to the debtor of its inability to pay nor the foreign policy or other repercussions of Jamaica's default. Such considerations are properly the concern of other governmental institutions. When counsel for Jamaica first raised these concerns with the Court at a pretrial conference, we urged Jamaica to seek the intervention of such concerned governmental agencies that might wish to communicate their views to the Court. No such intervention has occurred.[5]

## Lloyds Bank PLC v. Republic of Ecuador
— F. Supp. —, 1998 WL 118170 (S.D.N.Y. 1998)

Chin, J.

    In these seven interpleader actions, the plaintiff, stakeholders hold approximately $9.8 million in Past Due Interest Bonds ("PDI Bonds"). These bonds represent the unpaid, past due interest associated with certain debt either owed or guaranteed by the Republic of Ecuador ("Ecuador"). Various creditors, including the creditors named in these interpleader actions, (1) Banco del Pacifico (Panama), S.A. ("BDP-Panama") and Banco del Pacifico, S.A. ("BDP-Ecuador") (collectively, the "BDP Entities"); (2) Latin American Financial Services Corp. ("Lafise"); (3) Ecuatoriana de Financiamiento, S.A. ("Ecufinsa"); and (4) Fundacion Offsetec, Fundacion Capacitar, Fundacion Chicos de la Calle, and SOS Aldea de Ninos Ecuador (collectively, the "Foundations"),[1] lay claim to the PDI Bonds pursuant to a syndicated foreign debt agreement entered into among Ecuador and more than 250

---

5. The sole communication that has been furnished to the Court is a copy of an IMF Official Message to the Governor of the Bank of Jamaica dated July 30, 1987, which reads in pertinent part: "[o]n the basis of the information available to us, a judgment against a debtor country in this kind of case could create problems for the implementation of the international debt strategy that is supported by member governments of the International Monetary Fund."

1. Hereinafter, the BDP Entities, Lafise, Ecufinsa, and the Foundations shall be referred to collectively as the "Creditors."

financial institutions from around the world. Ecuador, on the other hand, seeks a declaration by the Court that it may cancel the PDI Bonds or transfer them to itself. Hence, these interpleader actions were commenced to determine how the PDI Bonds should be distributed among the Creditors, if at all.

Before the Court are cross-motions for summary judgment brought by Ecuador, the BDP Entities, Ecufinsa, and the Foundations. Lafise does not move for summary judgment, but opposes the entry of summary judgment against it in favor of either Ecuador or the EDP Entities.

The Court heard oral argument on the motions on February 10, 1998. For the following reasons, Ecuador's motions for summary judgment are denied; the BDP Entities' cross-motion for summary judgment against Ecuador is granted, but their cross-motion for summary judgment against Lafise is denied; Ecufinsa's cross-motion for summary judgment against Ecuador is granted; and the Foundations' cross-motions for summary judgment against Ecuador are granted. . . .

A. The Facts

In the early 1980s, the Central Bank of Ecuador (the "Central Bank") assumed certain foreign debt obligations of members of Ecuador's private sector. The debtors agreed to pay the equivalent value of the debt to the Central Bank in sucres (Ecuadorian currency). In return, the debtors were released from their debts to the foreign creditors, and the Central Bank became indebted to the foreign creditors in their place. The Central Bank's assumption of this debt was set forth in separate agreements between the Central Bank and each foreign creditor, called Deposit Facility and Loan Agreements ("DFLAs").

1. The Consolidation Agreement

Between 1985 and 1986, Ecuador and its foreign creditors renegotiated the DFLAs. These negotiations culminated in the execution of a Consolidation Agreement dated August 15, 1986 (the "Consolidation Agreement"), by which Ecuador's foreign debt was consolidated and restructured. The parties to the Consolidation Agreement were the Central Bank (as obligor), Ecuador (as guarantor), Citibank (as servicing bank), and the various foreign creditors, some of which are defendants in the present interpleader actions.

Pursuant to the Consolidation Agreement, the debt principal ("Consolidation Agreement Debt") was divided into various "tranches," each of which had a different maturity date and bore an interest rate provided for in the Consolidation Agreement. Most of the debt was payable in U.S. dollars, although some was payable in other currencies. The Consolidation Agreement further provided for the payment of the interest that accrued on its various tranches of principal, in quarterly installments.

2. Conversions of Consolidation Agreement Debt

Section 5.11 of the Consolidation Agreement provided an avenue through which Consolidation Agreement Debt could be converted into new obligations, payable in sucres. Three forms of conversion were available under the Consolidation Agreement: (1) debt-for-debt conversions; (2) capitalizations; and (3) compensation-for-liabilities conversions.

Regardless of the form of conversion used, the converting parties could acquire the debt at a discount, but convert it at face value, thereby realizing a substantial profit. Consequently, not long after execution of the Consolidation Agreement, a secondary market developed for the trading of Consolidation Agreement Debt. Upon obtaining prior approval from the Monetary Board of the Central Bank and giving proper notification to Citibank, a debtholder could assign its debt to another party, and the assignee then became a party to the Consolidation Agreement and could assign it further or convert it pursuant to section 5.11. Whether the assignor or the assignee retained the right to collect the interest on the debt principal was a matter left to the private agreement of the parties involved. Hence, through assignment, virtually any entity could acquire Consolidation Agreement Debt and convert it pursuant to section 5.11 of the Consolidation Agreement, and in fact, between August 1986 and January 1993, $550,000,000 worth of Consolidation Agreement Debt was converted by over 90 different entities worldwide.

Following execution of the Consolidation Agreement in August of 1986, Ecuador remained current on its obligation to pay interest on the foreign currency debt until late 1986/early 1987. In March of 1987, however, due to a drop in oil prices, exacerbated by an earthquake that damaged the country's oil pipelines, Ecuador was forced to declare a moratorium on its debt service. Ecuador remained in default on its interest obligations until May of 1994, and during this time, substantial amounts of interest on Consolidation Agreement Debt accrued but was not paid. Ecuador's default presented a serious dilemma: how to handle the accrued interest on Consolidation Agreement Debt once that debt was converted.

3. The 1994 Financing Plan and the PDI Bond Exchange Agreement

Finally, in 1994, in accordance with the Brady Plan,[2] Ecuador and its creditor banks entered into an agreement to restructure over $7 billion of Ecuador's foreign debt (the "1994 Financing Plan"). Pursuant to the 1994 Financing Plan, Ecuador's foreign creditors could exchange outstanding principal amounts of Ecuadorian loans for new U.S. dollar-denominated bonds issued by Ecuador.

It is Ecuador's position that the purpose of the 1994 Financing Plan was to permit the parties to renegotiate their respective obligations that had been formalized in the Consolidation Agreement. In other words, all existing obligations were to be eliminated, and essentially, the Consolidation Agreement was to be superseded by the 1994 Financing Plan. The Creditors maintain that, under the 1994 Financing Plan, no new agreement was reached concerning interest on converted debt, and that, therefore, Ecuador's obligations under the Consolidation Agreement with respect to past due interest on Consolidation Agreement Debt remained unchanged.

The 1994 Financing Plan was also intended to address the dilemma posed by Ecuador's default on its interest obligations. As an additional component of the 1994 Financing Plan, Ecuador and many of its creditors entered into the Past Due Interest Bond Exchange Agreement (the "PDI Bond Exchange Agreement"), dated October 4, 1994, which provided the means by which Ecuador would pay the interest arrears that had accrued over the years on the tranches of outstanding Consolidation Agreement Debt. Holders of debt owed or guaranteed by Ecuador could receive PDI Bonds in exchange for cancellation of their original obligations. Lloyds Bank was appointed to act as Closing Agent under the PDI Bond Exchange Agreement and was responsible for calculating the aggregate amount of outstanding interest.

The PDI Bond Exchange Agreement provided for recalculation of past due interest at rates lower than those that originally applied to Ecuador's sovereign debt. Past due interest was composed of two elements: (1) interest on principal, representing interest on the principal component of the outstanding debt, and (2) interest on interest, reflecting

---

2. In 1989, in response to growing concern over escalating international insolvency, United States Treasury Secretary Nicholas Brady announced a plan (the "Brady Plan") to restabilize the international financial system by encouraging banks around the world to reduce the debt obligations of lesser developed countries by restructuring old debt and providing new loans. *See Elliott Assocs., L.P. v. Republic of Panama*, 975 F.Supp. 332, 334 (S.D.N.Y.1997). Ecuador was one of the countries that took advantage of the Brady Plan, restructuring over $7 billion of its external debt. [For discussion of the Brady Plan, see Chapter 8, Note 8.2, *infra*.]

compensation to creditors for Ecuador's late payment of the interest arrears. Once computed, past due interest was payable to creditors in the form of PDI Bonds. Calculation of past due interest, the determination of which creditors were entitled to PDI Bonds, and the amounts to which each creditor was entitled required a process called "reconciliation." Reconciliation began in late 1994 and continued through most of 1995. At the end of the reconciliation process, a substantial amount of PDI Bonds was listed by Lloyds as "unreconciled" due to potential disputes among creditors that could claim entitlement to the same interest.

4. Ecuador's Adoption of a New Policy

Eventually, the issue arose of how to deal with the accrued interest associated with Consolidation Agreement Debt that had been converted. On February 27, 1995, Ecuador issued a memorandum outlining its newly-adopted policy regarding this issue. The policy, developed primarily by Dr. Augusto de la Torre, General Manager of the Central Bank, effectively eliminated creditors' rights to collect the unpaid, past due interest on converted debt principal unless they could prove that they expressly reserved this right at the time of conversion of debt, which conversions had occurred years earlier.

Ecuador justified its new policy on the grounds that (1) the conversions themselves involved the negotiation of new agreements, and that Ecuador had the strongest ties with the subject matter of and parties to these agreements and therefore Ecuadorian law should govern them, (2) under Ecuadorian law, the new conversion agreements constituted novations extinguishing any prior obligations, and (3) the legal conclusions underlying the policy were based on the law of Ecuador, and the Central Bank was obligated to comply with its country's laws. The Creditors insist that Ecuador adopted this policy in an effort to unilaterally re-write the Consolidation Agreement to avoid paying the interest arrears.

In implementing its new policy, Ecuador required parties claiming entitlement to PDI Bonds to present sufficient evidence demonstrating that they had expressly and contemporaneously reserved their right to receive the unpaid, past due interest on Consolidation Agreement Debt that had been converted by them or by their assignees. The parties charged with the reconciliation process had to determine whether these claims were adequately documented before PDI Bonds would be issued.

Ultimately, it became apparent that a portion of the PDI Bonds were unreconcilable. Yet, many converters of debt still pursued claims for those bonds. In August of 1995, Ecuador held a special meeting at which it explained the new policy to converters of debt. Ecuador urged them to drop their claims to PDI Bonds, and most of the converters acquiesced. Several, however, including the Creditors, refused to renounce their claims. Consequently, the unreconciled PDI Bonds were placed in an interpleader fund, and this litigation was commenced.

B. The Interpleader Actions

The Creditors claim they are each entitled to a portion of the PDI Bonds in the interpleader fund currently held by Lloyds Bank and Chase Manhattan Bank. The seven consolidated actions all involve the same fund consisting of approximately $9.8 million in PDI Bonds. . . .

Ecuador seeks summary judgment against all other parties. Its main arguments in support of summary judgment are that (1) Ecuadorian law governs the conversions of Consolidation Agreement Debt and that, under Ecuadorian law, the conversions were novations that extinguished the interest on debt principal, and (2) the 1994 Financing Plan and its own internal policy adopted in 1995 left the Central Bank with no choice but to deny creditors' claims for PDI Bonds without proper proof of entitlement thereto. . . .

The BDP Entities, Ecufinsa, and the Foundations all seek summary judgment against Ecuador. The BDP Entities also move for summary judgment on their claim for declaratory relief against Lafise. Lafise does not move for summary judgment, but opposes the entry of summary judgment against it in favor of either Ecuador or the BDP Entities. The Creditors as a group reject Ecuador's principal arguments. They contend that Ecuador's obligation under the Consolidation Agreement to pay interest on Consolidation Agreement Debt was unaffected by conversions of debt principal. In addition, they maintain that Ecuador devised and implemented its so-called "policy" in 1995 merely to avoid paying the interest arrears as it was obligated to do under the earlier Consolidation Agreement. . . .

The facts in these consolidated actions are largely undisputed. Indeed, the parties agree that most of the claims are properly decided by the Court as a matter of law, for the Court's decision turns on resolution of one central issue: whether Ecuador's obligation to pay the interest that accrued on Consolidation Agreement Debt was extinguished, as Ecuador contends. Ecuador advances two arguments in support of summary judgment. First, Ecuador argues that conversions of Consolidation Agreement Debt extinguished its obligation to pay the accrued interest associated with that debt principal. Second, Ecuador relies on the 1994 Financing Plan and the adoption of its internal policy in 1995 to justify its refusal to pay the interest arrears as required by the Consolidation Agreement.

1. Conversions of Consolidation Agreement Debt

Ecuador's principal argument is that its obligation to pay the interest on each tranche of debt principal was immediately extinguished upon conversion of that tranche. Ecuador engages in a complex analysis to reach this conclusion, which can be summarized as follows: (1) all three types of conversions were effectuated by new agreements, separate and distinct from the Consolidation Agreement, and, therefore, the conversions should be analyzed separately from the Consolidation Agreement; (2) because these separate agreements involved Ecuadorian parties, were negotiated in Ecuador, and were prepared and executed in Ecuador, they are governed by Ecuadorian law; (3) under Ecuadorian law, the conversions constituted novations, and, consequently, any rights creditors possessed under the Consolidation Agreement to receive unpaid, past due interest associated with converted debt principal were extinguished upon conversion absent an express, contemporaneous reservation of those rights; and (4) because the BDP Entities, Lafise, Ecufinsa, and the Foundations all failed to make an express, contemporaneous reservation of their rights, Ecuador's obligation to pay the interest was extinguished upon conversion of the debt.

This argument fails, for, as a matter of law, conversions of Consolidation Agreement Debt did not extinguish the interest that had accrued on the debt principal prior to conversion. First, a choice-of-law analysis leads to the conclusion that conversions of Consolidation Agreement Debt should not be analyzed separately from the Consolidation Agreement itself, and that New York law, not Ecuadorian law, governs all disputes arising out of the Consolidation Agreement. Second, under New York law, conversions of debt principal did not result in novations that canceled the right to collect the interest on the debt that existed under the Consolidation Agreement. Indeed, basic principles of contract interpretation make clear that the right to receive interest on Consolidation Agreement Debt remained intact notwithstanding conversions of such debt, and that the parties to that agreement intended to preserve creditors' rights to the interest under any and all circumstances. . . .

. . . I hold that section 5.11 of the Consolidation Agreement unambiguously provides that conversions of Consolidation Agreement Debt affected principal only. It therefore follows that the right to collect interest on converted debt remained intact upon conversion. Section 5.11 states as follows:

[E]ach Tranche (or portion thereof) in respect of which such Qualified Investment is delivered shall cease to be a "Tranche" and "External Indebtedness" for all purposes of this Agreement and the Obligor shall have no further obligations under this Agreement in respect of any such Tranche (or portion thereof). . . .

(Consol. Agmt. § 5.11(a)(i)). Elsewhere in the Consolidation Agreement, the term "Tranche" is defined as "the aggregate unpaid principal amount . . . payable to a Lender." . . . Thus, section 5.11(a)(i) is clear that only debt principal was meant to be extinguished upon conversion.

Ecuador argues that reference to "External Indebtedness" in the first clause of section 5.11(a)(i) means that the interest on each converted tranche was intended to be extinguished, too. This interpretation arguably would be reasonable but for the clause that follows, which explicitly states that Ecuador "shall have no further obligations under this Agreement in respect of any such Tranche." . . . The first clause of section 5.11(a)(i) is purely definitional, stating the change in terminology for purposes of the Consolidation Agreement upon conversion of a tranche of principal. The second clause of section 5.11(a)(i), on the other hand, contains the operative language, setting forth Ecuador's obligation after conversion and confirming that Ecuador was no longer required to repay that tranche after conversion took place. The second clause, however, says nothing about interest. If the drafters had intended for Ecuador to have no further obligation with respect to each tranche and the "External Indebtedness," associated therewith, they would have included the words "External Indebtedness" in the second clause of section 5.11(a)(i) as well.

While section 5.11(a) makes no mention of how interest on converted principal was to be treated, payment of interest on tranches of debt principal is addressed in Article III.A of the Consolidation Agreement. For example, section 3.06 provides: "Interest on the unpaid principal amount of each Tranche from time to time shall accrue under this Agreement from and including July 31, 1986 until such Tranche is paid in full. Interest on each Tranche shall be paid in arrears on each Interest Payment Date for such Tranche and on the date of payment in full." (Consol. Agmt. § 3 .06(a)). Similarly, section 3.07 of the Consolidation Agreement provides: "From and after the Effective Date, in the event that any principal amount of any Tranche, or any interest on any Tranche, is not paid when due, the Obligor shall pay interest on such unpaid principal amount or . . . [on] such interest from the date when due until the date of payment in full." (Consol. Agmt. § 3.07(a)).

There is no indication in either Article III.A or section 5.11(a) that Ecuador's duty to make interest payments on debt principal was extinguishable under any circumstances. Indeed, the cited provisions from Article III.A suggest that the parties intended Ecuador to be required to make its interest payments under any and all circumstances. Interpretation of section 5.11(a) in the manner that Ecuador suggests would render ineffective the earlier provisions regarding the payment of interest, and I am obligated to interpret the agreement so as to give effect to all of its provisions. . . . Accordingly, I hold as a matter of law that, under section 5.11(a), conversion eliminated Ecuador's obligations with respect to principal only, and that the accrued interest on tranches of Consolidation Agreement Debt was not extinguished upon conversion.

(2) Novation

Finally, conversions of debt principal could not have constituted novations because the "agreements" through which conversions were effectuated do not satisfy the elements for a novation under New York law. Under New York law, the following elements are required for a novation: (1) a previous valid obligation; (2) agreement of all parties to a new obligation; (3) extinguishment of the previous obligation; and (4) a valid new contract. ... The parties must have "clearly expressed or manifested their intention that a subsequent agreement supersede or substitute for an old agreement." . . . The burden of proving a novation rests with the party asserting the defense. . . . Ecuador cannot establish that the conversions constituted novations because it fails to offer any evidence of a "clear and definite" intent to extinguish the parties' prior obligations under the Consolidation Agreement. Acknowledging that no such proof exists, Ecuador argues that the parties' consent to a novation can be inferred under New York law, and that the parties' consent can be inferred here from their act of converting debt principal. This argument fails. "While consent to a novation need not be express and may be implied from all the facts and circumstances . . . a novation [must] never . . . be presumed." . . . Ecuador's sole evidence is the mere fact that the Creditors converted Consolidation Agreement Debt. Ecuador has simply failed to offer sufficient "facts and circumstances" from which a reasonable jury could conclude that parties who converted Consolidation Agreement intended the act of conversion to constitute a novation of the prior Consolidation Agreement. If the parties had intended to extinguish all rights and obligations under the Consolidation Agreement, surely they would have provided some indication that that was their intent. Accordingly, I hold that conversions of debt principal did not constitute novations extinguishing Ecuador's obligation to pay the interest arrears.

Ecuador argues that this case is about the effect of conversions on accrued interest, but in actuality, it is a case about interpretation of a contractual provision. The bottom line is that Ecuador's obligation to pay interest in the first place arose under the Consolidation Agreement. Thus, it is interpretation of that agreement that is relevant, not the individual conversion agreements. Ecuador obfuscates the issues by arguing that the agreements through which conversions were effectuated somehow altered its prior obligation to pay interest on debt principal. In fact, however, conversions of Consolidation Agreement Debt had no effect on Ecuador's obligation to pay the accrued interest, as discussed above, and Ecuador's argument to the contrary is without merit.

## Kahale, *Does a choice-of-law clause waive immunity?*
### Int'l. Fin. L. Rev. 28 (July 1988)

'This Agreement shall be governed by and interpreted in accordance with the laws of the State of New York'.
P.S. It is also silent on the question of immunity.

Assuming that the agreement containing the above clause has little, if any, connection with New York, can such language result in suit being brought in New York against a foreign state party to the contract? An affirmative answer is indicated by a brief passage in the legislative history of the Foreign Sovereign Immunities Act 1976 (FSIA 28 USC §§ 1602), the governing statute in the United States on questions of immunity and jurisdiction in actions against foreign states.[a] The impact of the legislative history continues to be felt today. Nevertheless, it is highly questionable whether a choice-of-law clause should be construed as a waiver of jurisdictional immunity in a US court.

When suit is brought against a foreign state which has agreed to a choice-of-law clause, the FSIA's waiver exception to jurisdictional immunity is typically invoked as a basis

---

a. For the text of the FSIA and materials on its effect on international banking, see Chapter 8, § 3, *infra*.

for jurisdiction. That exception provides simply that a foreign state may not claim jurisdictional immunity in any case in which it has waived its immunity, 'either explicitly or by implication' (§ 1605(a)(1)). Since a choice-of-law clause is not an express waiver of immunity, the key issue is the status of such a clause as an implicit waiver.

The following passage from the House of Representatives Report is often quoted: 'With respect to implicit waivers, the courts have found such waivers in cases where a foreign state . . . has agreed that the law of a particular country should govern a contract'. This passage is at once ambiguous, unsupported, and inconsistent with the jurisdictional framework of the FSIA.

A choice-of-law clause is hardly an unusual feature of a transnational contract, whether it be a state contract or one between private parties. In a state contract, the clause might refer to the law of the foreign state itself, the law of another country other than the United States, or the law of a jurisdiction within the United States. All possibilities would appear to be within the scope of the sweeping language of the House Report.

However, it is difficult to argue that a foreign state's choice of its own law waives immunity in the United States or anywhere else. While it may be somewhat less of a leap to infer a waiver from a choice of another country's law, the lack of any link between the purported waiver and the United States remains an obstacle to jurisdiction. When the clause actually refers to a jurisdiction within the United States, a closer question is raised. Yet it is not clear that even a US choice-of-law clause should be construed as a waiver of jurisdictional immunity under the FSIA.

Notwithstanding the language of the House Report, there does not appear to be any clear precedent for the proposition that a foreign state waives immunity by agreeing to a choice-of-law clause. *See Frazier v Hanover Bank*, 19 NYS 2d 319 (1953) where the argument that a New York choice-of-law clause was a waiver of immunity and consent to suit in New York was considered 'patently untenable'. (Compare the State Immunity Act of the United Kingdom, § 2(2), specifying that a choice- of-law clause is not a submission). This may be due to the fact that such a clause, unlike a choice-of-forum clause, relates to the substantive legal issues arising out of a contractual relationship, that is, issues relating to the validity and interpretation of the contract and the rights and obligations of the parties thereunder; it does not usually refer to the procedure for enforcing those rights and obligations or the forum in which suit is to be brought. . . .

Contracts must be governed by some law. A choice- of-law clause is designed to take the determination of which law that will be out of the hands of the courts and to afford the parties a measure of certainty that their substantive rights and obligations will be determined in accordance with their own choice of law. However, while the parties may feel comfortable in referring to the law of a particular country or state to govern their contract, they may not be as comfortable in having disputes determined in the courts of that jurisdiction. In fact, parties to a transnational contract frequently combine a choice-of-law clause with a clause designating, for example, international arbitration as the means of dispute resolution.

Another, more technical reason exists for rejecting the theory that a choice-of-law clause waives immunity. Under the FSIA, the issues of immunity, subject matter jurisdiction and personal jurisdiction are linked. The statute sets forth the rules governing the defence of sovereign immunity in the form of a general rule of immunity, followed by a series of exceptions. If any of the exceptions, such as the waiver provision, is applicable, sovereign law is denied. Federal district courts automatically have subject matter jurisdiction over any suit against a foreign state in respect of which the state is not entitled to immunity. Personal jurisdiction may be obtained over the foreign state in any case in which subject matter jurisdiction exists, provided that service of process is made in the manner prescribed by the FSIA. Thus, the applicability of an immunity exception results at once in the denial of immunity and the assertion of both subject matter and personal jurisdiction. It is therefore not possible to examine the immunity issue in the abstract, without appreciation of its jurisdictional ramifications.

Because the FSIA links the jurisdictional issues to immunity, Congress took pains to ensure that immunity would not be denied in any case lacking a jurisdictional nexus with the United States. Each immunity exception, other than the waiver provision, requires specific contacts with the United States in order to satisfy the constitutional due process standard that a defendant should not be subjected to suit unless it has such 'minimum contacts' with the forum that the maintenance of the suit would not offend 'traditional notions of fair play and substantial justice'. *International Shoe Co v Washington*, 326 US 310 (1945). Viewed in this context, the absence of required US contacts in the waiver provision can be explained by the fact that the jurisdictional concept embodied in the provision is based on consent, not contacts. When a defendant consents to suit in the United States, additional contacts are not necessary to satisfy due process. *See National Equipment Rental Ltd v. Szukhent*, 375 US 311 (1964). . . .

However, in such cases, it must be quite clear that the defendant has consented to suit in the United States. The courts have consistently held that a choice-of-law clause in a contract entered into by a foreign private defendant, even one referring to the law of a state of the United States, does not constitute a consent of that defendant to suit in the United States. *McShan v Omega Louis Brandt et Frere, SA*, 536 F2d 516 (2d Cir 1976); *Misco Leasing Inc v Vaughn*, 450 F2d 257 (10th Cir 1971). It seems logical that the rule should be the same when the defendant happens to be a foreign state.

The cases under the FSIA indicate that the courts generally have relied heavily on the House Report concerning the issue of choice-of-law clauses as waivers of jurisdictional immunity, sometimes at the expense of further inquiry into the merits of the issue. An early decision, one of the many cases spawned by the Nigerian purchases of cement in the 1970s, involved a petition to confirm a foreign arbitral award arising out of dispute under a contract containing both an arbitration and a choice-of-law clause. *Ipitrade International SA v Federal Republic of Nigeria*, 465 F Supp 824 (DDC 1978). Nigeria had agreed that disputes would be submitted to arbitration under the rules of the International Chamber of Commerce and that the contract would be governed by Swiss law. Relying on the legislative history, the Court held that Nigeria had waived immunity under 28 USC § 1605(a)(1) by virtue of the arbitration and choice-of-law clause.

*Ipitrade* was a default proceeding. Under the FSIA, US courts may not enter default judgments against foreign states unless the plaintiff establishes its right to relief by evidence satisfactory to the court. The decision in *Ipitrade* is therefore not technically attributable to Nigeria's default. Nevertheless, due to Nigeria's absence, there was no party in the proceedings to offer effective rebuttal to the petitioner's arguments, particularly with respect to the House Report. Consequently, the House Report passed its first test without much opposition and a new line of cases was begun.

In another Nigerian cement case, *Verlinden BV v Central Bank of Nigeria*, 488 F Supp 1284 (SDNY 1980), the Court exhibited skepticism toward both *Ipitrade* and the legislative history. There the contract involved both an arbitration and a Dutch choice-of-law clause. Expressing concern over the implication of basing jurisdiction in the United States on a choice of foreign law (or forum), the Court stated:

'The Congressional history cited by the plaintiff is not dispositive of this issue, in-

deed, it is at most ambiguous. The comment in the Congressional report . . . that
the courts had found an implicit waiver 'where a foreign state has . . . agreed that
the law of a particular country' would apply, does not necessarily constitute an
endorsement of that result'.

The Court in *Verlinden* questioned whether the reference in the legislative history
to the law of a particular country was meant to include a third-party country. It noted that
while it may be reasonable to suggest that a choice of US law waives sovereign immunity
in a US court, 'it is quite another matter to suggest, as did the Court in *Ipitrade*, that a
sovereign state which agrees to be governed by the laws of a third-party country–such as
The Netherlands–is thereby precluded from asserting its immunity in an American court'.
As reasoned in *Verlinden*, such a view would lead to a result Congress is not likely to have
intended: 'whenever a foreign sovereign had contracted with a private party anywhere in the
world, and chose to be governed by the laws or answer in the forum of any country other
than its own, it would expose itself to personal liability in the courts of the United States'.

Although the *Verlinden* Court approached the legislative history with a critical eye
and was sensitive to the jurisdictional issues inherent in an argument of waiver based on a
choice-of-law clause, it did indicate receptiveness to such an argument when the clause refers to US law. A similar approach was adopted in *Ohntrup v Firearms Center Inc*, 516 F
Supp 1281 (EDPa 1981), an action involving claims against a Turkish state company which
had manufactured a gun that allegedly malfunctioned and caused injury. The plaintiffs
argued that a forum selection clause in the contract between the manufacturer and another
defendant waived immunity under Section 1605(a)(1). The clause did not refer to the United
States and the plaintiffs in any event were not even parties to that contract. Under those
circumstances, the Court found that no waiver existed, notwithstanding language in the
House Report indicating that an agreement to arbitrate in another country constitutes a
waiver of immunity. The Court stressed that a 'waiver of immunity by a state as to one
jurisdiction cannot be interpreted to be a waiver as to all jurisdictions'. Nevertheless, it
indicated in passing that a waiver could reasonably be found where a foreign state agreed
to be governed by US law.

In *Resource Dynamics International Ltd v General People's Committee for Communications & Maritime Transport*, 593 F Supp 572 (NDGa 1984), the Court was faced
with a contract which did contain a US choice-of-law clause. The contract, which provided
for civil aviation training, was 'governed by the procedural and substantive laws in effect in
the State of Virginia'. Without elucidation of the waiver issue, the Court simply quoted the
legislative history and cited *Ohntrup* in concluding that the Libyan defendant had waived
immunity under Section 1605(a)(1). . . .

Arguably, *Resource Dynamics* may be distinguished from other choice-of-law cases
in that the contractual provision specified the applicability of the procedural as well as
substantive law of Virginia. The reference to procedural law is unclear and could possibly
be construed as an indirect reference to the court procedures for enforcing the contract in
Virginia, placing the clause one step closer to an actual choice-of-forum clause. However,
there is no indication in the Court's opinion that such language played any role in the
decision and, except for the citation of *Ohntrup*, there is no indication that the decision
turned upon the selection of US law. The Court underscored the part of the House Report
referring to the law of a particular country without mentioning any requirement that the
particular country be the United States.

*Marlowe v Argentine Naval Commission*, 604 F Supp 703 (DDC 1985), was an
action for breach of a contract which contained a clause providing that the contract was to

be governed by the laws of the District of Columbia. The Court held that the defendant had waived immunity under Section 1605(a)(1) and that subject matter and personal jurisdiction therefore existed, service of process having been made. . . .

Although *Marlowe* involved a US choice-of-law clause, it is not clear that this was the determinative factor. The *Ohntrup*, *Resource Dynamics*, and *Ipitrade* cases were all cited with approval. No clear distinction was made between cases involving US choice-of-law clauses and those where the applicable law was that of another country. Indeed, the Court was well aware that the clause in *Ipitrade* referred to Swiss law. . . .

Significantly, unlike the case in *Verlinden* and even *Ohntrup*, the Court in *Marlowe* exhibited no reluctance to embrace the House Report, stating, 'This House Report has been generally noted as authoritative legislative history'. Responding to the defendant's argument that the House Report was 'singularly devoid of any authoritative support', the Court observed that more than adequate authority had developed by that time in the form of the cases referred to above and that it was defendant's position 'which now seems to lack support'. Ironically, a series of decisions influenced by a passage in the House Report erroneously reporting the state of prior law had created impressive precedent in favour of the view that a choice-of-law clause waives immunity.

*Marlowe* also specifically addressed the jurisdictional implications of applying the waiver exception to immunity, recognising that personal jurisdiction could not be exercised over the defendant unless due process were satisfied. . . . In order to overcome this hurdle, the Court reasoned that the defence of lack of personal jurisdiction may be waived, and that since the FSIA governs both personal and subject matter jurisdiction, the defendant's 'implicit waiver of immunity under 1605(a)(1) constituted a waiver of the defence of lack of personal jurisdiction'.

However, while it is clear that a defendant may waive the jurisdictional defence, it is not clear how the Court drew its conclusion. It acknowledged the integration of the issues of immunity and jurisdiction in the FSIA, but did not complete the circle in analysing the issues. In effect, the Court's reasoning seemed to be that since a choice-of-law clause waived immunity and a denial of immunity results in jurisdiction, it follows that a choice-of-law clause waives jurisdictional objections as well. . . .

# 4. Lending Limitations

**Notes and Comments 7.7.** Banks are often limited in their ability to lend by a fixed limitation on the amount of outstanding loans and extensions of credit to any one borrower at any one time. This limitation is sometimes expressed as an amount equivalent to a specified percentage of the bank's capital and surplus. One example of this is the provision in the National Bank Act, 12 U.S.C. § 84. Review that provision and consider whether it applies to international lending by national banks.

**7.8.** In lending to foreign sovereigns, governmental entities, and other entities owned or controlled by the foreign government, the question may naturally arise whether all such loans should be treated as if they were loan to one "person" for purposes of lending limitations. Some guidance in this regard is offered by the Comptroller's regulations, an excerpt from which follows.

## Comptroller of the Currency
12 C.F.R. § 32.5

§ 32.5 Combination rules.

(a) General rule. Loans or extensions of credit to one borrower will be attributed to another person and each person will be deemed a borrower–

(1) When proceeds of a loan or extension of credit are to be used for the direct benefit of the other person, to the extent of the proceeds so used; or

(2) When a common enterprise is deemed to exist between the persons.

(b) Direct benefit. The proceeds of a loan or extension of credit to a borrower will be deemed to be used for the direct benefit of another person and will be attributed to the other person when the proceeds, or assets purchased with the proceeds, are transferred to another person, other than in a bona fide arm's length transaction where the proceeds are used to acquire property, goods, or services.

(c) Common enterprise. A common enterprise will be deemed to exist and loans to separate borrowers will be aggregated:

(1) When the expected source of repayment for each loan or extension of credit is the same for each borrower and neither borrower has another source of income from which the loan (together with the borrower's other obligations) may be fully repaid. An employer will not be treated as a source of repayment under this paragraph because of wages and salaries paid to an employee, unless the standards of paragraph (c)(2) of this section are met;

(2) When loans or extensions of credit are made–

(i) To borrowers who are related directly or indirectly through common control, including where one borrower is directly or indirectly controlled by another borrower; and

(ii) Substantial financial interdependence exists between or among the borrowers. Substantial financial interdependence is deemed to exist when 50 percent or more of one borrower's gross receipts or gross expenditures (on an annual basis) are derived from transactions with the other borrower. Gross receipts and expenditures include gross revenues/expenses, intercompany loans, dividends, capital contributions, and similar receipts or payments;

(3) When separate persons borrow from a bank to acquire a business enterprise of which those borrowers will own more than 50 percent of the voting securities or voting interests, in which case a common enterprise is deemed to exist between the borrowers for purposes of combining the acquisition loans; or

(4) When the OCC determines, based upon an evaluation of the facts and circumstances of particular transactions, that a common enterprise exists.

(d) Special rule for loans to a corporate group.

(1) Loans or extensions of credit by a bank to a corporate group may not exceed 50 percent of the bank's capital and surplus. This limitation applies only to loans subject to the combined general limit. A corporate group includes a person and all of its subsidiaries. For purposes of this paragraph, a corporation or a limited liability company is a subsidiary of a person if the person owns or beneficially owns directly or indirectly more than 50 percent of the voting securities or voting interests of the corporation or company.

(2) Except as provided in paragraph (d)(1) of this section, loans or extensions of credit to a person and its subsidiary, or to different subsidiaries of a person, are not combined unless either the direct benefit or the common enterprise test is met.

(e) Special rules for loans to partnerships, joint ventures, and associations–

(1) Partnership loans. Loans or extensions of credit to a partnership, joint venture, or association are deemed to be loans or extensions of credit to each member of the partnership, joint venture, or association. This rule does not apply to limited partners in limited partnerships or to members of joint ventures or associations if the partners or members, by the terms of the partnership or membership agreement, are not held generally

liable for the debts or actions of the partnership, joint venture, or association, and those provisions are valid under applicable law.

(2) Loans to partners.

(i) Loans or extensions of credit to members of a partnership, joint venture, or association are not attributed to the partnership, joint venture, or association unless either the direct benefit or the common enterprise tests are met. Both the direct benefit and common enterprise tests are met between a member of a partnership, joint venture or association and such partnership, joint venture or association, when loans or extensions of credit are made to the member to purchase an interest in the partnership, joint venture or association.

(ii) Loans or extensions of credit to members of a partnership, joint venture, or association are not attributed to other members of the partnership, joint venture, or association unless either the direct benefit or common enterprise test is met.

(f) Loans to foreign governments, their agencies, and instrumentalities–

(1) Aggregation. Loans and extensions of credit to foreign governments, their agencies, and instrumentalities will be aggregated with one another only if the loans or extensions of credit fail to meet either the means test or the purpose test at the time the loan or extension of credit is made.

(i) The means test is satisfied if the borrower has resources or revenue of its own sufficient to service its debt obligations. If the government's support (excluding guarantees by a central government of the borrower's debt) exceeds the borrower's annual revenues from other sources, it will be presumed that the means test has not been satisfied.

(ii) The purpose test is satisfied if the purpose of the loan or extension of credit is consistent with the purposes of the borrower's general business.

(2) Documentation. In order to show that the means and purpose tests have been satisfied, a bank must, at a minimum, retain in its files the following items:

(i) A statement (accompanied by supporting documentation) describing the legal status and the degree of financial and operational autonomy of the borrowing entity;

(ii) Financial statements for the borrowing entity for a minimum of three years prior to the date the loan or extension of credit was made or for each year that the borrowing entity has been in existence, if less than three;

(iii) Financial statements for each year the loan or extension of credit is outstanding;

(iv) The bank's assessment of the borrower's means of servicing the loan or extension of credit, including specific reasons in support of that assessment. The assessment shall include an analysis of the borrower's financial history, its present and projected economic and financial performance, and the significance of any financial support provided to the borrower by third parties, including the borrower's central government; and

(v) A loan agreement or other written statement from the borrower which clearly describes the purpose of the loan or extension of credit. The written representation will ordinarily constitute sufficient evidence that the purpose test has been satisfied. However, when, at the time the funds are disbursed, the bank knows or has reason to know of other information suggesting that the borrower will use the proceeds in a manner inconsistent with the written representation, it may not, without further inquiry, accept the representation.

(3) Restructured loans–

(i) Non-combination rule. Notwithstanding paragraphs (a) through (e) of this section, when previously outstanding loans and other extensions of credit to a foreign government, its agencies, and instrumentalities (i.e., public-sector obligors) that qualified for a separate lending limit under paragraph (f)(1) of this section are consolidated under a central obligor in a qualifying restructuring, such loans will not be aggregated and attributed to the central obligor. This includes any substitution in named obligors, solely because of the restructuring. Such loans (other than loans originally attributed to the central obligor in their own right) will not be considered obligations of the central obligor and will continue to be attributed to the original public-sector obligor for purposes of the lending limit.

(ii) Qualifying restructuring. Loans and other extensions of credit to a foreign government, its agencies, and instrumentalities will qualify for the non-combination process under paragraph (f)(3)(i) of this section only if they are restructured in a sovereign debt restructuring approved by the OCC, upon request by a bank for application of the non-combination rule. The factors that the OCC will use in making this determination include, but are not limited to, the following:

(A) Whether the restructuring involves a substantial portion of the total commercial bank loans outstanding to the foreign government, its agencies, and instrumentalities;

(B) Whether the restructuring involves a substantial number of the foreign country's external commercial bank creditors;

(C) Whether the restructuring and consolidation under a central obligor is being done primarily to facilitate external debt management; and

(D) Whether the restructuring includes features of debt or debt-service reduction.

(iii) 50 percent aggregate limit. With respect to any case in which the non-combination process under paragraph (f)(3)(i) of this section applies, a national bank's loans and other extensions of credit to a foreign government, its agencies and instrumentalities, (including restructured debt) shall not exceed, in the aggregate, 50 percent of the bank's capital and surplus.

§ 32.6    Nonconforming loans.

(a) A loan, within a bank's legal lending limit when made, will not be deemed a violation but will be treated as nonconforming if the loan is no longer in conformity with the bank's lending limit because–

(1) The bank's capital has declined, borrowers have subsequently merged or formed a common enterprise, lenders have merged, the lending limit or capital rules have changed; or

(2) Collateral securing the loan to satisfy the requirements of a lending limit exception has declined in value.

(b) A bank must use reasonable efforts to bring a loan that is nonconforming as a result of paragraph (a)(1) of this section into conformity with the bank's lending limit unless to do so would be inconsistent with safe and sound banking practices.

(c) A bank must bring a loan that is nonconforming as a result of circumstances described in paragraph (a)(2) of this section into conformity with the bank's lending limit within 30 calendar days, except when judicial proceedings, regulatory actions or other extraordinary circumstances beyond the bank's control prevent the bank from taking action.

**Notes and Comments 7.9.** Assume that an examination of the balance sheet of Quarter National Bank (QNB) indicates that it has unimpaired capital and surplus totalling $200 million. It has lent $25 million to the Nusquami Ministry of Development (NMD) in connection with a development project in which QNB, several other commercial banks, and the NMD itself are participating. Can QNB also make any or all of the following loans or extensions of credit:

   **a.** A short term credit of $10 million to NusBank, a Nusquami commercial bank 80%-owned by the Government of Nusquam, through the Nusquami

Ministry of Finance (NMF);

> **b.** A similar short term credit, secured by bonds of the Nusquami Port Authority (NPA), with a face value of $10 million;

> **c.** A similar short term credit, secured by a deposit in QNB, in the name of NusBank;

> **d.** A long-term project loan, in the amount of $20 million, to the NPA.

What other information, if any, do you require to answer this question?

# 5. Lending Supervision

**Notes and Comments 7.10.** Lending, whether domestic or international, also raises concerns about its effects on the safety and soundness of the lending bank. In general, such concerns are dealt with under the enforcement provisions of 12 U.S.C. § 1818.[3] However, in the case of international loans, another statutory enactment, the International Lending Supervision Act of 1983 (ILSA),[4] specifically addresses such concerns, among others. Compare section 1818(b), for example, with 12 U.S.C. §§ 3901-3904, 3907, and consider how they might differ in their approaches to lending supervision.

**7.11.** The following excerpts from the Comptroller's regulations are representative of the bank regulators' approach to lending supervision mandated by the ILSA.

## Comptroller of the Currency
### 12 C.F.R. pt. 28

§ 28.50 Authority, purpose, and scope.

(a) Authority. This subpart is issued pursuant to 12 U.S.C. 1 et seq., 93a, 161, and 1818; and the International Lending Supervision Act of 1983 (Pub.L. 98-181, title IX, 97 Stat. 1153, 12 U.S.C. 3901 et seq.). . . .

(c) Scope. This subpart requires national banks and District of Columbia banks to establish reserves against the risks presented in certain international assets and sets forth the accounting for various fees received by the banks when making international loans.

§ 28.51 Definitions.

For the purposes of this subpart:

(a) Banking institution means a national bank or a District of Columbia bank.

(b) Federal banking agencies means the OCC, the FRB, and the FDIC. . . .

(d) International loan means a loan . . . made to a foreign government, or to an individual, a corporation, or other entity not a citizen of, resident in, or organized or incorporated in the United States.

(e) International syndicated loan means a loan characterized by the formation of a group of managing banking institutions and, in the usual case, assumption by them of underwriting commitments, and participation in the loan by other banking institutions.

(f) Loan agreement means the document signed by all of the parties to a loan, containing the amount, terms, and conditions of the loan, and the interest and fees to be paid

---

3. *See, e.g.*, 12 U.S.C. § 1818(b) (administrative cease and desist order available to address unsafe and unsound practices).

4. Pub. L. No. 98-181, 97 Stat. 1153 (1983) (codified at 12 U.S.C. §§ 3901-3912).

by the borrower.

(g) Restructured international loan means a loan that meets the following criteria:

(1) The borrower is unable to service the existing loan according to its terms and is a resident of a foreign country in which there is a generalized inability of public and private sector obligors to meet their external debt obligations on a timely basis because of a lack of, or restraints on the availability of, needed foreign exchange in the country; and

(2) The terms of the existing loan are amended to reduce stated interest or extend the schedule of payments; or

(3) A new loan is made to, or for the benefit of, the borrower, enabling the borrower to service or refinance the existing debt.

(h) Transfer risk means the possibility that an asset cannot be serviced in the currency of payment because of a lack of, or restraints on the availability of, needed foreign exchange in the country of the obligor.

§ 28.52 Allocated transfer risk reserve.

(a) Establishment of allocated transfer risk reserve. A banking institution shall establish an allocated transfer risk reserve (ATRR) for specified international assets when required by the OCC in accordance with this section.

(b) Procedures and standards–

(1) Joint agency determination. At least annually, the Federal banking agencies shall determine jointly, based on the standards set forth in paragraph (b)(2) of this section, the following:

(i) Which international assets subject to transfer risk warrant establishment of an ATRR;

(ii) The amount of the ATRR for the specified assets; and

(iii) Whether an ATRR established for specified assets may be reduced.

(2) Standards for requiring ATRR–

(i) Evaluation of assets. The Federal banking agencies shall apply the following criteria in determining whether an ATRR is required for particular international assets:

(A) Whether the quality of a banking institution's assets has been impaired by a protracted inability of public or private obligors in a foreign country to make payments on their external indebtedness as indicated by such factors, among others, as whether:

(1) Such obligors have failed to make full interest payments on external indebtedness;

(2) Such obligors have failed to comply with the terms of any restructured indebtedness; or

(3) A foreign country has failed to comply with any International Monetary Fund or other suitable adjustment program; or

(B) Whether no definite prospects exist for the orderly restoration of debt service.

(ii) Determination of amount of ATRR.

(A) In determining the amount of the ATRR, the Federal banking agencies shall consider:

(1) The length of time the quality of the asset has been impaired;

(2) Recent actions taken to restore debt service capability;

(3) Prospects for restored asset quality; and

(4) Such other factors as the Federal banking agencies may consider relevant to the quality of the asset.

(B) The initial year's provision for the ATRR shall be 10 percent of the principal amount of each specified international asset, or such greater or lesser percentage determined by the Federal banking agencies. Additional provision, if any, for the ATRR in subsequent years shall be 15 percent of the principal amount of each specified international asset, or such greater or lesser percentage determined by the Federal banking agencies.

(3) Notification. Based on the joint agency determinations under paragraph (b)(1) of this section, the OCC shall notify each banking institution holding assets subject to an ATRR:

(i) Of the amount of the ATRR to be established by the institution for specified international assets; and

(ii) That an ATRR to be established for specified assets may be reduced.

(c) Accounting treatment of ATRR–

(1) Charge to current income. A banking institution shall establish an ATRR by a charge to current income and the amounts so charged shall not be included in the banking institution's capital or surplus.

(2) Separate accounting. A banking institution shall account for an ATRR separately from the Allowance for Possible Loan Losses, and shall deduct the ATRR from "gross loans and leases" to arrive at "net loans and leases." The ATRR must be established for each asset subject to the ATRR in the percentage amount specified.

(3) Consolidation. A banking institution shall establish an ATRR, as required, on a consolidated basis. . . .

(4) Alternative accounting treatment. A banking institution need not establish an ATRR if it writes down in the period in which the ATRR is required, or has written down in prior periods, the value of the specified international assets in the requisite amount for each such asset. For purposes of this paragraph, international assets may be written down by a charge to the Allowance for Possible Loan Losses or a reduction in the principal amount of the asset by application of interest payments or other collections on the asset. However, the Allowance for Possible Loan Losses must be replenished in such amount necessary to restore it to a level which adequately provides for the estimated losses inherent in the banking institution's loan portfolio.

(5) Reduction of ATRR. A banking institution may reduce an ATRR when notified by the OCC or, at any time, by writing down such amount of the international asset for which the ATRR was established.

§ 28.54  Reporting and disclosure of international assets.

(a) Requirements.

(1) Pursuant to section 907(a) of the International Lending Supervision Act of 1983 (title IX, Pub.L. 98-181, 97 Stat. 1153, 12 U.S.C. 3906) (ILSA) a banking institution shall submit to the OCC, at least quarterly, information regarding the amounts and composition of its holdings of international assets.

(2) Pursuant to section 907(b) of ILSA (12 U.S.C. 3906), a banking institution shall submit to the OCC information regarding concentrations in its holdings of international assets that are material in relation to total assets and to capital of the institution, such information to be made publicly available by the OCC on request. . . .

(c) Reservation of authority. Nothing contained in this part shall preclude the OCC from requiring from a banking institution such additional or more frequent information on the institution's holdings of international assets as the OCC may consider necessary.

**Notes and Comments 7.12.** Assume that a volcanic eruption and subsequent mudslides have resulted in Nusquam's major port facility now being located some three miles from the sea. This natural phenomenon has caused a financial and commercial collapse within the Nusquami economy. There appears to be serious question whether the Nusquami Government, its agencies and instrumentalities will be able to meet their quarterly interest payments on outstanding foreign debt (including QNB's loans and extensions of credit). When the Office of the Comptroller of the Currency discovers this, what supervisory steps will or should it take?

    **7.13.** Snitty Bank, N.A., has been a major lender to Nusquam, and the loans to the Government of Nusquam, and to various Nusquami commercial enterprises now makes up approximately 25 percent of Snitty's loan portfolio. Current indications are that many, if not all of these loans, will default over the next one to five years. Would there be any advantage to Snitty in establishing loan loss reserves to account for these expected losses now, or should Snitty simply wait until such time, if any, that the Comptroller requires the establishment of an ATRR?

# Chapter 8

# Problems of Less-Developed-Country ("LDC") Debt

## 1. Introduction

LDC debt is now, and has been for some time, in a period of serious crisis. One dimension of the problem is simply the magnitude of the total debt involved. In addition, from the point of view of U.S. international lenders, a high degree of concentration is also evident. For example, total foreign lending by U.S. commercial banks amounted to approximately $297 billion in 1986, with over 90 percent extended by a handful of the largest U.S. banks (i.e., those with assets over $10 billion). Nearly one-third of this debt was extended to borrowers that had restructured their debt within the past five years.

In short, what we have is a situation ripe for disaster: significant amounts of debt of LDCs with delicate economies concentrated in the loan portfolios of a relatively small number of lenders. Various strategies have traditionally been employed to avoid, or at least postpone, this potential for disaster. These strategies include, for example, debt refinancing (rollover of maturing debt or conversion of existing debt service payments into new medium-term debt) and debt rescheduling (formal deferment of debt-service payments, with new maturities applying to the deferred amounts).[1]

Various novel arrangements to resolve LDC debt crises have been implemented or proposed in recent years. Among these may be included spin-off "problem loan banks" to hold the questionable debt separate from a parent bank's ongoing operations,[2] aggressive use of loan loss reserves,[3] or the establishment of an international debt facility to broker relief

---

1. Some of these rescheduling arrangements can be quite complicated, involving a global understanding among a group of creditors. This is the approach in multiyear rescheduling arrangements, the so-called MYRAs, where creditors will negotiate consolidation periods of two or more years through the succession of shorter consolidations, coming into effect automatically after certain specified conditions are satisfied.

2. Indeed, this approach has been utilized in domestic problem bank situations since the mid-1980s. *See, e.g.*, Berg, *A New Way to Shed Bad Loans*, N.Y. Times, Jan. 16, 1988, at 35, col. 3.

3. *See, e.g.*, Bennett, *Banks Split On 3d-World Loan Issue*, N.Y. Times, Jan. 20, 1988, at D1, col. 6.

and renegotiation of LDC debt.[4] Nevertheless, by June 1999, total foreign debt of just the 33 *least* developed states amounted to approximately $127 billion.[5]

**Notes and Comments 8.1.** *Alternative Approaches to Official Debt Default.* Approximately 25 percent of the international loan portfolio of Quarter National Bank (QNB) is concentrated in loans to the Government of Nusquam, its agencies, instrumentalities, and corporations owned or controlled by the government. Several of its loans to the government itself are now in default, and QNB fears that this is the beginning of a trend. What alternative approaches to this problem are available to QNB? Consider the following excerpt.

### Walker F. Todd, A Brief History of International Lending, From a Regional Banker's Perspective
11 Geo. Mason U. L. Rev. 1 (1989)

In December 1987, the United States financial services industry passed the fourth of four significant milestones within one year in the evolution of the developing country debt problem or 'LDC' debt crisis. In February, Brazil announced a unilateral suspension of debt service to banks. Then, in May, Citicorp announced the creation of special loan loss reserves equal to about twenty-five percent of its Brazilian and selected other LDC credit exposure. Subsequently, forty-three of the fifty largest United States bank holding companies created similar reserves, principally to cover LDC exposures. Third, in mid-December, several large regional banks in the United States announced the first actual charge-offs of portions of their LDC credit exposures and the creation of enough additional loan loss reserves to bring remaining LDC credit exposures into line with current secondary market prices for LDC debt, generally in the neighborhood of fifty to sixty percent reserved or charged off.[14]

Finally, at year-end 1987, press reports indicated that the Government of Mexico, the United States Treasury, and J. P. Morgan had agreed on a proposal to exchange up to $10 billion of new, 20-year, interest-bearing Mexican bonds for up to $20 billion of outstanding Mexican loans owed to the banks participating in the arrangement. After the press statements, several large United States regional banks and foreign banks indicated their willingness to make tenders for bonds under the plan. Mexico proposed to use up to $2 billion of its $11 to $13 billion of foreign currency reserves to purchase a new issue of 20-year, zero-coupon United States treasury bonds with a value at maturity equal to the principal value of the Mexican bonds and to place the United States bonds in escrow inside

---

4. *See, e.g.*, Farnsworth, *Plan Is Offered to Ease Debt-Crisis Threat*, N.Y. Times, Mar. 1, 198, at D2, col. 1 (American Express "I2D2" proposal); Farnsworth, *I.M.F. Studying Plan to Ease Debt Burden*, N.Y. Times, Mar. 8, 1988, at D2, col. 5.

5. Roger Cohen, *An Agreement On Debt Relief For Poor Lands*, N.Y. Times, June 19, 1999, at A1, col. 6.

14. . . . With the exception of two large regional bank holding companies that have only 20 and 25 percent reserves for LDC debt exposure, and three large regional bank holding companies that have only negligible LDC debt exposure and no LDC debt reserves, the range of reserves among 23 large regional bank holding companies is from 43 to 100 percent of exposure, with a central tendency around 55 percent reserves. In contrast, among ten large New York City and Chicago bank holding companies, the range of LDC debt reserves is from 22 to 40 percent, with a central tendency around 25 percent.

the United States to secure the Mexican bonds, thereby insuring investors of repayment of principal at maturity. Some interest rate risk would remain for investors because the Mexican bonds would bear floating interest rates at a margin above LIBOR (London interbank offered rate) that is about twice the current interest margin for rescheduled Mexican debt. . . . In fact, press reports following the Mexican debt exchange indicated that only 139 of the estimated 560 banks eligible to submit bids actually did so. Only ninety-five bids were accepted, with an estimated value of $2.56 billion, in exchange for $3.67 billion of Mexican debt. . . .

United States banks' loans to all of Latin America, including Mexico, were only $8 billion at year-end 1973, but those loans nearly doubled, to $15 billion, by year-end 1974 and increased to $72.2 billion by year-end 1982. The June 1987 estimate for all of Latin America was $83.7 billion.

The official beginning of the LDC debt crisis was the public announcement of the Mexican payment difficulties in 1982. On August 15, 1982, the Mexican Finance Minister, Jesus Silva Herzog, met a group of more than 100 United States and foreign bankers in New York City and announced the end of Mexico's capacity to service its external, hard-currency debt obligations. Mexico's currency reserves were completely exhausted, and there was a scarcity of available, unpledged foreign assets that Mexico could use to secure new borrowings, but such assets somehow were found anyway. For a time, after the Mexican interruption of debt service, some large LDC debtors still were able to maintain debt service on a country-by-country basis. Brazil still could roll over maturing short-term bank credits until early December 1982, but then Brazil also temporarily interrupted its debt service, due to what was then characterized as short-term liquidity crisis. Then one by one, Argentina, Venezuela, and eventually every continental country in Latin America except Colombia and Paraguay, interrupted their foreign debt service. Each of those countries arranged restructurings of its external debt, usually under the auspices of the International Monetary Fund (IMF). . . .

The 1982-1985 era is remembered in commercial and central banking circles as the era of the initial reschedulings and new money loans. The principal justification for temporizing, advanced in official circles at the outset of the crisis, was to buy time, which made apparent good sense if all that was involved was a short-term liquidity crisis. However, when Poland suspended its external debt service in April 1981, a signal was sent that should have been hard to ignore regarding the future course of the LDC debt crisis. Procedures followed during the Polish debt crisis, which lasted five years before there was movement in the direction of an IMF program for Poland, proved to be leading indicators of actions taken with other LDCs and should have indicated whether the normal, so-called 'orthodox' approach to adjustment by LDCs was going to succeed over the long haul.

The use of the new money loan, attributed in the literature to Jacques de Larosiere, then head of the IMF, staved off legal default by roughly but just barely keeping interest payments current for a host of third world debtors in the 1982-1985 era. Unfortunately, new money lending also unwittingly and inexorably increased the outstanding principal owed by the debtors. The foreign debts of Mexico and Brazil increased from about $80 billion in 1982 to about $105 billion for Mexico and $114 billion for Brazil at year-end 1987, with very little in the way of useable funds provided in the interim. In the $4 billion and $5 billion new money credits arranged for Mexico and Brazil in 1983-85, as many as 530 banks were requested to act in unison—a difficult task in the best of times, and a nearly impossible one in those circumstances. Somehow this task was completed, but with progressively less participation by United States regional and some foreign banks, which contributed to the increased concentration of LDC loan problems in United States money center banks after 1982.

. . . The nine largest money center banks (excluding Continental Illinois) had total capital then of $27.1 billion, but their exposure to developing countries was $54.3 billion, more than twice their capital. Total United States bank claims on the fifteen countries later declared eligible for the Baker Plan were $90.2 billion in 1982. Thus, sixty percent of all United States banks' exposure to the most troubled developing countries was held by the nine largest banks. While most LDC debt exposure of European banks was in Africa, Asia, and Eastern Europe, the bulk of United States banks' exposure was in Latin America. Four debtor nations alone, Mexico ($23.6 billion), Brazil ($23.0 billion), Argentina ($9.1 billion), and Venezuela ($8.4 billion), accounted for three-fourths of all United States banks' exposure to the fifteen heavily indebted countries by June 1987. . . .

After the initial round of reschedulings in 1982-1984, a generally improved world economic outlook made bankers and central bankers optimistic that the new money lending approach might work after all. By early 1985, Mexico and Brazil had accumulated modest or, in Brazil's case, significant surpluses in their current account balances due to the application of the classic IMF formulas for adjustment–suitably modified, of course, because domestic inflation never really was controlled in either country. But exports were stimulated, imports were reduced drastically, and enough new money loans were provided to cover debt service needs. However, the original, orthodox plan seemed to be faltering as the year 1985 progressed. The Baker Plan, announced in October 1985, had the effect of relieving an immediate financial crisis in Mexico, created by an earthquake in Mexico City and other heavily populated areas, for which there were insufficient reconstruction funds. The Baker Plan contemplated enough advances of new money to provide growth in debtor economies above the level merely required to sustain interest payments on external borrowings. The Baker Plan is credited with enabling bankers and central bankers to have additional time to arrange longer-term solutions to the LDC debt crisis. . . .

The next phase of the LDC debt crisis began in May 1987, when the largest United States bank holding company[, Citicorp,] announced the creation of up to $3 billion of loan loss reserves for LDC debt, about twenty-five percent of its LDC exposure. Within a week, its share value increased $5 per share, about 10 percent of the value prior to the announcement. Other bank holding companies followed suit, including, in all, forty-three of the fifty largest bank holding companies in the United States. The initial round of provisionings occurred because, by year-end 1986, oil prices had fallen so low (about $9 per barrel) that Mexico's foreign exchange reserves (calculated at the last prior new money loan with an assumed price of $15 per barrel) were at negligible levels, the Austral (Argentina) and Cruzado (Brazil) currency reform plans were encountering difficulty, and Brazil suspended foreign exchange interest payments to conserve reserves in February 1987.

During 1987, the amount of loan loss reserves, usually only one or two percent of total loans at the largest banks since 1975, became much larger (three to five percent). This provisioning encouraged market analysts, and most money center banks' shares were traded consistently above book value from the spring until the autumn of 1987, one of the two times since 1974 that this situation occurred. The future exclusion of the LDC loss reserves from primary (Tier 1) capital for supervisory capital adequacy ratios, however, will require additional capital increases for some of the banks involved. . . .

The new loan-loss reserve ratios are surprisingly large, in the historical context. These higher levels of loan-loss reserves are all the more surprising because there are no special tax benefits for creating such large reserves. Under the 1986 tax law, banks' loan loss reserves are deductible from taxable income only to the extent that a bad-debt deduction (charge-off) actually is taken during the same tax year. As of this writing, seven of the ten largest United States banks had only about twenty-five percent of their LDC debt exposure reserved for; two large California bank holding companies and one large Chicago bank holding company were reserved for at least fifty percent of their LDC debt exposures in January 1988.

Foreign banks have not been idle in reserving against LDC exposure, either. Stimulated in part by generous tax allowances for loan loss provisions, continental European banks were between thirty percent and seventy percent reserved (provisioned), including East European and African exposures, as early as mid-1984. Kredietbank of Belgium announced in September 1987 that it would be 100 percent provisioned for LDC exposure by year-end 1987. Japanese and British banks, previously feeling themselves restrained by tax treatment of provisions that was similar to United States tax treatment (no deduction for provisions, but deductions for actual charge-offs), have begun to create special loan loss reserves for LDC exposure. British clearing banks are provisioned to the same general extent (about twenty-five to thirty-three percent of LDC exposure) as United States money center banks.

The round of special LDC loan provisioning initiated in March 1987 has not yet played itself out. More provisioning occurred in December 1987 and January 1988, and still more probably is in store, regardless of any new money loans made in the future, because of ongoing or recurring payments arrears. Brazil, Ecuador, and Argentina have been negotiating with bank creditors in late 1987 and early 1988, and officials are justifiably optimistic that agreements will be reached to provide new money loans to them during 1988, but it should be remembered that those countries have had frequent payments arrears during the 1982-1987 era. . . .

Bank supervisors may be expected to continue to press for both more capital and capital of better quality. The 1987 special provisions for LDC debt were taken almost entirely from the equity accounts (paid-in common share capital, perpetual preferred shares, and retained earnings or surplus) of the bank holding companies. Temporarily, at least, because 100 percent of the LDC loan loss provisions still count as primary supervisory capital, the primary capital ratios of the bank holding companies have not been weakened, but the common equity ratios are as low as they have been since the early 1980s, typically between two and four percent of total assets, at the largest companies.

Debt-for-equity swaps[a] and securitization of LDC debt are other options frequently mentioned for improving banks' capacity to manage the payments arrears problem on LDC debt. It has been difficult to find acceptable projects for such swaps, but at least a few billion dollars of debt per year should be capable of disposition in that manner. Securitization may offer limited options because institutional investors might have to comply with 'prudent man' fiduciary standards for purchases of packages of LDC debt that did not have third-party guarantees of payment.

Outright secondary market loan sales are another option, although not an option specifically approved for the Baker Plan. Bid prices in the London secondary market (March 1988) for Brazilian (forty-six percent), Argentine (twenty-seven percent), Mexican (forty-eight percent) and Venezuelan (fifty-two percent) debt were at such substantial discounts from face value, in admittedly thin trading, as to suggest that the market questions the eventual repayment capacities, or willingness to pay, of the debtors, notwithstanding any mathematical demonstration of their current or future capacities to pay. . . .

Failure of United States bankers and bank supervisory authorities to implement any of the market-oriented alternatives inevitably shifts the ball into the debtors' half of the field. As time passes, debtors like Brazil, who have benefitted handsomely from the 1986-1987 decline in oil prices and whose mathematical capacity to pay never was much in doubt, nevertheless could lose the willingness or domestic political capacity to pay. Long-term

---

a. On Debt-for-equity swaps, see § 2, *infra*.

stretch-outs of maturities in principal, reductions of interest rates below market rates (and even below costs of funds), partial repudiations, extensive accumulations of arrears, partial reductions, cancellations, forgiveness, and the like, probably will increase the longer that the principal value of the LDC debt continues at anything like the current level. Historical and market forces will drive the debt crisis in this direction, even if the United States authorities and the IMF do not.

No matter how it is measured, United States money center banks' exposure to LDCs is greater than the exposure for anyone else. Most of the large regional banks in the United States do not have excessively large, unprovisioned LDC debt exposures, while that exposure still is concentrated and only marginally provisioned for at the money center banks. Even after all the loan-loss reserving and provisioning for LDC debt, and even after retaining seventy percent of earnings for equity accounts, then deducting LDC exposure, Salomon Brothers has estimated that the United States money center banks would be barely solvent, with aggregate net worth of 0.1 percent of assets, while other creditor nations' banks are substantially stronger. . . .

The orthodox IMF three-year austerity cure for LDC overindebtedness is useful in the short term, in the absence of additional external stresses like earthquakes or mudslides, especially for normally profligate debtors with long and deep-rooted traditions of domestic inflation or capital flight. However, it is far from clear that new money lending, on the scale usually proposed in rescheduling and restructuring programs, can be implemented safely by commercial banks. . . .

In the absence of any effective, sustainable action by creditors, governments, or multilateral lending agencies to relieve the stresses of the LDC debt crisis, financial markets inevitably find their own solutions. Thus far, no market-driven solution has emerged that effects a global restructuring of LDC debts. Instead, a series of market alternatives have emerged, each dealing with comparatively small pieces of the total puzzle. For example, active, but still thin, trading in a secondary market for LDC debt of banks emerged in London in 1982 at discounts from par value that currently have a central tendency around fifty percent. The 1988 Morgan Guaranty-Mexico-United States Treasury bonds-for-debt auction is another illustration of market-driven solutions, as are debt-for-equity swaps. Most of such market-driven solutions to the LDC debt problem have been approved by the United States Treasury as acceptable alternatives ('menu options') under the Baker Plan. In any event, the longer that the problem persists without a global solution, the greater will be the number and amount of market-oriented proposals that will surface.

A steady decline in the overall value of LDC debt in the secondary market seems to have set in. The central tendency a year ago (March 1987) was in the sixty percent range, and a year earlier, it was close to seventy percent. If the fairly steady rate of decline persists for two to three more years, which is likely to happen unless debtor economies revive, the markets themselves may create an atmosphere in which general debt reduction or cancellation could flourish because, at twenty to thirty percent of par value, debtor countries themselves might find it a profitable use of foreign exchange to buy in their own debt. Thus, if anything other than a general muddling-through toward a debtor-funded cancellation of the LDC debt in two to three years is to emerge from the present crisis, the necessary reforms must begin to operate now, because there is not much time left. To some extent, Bolivia (eleven percent) and Peru (five percent) already have begun to operate on the 'debtor-funded cancellation' principle, and Argentina (twenty-seven percent) and Ecuador (twenty-nine percent) are beginning to reach market price levels at which such cancellations become feasible. . . .

An option frequently discussed, but still resisted by the United States government, is third-party guarantees of LDC debt. Initially, about three years ago, such discussions involved purchase of LDC debt from banks at about ninety percent of par. The secondary market price declines for LDC debt since 1984 have made such proposals distinctly less attractive to both official purchasers and LDC debtors who would have to maintain debt service on the remaining debt. Recent proposals of this type, such as one presented by the chairman of American Express in February 1988, would create a new entity, the Institute of International Debt and Development, a kind of international joint venture funded by sponsoring governments and operated by the IMF and the World Bank, to purchase up to $230 billion of debt from the fifteen countries eligible for the Baker Plan. The proposal assumes that the debt thus purchased can be serviced or sold for at least fifty percent of par value.

. . . [T]he United States tradition is distinctly different. Moreover, it is not clear whether the United States, as distinguished from large surplus countries like Japan and West Germany, should provide the bulk of the assumptions or guarantees. . . .

**Notes and Comments 8.2.** *The Brady Plan to the Rescue.* Nevertheless, by mid-1989, the challenge of LDC debt and the need for debt reduction remained serious concerns.[6] In March 1989, U.S. Treasury Secretary Brady proposed steps to strengthen debt reduction strategies and to provide financial support for efforts by debtor countries to reform their economies and to achieve sustainable growth, a proposal commonly known as the "Brady Plan." The plan emphasized debt and debt-service reduction as a complement to new private lending, and it also stressed investment and "flight capital" repatriation as sources of capital for developing countries. Thus, the three principal elements of the plan involved (*i*) a commitment on the part of debtors to a stronger emphasis on economic measures to increase and encourage foreign and domestic investment and repatriation of flight capital; (*ii*) support from the IMF and the World Bank, through financing and guarantees, for such economic reform measures; and, (*iii*) active support from private commercial banks, through negotiation of debt and debt-service reduction and through new lending.[7] Each of these elements is in effect a quid pro quo for the other two. Under the rubric of the Brady Plan, renegotiation of debt and debt-service requirements was finalized between Mexico and its U.S. creditor banks. What are the disadvantages to this approach? Consider the following cases.

## Lloyds Bank PLC v. Republic of Ecuador
— F. Supp. —, 1998 WL 118170 (S.D.N.Y. 1998)

Chin, J.

[For the facts involved, see the excerpt from the case in Chapter 7, § 3 *supra*.]

. . . Ecuador attempts to persuade the Court that either the 1994 Financing Plan and/or its internal "policy," adopted in 1995, regarding the treatment of the unpaid, past due interest, justifies its refusal to pay the interest arrears. Both contentions are rejected. First, to the extent that Ecuador relies on the 1994 Financing Plan, negotiated under the auspices

---

6. *See* INTERNATIONAL MONETARY FUND, 1989 ANNUAL REPORT 23-28 (discussing external debt situation and current strategies).

7. *See id.* at 24.

of the Brady Plan, as justification for its refusal to pay the interest arrears, authority in this circuit is clear that international debt resolution measures, such as the Brady Plan and those guided by the International Monetary Fund ("IMF"), do not alter prior obligations of the participating states. . . . *Pravin Banker Assocs., Ltd. v. Banco Popular del Peru*, 895 F.Supp. 660, 666 (S.D.N.Y. 1995) ("The Brady Plan does not abrogate the contractual rights of creditor banks, nor does it compel creditors to forbear from enforcing those rights while debt restructuring negotiations are ongoing."), *aff'd*, 109 F.3d 850 (2d Cir. 1997).

## Pravin Banker Associates, Ltd. v. Banco Popular del Peru
### 109 F.3d 850 (2d Cir. 1997)

Calabresi, Circuit Judge:

The reverberations of the international sovereign debt crisis of the 1980's are still being felt. Banco Popular del Peru ("Banco Popular") and the Republic of Peru ("Peru") appeal from a decision of the United States District Court for the Southern District of New York . . . granting summary judgment against them and denying their motion for . . . dismissal, or for a stay, of these proceedings pending completion of Peru's efforts to renegotiate its commercial debt under the Brady Plan. They seek a reversal of summary judgment or a stay of the execution of that judgment until Peru's renegotiation efforts are complete, arguing that the judgment for the appellee, Pravin Banker Associates, Ltd. ("Pravin"), threatens those negotiations and, hence, the successful economic rehabilitation of Peru. We find that the district court properly weighed America's competing interests in: a) ensuring the successful, voluntary resolution of past-due foreign sovereign debt and b) maintaining the enforceability of contracts under United States law. It then appropriately concluded that using principles of international comity to defer further the enforceability of Pravin's debt would violate United States policy. Accordingly, we affirm the district court's judgment. ...

Banco Popular, a state-owned bank since 1970, provided loans and credit to public and private companies and individuals in Peru. In order to do so, it borrowed funds from many foreign financial institutions. This action concerns the small part of Peru's foreign debt that was borrowed by Banco Popular from Mellon Bank, N.A. of Pittsburgh, PA ("Mellon") and later sold to Pravin. Following Mexico and a number of other Latin American countries, Peru announced in March 1983 that it had insufficient foreign exchange reserves to service its foreign debt, and that it was unable to get credit to do so. After its announcement, Peru negotiated with its creditors a series of agreements that stated terms for the settlement of various categories of Peruvian debt. Two of these, the Mellon Letter Agreements, attempted to resolve more than $14 million owed as a result of over thirty separate short-term working capital loans that Mellon had made to Banco Popular. The agreements, signed by Mellon Bank and Banco Popular, extended the due dates on these loans for 360 days. In exchange, the government of Peru itself guaranteed the loans.

In 1984, a round of negotiations intended to provide a longer-term solution to Peru's liquidity crisis failed, and Peru imposed new restrictions on the payment of foreign exchange in order to prevent the depletion of its external reserves. As a result, Banco Popular stopped making the principal payments on the Mellon debt that were required by the Letter Agreements, and from 1984 until 1992, only paid interest. This put Banco Popular in default on the loans. In 1989, many of Peru's commercial lenders, including Mellon, filed lawsuits to preserve their legal claims because they worried that, if they did not do so, the statute of limitations would expire on the outstanding debts.

In 1990, after Alberto Fujimori was elected President of Peru, Peru's economic policies changed dramatically. President Fujimori began a major reform of the Peruvian economy and in doing so attempted to comply with International Monetary Fund ("IMF") policies. Following these changes, the Bank Advisory Committee, a committee of Peru's creditors headed by Citibank, N.A., signed an agreement with Peru to stay all pending lawsuits in order to promote negotiations to resolve the entire problem of the unpaid foreign debts. The stay was conditioned on Peru's continued efforts to maintain fiscally sound economic policies, and on none of the individual lawsuits being permitted to go forward alone. Mellon participated in these meetings and agreed to a stay of its own lawsuit on analogous terms. Since then, Peru has made significant strides in restructuring its economy, reducing inflation, and decreasing the government deficit.

Since 1990, the Bank Advisory Committee has continued negotiations with Peru with the aim of reaching a restructuring agreement, under the auspices of the IMF, that would be consistent with the Brady Plan. Before the Brady Plan, announced by then United States Secretary of the Treasury Nicholas Brady in March of 1989, United States policy mainly encouraged additional lending to developing countries that were unable to service their sovereign debt. Under the Brady Plan, banks were, instead, urged voluntarily: (1) to reduce the foreign countries' debt burdens; (2) to restructure old debts; and, (3) as before, to provide additional loans. Countries entering Brady Plan negotiations are expected to conform to IMF requirements for restructuring their economy, and the IMF is charged with overseeing the negotiations between each country and its creditors. Thus, the plan contemplates a sharing of financial sacrifices between sovereign debtors and their commercial creditors in the context of negotiated and mutually agreed-upon terms.

The appellee, Pravin, acquired, at a discount in the secondary market for sovereign debt, $9 million (face value) of Banco Popular's debt to Mellon in 1990. Pravin resold most of this debt almost immediately, but continues to hold $1,425,000. Peru and Banco Popular were notified of the assignment from Mellon to Pravin, and Banco Popular, thereafter, made interest payments directly to Pravin.

Subsequently, Pravin alleges, Banco Popular stopped making interest payments, in violation of a new agreement between Pravin and the bank. Pravin contends that it then made a demand on Banco Popular for the principal and unpaid interest. When this demand was not met in February of 1992, Pravin declared Banco Popular in default on the debt. Later that year, since Banco Popular was unable to pay its creditors, Peru's central bank appointed a committee of liquidators to dissolve Banco Popular and to distribute its liquidated assets.

Pravin refused to join either the Peruvian liquidation proceedings or the Brady Plan negotiations. Instead, Pravin brought this suit against Banco Popular, and its guarantor, Peru, for non-payment of the debt. The defendants cross-moved to dismiss, stay, or deny Pravin's motion for summary judgment arguing that allowing the action to go forward would reawaken all of the other lawsuits that the Bank Advisory Committee had succeeded in having stayed. It would, Peru contends, result in a creditor stampede to find and attach Peruvian assets, and such a stampede would, in turn, disrupt Peru's structural reform efforts.

The district court granted a six-month stay to allow the orderly completion of Banco Popular's Peruvian liquidation proceedings. . . . After the six-month stay elapsed, Pravin renewed its motion for summary judgment and Banco Popular and Peru renewed their cross-motions for a stay or for dismissal of the complaint. They argued that this was essential to facilitate Peru's ongoing negotiations with the Bank Advisory Committee under the Brady Plan. The district court, thereupon, granted an additional two-month stay to permit the parties to submit further information to the court relating to: (1) the extent of Peru's debt problem, (2) Peru's efforts to resolve the problem through negotiations with its creditors, (3) whether there were other foreign debt actions pending against Peru, and (4) whether Peru had entered into any agreements that would toll the statute of limitations on Pravin's debt if Pravin did not continue its lawsuit against Peru. . . .

When this further stay expired, Pravin again renewed its motion for summary judgment, and the defendants again renewed their cross-motion for a stay or for dismissal. At this time, Peru and Banco Popular also advanced for the first time the argument that Pravin was not a proper assignee because, allegedly not being a financial institution, it was prohibited from buying the Mellon debt. The court rejected this claim, denied the motion of Banco Popular and Peru to dismiss or stay the action, and granted Pravin's motion for summary judgment, thereby allowing enforcement of the debt. . . . On January 19, 1996, it entered judgment for Pravin in the amount of $2,161,539.78, plus pre-judgment simple interest accrued from October 26, 1995 through the date of judgment, plus post-judgment interest. . . .

After this decision issued, the defendants once again moved to stay the judgment pending the resolution of their Brady negotiations with creditors. The district court rejected the motion, but stayed the judgment for 30 days to allow the defendants to appeal the denial. This court thereupon denied the motion to stay unless a bond were posted in the full amount of the judgment. . . . Before doing so, however, we asked the United States to express its views as to whether either denial of the motion to stay (or denial of the motion unless bond were posted) would contravene United States policy. The United States Attorney's office declined to submit a statement of interest, but sent a letter, . . . which indicated various sources of United States policy on foreign sovereign debt.

Peru and Banco Popular now appeal the denial of the motions to stay the proceedings and the grant of summary judgment. They argue that the court erred in failing to extend international comity to Peru's negotiations with the Bank Advisory Committee and in concluding that Pravin is a proper assignee of the Mellon debt. . . .

International comity is "the recognition which one nation allows within its territory to the legislative, executive or judicial acts of another nation." *Hilton v. Guyot*, 159 U.S. 113, 164 (1895). Under the principles of international comity, United States courts ordinarily refuse to review acts of foreign governments and defer to proceedings taking place in foreign countries, allowing those acts and proceedings to have extraterritorial effect in the United States. . . .

Although courts in this country have long recognized the principles of international comity and have advocated them in order to promote cooperation and reciprocity with foreign lands, comity remains a rule of "practice, convenience, and expediency" rather than of law. . . . And courts will not extend comity to foreign proceedings when doing so would be contrary to the policies or prejudicial to the interests of the United States. . . .

Peru's efforts to negotiate a settlement of its unpaid debt to foreign creditors are acts by a foreign government that have extraterritorial effect in the United States. Because Peru contends that this suit, and the district court's grant of summary judgment, is inconsistent with and disruptive to those efforts, the grant of summary judgment must be evaluated in the light of principles of international comity. . . .

As the district court recognized, however, extending comity to Peru's debt negotiations is only appropriate if it is consistent with United States government policy. The district court correctly identified two substantial aspects of United States policy that are implicated by this suit. First, the United States encourages participation in, and advocates the success of, IMF foreign debt resolution procedures under the Brady Plan. . . . Second, the United States has a strong interest in ensuring the enforceability of valid debts under the principles of contract law, and in particular, the continuing enforceability of foreign debts owed to United States lenders. . . . This second interest limits the first so that, although the United States advocates negotiations to effect debt reduction and continued lending to defaulting foreign sovereigns, it maintains that creditor participation in such negotiations should be on a strictly voluntary basis. It also requires that debts remain enforceable throughout the negotiations. . . .

. . . [T]he district court found that a six-month stay to allow the completion of the on-going liquidation proceedings for Banco Popular would not significantly harm United States interests, and the court therefore granted the stay. [In its third opinion,] however, the court found that an indefinite stay to allow Peru to complete its efforts to renegotiate its foreign debt would prejudice United States interests, and it refused to grant one, instead granting summary judgment in favor of Pravin. We agree with the court's conclusion in both instances.

The six-month stay . . . allowed Banco Popular's liquidation proceedings to be concluded. As such it followed the federal courts' long-standing recognition of foreign bankruptcy proceedings, . . . and did not threaten the long-term enforceability of the debt. To deny summary judgment . . . however, would have had a very different effect. It would first have denied Pravin its right to enforce the underlying debt–despite clear United States policy that it be able to do so–by making Pravin's rights conditional on the completion of a process which had no obvious (and reasonably proximate) termination date.[1] Second, it would have converted what the United States intended to be voluntary and open-ended negotiations between Peru and its creditors into the equivalent of a judicially-enforced bankruptcy proceeding, for it would, in effect, have prohibited the exercise of legal rights outside of the negotiations. . . . Under the circumstances, the district court correctly ruled that summary judgment was appropriate.

An argument might be made that, although summary judgment was appropriate, the circumstances of this case justified a stay of the proceedings or, in the alternative, a stay of the execution of the judgment because either stay might allow the completion of Peru's negotiations with its creditors without unduly threatening the ultimate enforceability of the debt. The district court's denial of the motions by Peru and Banco Popular to stay the proceedings or execution of the judgment, however, are reviewed only for abuse of discretion. . . . Since Banco Popular and Peru do not argue that the district court abused its discretion in denying the motion to stay the proceedings or execution of the judgment, and there is no evidence that the court failed to consider the proper facts in evaluating whether to grant a stay, we affirm the district court's denial. . . .

The district court correctly concluded that extending international comity to Peru's Brady agreement negotiations would be contrary to United States policy, and therefore properly refused to dismiss or stay the proceedings below until the completion of those negotiations. Similarly, the district court did not abuse its discretion in failing to stay the proceedings or the execution of the judgment during the course of the Brady negotiations.

## Elliott Associates, L.P. v. The Republic of Panama
975 F. Supp. 332 (S.D.N.Y. 1997)

Chin, District Judge.

In the 1980's, a number of countries–including the defendant Republic of Panama ("Panama")–encountered serious difficulties in servicing their foreign debt. As a consequence, and because of growing concern over the continued stability of the international

---

1. Although Peru's Brady agreement finally closed in early March 1997, see Sally Bowen, *Peru Completes Brady Deal*, Financial Times, Mar. 10, 1997, at 28, we note that the planned closing date had been delayed many times since the case was argued.

financial system, United States Treasury Secretary Nicholas Brady announced a plan (the "Brady Plan") in 1989 encouraging bank creditors to reduce the debt obligations of lesser developed countries by restructuring old debt and providing new loans.

Panama took advantage of the Brady Plan and restructured much of its external debt in 1995 pursuant to what became known as the "1995 Financing Plan." The restructured debt included balances due under loan agreements entered into with certain banks and financial institutions in 1978 for $300 million (the "1978 Agreement") and in 1982 for $225 million (the "1982 Agreement").

At issue in the instant case is a portion of the 1982 debt. In late 1995, two of the banks that had participated in the 1982 loan, Citibank, N.A. ("Citibank") and Swiss Bank Corporation ("Swiss Bank") (together, "the Banks"), assigned their interest in $12,242,018.21 of the debt to plaintiff Elliott Associates, L.P. ("Elliott") for approximately $8 million. After the assignments, Panama (through its Agent) made some interest payments to Elliott, but the payments eventually stopped. For its part, Elliott refused to restructure its debt in accordance with the 1995 Financing Plan, even though all the other creditors under the 1982 Agreement agreed to do so.

Instead, on July 15, 1996, Elliott commenced this breach of contract action, seeking judgment against Panama for the amounts due under the 1982 Agreement. Panama responded by asserting a counterclaim against Elliott for tortious interference with Panama's contractual relations with the Banks.

Before the Court is Elliott's motion for summary judgment, both for judgment on its breach of contract claim and for dismissal of Panama's counterclaim for tortious interference with contract. . . .

Panama contends that summary judgment must be denied because the assignments of the loans to Elliott were improper under the terms of the 1982 Agreement and the 1995 Financing Plan. . . .

. . . I . . . conclude that the defenses must be rejected as a matter of law. The assignments to Elliott were permitted by the agreements in question. . . .

In moving for summary judgment, Elliott argues that it has a valid assignment of the Banks' interests under the 1982 Agreement, that Panama thus has a contractual obligation to Elliott, and that Panama is in breach of that obligation by failing to repay its debt. Panama argues that the 1982 Agreement has been amended by the 1995 Financing Plan (which was agreed to by both Citibank and Swiss Bank, among others) to prohibit the assignment of debt in the manner in which the loans in question were assigned to Elliott. Moreover, Panama asserts that Elliott tortiously interfered with the implementation of the 1995 Financing Agreement by knowingly seeking assignment of debt contrary to its terms.

Section 14.08 of the 1982 Agreement provides that the Agreement can be "amended, modified or waived" upon the written consent of "the Borrower, the Agent and the Majority Lenders." . . . Section 1.01 defines "the Majority Lenders" as those "Lenders" who "at any time on or prior to the Commitment Termination Date . . . have more than 50% of the aggregate amount of the Commitments and, at any time thereafter, Lenders who at such time hold 50% of the aggregate unpaid principal amount of the Loans." . . . According to Panama, these conditions were met when Panama and Citibank, Swiss Bank, and other participating banks entered into the 1995 Financing Plan.

In general, the 1995 Financing Plan sets forth the terms of Panama's debt restructuring, including the exchange of principal for new bonds and new arrangements for interest payments. To maintain an orderly process pending its implementation, the Plan also included "Interim Measures," by which each creditor holding debt eligible for restructuring agreed not to "recognize or record any assignment of Eligible Principal or Eligible Interest made after the Final Trading Date" of October 20, 1995. . . . Panama was particularly concerned with establishing a "Final Trading Date" so that it would have a firm date by which it would know which creditors had committed to the Plan. The settlement of such assignments made before the Final Trading Date was to be completed on or before November 10, 1995. . . .

The 1995 Financing Plan also required that all creditors participating in the debt restructuring submit a Commitment Letter to Panama no later than November 14, 1995, agreeing: (1) not to assign any debt eligible for restructuring after October 20, 1995; (2) to complete the settlement of all such assignments on or before November 10, 1995; and (3) not to assign any such debt after signing the Commitment Letter except to an assignee who (a) completed the settlement of the assignment on or before November 10, 1995 and (b) agreed (i) to assume the obligations under the Commitment Letter and (ii) to submit a Commitment Letter on or before November 14, 1995. . . .The Commitment Letter also required that each Lender consent to the Interim Measures described in Part V of the Financing Plan.

According to Panama, after receiving Commitment Letters from "institutions holding more than 50 percent of the then-outstanding amounts under the 1982 Agreement," the 1982 Agreement was amended and modified retroactively to prohibit any assignments after October 20, 1995. . . . It is undisputed that Citibank and Swiss Bank each submitted a Commitment Letter to Panama on November 14, 1995. . . . In fact, Panama alleges that it received Commitment Letters from all of the other banks that held interests in the 1982 Agreement debt. . . . Thus, the 1982 Agreement was amended to include the terms of the 1995 Financing Plan. . . .

Elliott's entitlement to recover the amounts due under the 1982 Agreement turns on the validity of the assignments of the debt to Elliott from the Banks. Panama contends that the assignments were invalid because: (1) they were obtained after the Final Trading Date established in the 1995 Financing Plan; [and] (2) Elliott is not a proper assignee under the 1982 Agreement. . . .

Under the 1995 Financing Plan, banks could not "recognize or record" any assignments of debt "made after the Final Trading Debt" of October 20, 1995. . . . The 1995 Financing Plan gave the banks until November 10, 1995 to complete the "settlement" of assignments made by October 20, 1995. . . . As summarized in Annex B:

> Pursuant to the Commitment Letter, each Lender will agree not to assign any of its Eligible Debt after October 20, 1995 (the "Final Trading Date ") and to complete the settlement of all such assignments on or before November 10, 1995.
> . . .

. . . Hence, the 1995 Financing Agreement contemplated two different dates for trading–or assigning–eligible debt: the date the trade was made and the date the trade was settled.

The evidence submitted by Elliott shows unequivocally that the assignments were timely because both dates were met. . . . Moreover, it is undisputed that after Panama was notified in December 1995 by the Agent that Citibank and Swiss Bank assigned their interests to Elliott, the Agent acknowledged Elliott's assignments and registered Elliott as a creditor of Panama under the 1982 Agreement. . . . The Agent further demonstrated its acknowledgement of the validity of the assignments by subsequently paying, with Panama's knowledge, $973,289 in interest on the 1982 debt to Elliott. . . . Finally, Panama has not disputed that all 48 trades involving the 1982 Agreement were settled by assignment notices that were "effective" after October 20, 1995 and that all of these assignments–except for the two involving Elliott–were accepted by the Agent and Panama. . . . On this record, a reasonable factfinder could only conclude that the assignments were timely: that they were made before October 20, 1997 and that they were "settled" before November 10, 1997.

Panama's contention that the assignments to Elliott at issue in this case were not made until after October 20, 1995 is based solely on the two "Assignment Notices" submitted to Panama and the Agent from the Banks and Elliott. . . . Both of these Assignment Notices are dated after October 20, 1995 and state that the assignments to Elliott take effect on dates after the Final Trading Date. . . . The assignment from Swiss Bank is dated October 31, 1995 and states that the assignment "is effective October 31, 1995." The assignment from Citibank is dated November 6, 1995 and states that it "is effective from November 6, 1995." Panama argues that these documents show that Elliott and the Banks acknowledge that "they had assigned an interest in the 1982 Agreement after October 20, 1995." . . .

The two assignment notices are insufficient to raise a genuine issue of fact, for the record shows clearly that the dates of the assignment notices are the dates the assignments were "settled." The dates of both notices, of course, precede the November 10, 1995 "settlement" date. A reasonable factfinder could only conclude that the assignment notices merely consummated–or made effective–trades that were made before the Final Trading Date. . . .

Panama also alleges that even if the assignments were completed before the Final Trading Date, Elliott would then be required to restructure because it would then be bound by the 1995 Financing Plan. . . . This argument, however, is simply wrong, as the plain language of the Commitment Letters makes clear. Citibank and Swiss Bank both executed Commitment Letters on November 14, 1995 stating in pertinent part:

> We further agree that after the date of this Commitment Letter, we will only assign our Eligible Debt to an assignee that ... agrees ... to assume our commitment and related obligations [under the 1995 Financing Plan]. . . .

. . . [T]his obligation existed only with respect to assignments made "after the date of [the] Commitment Letter[s]." Because the assignments were made to Elliott and settled before the Commitment Letters were executed, Elliott was not required to assume the Banks' obligations under the 1995 Financing Plan and thus Elliott was not bound to restructure. . . .

The final issue is the viability of Panama's counterclaim for tortious interference with contract. Under New York law, to establish a claim of tortious interference with contract, a plaintiff must prove: (1) the existence of a contract; (2) defendant's knowledge thereof; (3) defendant's intentional inducement of a breach of that contract; and (4) damages. . . .

Elliott argues that Panama's claim for tortious interference must be dismissed because Panama has failed, among other things, to demonstrate the existence of a genuine issue of fact with respect to the intent aspect of the third element. I agree. Hence, Elliott's motion for summary judgment is granted.

The intent required to sustain a claim for tortious interference with contract is "exclusive malicious motivation." . . . The action must have been taken by the defendant "without justification, for the sole purpose of harming the plaintiffs." . . .

Here, a reasonable factfinder could only conclude that Elliott was not acting with "exclusive malicious motivation" or for the "sole purpose" of harming Panama. To the contrary, Elliott spent some $8 million. It did that not because it wanted to hurt Panama or interfere with Panama's contracts, but because of the most basic of motivations–it wanted to make money. Elliott invested in the foreign debt because it was hoping to turn a profit.

Hence, no genuine issue of material fact exists as to the third element of tortious interference with contract and the counterclaim must be dismissed.

**Notes and Comments 8.3:** *Proposal for debt relief for least developed countries.* International charitable organizations have been advocating broad debt forgiveness for the world's poorest, or least developed, countries at the threshold of the new millennium.[8] Leaders of the G-7, the group of seven largest western industrialized democracies, announced in June 1999 a plan for debt relief for the 33 least developed countries.[9] The relief could affect $60 billion in foreign debt, and possibly as much as $90 billion in foreign debt if other creditor states joined in the plan. This plan, which still requires approval and implementation of the individual G-7 member states, is actually an assemblage of several disparate elements. Approximately $15 to $20 billion of the plan would involve cancellation of official development assistance debt extended mainly by the IMF and the World Bank. Other forms of debt relief would be tied to future economic reforms undertaken by the debtor states. These other forms of relief would include: new financial assistance by the IMF and the World Bank, cancellation of trade-related debt underwritten by government guarantees, and debt concessions by private creditors of the least developed countries. The various elements of this stitched-together plan obviously require approvals differing constituencies, public, private and multilateral.

# 2. Debt-for-Equity Swaps: Federal Reserve Amendments

**Notes and Comments 8.4.** The material that follows examines one regulatory response to the LDC debt crisis, the initiative of the Fed to permit conversion of debt into equity investments on the part of former international lenders. Review the loan transactions proposed in Chapter 7, Note 7.9, *supra*. Assume that all of these loans have been made by QNB. Under what circumstances could QNB exchange, or "swap," these loans for related equity investments under the successive amendments to Reg K? (These amendments were originally codified as § 211.5(f), but are now embodied in the revised § 211.8(g).)

## Federal Reserve Board, Amendments to Regulation K
52 Fed.Reg. 30,912 (1987) (codified at 12 C.F.R. § 211.5)

The Board has revised its regulation governing permissible foreign investments of U.S. banking organizations to permit investors to acquire from foreign governments ownership of certain foreign companies engaged in nonfinancial activities in the context of exchanging debt obligations of the government for equity ownership interests in the companies. The Board is continuing its examination of regulations governing debt-for-equity investments in heavily indebted countries and requests comments on issues related to such investments. . . .

---

8. *See* Roger Cohen, *An Agreement On Debt Relief For Poor Lands*, N.Y. Times, June 19, 1999, at A8, col. 5 (discussing position of OxFam).

9. *Id.* at A1, col. 6.

Under the Board's regulations, U.S. banking authorities have substantial authority to make investments in foreign financial companies, including investments resulting from debt-for-equity swaps. Generally under Regulation K, a U.S. banking organization may hold as much as 100 percent of the shares of nonfinancial companies. . . .

Involvement by U.S. banking organizations in debt- for-equity transactions has taken three forms. First, U.S. banks have earned fees by acting as brokers between other banks and multinational companies seeking to make equity investments in developing countries. Second, some U.S. and foreign banking organizations making portfolio adjustments have sold loans to other potential investors, usually multinational corporations that have in turn used them to make debt-for-equity investments in developing countries. Substantial debt-for-equity investment have been made by multinational companies because such investments have been viewed as a natural extension of their business operations. Finally, U.S. banking organizations have themselves made limited debt-for-equity investments under Regulation K.

Some countries with substantial debts to foreign creditors allow or encourage a portion of those debts to be converted into equity investments in those countries. The companies available for investment include nonfinancial companies that are currently state-owned. Private investment in such companies may provide some benefits to the countries by reducing economic inefficiencies and governmental subsidies. . . .

The liberalizing amendment would permit investments to be made in companies being privatized by a foreign government using sovereign debt held by the banking organization. If there are instances in which a program of debt-for-equity conversions established by the government of a heavily indebted developing country requires that new money be invested in addition to the proceeds of the debt obligation that is swapped, the Board will consider such investments on a case-by-case basis.

Under the amendment to Regulation K, U.S. banking organizations will be able to make investments in companies being privatized in eligible countries. These would include countries that since 1980 have rescheduled external sovereign debt. The amendment would not allow, for example, a U.S. banking organization to buy a controlling interest in a company in an industrialized country where the company is engaged in activities other than those permissible under Regulation K, even if that company is in the process of being privatized.

Because the amendment is intended to provide flexibility in managing portfolios of loans to heavily indebted countries and is not intended to permit permanent investments in nonbank concerns, the equity interests acquired under this proposal must be divested after a temporary period when it becomes feasible. The debt-for-equity conversion programs usually have restrictions on repatriation of dividends and capital; the repatriation restrictions do not, however, prevent the sale of such companies to other foreign non-residents. In light of the ability to divest the company even within the period of repatriation restrictions, the Board has determined that a reasonable holding period appears to be five years. The Board retains the discretion to grant additional extensions of time totalling five additional years for good cause, normally in one-year increments.

Because this amendment would permit a banking organization to take controlling interests in commercial and industrial companies, even if only for a limited period of time, the Board determined that such investments should be through the bank holding company and not through the bank itself. This form of ownership attempts to erect an effective barrier between the bank and the commercial and industrial activities of the companies to be acquired. It does this in several ways: the nonbanking activity is further isolated from the bank; ownership through the bank holding company is intended to indicate that the nonbank is not protected by the federal safety net available to banks. . . .

## Federal Reserve Board, Amendments to Regulation K
53 Fed. Reg. 5358 (1988) (codified at 12 C.F.R. § 211.5)

After further review of its regulations and consideration of public comment, the Board has revised Regulation K governing foreign investments of U.S. banking organizations. The new regulation permits investors to acquire up to 40 percent of the shares of foreign nonfinancial companies where sovereign debt obligations are being exchanged for ownership interests in the companies. The Board also revised the regulation to permit companies acquired through debt-for-equity conversions in heavily indebted developing countries to be held for up to 15 years and liberalized the investment procedures for such investments. . . .

. . . [T]here are not a significant number of opportunities for investment in privatizations because many governments are reluctant to give up control of important state-owned enterprises and to allow important sectors of the economy to pass into foreign control. The amount of equity being made available for investment under privatization programs is small in relation to the amount of sovereign debt outstanding. Therefore, [public comments received concerning the 1987 amendments] stated that, in order for the regulation to be meaningful, private sector companies must be eligible for investment. ...

Regulation K as revised in August permitted debt-for-equity investments in nonbank companies to be held for a period of five years with the possibility of an extension for an additional five years. All comments received stated that the time period for divestiture is too short and asked that the holding period be long enough to permit the investor to maximize recovery on investments. The comments noted that all of the debt-for-equity programs in heavily indebted countries include restrictions on repatriation of dividends and on the investor's ability to sell the investment to local investors and repatriate the capital. These restrictions extend beyond the initial five years provided in the Board's regulation and in many cases beyond the 10-year maximum available with extensions under the Board's regulation.

After further review, the Board determined to permit investments made under the revised regulation to be held for the lesser of 15 years or two years beyond the end of the period established by the country restricting repatriation of the investment. This liberalization would apply to investments in public sector companies being privatized as well as to private sector companies. Extending the period to 15 years would respond to the concerns of those banking organizations that believe that divestiture will be difficult and costly if required within the period during which repatriation of the capital investments restricted by the foreign country. Under the debt-for-equity programs of the major Latin American countries 13 years is currently the longest period during which repatriation of the investment is restricted. As a result, a maximum holding period of 15 years (or two years beyond the restricted period if shorter than 13 years) should give U.S. banking organizations greater opportunity to sell such investments. . . .

The Board determined that additional flexibility should be available in the investment procedures for debt-for-equity swaps. The regulation grants the Board's general consent for investments that do not exceed the greater of $15 million or one percent of the equity of the investing bank holding company. The Board determined that, in the context of making debt-for-equity investments where funds are already committed to a country, a percentage of the investor's equity capital is a reasonable measure of the need for review of the investments. This new limit would also apply to investments made under the previous amendment to Regulation K permitting controlling investments to be made in public sector companies.

Under the liberalized regulation, prior notice to or the specific consent of the Board will be required where (1) the amount to be invested exceeds the greater of $15 million or one percent of the investor's equity capital after the deduction of goodwill; (2) the country's debt-for-equity swap program requires the investor to invest new money in addition to swapping debt obligations, and then only if the new money portion of the investment exceeds $15 million; or (3) the investment is to be made through an insured bank or its subsidiary.

## Board of Governors of the Federal Reserve System, International Banking Operations,
66 Fed. Reg. 54,346 (2001) (codified at 12 C.F.R. § 211.8)

Regulation K currently permits banking organizations to swap certain developing country debt for equity interests in companies of any type. Established in 1987 to assist banking organizations in managing large amounts of nonperforming, illiquid sovereign debt, these foreign investment provisions are more liberal than Regulation K's other investment provisions. Under certain conditions set out in Regulation K, investors may invest under general consent authority up to one percent of their tier 1 capital in up to 40 percent of the shares, including voting shares, of private sector companies in eligible countries. Such an investment must be held through the bank holding company, unless the Board specifically permits it to be held through the bank or a bank subsidiary. Eligible countries are defined as those that have rescheduled their debt since 1980, or any country the Board deems to be eligible.

Since the debt/equity swap provisions were introduced, a well developed secondary market in developing country debt has emerged. The vast bulk of developing country problem debt has been repackaged in the form of long-term Brady bonds, mostly denominated in U.S. dollars and fully collateralized as to principal by U.S. government bonds. Many banking organizations actively trade these instruments in the secondary market.

Due to the development of the secondary markets for emerging market debt, U.S. banks now have the same options with regard to many of these assets as they have with other bank assets–namely, they can hold the asset with a view toward collecting at maturity or sell the asset for cash to invest in other bank eligible assets. Indeed, the sovereign debt of most of the historically "eligible countries" is no longer illiquid, and those eligible countries that account for the vast share of rescheduled debt have largely regularized their relations with commercial banks.

In light of these changed circumstances and to redirect this special authority to the asset quality problem it was originally intended to help resolve, in the [1997] Proposal[, 62 Fed. Reg. 68,423 (1997)] the Board proposed to redefine the term "eligible country." Under the proposed definition, only countries with currently impaired sovereign debt (i.e., debt for which an allocated transfer risk reserve would be required under the International Lending Supervision Act and for which there is no liquid market) would be eligible for investments through debt/equity swaps under Regulation K. Existing holdings of such investments would be grandfathered, subject to the existing divestiture periods applicable to such investments (i.e., generally, 10 years from the date of acquisition).

Several commenters supported the proposed changes. Only one comment opposed the change to the definition of an "eligible country". Another commenter urged the Board to extend the general consent authority for debt/equity swaps to such investments made by banks and bank subsidiaries. The Board continues to believe the additional authority granted under the debt/equity swap provisions should be limited to countries with currently impaired debt, in light of the developments described above and, accordingly, adopts the proposed change to the definition of an "eligible country." The Board also considers that general consent authority for engaging in debt/equity swaps under the bank continues to be inappropriate. As at present, a bank or bank subsidiary may seek authority from the Board to hold such an investment on a case-by-case basis.

[The current version of the debt-eqity swap provision, formerly § 211.5(f), reads as follows. For excerpts from other pertinent provisions of Reg K, see Chapter 5, § 2, *supra* and especially the excerpts from § 211.8.]

§ 211.8   Investments and activities abroad
. . .
(g) Investments made through debt-for-equity conversions.

(1) Permissible investments. A bank holding company may make investments through the conversion of sovereign-or private-debt obligations of an eligible country, either through direct exchange of the debt obligations for the investment, or by a payment for the debt in local currency, the proceeds of which, including an additional cash investment not exceeding in the aggregate more than 10 percent of the fair value of the debt obligations being converted as part of such investment, are used to purchase the following investments:

(i) Public-sector companies. A bank holding company may acquire up to and including 100 percent of the shares of (or other ownership interests in) any foreign company located in an eligible country, if the shares are acquired from the government of the eligible country or from its agencies or instrumentalities.

(ii) Private-sector companies. A bank holding company may acquire up to and including 40 percent of the shares, including voting shares, of (or other ownership interests in) any other foreign company located in an eligible country subject to the following conditions:

(A) A bank holding company may acquire more than 25 percent of the voting shares of the foreign company only if another shareholder or group of shareholders unaffiliated with the bank holding company holds a larger block of voting shares of the company;

(B) The bank holding company and its affiliates may not lend or otherwise extend credit to the foreign company in amounts greater than 50 percent of the total loans and extensions of credit to the foreign company; and

(C) The bank holding company's representation on the board of directors or on management committees of the foreign company may be no more than proportional to its shareholding in the foreign company.

(2) Investments by bank subsidiary of bank holding company. Upon application, the Board may permit an indirect investment to be made pursuant to this paragraph (g) through an insured bank subsidiary of the bank holding company, where the bank holding company demonstrates that such ownership is consistent with the purposes of the FRA. In granting its consent, the Board may impose such conditions as it deems necessary or appropriate to prevent adverse effects, including prohibiting loans from the bank to the company in which the investment is made.

(3) Divestiture--(i) Time limits for divestiture. A bank holding company shall divest the shares of, or other ownership interests in, any company acquired pursuant to this paragraph (g) within the longer of:

(A) Ten years from the date of acquisition of the investment, except that the Board may extend such period if, in the Board's judgment, such an extension would not be detrimental to the public interest; or

(B) Two years from the date on which the bank holding company is permitted to repatriate in full the investment in the foreign company.

(ii) Maximum retention period. Notwithstanding the provisions of paragraph (g)(3)(i) of this section:

(A) Divestiture shall occur within 15 years of the date of acquisition of the shares of, or other ownership interests in, any company acquired pursuant to this paragraph (g); and

(B) A bank holding company may retain such shares or ownership interests if such retention is otherwise permissible at the time required for divestiture.

(iii) Report to Board. The bank holding company shall report to the Board on its plans for divesting an investment made under this paragraph (g) two years prior to the final date for divestiture, in a manner to be prescribed by the Board.

(iv) Other conditions requiring divestiture. All investments made pursuant to this paragraph (g) are subject to paragraph (e) of this section requiring prompt divestiture (unless the Board upon application authorizes retention), if the company invested in engages in impermissible business in the United States that exceeds in the aggregate 10 percent of the company's consolidated assets or revenues calculated on an annual basis; provided that such company may not engage in activities in the United States that consist of banking or financial operations (as defined in § 211.23(f)(5)(iii)(B)) of this part, or types of activities permitted by regulation or order under section 4(c)(8) of the BHC Act (12 U.S.C. 1843(c)(8)), except under regulations of the Board or with the prior approval of the Board.

(4) Investment procedures--(i) General consent. Subject to the other limitations of this paragraph (g), the Board grants its general consent for investments made under this paragraph (g) if the total amount invested does not exceed the greater of $25 million or 1 percent of the tier 1 capital of the investor.

(ii) All other investments shall be made in accordance with the procedures of § 211.9(f) and (g) of this part, requiring prior notice or specific consent.

(5) Conditions--(i) Name. Any company acquired pursuant to this paragraph (g) shall not bear a name similar to the name of the acquiring bank holding company or any of its affiliates.

(ii) Confidentiality. Neither the bank holding company nor its affiliates shall provide to any company acquired pursuant to this paragraph (g) any confidential business information or other information concerning customers that are engaged in the same or related lines of business as the company.

# 3. Sovereign Immunity Issues

**Notes and Comments 8.5.** Assume that the Nusquami Port Authority (NPA) has been facing a financial crisis. The volcanic eruption and mudslides have eliminated any prospect of income from a major port facility. NPA bonds are now worthless, and so there is at present no collateral for a $10 million loan which QNB had extended to the NPA. In accordance with the terms of the loan agreement as QNB understands them, the bank has demanded replacement of the collateral for this loan, and the NPA has categorically refused to provide additional collateral. QNB has now declared the loan in default. In light of the material that follows, consider the following questions:

**a.** May QNB validly initiate a civil suit against the NPA in U.S. federal district court for recovery of principal and interest under the loan? If so, what is the procedure to be followed in doing so?

**b.** What defenses might be available to the NPA against this suit?[10] What is the likelihood of success with respect to any such defense?

**c.** Assume that QNB has obtained judgment in its favor. May it execute the judgment against bank accounts held by First Credulity Bank of Philadelphia in the name of the Nusquami Government?[11] May it execute against a cargo crane now in storage in a warehouse in San Diego, which had been purchased by the NPA for installation at the now abandoned port facility in Nusquam?

**d.** Would it make any difference to any of your answers to a-c, *supra*, if the defendant in QNB's suit had been the Nusquami Ministry of Development, rather than the NPA?

## Foreign Sovereign Immunities Act
Pub. L. No. 94-583, Oct. 21, 1976, 90 Stat. 2891(1976)
(codified at 28 U.S.C. §§ 1330, 1602-1611), *as amended*

§ 1330. Actions against foreign states

(a) The district courts shall have original jurisdiction without regard to amount in controversy of any nonjury civil action against a foreign state as defined in section 1603(a) of this title as to any claim for relief in personam with respect to which the foreign state is not entitled to immunity either under sections 1605-1607 of this title or under any applicable international agreement.

(b) Personal jurisdiction over a foreign state shall exist as to every claim for relief over which the district courts have jurisdiction under subsection (a) where service has been made under section 1608 of this title.

(c) For purposes of subsection (b), an appearance by a foreign state does not confer personal jurisdiction with respect to any claim for relief not arising out of any transaction or occurrence enumerated in sections 1605-1607 of this title.

§ 1602. Findings and declaration of purpose

The Congress finds that the determination by United States courts of the claims of foreign states to immunity from the jurisdiction of such courts would serve the interests of justice and would protect the rights of both foreign states and litigants in United States courts. Under international law, states are not immune from the jurisdiction of foreign courts insofar as their commercial activities are concerned, and their commercial property may be levied upon for the satisfaction of judgments rendered against them in connection with their commercial activities. Claims of foreign states to immunity should henceforth be decided by courts of the United States and of the States in conformity with the principles set forth in this chapter.

---

10. *Cf. Croesus EMTR Master Fund L.P. v. Federative Republic of Brazil*, 212 F.Supp.2d 30 (D.D.C. 2002) (holding, in breach of contract action against state, FSIA commercial activity exception not triggered by state's purported promotion of bonds in U.S. bond market; commercial activity and direct effect exceptions not triggered by alleged omissions concerning value of bonds or by failure to pay interest and principal; dismissal on *forum non conveniens* grounds appropriate).

11. *See, e.g., Flatow v. Islamic Republic of Iran*, 308 F.3d 1065 (9th Cir. 2002), *cert. denied*, 538 U.S. 944 (2003) (upholding presumption that bank wholly owned by state was still juridical entity separate from state and not subject to execution of judgment entered against state).

§ 1603.  Definitions

For purposes of this chapter–

(a) A "foreign state," except as used in section 1608 of this title, includes a political subdivision of a foreign state or an agency or instrumentality of a foreign state as defined in subsection (b).

(b) An "agency or instrumentality of a foreign state" means any entity–

(1) which is a separate legal person, corporate or otherwise, and

(2) which is an organ of a foreign state or political subdivision thereof, or a majority of whose shares or other ownership interest is owned by a foreign state or political subdivision thereof, and

(3) which is neither a citizen of a State of the United States as defined in section 1332(c) and (d) of this title, nor created under the laws of any third country.

(c) The "United States" includes all territory and waters, continental or insular, subject to the jurisdiction of the United States.

(d) A "commercial activity" means either a regular course of commercial conduct or a particular commercial transaction or act. The commercial character of an activity shall be determined by reference to the nature of the course of conduct or particular transaction or act, rather than by reference to its purpose.

(e) A "commercial activity carried on in the United States by a foreign state" means commercial activity carried on by such state and having substantial contact with the United States.

§ 1604.  Immunity of a foreign state from jurisdiction

Subject to existing international agreements to which the United States is a party at the time of enactment of this Act a foreign state shall be immune from the jurisdiction of the courts of the United States and of the States except as provided in sections 1605 to 1607 of this chapter.

§ 1605.  General exceptions to the jurisdictional immunity of a foreign state

(a) A foreign state shall not be immune from the jurisdiction of courts of the United States or of the States in any case–

(1) in which the foreign state has waived its immunity either explicitly or by implication, notwithstanding any withdrawal of the waiver which the foreign state may purport to effect except in accordance with the terms of the waiver;

(2) in which the action is based upon a commercial activity carried on in the United States by a foreign state; or upon an act performed in the United States in connection with a commercial activity of the foreign state elsewhere; or upon an act outside the territory of the United States in connection with a commercial activity of the foreign state elsewhere and that act causes a direct effect in the United States;

(3) in which rights in property taken in violation of international law are in issue and that property or any property exchanged for such property is present in the United States in connection with a commercial activity carried on in the United States by a foreign state; or that property or any property exchanged for such property is owned or operated by an agency or instrumentality of the foreign state and that agency or instrumentality is engaged in a commercial activity in the United States;

(4) in which rights in property in the United States acquired by succession or gift or rights in immovable property situated in the United States are in issue;

(5) not otherwise encompassed in paragraph (2) above, in which money damages are sought against a foreign state for personal injury or death, or damage to or loss of

property, occurring in the United States and caused by the tortious act or omission of that foreign state or of any official or employee of that foreign state while acting within the scope of his office or employment; except this paragraph shall not apply to–

(A) any claim based upon the exercise or performance or the failure to exercise or perform a discretionary function regardless of whether the discretion be abused, or

(B) any claim arising out of malicious prosecution, abuse of process, libel, slander, misrepresentation, deceit, or interference with contract rights; [or,]

(6) in which the action is brought, either to enforce an agreement made by the foreign State with or for the benefit of a private party to submit to arbitration all or any differences which have arisen or which may arise between the parties with respect to a defined legal relationship, whether contractual or not, concerning a subject matter capable of settlement by arbitration under the laws of the United States, or to confirm an award made pursuant to such an agreement to arbitrate, of (A) the arbitration takes place or is intended to take place in the United States, (B) the agreement or award is or may be governed by a treaty or other international agreement in force for the United States calling for the recognition and enforcement of arbitral awards, (C) the underlying claim, save for the agreement to arbitrate, could have been brought in a United States court under this section or section 1607, or (D) paragraph (1) of this subsection is otherwise applicable. ...

§ 1606. Extent of liability

As to any claim for relief with respect to which a foreign state is not entitled to immunity under section 1605 or 1607 of this chapter, the foreign state shall be liable in the same manner and to the same extent as a private individual under the circumstances; but a foreign state except for an agency or instrumentality thereof shall not be liable for punitive damages . . . ; if, however, in any case wherein death was caused, the law of the place where the action or omission occurred provides, or has been construed to provide, for damages only punitive in nature, the foreign state shall be liable for actual or compensatory damages measured by the pecuniary injuries resulting from such death which were incurred by the persons for whose benefit the action was brought.

§ 1607. Counterclaims

In any action brought by a foreign state, or in which a foreign state intervenes, in a court of the United States or of a State, the foreign state shall not be accorded immunity with respect to any counterclaim–

(a) for which a foreign state would not be entitled to immunity under section 1605 of this chapter had such claim been brought in a separate action against the foreign state; or

(b) arising out of the transaction or occurrence that is the subject matter of the claim of the foreign state; or

(c) to the extent that the counterclaim does not seek relief exceeding in amount or differing in kind from that sought by the foreign state.

§ 1608. Service; time to answer; default

(a) Service in the courts of the United States and of the States shall be made upon a foreign state or political subdivision of a foreign state:

(1) by delivery of a copy of the summons and complaint in accordance with any special arrangement for service between the plaintiff and the foreign state or political subdivision; or

(2) if no special arrangement exists, by delivery of a copy of the summons and complaint in accordance with an applicable international convention on service of judicial

documents; or

(3) if service cannot be made under paragraphs (1) or (2), by sending a copy of the summons and complaint and a notice of suit, together with a translation of each into the official language of the foreign state, by any form of mail requiring a signed receipt, to be addressed and dispatched by the clerk of the court to the head of the ministry of foreign affairs of the foreign state concerned, or

(4) if service cannot be made within 30 days under paragraph (3), by sending two copies of the summons and complaint and a notice of suit, together with a translation of each into the official language of the foreign state, by any form of mail requiring a signed receipt, to be addressed and dispatched by the clerk of the court to the Secretary of State in Washington, District of Columbia, to the attention of the Director of Special Consular Services -- and the Secretary shall transmit one copy of the papers through diplomatic channels to the foreign state and shall send to the clerk of the court a certified copy of the diplomatic note indicating when the papers were transmitted.

As used in this subsection, a "notice of suit" shall mean a notice addressed to a foreign state and in a form prescribed by the Secretary of State by regulation.

(b) Service in the courts of the United States and of the States shall be made upon an agency or instrumentality of a foreign state:

(1) by delivery of a copy of the summons and complaint in accordance with any special arrangement for service between the plaintiff and the agency or instrumentality; or

(2) if no special arrangement exists, by delivery of a copy of the summons and complaint either to an officer, a managing or general agent, or to any other agent authorized by appointment or by law to receive service of process in the United States; or in accordance with an applicable international convention on service of judicial documents; or

(3) if service cannot be made under paragraphs (1) or (2), and if reasonably calculated to give actual notice, by delivery of a copy of the summons and complaint, together with a translation of each into the official language of the foreign state–

(A) as directed by an authority of the foreign state or political subdivision in response to a letter rogatory or request or

(B) by any form of mail requiring a signed receipt, to be addressed and dispatched by the clerk of the court to the agency or instrumentality to be served, or

(C) as directed by order of the court consistent with the law of the place where service is to be made. . . .

(e) No judgment by default shall be entered by a court of the United States or of a State against a foreign state, a political subdivision thereof, or an agency or instrumentality of a foreign state, unless the claimant establishes his right or claim to relief by evidence satisfactory to the court. A copy of any such default judgment shall be sent to the foreign state or political subdivision in the manner prescribed for service in this section.

§ 1609. Immunity from attachment and execution of property of a foreign state

Subject to existing international agreements to which the United States is a party at the time of enactment of this Act the property in the United States of a foreign state shall be immune from attachment arrest and execution except as provided in sections 1610 and 1611 of this chapter.

§ 1610. Exceptions to the immunity from attachment or execution

(a) The property in the United States of a foreign state, as defined in section 1603(a) of this chapter, used for a commercial activity in the United States, shall not be immune from attachment in aid of execution, or from execution, upon a judgment entered by a court of the United States or of a State after the effective date of this Act, if–

(1) the foreign state has waived its immunity from attachment in aid of execution or from execution either explicitly or by implication, notwithstanding any withdrawal of the waiver the foreign state may purport to effect except in accordance with the terms of the waiver, or

(2) the property is or was used for the commercial activity upon which the claim is based, or

(3) the execution relates to a judgment establishing rights in property which has been taken in violation of international law or which has been exchanged for property taken in violation of international law, or

(4) the execution relates to a judgment establishing rights in property–

(A) which is acquired by succession or gift, or

(B) which is immovable and situated in the United States: Provided, That such property is not used for purposes of maintaining a diplomatic or consular mission or the residence of the Chief of such mission, or

(5) the property consists of any contractual obligation or any proceeds from such a contractual obligation to indemnify or hold harmless the foreign state or its employees under a policy of automobile or other liability or casualty insurance covering the claim which merged into the judgement, or

(6) the judgment is based on an order confirming an arbitral award rendered against the foreign State, provided that attachment in aid of execution, or execution, would not be inconsistent with any provision in the arbitral agreement. . . .

(b) In addition to subsection (a), any property in the United States of an agency or instrumentality of a foreign state engaged in commercial activity in the United States shall not be immune from attachment in aid of execution, or from execution, upon a judgment entered by a court of the United States or of a State after the effective date of this Act if–

(1) the agency or instrumentality has waived its immunity from attachment in aid of execution or from execution either explicitly or implicitly may purport to effect except in accordance with the terms of the waiver, or

(2) the judgment relates to a claim for which the agency or instrumentality is not immune by virtue of section 1605(a)(2), (3), [or] (5) . . . , or 1605(b) of this chapter, regardless of whether the property is or was involved in the act upon which the claim is based.

(c) No attachment or execution referred to in subsections (a) and (b) of this section shall be permitted until the court has ordered such attachment and execution after having determined that a reasonable period of time has elapsed following the entry of judgment and the giving of any notice required under section 1608(e) of this chapter.

(d) The property of a foreign state, as defined in section 1603(a) of this chapter, used for a commercial activity in the United States, shall not be immune from attachment prior to the entry of judgment in any action brought in a court of the United States or of a State, or prior to the elapse of the period of time provided in subsection (c) of this section, if–

(1) the foreign state has explicitly waived its immunity from attachment prior to judgment, notwithstanding any withdrawal of the waiver the foreign state may purport to effect except in accordance with the terms of the waiver, and

(2) the purpose of the attachment is to secure satisfaction of a judgment that has been or may ultimately be entered against the foreign state, and not to obtain jurisdiction....

§ 1611. Certain types of property immune from execution

(a) Notwithstanding the provisions of section 1610 of this chapter, the property of those organizations designated by the President as being entitled to enjoy the privileges, exemptions, and immunities provided by the International Organizations Immunities Act shall not be subject to attachment or any other judicial process impeding the disbursement of funds to, or on the order of, a foreign state as the result of an action brought in the courts of the United States or of the States.

(b) Notwithstanding the provisions of section 1610 of this chapter, the property of a foreign state shall be immune from attachment and from execution, if–

(1) the property is that of a foreign central bank or monetary authority held for its own account, unless such bank or authority, or its parent foreign government, has explicitly waived its immunity from attachment in aid of execution, or from execution, notwithstanding any withdrawal of the waiver which the bank, authority or government may purport to effect except in accordance with the terms of the waiver; or

(2) the property is, or is intended to be, used in connection with a military activity and

(A) is of a military character, or

(B) is under the control of a military authority or defense agency.

### Kahale, Does a Choice-of-Law Clause Waive Immunity?
Int'l. Fin. L. Rev. 28 (July 1988)

[Reread the excerpt from Kahale reproduced in Chapter 7, § 3, *supra*.]

### Callejo v. Bancomer, S.A.
764 F.2d 1101 (5th Cir. 1985)

Goldberg, Circuit Judge:

This suit is one of several arising from the promulgation by Mexico of exchange control regulations on August 13, 1982, and from the subsequent nationalization of privately-owned Mexican banks on September 1, 1982. The exchange control regulations mandated that all deposits in Mexican banks, however denominated, be repaid in Mexican pesos at specified rates of exchange. Because the dollar rate of exchange was well below the market rate, the regulations constituted a Montezuma's revenge on American depositors who had dollar deposits in Mexican banks. A number of these indisposed investors, including the plaintiffs in the present suit, have brought claims against Mexican banks for breach of contract.

Thus far, the courts that have passed on these cases have been unanimous in dismissing the plaintiffs' claims, either on the ground that the banks are immune from suit under the doctrine of sovereign immunity, *Braka v. Nacional Financiera*, N. 83-4161 (S.D.N.Y. July 8, 1984); *Frankel v. Banco Nacional de Mexico*, No. 82- 6457 (S.D.N.Y. May 31, 1983), or on the ground that suit is barred by an act of state doctrine, *Braka v. Bancomer*, S.A., 589 F. Supp. 1465 (S.D.N.Y. 1984), *aff'd*, 762 F.2d 222 (2d Cir. 1985); *Braka v. Multibanco Comermex*, 589 F. Supp. 802 (S.D.N.Y. 1984). In the present case, the district court relied on sovereign immunity, holding that Bancomer is an instrumentality of the Mexican Government, that the Callejos' suit is based on sovereign not commercial activities, and that therefore Bancomer is immune from suit under the Foreign Sovereign Immunities Act ("FSIA"), 28 U.S.C. §§ 1330, 1332(a)(2)-(4), 139(f), 1441(d), 1602-1611 (1982). Because the district court dismissed the Callejos' claim for lack of jurisdiction, it did not reach the act of state question.

We agree with the result reached by the district court, but disagree with its rationale. We believe that Bancomer is not immune from suit under the FSIA and that the case is properly analyzed in act of state terms. Because we are barred under the act of state doctrine for inquiring into the validity of acts of foreign state performed in their own territory–including the validity of Mexico's exchange control regulations–we affirm the district court's dismissal of the present suit.

I. Facts

William Callejo and his wife Adelfa are United States citizens who reside in Texas. Beginning in 1979 or 1980, the Callejos purchased certificates of deposit ("CDs") issued by Bancomer, S.A., a then privately- owned Mexican bank.[1] The record is unclear about how this business relationship originated–in particular, whether it resulted from Bancomer's solicitations in Texas. During the court of the Callejos' relationship with Bancomer, however, Bancomer regularly engaged in commercial activity in the United States, operating a branch office in Los Angeles and an agency in New York City. In Texas, Bancomer maintained accounts with both Republic Bank Dallas and Laredo National Bank.

The procedure used by the Callejos and Bancomer to make deposits and payments, although labrynthine in course, is fairly clear in outline. To make deposits, the Callejos would direct their bank in Dallas to wire funds to Laredo National Bank in Laredo, Texas, where they would be credited to Bancomer's account. Bancomer would then direct Laredo National to debit Bancomer's account in the same amount, and would credit the amount to the Callejos' account at Bancomer's branch in Nuevo Laredo, Mexico. To cover this credit by Bancomer to the Callejos' account, Laredo National would transfer the funds (by an undisclosed mechanism) to Bancomer's Nuevo Laredo branch. It is undisputed that Laredo National acted as a correspondent bank in effectuating these deposits, that Bancomer's account with Laredo National did not show a net increase as a result of the transactions, and that the Callejos' money was deposited in an account in Bancomer's Nuevo Laredo branch, where the certificates of deposit were issued.

The means by which Bancomer paid interest and principal to the Callejos are the subject of somewhat greater dispute. The Callejos claim that Bancomer effectuated the payments by directing Laredo National to draw funds from Bancomer's Laredo National Account and to transfer them to the Callejos' bank in Dallas. According to the Callejos, this method of payment was established specifically to ensure that they would receive the payments in Texas rather than Mexico. Bancomer, in contrast, claims that it would issue cashier's checks in Mexico payable to the Callejos and would hold the checks at its Nuevo Laredo branch pending receipt of instructions from the Callejos as to how the funds should be remitted. Usually, the funds would be remitted my means of interbank transfers; on occasion, however, they would be redeposited in Mexico, or would be sent in the form of a cashier's check to a third person, or would be remitted to one of the Callejos' accounts with another Mexican bank. Although these descriptions of the method of payment differ in emphasis, they are directly contradictory; the payments drawn on Bancomer's account with Laredo National, which the Callejos highlight, were merely one link in a larger chain by which Bancomer transferred funds from its Nuevo Laredo branch to the Callejos' American accounts. As with the method of making deposits, Laredo National's role appears to have been that merely of a correspondent bank.

---

1. The CDs purchased by the Callejos included both dollar- and peso-denominated certificates. The Callejos bought these certificates on their own behalf and as trustees for undisclosed principals.

The four certificates of deposit at issue in the present suit were purchased by the Callejos on May 31 and June 2, 1982. Two were renewals of prior certificates and two were new certificates; all had terms of three months, were denominated in United States dollars, and called for payment of principal and interest in United States dollars. Together, they had a value of approximately $300,000. Like the other certificates of deposit purchased by the Callejos, they specified on their face Mexico City as the place of payment.

In August 1982, facing a severe monetary crisis brought on by a decline in the world price of oil, the Government of Mexico promulgated exchange control regulations. These were supplemented by further regulations in September 1982. The regulations required Mexican banks to pay principal and interest in U.S. dollar-denominated certificates of deposit in pesos rather than dollars, at a specified rate of exchange.[2] The regulations also required that payment be made in Mexico and limited the number of pesos that foreigners could remove from the country. On September 1, 1982, the Government of Mexico nationalized all privately- owned Mexican banks, including Bancomer.

Pursuant to the new exchange control regulations, on August 13, 1982, Bancomer notified the Callejos that it would pay the principal and interest on the Callejos' four certificates of deposit in pesos at a rate of exchange substantially below the market rate. To forestall this, the Callejos renewed the two certificates of deposit due to mature on August 31, 1982, and filed the present suit. . . .

Along with other privately-owned Mexican banks, Bancomer was nationalized by the Mexican Government on September 1, 1982. Consequently, Bancomer is now an "agency or instrumentality of a foreign state" within the meaning of 28 U.S.C. § 1603(b)(2), and would ordinarily be entitled to immunity from the jurisdiction of American courts under the FSIA, 28 U.S.C. § 1604. The FSIA, however, contains a number of exceptions to the jurisdictional immunity of foreign states. One of these is found in 28 U.S.C. § 1605(a)(2). . . .[5]

---

2. The governmentally-established exchange rate was 70 pesos to the dollar for all non-priority transactions. According to the Callejos, the market exchange rate in August 1982 was 114 pesos to the dollar. This rate subsequently rose to more than 130 pesos to the dollar in November 1982.

5. Under the FSIA, where an exception to sovereign immunity applies, the federal courts have subject- matter jurisdiction over the dispute. 28 U.S.C. § 1330(a); see *Verlinden B.V. v. Central Bank of Nigeria*, 461 U.S. 480 (1983) (subject-matter jurisdiction over FSIA suits does not depend on diversity of citizenship; instead, FSIA claims fall within the judicial power of the United States because they "arise under" the laws of the United States, i.e., the FSIA itself). Moreover, where subject matter jurisdiction exists and where service of process is made pursuant to 28 U.S.C. § 1608, then personal jurisdiction exists. 28 U.S.C. § 1330(b). As with all suits, however, the exercise of personal jurisdiction must comply with the due process clause. *See Texas Trading & Milling Corp. v. Federal Republic of Nigeria*, 647 F.2d 300, 308 (2d Cir. 1981), *cert. denied*, 454 U.S. 1148 (1982).

Here, Bancomer appears to concede that, if subject matter jurisdiction exists, then personal jurisdiction also exists. Although Bancomer initially claimed that the Callejos failed to serve process in compliance with 28 U.S.C. § 1608, the Callejos reserved Bancomer by delivering a summons and a copy of their complaint both to the manager of Bancomer's New York agency and to the Subdirector/General Manager of Bancomer's Los Angeles branch office. On appeal, Bancomer has not reiterated its claim that the Callejos failed to comply with 28 U.S.C. § 1608, nor has it raised as a separate defense the argument that the exercise of personal jurisdiction would violate due process. To the extent that Bancomer contends that there are insufficient contacts for the exercise of personal jurisdiction, . . . we hold that the contacts discussed in Part II(B) below are sufficient to satisfy the requirements of due process.

The Callejos claim that this exception applies in the present case, since their suit is based upon a commercial activity by Bancomer that was both carried on and caused a direct effect in the United States.

The FSIA has aptly been called a "remarkably obtuse" document, a "statutory labyrinth that, owing to the numerous interpretive questions engendered by its bizarre structure and its many deliberately vague provisions, has during its brief lifetime been a financial boom for the private bar but a constant bane of the federal judiciary." *Gibbons v. Udaras na Gaeltachta*, 549 F.Supp. 1094, 1105, 1106 (S.D.N.Y. 1982), *quoted in Vencedora Oceanica Navigacion v. Compagnie Nationale Algerienne de Navigation*, 730 F.2d 195, 205 (5th Cir. 1984) (Higginbotham, J., dissenting). Although the FSIA was intended to introduce uniformity into the process of granting sovereign immunity, *see* H.R.Rep. No. 1487, 94th Cong., 2d Sess. 7, *reprinted in* 1976 U.S.Code Cong. & Ad.News 6604, 6605-06 ("House Report"), Congress, rather than provide explicit direction, paradoxically put its faith in the courts to develop guidelines on a case-by-case basis. *Texas Trading & Milling Corp. v. Federal Republic of Nigeria*, 647 F.2d 300, 308-09 (2d Cir. 1981), *cert. denied*, 454 U.S. 1148 (1982). Thus, while the outer limits of our analysis are defined by the Act itself, the specific path we take must be guided by the general purposes underlying the Act.

In determining whether Section 1605(a)(2) applies, two questions are relevant:

(1) Is the Callejos' suit "based upon a commercial activity" by Bancomer?

(2) If so, did this commercial activity have the required jurisdictional nexus with the United States?

In the present case, the district court answered the first of these questions in the negative and therefore never reached the second. It held that the action was "based upon" the promulgation by Mexico of exchange control regulations–a sovereign act–not upon Bancomer's banking activities. We disagree. In our view, the Callejos' action arose as a result of Bancomer's commercial banking activities. Moreover, these banking activities had a direct effect in the United States, thus satisfying the jurisdictional-nexus requirement of Section 1605(a)(2). For these reasons, we hold that Bancomer is not entitled to sovereign immunity under the FSIA.

A. Commercial Activity

In determining whether the commercial activity exception applies, the critical question is usually whether the relevant activity is commercial or sovereign in nature–whether it is a *jure gestionis* or a *jure imperii*, a private or a public act.[6] Here, however, there is little doubt about how to characterize the activities at issue: Bancomer's actions in selling the certificates of deposit were clearly commercial in nature. . . . The question, instead, is defining with precision which of these activities is the *relevant* activity–that is, the activity on which the Callejos' suit is "based"?

The district courts that have considered this question have given different answers.

---

6. The FSIA provides little guidance on this issue. The only discussion occurs in 28 U.S.C. § 1603 (d). . . .

While this is helpful so far as it goes, it is somewhat circular, since it defines "commercial activity" in terms of "commercial conduct" and "commercial transaction" but contains no independent definition of "commercial." Generally, however, if an activity is of a type that a private person would customarily engage in for profit, it is clearly commercial. *See Letelier v. Republic of Chile*, 748 F.2d 790, 796-97 (2d Cir. 1984); *International Ass'n of Machinists & Aerospace Workers v. OPEC*, 649 F.2d 1354, 1357 (9th Cir. 1981), *cert. denied*, 454 U.S. 1163 (1982); House Report, *supra*, at 6614-15.

The court below followed *Frankel v. Banco Nacional de Mexico*, No. 82- 6457 (S.D.N.Y. May 31, 1983), in finding that the relevant activity was the promulgation by Mexico of exchange control regulations. As the *Frankel* court noted,

> [P]laintiffs allege no conduct on the part of Banco Nacional in breach of its obligations to plaintiffs other than measures taken by Banco Nacional to comply with the currency control rules and regulations promulgated by the Mexican Government. . . .

In contrast, the court in *Braka v. Bancomer* focused on the defendant bank's actions in selling the certificates of deposit:

> Although a foreign sovereign's internal currency regulation "is precisely the type of governmental activity that cannot be subjected to judicial scrutiny," . . . the Ministry of Treasury, not Bancomer, was responsible for the exchange controls. The issue under the FSIA is to determine whether the act of the named defendant was performed in a sovereign or a commercial capacity; analysis must focus on the named defendant's acts which are the basis of the action and not on the separate acts of other sovereign instrumentalities or agencies.

589 F.Supp. at 1469. Applying this test, the *Braka* court concluded, "Here, the activity at issue is Bancomer's issuance of CDs to attract time deposits. The act that gave rise to plaintiffs' claim was Bancomer's breach of its contractual obligation to repay the deposit and any interest due in United States dollars." *Id.*

We agree with the conclusion of the *Braka* court rather than the conclusion reached in *Frankel*. Under the FSIA, sovereign immunity depends on the nature of those acts of the defendant that form the basis of the suit. Here, the act complained of was Bancomer's breach of its contractual obligations to the Callejos, not the promulgation by Mexico of exchange control regulations. . . . These contractual obligations were commercial in nature; they were of a kind that a private individual would customarily enter into for profit. Indeed, at the time that Bancomer sold the certificates of deposit, it was a private entity and did so as part of its general commercial activities. The fact that Bancomer was later nationalized is, in the current context, irrelevant. Even if Bancomer had remained a private entity, it would have been obligated under Mexican law to breach its contractual obligations to the Callejos. Its actions in doing so were not actions that only a sovereign could perform, but were instead commercial. . . .

Bancomer nevertheless contends that the Callejos' suit was based upon the Mexican exchange regulations since, but for these regulations, it would not have breached the terms of the CDs and the Callejos' suit would not have arisen. We do not read Section 1605(a)(2)'s "based upon" requirement, however, to be equivalent merely to a requirement of causation. In most instances, a suit results from a variety of factors; it is no more the result of a single cause than was the Civil War. To say that the commercial activity exception does not apply whenever a suit is caused by a sovereign act would, in large measure, read the exception out of the law. We believe, instead, that the focus should be on the elements of the cause of action itself: Is the gravamen of the complaint a sovereign activity by the defendant? Here, the answer is clearly no: The activities of Bancomer that are the basis of the Callejos' complaint–the sale of the certificates of deposit and the subsequent payments in pesos rather than dollars–were commercial in nature.[7]

Nor does Bancomer acquire any derivative immunity by virtue of the fact that, in breaching the terms of the certificates of deposit, it was merely complying with the sovereign decrees of the Mexican Government. In *Arango v. Guzman Travel Advisors Corp.*, 621 F.2d 1371 (5th Cir. 1980), we rejected this view of derivative immunity. There, the plaintiffs brought breach of contract, negligence, battery, and false imprisonment claims against the Dominican national airline after they had been denied entry as vacationers in the Dominican Republic. We held that the airline was not entitled to sovereign immunity on the breach of contract and tort claims, even though, in breaching the tour contract, it was merely complying with the government's sovereign decision to exclude the plaintiffs. *Id.* at 1379-80. Instead, the airline was entitled to sovereign immunity only on the battery and false imprisonment claims, where it had acted "as an arm or agent of the Dominican government." *Id.* at 1379. The airline acquired immunity not derivatively from the government's sovereign acts, but only by participating directly in those acts–that is, by acting as a sovereign itself. In the present case, Bancomer did not act as an agent of the Mexican Government in implementing the exchange regulations; instead, it acted as any private party would in complying with the law. As the *Braka* court noted,

> [Bancomer] was not the central bank and it had no special role in effectuating the monetary controls beyond complying with the decrees. Bancomer's act in paying pesos instead of dollars was not 'peculiarly within the realm of the government,' and its breach was no more a sovereign act than that of any other debtor, private or public, that had contracted to repay in dollars rather than pesos. That it was prevented from complying with its contract by a governmental decree flatly prohibiting the use of dollars as legal tender does not make it immune from suit as an agent of the Republic of Mexico.

589 F.Supp. at 1470.

Because we hold that Bancomer's activities were neither themselves sovereign nor entitled to any derivative immunity by virtue of being compelled by Mexican law, we conclude that the court erred in dismissing the suit on the ground that the suit was based on sovereign, not commercial, activity. We therefore turn to the other prong of Section 1605(a)(2): that the commercial activity have the required jurisdictional nexus with the United States.

B. Jurisdictional Nexus

Section 1605(a)(2) grants an exception from sovereign immunity for suits based upon a commercial activity by an instrumentality of a foreign state, but only if the commercial activity had a sufficient connection with the United States. Section 1605(a)(2) identifies three such connections. . . .

The Callejos claim that Bancomer's commercial activities were carried on and had direct effects in the United States, and that therefore the first and third of these jurisdictional bases exist. We agree with the latter claim–namely, that the breach of the certificates of

---

7. This interpretation is supported by the language of § 1603(d), that "[t]he commercial character of an activity shall be determined by reference to [its] *nature* . . . rather than be reference to its *purpose*." (Emphasis added). Here, the nature of Bancomer's breach of contract was commercial even though its purpose was to comply with the sovereign decrees of the Mexican Government. *Cf. Arango v. Guzman Travel Advisors Corp.*, 621 F.2d 1371, 1379-80 (5th Cir. 1980) (holding that commercial activity exception applied to plaintiff's contract claim, even though suit arose as a result of the Dominican Republic's sovereign decision to deny plaintiffs entry).

deposit had direct effects in the United States–and therefore do not address whether Banco-mer's activities in connection with the certificates were "carried on in the United States" within the meaning of the FSIA.[8]

Determining whether a commercial activity abroad has a "direct effect in the United States" is "an enterprise fraught with artifice." *Texas Trading & Milling Corp. v. Federal Republic of Nigeria*, 647 F.2d 300, 312 (2d Cir. 1981), *cert. denied*, 454 U.S. 1148 (1982). "The question is, was the effect sufficiently 'direct' and sufficiently 'in the United States' that Congress would have wanted an American court to hear the case? No rigid parsing of § 1605(a)(2) should lose sight of that purpose." *Id.* at 313.

The legislative history of the FSIA directs us to look to Section 18 of the Restate-ment (Second) of Foreign Relations Law of the United States (1965), when interpreting the "direct effects" clause. House Report, *supra*, at 6618. This section governs the extent to which American law may be applied to conduct overseas, and states that the conduct must have a "substantial" effect in the United States, "as a direct and foreseeable result of the con-duct outside the territory" of the United States. RESTATEMENT, *supra*, at § 18(b)(ii)-(iii). In several cases where an American plaintiff was injured overseas, this rule has been held to preclude recovery, since the effects in the United States, although potentially substantial, were not "direct and foreseeable." . . . In these cases, the contacts with the United States were purely fortuitous in that they depended solely on the fact that the injured persons happened to be American. . . .

However, where the effects in the United States of an activity abroad are less fortui-tous, courts have been much more willing to characterize them as "direct." For example, nonpayment of a note payable in the United States to a United States company has been held to cause a direct effect in the United States for the purposes of Section 1605(a)(2). . . . Similarly, a demand for payment on a letter of credit issued by an American bank has been held to have a direct effect in the United States since it causes a depletion of funds in the American bank. . . .

Here there is considerable controversy over where the certificates of deposit were payable. The Callejos claim that the place of payment was Texas, where they received the

---

8. Although the facts necessary to determine that the breach had direct effects in the United States are undisputed, this is not true of the question of whether the activities on which the suit is based were "carried on in the United States." The fact that Bancomer does business in the United States is insufficient to support a finding of jurisdiction under the first clause of § 1605(a)(2). *Vencedora Oceanica Navigacion v. Compagnie Nationale Algerienne de Navigation*, 730 F.2d 195, 202 (5th Cir. 1984). Instead, Bancomer's commercial activities in the United States must have a nexus with the act complained of in this lawsuit. *Id.* A defendant's general business activities in the forum may be suffi-cient to establish his "presence" for purposes of personal jurisdiction, but they are insufficient to establish the contacts necessary for the exercise of jurisdiction under the FSIA. *Harris v. VAO Intourist*, 481 F.Supp. 1056, 1059-61 (E.D.N.Y. 1979). In the present case, it is unclear whether the act complained of grew out of Bancomer's commercial activities within the United States. On the one hand, Bancomer utilized the services of American correspondent banks and the U.S. mails, and placed telephone calls to the Callejos in Texas regarding the purchase and renewal of the CDs. On the other hand, Bancomer does not appear to have advertised or otherwise solicited business in the United States in connection with the sale of the certificates. *Cf. Wolf v. Banco Nacional de Mexico*, 739 F.2d 1458, 1460 (9th Cir. 1984) (holding that where plaintiff purchased CDs as a result of defendant's advertisements in the U.S., the sale of the CDs was a commercial activity carried on in the U.S.), *cert. denied*, --- U.S. ---, 105 S.Ct. 784 (1985). Given the undeveloped state of the record and the fact that we need not reach this issue, we express no opinion about what activities in the United States would be sufficient to satisfy the first clause of § 1605(a)(2).

funds; Bancomer claims that it was Mexico, as specified on the certificates themselves. In the present context, however, the question of whether there was a direct effect in the United States can be resolved without reference to the place of payment. Since the Callejos were located in the United States, the effects of Bancomer's breach were inevitably felt in by them there. Moreover, these effects in the United States were foreseeable. Unlike the cases where an American was injured abroad, here the fact that effects were felt in the United States were not fortuitous. Bancomer has engaged in a regular course of business conduct with the Callejos over a several-year period. It was well-aware that it was dealing with American investors–it called them in the United States, mailed the certificates to them there, and remitted payments through an American correspondent bank. Given these factors, we do not perceive any material difference whether the legal place of payment was Mexico or the United States. In either case, Bancomer's breach was closely and foreseeably tied to the effects felt by the Callejos in the United States.

Our conclusion that the place of payment is not decisive is supported by the policies underlying the FSIA. The doctrine of sovereign immunity is one of a number of doctrines that attempt to regulate the relations between sovereign states. The essence of sovereignty is supremacy of authority–one sovereign rarely likes to be told what to do by another. Consequently, the exercise of jurisdiction over a foreign state is, as Chief Justice Marshall recognized when introducing the doctrine of sovereign immunity into American jurisprudence, a "delicate and important inquiry." *Schooner Exchange v. McFaddon*, 11 U.S. (7 Cranch) 116 (1812). By declining to exercise jurisdiction over foreign states where the activities in question either are sovereign in nature or have an insufficient connection with the United States, the United States recognizes that its interest in providing a forum for litigation by aggrieved parties must often yield to the foreign state's interest in its independence. Where either the foreign state's interest in independence is great or the United States's interest in asserting jurisdiction is weak, the FSIA grants sovereign immunity in order to serve our larger interest in preserving international amity.

In weighing these competing interests, arcane doctrines regarding the place of payment are largely irrelevant. In the ever more complex world of international banking, these doctrines doubtless serve a useful function. However, in ordering relations between sovereign states, a larger perspective is appropriate. As the court in *Texas Trading* noted, "Congress in writing the FSIA did not intend to incorporate into modern law every ancient sophistry concerning 'where' an act or omission occurs. Conduct crucial to modern commerce telephone calls, telexes, electronic transfers of intangible debits and credits–can take place in several jurisdictions. Outmoded rules placing such activity 'in' one jurisdiction or another are not helpful here." 647 F.2d at 311 n. 30.

In the present case, we fail to perceive why jurisdiction should not be exercised. Mexico's interest is not so great–the suit is based on commercial not sovereign acts–nor America's interest so weak–Bancomer had engaged in a long-standing business relationship with residents of the United States which caused them substantial financial harm–that the United States must defer to Mexico. Under these circumstances, we believe that Section 1605(a)(2) applies and that jurisdiction is consequently not barred by sovereign immunity.

## De Sanchez v. Banco Central de Nicaragua
770 F.2d 1385 (5th Cir. 1985)

Goldberg, Circuit Judge:
In July 1979, the Nicaraguan government of General Anastasio Somoza fell to the Sandinista revolutionaries. As usually occurs, members of the old regime fled the country

to escape the reach of "revolutionary justice." But where defeated aristocracies once emigrated to London or Paris, now they seem to wind up in Miami. One of these emigres–Mrs. Josefina Navarro de Sanchez, the wife of President Somoza's former Minister of Defense–brought the present suit to collect on a check for $150,000 issued to her by the Nicaraguan Central Bank (Banco Central de Nicaragua) shortly before Somoza's fall. Mrs. Sanchez was unable to cash this check after the new government assumed power and placed a stop-payment order on it. . . .

I.

On September 7, 1978, Mrs. Josefina Najarro [*sic*] de Sanchez, a Nicaraguan national, purchased a certificate of deposit worth $150,000 from Banco Nacional de Nicaragua, a then privately-owned commercial Nicaraguan bank. The certificate was payable in United States dollars and had a scheduled maturity date of October 6, 1982. It specified that Banco Nacional would redeem the certificate only at or after this date.

In June 1979, the Nicaraguan government of General Somoza was on the verge of collapse. Mrs. Sanchez left Nicaragua for Miami, Florida. To raise money for her resettlement expenses, Mrs. Sanchez decided to redeem her certificate of deposit three years prior to its maturity date. She therefore contacted her husband, General Herberto Sanchez, who was still in Nicaragua, and requested that he redeem the certificate.

At the time, Nicaragua was suffering from a critical shortage of foreign exchange. In September 1978, the Nicaraguan government had adopted exchange control regulations limiting sales of foreign exchange by Banco Central to ten specific purposes and requiring that sales of foreign exchange for other purposes be authorized by Banco Central's Board of Directors. Decree No. 332-MEIC, 4 Rec. at 273-74, 278-80. In May 1979, even tighter restrictions on the use of foreign exchange were imposed pursuant to a standby agreement between Nicaragua and the International Monetary Fund. Despite these restrictions, by July 1979 the national had a net foreign exchange deficit of over $200 million, barely enough to meet one average day's worth of import requirements.

Because of the shortage of foreign exchange, redeeming Mrs. Sanchez's certificate of deposit was easier said than done. President Somoza himself, two weeks before fleeing the country, took time from his presumably busy schedule to write a personal letter to the President of Banco Nacional recommending that the certificate be redeemed "as a special case" and stating that he would be "grateful . . . for a favorable decision."[1] . . . When this proved unavailing due to Banco Nacional's shortage of dollars, the President of Banco Nacional contacted Banco Central requesting that Banco Central sell the dollars necessary to redeem the certificate. Dr. Roberto Incer, the President of Banco Central and a cousin of General Sanchez, personally authorized the sale of the dollars by telephone from Guatemala, where he was negotiating a line of credit to a National Guard officer from the Guatemalan Central Bank. Pursuant to Dr. Incer's instructions, Banco Central issued a check directly in favor of Mrs. Sanchez for $150,000, drawn on Banco Central's account with Citizens and Southern International Bank ("C & S Bank") in New Orleans, Louisiana. Although it is unclear whether Banco Nacional ever reimbursed Banco Central for this money, Banco Nacional did cancel Mrs. Sanchez's certificate after the check to Mrs. Sanchez was issued by Banco Central.

By the time the check reached Mrs. Sanchez in Miami, however, the political situation in Nicaragua had deteriorated even further. Although the new government did not

---

1. Apparently, General Sanchez was a close personal friend and associate of President Somoza. Indeed, when the Somoza government finally fell on July 17, 1979, General Sanchez was among the handful who departed with Somoza on the same plane.

formally come to power in Nicaragua until July 19, 1979, persons purporting to represent the Sandinista government contacted C & S Bank on July 11-13, claiming control over Banco Central's account. To protect the Bank, the President of C & S decided on July 13 not to clear further checks issued by Banco Central. Dr. Arturo Cruz, the new President of Banco Central, telephoned C & S on July 17, reiterating that C & S should freeze Banco Central's account. He confirmed this stop-payment order by telex on July 23, the day after being formally appointed to office.

As a result of these events, when Mrs. Sanchez attempted to cash the check first at C & S's Miami office and later at C & S's New Orleans office, the Bank would not honor it. In Miami, Mrs. Sanchez's son, despite being accompanied by Dr. Incer, the outgoing President of Banco Central, was told on July 16 that the check must be deposited at C & S's New Orleans office, where Mrs. Sanchez had her account. In New Orleans, however, the bank informed her on the following day that there were insufficient funds in Banco Central's account to cover the check. When Mrs. Sanchez re-presented the check three days later on July 20, it was returned to her marked "refer to maker." That day, Mr. Kenneth Moore, President of the C & S Bank in New Orleans, wrote to Mrs. Sanchez:

> In reference to Banco Central de Nicaragua check number 20110 payable to you in the amount of U.S.Dlrs. 150,000.00, the check payment was refused by us on presentation on July 17, 1979. Due to the fact we had no knowledge of the country on that date due to the civil war in the country, we suspended all payments from [Banco Central's] account, our legal right under the terms of the Uniform Commercial Code of the United States. We were subsequently instructed by Dr. Arturo Cruz, President of the Central Bank, to suspend all payments.

After Dr. Cruz's telephone call was confirmed by the July 23 telex, payment was indefinitely stopped on Mrs. Sanchez's check.

Upon assuming power, the new government of Nicaragua immediately began to establish priorities to govern the use of the country's remaining foreign exchange resources. These priorities were enumerated in a regulation adopted by Banco Central on September 6, 1979. . . . In addition, Dr. Cruz ordered the staff of Banco Central to conduct an audit of each check on which payment had been stopped. The purpose was to determine which checks were properly issued and consistent with the national priorities for the use of foreign exchange. Based on this audit, Mrs. Sanchez's check was placed in the category, "[s]ales of foreign exchange to the National Guard . . . and to those who are associated or friends of the National Guard." . . . Although the auditors found that the check was correct "from a purely accounting point of view," . . . Dr. Cruz determined that the check to Mrs. Sanchez should not be paid since payment would be inconsistent with the national priorities governing the use of foreign exchange. He made this recommendation to the Government Junta–a three-member board that exercise the role of chief executive in the Nicaraguan government–and the Junta agreed. . . .

The district court initially determined that it had jurisdiction over the suit under the FSIA and denied Banco Central's motion to dismiss. Specifically, the court found that two exceptions to the doctrine of sovereign immunity applied: first, the "expropriation exception," under which a state is not immune from claims involving "rights in property taken in violation of international law," 28 U.S.C. § 1605(a)(3); and second, the tortious activity exception, which denies immunity to foreign states sued for tortious conduct that causes damage to property in the United States, *id.* § 1065(a)(5). . . . The district court also held, in passing, that the act of state doctrine did not apply. *Id.* at 910 n. 10.

After discovery was completed, Banco Central moved for summary judgement, reiterating its sovereign immunity claim and arguing additionally that the act of state doctrine applied. The district court agreed with the second of these arguments–namely, that the suit is barred by the act of state doctrine–and therefore found it unnecessary to review its earlier ruling regarding sovereign immunity. After the district court entered its final order of dismissal on March 16, 1984, Mrs. Sanchez filed the present appeal.

II.

. . . The FSIA was enacted in 1976 to bring uniformity to determinations of sovereign immunity. H.R.Rep. No. 1487, 94th Cong., 2d Sess. 7, *reprinted in* 1976 U.S. Code Cong. & Admin.News 6604, 6605-06 ("House Report"). It initially grants immunity to foreign states and their instrumentalities, 28 U.S.C. § 1604, and then carves out certain exceptions to this grant of immunity, *id.* §§ 1605-07. Unless one of these exceptions applies, then the federal courts lack both subject matter, *id.* § 1330(a), and personal jurisdiction, *id.* § 1330(b).[4]

In the present case, Mrs. Sanchez does not contest that the defendant–Banco Central–is an instrumentality of a foreign state within the meaning of 28 U.S.C. § 1603(b)(2), since it is an organ of the Nicaraguan government. *See* House Report, *supra,* at 6614 ("As a general matter, entities which meet the definition of an 'agency or instrumentality of a foreign government' could assume a variety of forms, including . . . a central bank. . . ."). Ordinarily, therefore, it would be entitled to sovereign immunity under Section 1604 of the FSIA. Mrs. Sanchez argued to the district court, however, that three exceptions to sovereign immunity apply: (1) the commercial activity exception, § 1605(a))(2); (2) the expropriation in violation of international law exception, § 1605(a)(3); and (3) the tortious activity exception, § 1605(a)(5). The district court disagreed with Mrs. Sanchez regarding the first of these exceptions, holding that the suit is based on sovereign, not commercial, activity. It agreed, however, that both the expropriation and tortious activity exceptions apply, and therefore concluded that it had jurisdiction over the suit. Because we disagree that either of these exceptions to sovereign immunity applies, we hold that Banco Central is immune from suit under Section 1604 of the FSIA.

A.

The commercial activity exception is the most frequently argued of the sovereign-immunity exceptions. It antedates the FSIA and embodies the "restrictive theory" of sovereign immunity, under which a foreign state is immune only from suits based on their public as opposed to their commercial acts–their *jure imperii* as opposed to their *jure gestionis*. But whereas prior to the FSIA, the Department of State determined whether the commercial activity exception applied, the FSIA vests this power in the courts to shield the inquiry from political considerations. House Report, *supra,* at 6606. Under the Act, sovereign immunity determinations are to be made on "purely legal grounds", *id.,* rather than on an ad hoc, diplomatic basis.

Like the other exceptions to sovereign immunity, the commercial activity exception attempts to accommodate the interest of private parties in bringing suit with the interest of foreign states in immunity from suit. Where a foreign state's sovereign acts are the basis of a suit, the United States refrains from exercising jurisdiction out of respect for the defendant's

---

4. Under § 1330(b), personal jurisdiction depends not only on the applicability of an exception to sovereign immunity but also on service of process in compliance with 28 U.S.C. § 1608. In addition, the exercise of personal jurisdiction must meet the constitutional requirements of due process. *Texas Trading & Milling Corp. v. Federal Republic of Nigeria,* 647 F.2d 300, 308 (2d Cir. 1981), *cert. denied,* 454 U.S. 1148 (1982).

coequal sovereign status. Where a suit arises from a foreign state's commercial acts, however, the state's interest in immunity is much weaker. . . .

In ascertaining whether the commercial activity exception applies, three questions are involved. First, we must define with precision the relevant activity. This requires focusing on the acts of the named defendant, not on other acts that may have had a casual connection with the suit. . . . In particular, we must isolate those specific acts of the named defendant that form the basis of the plaintiff's suit. "The focus of the exception to immunity recognized in § 1605(a)(2) is not on whether the defendant generally engages in a commercial enterprise or activity . . . ; rather, it is on whether the particular conduct giving rise to the claim in question constitutes or is in connection with commercial activity, regardless of the defendant's generally commercial or governmental character." *Arango v. Guzman Travel Advisors Corp.*, 621 F.2d 1371, 1379 (5th Cir. 1980). Second, we must determine whether the relevant activity is sovereign or commercial–a label which depends on the nature of the activity rather than on its purpose. 28 U.S.C. § 1603(d). Finally, if the activity is commercial in nature, we must determine whether it had the requisite jurisdictional nexus with the United States. Section 1605(a)(2) identifies three such connections. . . .

Here, the activity giving rise to the suit was the issuance of the check to Mrs. Sanchez and the specific act complained of was the failure by Banco Central to honor that check. . . . [W]e must examine the nature of that activity and act, not the connected activities of either the Nicaraguan government or Banco Nacional. If Banco Central's actions were commercial, then it is subject to suit regardless of the fact that it may have acted pursuant to a sovereign decision of the Nicaraguan government to preserve Nicaragua's foreign exchange reserves. . . . Conversely, if its actions were sovereign, then the fact that Banco Nacional's initial sale of the certificate to Mrs. Sanchez was commercial does not infect Banco Central. . . . We turn first to Banco Central's issuance of the check to determine whether it was commercial or sovereign in nature.

Although ascertaining the commercial or sovereign nature of a given activity is usually the critical question in a sovereign immunity case, the FSIA provides distressingly little guidance. The only discussion of the issue occurs in 28 U.S.C. § 1603(d). . . .

The legislative history of the FSIA provides more guidance. As examples of commercial activities, the House Report lists "a foreign government's sale of a service or a product, its leasing of property, its borrowing of money, its employment or engagement of laborers, clerical staff or public relations or marketing agents, [and] its investment in a security of an American corporation." House Report, *supra*, at 6615. More generally, the legislative history suggests that courts should "inquire whether the activity in question is one which private persons ordinarily perform or whether it is peculiarly within the realm of governments." *Jurisdiction of U.S. Courts in Suits Against Foreign States: Hearings on H.R. 11315 Before Subcomm. on Administrative Law and Governmental Relations of the House Comm. on the Judiciary*, 94th Cong., 2d Sess. 53 (1976) (statement of Monroe Leigh, Legal Advisor, U.S. Dep't of State). However, Congress recognized that by not defining "commercial activity" with precision, the courts would have "a great deal of latitude" in interpreting the exception. House Report, *supra*, at 6615.

The principal obstacle in determining whether an activity is commercial or sovereign in nature is that the same activity can often be characterized in a number of different ways. A federal trial, for example, could be characterized in the broadest, generic terms as a form of dispute resolution, or, more specifically, as government-sponsored adjudication. But whereas the broad category of dispute resolution encompasses activities that might be considered commercial, such as paid-for arbitration, the narrower category of adjudication defines an intrinsically public activity, invested with the sovereign authority of the state.

Here, a similar quandary arises. Banco Central's issuance of the check could be characterized either as a sale of foreign currency or as the regulation and supervision of Nicaragua's foreign exchange reserves. The former is a commercial activity: Private banks often sell foreign currency to one another, particularly if they have a correspondent-bank relationship.[9] The regulation and supervision of a nation's foreign exchange reserves, however, is a sovereign activity. It is one aspect of a government's sovereign function of regulating the monetary system.

Despite these difficulties, we have little trouble characterizing Banco Central's issuance of the check as sovereign. Under Nicaragua's foreign exchange regulations, Banco Central's actions in selling foreign exchange reserves were not the same as those of a private bank. By law, Banco Central had overall responsibility for the control and management of Nicaragua's money reserves. Decree 525 of August 23, 1960, art. 4(h). . . . It was permitted to sell foreign exchange only for certain limited purposes. Indeed, by June of 1979, Nicaragua's dollar holdings had become so depleted that the President of Banco Central ordered his foreign exchange manager to clear every sale of dollars personally with him. ... Unlike Banco Nacional, which sold the certificate of deposit to Mrs. Sanchez in order to earn profits, Banco Central did not enter the marketplace as a commercial actor, nor did it earn any fee by issuing the check to Mrs. Sanchez. . . . Instead, Banco Central became involved with Mrs. Sanchez only in its official role of regulating the sale of foreign exchange. Its only authorized purpose in issuing the check was to maintain stable exchange rates and to allocate scarce foreign exchange reserves among competing uses. Consequently, in the current context, characterizing Banco Central's action as a sale of dollars is not merely incomplete–it is incorrect. . . .

We recognize that in differentiating sales of dollars by Banco Central from sales by private banks, we rely on the different purposes motivating the sales. This might seem to contravene the requirement that, in determining whether an activity is commercial or sovereign, we examine its "nature" rather than its "purpose." 28 U.S.C. § 1603(d). We do not interpret this provision, however, to bar us totally from considering the purposes of different types of activities. Indeed, we do not believe that an absolute separation is always possible between the ontology and the teleology of an act. Often, the essence of an act is defined by its purpose–gift-giving, for example. Unless we can inquire into the purposes of such acts, we cannot determine their nature. Indeed, commercial acts themselves are defined largely by references to their purpose. What makes these acts commercial is not some ethereal essence inhering in the conduct itself; instead, as Congress recognized, acts are commercial because they are generally engaged in for profit. House Report, *supra*, at 6615.

Congress's intent in instructing us to focus on the nature of an activity rather than on its purpose was to preclude foreign governments from always being able to claim sovereign immunity. Whenever a government enters the marketplace to buy or sell goods, its purpose ultimately is not to earn profits; in some sense, its motivation is the public good. Consequently, if the purpose of an activity defined in full whether the activity was sovereign or commercial, all governmental activities would be sovereign.

---

9. The commercial activity issue would be much easier if the sale of dollars had not been an ordinary banking function at the time -- that is, if Banco Central had had exclusive authority over all sales of foreign exchange. In that event, the sale by Banco Central would have been uniquely governmental. Here, however, this was not true. If other commercial banks had had dollars on hand, they could have sold them to Banco Nacional. *See* Decree 332-MEIC art. 4. . . . Banco Nacional was forced to go to Banco Central to purchase the necessary dollars not due to any legal requirement but only because, as a practical matter, no other bank had any dollar reserves.

Here, Banco Central's purpose in selling dollars–namely, to regulate Nicaragua's foreign exchange reserves–was not ancillary to its conduct; instead, it defined the conduct's nature. Banco Central was not merely engaging in the same activity as private banks with a different purpose; in a basic sense, it was engaging in a different activity. It was performing one of its intrinsically governmental functions as the Nicaraguan Central Bank.[10] *See Braka v. Bancomer, S.A.*, 589 F.Supp. 1465, 1469 (S.D.N.Y. 1984), *aff'd*, 762 F.2d 222 (2d Cir. 1985). As such, it was wearing its sovereign rather than its commercial hat. If we were to hold that a central bank is subject to suit for its actions in regulating its foreign exchange reserves, we would interfere with this basic governmental function and would thereby touch sharply on "national nerves," contrary to the policies underlying the FSIA. . . .

B.

Section 1605(a)(3) of the FSIA provides that a foreign state shall not be immune from suit in any case "in which rights in property taken in violation of international law are in issue." . . .

Precisely what types of "rights in property" fall within the compass of Section 1605(a)(3) has been the subject of some dispute. . . .

We need not decide here, however, whether Mrs. Sanchez's contractual right to receive payment on Banco Central's check is a "right in property" within the meaning of Section 1605(a)(3). Instead, there is a more basic reason why Nicaragua's actions are not subject to review: the breach by Nicaragua of Mrs. Sanchez's contractual rights did not violate international law, since it affected only a Nicaraguan national, Mrs. Sanchez. With a few limited exceptions, international law delineates minimum standards for the protection only of aliens; it does not purport to interfere with the relations between a national and its own citizens. Thus, even if Banco Central's actions might have violated international law had they been taken with respect to an alien's property, the fact that they were taken with respect to the intangible property rights of a Nicaraguan national means that they were outside the ambit of international law.

In applying Section 1605(a)(3), our inquiry is narrowly circumscribed. The question is not whether a foreign state's actions are consistent with United States law or United States conceptions of public policy. Nor are we concerned with whether, on the merits, we should recognize or assist the taking of property by the foreign state. Instead, the question is solely whether any generally accepted norm of *international* law prohibits the defendant's actions. If not, then unless another exception to sovereign immunity applies, the foreign state is immune from suit and we lack jurisdiction to inquire into the validity of its conduct.

International law, as its name suggests, deals with relations between sovereign states, not between states and individuals. . . . Nations not individuals have been its traditional subjects. . . . Injuries to individuals have been cognizable only where they implicate two or more different nations: if one state injures the national of another state, then this can give rise to a violation of international law since the individual's injury is viewed as an injury to his state. As long as a nation injures only its own nationals, however, then no other state's interest is involved; the injury is a purely domestic affair, to be resolved within the confines

---

10. In this respect, Banco Central's action differ from those of a government agency that purchases cement or bullets, both of which are considered to be commercial acts. *Texas Trading & Milling Corp. v. Federal Republic of Nigeria*, 647 F.2d 300, 310 & n. 27 (2d Cir. 1981), *cert. denied*, 454 U.S. 1148 (1982); House Report, *supra*, at 6615. In purchasing cement or bullets, a government agency does not perform an intrinsically governmental function; instead, it performs acts that are ancillary to the independently identifiable governmental functions of building harbors and fighting wars.

of the nation itself.[14] . . .

. . . At present, the taking by a state of its national's property does not contravene the international law of minimum human rights.[15] This has been held to be true in much more egregious situations than the present, including cases where the plaintiff had his own property taken pursuant to Nazi racial decrees. *Dreyfus*, 534 F.2d at 30-31. It is certainly true here. . . .

## C.

The final exception to sovereign immunity invoked by Mrs. Sanchez is the tortious activity exception. 28 U.S.C. § 1605(a)(5). Under this exception, a foreign state is not immune from suit where money damages are sought for losses of property caused by the tortious act or omission of the foreign state. Although the exception was directed primarily at traffic accidents, *see* House Report, *supra*, at 6619, it is cast in general terms that apply to all tort actions for money damages.

We need not pause long over this argument. Mrs. Sanchez brought two claims in tort against Banco Central, one for misrepresentation and one for conversion of property. The first of these is explicitly exempted from the tortious activity exception. 28 U.S.C. § 1605(a)(5)(B) ("this paragraph shall not apply to . . . any claim arising out of . . . misrepresentation"). The second, although nominally within the ambit of the exception, is not the type of tort claim that the exception was intended to cover. Mrs. Sanchez's claim, although sounding in tort, is essentially a claim for an unjust taking of property. As noted, Congress has provided an exception in Section 1605(a)(5) for takings of property that violate international law. We do not believe that Congress intended plaintiffs to be able to rephrase their takings claims in terms of conversion and thereby bring the claims even where the takings are permitted by

---

14. Potentially, an injury by a state to its own national might implicate international law if the injury occurred with another state's territory. In that event, the state where the injury occurred might have an interest if the injury affected its territorial sovereignty. International law would become involved not because of the status of the injured party but because of the location of the injury.

In the present case, Mrs. Sanchez claims that her injury occurred in the United States, since that is where Banco Central's check was made payable. We need not decide here whether Banco Central's contractual obligations were "located" in the United States. Even if they were, the breach of these obligations was not of such a nature as to affront the territorial sovereignty of the United States. The situation might be different if Nicaragua had attempted to expropriate a piece of real property owned by Mrs. Sanchez in the United States. Then, Nicaragua's actions could be seen as literally challenging the authority of the United States over its own territory. We decide here only that taking of *intangible* property rights–including breaches of contract–do not violate international law where the injured party is a national of the acting state, regardless of the property's location.

15. *Verlinden B.V. v. Central Bank of Nigeria*, 647 F.2d 320, 325 n. 16 (2d Cir. 1981), *rev'd on other grounds*, 461 U.S. 480 (1983); *Dreyfus*, 534 F.2d at 30- 31; *Vencap*, 519 F.2d at 1015 ("We cannot subscribe to plaintiffs' view that the Eighth Commandment 'Thou shalt not steal' is part of the law of nations."); *Jafari v. Islamic Republic of Iran*, 539 F.Supp. 209, 215 (N.D. Ill. 1982); *cf. United States v. Belmont*, 301 U.S. 324, 332 (1937) ("What another country has done in the way of taking over property of its nationals . . . is not a matter for judicial consideration here. Such national must look to their own government for any redress to which they may be entitled."); *F. Palicio y Compania, S.A. v. Brush*, 256 F.Supp. 481, 487 (S.D.N.Y. 1966) ("[C]onfiscations by a state of the property of its own nationals, no matter how flagrant and regardless of whether compensation has been provided, do not constitute violations of international law."), *aff'd mem.*, 375 F.2d 1011 (2d Cir.), *cert. denied*, 389 U.S. 830 (1967); *Salimoff & Co. v. Standard Oil Co.*, 262 N.Y. 220, 227, 186 N.E. 697, 682 (1933) ("According to the law of nations, [the Soviet Union] did no legal wrong when it confiscated the oil of its own nationals and sold it in Russia to the defendants."); RESTATEMENT (REVISED), *supra*, § 702 comment a.

international law. . . .

## Croesus EMTR Master Fund L.P. v. Federative Republic of Brazil
212 F.Supp.2d 30 (D.D.C. 2002)

BATES, District Judge.

[Three hedge funds brought a breach of contract action against the Republic of Brazil alleging failure to pay principal and interest on bonds issued by Brazil in 1902 and 1911 (the "1902 and 1911 Bonds" or the "Bonds"), purchased by them in secondary markets in the United States. Brazil moved to dismiss on sovereign immunity grounds.]

### FACTUAL AND PROCEDURAL BACKGROUND

. . . In support of its motion, Brazil submits a declaration from Fabio Barbosa, the Secretary of Brazil's National Treasury Secretariat, Ministry of Finance. . . . Mr. Barbosa notes that the Bonds are registered bonds stated in Brazilian currency, that transfers of ownership of the Bonds could be effected only in Brazil where the records of ownership are maintained, and that payment of interest could be accomplished in person only at Brazil's Public Debt Office. . . . Mr. Barbosa explains that, in an effort to retire Brazil's outstanding internal debt obligations, Brazil in 1962 allowed for a five-year period during which the 1902 and 1911 Bonds could be exchanged for different securities, and at the end of which the Bonds were to become valueless. . . . In 1967, Brazil also issued a decree redeeming a certain category of bonds, including the 1902 and 1911 Bonds. . . . Pursuant to this and other decrees, any Bonds that had not been presented for redemption by July 1, 1969, were deemed invalid by Brazil. . . . Accordingly, Mr. Barbosa asserts, not only were the payment obligations at issue extinguished, but also plaintiffs could not be proper owners of the Bonds, because Brazil stopped accepting transfers of ownership once the Bonds were redeemed and the transfer books were closed in 1969. . . . Mr. Barbosa denies that Brazil had any role in facilitating plaintiffs' purchase of the Bonds, and notes that speculators in recent years "have purportedly 'acquired' bonds at minimal values, hoping through litigation or otherwise to increase the value of those bonds and profit thereby." . . .

Upon consideration of the parties' submissions, and the hearing on May 30, 2002, the Court concludes that the Foreign Sovereign Immunities Act ("FSIA"), 28 U.S.C. §§ 1602, et seq., is a bar to jurisdiction here. Plaintiffs have failed to identify factual issues requiring discovery at this time, and even if they did, the Court would dismiss this case under the principles of forum non conveniens rather than subject Brazil to intrusions upon its apparent immunity.

### ANALYSIS

I. Lack of Subject Matter Jurisdiction Under the FSIA

Section 1604 of the FSIA provides that "a foreign state shall be immune from the jurisdiction of the courts of the United States and of the States except as provided in sections 1605 to 1607 of this chapter." Section 1605(a)(2), in turn, specifies that immunity does not apply in any case:

> in which the action is based upon [1] a commercial activity carried on in the United States by the foreign state; or [2] upon an act performed in the United States in connection with a commercial activity of the foreign state elsewhere; or [3] upon an act outside the territory of the United States in connection with a commercial activity of the foreign state elsewhere and that act causes a direct

effect in the United States.

Brazil moves to dismiss the complaint on the basis that Brazil is immune from suit and that none of the "commercial activity" exceptions in § 1605(a)(2), or any other exceptions to immunity, apply to plaintiffs' action.[2] Plaintiffs, in turn, contend that both the first and third clauses of § 1605(a)(2) are implicated by the complaint.

A. The First Clause of § 1605(a)(2)

Under the first clause of § 1605(a)(2), a sovereign is not entitled to immunity when the "action is based upon a commercial activity carried on in the United States by the foreign state." Plaintiffs offer a rather complex theory for why this exception applies here. As a starting point, they argue that Brazil currently offers and sells "Global bonds" through primary markets in the United States. In addition, they argue, there are secondary markets for various Brazilian securities, including the 1902 and 1911 Bonds, in the United States. According to plaintiffs, the "secondary markets and the primary markets are linked as one commercial activity" because "[s]econdary markets are essential to the proper functioning of the primary markets for foreign sovereign debtors." . . . The existence of a smoothly functioning secondary market for one security, plaintiffs argue, leads to better primary and secondary markets for a sovereign's other securities, with higher trading prices, because investors have confidence that they will be able to resell any securities that they purchase. Based on this logic, plaintiffs speculate that, in an effort to promote sales of its "Global bonds" and other securities, Brazil fostered the secondary markets for the 1902 and 1911 Bonds in the United States (where the plaintiffs allegedly purchased some of their Bonds). Accordingly, plaintiffs argue, Brazil engaged in the "commercial activity of issuing securities and promoting secondary markets for its securities to and by persons in the United States."
. . .

Plaintiffs' theory, although creative, is ultimately unpersuasive. Even if Brazil knew that there was a secondary market for the Bonds in the United States, and even if Brazil fostered that market, plaintiffs' action is not "based upon" that conduct, as required by the language of the first clause of § 1605(a)(2). The Supreme Court explained in *Saudi Arabia v. Nelson,* 507 U.S. 349, 357 (1993), that the phrase "based upon" in § 1605(a)(2) means "those elements of a claim that, if proven, would entitle a plaintiff to relief under his theory of the case." "Based upon" thus "calls for something more than a mere connection with, or relation to, commercial activity." *Id.* at 358. . .

The claim stated in plaintiffs' complaint is a straight-forward breach of contract claim for non-payment. It is "based upon" Brazil's failure to pay the principal and interest on the Bonds. Although plaintiffs allege in their complaint that Brazil knows of U.S. secondary markets for the Bonds, the complaint is certainly not "based upon" Brazil's purported promotion of these markets. Even if proven, then, the allegation that Brazil fostered secondary markets would not "entitle ... plaintiff[s] to relief under [their] theory of the case." *Id.* at 357. To the contrary, the secondary market allegations "are legally irrelevant to [plaintiffs'] right of recovery." *Goodman Holdings v. Rafidain Bank,* 26 F.3d 1143, 1146 (D.C.Cir.1994).

Plaintiffs attempt to bolster their position by alleging that "Brazil had a contractual duty under Brazilian law to make reasonable efforts to inform traders in the United States

---

2. Brazil also argues that it is immune from suit because it issued the Bonds in 1902 and 1911, before the FSIA was enacted and while the United States had a policy of absolute immunity for foreign sovereigns. Because the Court finds that even if the FSIA does apply Brazil is immune from suit, it need not consider the parties' arguments concerning retroactivity.

that Brazil's position was that it viewed the Bonds as redeemed and invalid and that it had no intention of making further payments under the Bonds." . . . In support of this allegation, plaintiffs submit a declaration from a Brazilian law professor who opines that, under Brazilian law, Brazil has a duty when it issues securities to inform the financial markets of any relevant fact which could reasonably affect the investors' decision to sell or buy the securities. . . . This duty, as well as the "duty to make only truthful representations to other parties," are related to the general duty of " 'good faith' ... applicable to all legal obligations [under Brazilian law], including contracts between ... the Government and its citizens and companies." . . . According to plaintiffs' legal expert, then, Brazil violated these duties because it failed to inform investors adequately: 1) that the public works financed by the Bonds had been completed; 2) that Brazil redeemed the Bonds in 1967; and 3) that Brazil considered the Bonds valueless. . . .

Plaintiffs' theory is insufficient to support jurisdiction here. The only claim brought by plaintiffs is for "Breach of Contract" and the only contractual breach identified in the complaint is Brazil's failure to pay principal and interest. As the complaint states:

> Brazil has not made any interest payments or repayments of the principal to the Plaintiffs. These failures breached Brazil's contractual obligation to repay the Plaintiffs Croesus, Polaris, and Select Capital as bearers of the Bonds.

. . . The complaint does not purport to set forth a claim for fraud or misrepresentation, nor does it even suggest that Brazil has violated any duty of "good faith" under Brazilian law or any related duties to inform investors or make truthful representations.

In fact, the only allegations in the complaint even alluding to representations made by Brazil about the Bonds are: 1) that "[o]n at least two occasions, once in 1967 and once in 1995, Brazil reaffirmed the validity of the 1902 Bonds and the 1911 Bonds notwithstanding that the relevant infrastructure projects were not completed"; and 2) that "[n]otwithstanding earlier actions to reaffirm the validity of the Bonds, Brazil refused to pay the bondholders after presentment and has publicly stated that it will not pay the 1902 Bonds or the 1911 Bonds." . . . The context of the complaint makes clear that the purpose of these allegations is not to support a cause of action for fraud, misrepresentation or breach of any duty of good faith, but rather to support plaintiffs' assertions that the Bonds are valid and that presentment by plaintiffs would be futile. . . .Thus, even liberally construed, the complaint fails to indicate that plaintiffs are attempting to state a claim "based upon" any misrepresentations or omissions about the validity of the Bonds. *See Conley v. Gibson,* 355 U.S. 41, 47 (1957) (complaint must "give the defendant fair notice of what the plaintiff's claim is and the grounds upon which it rests").

Accordingly, on these facts and allegations, there is no exception to immunity under the first clause of § 1605(a)(2). *See Nelson,* 507 U.S. at 357.[3] Moreover, because plaintiffs' theories concerning secondary markets and alleged failures to inform investors are legally irrelevant, there is no need for discovery on those issues.

B. The Third Clause of § 1605(a)(2)

The third clause of § 1605(a)(2) provides an exception to immunity where a case is "based upon ... an act outside the territory of the United States in connection with a commercial activity of the foreign state elsewhere and that act causes a direct effect in the

---

3. Because the Court finds that plaintiffs' case is not "based upon" any allegation of misrepresentation or omission, the Court need not reach the question whether such alleged conduct can constitute a "commercial activity" under § 1605(a)(2).

United States." Plaintiffs identify two "acts" by Brazil allegedly fitting within this clause–Brazil's alleged failure to "keep market participants informed of actions affecting the value of the [B]onds" and Brazil's failure to repay the principal and interest on the Bonds. . . .

The first alleged act cannot provide a basis for an exception. As discussed above, plaintiffs' action is not "based upon" an alleged failure to inform market participants.

The second alleged act, the non-payment of principal and interest, is the basis for plaintiff's claim. The relevant question therefore is whether the non-payment had a "direct effect" in the United States. According to plaintiffs, a "direct effect" occurred because plaintiffs (two of whom are U.S. entities, and all of whom have U.S. investors) did not receive payments into their U.S. bank accounts. The Court disagrees.

In this context, the Supreme Court has held that an effect is direct if it follows as an "immediate consequence" of a defendant's activity. *Republic of Argentina v. Weltover,* 504 U.S. 607, 618 (1992). As further explained by the D.C. Circuit, an effect is direct if it " 'has no intervening element, but rather, flows in a straight line without deviation or interruption.' " *Princz v. Federal Republic of Germany,* 26 F.3d 1166, 1172 (D.C.Cir.1994) (quoting *Upton v. Empire of Iran,* 459 F.Supp. 264, 266 (D.D.C.1978)).

It is clear enough that non-payment of funds into a U.S. bank can constitute a "direct effect." In *Weltover,* for example, the Supreme Court found that, where a party had designated accounts in New York as the place of payment on interest payments owed by Argentina, Argentina's failure to pay satisfied the "direct effect" standard:

> Because New York was thus the place of performance for Argentina's ultimate contractual obligations, the rescheduling of those obligations necessarily had a "direct effect" in the United States: Money that was supposed to have been delivered to a New York bank for deposit was not forthcoming.

504 U.S. at 619 (1992).

But in *Goodman Holdings v. Rafidain Bank,* 26 F.3d 1143 (D.C.Cir.1994), the D.C. Circuit clarified that a "direct effect" in the United States occurs only where payment was"supposed" to have been made or received in the United States:

> The situation here is quite different [than in *Weltover* ]. There has been no " 'immediate consequence' " in the United States of Rafidain's failure to honor the letters [of credit]. Neither New York nor any other United States location was designated as the "place of performance" where money was "supposed" to have been paid by Rafidain or to Goodman. Rafidain might well have paid them from funds in United States banks but it might just as well have done so from accounts located outside of the United States, as it had apparently done before. Thus, Rafidain does not lose its immunity under the direct effect exception.

*Id.* at 1146-47.

Here, the parties disagree on whether payment was ever "supposed" to have been made in the United States. It is undisputed that up through the 1960s, payments were made at "empowered branch[es]," none of which was located in the United States, and that, under the terms of the Bonds, a bondholder had no right to designate a place of payment in the United States. . . . But plaintiffs contend that because Brazil's Public Debt Office (which formerly served as an "empowered branch" for payment) no longer exists, "the creditor has the right to choose between any of the existent systems of payment that today Brazil utilizes to pay interest in its debt securities." . . . Because Brazil currently uses agents in the United

States for payments on some of its other financial obligations, plaintiffs argue, "Brazil likely would have honored a designation by the Plaintiffs of a place in the United States as the place of payment." . . .

Plaintiffs' argument fails. First, plaintiffs do no more than speculate that Brazil would "likely" have honored a designation of the United States as the place of payment. Second, plaintiffs never did designate the United States as the place of payment. Instead, they determined that presentment of the Bonds for payment would be futile and they proceeded to file this lawsuit. Thus the Court is left with mere conjecture–that if plaintiffs had presented the Bonds for payment, they would have designated the United States as the place for payment, and that, under a hypothetical Brazilian regime that recognized the validity of the Bonds (which were formerly payable only in Brazil), Brazil would "likely" agree to plaintiffs' designation. This scenario is too full of contingencies to support the conclusion that payment was "supposed" to have been made in the United States. The non-payment could have had no "immediate consequences"–and thus no "direct effect"–in the United States where there was never any designation of a place in the United States where payment was to be received, much less any firm basis to believe that such a designation would have been accepted by Brazil and proper as a matter of Brazilian law.[5]

Accordingly, plaintiffs cannot identify a "direct effect" in the United States and there is no exception to immunity under the third clause of § 1605(a)(2). Moreover, plaintiffs are not entitled to discovery on the issue of "direct effect," as plaintiffs present no facts suggesting that Brazil has recently made payments in the United States on the 1902 or 1911 Bonds.

II. Forum Non Conveniens

The Court therefore concludes that there are no grounds for an exception to immunity under any clause in § 1605(a)(2), and that discovery is not necessary before making a determination on that issue. Hence, the complaint must be dismissed on that basis. Even if there were grounds for discovery, however, the Court would dismiss the complaint at this time. Under controlling precedent in this Circuit, jurisdictional discovery on FSIA issues "should not be authorized at all if the defendant raises either a different jurisdictional or an 'other non-merits ground[ ] such as form non conveniens [or] personal jurisdiction' the resolution of which would impose a lesser burden on the defendant." *Phoenix Consulting v. Republic of Angola*, 216 F.3d at 40 (quoting *In re Papandreou*, 139 F.3d 247, 254-55 (D.C.Cir.1998)). Here, the Court finds that there are compelling grounds for dismissal under the doctrine of forum non conveniens.[6] . . .

---

5. It is not clear whether plaintiffs are arguing that a "direct effect" in the United States occurred merely by virtue of the fact that U.S. entities allegedly suffered losses resulting from Brazil's non- payment. Plaintiffs have not identified any precedent in this Circuit supporting such a position, and the Court sees no basis for extending the meaning of "direct effect" that far. Indeed, loss to a U.S. plaintiff would not necessarily constitute "direct effect" even under the expansive approach of the Fifth Circuit that plaintiffs ask the Court to employ here. *See Voest-Alpine Trading USA Corp. v. Bank of China*, 142 F.3d 887, 896 n. 11 (5th Cir.1998) (declining to reach question as to whether "any financial loss suffered by an American plaintiff, regardless of where that loss was incurred, is alone sufficient to constitute a direct effect under the third clause").

6. Plaintiffs argue that a court may not dismiss a case under the FSIA on the basis of forum non conveniens. But the cases cited by plaintiffs for this proposition involve the state sponsored terrorism exception to the FSIA, which does not apply here. *See, e.g., Daliberti v. Republic of Iraq*, 97 F.Supp.2d 38, 54 n. 7 (D.D.C.2000); *Flatow v. Islamic Republic of Iran*, 999 F.Supp. 1, 25 (D.D.C.1998). Moreover, *Phoenix Consulting*, 216 F.3d at 40, and *In re Papandreou*, 139 F.3d at 254-55, clearly permit courts to consider forum non conveniens as a basis for dismissal where the

# 4. Act of State Doctrine

**Notes and Comments 8.6.** What is the difference between the concept of sovereign immunity and the "Act of State" doctrine? Historically, claims of sovereign immunity typically arose as defenses raised by an alleged sovereign or its agencies or instrumentalities, which appeared as defendant in litigation. An act of state argument was a device of issue preclusion–not, strictly speaking, a defense, raised by a private defendant in litigation, whose title to disputed property depended upon some act of an alleged sovereign that was not a party to the litigation.

Thus, if a fur trapper attempted to sue a governmental agency that had contracted to purchase pelts, the latter might raise a defense of sovereign immunity. Today, under the "restrictive theory" of sovereign immunity endorsed by the Foreign Sovereign Immunities Act, that defense might or might not cover the transaction in question. In contrast, if the pelts were expropriated by the government, which then sold them to a third party, the third party might find itself sued by the fur trapper, in the former owner's home country, in an action for unlawful conversion of the pelts. If the validity of the government's passage of title to third party were an issue in the case, as it would almost certainly be, the third party might raise the Act of State doctrine, namely, that the courts of one country ought not to sit in judgment on the validity of the acts of the government of another country effected within the territory of that other government. *See, e.g., Underhill v. Hernandez*, 168 U.S. 250 (1897). If successful, this would preclude judicial consideration of that issue.

**8.7.** These historical assumptions have blurred because of the increasing involvement of foreign governments, their agents and instrumentalities in commercial transactions. Today a foreign government instrumentality might therefore be a defendant in an action where both the act of state doctrine and the defense of sovereign immunity are relevant. The restrictive theory of sovereign immunity make that defense less useful, but the Act of State doctrine is not directly affected by these modification in sovereign immunity law.[12]

**8.8.** The Supreme Court has traditionally taken a case-by-case approach to the question of what sort of act qualifies as an "act of state." *See generally Underhill, supra*; *First National City Bank v. Banco Nacional de Cuba*, 406 U.S. 759 (1972) (plurality opinion); *Alfred Dunhill, supra* note 1 (plurality opinion). It seems clear that the act in question should reflect an actual exercise of sovereign power, and probably should not consist solely of preexisting legislation intended to be triggered by subsequent events. *See, e.g., Industrial Inv. Dev. Corp., supra* note 12. *But cf. Alfred Dunhill*, 425 U.S. at 718 (dissent) (arguing act need not be formalized). The act must take place and have its effect within the actual territory of the foreign state. *See, e.g., Banco Nacional de Cuba v. Sabbatino*, 376 U.S. 398, 427-028, 431-32 (1964); *Alfred Dunhill*, 425 U.S. at 697; *United Bank Ltd. v. Cosmic International, Inc.*, 542 F.2d 868, 872-74 (2d Cir. 1976); *Republic of Iraq v. First National City Bank*, 353 F.2d 47 (2d Cir. 1965), *cert. denied* 382 U.S. 1027 (1966).

**8.9.** Consider the cases excerpted below in order to resolve the following problems:

---

FSIA applies. *See also Verlinden B.V. v. Central Bank of Nigeria,* 461 U.S. 480, 490 n. 15 (1983) (the FSIA "does not appear to affect the traditional doctrine of forum non conveniens").

12. For example, it is unsettled whether the doctrine should be restricted, as sovereign immunity is, by an exception for "commercial acts." *Alfred Dunhill of London, Inc. v. Republic of Cuba*, 425 U.S. 682, 703-704 (1976) (plurality opinion); *id.* at 725 (dissent) (citing *Sabbatino*). *See also Industrial Inv. Dev. Corp. v. Mitsui & Co.*, 594 F.2d 48, 52 (5th Cir. 1979), *cert. denied*, 445 U.S. 903 (1980); *IAM v. OPEC*, 649 F.2d 1354, 1360 (9th Cir. 1981).

**a.** Following the earthquakes and mudslides in Nusquam, the Central Bank of Nusquam has declared an "emergency moratorium" on foreign exchange transactions. Consequently, the NPA has informed QNB that it will not be able to make payments of interest and principal on its loan, which is denominated in dollars. In the loan agreement, the NPA waived claims of sovereign immunity. If QNB sues, will the NPA be able to interpose the Act of State doctrine successfully?

**b.** Melvin S. Witless received a check from Gollijee Importers Ltd. (GIL), in payment of a shipment of widgets that Witless had exported to Gollijee in Nusquam. The check had been certified by Gollijee's bank, NusBank. The Nusquami Ministry of Justice (NMJ), acting on suspicions that Daza Gollijee was a close collaborator of the since deposed "Supreme Leader" of Nusquam, has seized his Nusquami assets, including his company GIL. The NMJ has instructed the Los Angeles branch of NusBank to refuse payment of the check received by Witless, and the branch has since informed Witless that it will not pay on the check. If Witless sues the NusBank branch, will it be able to interpose the Act of State doctrine successfully?

## Libra Bank Ltd. v. Banco Nacional de Costa Rica
### 570 F.Supp. 870 (S.D.N.Y. 1983)

[For the factual background of this case and the court's discussion of the pertinent provisions of the loan agreement at issue, see § 3, *supra*.]

### I.

Banco Nacional has submitted the affidavit of its Assistant General Manager, Alvara Santisteban Castro, in opposition to plaintiffs' motion for summary judgment. An examination of Santisteban's affidavit and defendant's memoranda indicates that Banco Nacional's opposition to the motion is based on its view that the events occurring on August 27 and November 24, 1981, in Costa Rica constitute a defense to repayment under the act of state doctrine and that in any event material issues of fact exist with respect to these events. Plaintiffs claim that any factual disputes with respect to these events are immaterial. They claim that even if the court credits Banco Nacional's version of the facts that the Costa Rican decrees prevented it from obtaining foreign currency, the act of state doctrine is no defense to liability in this case because 1) the act of state doctrine applies only when the foreign state expropriates property within its own territorial boundaries–since the situs of the property in question is in the United States this court need not abstain from examining the acts' validity; and 2) even if the act of state doctrine does apply, this case falls within the commercial activity exception to that doctrine so that the court need not abstain from examining those acts.

A. The Act of State Doctrine

. . .

Under *Sabbatino*'s formulation, the act of state doctrine forecloses judicial inquiry into the validity of foreign seizures only when there is "*a taking of property within its own territory by a foreign sovereign government,*" *id.* at 428 (emphasis added). This "territorial corollary," . . . goes to the applicability of the act of state doctrine. Unless the expropriation occurs within the foreign state, this court is free to inquire into the validity of the acts of the foreign nation. This important limitation on the preclusive scope of the doctrine was recently stated by the Second Circuit:

Under the traditional application of the act of state doctrine, the principle of judicial refusal of examination applies only to a taking by a foreign sovereign of property within its own territory . . . ; when property confiscated is within the United States at the time of the attempted confiscation, our courts will give effect to acts of state "only if they are consistent with the policy and law of the United States." *Banco Nacional de Cuba v. Chemical Bank of New York*, 658 F.2d 903, 908 (2d Cir. 1981) (Kearse, J.) (quoting *Republic of Iraq v. First National City Bank*, 353 F.2d 47, 51 (2d Cir. 1965) (Friendly, J.), *cert. denied*, 382 U.S. 1027 (1966)). . . .

In *Republic of Iraq v. First National City Bank*, 353 F.2d 47 (2d Cir. 1965) (*Republic of Iraq*), the Republic of Iraq confiscated the assets of its deposed monarch, King Faisal II, held in deposit and custody accounts with a bank in New York City. Judge Friendly stated that in determining whether to question the validity of the confiscation decree, a court must first determine whether the property was located in the United States at the time of the attempted act of confiscation. 353 F.2d at 51. If the property is located in this country, a court must examine that act of seizure within the framework of our own policies and laws and must enforce it only if it is consistent with our system of jurisprudence. Because the Second Circuit concluded that King Faisal's assets were located in the United States, it refused to give effect to the foreign decree.

In the instant case, defendant argues that the acts of state in question occurred in Costa Rica. Defendant also argues that the acts in question are the August 27, 1981 and the November 24, 1981 decreed passed by the Costa Rican government regulating the conduct of its banks with the effect that the loan cannot be repaid in New York. This case, according to the defendant, is to be distinguished from *Republic of Iraq* where the decree stated that the foreign nation was seizing property located in New York. The court finds this argument to be without merit. First, the acts in question are not the resolutions passed by the Costa Rican government. As Judge Wisdom has stated, the act of state "refers to full exercise by the foreign state of dominion over the property in question, *not to the documentary execution of whatever legal action the foreign state takes toward the property or its own national* . . . it looks not to the execution of a nationalization decree but rather to exercise of dominion over real property located in the United States." *Maltina Corporation v. Cawy Bottling Company*, 462 F.2d 1021, 1025 n. 3 (5th Cir.) (emphasis added), *cert. denied*, 409 U.S. 1060 (1972). Second, defendant's argument that the Costa Rican decrees do not confiscate property but merely prevented defendant from repayment is also without merit. The property in question in this case is plaintiffs' legal right to repayment of the debt owed by the defendant. The Costa Rican decrees purport to alter the legal relations of the parties because they attempt to extinguish plaintiffs' rights. That act is as much an attempt to confiscate plaintiffs' property in this case as was the attempt to confiscate King Faisal's accounts in *Republic of Iraq*. That tangible property may have been involved in *Republic of Iraq* as opposed to intangible property here is a distinction without legal significance since in a strict legal sense all property is intangible. The American legal concept of property refers not to possession of "things," but to certain legal rights among persons with respect to "things." *See generally* B. ACKERMAN, PRIVATE PROPERTY AND THE CONSTITUTION, 26-27 (1977). Since the court finds defendant's attempts to distinguish this case from *Republic of Iraq* to be unavailing, the court turns now to an examination of cases illuminating Judge Friendly's two step analysis.

In *Menendez v. Saks*, 485 F.2d 1355 (2d Cir. 1973) (*Menendez*), the Second Circuit stated that "[f]or purposes of the act of state doctrine, a debt is not 'located' within a foreign state unless that state has the power to enforce or collect it." 485 F.2d at 1364. The court further stated that "the power to enforce payment of a debt, . . . the basis of our decision in

*Republic of Iraq*[,] . . . generally depends on jurisdictions over the person of the debtor." *Id.* at 1365 (citing *Harris v. Balk*, 198 U.S. 215 (1904)).

*Menendez* involved a dispute between former owners of a cigar manufacturing business and agents of the Cuban government or "interventors" who had been placed in charge of operating these businesses after their nationalization by the Cuban government. Both the former owners and the interventors asserted rights to pre-seizure debts owed by cigar importers in New York City. The court held that the doctrinal obstacle of the act of state did not bar judicial inquiry:

> Application of the principles of [*Republic of Iraq*] satisfies us that since the owners' accounts receivable had their situs in the United States rather than in Cuba at the time of intervention and since the Cuban government's purported seizure of them without compensation is contrary to our own domestic policy, the act of state doctrine does not apply, the confiscation was ineffective, and the interventors' claim must be rejected. The owners rather than the interventors therefore remain entitled to collect these accounts.

485 F.2d at 1364.

In *United Bank, Ltd. v. Cosmic International, Inc.*, 542 F.2d 868 (2d Cir. 1976), Bangladesh and Pakistani plaintiffs asserted conflicting rights to payment for jute products exported from East Pakistan and resold in the United States prior to the March 26, 1971 "Proclamation of Independence" declaring East Pakistan to be the sovereign state of Bangladesh. The defendant, Cosmic International, Inc., a Delaware corporation with its principal place of business in New York, held two funds amounting to $97,043.50 and $433,365.96 which represented the proceeds from the sale of the jute products in question. The defendant admitted that it owed the money but sought judicial clarification as to whom it should pay. In sum, the issue was whether the pre-revolution owners or the post-revolution successors owned the debt. The District Court, relying on *Republic of Iraq* and *Menendez*, held that the situs of the debt was in New York:

> [I]t is clear the sales transactions were complete and all that remained was the right to receive payment, which was to be made in New York City. This right existed before December 16, 1971, the date the new Bangladesh government gained control of East Pakistan. The act of state doctrine is inapplicable because the situs of the debts was New York at the time the Bangladesh government attempted to seize them.

*United Bank, Ltd. v. Cosmic International, Inc.*, 392 F.Supp 262, 265 (S.D.N.Y. 1975). The Second Circuit affirmed the District Court's analysis of the act of state doctrine, 542 F.2d at 872, and rejected each of the Bangladesh plaintiffs' arguments placing the situs of the debt in Bangladesh. *Id.* at 873-77. *See also Vishipco Line v. Chase Manhattan Bank, N.A.*, 660 F.2d 854, 862 (2d Cir. 1981) (*Vishipco Line*) (for purposes of act of state doctrine, "[t]he rule announced in *Harris v. Balk*, 198 U.S. 215 (1905), continues to be valid on this point: the power to enforce payment of a debt depends on jurisdiction over the debtor), *cert. denied*, — U.S. —, 103 S.Ct. 313 (1982).

The territorial limitation on the act of state doctrine was recognized recently by the New York Court of Appeals in *Weston Banking Corporation v. Turkiye Garanti Bankasi*, 57 N.Y.2d 315, 442 N.E.2d 1195, 456 N.Y.S.2d 684 (1982) (*Weston Banking*). In *Weston Banking*, the plaintiff, a Panamanian bank, sought to enforce a promissory note that was signed by the representative of the defendant, a Turkish bank, on July 9, 1976, in Istanbul, Turkey.

According to the terms of the note, defendant undertook an obligation to repay plaintiff principal in the amount of 500,000 Swiss francs, plus interest calculated at 9% per annum. The note provided that all payments were to be made at the offices of Chemical Bank (Chemical) in New York City. The note designated New York as the proper jurisdiction for the resolution of any disputes and, under the terms of the note, the defendant consented to the jurisdiction of the New York courts. 442 N.E.2d at 1196, 456 N.Y.S.2d at 685. The defendant bank duly borrowed the 500,000 Swiss francs. As the interest became due, defendant made payments in Swiss francs at Chemical's International Division in New York City. When the note was presented for repayment of the principal, defendant refused to pay on the grounds that the then existing Turkish banking regulations barred it from repaying the note in Swiss francs. Plaintiff moved for summary judgment. The trial court denied the motion. The Appellate Division modified, on the law, and granted plaintiff's motion for summary judgment. On appeal, the New York Court of Appeals affirmed. Noting that "the note requires payment to be made at Chemical Bank in New York City and designates New York banking law to be controlling," 442 N.E.2d at 1199, 456 N.Y.S.2d at 688, the court stated:

> We conclude that on these facts the Act of State doctrine does not constitute a defense to plaintiff's actio to recover on this note. A debt is not located within a foreign State unless it has the power at the instance of an interested party to enforce or collect it. . . . Here, the debt is equally capable of being enforced against the defendant's assets in New York as it is capable of being enforced against its assets in Turkey, and the state of Turkey has no power to enforce collection of this debt. The mere fact that this suit might have been commenced in Turkey, instead of New York, does not bar this action. Indeed, the note provides that New York shall be the proper jurisdiction for dispute resolution. Such a provision naturally contemplates enforcement of any judgment which would resolve the dispute. Thus, the Act of State doctrine does not bar this action.

*Id.* (citations omitted). *See also Manas y Pineiro v. Chase Manhattan Bank, N.A.*, 106 Misc.2d 660, 434 N.Y.S.2d 868, 8772 (Sup. Ct. 1980) (act of state doctrine applicable where both the res and the persons were inside foreign country at time of seizure).

C. Applying the Extraterritorial Standards

Unlike the majority of the act of state cases involving debts, this case does not involve the attempt by a foreign nation to confiscate a debt *owed* by a United States national to a foreign national, *see Republic of Iraq*; (attempt to seize accounts owed by New York City bank to King Faisal); *Menendez* (Cuban interventors claiming New York debts owed to former owners of cigar manufacturing business); *United Bank Ltd. v. Cosmic International, Inc.*, (attempt by newly spawned nation to seize New York debts owed to pre-revolution owners). Instead, this case involves the attempt by a foreign nation to avoid payment of a debt which *it* concededly owes to its creditors. The posture of this case makes it somewhat difficult to apply the form of the test posed by the Second Circuit, that "a debt is not 'located' within a foreign state unless that state has the power to enforce or collect it." *Menendez*, 485 F.2d at 1364. That formula was composed in the factual context of attempts by a foreign state to seize for itself a debt owed to another. Applying it in this context, as did the court in *Weston Banking*, presents certain obvious difficulties. This is because the foreign state in almost all instances can in theory enforce a debt since the foreign national will in most instances be domiciled in the foreign nation; if a foreign corporation or bank is involved that entity will almost always have a branch in its home nation. The *Weston Banking* court hurdled this obstacle as follows:

Here, the debt is equally capable of being enforced against the defendant's assets in New York as it is capable of being enforced against its assets in Turkey, and the State of Turkey has no power to enforce collection of this debt. The mere fact that this suit might have been commenced in Turkey, instead of New York, does not bar the action. Indeed, the note provides that New York shall be the proper jurisdiction for dispute resolution. Such a provision naturally contemplates enforcement of any judgment which would resolve the dispute.

442 N.E.2d at 1199, 456 N.Y.S.2d at 688. The *Weston Banking* court's underlying rationale, one that this court believes is sound, is that although a debtor may in theory be sued at the creditor's choice in either of two jurisdictions, the legal incidents of the debt may nevertheless place it, for the purposes of the act of state doctrine, in this nation rather than in the foreign nation. This is so because when the creditor proceeds against the debtor in the place of his home, he does so upon the theory that a creditor may always sue the person of the debtor in the place of his domicile upon the asserted jurisdictional basis that the courts there have personal jurisdiction over the debtor. The creditor may also sue the debtor wherever the debtor is found upon the different legal theory that the debt is located in that jurisdiction. The court notes this analysis is consistent with the historical formula set forth in *Harris v. Balk*, 198 U.S. 215, 222-23 (1905) ("The obligation of the debtor to pay his debt clings to and accompanies him wherever he goes. He is as much bound to pay his debt in a foreign state when therein sued upon his obligation by his creditor, as he was in the state where the debt was contracted. . . . This obligation can be enforced by the courts of the foreign state after personal service of process therein, just as well as by the courts of the domicile of the debtor."). Thus, this court believes that even if a creditor can sue a debtor in his home in a foreign state that has the power to compel the indigenous debtor to pay his debt, a United States court may still find that the situs of the debt was in this nation at the time of the attempted confiscation.

. . . [T]he situs of the debt owed by Banco Nacional was in this nation at the time that the foreign currency decrees were enacted. Under the terms of the loan agreement, Banco Nacional consented to the jurisdiction of this court, *see National Equipment Rental Ltd. v. Szukhent*, 375 U.S. 311, 315-16 (1965); and thus this court has jurisdiction over the debtor. *See Harris v. Balk*, 198 U.S. at 222-23; *Vishipco Line*, 660 F.2d at 684. Banco Nacional also consented to have the letter agreement construed in accordance with New York law. Under the terms of the loan agreement, Banco Nacional was to make all payments to the Chase Manhattan Bank ("Chase") in New York City. The promissory notes executed upon the loan agreement also provide that payment is to be made in Chase's New York branch. The notes further provide that Banco Nacional shall make all payments "free and clear of and exempt from . . . any other charges and withholdings whatsoever imposed . . . with respect to the . . . performance . . . of this Promissory Note." The court further notes that at the time that the Costa Rican decrees were enacted, Banco Nacional had $2.5 million in various New York City bank accounts. Of those assets, plaintiffs succeeded in attaching over $800,000 in connection with this lawsuit. Moreover, Banco Nacional appears to have other considerable assets located in the United States including a majority ownership interest in Banco Internacional de Costa Rica which has a branch in Miami, Florida.

Under these circumstances, this court holds that the situs of the debt was in New York at the time of the attempted confiscation by the Costa Rican government. The Costa Rican decrees attempted to alter the legal relations between the parties with respect to the debt by extinguishing the legal right to repayment, the only property in question, whose situs was in New York. The circumstances of this case are similar to those in *United Bank, Ltd.*

*v. Cosmic International, Inc.*, 392 F.Supp. 262 (S.D.N.Y. 1975) where Judge Brieant ruled, "[A]ll that remained was the right to repayment, which was to be made in New York City. This right existed before December 16, 1971, the date the new Bangladesh government gained control of East Pakistan. The act of state doctrine is inapplicable because the situs of the debts was New York . . . ," *id.* at 265.

Since the act of state doctrine is inapplicable, this court may examine the validity of the Costa Rican decrees and need "give effect to [these] acts of state 'only if they are consistent with the policy and law of the United States.'" *Republic of Iraq*, 353 F.2d at 51 (citation omitted). The court holds that it shall not give effect to the Costa Rican decrees since a foreign state's effective confiscation of property, without compensation, is repugnant to the Constitution and laws of this nation. *See United Bank, Ltd. v. Cosmic International, Inc.*, 542 F.2d at 873; *Menendez*, 485 F.2d at 1354; *Republic of Iraq*, 353 F.2d at 51.

The court is not unmindful that the effect of its judgment is to reverse the Costa Rican decrees. The court believes, however, that in this situation, because its judgment is unlikely to "'vex the peace of nations.' . . . there is less need for judicial deference to the foreign affairs competence of the other branches of government." *United Bank, Ltd. v. Cosmic International, Inc.*, 542 F.2d at 875 (citation omitted) (quoting *Maltina Corp. v. Cawy Bottling Co. (Maltina Corp.)*, 462 F.2d at 1028-29). As the Court noted in *Sabbatino*:

> It is also evident that some aspects of international law touch much more sharply on national nerves than do others; the less important the implications of an issue are for our foreign relations, the weaker the justification for exclusivity in the political branches.

376 U.S. at 428. *Cf. Baker v. Carr*, 369 U.S. 186, 211- 12 (1962) ("[I]t is error to suppose that every case or controversy which touches foreign relations lies beyond judicial cogniz-ance. Our cases in this field seem invariably to show a discriminating analysis of the par-ticular question posed . . . , of its susceptibility to judicial handling in the light of its nature and posture in the specific case, and of the possible consequences of judicial action.").

The Second Circuit has indicated that "the underlying rationale of the act of state doctrine should be considered when determining situs in a situation involving a purported extraterritorial seizure." *United Bank Ltd. v. Cosmic International, Inc.*, 542 F.2d at 874 (citing *Tabacalera Severiano Jorge, S.A. v. Standard Cigar Co.*, 392 F.2d 706, 714-15 (5th Cir.) (*Tabacalera*), *cert. denied*, 393 U.S. 924 (1968)). In its discussion of the underlying rationale of the territorial limitation to the act of state doctrine, the *Tabacalera* court stated:

> The underlying thought expressed in all of the cases touching on the Act of State Doctrine is a common-sense one. It is that when a foreign government performs an act of state which is an accomplished fact, that is when it has the parties and the *res* before it and acts in such a manner as to change the relationship between the parties touching the *res*, it would be an affront to such foreign government for courts of the United States to hold that such act was a nullity. Furthermore, it is plain that the decisions took into consideration the realization that in most situations there was nothing the United States courts could do about it in any event.

392 F.2d at 715 (emphasis in original). The Second Circuit has stated that the *Tabacalera* court "recogniz[ed] that the act of state doctrine reflects at least in part the realization that in most cases there is nothing that an American court can do to rectify a foreign seizure which has been fully effected within the territory of the expropriating state. . . ." *United*

*Bank, Ltd. v. Cosmic International, Inc.*, 542 F.2d at 874 (citing *Tabacalera*, 392 F.2d at 715). On the other hand, "[w]here an act of state has not 'come to complete fruition within the dominion of . . . [a foreign] government, '. . . no *fait accompli* has occurred . . . [I]n the absence of such a *fait accompli*, there is less likelihood that any ensuing judicial review would jeopardize this country's foreign relations . . . ." *Id.* at 874 (quoting *Tabacalera*, 392 F.2d at 715-16). The Second Circuit then explicated the relationship between the territorial limitation and the legal source of the act of state doctrine:

> This emphasis on the completion of the Act of State squares with the policy con-
> siderations articulated in the *Sabbatino* decision . . . . The obvious inability of a
> foreign state to complete an expropriation of property beyond its borders reduces
> the foreign state's expectations of dominion over that property; "the concept of
> territorial sovereignty is . . . deep seated . . ." *Sabbatino, supra*, 376 U.S. at
> 431-32. Consequently, [since] the potential for offense to the foreign state is
> reduced, there is less danger that judicial disposition of the property will "vex the
> peace of nations." . . .

542 F.2d at 874-75 (quoting *Maltina Corp.*, 462 F.2d at 1028-29).

As *Sabbatino* indicates, the underlying rationale of the act of state doctrine is that the judicial branch may not pass upon the validity of foreign acts when to do so would vex the harmony of our international relations with that foreign nation. Rather, it is for the political branch, in the exercise of its considered judgment, to engage in acts which may have the possible consequence of significantly altering our relationship with a foreign nation. As the Second Circuit indicates, whether the act of the judicial branch will vex our relations with a foreign state depends on the "foreign state's expectations of dominion over [the] property [in question]," *United Bank, Ltd. v. Cosmic International, Inc.*, 542 F.2d at 875 (quoting *Maltina Corp.*, 462 F.2d at 1028). Within its territorial boundaries, the foreign state has reasonable expectations of complete dominion over property and acts by courts of this nation declaring confiscation decrees invalid would "often be likely to give offense to the expropriating country; since the concept of territorial sovereignty is so deep seated, any state may resent the refusal of the courts of another sovereign to accord validity to acts within its territorial borders." *Sabbatino*, 376 U.S. at 432. On the other hand, a foreign state cannot be said to have reasonable expectations of dominion over property located in this nation because of "[t]he obvious inability of a foreign state to complete an expropriation of property beyond its borders. . . ." *United Bank, Ltd. v. Cosmic International, Inc.*, 542 F.2d at 875 (quoting *Maltina Corp.*, 462 F.2d at 1028). As these cases suggest, the territorial limitation to the act of state doctrine embodies the considered judgment of the judicial branch that a foreign state can be said to have reasonable expectations of dominion only with respect to property located within its own boundaries. In such circumstances, courts may not act because to do so would frustrate the foreign nation's reasonable expectations so as to vex our relationship with that foreign government.

These cases, discussed above, clarify the relationship between the territorial limit-ation and the ultimate source of the act of state doctrine's binding legal power, the constitu-tional principles of separation of powers. The territorial limitation is a judicially created device which serves to regulate the proper distribution of functions between the judicial and political branches. *Sabbatino*, 376 U.S. at 427-28. The underlying notion embodied in the territorial limitation is the considered judgment of the judicial branch that courts will vex our relations with foreign governments only when they act to frustrate the foreign nation's reasonable expectations of dominion. On the other hand, a foreign nation cannot be said to entertain reasonable expectations of dominion over the property located in this nation at the time of the attempted confiscation.

As the *Tabacalera* court stated, "[t]he situs of intangible property is about as intangible a concept as is known to the law." 392 F.2d at 714. This court is, of course, constrained to follow the teachings of *Republic of Iraq* and determine the situs of the debt at issue in this case. Having applied the tests set forth in *Harris v. Balk* and *Republic of Iraq* and their progeny, this court concluded that the situs of the debt at issue in the instant case was in this nation and that the act of state doctrine is inapplicable to this case. Yet, the tests fashioned to determine the situs of a debt are rigid and mechanical and can be difficult to apply. More importantly, this inflexible approach, focusing on a somewhat formalistic analysis of the situs of the debt, may not be an accurate measure of the foreign state's reasonable expectations which appears to be the root notion underlying the regulatory purpose of the territorial limitation to the act of state doctrine. This court believes, therefore, that the inapplicability of the act of state doctrine is more clearly seen when the principle of objective reasonableness underlying the territorial limitation is applied directly to the facts of this case.

In this case, the act of state was incomplete at the time of the attempted confiscation. Since Banco Nacional was found here and had considerable assets here, "the Act of State itself remain[ed] incomplete in the absence of acquiescence by the forum state," *Maltina Corp.*, 462 F.2d at 1028, and in such a case as this, "[t]he obvious inability of a foreign state to complete an expropriation of property beyond its borders reduces the foreign state's expectations of dominion over that property," *id*. In this case, where a foreign government contracts to repay a debt in New York City, consents to the jurisdiction of our courts, waives its sovereign immunity with respect to legal proceedings concerning that debt, and continues to maintain considerable assets in this nation, it can hardly be said that this court's judgment shall frustrate the foreign state's reasonable expectations of dominion over the legal rights involved therein so as to vex our amicable relations with that foreign nation. Accordingly, the court concludes that its exercise of its judicial power is appropriate in this case and is fully consistent with the proper distribution of functions in our system of separation of powers between the "judicial and political branches of the Government on matters bearing upon foreign affairs." *Sabbatino*, 376 U.S. at 427-28.


## Callejo v. Bancomer, S.A.
### 764 F.2d 1101 (5th Cir. 1985)

[For the background of this case, see the excerpt from the case in § 3, *supra*.]

Like the doctrine of sovereign immunity, the act of state doctrine springs "from the thoroughly sound principle that on occasion individual litigants may have to forego decision on the merits of their claims because the involvement of the courts in such a decision might frustrate the conduct of the Nations' foreign policy." *First National City Bank v. Banco Nacional de Cuba*, 406 U.S. 759, 769 (1972); *see also Banco Nacional de Cuba v. Sabbatino*, 376 U.S. 398, 438 (1964) (act of state doctrine "shares with the immunity doctrine a respect for sovereign states"). Thus, in considering the act of state issue, we traverse much of the same path that we did in the sovereign immunity context—again, our focus is on preventing friction with coequal sovereigns. However, if the Foreign Service Immunities Act is a tangled web of statutory ambiguities, the act of state doctrine is an airy castle. Rather than narrowly focusing on the status of the act and actor complained of, we examine more generally the underlying acts of the foreign state. In the act of state context, even if the defendant is a private party, not an instrumentality of a foreign state, and even if the suit is not based specifically on a sovereign act, we nevertheless decline to decide the merits of the case if in doing so we would need to judge the validity of the public acts of a sovereign state performed within its own territory. *Sabbatino*, 376 U.S. at 428; *Compania de Gas de Nuevo Laredo v. Entex, Inc.*, 686 F.2d 322, 325-26 (5th Cir. 1982) (applying act of state doctrine in suit between private parties), *cert. denied*, 460 U.S. 1041; (1983); *Tabacalero Severiano Jorge, S.A. v. Standard Cigar Co.*, 392 F.2d 706 (5th Cir.) (same), *cert. denied*, 393 U.S. 924 (1968). . . .

In essence, the act of state doctrine operates as a super-choice-of-law rule, requiring that foreign law be applied in certain circumstances. . . . Normally, a court will only apply foreign law if it is compatible with the public policy of the forum. . . . The act of state doctrine recognizes, however, that in the international context, refusing to enforce foreign law because it is contrary to U.S. conceptions of public policy is unduly parochial and is likely to insult the foreign sovereign, thereby embarrassing the foreign policy of the United States.[13] . . .

In the present case, Bancomer claims that Mexico's promulgation of exchange control regulations constituted an act of state, and that consideration of the Callejos' claims would require us to inquire into the validity of those regulations The Callejos argue, in response, that the act of state doctrine is inapplicable for three reasons: (1) Mexico's promulgation of the exchange control regulations was a commercial act, not an act of state; (2) the "treaty exception" to the act of state doctrine applies, since the exchange control regulations violate Mexico's obligations under the Articles of Agreement of the International Monetary Fund;[a] and (3) the situs of the certificates of deposit was Texas rather than Mexico, and therefore the certificates are not governed by the Mexican decrees. We consider each of these arguments in turn.

A.  The Commercial Activity Exception

In Part III of *Alfred Dunhill of London, Inc. v. Republic of Cuba*, 425 U.S. 682 (1976), a plurality of the Court enunciated a commercial activity exception to the act of state doctrine.[15] *Id.* at 695-706; *cf. Texas Trading & Milling Corp. v. Federal Republic of Nigeria*, 647 F.2d 300, 316 n. 38 (2d Cir. 1981) (declining to apply act of state doctrine to Nigeria's breach of cement-purchase contracts), *cert. denied*, 454 U.S. 1148 (1982). This exception states that the act of state doctrine does not apply to "the repudiation of a purely commercial

---

13. Although the act of state doctrine is not prescribed by international law, *Sabbatino*, 376 U.S. at 421-22, most other nations have shown a similar solicitude for the feelings of their fellow states. *See* RESTATEMENT (REVISED) OF FOREIGN RELATIONS LAW OF THE UNITED STATES § 469 reporters' note 12 (Tent. Draft No. 6, 1985).

a. On the effect of the IMF Charter on the Act of State doctrine and related issues, see question 8.10, *infra*, and accompanying excerpts.

15. Only four judges joined in this part of the Court's opinion. The majority decided the case on the ground that Cuba's actions in repudiating a commercial debt were not invested with the sovereign authority of the state and hence were not acts of state at all. *Id.* at 694-95. As the Court noted, "No statute, decree, order, or resolution of the Cuban Government itself was offered in evidence indicating that Cuba had repudiated its obligations in general or any class thereof or that it had as a sovereign matter determined to confiscate the amounts due three foreign importers." *Id.* at 695. Here, there is no question that Mexico's promulgation of the exchange control regulations was invested with the sovereign authority of the state. The decrees were issued by the Mexican Ministry of Treasury and Public Credit and by President Lopez Portillo, and were later reiterated in legislative enactments.

obligation owed by a foreign sovereign or by one of its commercial instrumentalities." *Dunhill*, 425 U.S. at 695. The plurality saw the exception as a corollary of the commercial immunity doctrine, with similar policy justifications.[16] *Id.* at 705-06 & n. 18. As the plurality noted, "[T]he mere assertion of sovereignty as a defense to a claim arising out of purely commercial acts by a foreign sovereign is no more effective if given the label 'Act of State' than if it is given the label 'sovereign immunity.'" *Id.* at 705.

In the present case, we need not decide whether to adopt the commercial activity exception, since Mexico's actions were clearly sovereign and not commercial in nature.[17] For act of state (as opposed to sovereign immunity) purposes, the relevant acts are not merely those of the named defendants, but any governmental acts whose validity would be called into question by adjudication of the suit. Here, although the specific act complained of by the Callejos was Bancomer's breach of contract, not Mexico's promulgation of the exchange control regulations, adjudication of the breach of contract claim would necessarily call into question the Mexican regulations. Under these regulations, Bancomer has discharged its obligation to the Callejos by paying off the certificates in pesos at the established rate of exchange. Thus, we could require Bancomer to honor the terms of the certificates only by disregarding the regulations. *See Braka v. Bancomer, S.N.C.*, 762 F.2d 222, 225-26 (2d Cir. 1985).

The power to issue exchange control regulations is paradigmatically sovereign in nature; it is not of a type that a private person can exercise. Unlike in *Dunhill*, where Cuba repudiated a single debt, here Mexico promulgated comprehensive, national decrees in response to a national monetary crisis. As the court noted in *Braka v. Bancomer, S.A.*, 589 F.Supp. 1465 (S.D.N.Y. 1984), *aff'd*, 762 F.2d 222 (2d Cir. 1985),

Mexico's act in this instance cannot be construed as a simple repudiation of a

---

16. Writing for the plurality, Justice White justified the commercial activity exception by stating, "[S]ubjecting foreign governments to the rule of law in their commercial dealings presents a much smaller risk of affronting their sovereignty than would an attempt to pass on the legality of their governmental acts. In their commercial capacities, foreign governments do not exercise powers peculiar to sovereigns. Instead, they exercise only those powers that can also be exercised by private persons. Subjecting them in connection with such acts to the same rules of law that apply to private citizens is unlikely to touch very sharply on 'national nerves.'" *Id.* at 703-04.

17. The articulation in *Dunhill* of a commercial activity exception to the act of state doctrine has engendered considerable debate. *Compare International Ass'n of Machinists & Aerospace Workers v. OPEC*, 649 F.2d 1354, 1360 (9th Cir. 1981) (declining to adopt commercial activity exception), *cert. denied*, 454 U.S. 1163 (1982), *with* Note, *Foreign Sovereign Immunity and Commercial Activity*, 83 Colum.L.Rev. 1440, 1445-51 (1983) (arguing in favor of commercial activity exception).

Although we have cited *Dunhill* on a number of occasions, *see Compania de Gas de Nuevo Laredo v. Entex, Inc.*, 686 F.2d 322, 326 (5th Cir. 1982), *cert. denied*, 460 U.S. 1041 (1983); *Arango v. Guzman Travel Advisors Corp.*, 621 F.2d 1371, 1380 n. 11 (5th Cir. 1980); *Industrial Inv. Dev. Corp. v. Mitsui & Co.*, 594 F.2d 48, 52 (5th Cir. 1979), *cert. denied*, 445 U.S. 903 (1980), thus far we have not actually adopted the commercial activity exception, *Airline Pilots Ass'n v. Taca Int'l Airlines*, 748 F.2d 965, 970 n. 2 (5th Cir. 1984), *cert. denied*, — U.S. —, 105 S.Ct. 2324 (1985). In *Entex*, we held that the actions in question were governmental rather than commercial, and thus never had the opportunity to determine whether, if they were commercial, the act of state doctrine would apply. 686 F.2d at 326. Similarly, we held in *Mitsui* that the act of state doctrine did not apply for other reasons and thus did not reach the commercial activity exception issue. 594 F.2d at 52. Finally, in *Arango*, the commercial activities in question were not invested with the sovereign authority of the state; they consisted merely of the sale of airline tickets and tourist cards, and the activities in connection therewith. 621 F.2d at 1380 n. 11.

> government entity's commercial debt. While the ultimate result may seem similar --i.e. Mexico has enriched itself at plaintiff's expense–the mechanisms used by Mexico are conventional devices of civilized nations faced with severe monetary crises, rather than the crude and total confiscation by force of a private person's assets.

*Id.* at 1472. Were we to disregard the exchange regulations by enforcing the Callejos' certificates of deposit, we would render nugatory the attempts by Mexico to protect its foreign exchange reserves. While we are doubtful of our ability to foresee what will vex the peace of nations, we have no doubt that disregarding the Mexican regulations would be very vexing indeed. We therefore reject the Callejos' commercial activity argument. . . .

[The court then turned to the Callejos' argument concerning the so-called "treaty exception." The court held that the treaty exception did not render the doctrine inapplicable to the Callejos' claims. The court's discussion of this issue is excerpted following Note 8.10, *infra.*]

C. The Situs of the Deposits

The final argument advanced by the Callejos for not applying the act of state doctrine is that the situs of their CDs was Texas rather than Mexico. The Callejos argue that under traditional choice-of-law rules pegging the choice of law to the situs of the property, Texas law should govern the certificates. Application of the act of state doctrine, they contend, would improperly give extraterritorial effect to the Mexican decrees.

In *Sabbatino*, the Court limited the act of state doctrine to takings of property "within its own territory by a foreign government." 376 U.S. at 428. Consistent with this limitation, we have refused to give effect to foreign acts of state that affected property whose situs was the United States. *See Maltina Corp. v. Cawy Bottling Co.*, 462 F.2d 1021 (5th Cir.), *cert. denied*, 409 U.S. 1060 (1972); *Tabacalera Severiano Jorge, S.A. v. Standard Cigar Co.*, 392 F.2d 706 (5th Cir.), *cert. denied*, 393 U.S. 924 (1968).[29]

The theory underlying the territorial limitation to the act of state doctrine is that a

---

29. Even when an act of a foreign state affects property outside of its territory, however, we may still give effect to the act if doing so is consistent with United States public policy. *Maltina*, 462 F.2d at 1026-27; *accord Banco Nacional de Cuba v. Chemical Bank New York Trust Co.*, 658 F.2d 903, 908-09 (2d Cir. 1981); *United Bank Ltd. v. Cosmic Int'l, Inc.*, 542 F.2d 868, 872-73 & n. 7 (2d Cir. 1976); *Republic of Iraq v. First Nat'l City Bank*, 353 F.2d 47, 51 (2d Cir. 1965), *cert. denied*, 382 U.S. 1027 (1966); *see also Libra Bank Ltd. v. Banco Nacional de Costa Rica*, 570 F.Supp. 870, 877, 882 (S.D.N.Y. 1983); RESTATEMENT (SECOND), *supra* note 12, at § 43(2) ("A court in the United States will give effect to an act of a foreign state [with respect to a thing located, or an interest localized, outside of its territory] . . . only if to do so would be consistent with the policy and law of the United States."); *cf. United States v. Belmont*, 301 U.S. 324, 332 (1937) (applying Russian governmental decree to bank deposits in New York on ground that this furthered United States policy). Although the fact that the property is located outside of the foreign state reduces the potential for offense, the considerations underlying the act of state doctrine may still be present. *See Maltina*, 462 F.2d at 1029 (differences are only of degree). A foreign state's interest in the enforcement of its laws does not always end at its borders. In the present case, however, since we find that the situs of the certificates was Mexico and not the United States, we do not reach the second prong of the territorial limitation test, namely, whether recognizing the Mexican decrees would be consistent with the policy and law of the United States. *Cf. Allied Bank Int'l v. Banco Credito Agricola*, 757 F.2d 516, 519-20 (2d Cir. 1985) (on rehearing) (holding that Costa Rican regulations suspending the repayment of external debt were contrary to American public policy).

foreign state is less concerned about the effect of its acts on property outside of its territory than within. . . .

In determining whether the situs of foreign property is the United States or a foreign state, federal rather than state law governs. *Tabacalera*, 392 F.2d at 715; *cf. Sabbatino*, 376 U.S. at 425 (issues regarding application of act of state doctrine must be treated as aspects of federal law). This is true even if the plaintiff's underlying claim is based on state law. . . .
.

On a previous occasion, we noted that "[t]he situs of intangible property is about as intangible a concept as is known to the law." *Tabacalera*, 392 F.2d at 714. "The situs may be in one place for ad valorem tax purposes, . . . ; it may be in another place for venue purposes, i.e., garnishment . . . ; it may be in more than one place for tax purposes in certain circumstances . . . ; it may be in still a different place when the need for establishing its true situs is to determine whether an overriding national concern, like the application of the Act of State Doctrine is involved." *Id.* at 714-15 (citations omitted). In determining the situs of an obligation, we take as our guide the general policies of the act of state doctrine rather than narrow rules developed in other contexts. *See Maltina*, 462 F.2d at 1027 ("[T]he federal courts are to take a pragmatic view of what constitutes an extraterritorial action by a foreign state.").

Over the years, several tests have been developed to determine the situs of intangible property. One was elaborated by this court in *Tabacalera*, where we stated,

> [W]e think it clear that whatever efforts were made by the Cuban government dealing with Tabacalera, these acts are to be recognized under the Act of State Doctrine only insofar as they were able to come to complete fruition within the dominion of the Cuban government. As to other matters we conclude that they were not a 'taking of a property *within its own territory*' within the language used by the Supreme Court in *Sabbatino*.

392 F.2d at 715-16 (emphasis in original). Under this test, the situs of an obligation is determined not by the domicile of the creditor, as it is in other contexts, but by whether the foreign state is in a position to perform a *fait accompli*. *Id*. The policy considerations underlying this conclusion were elaborated by the court as follows: "[W]hen a foreign government performs an act of state which is an accomplished fact, that is when it has the parties and the *res* before it and acts in such a manner as to change the relationship between the parties touching the *res*, it would be an affront to such foreign government for courts of the United States to hold that such act was a nullity." *Id*. at 715. Because the property in question in *Tabacalera* consisted of a credit that was owed by an American company in Florida and that Cuba therefore was not in a position to seize, the court held that the property was located in the United States and declined to apply the act of state doctrine.

Although the *Tabacalera* test has been applied in a number of cases, . . . we do not find it helpful here. In *Tabacalera*, the foreign government was attempting to collect a debt rather than attempting to avoid paying it; the question was whether the foreign decrees applied to an obligation owed by an American debtor. Here, in contrast, the situation is reversed: the foreign national is the debtor and the American national the creditor. If we simply applied the *Tabacalera* test, the situs of the certificates would clearly be Mexico, since Mexico can enforce the collection of debts owed by Bancomer, a Mexican domiciliary. . . . In that event, the act of state doctrine would apply whenever a foreign state seized debts owed by its banks, no matter how many ties the debts had to this country.

We do not think that *Tabacalera* intended such results. The power to collect a debt is for the benefit of the creditor, not the debtor; the fact that a debt can be enforced by the creditor in one forum should not be the basis of depriving him of his ability to enforce the debt in a different forum. Otherwise, the sword of the creditor would become a shield for the debtor. Since we do not believe that debts owed by foreign banks to American nationals are always sitused [*sic*]in the foreign country–and consequently do not believe that the act of state doctrine always applied to such debts–we do not apply the *Tabacalera* test here. ...

Instead, for debts owed by foreign banks to American nationals, the proper test for determining situs is where the incidents of the debt, as a whole, place it. One relevant factor is the place where the deposit is carried, but this is not the only factor. In addition, we must examine the place of payment, the intent of the parties (if any) regarding the applicable law, and the involvement of the American banking system in the transaction. Together, these factors help us to determine the extent of the foreign government's interest in the debt. They therefore help to answer the ultimate question in the act of state context: Are the ties of the debt to the foreign country sufficiently close that we will antagonize the foreign government by not recognizing its acts? . . .

Here, the incidents of the certificates of deposit clearly place them in Mexico. The certificates of deposit were issued by Bancomer's Nuevo Laredo branch, where the Callejos' deposits were carried, and called for payment in Mexico. This grouping of contracts, when viewed through the gloss of the policies underlying the act of state doctrine, places the debt in Mexico and calls for the application of Mexican law.

The Callejos contend, however, that although the specified place of payment was Mexico, the course of conduct of the parties altered this agreement since the Callejos regularly received their payments in Texas. The Callejos, however, mistake remittances for payments. Although Bancomer remitted its payments to the Callejos in Texas, this did not mean that the place of payment was Texas. Unlike in *Garcia*, where the certificates of deposit issued by the Cuban branch bank were guaranteed by Chase Manhattan's New York office and payable upon presentation at any Chase Manhattan branch worldwide, 735 F.2d at 646, here the Callejos could not receive payment simply by presenting the certificates at one of Bancomer's correspondent banks in Texas. They had no right to draw directly upon Bancomer's accounts with Texas banks. Although the money was transferred to them through the services of a Texas correspondent bank, and although they were in Texas when they actually received the payments, this does not alter the fact that the only place where they had a legal right to be paid was at Bancomer's office in Mexico. . . .

The Callejos make much of the fact that when they made deposits, the money was in the first instance transferred to Bancomer's account at Laredo National Bank in Laredo, Texas. They contend, on this basis, that the deposits were made in Texas, where Bancomer first received control over the money, not in Mexico. We take a less formalistic approach to the problem of determining where a deposit is made. Here, the evidence was undisputed that, after receiving the money in its account at Laredo National Bank, Bancomer promptly transferred the money to its Nuevo Laredo branch; at the end of each business day its balance with Laredo National remained unchanged. Under these circumstances, Laredo National acted merely as a conduit for the deposits, not as their repository. . . . To hold otherwise would throw a monkeywrench into the wheels of international finance, whose smooth operation depends in large part on the lubricating influence of correspondent banks. It would mean that the deposits held by a bank would have different situses depending on the locations of the correspondent banks that first received them. Potentially a bank would have to comply with different laws for different deposits at a single branch. Rather than open this Pandora's box, banks would almost certain attempt to receive deposits directly, without the services of a correspondent bank.

## Allied Bank Int'l v. Banco Credito Agricola de Cartago
757 F.2d 516 (2d Cir. 1985)

Meskill, Circuit Judge:

I.

Allied is the agent for a syndicate of thirty-nine creditor banks. Defendants-appellees are three Costa Rican banks that are wholly owned by the Republic of Costa Rica and subject to the direct control of the Central Bank of Costa Rica (Central Bank). Allied brought this action in February 1982 to recover on promissory notes issued by the Costa Rican banks. The notes, which were in default, were payable in United States dollars in New York City. The parties' agreements acknowledged that the obligations were registered with Central Bank which was supposed to provide the necessary dollars for payment.

The defaults were due solely to actions of the Costa Rican government. In July 1981, in response to escalating national economic problems, Central Bank issued regulations which essentially suspended all external debt payments. In November 1981, the government issued an executive decree which conditioned all payments of external debt on express approval from Central Bank. Central Bank subsequently refused to authorize any foreign debt payments in United States dollars, thus precluded payment on the notes here at issue. In accordance with the provisions of the agreements, Allied accelerated the debt and sued for the full amount of principal and interest outstanding.

. . . The sole defense raised by [the Costa Rican banks] in response was the act of state doctrine.

. . . Reasoning that a judicial determination contrary to the Costa Rican directives could embarrass the United States government in its relations with the Costa Rican government, the [district court] held that the act of state doctrine barred entry of summary judgment for Allied. . . .

II.

In our previous decision, we affirmed the district court's dismissal. We did not address the question of whether the act of state doctrine applied because we determined that the actions of the Costa Rican government which precipitated the default of the Costa Rican banks were fully consistent with the law and policy of the United States. We therefore concluded that principles of comity compelled us to recognize as valid the Costa Rican directives. [The court then explained why it now believed that its interpretation of U.S. policy had been mistaken. That and related portions of the court's opinion is excerpted *infra* at 346.]

In light of the government's elucidation of its position, we believe that our earlier interpretation of United States policy was wrong. Nevertheless, if . . . the act of state doctrine applies, it precludes judicial examination of the Costa Rican decrees. Thus we must first consider that question.

III.

. . .

The extraterritorial limitation, an inevitable conjunct of the foreign policy concerns underlying the doctrine, dictates that our decision herein depends on the situs of the property at the time of the purported taking. The property, of course, is Allied's right to receive repayment from the Costa Rican banks in accordance with the agreements. The act of state doctrine is applicable to this dispute only if, when the decrees were promulgated, the situs of the debts was in Costa Rica. Because we conclude that the situs of the property was in the United States, the doctrine is not applicable.

As the Fifth Circuit explained in *Tabacalera*, the concept of the situs of a debt for act of state purposes differs from the ordinary concept. . . .

In this case, Costa Rica could not wholly extinguish the Costa Rican banks' obligation to timely pay United States dollars to Allied in New York. Thus the situs of the debt was not Costa Rica.

The same result obtains under ordinary situs analysis. The Costa Rican banks conceded jurisdiction in New York and they agreed to pay the debt in New York City in United States dollars. Allied, the designated syndicate agent, is located in the United States, specifically in New York; some of the negotiations between the parties took place in the United States. The United States has an interest in maintaining New York's status as one of the foremost commercial centers in the world. Further, New York is the international clearing center for United States dollars. In addition to other international activities, United States banks lend billions of dollars to foreign debtors each year. The United States has an interest in ensuring that creditors entitled to payment in the United States in United States dollars under contracts subject to the jurisdiction of United States courts may assume that, except under the most extraordinary circumstances, their rights will be determined in accordance with recognized principles of contract law.

In contrast, while Costa Rica has a legitimate concern in overseeing the debt situation of state-owned banks and in maintaining a stable economy, its interest in the contracts at issue is essentially limited to the extent to which it can unilaterally alter the payment terms. Costa Rica's potential jurisdiction over the debt is not sufficient to locate the debt there for the purposes of act of state doctrine analysis. . . .

Thus, under either analysis, our result is the same: the situs of the debt was in the United States, not in Costa Rica. Consequently, this was not "a taking of property within its own territory by [Costa Rica]." *Sabbatino*, 376 U.S. at 428. The act of state doctrine is, therefore, inapplicable.

## Lloyds Bank PLC v. Republic of Ecuador
— F. Supp. —, 1998 WL 118170 (S.D.N.Y. 1998)

Chin, J.

[For a discussion of the facts underlying this dispute, see the portion of the opinion excerpted in Chapter 7, § 3, *supra*.]

. . . [W]hile Ecuador does not affirmatively rely on the act of state doctrine to justify its refusal to pay the interest arrears, it does use its 1995 internal policy to reinforce its position that the interest was extinguished. Ecuador is well aware that any argument under the act of state doctrine would fail in these actions, for courts in this circuit have rejected the act of state defense in virtually identical cases. . . . As a result, Ecuador takes a different approach. It argues instead that its 1995 policy was based on principles of Ecuadorian law already in existence, and that the Central Bank had no choice but to comply with the laws of its own country. Ecuador contends that its actions here are therefore distinguishable from the actions taken by other sovereigns in the act of state doctrine cases because it did not pass a new law ex post facto, but rather devised its policy based on existing law.

I am unpersuaded by Ecuador's attempt to distinguish these cases from the act of state doctrine cases because, in essence, an act of state defense is precisely what Ecuador is asserting. Ecuador is asking this Court to bless its refusal to live up to its obligations under the Consolidation Agreement, entered into in 1986, by giving force and effect to a policy devised and implemented in 1995, which effectively deprives Ecuador's creditors of rights they had under an earlier agreement.

In both *Allied Bank* and *Libra Bank*, the Second Circuit and this Court, respectively, refused to hold that a sovereign's ex post facto decree excuses the prior obligations of the sovereign's debtor banks. . . . Based on the similarity between these two decisions and the cases at bar, I conclude that the reasoning of *Allied Bank* and *Libra Bank* apply with equal force here. . . . While Ecuador's obligations with respect to Consolidation Agreement Debt principal were indeed extinguished upon conversion, its interest obligations clearly remained intact, and Ecuador's "unilateral attempt to repudiate" this obligation is "inconsistent with the orderly resolution of international debt problems." . . . Implementation of the 1995 policy can be viewed as nothing more than an attempt by Ecuador to circumvent its obligation to pay interest by passing a law eliminating that obligation after the fact, in contravention of both the laws and policies of the United States. . . . Accordingly, I hold that Ecuador's prior obligation under the Consolidation Agreement to pay interest on converted debt was unaffected by implementation of either the 1994 Financing Plan or its own policy in 1995, and its attempt to justify its refusal to pay the interest arrears on either basis fails as a matter of law.

**Notes and Comments 8.10.** *Effect of IMF Policy on the Application of the Act of State Doctrine.* In several ways, the policies implemented by the International Monetary Fund (IMF)[13] under its charter may affect the applicability of the Act of State doctrine or other aspects of litigation. For example, it may be argued that acts of a state consistent with its rights and obligations under the IMF Charter should not be subject to review by a court, even if the Act of State doctrine would otherwise permit such review. Similarly, if the IMF itself has endorsed (or perhaps even required) the state to take the steps that are now being challenged, a court may be reluctant to intervene. In contrast, there is also an inverse use of IMF policy, under the so-called "treaty exception" to the Act of State doctrine. The exception states that, if the act of a state violates a clear treaty obligation, the doctrine may be inapplicable, and a court may then subject the state's act to review. In the following excerpts, consider how and why IMF policies are being invoked. Are the arguments successful?

## Gerhard Wegen, 2(b) or Not 2(b): Fifty Years of Questions– The Practical Implications of Article VIII Section 2(b)
### 62 Fordham L. Rev. 1931 (1994)

. . . Interpretation of section 2(b) is greatly complicated by the fact that the clause is contained in a multilateral agreement under public international law that was drafted in a very short period of time, and then only in the English language, which is uncommon with multilateral documents. I believe that it was drafted within two or three days, and in a peculiar type of language which resembles neither that of the common law lawyer nor that of the continental lawyer. The first sentence of section 2(b) states:

> Exchange contracts which involve the currency of any member and
> which are contrary to the exchange control regulations of that member maintained
> or imposed consistently with this Agreement shall be unenforceable in the

---

13. On the history of the IMF and its role in regulating international financial relations among states, see Michael P. Malloy, *Shifting Paradigms: Institutional Roles in a Changing World*, 62 FORDHAM L. REV. 1911 (1994).

territories of any member.[2]

It is worthwhile to compare non-official German and French versions. The unofficial German text reads:

> *Aus Devisenkontrakten, welche die Wahrung eines Mitglieds der führen*
> *und den von diesem Mitglied in Übereinstimmung mit diesem Übereinkommen*
> *aufrechterhaltenen oder eingeführten Devisenkontrollbestimmungen*
> *zuwiderlaufen, kann in den Hoheitsgebieten der Mitglieder nicht geklagt werden.*[3]

A French translation, upon which the Belgian, French, and Swiss authorities agreed, reads:

> *Les contrats relatifs aux devises qui portent sur la monnaie d'un membre*
> *et qui sont en opposition avec la réglementation du contrôle des changes de ce*
> *membre maintenue ou imposée conformément au présent accord n'auront pas*
> *force obligatoire dans les territoires de tout membre.*[4]

It is obvious that while the English version talks about "exchange contracts which are unenforceable," the German version says "contracts which cannot be put before the court," and the French version says "contracts which have no binding force." Therefore, on the very basic level of language, the various versions are inconsistent. Adding to this difficulty, no single international court interprets this clause, and thus no one single authoritative interpreter exists.

It is also important to realize that different countries may view this clause in different ways. On the one hand, a court might judge the clause under principles of public international law, which are typically used to interpret the instruments of public international law, and which are familiar to public international lawyers. On the other hand, a court may evaluate it under a conflict of laws approach . . . as a question of what law to apply to a transaction, or which substantive law holds contracts to be unenforceable.

The distinction between public law and private law, which is very pronounced in the German system, is also relevant to interpreting section 2(b) with regard to national exchange control regulations. The section might be considered to fall either under public law as an exchange control regulation imposed by the state, or under private law because it provides that private contracts may be found unenforceable. Elements of public policy further complicate the construction of section 2(b). These elements include protecting the forum state's status as a financial center and safeguarding the rights of both debtors and creditors.

. . .

Even though the Bretton Woods Agreement is a treaty under public international law, one of its main purposes was to deal, for the first time, with exchange control regulations on a private basis. Prior to Bretton Woods, exchange control regulations were looked at from a perspective of public law only. The so-called "revenue rule" has traditionally provided that rules of public law are only applicable within the territory of

---

2. [Second Amendment of Articles of Agreement of the International Monetary Fund, Apr. 30, 1976, 29 U.S.T. 2203,] art. VIII § 2(b) [hereinafter Articles of Agreement].

3. This version appears in Bundesgesetzblatt, Teil II BGBl.II 1978, 13, 34-35.

4. This translation is quoted in 3 SIR JOSEPH GOLD, THE FUND AGREEMENT IN THE COURTS 629 (1986).

the state in which they were created, and do not have extra-territorial application. The parties to the Bretton Woods Agreement, how-ever, wanted to establish a regime in which exchange control regulations of one state could be enforced in other states. In other words, section 2(b) is intended to establish extra-territorial recognition of foreign exchange controls in the member states to the International Monetary Fund.

Of course, in order to make section 2(b) effective with regard to individuals, it was necessary to implement it in the national legal systems of each member state. This was accomplished by obligating the member states in the Agreement to do so in such a way that it would be enforced in their legal systems.[8] Implementation of a rule that is contained in a multilateral agreement under public international law can be accomplished in different ways. One alternative is simply to enact the text into national law. The second alternative is to state in national law that Article VIII, section 2(b) of the Bretton Woods Agreement will be given effect within the country. The third alternative is to ratify the Agreement and leave open the specific means for providing for its effectiveness in the country. The United States, which falls into the second category, deals with the problem through section 11 of the Bretton Woods Agreement Act of 1945:

> The provisions of article IX, sections 2 to 9, both inclusive, and the first sentence of article VIII, section 2(b), of the Articles of Agreement of the Fund . . . shall have full force and effect in the United States and its Territories and possessions upon acceptance of membership by the United States in, and the establishment of, the Fund and the Bank, respectively.[9]

By contrast, in states such as Australia, Mexico, and Sweden, it is still not clear from the ratification process whether Article VIII, section 2(b) was actually adopted into domestic law.[10] It could be argued, however, that such implementation is not actually necessary because the states falling into this category have ratified the instruments as such.

A consequence of adoption into domestic law is that, although enacted on an international level, no international court has jurisdiction to interpret section 2(b). Instead, it is the national courts of the member states which have construed it. The writings of scholars such as Sir Joseph Gold,[11] F.A. Mann,[12] Professor Arthur Nussbaum,[13] and, most recently, Professor Werner Ebke[14] have also impacted greatly on the clause's interpretation; this is one of the few instances where scholarly writing has impacted national jurisprudence

---

8. *See* Articles of Agreement, . . . art. XX § 2a; Werner F. Ebke, *Article VIII, Section 2(b), International Monetary Cooperation, and the Courts*, 23 INT'L LAW. 677, 684 & n.39 (1989) [hereinafter International Monetary Cooperation].

9. 22 U.S.C. § 286h (1988).

10. For a discussion regarding the legal status of § 2(b) in these three countries, see WERNER F. EBKE, INTERNATIONALES DEVISENRECHT 162-63 (1991) [hereinafter Internationales Devisenrecht].

11. *See* Gold, *supra* note 4; SIR JOSEPH GOLD, EXCHANGE RATES IN INTERNATIONAL LAW AND ORGANIZATION (1988); Sir Joseph Gold, *Developments in the International Monetary System, the International Monetary Fund, and International Monetary Law since 1971*, 174 Recueil des Cours 107 (1982).

12. *See* FREDERICK A. MANN, THE LEGAL ASPECT OF MONEY (5th ed. 1992).

13. *See* ARTHUR NUSSBAUM, MONEY IN THE LAW, NATIONAL AND INTERNATIONAL (2d ed. 1950).

14. For a detailed study which has begun to impact German jurisprudence on the subject, see Internationales Devisenrecht, *supra* note 10.

directly. Indeed, it is mainly due to such scholars that the courts have become aware of the clause at all.

... [I]n many instances over the last fifty years courts have simply disregarded the rules on a systematic level because neither the parties, counsel, nor the court thought of invoking section 2(b). Thus, it is difficult to assess the true applicability of the clause. In the early years, there was a great reluctance to deal with the clause at all. In the United States, the first wave of cases came about due to war-related immigration matters, in which U.S. institutions sued non-U.S. citizens, or vice-versa.[15] The second series of cases developed around the Cuban socialist revolution, in particular the so-called Cuban insurance cases.[16] Since the late 1970s, the clause has become very important in international finance transactions, particularly those involving U.S. citizens dealing with foreign banks and foreign countries.[17] European case law, including Germany's, developed mainly in international trade cases.[18] Thus, a certain case law did develop in all major jurisdictions. But no cases appear to have arisen in smaller countries, such as Switzerland, which of course is an important jurisdiction in international banking transactions. . . .

The first issue concerning section 2(b)'s interpretation is how to characterize it–that is, whether it should be considered a rule of conflict of laws or a rule of substantive law. In Germany, the question also arises whether it is a rule of civil procedure or of substantive law. In general, section 2(b) has characteristics of its own that impact public law, private law, and substantive law.

Germany characterizes section 2(b) in accordance with the law of each member state that applies it. Because section 2(b) has been implemented into the laws of the various member states on a domestic level, Germans leave its characterization to the respective legal system that applies in a particular case. Thus, German law views section 2(b) as a conflict of laws rule that preempts rules for special statutory choice of law and general conflict of laws.[19] On the other hand, it could also be characterized under German law as a substantive law rule with procedural implications. As a choice of law rule, section 2(b) preempts other choice of law rules. In Germany, "due regard for the foreign exchange regulations of other countries" means that when such regulations are in place and in conformity with the Agreement, German public policy will not be invoked to disregard them. German law will, therefore, construe duly-promulgated foreign exchange control regulations to hold contracts unenforceable when appropriate; no recourse may be had to other German conflict of laws rules.

While this question may seem fairly esoteric, it actually has important practical consequences. Construing section 2(b) as a conflict of laws rule requires the application of

---

15. *See, e.g., Southwestern Shipping Corp. v. National City Bank*, 160 N.E.2d 836 (N.Y.) (resolving a contract dispute between Italian concerns and an American bank, which implicated foreign exchange regulations of the Bretton Woods Agreement), *cert. denied* 361 U.S. 895 (1959); *Perutz v. Bohemian Discount Bank in Liquidation*, 110 N.E.2d 6 (N.Y. 1953) (deciding a suit between a U.S. citizen and a Czech bank); *Cermak v. Bata Akciova Spolecnost*, 80 N.Y.S.2d 782, 783 (Sup. Ct. 1948) (deciding an action by U.S. assignees to recover a deposit from a Czech corporation), *aff'd*, 90 N.Y.S.2d 680 (App. Div. 1949).

16. *See Varas v. Crown Life Ins. Co.*, 203 A.2d 505 (Pa. Super. Ct. 1964), *cert. denied*, 382 U.S. 827 (1965).

17. *See Libra Bank Ltd. v. Banco Nacional de Costa Rica*, 570 F. Supp. 870 (S.D.N.Y. 1983).

18. *See* Internationales Devisenrecht, *supra* note 10, at 173.

19. *See* International Monetary Cooperation, *supra* note 8, at 684.

the exchange control regulations of third states in Germany. But then the question arises as to what the legal consequences are when the rule ceases to be in force. For instance, a contract may be concluded under a foreign exchange control regulation which is later revoked by the state. Thus, at the time the contract was concluded, it was contrary to the foreign exchange control regulations of another state, but is no longer so. If section 2(b) is considered a rule of substantive law, however, then two alternatives exist: either the contract will be considered invalid and unenforceable from the beginning, or the exchange control regulation constitutes a condition which was present but has now disappeared, so that the contract was unenforceable but has now become enforceable.

In the United States, courts have sometimes refused to enforce contracts that are contrary to the exchange control regulations of other countries not based on the language of section 2(b), but on the act of state doctrine.[20] This is uncommon for us on the Continent of Europe, because we do not recognize an act of state doctrine to the same extent as the United States. Another important question that sometimes arises is whether a member state's public policy considerations may override section 2(b). The basic problem in this regard is whether foreign exchange control regulations may be denied enforcement in the forum state based on that state's public policy.

Although no German case has been decided on this point, Germans would argue that once section 2(b) finds an application, the public policy of the forum state cannot override it. It could, however, be argued that public policy should come into play where basic notions of justice and fairness are concerned; one example would be when foreign exchange control regulations of another state are promulgated in conformity with the Agreement, but violate basic notions of justice recognized in Germany, such as discrimination on the basis of race or religion. . . .

Another problem that arises concerns arbitrability–that is, whether the parties can submit to arbitration the question of whether a contract is an exchange contract under Article VIII, section 2(b), and whether section 2(b) should be taken into account by arbitral tribunals. There has been some debate on this issue, and a case has even come up before the International Chamber of Commerce.[21] Though in that case the arbitral tribunal unfortunately misconstrued the nature of section 2(b) and stated that it should only apply to state contracts, it is generally accepted that arbitral tribunals should take note of section 2(b) if the facts indicate that section 2(b) may be involved. Thus, the arbitral tribunal should raise the issue on its own motion if it is appropriate, even if the parties do not raise it.

Finally, questions arise under section 2(b) with regard to the recognition and enforcement of judgments. For example, in an English case, the court took the position that only currency contracts, *i.e.*, contracts to exchange one currency against another, could be considered exchange contracts.[23] That case concerned a futures contract. The English plaintiff, a brokerage firm, prevailed against an Italian defendant. As the Italian defendant had no assets in England, the English plaintiff attempted to enforce the judgment in Italy, but the Italian court refused, based on public policy grounds and a narrow interpretation of section 2(b). . . .

[The concept of an "exchange control"] has given rise to much debate and diversity of opinion between the legal systems of the United States/United Kingdom and those of

---

20. *See, e.g., Allied Bank Int'l v. Banco Credito Agricola de Cartago*, 566 F. Supp. 1440 (S.D.N.Y. 1983) (holding the act of state doctrine as meritorious in defending against a suit for a loan default), *rev'd*, 757 F.2d 516 (2d Cir.), *cert. denied*, 473 U.S. 934 (1985). . . .

21. This case is described in Internationales Devisenrecht, *supra* note 10, at 164.

23. *See Wilson, Smithett & Cope Ltd. v. Terruzzi*, 1976 1 Q.B. 703, 713 (C.A.).

continental Europe. The United States and the United Kingdom, following Professor Nuss-baum's lead, define exchange contracts as contracts that have as their subject the exchange of currency, meaning currency contracts in the narrowest sense.[24] On the other hand, the continental systems, and particularly Germany, define exchange contracts as contracts that have as their essential nature an exchange of goods or services that has an impact on the foreign exchange reserves available in that country.[25] Thus, on the Continent, any contract for the sale of goods or for services involving a currency and which would lead to a decrease or increase in the foreign exchange funds of the member states is considered an exchange contract. In this broad notion of exchange contracts, virtually all contracts between parties residing in member states potentially have such an impact, and thus could be considered exchange contracts. This broader interpretation, which was developed in particular by F.A. Mann,[26] seems to further the goals of the Agreement more effectively, since it subjects more contracts to section 2(b). Thus more transactions will have to be concerned with the foreign exchange regulations of member states and their impact in the forum state.

In Germany, the U.S./U.K. view has traditionally been incomprehensible. Germany regards contracts such as those for the sale of goods, for services, life insurance contracts, surety contracts, guarantees, and so-called "acknowledgments of debt" (*Schuldanerkennt-nisse*) all as potential exchange contracts. This is also true for contracts regarding interna-tional monetary commitment agreements and international money collection agreements. One current problem concerns international loan agreements. Common law courts, for instance a federal court in the Southern District of New York, have explicitly stated that international loan agreements are not to be considered exchange contracts, based on their desire to maintain the position of the forum as an international financial center.[27] By contrast, Germany generally considers international loan agreements to be exchange contracts under section 2(b), which may account for the reluctance to select the application of German law in international loan agreements.

But a recent case indicates that the German courts are becoming slightly more flexible with regard to the types of contracts that are considered "exchange contracts" under section 2(b). In a case involving a Bulgarian limited partner that had attempted to rely on the provision as grounds for refusing to pay an increased capital contribution to a German limited partnership, the German Federal Supreme Court (*Bundesgerichtshof*) ruled for the first time that international capital transfers do not fall under section 2(b).[29] . . .

Determining whether particular exchange control regulations are maintained or imposed consistently with the Agreement is obviously a difficult assessment for a court to make. Since most courts, not to mention most attorneys, are hardly experts in the technical-ities of foreign exchange regulations, under the Bretton Woods Agreement it is possible to

---

24. *See* International Monetary Cooperation, *supra* note 8, at 687.

25. *See id.* at 687-89.

26. *See* Mann, *supra* note 12, at 378-86.

27. *See, e.g., Libra Bank Ltd. v. Banco Nacional de Costa Rica*, 570 F. Supp. 870, 900 (S.D.N.Y. 1983) (holding that a contract to borrow U.S. currency, which requires U.S. currency, and which designates New York as the situs of repayment, was not an exchange contract within the meaning of § 2(b)); *see also* International Monetary Cooperation, *supra* note 8, at 687.

29. *See* Judgment of Nov. 8, 1993, BGH, W. Ger., 1994 Recht der internationalen Wirtschaft RIW 151; Judgment of Feb. 22, 1994, BGH, W. Ger., 1994 RIW 327.

request the executive board of the International Monetary Fund to make this assessment.[30]
. . .

The . . . legal consequence that such contract is unenforceable[,] [t]ogether with the
question of what is an exchange contract, . . . is one of the areas in which common law
countries diverge most sharply from the continental legal systems. The concept of unenforceability is a common law concept deriving from the system of actions under Roman law,
and it is fairly obvious to a common law lawyer that there are obligations or contracts which
may be unenforceable in court. This concept is difficult for a continental lawyer, who instead
speaks of the "voidness" of a contract.

Shortly after World War II, F.A. Mann, among others, proposed that an exchange
contract that violates foreign exchange regulations should be considered void. But this result
is highly questionable because foreign exchange regulations may be imposed at one time and
terminated later, just as states may join the Agreement and then leave it later. Thus, the
problem with Mann's view is that the contract would be void *ab initio*, and therefore could
not be void later.

The German courts have gone in a completely different direction by deciding that
contracts which were contrary to foreign exchange control regulations could be valid, but
could not be enforced in court.[31] This view postulates the existence of a new procedural
requirement for a contract to be sued upon in court–that is, that it does not violate exchange
control regulations. Thus, a German court, in entertaining a suit, may decide, either upon
motion by the parties or upon its own motion, that section 2(b) is implicated and that the
contract violates it. In such a case, the court would dismiss the suit and find the contract
inadmissible on procedural grounds; it would not reach a decision on the merits. Germany's
trend seems to be that such contracts should be regarded, as they are in the common law
world, as imperfect, even though they continue to be binding obligations. The result is that
there may be a kind of conditional validity of the contract, *i.e.*, that the contract may exist,
but that its existence is conditional on not being contrary to foreign exchange control regulations.[32] This concept is otherwise unknown to both continental and common law lawyers.

One important question that arises in practice concerns the status of accessory
security taken under an exchange contract which is then not enforceable. This question also
arises with regard to sureties and guaranties, and with set-offs, when the claim which may
be set off is unenforceable under section 2(b). Or, what are the consequences when one of
the parties claims damages under a contract which is declared unenforceable under section
2(b)? All of these incidental problems are basically decided along the same split we have
seen earlier: the U.S./U.K. courts and scholars would tend to narrowly construe section 2(b),
saying that the section applies to exchange contracts only, and not to other instruments of
international trade such as letters of credit, sureties, and the like. German courts, however,
would state that "full faith and credit" should be given to section 2(b), and that if a contract
is declared unenforceable, then any legal transaction immediately prior to that contract must
also be unenforceable. This would also apply to a surety or guaranty which is tainted by the
contract's unenforceability. . . .

A few matters concerning section 2(b) that are important under German law remain.

---

30. *See* Articles of Agreement, . . . at art. XXIX. For a discussion of this procedure, see
International Monetary Cooperation, *supra* note 8, at 697-98.

31. *See* Judgment of Apr. 27, 1970, BGH, W. Ger., 1970 Wertpapiermitteilungen WM 785,
786; Order of Dec. 21, 1976, BGH, W. Ger., 1976 Die deutsche Rechtssprechung auf dem Gebiete des
internationalen Privatrechts IPRspr 342, 343.

32. *See* Judgment of Apr. 27, 1970, BGH, W. Ger., 1970 WM 785, 786.

The first is the concept of enforceability as a procedural requirement that the court must examine on its own motion. Up until the time at which a judgment is rendered, the court may examine the concept of the enforceability of a contract based on foreign exchange controls. There are three instances of such examination in Germany: the lower court, the appellate level, and the federal level.

Typically, section 2(b) defenses come into play at the appellate or the federal levels only, because at these levels both counsel and the courts tend to be more sophisticated. In many instances, defenses based on section 2(b) are often brought in as a last resort, sometimes after many years of litigation. It often happens that the first two levels fully litigated the matter and made findings of fact, and then one of the parties raises the issue of section 2(b) at the last moment at the federal level. In such a case, the party making the submission may invoke the lack of a procedural requirement (namely, that of an enforceable contract), causing the whole case to fall apart. This is a real problem in Germany, and one which does justice to neither the plaintiff nor the defendant.

Secondly, Germany procedurally requires the plaintiff to substantiate and put forward all of his arguments. So section 2(b) is not viewed as a defense that must be invoked by the defendant, but as a procedural requirement requiring the plaintiff to prove its non-application.[33] The common law system, by contrast, views section 2(b) as a defense that must be raised by the defendant.[34] Under the German view, therefore, if the plaintiff fails to substantiate its claim that the court should not apply section 2(b), the complaint would be dismissed without the court having reached a decision on the merits. This can have practical implications with regard to the issuance of international bonds. Germany is a major provider of capital in the international markets, which involves issuing Deutsche Mark bonds under German law. If litigation is then brought before the German courts and the plaintiff fails to meet its burden, the bondholders are at risk of not having their money repaid. Luckily there are signs that the situation may change in Germany, particularly due to the scholarly work of Professor Ebke[35]–that is, that section 2(b) may be looked upon as a defense which is based on the concept of an imperfect obligation. . . .

Section 2(b) will likely play an ever-increasing role in international loans and international bonds. There are certainly problems in this regard on the European Continent caused by the broad interpretation of section 2(b). The fall of eastern Europe's socialist countries and the rise of a host of new states which are becoming members of the Agreement, together with a scarcity of capital and the problems of many of these states, will also likely lead to a host of new foreign exchange regulations, which can only increase the importance of section 2(b) in the future.

## Libra Bank Ltd. v. Banco Nacional de Costa Rica
### 570 F.Supp. 870 (S.D.N.Y. 1983)

[After the court had entered its order in *Libra Bank Ltd.*, *supra*, defendant Banco

---

33. *See* Judgment of Apr. 27, 1970, BGH, W. Ger., 1970 WM 785, 786-87; *see also* International Monetary Cooperation, *supra* note 8, at 700-01.

34. *See, e.g., Libra Bank Ltd. v. Banco Nacional de Costa Rica*, 570 F. Supp. 870, 902 (S.D.N.Y. 1983) (finding that the defendant failed to sustain its burden of proof that its currency restrictions were exempt from IMF approval requirements); *see also* International Monetary Cooperation, *supra* note 8, at 701.

35. For Professor Ebke's criticism of the German view, see International Monetary Cooperation, *supra* note 8, at 700-03.

Nacional attempted to raise the treaty exception to defeat the enforceability of the agreement. The following excerpt provides the court's analysis of this argument.]

This court's opinion and order of July 11, 1983 granted plaintiffs' motion for summary judgment. On July 15, 1983, the date this court was prepared to enter judgment in this case, defendant Banco Nacional de Costa Rica, S.A. (Banco Nacional) moved to reargue the motion. In its July 11, 1983 opinion, this court held that since the act of state doctrine was inapplicable to this case, this court would give no effect to the Costa Rican decrees because "they [were not] consistent with the policy and law of the United States." . . . Defendant now contends that the nonenforcement of the loan agreement is consistent with the policies and laws of this nation as evidenced by Article VIII, section 2(b) of the Articles of Agreement of the International Monetary Fund. . . . After considering the briefs of the parties on this newly raised question of law, the court reaffirms its decision granting plaintiffs' motion for summary judgment and denies defendant's motion to reargue. . . .

Defendant contends that both the United States and Costa Rica are signatories of the Agreement, that each element of Article VIII, section 2(b) is present in this case, and that the loan agreement is unenforceable.

By definition, Article VIII, section 2(b) applies only to "exchange contracts." Relying primarily upon the views of a commentator, defendant urges this court to adopt a broad definition of these terms, sufficiently expansive to include international loans. *See* Williams, *Extraterritorial Enforcement of Exchange Control Regulations Under the International Monetary Fund Agreement*, 15 Va. J. Int'l Law 319, 338 (1975) (Williams). However, Williams himself acknowledges that he advocates a broad interpretation of the terms and that "[n]o American decision unequivocally supports a liberal interpretation of the term 'exchange contract.'" *Id.* at 342.

The broad view and narrow interpretations of "exchange contracts" are set forth by a leading commentator as follows:

> The narrow view of "exchange contracts" in Article VIII, Section 2(b) is that they are contracts for the exchange of one currency against another or one means of payment against another. The broad view is that they are contracts involving monetary elements.

J. GOLD, THE FUND AGREEMENT IN THE COURTS: VOLUME II (1982) (Gold). A review of the decisions that have directly addressed the meaning of these terms reveals that they consistently adhere to the narrow interpretation of the terms "exchange contracts."

In *Banco do Brasil, S.A. v. A.C. Israel Commodity Co. Inc.*, 12 N.Y.2d 371, 190 N.E.2d 235, 239 N.Y.S.2d 872 (1963), *cert. denied*, 376 U.S. 906 (1964), the Court of Appeals endorsed a narrow view of the terms "exchange contracts" as contracts which have as their immediate object the exchange of international media of payment, *viz*, the exchange of one currency for another:

> It is far from clear whether this sale of coffee is covered by subdivision (b) of section 2. . . . Subdivision (b) of section 2 has been construed as reaching only "transactions which have as their immediate object 'exchange,' that is, international media of payment" . . . , or a contract where the consideration is payable in the currency of the country whose exchange controls are violated. . . . More recently, however, it has been suggested that it applies to "contracts which in any way affect a country's exchange resources" . . . . A similar view has been advanced to explain the further textual difficulty existing with respect to whether

a sale of coffee in New York for American dollars "involves the currency" of Brazil, the member whose exchange controls were allegedly violated. Again it is suggested that adverse effect on the exchange resources of a member *ipso facto* "involves" the "currency" of that member. . . . *We are inclined to view an interpretation of subdivision (b) of section 2 that sweeps in all contracts affecting any members' exchange resources as doing considerable violence to the test of the section. It says "involve the currency" of the country whose exchange controls are violated; not "involve the exchange resources".*

12 N.Y.2d at 375-76, 1980 N.E.2d at 236, 239 N.Y.S.2d at 873-74 (emphasis added; citations omitted).

In *J. Zeevi & Sons, Ltd. v. Grindlays Bank (Uganda), Limited*, 37 N.Y.2d 220, 333 N.E.2d 168, 371 N.Y.S.2d 892 (*Zeevi*), *cert. denied*, 423 U.S. 866 (1975), the Court of Appeals adhered to its narrow interpretation of the terms "exchange contracts." On March 24, 1972, Hiram Zeevi & Company (Uganda) Ltd., an Israeli corporation, deposited with defendant Grindlays Bank (Uganda) Ltd., local currency valued at $406,864.80 in American dollars. The purpose of the deposit was to provide an account against which plaintiff J. Zeevi & Sons, Ltd., a partnership, could draw money. Defendant subsequently issued a letter of credit acknowledging that it had opened its irrevocable credit No. 110/84 for $406,846.80 in favor of the partnership.

By official directive, the Uganda government subsequently notified defendant that foreign exchange allocations in favor of Israeli companies and nationals should be cancelled and ordered defendant to make no foreign exchange payments pursuant to the letter of credit. Thereafter, when plaintiff presented for reimbursement 10 drafts drawn under the letter of credit at defendant's New York agent bank, the bank refused to honor the drafts. Plaintiffs brought suit. The Supreme Court held that the letter of credit was enforceable and granted plaintiff's motion for partial summary judgment. The Appellate Division confirmed.

On appeal, the Court of Appeals affirmed the lower courts and specifically rejected defendant's contention that enforcement of the letter of credit violated Article VIII, section 2(b) of the Bretton Woods Agreement. Judge Cooke held:

> Contrary to defendants' position, the agreement, even when read in its broadest sense, fails to bring the letter of credit within its scope, since said letter of credit is not an exchange contract. In *Banco do Brasil, S.A. v. Israel Commodity Co.*, 12 N.Y.2d 371, 375-376, 239 N.Y.S.2d 872, 874, 190 N.E.2d 234, 236, this court frowned on an interpretation of the Bretton Woods Agreement which "sweeps in all contracts affecting any members' exchange resources as doing considerable violence to the test of the section".

37 N.Y.2d at 229, 333 N.E.2d at 174, 371 N.Y.S.2d at 900. . . .

Other cases that have squarely addressed the issue also adhere to a narrow interpretation of the terms "exchange contracts." . . .

The authorities relied upon by defendant do not persuade this court to adopt a broad interpretation of the terms "exchange contracts."[4] The advocates of the broad view in this

---

4. Defendant relies primarily upon the view of a single commentator who defines an exchange contract to include "international loan agreements." Williams, *Extraterritorial Enforcement of Exchange Control Regulations Under the International Monetary Fund Agreement*, 15 Va.J. Int'l L. 319, 338 (1975). However, the commentator himself acknowledges that this broad interpretation has never been "unequivocally" supported by an American court, *id.* at 342, and has been explicitly rejected by the New York courts. *Id.* at 335. Indeed, the broad interpretation has been advocated in the

nation are primarily commentators. *See* GOLD, *supra*, at 92; Williams, *supra*, at 337-44; Meyer, *Recognition of Exchange Controls After the International Monetary Fund Agreement*, 62 Yale L.J. 867, 885-88 (1953). At least one commentator, in urging the broad view, argues that the term "exchange" should be deleted from Article VIII, section 2(b). *See* Williams, *supra*, at 395 (suggesting the terms "exchange" and "involve the currency" be deleted from Article VIII, section 2(b) in order to "establish that a broad interpretation of this provision is correct . . ."). As the provision is presently written, however, a broad interpretation of "*exchange* contracts," sufficiently expansive to include international loans, does violence to the text of the section. . . .

The court declines to depart from the interpretation of exchange contracts consistently propounded by the courts that have directly addressed the issue. The court holds that a contract to borrow United States currency, which requires repayment in United States currency, and which designates New York as the situs of repayment, is not an exchange contract within the meaning of Article VIII, section 2(b).[5] The Bretton Woods Agreement

---

United States only by commentators. *See id.* at 344; GOLD, THE FUND AGREEMENT IN THE COURTS: VOLUME II at 92 (1982); Meyer, *Recognition of Exchange Controls After the International Monetary Fund Agreement*, 62 Yale L.J. 867, 886 (1953).

Defendant also cites three New York cases to support this broad interpretation. A careful examination of these cases demonstrates that they do not directly support defendant's position. In *Brill v. Chase Manhattan Bank*, 14 A.D.2d 852, 220 N.Y.S.2d 903 (1st Dep't 1961), two dissenting judges argued that a check by a bank in Cuba for a deposit in pesos, was, if payable in United States currency, an exchange contract. *Id.* at 852, 220 N.Y.S.2d at 904 (Botein & Stever, JJ., dissenting in part). However, the argument of the dissenting judges supports the narrow interpretation because it interpreted the check to be an exchange contract if the object of the contract were to exchange one nation's currency for that of another. Indeed, the dissent has been cited by Williams as support for the narrower interpretation. *See* Williams, *supra*, at 334 n. 65.

Neither does *Southwestern Shipping Corp. v. National City Bank*, 11 Misc.2d 397, 173 N.Y.S.2d 509 (Sup.Ct.) (*Southwestern*), *aff'd*, 6 A.D.2d 1036, 178 N.Y.S.2d 1019 (1st Dep't 1958), *rev'd on other grounds*, 6 N.Y.S.2d 454, 160 N.E.2d 836, 190 N.Y.S.2d 352, *cert. denied*, 361 U.S. 895 (1959) support the narrow interpretation. *Southwestern* involved not a loan but an exchange of lire for dollars, which is clearly within the narrow view of "exchange contracts."

Furthermore, although the court did find that the Bretton Woods Agreement barred enforcement, the court did so without any discussion of the terms "exchange contracts." Moreover, the court also focused on the illegality *ab initio* of the contract and stated that even in the absence of the Bretton Woods Agreement, it would not enforce an illegal contract. 11 Misc.2d at 411, 173 N.Y.S.2d at 523.

The final case, *Perutz v. Bohemian Discount Bank in Liquidation*, 304 N.Y. 533, 110 N.E.2d 6 (1953) (*Perutz*) also gives no support to defendant's position. In *Perutz*, a Czechoslovakian who became a United States citizen sued to recover his pension from his former employer, a Czechoslovakian banking corporation. Czechoslovakian law prohibited payment in foreign currency to a nonresident. The court held that the Bretton Woods Agreement barred enforcement of the payment of the pension in this nation in United States currency. 304 N.Y. at 537, 110 N.E.2d at 7-8. However, as in *Southwestern*, the *Perutz* court did not discuss the interpretation of "exchange contracts." Moreover, a leading advocate of the broad interpretation of "exchange contracts" has stated that the *ratio descendi* of *Perutz* is "obscure," GOLD, *supra*, at 30, and "not clear." *Id.* at 200. Under these circumstances, *Perutz* is hardly persuasive authority for the broad interpretation.

Finally, these cases are all at least twenty years old and would appear to be superseded, insofar as they express contrary views, by the Court of Appeals' ruling in the *Zeevi* case.

5. Research has disclosed only one case that could be viewed as contra to this narrow interpretation of exchange contracts. In *Confederation Life Association v. Ugalde*, 164 So.2d 1 (S.Ct.Fla.), *cert. denied*, 379 U.S. 915 (1964), the Florida Supreme Court ruled that an insurance contract issued

is therefore inapplicable to this case.

Moreover, assuming *arguendo* that the loan agreement is an exchange contract, defendant has submitted no authority for its view that a contract, valid and enforceable when made, may be rendered unenforceable by an intervening currency regulation. Indeed, there is authority in support of the contrary view. *See Blanco v. Pan-American Life Insurance Company*, 221 F.Supp. 219, 229 (S.D.Fla. 1963) ("[T]hese [foreign currency regulations] do not apply to cover the situation of a Cuban national enforcing an executory contract in the forum of another jurisdiction according to the terms of an obligation existing prior to the passage of those laws."), *aff'd on other grounds*, 362 F.2d 167, 171 (5th Cir. 1966) (holding that because Cuba had since withdrawn from International Monetary Fund, Cuba was no longer entitled to protection of Agreement but also noted that "[e]ven if this were not so, the Bretton Woods Agreement would not be applicable to contracts such as insurance policies here involved."); *Theye*, 161 So.2d at 72-73 (in reversing lower court that gave effect to intervening currency regulations under Bretton Woods Agreement, court held that where currency regulations permitted payment in United States currency at time insurance policy was executed, subsequent currency regulation requiring payment in pesos had no effect on existing obligation); *see also* F. MANN, THE LEGAL ASPECT OF MONEY 377-78 (4th ed. 1982) ("In short, Art. VIII(2)(b) gives international recognition to the original ineffectiveness of an exchange contract, but does not touch a contract which during its life [becomes] an exchange contract contrary to regulations."); *but see* GOLD, *supra*, at 91-92; Williams, *supra*, at 364-67.[6]

Finally, this court concludes that defendant has not demonstrated that these currency

---

to a Cuban resident fell within the scope of the Articles of the International Monetary Fund. 164 So.2d at 2. The insurance policy was unenforceable under Cuban law and the Florida court refused to enforce it in the United States. *Id*. In *Ugalde*, however, the policy was payable in Cuba itself, not in the United States. *Id*. In the instant case, payment is due in the United States not in Costa Rica. Furthermore, the *Ugalde* court reached its conclusion of unenforceability in a single paragraph without any reference to or discussion of the terms "exchange contracts" or Article VIII, section 2(b). Two later Florida cases following *Ugalde* were summarily decided relying solely upon that case and contained no discussion of Article VII, section 2(b). *See Crown Life Insurance Co. v. Calvo*, 1654 So.2d 813 (S.Ct.Fla.), *cert. denied*, 379 U.S. 915 (1964); *Sun Life Assurance Co. v. Klawans*, 165 So.2d 166 (S.Ct.Fla. 1964).

These cases, decided almost twenty years ago in the context of insurance policies, appear to be the only judicial authority for an expansive reading of Article VIII, section 2(b). For the reasons already discussed, however, the court finds them unpersuasive and declines to follow them.

6. The International Monetary Fund's official interpretation of Article VIII, Section 2(b) reads in relevant part:

> Parties entering into exchange contracts involving the currency of any member of the Fund and contrary to exchange control regulations of that member which are maintained or imposed consistently with the Fund Agreement will not receive the assistance of the judicial or administrative authorities of other members in obtaining the performance of such contracts.

14 M. WHITEMAN, DIGEST OF INTERNATIONAL LAW 155 (1970) (quoting International Monetary Fund, Annual Report, 1949 at 82-83). The phrases "parties entering into exchange contracts . . . contrary to exchange control regulations" suggests that Article VIII, section 2(b) applies only when the contract is illegal *ab initio*. Although leading commentators such as Gold believe that regulations which retroactively render exchange contracts unenforceable do not pose a problem, *see* GOLD at 92, this court is not persuaded on the basis of these arguments alone that Article VIII, section 2(b) applied to currency regulations which retroactively render contracts unenforceable.

regulations are "maintained or imposed consistently with [the Fund] Agreement. ..." In its attempt to discharge this burden, defendant makes the bland assertion that

> [t]he decrees of the Costa Rican government are imposed and maintained "consistently" with the Bretton Woods Agreement inasmuch as they fulfill the purposes of the Agreement, namely, to promote exchange stability and to maintain orderly arrangements. . . .

About the task of demonstrating consistency, a leading commentator has written:

> [A] defendant who relies on Article VIII, Section 2(b) necessarily asserts that exchange controls are maintained or imposed consistently with the Articles, and he should have the burden of proving this fact.

GOLD, *supra*, at 334; *see also id.* at 358 (urging that in determining consistency the "only safe course is to seek the advice of the [International Monetary] Fund."). . . .

A careful examination of the Articles of Agreement of the International Monetary Fund demonstrates that defendant's simple statement hardly suffices to demonstrate consistency with the Fund Agreement.

Article VIII, section 2(a) provides:

> (a) Subject to the provisions of Article VII, Section 3(b) and Article XIV, Section 2, no member shall, without the approval of the Fund, impose restrictions on the making of payments and transfers for current international transactions.[7]

Article XXX defines "current transactions" as follows:

> (d) *Payments for current transactions means payments which are not for the purpose of transferring capital, and includes*, without limitation:
> (1) *all payments due in connection with* foreign trade, other current business, including services, and *normal short-term banking and credit facilities*;
> (2) *payments due as interest on loans* and as net income from other investments;
> (3) payments of moderate amount for amortization of loans or for depreciation of direct investments; and

---

7. Article VII, section 3(b) provides in pertinent part:

> (b) A formal declaration [by the Fund] under (a) above shall operate as an authorization to any member, after consultation with the Fund, temporarily to impose limitations on the freedom of exchange operations in the scarce currency.

Article XIV, section 2 provides in pertinent part:

> Section 2. *Exchange Restrictions.*
> A member that has notified the Fund that it intends to avail itself of transitional arrangements under this provision may, notwithstanding the provisions of any other articles of this Agreement, maintain and adapt to changing circumstances the restrictions on payments and transfers for current international transactions that were in effect on the date on which it became a member.

Defendant has made no attempt to demonstrate that it has complied with these provisions.

(4) moderate remittances for family living expenses.

The Fund may, after consultation with the member concerned, determine whether certain specific transactions are to be considered current transactions or capital transactions. (Emphasis added.)

The distinction between current or capital transactions can be a crucial one since a member of the International Monetary Fund (the Fund) is free to impose restrictions on capital transactions without the approval of the Fund. Article VI, section 3 provides:

> Section 3. *Controls of capital transfers.*
>
> Members may exercise such controls as are necessary to regulate international capital movements, but no member may exercise these controls in a manner which will restrict payments for current transactions or which will unduly delay transfers of funds in settlement of commitments, except as provided in Article VII, Section 3(b) and in Article XIV, Section 2.

With these provisions in mind, the court concludes that a showing that these currency restrictions are maintained or imposed consistently with the Fund includes the following: defendant may show that it has obtained Fund approval for these restrictions. Alternatively, defendant may demonstrate that these are restrictions upon capital as opposed to current transactions and that the Fund's approval is therefore unnecessary. Defendant has failed to sustain its burden by accomplishing either task, and its bland assertion alone does not suffice to discharge its burden. . . .

## Callejo v. Bancomer, S.A.
### 764 F.2d 1101 (5th Cir. 1985)

The act of state doctrine is premised not only on an unwillingness to apply American public policy to invalidate foreign laws but also on a pessimism about the competence of the judiciary to ascertain norms of international law. Potentially, international law as well as American public policy could serve as a touchstone for evaluating foreign acts of state: if an act of state were contrary to international law we could treat the act as invalid and adjudicate the plaintiff's claim. This approach would allow us to review foreign acts of state without engaging in the dubious practice of evaluating these acts against the potentially parochial norms of American public policy.

The Court, however, in large part foreclosed this avenue of review in *Banco Nacional de Cuba v. Sabbatino*, 376 U.S. 398 (1964). There the Court was asked to review the validity of Cuba's expropriation of a Cuban sugar company owned by United States residents. The Court declined to do so, holding that this country's response to Cuba's acts should be fashioned and implemented by the executive, not the judiciary. *Id*. at 431-32. Although the Court admitted that Cuba's acts might have violated international law, it held that international opinion was sufficiently divided that international law did not provide a firm basis for adjudicating the validity of Cuba's acts. *Id*. at 428-31.[18] In essence, the Court held

---

18. Although the Court stated in a footnote that "[t]here are, of course, areas of international law in which consensus as to standards is greater and which do not represent a battleground for conflicting ideologies," and went on to state that "[t]his decision in no way intimates that the courts of this country are broadly foreclosed from considering questions of international law," *id*. at 430 n. 34, to our knowledge this caveat has never been pursued. We are unaware of any cases since *Sabbatino* that have construed customary international law to invalidate a foreign act of state. *See* RESTATEMENT

that international law generally does not provide "judicially discoverable and manageable standards for resolving" cases. . . .

In *Sabbatino*, however, the Court recognized that "the greater the degree of codification or consensus concerning a particular area of international law, the more appropriate it is for the judiciary to render decisions regarding it, since the courts can the focus on the application of an agreed upon principle to circumstances of fact rather than on the sensitive task of establishing a principle not inconsistent with national interest or with international justice." *Sabbatino*, 376 U.S. at 428. On this basis, the Court elaborated an exception to the act of state doctrine under which the doctrine may not apply if there is "a treaty or other unambiguous agreement regarding controlling legal principles." *Id.*

Here, the Callejos claim that the Mexican exchange control regulations violate the Articles of Agreement of the International Monetary Fund ("Fund Agreement"), . . . to which Mexico is a party. In particular, they claim that the regulations violate Article VIII, Section 2(a), which forbids members from imposing exchange control regulations on "current international transactions" without the prior approval of the International Monetary Fund ("IMF" or "Fund").[20] The Callejos argue that because the Fund Agreement is "a treaty or other unambiguous agreement," the act of state doctrine does not apply.[21]

In the twenty years that have elapsed since its inception in *Sabbatino*, the treaty exception to the act of state doctrine has been applied sparingly . . .–by this court not at all. Although *Sabbatino* refers merely to "treat[ies] or other unambiguous agreements," treaties are not all of a piece; they come in different sizes and shapes, ranging from the Convention for the Unification of Certain Rules Relating to International Transportation by Air ("Warsaw Convention") . . . to the United Nations Charter, . . . whose broad but vague pronouncements are more similar to those of the United States Bill of Rights. For this reason,

---

(REVISED), *supra* note 13, at § 469 comment b.

20. The Callejos also argue for the first time on appeal that the exchange regulations violate Art. VIII, § 3 of the Fund Agreement. Generally, we do not consider issues that were not raised before the district court unless our failure to do so would result in grave injustice, . . . or unless the issue can be resolved as a matter of law or is otherwise beyond doubt. . . . Here, the Callejos' failure to raise the Art. VIII, § 3 issue has prejudiced Bancomer by precluding it from obtaining evidence from the IMF that the exchange regulations do not violate that provision. Therefore, we decline to consider this argument.

21. Apart from the Fund Agreement, the Mexican exchange control regulations appear to be permissible under international law. The RESTATEMENT (SECOND), *supra* note 12, approves such measures when "reasonably necessary . . . to protect the foreign exchange resources of the state," and notes, "[T]he application to an alien of a requirement that foreign funds held within the territory of the state be surrendered against payment in local currency at the official rate of exchange is not wrongful under international law, even though the currency is less valuable on the free market than the foreign funds surrendered." *Id.* at § 198 & comment b; *see also* 8 M. WHITEMAN, DIGEST OF INTERNATIONAL LAW 981-92, 988-90 (1967). "This is not an era . . . in which there is anything novel or internationally reprehensible about even the most stringent regulation of national currencies and the flow of foreign exchange. Such practices have been followed, as the exigencies of international economics have required–and despite resulting losses to individuals–by capitalist countries and communist countries alike, by the United States and its allies as well as by those with whom our country has had profound differences. They are practices which are not even of recent origin but which have been recognized as a normal measure of government for hundreds of years, if not, indeed, as long as currency has been used as the medium of international exchange." *French v. Banco Nacional de Cuba*, 23 N.Y.2d 46, 63, 295 N.Y.S.2d 433, 242 N.E.2d 704 (1968); *accord Braka v. Bancomer, S.A.*, 589 F.Supp. 1465, 1473 (S.D.N.Y. 1984), *aff'd*, 762 F.2d 222 (2d Cir. 1985).

the treaty exception was not stated in *Sabbatino* as "an inflexible and all-encompassing rule," 376 U.S. at 428; instead, its application depends on pragmatic considerations, including both the clarity of the relevant principles of international law and the potential implications of a decision on our foreign policy. *Id.*[22]

In determining whether the Fund Agreement–and Article VIII, Section 2(a) in particular–warrant application of the treaty exception, we tread upon uncharted ground. Thus far, no court has passed on this issue, and commentators have made, at best, ambiguous pronouncements. . . . Initially, we note that it is unclear to what extent the Fund Agreement is unclear. Article VIII, Section 2(a) applies by its terms only to exchange control regulations governing "current international transactions" (as opposed to "capital transfers"). Under Article VI, Section 3 of the Fund Agreement, members may validly impose restrictions on international capital movements. Thus, determining whether a set of exchange control regulations requires approval by the Fund pursuant to Article VIII, Section 2(a) depends in part on determining whether they apply to "current" or "capital" transactions. Given the substantial uncertainty regarding the meanings of these terms,[23] we are doubtful that Article VIII, Section 2(a) is the type of "unambiguous agreement" referred to in *Sabbatino*. . . .

In the context of the present case, however, we need not pass on this question in the abstract, since the IMF has itself clarified the meaning of the Fund Agreement as it applies to the Mexican regulations by indicating that they are consistent with the Agreement. On May 3, 1983, in response to an inquiry from Bancomer's counsel, the Director of the Legal Department of the Fund specifically stated that "the 'provisions of Mexico's Currency Regulations (enacted in August and continuing in effect today) which require repayment of deposits in Mexican banks to be made in Mexican pesos regardless of the currency in which the deposits are denominated' . . . do not violate and are not inconsistent with the Articles of Agreement of the International Monetary Fund." . . .[25] This determination at once renders the

---

22. Significantly, the Court in *Sabbatino* articulated the treaty exception in negative rather than positive terms: It stated that "the Judicial Branch will not examine the validity of a [foreign act of state] . . . in the absence of a treaty or other unambiguous agreement," *id.*, but did not state the converse, namely, that if a treaty exists then the act of state doctrine does not apply.

23. *Compare* H. SMIT, N. GALSTON & S. LEVITSKY, INTERNATIONAL CONTRACTS § 6.05(1) (b), at 165-66 ("current transactions" include international deposits) *with* Evans, *Current and Capital Transactions: How the Fund Defines Them*, 5 Fin. & Dev. 30, 34 (1968) ("current transactions" are those arising from international trading activities). *See generally* F. MANN, THE LEGAL ASPECT OF MONEY 396 (4th ed. 1982) ("extremely difficult" to determine meaning of "'current transactions' which is only very inadequately defined" by the Fund Agreement); J. Gold, *The Cuban Insurance Cases and the Articles of the Fund* 37-45 (IMF Pamphlet Series no. 8, 1966) (discussing confusion surrounding terms "capital" and "current" transactions).

25. Although the Callejos did not question the sufficiency of the Fund's May 3 letter before the district court, they argue on appeal that the letter is inadequate evidence of the Fund's position since, under Art. VIII, § 2(a), and Art. XXIX, only the Executive Board of the Fund can approve exchange regulations and offer interpretations of the Fund Agreement. In response, Bancomer listed as appendices to its brief copies of two letters, one from the Secretary of the IMF, and the other from the Director of the Legal Department of the IMF stating that the Executive Board approved the Mexican exchange control regulations on December 23, 1982. Since these letters were not introduced into evidence in the court below, they cannot be considered by us on appeal. . . . By the same token, however, we cannot consider arguments raised for the first time on appeal, especially where, as here, the failure to raise them before the district court has prejudiced the other side's ability to respond. ...

Although the May 3 letter is not dispositive of the Fund's position, we believe that it is *prima facie* evidence. Because the Callejos failed to offer any evidence to rebut or otherwise undermine the

Fund Agreement unambiguous in its application to the present case, but also defeats, on the merits, the Callejos' Article VIII, Section 2(a) claim.

We consider the Fund's interpretations to be persuasive authority on the meaning of the Fund Agreement.[26] The Fund Agreement is a complex regulatory document whose sense is often obscure. In interpreting it, we defer to the greater expertise of the Fund. ... This deference is akin to the deference that we accord to an administrative agency's interpretations of its own statutory scheme. . . . Here, however, an additional policy counsels in favor of deference: promoting uniform interpretations of the Fund Agreement. In contrast to the domestic sphere, where the territorial reach of our jurisdiction is coextensive with that of the statutes that we interpret, here we cannot give interpretations of the Fund Agreement that are binding on other member nations. . . . If each member of the Fund were to interpret the Fund Agreement separately–deciding when and when not to follow the Fund's own interpretations–this would detract form the Fund Agreement's underlying policy of promoting uniformity in international finance. We do not believe that the act of state doctrine–the principal purpose of which is to prevent the courts from becoming embroiled in sensitive international disputes–would be served by challenging acts whose validity has not otherwise been questioned. The treaty exception was intended to allow courts to apply international law where consensus exists; it was not intended to allow courts to upset a preexisting consensus regarding the validity of a foreign act of state.[27]

The exact basis for the Fund's conclusion that the Mexican regulations are consistent with the Fund Agreement is somewhat unclear. The Fund's conclusion could be based (1) on its view that the Mexican regulations govern capital rather than current transactions, in which case Article VIII, Section 2(a) approval was not required, and/or (2) on its granting approval of the regulations pursuant to Article VIII, Section 2(a). If the Fund's conclusion is based on the first ground, then, at most, we can only review the Fund's interpretation to determine whether it is reasonable, since we consider the Fund's interpretation to be highly persuasive authority. Here this standard is clearly met, particularly given the uncertainty that exists regarding the dividing line between current and capital transactions. If, however, the

---

letter, we believe that they failed to raise a genuine issue of fact regarding the Fund's approval of the Mexican regulations. This result is buttressed by the IMF's general interpretive view that currency regulations should be presumed to be in conformity with the Fund Agreement unless the Fund indicates otherwise. See 1 J. HORSEFIELD, THE INTERNATIONAL MONETARY FUND, 1945-1965, at 210 (1969) (discussing the Legal Department's opinion letter of Oct. 29, 1948). Under this view, it is the plaintiff's burden to demonstrate that the IMF disapproved the currency regulations in question, rather than the defendant's burden to prove the converse. Here, the Callejos introduced no evidence that the Fund has disapproved the Mexican regulations.

26. According to some commentators, since Art. XXIX of the Fund Agreement makes interpretations by the Fund binding on signatory nations, they are subsidiarily binding on the courts of signatory nations, including those of the United States. See J. Gold, Interpretation by the Fund 31-42 (IMF Pamphlet Series No. 11, 1968) (discussing predecessor of Art. XXIX). We express no view on this question here, and employ the Fund's interpretation merely as persuasive rather than as binding authority. . . .

27. Bancomer contends that if the Mexican exchange control regulations were promulgated in conformity with the Fund Agreement, we must dismiss this case under Art. VIII, § 2(b) of that Agreement, which forbids courts from enforcing "exchange contracts" involving the currency of a Fund member that violate the member's currency regulations. See 22 U.S.C. § 286h (1982) (incorporating Art. VIII, § 2(b) into U.S. law). In essence, § 2(b) is an internationally imposed act of state doctrine. Since we already dismiss the case under our own domestic act of state doctrine, we need not consider this additional defense. . . .

Fund's conclusion rests on the latter ground, then we are precluded from exercising even this limited level of review. Article VIII, Section 2(a) only requires the approval of the Fund; once such approval is given, the regulations are by definition valid. The decision whether to approve exchange control regulations is committed to the discretion of the Fund. We have no power to review the Fund's exercise of this discretion. Thus, even if we did not accept the Fund's interpretation of the Fund Agreement as persuasive authority, its decision to approve exchange control regulations pursuant to Article VIII, Section 2(a) would be final.

The Callejos attempt to avoid this result by arguing that even if the Fund did approve the Mexican regulations, it failed to do so *prior* to their promulgation. . . . While such prior approval is technically required by Article VIII, Section 2(a), we do not believe that the violation of this requirement is of a magnitude sufficient to justify disregarding the act of state doctrine, particularly where approval is later given by the Fund.[28] The treaty exception to the act of state doctrine does not penalize a foreign country for every failure to "go by the book." The same prudential considerations that underlie the act of state doctrine apply to the treaty exception as well.

## Allied Bank Int'l v. Banco Credito Agricola de Cartago
### 757 F.2d 516 (2d Cir. 1985)

Meskill, Circuit Judge:

Our interpretation of United States policy [in an earlier opinion in the case], arose primarily from our belief that the legislative and executive branches of our government fully supported Costa Rica's actions and all of the economic ramifications. On rehearing, the Executive Branch of the United States joined this litigation as *amicus curiae* and respectfully disputed our reasoning. The Justice Department brief gave the following explanation of our government's support for the debt resolution procedure that operates through the auspices of the International Monetary Fund (IMF). Guided by the IMF, this long established approach encourages the cooperative adjustment of international debt problems. The entire strategy is grounded in the understanding that, while parties may agree to renegotiate conditions of payment, the underlying obligations to pay nevertheless remain valid and enforceable. Costa Rica's attempted unilateral restructuring of private obligations, the United States contends, was inconsistent with this system of international cooperation and negotiation and this inconsistent with United States policy.

The United States government further explains that its position on private international debt is not inconsistent with either its own willingness to restructure Costa Rica's intergovernmental obligations or with continued United States aid to the economically distressed Central American country. . . .

Acts of foreign governments purporting to have extraterritorial effect–and consequently, by definition, falling outside the scope of the act of state doctrine–should be recognized by the courts only if they are consistent with the law and policy of the United States. . . . Thus, we have come full circle to reassess whether we should give effect to the Costa Rican directives. We now conclude that we should not.

---

28. The Fund itself, in recognition of the fact that it is not always possible to obtain prior approval when exchange controls are imposed to preserve national security, has adopted more flexible procedures under which members must merely give notice to the Fund of the imposition of exchange controls. Unless the Fund specifically disapproves the controls, members are entitled to assume that the Fund approves the controls. *See* 3 INTERNATIONAL MONETARY FUND 1945-1965: Documents 257 (J. Horsefield ed. 1969).

The Costa Rican government's unilateral attempt to repudiate private, commercial obligations is inconsistent with the orderly resolution of international debt problems. It is similarly contrary to the interests of the United States, a major source of private international credit. The government has procedures for resolving intergovernmental financial difficulties. . . . With respect to private debt, support for the IMF resolution strategy is consistent with both the policy aims and best interests of the United States. . . .

The Costa Rican directives are inconsistent with the law and policy of the United States. We refuse, therefore, to hold that the directives excuse the obligations of the Costa Rican banks. The appellees' inability to pay United States dollars relates only to the potential enforceability of the judgment; it does not determine whether judgement should enter. . . .

# Chapter 9

# International Deposits and Other Activities

## 1. Introduction

While lending continues to occupy the central focus of regulatory concern with respect to international banking activity, other activities are nevertheless important both to banking enterprises and their regulators. This chapter examines some of these other activities. It begins with international deposit-taking, which is one of the two "core activities" of banking (along with lending). It then examines in brief succession other significant activities.

## 2. International Deposit-Taking

Deposit-taking is a traditional or "core" activity of commercial banking, and it is also a significant international banking activity. The following notes examine the distinct regulatory concerns raised by international deposit-taking.

**Notes and Comments 9.1.** To what extent are international-related deposits subject to the federal deposit insurance system? Consider CORE PRINCIPLES, *infra*, and the following situations.

> **a.** Quarter National Bank (QNB) holds deposits for non-U.S. customers both at its U.S. headquarters and at branches in other countries. To what extent are these deposits subject to the federal deposit insurance system? Review 12 U.S.C. §§ 1811, 1813-1816.
> **b.** NusBank, chartered under the laws of Nusquam, has a U.S. subsidiary, chartered under state law. To what extent is it subject to the federal deposit insurance system? Review *id.* §§ 1811, 1813-1816, 3104.
> **c.** NusBank also has a federal branch operating in another state. To what extent is it subject to the federal deposit insurance system?
> **d.** Aside from the cost of federal deposit insurance (*see id.* § 1817(a)-(b)), what other regulatory and supervisory consequences confront a banking enterprise subject to the federal deposit insurance system? Review *id.* §§ 1817(j), 1818.

**9.2.** *Examination cycle for banks operating in the United States.* In general, each national bank and insured state bank must be examined every twelve months by its primary federal regulator. However, section 111 of the Federal Deposit Insurance Corporation Improvement Act of 1991[1] authorized an eighteen-month examination cycle for certain banks with a composite rating of "1" (on a scale of 1-5) under the Uniform Financial Institutions Rating System (UFIRS) and total assets of $100 million or less. Later, section 306 of the Riegle Community Development and Regulatory Improvement Act of 1994[2] expanded the availability of the eighteen-month examination cycle to certain banks with a composite rating of "1" under UFIRS and total assets of less than $250 million, as well as to certain banks with a composite rating of "2" under UFIRS and total assets of $100 million or less. Finally, section 2221 of Economic Growth and Regulatory Paperwork Reduction Act of 1996 (EGRPRA) amended section 10(d) of the Federal Deposit Insurance Act (FDIA)[3] to provide that at any time after 23 September 1996, U.S. bank supervisory agencies could extend the eighteen-month examination cycle to certain banks with a composite rating of "2" and total assets of $250 million or less. Effective 2 April 1998, the bank regulatory agencies issued a final rule that extended the examination cycle to eighteen months for certain banks that satisfy the requirements of section 2221 of EGRPRA.[4] To be eligible for the extended cycle, a bank must:

> (*i*) Have total assets of $250 million or less;
> (*ii*) Be rated a composite rating of "2" or better under the UFIRS;
> (*iii*) Be well capitalized;
> (*iv*) Be well managed;
> (*v*) Not be subject to a formal enforcement action; and,
> (*vi*) Not have experienced a change of control during the preceding twelve-month period in which a full-scope, on-site examination would have been required but for section 10(d) of the FDIA.

To implement section 2214 of EGRPRA, the agencies issued a joint interim rule on 28 August 1998 that similarly extended the examination cycle for certain U.S. branches and agencies of foreign banks.[5] Under the joint interim rule, a U.S. branch or agency of a foreign bank may be considered for an eighteen-month examination cycle if the branch or agency meets certain criteria and if there are no other factors that cause the appropriate federal banking agency to conclude that more frequent examinations of the branch or agency are appropriate. To be eligible for an eighteen-month examination cycle, the U.S. branch or agency of a foreign bank must:

> (*i*) Have total assets of $250 million or less;
> (*ii*) Have received a composite ROCA[6] supervisory rating of "1" or "2" at its most recent examination;
> (*iii*) Satisfy *one* of the following requirements: (*A*) The foreign bank's most recently reported capital adequacy position consists of, or is equivalent to,

---

1. Pub. L. 102-242, 105 Stat. 2236 (1991) (codified at 12 U.S.C. § 1820(d)).

2. Pub. L. 103-325, 108 Stat. 2160 (1994).

3. 12 U.S.C. § 1820(d)(10).

4. 63 Fed. Reg. 16,377 (1998).

5. 63 Fed. Reg. 46,118 (1998).

6. The supervisory rating system for branches and agencies of foreign banks is referred to as ROCA. The four components of ROCA are: *R*isk management, *O*perational controls, *C*ompliance, and *A*sset quality.

Tier 1 and total risk-based capital ratios of at least 6 percent and 10 percent, respectively, on a consolidated basis; or, (*B*) The branch or agency has maintained, on a daily basis over the past three quarters, eligible assets in an amount not less than 108 percent of third party liabilities and sufficient liquidity is currently available to meet its obligations to third parties;

(*iv*) Not be subject to a formal enforcement action or order by the Board, FDIC, or OCC; and,

(*v*) Not have experienced a change in control during the preceding twelve-month period in which a full-scope, on-site examination would have been required but for section 3105(c)(1)(C) of the IBA.

The agencies noted in the joint interim rule that each agency retained the authority to examine a U.S. branch or agency of a foreign bank as frequently as deemed necessary. The joint interim rule also provided that, in determining whether a U.S. branch or agency of a foreign bank is eligible for an extended examination cycle, the agencies may consider additional factors, including whether:

(*i*) Any of the individual components of the ROCA rating of the U.S. branch or agency is rated "3" or worse;

(*ii*) The results of any off-site supervision indicate a deterioration in the condition of the U.S. branch or agency;

(*iii*) The size, relative importance, and role of a particular U.S. branch or agency when reviewed in the context of the foreign bank's entire U.S. operations otherwise necessitate an annual examination (including, for example, whether the office generates a significant level of assets that are booked elsewhere); and,

(*iv*) The condition of the foreign bank itself gives rise to a need to examine the U.S. branch or agency every twelve months.

The agencies also noted that they generally would determine whether to apply the eighteen-month examination cycle to a particular U.S. branch or agency based on the overall risk assessment for that office, as well as the factors noted in the joint interim rule. Since U.S. branches and agencies of foreign banks do not receive separate examination ratings of their management, the agencies stated in the joint interim rule that they would use certain criteria as a proxy for the well managed criterion applicable to U.S. banks, including the ROCA component and composite ratings, the existence of any formal enforcement action or order issued by an agency, and the other discretionary standards described above.

The joint interim rule became effective immediately, but the agencies invited public comment on any aspect of the joint interim rule. Commenters strongly favored adopting the rule on a final basis. The agencies did so in 1999.[7] The FDIC rule, excerpted *infra*, is representative. What would be the incentive for a U.S. branch or agency of a foreign bank to attempt to meet the criteria of § 347.214?

## Federal Deposit Insurance Corporation
### 12 C.F.R. Part 347  International Banking

§ 347.214  Examination of branches of foreign banks.

---

7. 64 Fed. Reg. 56,949 (1999) (codified at 12 C.F.R. §§ 4.7, 211.26, 347.214) (joint rulemaking by OCC, Fed and FDIC).

(a) Frequency of on-site examination. Each branch or agency of a foreign bank shall be examined on-site at least once during each 12-month period (beginning on the date the most recent examination of the office ended) by:

(1) The Board of Governors of the Federal Reserve System (Board);

(2) The FDIC, if an insured branch;

(3) The Office of the Comptroller of the Currency (OCC), if the branch or agency of the foreign bank is licensed by the Comptroller; or

(4) The state supervisor, if the office of the foreign bank is licensed or chartered by the state.

(b) 18-month cycle for certain small institutions. (1) Mandatory standards. The FDIC may conduct a full-scope, on-site examination at least once during each 18-month period, rather than each 12-month period as provided in paragraph (a) of this section, if the insured branch:

(i) Has total assets of $250 million or less;

(ii) Has received a composite ROCA supervisory rating (which rates risk management, operational controls, compliance, and asset quality) of 1 or 2 at its most recent examination;

(iii) Satisfies the requirement of either the following paragraph (b)(iii)(A) or (B):

(A) The foreign bank's most recently reported capital adequacy position consists of, or is equivalent to, Tier 1 and total risk-based capital ratios of at least 6 percent and 10 percent, respectively, on a consolidated basis; or

(B) The insured branch has maintained on a daily basis, over the past three quarters, eligible assets in an amount not less than 108 percent of the preceding quarter's average third party liabilities (determined consistent with applicable federal and state law) and sufficient liquidity is currently available to meet its obligations to third parties;

(iv) Is not subject to a formal enforcement action or order by the Board, FDIC, or the OCC; and

(v) Has not experienced a change in control during the preceding 12-month period in which a full-scope, on-site examination would have been required but for this section.

(2) Discretionary standards. In determining whether an insured branch that meets the standards of paragraph (b)(1) of this section should not be eligible for an 18-month examination cycle pursuant to this paragraph (b), the FDIC may consider additional factors, including whether:

(i) Any of the individual components of the ROCA supervisory rating of an insured branch is rated "3" or worse;

(ii) The results of any off-site monitoring indicate a deterioration in the condition of the insured branch;

(iii) The size, relative importance, and role of a particular insured branch when reviewed in the context of the foreign bank's entire U.S. operations otherwise necessitate an annual examination; and

(iv) The condition of the parent foreign bank gives rise to such a need.

(c) Authority to conduct more frequent examinations. Nothing in paragraphs (a) and (b) of this section limits the authority of the FDIC to examine any insured branch as frequently as it deems necessary.

**Notes and Comments 9.3.** Are international-related deposits subject to federal deposit reserve requirements? Review *id.* §§ 461, 3105(a). Consider also the following.

## Board of Governors of the Federal Reserve System

§ 204.1 Authority, purpose and scope.

(a) Authority. This part is issued under the authority of section 19 (12 U.S.C. 461 et seq.) and other provisions of the Federal Reserve Act and of section 7 of the International Banking Act of 1978 (12 U.S.C. 3105).

(b) Purpose. This part relates to reserves that depository institutions are required to maintain for the purpose of facilitating the implementation of monetary policy by the Federal Reserve System.

(c) Scope.

(1) The following depository institutions are required to maintain reserves in accordance with this part:

(i) Any insured bank as defined in section 3 of the Federal Deposit Insurance Act (12 U.S.C. 1813(h)) or any bank that is eligible to apply to become an insured bank under section 5 of such Act (12 U.S.C. 1815);

(ii) Any savings bank or mutual savings bank as defined in section 3 of the Federal Deposit Insurance Act (12 U.S.C. 1813(f), (g));

(iii) Any insured credit union as defined in section 101 of the Federal Credit Union Act (12 U.S.C. 1752(7)) or any credit union that is eligible to apply to become an insured credit union under section 201 of such Act (12 U.S.C. 1781);

(iv) Any member as defined in section 2 of the Federal Home Loan Bank Act (12 U.S.C. 1422(4)); and

(v) Any insured institution as defined in section 401 of the National Housing Act (12 U.S.C. 1724(a)) or any institution which is eligible to apply to become an insured institution under section 403 of such Act (12 U.S.C. 1726).

(2) Except as may be otherwise provided by the Board, a foreign bank's branch or agency located in the United States is required to comply with the provisions of this part in the same manner and to the same extent as if the branch or agency were a member bank, if its parent foreign bank (i) has total worldwide consolidated bank assets in excess of $1 billion; or (ii) is controlled by a foreign company or by a group of foreign companies that own or control foreign banks that in the aggregate have total worldwide consolidated bank assets in excess of $1 billion. In addition, any other foreign bank's branch located in the United States that is eligible to apply to become an insured bank under section 5 of the Federal Deposit Insurance Act (12 U.S.C. 1815) is required to maintain reserves in accordance with this part as a nonmember depository institution.

(3) Except as may be otherwise provided by the Board, an Edge Corporation (12 U.S.C. 611 et seq.) or an Agreement Corporation (12 U.S.C. 601 et seq.) is required to comply with the provisions of this part in the same manner and to the same extent as a member bank. . . .

(5) The provisions of this part do not apply to any deposit that is payable only at an office located outside the United States.

§ 204.2 Definitions.

For purposes of this part, the following definitions apply unless otherwise specified:

(a)(1) "Deposit" means:

(i) The unpaid balance of money or its equivalent received or held by a depository institution in the usual course of business and for which it has given or is obligated to give credit, either conditionally or unconditionally, to an account, including interest credited, or which is evidenced by an instrument on which the depository institution is primarily liable.

. . .

(2) "Deposit" does not include:

(xii) Any liability of a United States branch or agency of a foreign bank to another United States branch or agency of the same foreign bank, or the liability of the United States office of an Edge Corporation to another United States office of the same Edge Corporation.

(b)(1) "Demand deposit" means a deposit that is payable on demand, or a deposit issued with an original maturity or required notice period of less than seven days, or a deposit representing funds for which the depository institution does not reserve the right to require at least seven days' written notice of an intended withdrawal. . . .

(e) "Transaction account" means a deposit or account from which the depositor or account holder is permitted to make transfers or withdrawals by negotiable or transferable instrument, payment order of withdrawal, telephone transfer, or other similar device for the purpose of making payments or transfers to third persons or others or from which the depositor may make third party payments at an automated teller machine ("ATM") or a remote service unit, or other electronic device, including by debit card, but the term does not include savings deposits. . . .

(f)(1) "Nonpersonal time deposit" means:

(i) A time deposit . . . representing funds in which any beneficial interest is held by a depositor which is not a natural person. . . .

(h) "Eurocurrency liabilities" means:

(1) For a depository institution or an Edge or Agreement Corporation organized under the laws of the United States, the sum, if positive, of the following:

(i) Net balances due to its non-United States offices and its international banking facilities ("IBFs") from its United States offices;

(ii)(A) For a depository institution organized under the laws of the United States, assets (including participations) acquired from its United States offices and held by its non-United States offices, by its IBF, or by non-United States offices of an affiliated Edge or Agreement Corporation; or

(B) For an Edge or Agreement Corporation, assets (including participations) acquired from its United States offices and held by its non-United States offices, by its IBF, by non-United States offices of its U.S or foreign parent institution, or by non-United States offices of an affiliated Edge or Agreement Corporation; and

(iii) Credit outstanding from its non-United States offices to United States residents (other than assets acquired and net balances due from its United States offices), except credit extended (A) from its non-United States offices in the aggregate amount of $100,000 or less to any United States resident, (B) by a non-United States office that at no time during the computation period had credit outstanding, to United States residents exceeding $1 million, (C) to an international banking facility, or (D) to an institution that will be maintaining reserves on such credit pursuant to this part. Credit extended from non-United States offices or from IBFs to a foreign branch, office, subsidiary, affiliate of other foreign establishment ("foreign affiliate") controlled by one or more domestic corporations is not regarded as credit extended to a United States resident if the proceeds will be used to finance the operations outside the United States of the borrower or of other foreign affiliates of the controlling domestic corporation(s).

(2) For a United States branch or agency of a foreign bank, the sum, if positive, of the following:

(i) Net balances due to its foreign bank (including offices thereof located outside the United States) and its international banking facility after deducting an amount equal to 8 per cent of the following: the United States branch's or agency's total assets less the sum of (A) cash items in process of collection; (B) unposted debits; (C) demand balances due from depository institutions organized under the laws of the United States and from other foreign banks; (D) balances due from foreign central banks; and (E) positive net balances due from its IBF, its foreign bank, and the foreign bank's United States and non-United States offices; and

(ii) Assets (including participations) acquired from the United States branch or agency (other than assets required to be sold by Federal or State supervisory authorities) and held by its foreign bank (including offices thereof located outside the United States), by its parent holding company, by non-United States offices or an IBF of an affiliated Edge or Agreement Corporation, or by its IBFs. . . .

(j) "Net transaction accounts" means the total amount of a depository institution's transaction accounts less the deductions allowed under the provisions of § 204.3.

(k)(1) "Vault cash" means United States currency and coin owned and held by a depository institution that may, at any time, be used to satisfy depositors' claims. . . .

(*l*) "Pass through account" means a balance maintained by a depository institution that is not a member bank, by a U.S. branch or agency of a foreign bank, or by an Edge or Agreement Corporation, (1) in an institution that maintains required reserve balances at a Federal Reserve Bank, (2) in a Federal Home Loan Bank, (3) in the National Credit Union Administration Central Liquidity Facility, or (4) in an institution that has been authorized by the Board to pass through required reserve balances if the institution, Federal Home Loan Bank, or National Credit Union Administration Central Liquidity Facility maintains the funds in the form of a balance in a Federal Reserve Bank of which it is a member or at which it maintains an account in accordance with rules and regulations of the Board. . . .

(o) "Foreign bank" means any bank or other similar institution organized under the laws of any country other than the United States or organized under the laws of Puerto Rico, Guam, American Samoa, the Virgin Islands, or other territory or possession of the United States. . . .

(t) "Any deposit that is payable only at an office located outside the United States" means (1) a deposit of a United States resident[9] that is in a denomination of $100,000 or more, and as to which the depositor is entitled, under the agreement with the institution, to demand payment only outside the United States or (2) a deposit of a person who is not a United States resident[9] as to which the depositor is entitled, under the agreement with the institution, to demand payment only outside the United States. . . .

§ 204.3 Computation and maintenance.

(a) Maintenance and reporting of required reserves.

(1) Maintenance. A depository institution, a U.S. branch or agency of a foreign bank, and an Edge or Agreement corporation shall maintain reserves against its deposits and Eurocurrency liabilities in accordance with the procedures prescribed in this section and § 204.4 and the ratios prescribed in § 204.9. . . . For purposes of this part, the obligations of a majority-owned (50 percent or more) U.S. subsidiary (except an Edge or Agreement corporation) of a depository institution shall be regarded as obligations of the parent depository institution.

(2) Reporting.

---

9. A deposit of a foreign branch, office, subsidiary, affiliate or other foreign establishment ("foreign affiliate") controlled by one or more domestic corporations is not regarded as a deposit of a United States resident if the funds serve a purpose in connection with its foreign or international business or that of other foreign affiliates of the controlling domestic corporation(s).

(i) Every depository institution, U.S. branch or agency of a foreign bank, and Edge or Agreement corporation shall file a report of deposits (or any other required form or statement) directly with the Federal Reserve Bank of its District, regardless of the manner in which it chooses to maintain required reserve balances. A foreign bank's U.S. branches and agencies and an Edge or Agreement corporation's offices operating within the same state and the same Federal Reserve District shall prepare and file a report of deposits on an aggregated basis. . . .

(3) Allocation of low reserve tranche and exemption from reserve requirements. A depository institution, a foreign bank, or an Edge or Agreement corporation shall, if possible, assign the low reserve tranche and reserve requirement exemption prescribed in § 204.9(a) to only one office or to a group of offices filing a single aggregated report of deposits. The amount of the reserve requirement exemption allocated to an office or group of offices may not exceed the amount of the low reserve tranche allocated to such office or offices. If the low reserve tranche or reserve requirement exemption cannot be fully utilized by a single office or by a group of offices filing a single report of deposits, the unused portion of the tranche or exemption may be assigned to other offices or groups of offices of the same institution until the amount of the tranche (or net transaction accounts) or exemption (or reservable liabilities) is exhausted. The tranche or exemption may be reallocated each year concurrent with implementation of the indexed tranche and exemption, or, if necessary during the course of the year to avoid underutilization of the tranche or exemption, at the beginning of a reserve computation period.

(b) Form and location of reserves.

(1) A depository institution, a U.S. branch or agency of a foreign bank, and an Edge or Agreement corporation shall hold reserves in the form of vault cash, a balance maintained directly with the Federal Reserve Bank in the Federal Reserve District in which it is located, or, in the case of nonmember institutions, with a pass-through correspondent in accordance with § 204.3(i). . . .

(f) Deductions allowed in computing reserves.

(1) In determining the reserve balance required under this part, the amount of cash items in process of collection and balances subject to immediate withdrawal due from other depository institutions located in the United States (including such amounts due from United States branches and agencies of foreign banks and Edge and agreement corporations) may be deducted from the amount of gross transaction accounts. The amount that may be deducted may not exceed the amount of gross transaction accounts.

(2) United States branches and agencies of a foreign bank may not deduct balances due from another United States branch or agency of the same foreign bank, and United States offices of an Edge or Agreement Corporation may not deduct balances due from another United States office of the same Edge Corporation. . . .

(i) Pass-through rules.

(1) Procedure.

(i) A nonmember depository institution, a U.S. branch or agency of a foreign bank, or an Edge or Agreement corporation required to maintain reserve balances (respondent) may select only one institution to pass through its required reserve balances, unless otherwise permitted by Federal Reserve Bank in whose district the respondent is located. Eligible institutions through which respondent required reserve balances may be passed (correspondents) are Federal Home Loan Banks, the National Credit Union Administration Central Liquidity Facility, and depository institutions, U.S. branches or agencies of foreign banks, and Edge and Agreement corporations that maintain required reserve balances at a Federal Reserve office. In addition, the Board reserves the right to permit other institutions, on a case-by-case basis, to serve as pass-through correspondents. The correspondent chosen must subsequently pass through the required reserve balances of its respondents directly to a Federal Reserve Bank. . . .

§ 204.8 International banking facilities.

(a) Definitions. For purposes of this part, the following definitions apply:

(1) "International banking facility" or "IBF" means a set of asset and liability accounts segregated on the books and records of a depository institution, United States branch or agency of a foreign bank, or an Edge or Agreement Corporation that includes only international banking facility time deposits and international banking facility extensions of credit.

(2) "International banking facility time deposit" or "IBF time deposit" means a deposit, placement, borrowing or similar obligation represented by a promissory note, acknowledgment of advance, or similar instrument that is not issued in negotiable or bearer form, and

(i)(A) That must remain on deposit at the IBF at least overnight; and

(B) That is issued to

(1) Any office located outside the United States of another depository institution organized under the laws of the United States or of an Edge or Agreement Corporation;

(2) Any office located outside the United States of a foreign bank;

(3) A United States office or a non-United States office of the entity establishing the IBF;

(4) Another IBF; or

(5) A foreign national government, or an agency or instrumentality thereof, engaged principally in activities which are ordinarily performed in the United States by governmental entities;[10] an international entity of which the United States is a member; or any other foreign international or supranational entity specifically designated by the Board;[11] or

(ii)(A) That is payable

(1) On a specified date not less than two business days after the date of deposit;

(2) Upon expiration of a specified period of time not less than two business days after the date of deposit; or

(3) Upon written notice that actually is required to be given by the depositor not less than two business days prior to the date of withdrawal;

(B) That represents funds deposited to the credit of a non-United States resident or a foreign branch, office, subsidiary, affiliate, or other foreign establishment ("foreign affiliate") controlled by one or more domestic corporations provided that such funds are used only to support the operations outside the United States of the depositor or of its affiliates located outside the United States; and

(C) That is maintained under an agreement or arrangement under which no deposit or withdrawal of less than $100,000 is permitted, except that a withdrawal of less than $100,000 is permitted if such withdrawal closes an account.

(3) "International banking facility extension of credit or "IBF loan" means any transaction where an IBF supplies funds by making a loan, or placing funds in a deposit account. Such transactions may be represented by a promissory note, security, acknowledgment of advance, due bill, repurchase agreement, or any other form of credit transaction. Such credit may be extended only to:

---

10. Other than states, provinces, municipalities, or other regional or local governmental units or agencies or instrumentalities thereof.

11. The designated entities are specified in 12 CFR 204.125.

(i) Any office located outside the United States of another depository institution organized under the laws of the United States or of an Edge or Agreement Corporation;

(ii) Any office located outside the United States of a foreign bank;

(iii) A United States or a non-United States office of the institution establishing the IBF;

(iv) Another IBF;

(v) A foreign national government, or an agency or instrumentality thereof,[12] engaged principally in activities which are ordinarily performed in the United States by governmental entities; an international entity of which the United States is a member; or any other foreign international or supranational entity specifically designated by the Board;[13] or

(vi) A non-United States resident or a foreign branch, office, subsidiary, affiliate or other foreign establishment ("foreign affiliate") controlled by one or more domestic corporations provided that the funds are used only to finance the operations outside the United States of the borrower or of its affiliates located outside the United States.

(b) Acknowledgment of use of IBF deposits and extensions of credit. An IBF shall provide written notice to each of its customers (other than those specified in § 204.8(a)(2)(i)(B) and § 204.8(a)(3)(i) through (v)) at the time a deposit relationship or a credit relationship is first established that it is the policy of the Board of Governors of the Federal Reserve System that deposits received by international banking facilities may be used only to support the depositor's operations outside the United States as specified in s 204.8(a)(2)(ii)(B) and that extensions of credit by IBFs may be used only to finance operations outside of the United States as specified in § 204.8(a)(3)(vi). In the case of loans to or deposits from foreign affiliates of U.S. residents, receipt of such notice must be acknowledged in writing whenever a deposit or credit relationship is first established with the IBF.

(c) Exemption from reserve requirements. An institution that is subject to the reserve requirements of this Part is not required to maintain reserves against its IBF time deposits or IBF loans. Deposit-taking activities of IBFs are limited to accepting only IBF time deposits and lending activities of IBFs are restricted to making only IBF loans.

(d) Establishment of an international banking facility. A depository institution, an Edge or Agreement Corporation or a United States branch or agency of a foreign bank may establish an IBF in any location where it is legally authorized to engage in IBF business. However, only one IBF may be established for each reporting entity that is required to submit a Report of Transaction Accounts, Other Deposits and Vault Cash....

(e) Notification to Federal Reserve. At least fourteen days prior to the first reserve computation period that an institution intends to establish an IBF it shall notify the Federal Reserve Bank of the district in which it is located of its intent. Such notification shall include a statement of intention by the institution that it will comply with the rules of this Part concerning IBFs, including restrictions on sources and uses of funds, and recordkeeping and accounting requirements. Failure to comply with the requirements of this Part shall subject the institution to reserve requirements under this Part or result in the revocation of the institution's ability to operate an IBF.

(f) Recordkeeping requirements. A depository institution shall segregate on its books and records the asset and liability accounts of its IBF and submit reports concerning the operations of its IBF as required by the Board.

---

12. Other than states, provinces, municipalities, or other regional or local governmental units or agencies or instrumentalities thereof.

13. The designated entities are specified in 12 CFR 204.125.

§ 204.9 Reserve requirement ratios.

The following reserve requirement ratios are prescribed for all depository institutions, banking Edge and agreement corporations, and United States branches and agencies of foreign banks:

| Category | Reserve requirement |
| --- | --- |
| Net transaction accounts: | |
| $0 to $6.6 million.          .          . | 0 percent of amount. |
| Over $6.6 million and up to $45.4 million  .          .          . | 3 percent of amount. |
| Over $45.4 million          .          . | $1,164,000 plus 10 percent of amount over $45.4 million. |
| Nonpersonal time deposits.          . | 0 percent. |
| Eurocurrency liabilities    .          . | 0 percent. |

§ 204.122  Secondary market activities of International Banking Facilities.

(a) Questions have been raised concerning the extent to which International Banking Facilities may purchase (or sell) IBF-eligible assets such as loans (including loan participations), securities, CDs, and bankers' acceptances from (or to) third parties. Under the Board's regulations, as specified in § 204.8 of Regulation D, IBFs are limited, with respect to making loans and accepting deposits, to dealing only with certain customers, such as other IBFs and foreign offices of other organizations, and with the entity establishing the IBF. In addition, an IBF may extend credit to a nonbank customer only to finance the borrower's non-U.S. operations and may accept deposits from a nonbank customer that are used only to support the depositor's non-U.S. business.

(b) Consistent with the Board's intent, IBFs may purchase IBF-eligible assets[1] from, or sell such assets to, any domestic or foreign customer provided that the transactions are at arm's length without recourse. However, an IBF of a U.S. depository institution may not purchase assets from, or sell such assets to, any U.S. affiliate of the institution establishing the IBF; an IBF of an Edge or Agreement corporation may not purchase assets from, or sell assets to, any U.S. affiliate of the Edge or Agreement corporation or to U.S. branches of the Edge or Agreement corporation or to U.S. branches of the Edge or Agreement corporation other than the branch[2] establishing the IBF; and an IBF of a U.S. branch or agency of a foreign bank may not purchase assets from, or sell assets to any U.S. affiliates of the foreign bank or to any other U.S. branch or agency of the same foreign bank.[2] (This would not prevent an IBF from purchasing (or selling) assets directly from (or to) any IBF, including an IBF of an affiliate, or to the institution establishing the IBF;  such purchases from the institution establishing the IBF would continue to be subject to Eurocurrency reserve requirements except during the initial four-week transition period.) Since repurchase agree-

---

1. In order for an asset to be eligible to be held by an IBF, the obligor or issuer of the instrument, or in the case of bankers' acceptances, the customer and any endorser or acceptor, must be an IBF-eligible customer.

2. Branches of Edge or Agreement corporations and agencies and branches of foreign banks that file a consolidated report for reserve requirements purposes . . . are considered to be the establishing entity of an IBF.

ments are regarded as loans, transactions involving repurchase agreements are permitted only with customers who are otherwise eligible to deal with IBFs, as specified in Regulation D.

(c) In the case of purchases of assets, in order to determine that the Board's use-of-proceeds requirement has been met, it is necessary for the IBF (1) to ascertain that the applicable IBF notices and acknowledgments have been provided, or (2) in the case of loans or securities, to review the documentation underlying the loan or security, or accompanying the security (*e.g.*, the prospectus or offering statement), to determine that the proceeds are being used only to finance the obligor's operations outside the U.S., or (3) in the case of loans, to obtain a statement from either the seller or borrower that the proceeds are being used only to finance operations outside the U.S., or in the case of securities, to obtain such a statement from the obligor, (4) in the case of bankers' acceptances, to review the underlying documentation to determine that the proceeds are being used only to finance the parties' operations outside the United States.

(d) Under the Board's regulations, IBFs are not permitted to issue negotiable Euro-CDs, bankers' acceptances, or similar instruments. Accordingly, consistent with the Board's intent in this area, IBFs may sell such instruments issued by third parties that qualify as IBF-eligible assets provided that the IBF, its establishing institution and any affiliate of the institution establishing the IBF do not endorse, accept, or otherwise guarantee the instrument.

§ 204.125. Foreign, international, and supranational entities referred to in §§204.2 (c)(1)(iv)(E) and 204.8(a)(2)(i)(B)(5).

The entities referred to in §204.2(c)(1)(iv)(E) and §204.8(a)(2)(i)(B)(5) are:

Europe

Bank for International Settlements.
European Atomic Energy Community.
European Central Bank
European Coal and Steel Community.
The European Communities.
European Development Fund.
European Economic Community.
European Free Trade Association.
European Fund.
European Investment Bank.

Latin America

Andean Development Corporation.
Andean Subregional Group.
Caribbean Development Bank.
Caribbean Free Trade Association
Caribbean Regional Development Agency.
Central American Bank for Economic Integration.
The Central American Institute for Industrial Research and Technology.
Central American Monetary Stabilization Fund.
East Caribbean Common Market.
Latin American Free Trade Association.
Organization for Central American States.
Permanent Secretariat of the Central American General Treaty of Economic Integration.
River Plate Basin Commission.

Africa

    African Development Bank.

    Banque Centrale des Etats de l'Afrique Equatorial et du Cameroun.

    Banque Centrale des Etats d'Afrique del'Ouest.

    Conseil de l'Entente.

    East African Community.

    Organisation Commune Africaine et Malagache.

    Organization of African Unity.

    Union des Etats de l'Afrique Centrale.

    Union Douaniere et Economique de l'Afrique Centrale.

    Union Douaniere des Etats de l'Afrique de l'Ouest.

Asia

    Asia and Pacific Council.

    Association of Southeast Asian Nations.

    Bank of Taiwan.

    Korea Exchange Bank.

Middle East

    Central Treaty Organization.

    Regional Cooperation for Development.

§ 204.128 Deposits at foreign branches guaranteed by domestic office of a depository institution.

(a) In accepting deposits at branches abroad, some depository institutions may enter into agreements from time to time with depositors that in effect guarantee payment of such deposits in the United States if the foreign branch is precluded from making payment. The question has arisen whether such deposits are subject to Regulation D, and this interpretation is intended as clarification.

(b) Section 19 of the Federal Reserve Act which establishes reserve requirements does not apply to deposits of a depository institution "payable only at an office thereof located outside of the States of the United States and the District of Columbia" (12 USC 371a; 12 CFR 204.1(c)(5)). The Board ruled in 1918 that the requirements of section 19 as to reserves to be carried by member banks do not apply to foreign branches. . . . The Board has also defined the phrase "Any deposit that is payable only at an office located outside the United States," in § 204.2(t) of Regulation D, 12 CFR 204.2(t).

(c) The Board believes that this exemption from reserve requirements should be limited to deposits in foreign branches as to which the depositor is entitled, under his agreement with the depository institution, to demand payment only outside the United States, regardless of special circumstances. The exemption is intended principally to enable foreign branches of U.S. depository institutions to compete on a more nearly equal basis with banks in foreign countries in accordance with the laws and regulations of those countries. A customer who makes a deposit that is payable solely at a foreign branch of the depository institution assumes whatever risk may exist that the foreign country in which a branch is located might impose restrictions on withdrawals. When payment of a deposit in a foreign branch is guaranteed by a promise of payment at an office in the United States if not paid at the foreign office, the depositor no longer assumes this risk but enjoys substantially the same rights as if the deposit had been made in a U.S. office of the depository institution. To assure the effectiveness of Regulation D and to prevent evasions thereof, the Board considers that such guaranteed foreign-branch deposits must be subject to that regulation.

(d) Accordingly, a deposit in a foreign branch of a depository institution that is guaranteed by a domestic office is subject to the reserve requirements of Regulation D the same as if the deposit had been made in the domestic office. This interpretation is not designed in any respect to prevent the head office of a U.S. bank from repaying borrowings from, making advances to, or supplying capital funds to its foreign branches, subject to Eurocurrency liability reserve requirements.

**Notes and Comments 9.4.** *Effect of FDICIA on deposit-taking.* The Federal Deposit Insurance Corporation Improvement Act of 1991[8] imposes restrictions on the retail deposit-taking activities of U.S. branches of foreign-based banks. Generally, such deposit-taking is now required to be done through U.S. banking subsidiaries, which are required to carry federal deposit insurance. *See* Note 2.3, *supra.*

**9.5.** *Effect of IBBEA on deposit-taking.* The Interstate Banking and Branching Efficiency Act of 1994 (IBBEA)[9] primarily affects the interstate expansion of U.S.- and non-U.S.-based banking enterprises. *See* Note 6.7, *supra.* However, IBBEA also has an effect on the U.S. deposit-taking activities of non-U.S. banks. In answering the following questions, consider the excerpts from the FDIC regulations set forth *infra*:

> **a.** NusBank has a state-licensed branch that has accepted deposits in amounts less than $100,000 since its establishment in 1988. It is now proposing to sell the branch to Wholly Foreign Bank (WFB). If WFB purchases the NusBank branch, can it continue to maintain the deposits? Can it accept new deposits in amounts less than $100,000?
>
> **b.** NusBank has a state-licensed branch that has maintained deposits in amounts less than $100,000 for A Corp., a U.S. firm that is privately held by members of the Alfabett family. Can it continue to maintain these deposits?
>
> **c.** NusBank's state-licensed branch has average daily deposits of $1,000,000. Herman Alfabett, a Nusquami citizen who is resident in the United States, would like to open a personal checking account with the NusBank branch. He anticipates that the average daily balance in the account would be approximately $12,000. Can the branch open this account for Herman?

## Federal Deposit Insurance Corporation
### 12 C.F.R. Part 347  International Banking

§ 347.202  Definitions.

For the purposes of this subpart:

(a) Affiliate means any entity that controls, is controlled by, or is under common control with another entity. An entity shall be deemed to "control" another entity if the entity directly or indirectly owns, controls, or has the power to vote 25 percent or more of any class of voting securities of the other entity or controls in any manner the election of a majority of the directors or trustees of the other entity.

(b) Branch means any office or place of business of a foreign bank located in any state of the United States at which deposits are received. The term does not include any office or place of business deemed by the state licensing authority or the Comptroller of the Currency to be an agency.

(c) Deposit has the same meaning as that term in section 3(l) of the Federal Deposit

---

8. Pub. L. No. 102-242, 105 Stat. 2236 (December 19, 1991) (codified at scattered sections of 12 U.S.C.).

9. Pub. Law No. 103-328, Sept. 29, 1994, 108 Stat. 2338 (1994).

Insurance Act (12 U.S.C. 1813(*l*)).

(d) Depository means any insured state bank, national bank, or insured branch.

(e) Domestic retail deposit activity means the acceptance by a state branch of any initial deposit of less than $100,000.

(f) Federal branch means a branch of a foreign bank established and operating under the provisions of section 4 of the International Banking Act of 1978 (12 U.S.C. 3102).

(g) Foreign bank means any company organized under the laws of a foreign country, any territory of the United States, Puerto Rico, Guam, American Samoa, the Northern Mariana Islands, or the Virgin Islands, which engages in the business of banking. The term includes foreign commercial banks, foreign merchant banks and other foreign institutions that engage in banking activities usual in connection with the business of banking in the countries where such foreign institutions are organized and operating. Except as otherwise specifically provided by the Federal Deposit Insurance Corporation, banks organized under the laws of a foreign country, any territory of the United States, Puerto Rico, Guam, American Samoa, the Northern Mariana Islands, or the Virgin Islands which are insured banks other than by reason of having an insured branch are not considered to be foreign banks for purposes of §§ 347.208, 347.209, 347.210, and 347.211.

(h) Foreign business means any entity including, but not limited to, a corporation, partnership, sole proprietorship, association, foundation or trust, which is organized under the laws of a foreign country or any United States entity which is owned or controlled by an entity which is organized under the laws of a foreign country or a foreign national.

(i) Foreign country means any country other than the United States and includes any colony, dependency or possession of any such country.

(j) Home state of a foreign bank means the state so determined by the election of the foreign bank, or in default of such election, by the Board of Governors of the Federal Reserve System.

(k) Immediate family member of a natural person means the spouse, father, mother, brother, sister, son or daughter of that natural person.

(*l*) Initial deposit means the first deposit transaction between a depositor and the branch. The initial deposit may be placed into different deposit accounts or into different kinds of deposit accounts, such as demand, savings or time. Deposit accounts that are held by a depositor in the same right and capacity may be added together for the purposes of determining the dollar amount of the initial deposit. "First deposit" means any deposit made when there is no existing deposit relationship between the depositor and the branch.

(m) Insured bank means any bank, including a foreign bank having an insured branch, the deposits of which are insured in accordance with the provisions of the Federal Deposit Insurance Act.

(n) Insured branch means a branch of a foreign bank any deposits of which branch are insured in accordance with the provisions of the Federal Deposit Insurance Act.

(o) Large United States business means any entity including, but not limited to, a corporation, partnership, sole proprietorship, association, foundation or trust which is organized under the laws of the United States or any state thereof, and:

(1) Whose securities are registered on a national securities exchange or quoted on the National Association of Securities Dealers Automated Quotation System; or

(2) Has annual gross revenues in excess of $1,000,000 for the fiscal year immediately preceding the initial deposit.

(p) A majority owned subsidiary means a company the voting stock of which is more than 50 percent owned or controlled by another company.

(q) Noninsured branch means a branch of a foreign bank deposits of which branch are not insured in accordance with the provisions of the Federal Deposit Insurance Act.

(r) Person means an individual, bank, corporation, partnership, trust, association, foundation, joint venture, pool, syndicate, sole proprietorship, unincorporated organization, or any other form of entity.

(s) Significant risk to the deposit insurance fund shall be understood to be present whenever there is a high probability that the Bank Insurance Fund administered by the FDIC may suffer a loss.

(t) State means any state of the United States or the District of Columbia.

(u) State branch means a branch of a foreign bank established and operating under the laws of any state.

(v) A wholly owned subsidiary means a company the voting stock of which is 100 percent owned or controlled by another company except for a nominal number of directors' shares.

§ 347.203   Restriction on operation of insured and noninsured branches.

The FDIC will not insure deposits in any branch of a foreign bank unless the foreign bank agrees that every branch established or operated by the foreign bank in the same state will be an insured branch; provided, that this restriction does not apply to any branch which accepts only initial deposits in an amount of $100,000 or greater.

§ 347.204   Insurance requirement.

(a) Domestic retail deposit activity. In order to initiate or conduct domestic retail deposit activity which requires deposit insurance protection in any state a foreign bank shall:

(1) Establish one or more insured bank subsidiaries in the United States for that purpose; and

(2) Obtain deposit insurance for any such subsidiary in accordance with the Federal Deposit Insurance Act.

(b) Exception. For purposes of paragraph (a) of this section, "foreign bank" does not include any bank organized under the laws of any territory of the United States, Puerto Rico, Guam, American Samoa, or the Virgin Islands the deposits of which are insured by the Corporation pursuant to the Federal Deposit Insurance Act.

(c) Grandfathered insured branches. Domestic retail deposit accounts with balances of less than $100,000 that require deposit insurance protection may be accepted or maintained in a branch of a foreign bank only if such branch was an insured branch on December 19, 1991.

(d) Noninsured branches. A foreign bank may establish or operate a state branch which is not an insured branch whenever:

(1) The branch only accepts initial deposits in an amount of $100,000 or greater; or

(2) The branch meets the criteria set forth in §347.205 or §347.206.

§ 347.205   Branches established under section 5 of the International Banking Act.

A foreign bank may operate any state branch as a noninsured branch whenever the foreign bank has entered into an agreement with the Board of Governors of the Federal Reserve System to accept at that branch only those deposits as would be permissible for a corporation organized under section 25(a) of the Federal Reserve Act (12 U.S.C. 611 et seq.) and implementing rules and regulations administered by the Board of Governors (12 CFR part 211).

§ 347.206   Exemptions from the insurance requirement.

(a) Deposit activities not requiring insurance. A state branch will not be deemed to be engaged in domestic retail deposit activity which requires the foreign bank parent to establish an insured bank subsidiary in accordance with §347.204(a) if the state branch only accepts initial deposits in an amount of less than $100,000 which are derived solely from the following:

(1) Individuals who are not citizens or residents of the United States at the time of the initial deposit;

(2) Individuals who:

(i) Are not citizens of the United States;

(ii) Are residents of the United States; and

(iii) Are employed by a foreign bank, foreign business, foreign government, or recognized international organization;

(3) Persons (including immediate family members of natural persons) to whom the branch or foreign bank (including any affiliate thereof) has extended credit or provided other nondeposit banking services within the past twelve months or has entered into a written agreement to provide such services within the next twelve months;

(4) Foreign businesses, large United States businesses, and persons from whom an Edge Corporation may accept deposits under §211.4(e)(1) of Regulation K of the Board of Governors of the Federal Reserve System, 12 CFR 211.4(e)(1);

(5) Any governmental unit, including the United States government, any state government, any foreign government and any political subdivision or agency of any of the foregoing, and recognized international organizations;

(6) Persons who are depositing funds in connection with the issuance of a financial instrument by the branch for the transmission of funds or the transmission of such funds by any electronic means; and

(7) Any other depositor, but only if the branch's average deposits under this paragraph (a)(7) do not exceed one percent of the branch's average total deposits for the last 30 days of the most recent calendar quarter (de minimis exception). In calculating this de minimis exception, both the average deposits under this paragraph (a)(7) and the average total deposits shall be computed by summing the close of business figures for each of the last 30 calendar days, ending with and including the last day of the calendar quarter, and dividing the resulting sum by 30. For days on which the branch is closed, balances from the last previous business day are to be used. In determining its average branch deposits, the branch may exclude deposits in the branch of other offices, branches, agencies or wholly owned subsidiaries of the bank. In addition, the branch must not solicit deposits from the general public by advertising, display of signs, or similar activity designed to attract the attention of the general public. A foreign bank which has more than one state branch in the same state may aggregate deposits in such branches (excluding deposits of other branches, agencies or wholly owned subsidiaries of the bank) for the purpose of this paragraph (a)(7).

(b) Application for an exemption. (1) Whenever a foreign bank proposes to accept at a state branch initial deposits of less than $100,000 and such deposits are not otherwise excepted under paragraph (a) of this section, the foreign bank may apply to the FDIC for consent to operate the branch as a noninsured branch. The Board of Directors may exempt the branch from the insurance requirement if the branch is not engaged in domestic retail deposit activities requiring insurance protection. The Board of Directors will consider the size and nature of depositors and deposit accounts, the importance of maintaining and improving the availability of credit to all sectors of the United States economy, including the international trade finance sector of the United States economy, whether the exemption would give the foreign bank an unfair competitive advantage over United States banking organizations, and any other relevant factors in making this determination. . . .

(c) Transition period. A noninsured state branch may maintain a retail deposit lawfully accepted prior to April 1, 1996 pursuant to regulations in effect prior to July 1, 1998 . . . :

(1) If the deposit qualifies pursuant to paragraph (a) or (b) of this section; or

(2) If the deposit does not qualify pursuant to paragraph (a) or (b) of this section, no later than:

(i) In the case of a non-time deposit, five years from April 1, 1996; or

(ii) In the case of a time deposit, the first maturity date of the time deposit after April 1, 1996.

**Notes and Comments 9.6.** *Eurodollar deposits*. Special problems arise in connection with Eurodollar deposits, *i.e.*, "United States dollars that have been deposited with a banking institution located outside the United States, with a corresponding obligation on the part of the banking institution to repay the deposit in United States dollars."[10] In this regard, reconsider the Cuban branch cases, Chapter 4, § 2, *supra*. How would the opinions in the following decisions have affected the outcome in those cases? Consider also whether the following excerpts are consistent with the views expressed by Judge Kearse in her dissent in *Garcia, supra*.

## Citibank, N.A. v. Wells Fargo Asia Limited
### 495 U.S. 660 (1990)

Justice Kennedy delivered the opinion of the Court.

At issue here is whether the home office of a United States bank is obligated to use its general assets to repay a Eurodollar deposit made at one of its foreign branches, after the foreign country's government has prohibited the branch from making repayment out of its own assets.

I

The case arises from a transaction in what is known in the banking and financial communities as the Eurodollar market. . . . The banking institution receiving the deposit can be either a foreign branch of a United States bank or a foreign bank.

A major component of the Eurodollar market is interbank trading. In a typical interbank transaction in the Eurodollar market, the depositing bank (Bank A) agrees by telephone or telex, or through a broker, to place a deposit denominated in United States dollars with a second bank (Bank X). For the deposit to be a Eurodollar deposit, Bank X must be either a foreign branch of a United States bank or a foreign bank; Bank A, however, can be any bank, including one located in the United States. To complete the transactions, most banks that participate in the interbank trading market utilize correspondent banks in New York City, with whom they maintain, directly or indirectly, accounts denominated in United States dollars. In this example, the depositor bank, Bank A, orders its correspondent bank in New York (Bank B) to transfer United States dollars from Bank A's account to Bank X's account with Bank X's New York correspondent bank (Bank Y). The transfer of funds from Bank B to Bank Y is accomplished by means of a wire transfer through a clearing mechanism located in New York City and known as the Clearing House Interbank Payments System, or "CHIPS." . . . Repayment of the funds at the end of the deposit term is accomplished by having Bank Y transfer funds from Bank X's account to Bank B, through

---

10. *Citibank, N.A. v. Wells Fargo Asia Limited*, 495 U.S. 660, 663 (1990).

the CHIPS system, for credit to Bank A's account.

The transaction at issue here follows this pattern. Respondent Wells Fargo Asia Limited (WFAL) is a Singapore-chartered bank wholly owned by Wells Fargo Bank, N.A., a bank chartered by the United States. Petitioner Citibank, N.A. (Citibank), also a United States-chartered bank, operates a branch office in Manila, Philippines (Citibank/Manila). On June 10, 1983, WFAL agreed to make two $1 million time deposits with Citibank/Manila. The rate at which the deposits would earn interest was set at 10%, and the parties agreed that the deposits would be repaid on December 9 and 10, 1983. The deposits were arranged by oral agreement through the assistance of an Asian money broker, which made a written report to the parties that stated, inter alia:

> " 'Pay: Citibank, N.A. New York Account Manila
> " 'Repay: Wells Fargo International, New York Account Wells Fargo Asia Ltd., Singapore Account # 003-023645.' "

852 F.2d 657, 658-659 (2d Cir. 1988). The broker also sent WFAL a telex containing the following "'[i]nstructions'":

> " 'Settlement -- Citibank NA NYC AC Manila
> " 'Repayment -- Wells Fargo Bk Intl NYC Ac Wells Fargo Asia Ltd Sgp No 003- 023645,' "

*id.*, at 659. That same day, the parties exchanged telexes confirming each of the two deposits. WFAL's telexes to Citibank/Manila read:

> " 'We shall instruct Wells Fargo Bk Int'l New York our correspondent please pay to our a/c with Wells Fargo Bk Int'l New York to pay to Citibank NA customer's correspondent USD 1,000,000.' "

*Ibid.* The telexes from Citibank/Manila to WFAL read:

> " 'Please remit US Dlr 1,000,000 to our account with Citibank New York. At maturity we remit US Dlr 1,049,444.44 to your account with Wells Fargo Bank Intl Corp NY through Citibank New York.' "

*Ibid.*

A few months after the deposit was made, the Philippine government issued a Memorandum to Authorized Agent Banks (MAAB 47) which provided in relevant part:

> " 'Any remittance of foreign exchange for repayment of principal on all foreign obligations due to foreign banks and/or financial institutions, irrespective of maturity, shall be submitted to the Central Bank [of the Philippines] thru the Management of External Debt and Investment Accounts Department (MEDIAD) for prior approval.' "

*Ibid.* According to the Court of Appeals, "[a]s interpreted by the Central Bank of the Philippines, this decree prevented Citibank/Manila, an 'authorized agent bank' under Philippine law, from repaying the WFAL deposits with its Philippine assets, *i.e.*, those assets not either deposited in banks elsewhere or invested in non-Philippine enterprises." *Ibid.* As a result, Citibank/Manila refused to repay WFAL's deposits when they matured in December 1983.

WFAL commenced the present action against Citibank in the United States District Court for the Southern District of New York, claiming that Citibank in New York was liable for the funds that WFAL deposited with Citibank/Manila. While the lawsuit was pending, Citibank obtained permission from the Central Bank of the Philippines to repay its Manila depositors to the extent that it could do so with the non-Philippine assets of the Manila branch. It paid WFAL $934,000; the remainder of the deposits, $1,066,000, remains in dispute. During the course of this litigation, Citibank/Manila, with the apparent consent of the Philippine government, has continued to pay WFAL interest on the outstanding principal.
. . .

. . . [T]he District Court accepted WFAL's invitation to assume that Philippine law governs the action. The court saw the issue to be whether, under Philippine law, a depositor with Citibank/Manila may look to assets booked at Citibank's non-Philippine offices for repayment of the deposits. After considering affidavits from the parties, it concluded (1) that under Philippine law an obligation incurred by a branch is an obligation of the bank as a whole; (2) that repayment of WFAL's deposits with assets booked at Citibank offices other than Citibank/Manila would not contravene MAAB 47; and (3) that Citibank therefore was obligated to repay WFAL, even if it could do so only from assets not booked at Citibank/Manila. It entered judgment for WFAL, and Citibank appealed.

A panel of the United States Court of Appeals for the Second Circuit remanded the case to the District Court to clarify the basis for its judgment. The Second Circuit ordered the District Court to make supplemental findings of fact and conclusions of law on the following matters:

"(a) Whether the parties agreed as to where the debt could be repaid, including whether they agreed that the deposits were collectible only in Manila.
"(b) If there was an agreement, what were its essential terms?
"(c) Whether Philippine law (other than MAAB 47) precludes or negates an agreement between the parties to have the deposits collectible outside of Manila.
"(d) If there is no controlling Philippine law referred to in (c) above, what law does control?"
. . .

In response to the first query, the District Court distinguished the concepts of repayment and collection, defining repayment as "refer[ring] to the location where the wire transfers effectuating repayment at maturity were to occur," and collection as "refer[ring] to the place or places where plaintiff was entitled to look for satisfaction of its deposits in the event that Citibank should fail to make the required wire transfers at the place of repayment." . . . It concluded that the parties' confirmation slips established an agreement that repayment was to occur in New York, and that there was neither an express agreement nor one that could be implied from custom or usage in the Eurodollar market on the issue of where the deposits could be collected. In response to the second question, the court stated that "[t]he only agreement relating to collection or repayment was that repayment would occur in New York." . . . As to third query, the court stated that it knew of no provision of Philippine law that barred an agreement making WFAL's deposits collectible outside Manila. Finally, in response to the last query, the District Court restated the issue in the case as follows: "Hence, the dispute in this case . . . boils down to one question: is Citibank obligated to use its worldwide assets to satisfy plaintiff's deposits? In other words, the dispute is not so much about where repayment physically was to be made or where the deposits were collectible, but rather which assets Citibank is required to use in order to satisfy its obligation to plaintiff. As we have previously found that the contract was silent on this issue, we interpret query (d) as imposing upon us the task . . . of deciding whether New York or Philippine law controls the answer to that question." . . . The District Court held that, under either New York or federal choice-of-law rules, New York law should be applied. After reviewing New York law, it held that Citibank was liable for WFAL's deposits with Citibank/Manila, and that WFAL could look to Citibank's worldwide assets for satisfaction of its deposits.

The Second Circuit affirmed, but on different grounds. Citing general banking law principles, the Court of Appeals reasoned that, in the ordinary course, a party who makes a deposit with a foreign branch of a bank can demand repayment of the deposit only at that branch. In the court's view, however, these same principles established that this "normal limitation" could be altered by an agreement between the bank and the depositor: "If the parties agree that repayment of a deposit in a foreign bank or branch may occur at another location, they authorize demand and collection at that other location." 852 F.2d, at 660. The court noted that the District Court had found that Citibank had agreed to repay WFAL's deposits in New York. It concluded that the District Court's finding was not clearly erroneous . . . , and held that, as a result, WFAL was entitled "to collect the deposits out of Citibank assets in New York." 852 F.2d., at 661.

. . . We decide that the factual premise on which the Second Circuit relied in deciding the case contradicts the factual determinations made by the District Court, determinations that are not clearly erroneous. We vacate the judgment and remand the case to the Court of Appeals for further consideration of the additional legal questions in the case.

## II

Little need be said respecting the operation or effect of the Philippine decree at this stage of the case, for no party questions the conclusion reached by both the District Court and the Court of Appeals that Philippine law does not bar the collection of WFAL's deposits from the general assets of Citibank in the State of New York. . . . The question, rather, is whether Citibank is obligated to allow collection in New York, and on this point two principal theories must be examined. The first is that there was an agreement between the parties to permit collection in New York, or indeed at any place where Citibank has assets, an agreement implied from all the facts in the case as being within the contemplation of the parties. A second, and alternative, theory for permitting collection is that, assuming no such agreement, there is a duty to pay in New York in any event, a duty that the law creates when the parties have not contracted otherwise. . . .

The Court of Appeals appears to have relied upon the first theory we have noted, adopting the premise that the parties did contract to permit recovery from the general assets of Citibank in New York. Yet the District Court had made it clear that there is a distinction between an agreement on "repayment," which refers to the physical location for transacting discharge of the debt, and an agreement respecting "collection," which refers to the location where assets may be taken to satisfy it, and in quite specific terms, it found that the only agreement the parties made referred to repayment.

The Court of Appeals . . . appears to have viewed repayment and collection as interchangeable concepts, not divisible ones. It concluded that the agreement as to where repayment could occur constituted also an agreement as to which bank assets the depositor could look to for collection. . . .

That the Court of Appeals based its ruling on the premise of an agreement between the parties is apparent as well from the authorities upon which it relied to support its holding. The court cited three cases for the proposition that an agreement to repay at a particular location authorizes the depositor to collect the deposits at that location, all of which involve applications of the act of state doctrine: *Allied Bank International v. Banco Credito Agricola de Cartago*, 757 F.2d 516 (2d Cir.), *cert. dism'd*, 473 U.S. 934 (1985); *Garcia v. Chase*

*Manhattan Bank, N.A.*, 735 F.2d 645, 650-651 (2d Cir. 1984); and *Braka v. Bancomer, S.N.C.*, 762 F.2d 222, 225 (2d Cir. 1985). Each of these three cases turns upon the existence, or nonexistence, of an agreement for collection. In *Garcia* and *Allied Bank*, the agreement of the parties to permit collection at a location outside of the foreign country made the legal action of the foreign country irrelevant. . . . In *Braka*, the agreement between the parties was that repayment and collection would be permitted only in the foreign country, and so the foreign law controlled. . . . By its reliance upon these cases, the Court of Appeals, it seems to us, must have been relying upon the existence of an agreement between Citibank and WFAL to permit collection in New York. As noted above, however, this premise contradicts the express finding of the District Court.

. . . As the Court of Appeals itself acknowledged, the record contains ample support for the District Court's finding that the parties agreed that repayment, defined as the wire transfers effecting the transfer of funds to WFAL when its deposits matured, would take place in New York. . . .

As to collection, the District Court found that neither the parties' confirmation slips nor the evidence offered at trial with regard to whether "an agreement concerning the place of collection could be implied from custom and usage in the international banking field" established an agreement respecting collection. . . . Upon review of the record, we hold this finding . . . was not clearly erroneous. . . .

Nor does the evidence contradict the District Court's conclusion that the parties, in this particular case, failed to establish a relevant custom or practice in the international banking community from which it could be inferred that the parties had a tacit understanding on the point. Citibank's experts testified that the common understanding in the banking community was that the higher interest rates offered for Eurodollar deposits, in contrast to dollar deposits with United States banks, reflected in part the fact that the deposits were not subject to reserve and insurance requirements imposed on domestic deposits by United States banking law. This could only be the case, argues Citibank, if the deposits were "payable only" outside of the United States, as required by . . . 12 U.S.C. § 461(b) (6), and . . . 12 U.S.C. § 1813(*l*)(5). It argues further that higher rates reflected the depositor's assumption of foreign "sovereign risk," defined as the risk that actions by the foreign government having legal control over the foreign branch and its assets would render the branch unable to repay the deposit. . . .

WFAL's experts, on the other hand, testified that the identical interest rates being offered for Eurodollar deposits in both Manila and London at the time the deposits were made, despite the conceded differences in sovereign risk between the two locations, reflected an understanding that the home office of a bank was liable for repayment in the event that its foreign branch was unable to repay for any reason, including restrictions imposed by a foreign government. . . .

A fair reading of all of the testimony supports the conclusion that, at least in this trial, on the issue of the allocation of sovereign risk there was a wide variance of opinion in the international banking community. We cannot say that we are left with "the definite and firm conviction" that the District Court's findings are erroneous. . . . Because the Court of Appeals' holding relies upon contrary factual assumptions, the judgment for WFAL cannot be affirmed under the reasoning used by that court.

Given the finding of the District Court that there was no agreement between the parties respecting collection from Citibank's general assets in New York, the question becomes whether collection is permitted nonetheless by rights and duties implied by law. . . . It is unclear from the opinion of the Court of Appeals which law [New York or Philippine law] it found to be controlling; and we decide to remand the case for the Court of Appeals to determine which law applies, and the content of that law. . . .

One of WFAL's contentions is that the Court of Appeals' opinion can be supported on the theory that it is based upon New York law. We do not think this is a fair or necessary construction of the opinion. The Court of Appeals placed express reliance on its own opinion in *Garcia v. Chase Manhattan Bank, N.A.*, 735 F.2d 645 (2d Cir. 1984), without citing or discussing *Perez v. Chase Manhattan Bank, N.A.*, 61 N.Y.2d 460, 474 N.Y.S.2d 689, 463 N.E.2d 5 (1984). In that case, the New York Court of Appeals was explicit in pointing out that its decision was in conflict with that reached two days earlier by the Second Circuit in Garcia, . . . a case that the *Perez* court deemed "similar on its facts." . . . Given this alignment of authorities, we are reluctant to interpret the Court of Appeals' decision as resting on principles of state law. The opinion of the Court of Appeals, moreover, refers to "general banking law principles" and "United States law," . . . ; whether this is the semantic or legal equivalent of the law of New York is for the Court of Appeals to say in the first instance.

Alternatively, if the Court of Appeals, based upon its particular expertise in the law of New York and commercial matters generally, is of the view that the controlling rule is supplied by Philippine law or, as Citibank would have it, by a federal common-law rule respecting bank deposits, it should make that determination, subject to any further review we deem appropriate. In view of our remand, we find it premature to consider the other contentions of the parties respecting the necessity for any rule of federal common law, or the pre-emptive effect of federal statutes and regulations on bank deposits and reserves....

Justice STEVENS, dissenting.

The Court wisely decides this case on a narrow ground. Its opinion, however, ignores an aspect of the case that is of critical importance for me.

The parties agree that Citibank assumed the risk of loss caused by either the insolvency of its Manila branch, or by an act of God. Citibank argues that only the so-called "sovereign risk" is excluded from its undertaking to repay the deposit out of its general assets. In my opinion such a specific exclusion from a general undertaking could only be the product of an express agreement between the parties. The District Court's finding that no such specific agreement existed is therefore dispositive for me.

Accordingly, I would affirm the judgment of the Court of Appeals.

# Wells Fargo Asia Limited v. Citibank, N.A.
## 936 F.2d 723 (2d Cir. 1991)

Kearse, Circuit Judge:

This action, brought by plaintiff Wells Fargo Asia Limited ("WFAL") to recover funds deposited with the Philippine branch of defendant Citibank, N.A. ("Citibank"), returns to us on remand from the United States Supreme Court . . . for a determination of what law applies to the present controversy and the content of that law, and for resolution of the controversy in light of those determinations. For the reasons below, we affirm the district court's ruling that the law of New York is applicable and its award of judgment in favor of WFAL.
. . .

In response to this Court's earlier inquiry, the district court discussed the choice-of-law question as follows:

> The legal principles governing our determination are straightforward. Jurisdiction in this action is asserted both on the basis of diversity and federal question involving 12 U.S.C. § 632. In diversity cases, of course, we must apply

the conflict of law doctrine of the forum state. *Klaxon Co. v. Stentor Elec. Mfg. Co.* (1941) 313 U.S. 487. In federal question cases, we are directed to apply a federal common law choice of law rule to determine which jurisdiction's substantive law should apply. *Corporacion Venezolana de Fomento v. Vintero Sales Corp.* (2d Cir. 1980) 629 F.2d 786, 794-95, *cert. denied* (1981) 449 U.S. 1080. The rule in New York is that "the law of the jurisdiction having the greatest interest in the litigation will be applied and that the facts or contacts which obtain significance in defining State interests are those which relate to the purpose of the particular law in conflict." *Intercontinental Planning, Ltd. v. Daystrom, Inc.* (1969) 24 N.Y.2d 372, 382, 300 N.Y.S.2d 817, 825, 248 N.E.2d 576, 582. Federal law invokes similar considerations, . . . and the place of performance is considered an important factor. *Citibank, N.A. v. Benkoczy* (S.D.Fla. 1983) 561 F. Supp. 184, 186 and cases cited therein. Regardless of whether the New York or federal test is used, application of these standards leads us to the conclusion that New York law should be used to evaluate Wells Fargo's contention that Citibank's worldwide assets are available for repayment of the deposits. As the New York Court of Appeals has recognized, "New York . . . is a financial capital of the world, serving as an international clearing house and market place for a plethora of international transactions . . . [.] In order to maintain its preeminent financial position, it is important that the justified expectations of the parties to the contract be protected." *J. Zeevi and Sons, Ltd. v. Grindlays Bank (Uganda) Ltd.* (1975) 37 N.Y.2d 220, 227, 371 N.Y.S.2d 892, 898, 333 N.E.2d 168, 172. In our view, these expectations will be best promoted by applying a uniform rule of New York law where, as here, the transactions were denominated in United States dollars and settled through the parties' New York correspondent banks, and where the defendant is a United States bank with headquarters in New York. Since Eurodollar transactions denominated in U.S. dollars customarily are cleared in New York . . . , the rationale for application of New York law becomes even stronger. If the goal is to promote certainty in international financial markets, it makes sense to apply New York law uniformly, rather than conditioning the deposit obligations on the vagaries of local law, and requiring each player in the Eurodollar market to investigate the law of numerous foreign countries in order to ascertain which would limit repayment of deposits to the foreign branch's own assets. 695 F.Supp. at 1453-54.

As to the content of New York law on the matter, the district court noted that the most recent pronouncement of the New York Court of Appeals, see *Perez v. Chase Manhattan National Bank, N.A.*, 61 N.Y.2d 460, 468, 474 N.Y.S.2d 689, 691, 463 N.E.2d 5, 7, *cert. denied*, 469 U.S. 966 (1984), indicated that the parent bank is ultimately liable for the obligations of the foreign branch. Though the district court reasoned that an actual expropriation by the foreign government would be treated differently, it concluded that in the present case, there having been no expropriation and no limitation of the depositor's rights but only action affecting the assets of the branch, New York law would allow collection of the debt in New York:

> [I]f the Philippines had confiscated plaintiff's deposits, New York courts would interpret the expropriation as a compulsory assignment of the depositor's rights, so that payment to the Philippine assignee would discharge the debt. A New York court would further recognize such compulsory assignment as an act of a foreign sovereign unreviewable under the Act of State doctrine. *Perez, supra*, 61 N.Y.2d 460, 474 N.Y.S.2d 689, 463 N.E.2d 5. We believe New York would take a similar approach in the situation where a foreign government had effected a partial

confiscation in the form of a tax on a deposit made at a foreign branch. *See, Dunn v. Bank of Nova Scotia* (5th Cir.1967) 374 F.2d 876. However, we are aware of no persuasive authority to tell us to what extent, if any, a New York court would defer to local law in the situation here presented, where the foreign sovereign did not extinguish the branch's debt either in whole or in part but merely conditioned repayment on the obtaining of approval from a government agency. Fortunately, we need not resolve that troublesome question.

695 F.Supp. at 1454-55. The court found it unnecessary to determine whether New York law would hold that a foreign government's refusal to give the prerequisite consent constitutes an excuse for refusal to make repayment, in light of its earlier finding that Citibank "had not satisfied its good faith obligation to seek the [Philippine] government's consent to use the assets booked at Citibank's non-Philippine offices." . . . The court reaffirmed that finding.

We agree with the district court's analysis, and we conclude, substantially for the reasons that court stated, that New York law governs the present claim and that under New York law, Citibank was not excused from making repayment. In urging that we reach the contrary conclusion, Citibank argues that there is a clear federal policy placing the risk of foreign-law impediments to repayment on the depositor. In so arguing, it relies on federal banking rules such as 12 U.S.C. § 461(b)(6) (1988), which provides that banking reserve requirements "shall not apply to deposits payable only outside the States of the United States and the District of Columbia," and 12 C.F.R. § 204.128(c) (1990) (issued at 52 Fed.Reg. 47696, Dec. 16, 1987), which provides that "[a] customer who makes a deposit that is payable solely at a foreign branch of the depository institution assumes whatever risk may exist that the foreign country in which a branch is located might impose restrictions on withdrawals." Citibank's reliance on these provisions is misplaced. Federal law defines a deposit that is "payable only at an office outside the United States" as "a deposit . . . as to which the depositor is entitled, under the agreement with the institution, to demand payment only outside the United States." *Id.* § 204.2(t). The provisions relied on thus do not reveal a policy allocating the risk to depositors as a matter of law where there is no such agreement. So long as state law does not restrict a bank's freedom to enter into an agreement that allocates the risk of foreign sovereign restrictions, state law does not conflict with the federal policy reflected in current statutes or regulations. We see no such restriction in the law of New York, and hence there is no " 'significant conflict'," . . . between New York law and federal law such as would be necessary to justify the creation of a federal common law.

We conclude that under New York law, unless the parties agree to the contrary, a creditor may collect a debt at a place where the parties have agreed that it is repayable. In applying this principle to the circumstances of the present case to affirm the judgment in favor of WFAL, we do not assume the existence of an agreement between Citibank/Manila and WFAL to permit collection in New York; rather, in light of the express finding of the district court that the parties had no agreement as to permissible situses of collection, we rely on the absence of any agreement forbidding the collection in New York.

Finally, we note that on the present remand, WFAL urged us to affirm on the basis of recently submitted evidence that in fact Citibank, while refusing to use non-Manila assets to pay Citibank/Manila's debts, has received profits of at least $25 million from Citibank/Manila during the period 1984-1989. WFAL contends that it is entitled to have its deposits repaid out of these profits. Citibank does not dispute that it received these profits but takes the position that it is not required to use these profits to pay persons whose deposits in Citibank/Manila remain unpaid. We need not resolve this question. Suffice it to say that Citibank's acknowledged ability to obtain Philippine Central Bank approval of transfers to it of moneys as profits appears to support the district court's finding, if further support were needed, that Citibank in fact did not satisfy its good faith obligation to seek that government's approval of repayment. . . .

# 3. Letters of Credit

**Notes and Comments 9.7.** Letters of credit (L/Cs) come in two basic varieties, commercial (or "documentary" or "trade") L/Cs, and standby (or "guaranty") L/Cs. Despite apparent similarities, these two types perform quite different functions. One of the basic regulatory issues, therefore, is whether or not the two should be subject to distinct regulatory regimes. The following excerpt provides some general guidance as to the types of letters of credit used in banking practice.

## Comptroller's Handbook for National Bank Examiners,
Section 811.1

There are two major types of letters of credit used to finance foreign transactions: the commercial documentary letter of credit and the standby letter of credit. The commercial documentary letter of credit is most commonly used to finance a commercial contract for the shipment of goods from seller to buyer. This versatile instrument may be applied to nearly every type of foreign transaction and provides for the prompt payment of money to the seller when shipment is made as specified under its terms.

Although a standby letter of credit may arise from a commercial transaction, it is not linked directly to the shipment of goods from seller to buyer. It may cover performance of a construction contract, serve as an assurance to a bank that the seller will honor his or her obligations under warranties, or relate to the performance of a purely monetary obligation, for example, when the credit is used to guarantee payment of commercial paper at maturity. The role of the bank in issuing standby letters of credit differs from that used in issuing commercial letters of credit.

Under all letters of credit, the banker expects the customer to be financially able to meet his or her commitments. A banker's payment under a commercial credit for the customer's account is usually reimbursed immediately by the customer and does not become a loan. However, the bank only makes payment on a standby letter of credit when the customer, having defaulted on his or her primary obligation, will probably be unable to reimburse it. . . .

The importance of documentation is paramount in all letter of credit transactions. Many letters of credit are part of continuous transactions evolving from letters of credit to sight drafts or acceptances or to notes and advances, collateralized by trust receipts or warehouse receipts. Ultimate repayment often depends upon the eventual sale of the goods involved. Thus, although the transaction passes through various sections of the international banking division, the proper handling and accuracy of the documents required under the letter of credit, is of primary concern.

**Notes and Comments 9.8.** *Commercial Letters of Credit.* Commercial L/Cs have long been a traditional activity of commercial banks. They are a particularly important service of banks in support of international trade transactions. The nature of this type of transaction is illustrated in Figure 9.1, *infra*.

A documentary L/C is the commitment of the "issuing bank" (or "issuer," in the terminology of revised UCC Article 5[11]) that it will make payment to the L/C beneficiary on drafts drawn on the L/C under circumstances specified in the L/C. The customer of the bank who opens the L/C, known as the "account party" (or "applicant" in revised Article 5[12]), is usually the buyer of goods. The L/C beneficiary is usually the seller of those goods, or a bank specified by the seller. The typical condition under which the issuing bank will make payment is the presentation to issuing bank of specified documents, such as the bill of lading for the goods sold and shipped, or other evidences of title, as well as insurance certificates, customs documents, and any other documents specified by the parties in their negotiations.

Often another bank, known as the "confirming bank" (or "confirmer"[13]), is used to "confirm" the L/C, which means that it takes on the obligation to make payment to the beneficiary under the L/C, with subsequent presentation of demand to the issuing bank. A confirming bank may be used where the issuing bank is unknown to the beneficiary/seller, or where it is not convenient for the beneficiary to deal directly with an issuing bank in the buyer's home country.

A confirming bank should not be confused with an "advising bank" (or "adviser"[14]), which merely undertakes to inform the beneficiary/seller that an issuing bank has established an L/C in seller's favor. An advising bank does not undertake any obligation itself to make payment under the L/C.

Problems may arise, exposing the issuing or confirming bank to risk, if there is any break in the pattern of behavior and expectations from account party to issuing bank, issuing bank to confirming bank, confirming bank to beneficiary, and so forth. In the following cases, what went wrong with the L/C transaction, and why should regulators–as opposed to the private parties involved in the transaction–have any interest in the resolution of the situation?

Figure 9.1
Typical Documentary Letter of Credit

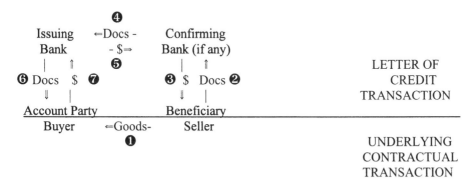

SELLER PERFORMS ⇒ LETTER OF CREDIT TRIGGERED

❶ Seller ships goods; obtains necessary documents ("docs") from shipper

---

11. UCC § 5-102(a)(9) (1995 Rev.).

12. *Id.* § 5-102(a)(2).

13. *Id.* § 5-102(a)(4).

14. *Id.* § 5-102(a)(1).

Seller submits docs and draft to C bank
C bank pays Seller on draft
C bank submits docs and draft to I bank
I bank reimburses C bank
I bank makes docs available to Buyer
Buyer reimburses I bank in exchange for docs

*Source*: MICHAEL P. MALLOY, PRINCIPLES OF BANK REGULATION § 9.20 (2d ed. 2003).

---

## Maurice O'Meara Co. v. National Park Bank of New York
### 239 N.Y. 386, 146 N.E. 636 (N.Y. Ct. App. 1925)

McLaughlin, J.

This action was brought to recover damages alleged to have been sustained by the plaintiff's assignor, Ronconi & Millar, by defendant's refusal to pay three sight drafts against a confirmed irrevocable letter of credit. The letter of credit was in the following form:

The National Park Bank of New York

Our Credit No. 14956                                 October 28, 1920.

Messrs. Ronconi & Millar, 49 Chambers Street, New York City, N.Y.–Dear Sirs:
In accordance with instructions received from the Sun-Herald Corporation of this city, we open a confirmed or irrevocable credit in your favor for account of themselves, in amount of $224,853.30, covering the shipment of 1,322-2/3 tons of newsprint paper in 72- 12/" and 36-1/2" rolls to test 11-12, 32 lbs. at 8-1/2c/ per pound net weight–delivery to be made in December, 1920, and January, 1921.
Drafts under this credit are to be drawn at sight on this bank, and are to be accompanied by the following documents of a character which must meet with our approval:

> Commercial invoice in triplicate.
> Weight returns.
> Negotiable dock delivery order actually carrying
> with it control of the goods.

This is a confirmed or irrevocable credit, and will remain in force to and including February 15, 1921, subject to the conditions mentioned herein.
When drawing drafts under this credit, or referring to it, please quote our number as above.

> Very truly yours,
> R. Stuart, Assistant Cashier.
> (R.C.)

The complaint alleged the issuance of the letter of credit; the tender of three drafts, the first on the 17th of December, 1920, for $46,301.71, the second on January 7, 1921, for $41,416.34, and the third on January 13, 1921, for $32,968.35. Accompanying the first draft were the following documents:

> 1. Commercial invoice of the said firm of Ronconi & Millar in triplicate, covering three hundred (300) thirty-six and one-half (36-1/2) inch rolls of newsprint paper and three hundred (300) seventy-two and one-half (72-1/2) inch rolls of newsprint paper, aggregating a net weight of five hundred and forty-four

thousand seven hundred and twenty-six pounds (544,726), to test eleven (11), twelve (12), thirty-two (32) pounds.

    2.  Affidavit of Elwin Walker, verified December 16, 1920, to which were annexed samples of newsprint paper, which the said affidavit stated to be representative of the shipment covered by the accompanying invoices and to test twelve (12) points, thirty-two (32) pounds.

    3.  Full weight returns in triplicate.

    4.  Negotiable dock delivery order on the Swedish American Line, directing delivery to the order of the National Park Bank of three hundred (300) rolls of newsprint paper seventy-two and one-half (72-1/2) inches long and three hundred (300) half rolls of newsprint paper.

    The documents accompanying the second draft were similar to those accompanying the first. . . . The complaint also alleged defendant's refusal to pay, a statement of the amount of loss upon the resale of the paper due to a fall in the market price, expenses for lighterage, cartage, storage, and insurance amounting to $3,045.02, an assignment of the cause of action by Ronconi & Millar to the plaintiff, and a demand for judgment.

    The answer . . . and set up (a) as an affirmative defense, that plaintiff's assignor was required by the letter of credit to furnish to the defendant "evidence reasonably satisfactory" to it that the paper shipped to the Sun-Herald Corporation was of a bursting or tensile strength of 11 to 12 points at a weight of paper of 32 pounds; that neither the plaintiff nor its assignor, at the time the drafts were presented, or at any time thereafter, furnished such evidence; (b) as a partial defense, that, when the draft for $46,301.71 was presented, the defendant notified the plaintiff there had not been presented "evidence reasonably satisfactory" to it, showing that the newsprint paper referred to in the documents accompanying said drafts was of the tensile or bursting strength specified in the letter of credit; that thereupon an agreement was entered into between plaintiff and defendant that the latter should cause a test to be made of the paper represented by the documents then presented, and, if such test showed that the paper was up to the specifications of the letter of credit, defendant would make payment of the draft; (c) for a third separate and distinct defense that the paper tendered was not, in fact, of the tensile or bursting strength specified in the letter of credit; . . .

    After issue had been joined the plaintiff moved . . . for summary judgment. . . .

    The motion for summary judgment was denied and the defendant appealed to the Appellate Division, where the order denying the same was unanimously affirmed. . . .

    I am of the opinion that the order of the Appellate Division and the Special Term should be reversed and the motion granted. The facts set out in defendant's answer and in the affidavits used by it in opposition to the motion are not a defense to the action.

    The bank issued to plaintiff's assignor an irrevocable letter of credit, a contract solely between the bank and plaintiff's assignor, in and by which the bank agreed to pay sight drafts to a certain amount on presentation to it of the documents specified in the letter of credit. This contract was in no way involved in or connected with, other than the presentation of the documents, the contract for the purchase and sale of the paper mentioned. That was a contract between buyer and seller, which in no way concerned the bank. The bank's obligation was to pay sight drafts when presented if accompanied by genuine documents specified in the letter of credit. If the paper when delivered did not correspond to what had been purchased, either in weight, kind or quality, then the purchaser had his remedy against the seller for damages. Whether the paper was what the purchaser contracted to purchase did not concern the bank and in no way affected its liability. It was under no obligation to ascertain, either by a personal examination or otherwise, whether the paper conformed to the contract between the buyer and seller. The bank was concerned only in the drafts and the documents accompanying them. This was the extent of its interest. If the drafts, when presented, were accompanied by the proper documents, then it was absolutely bound to make the payment under the letter of credit, irrespective of whether it knew, or had reason to believe, that the paper was not of the tensile strength contracted for. This view, I think, is the one generally entertained with reference to a bank's liability under an irrevocable letter of credit of the character of the one here under consideration. . . .

The defendant had no right to insist that a test of the tensile strength of the paper be made before paying the drafts; nor did it even have a right to inspect the paper before payment, to determine whether it in fact corresponded to the description contained in the documents. The letter of credit did not so provide. All that the letter of credit provided was that documents be presented which described the paper shipped as of a certain size, weight, and tensile strength. To hold otherwise . . . would impose upon a bank a duty which in many cases would defeat the primary purpose of such letters of credit. This primary purpose is an assurance to the seller of merchandise of prompt payment against documents.

It has never been held, so far as I am able to discover, that a bank has the right or is under an obligation to see that the description of the merchandise contained in the documents is correct. A provision giving it such right, or imposing such obligation, might, of course, be provided for in the letter of credit. The letter under consideration contains no such provision. If the bank had the right to determine whether the paper was of the tensile strength stated, then it might be pertinent to inquire how much of the paper must it subject to the test. If it had to make a test as to tensile strength, then it was equally obligated to measure and weigh the paper. No such thing was intended by the parties and there was no such obligation upon the bank. . . .

Cardozo, J. (dissenting).

. . . I dissent from the view that, if [the bank] chooses to investigate and discovers thereby that the merchandise tendered is not in truth the merchandise which the documents describe, it may be forced by the delinquent seller to make payment of the price irrespective of its knowledge. We are to bear in mind that this controversy is not one between the bank on the one side and on the other a holder of the drafts who has taken them without notice and for value. The controversy arises between the bank and a seller who has misrepresented the security upon which advances are demanded. Between parties so situated payment may be resisted if the documents are false.

. . . I cannot accept the statement of the majority opinion that the bank was not concerned with the with any question as to the character of the paper. If that is so, the bales tendered might have been rags instead of paper, and still the bank would have been helpless, though it had knowledge of the truth, if the documents tendered by the seller were sufficient on their face. A different question would be here if the defects had no relation to the description in the documents. In such circumstances it would be proper to say that a departure from the terms of the contract between the vendor and the vendee was of no moment to the bank. That is not the case before us. If the paper was of the quality stated in the defendant's answer the documents were false.

## United Bank Ltd. v. Cambridge Sporting Goods Corp.
41 N.Y.2d 254, 360 N.E.2d 943 (1976)

Gabrielli, Justice.

. . .

In April, 1971, appellant Cambridge Sporting Goods Corporation (Cambridge) entered into a contract for the manufacture and sale of boxing gloves with Duke Sports (Duke), a Pakistani corporation. Duke committed itself to the manufacture of 27,936 pairs of boxing gloves at a sale price of $42,576.80; and arranged with its Pakistani bankers, United Bank Limited (United) and The Muslim Commercial Bank (Muslim), for the financing of the sale. Cambridge was requested by these banks to cover payment of the purchase price by opening an irrevocable letter of credit with its bank in New York, Manufacturers Hanover Trust Company (Manufacturers). Manufacturers issued an irrevocable letter of credit obligating it, upon the receipt of certain documents indicating shipment of the merchandise pursuant to the contract, to accept and pay, 90 days after acceptance, drafts drawn upon Manufacturers for the purchase price of the gloves. . . .

An inspection of the shipments upon their arrival revealed that Duke had shipped old, unpadded, ripped and mildewed gloves rather than the new gloves to be manufactured as agreed upon. Cambridge then commenced an action against Duke . . . joining Manufacturers as a party, and obtained a preliminary injunction prohibiting the latter from paying drafts drawn under the letter of credit. . . . Duke ultimately defaulted in the action and judgment against it was entered in the amount of the drafts, in March, 1972. . . .

. . . Because Cambridge obtained an injunction against payment of the drafts and has levied against the proceeds of the drafts, it stands in the same position as the issuer, and, thus, the law of letters of credit governs the liability of Cambridge to the Pakistani banks. Article 5 of the Uniform Commercial Code, dealing with letters of credit, and the Uniform Customs and Practice for Documentary Credits promulgated by the International Chamber of Commerce set forth the duties and obligations of the issuer of a letter of credit.[2] A letter of credit is a commitment on the part of the issuing bank that it will pay a draft presented to it under the terms of the credit, and if it is a documentary draft, upon presentation of the required documents of title (*see* Uniform Commercial Code, § 5-103). Banks issuing letters of credit deal in documents and not in goods and are not responsible for any breach of warranty or nonconformity of the goods involved in the underlying sales contract (see Uniform Commercial Code, § 5-114, subd. [1]; Uniform Customs and Practice, General Provisions and Definitions [c] and article 9; *O'Meara Co. v. National Park Bank of N.Y.*, 239 N.Y. 386, 146 N.E. 636. . . . Subdivision (2) of section 5-114, however indicates certain limited circumstances in which an issuer *may* properly refuse to honor a draft drawn under a letter of credit or a customer may enjoin an issuer from honoring such a draft.[3] Thus, where

---

2. It should be noted that the Uniform Customs and Practice controls, in lieu of article 5 of the code, where, unless otherwise agreed by the parties, a letter of credit is made subject to the provisions of the Uniform Customs and Practice by its terms or by agreement, course of dealing or usage of trade (Uniform Commercial Code, § 5-102, subd. [4]). No proof was offered that there was an agreement that the Uniform Customs and Practice should apply, nor does the credit so state. . . . Neither do the parties otherwise contend that their rights should be resolved under the Uniform Customs and Practice. However, even if the Uniform Customs and Practice were deemed applicable to this case, it would not, in the absence of a conflict, abrogate the precode case law (now codified in Uniform Commercial Code, § 5-114) and that authority continues to govern even where article 5 is not controlling. . . . Moreover, the Uniform Customs and Practice provisions are not in conflict nor do they treat with the subject matter of § 5-114 which is dispositive of the issues presented on this appeal. . . . Thus, we are of the opinion that the Uniform Customs and Practice, where applicable, does not bar the relief provided for in § 5-114 of the code.

3. Subdivision (2) of section 5-114 of the Uniform Commercial Code provides that,

[u]nless otherwise agreed when documents appear on their fact to comply with the terms of

"fraud in the transaction" has been shown and the holder has not taken the draft in circumstances that would make it a holder in due course, the customer may apply to enjoin the issuer from paying drafts drawn under the letter of credit. . . . This rule represents a codification of precode case law most eminently articulated in the landmark case of *Sztejn v. Schroder Banking Corp.*, 177 Misc. 719, 31 N.Y.S.2d 631, . . . where it was held that the shipment of cowhair in place of bristles amounted to more than mere breach of warranty but fraud sufficient to constitute grounds for enjoining payment of drafts to one not a holder in due course. . . . Even prior to the *Sztejn* case, forged or fraudulently procured documents were proper grounds for avoidance of payment of drafts drawn under a letter of credit . . . ; and cases decided after the enactment of the code have cited *Sztejn* with approval. . . .

The petitioning banks do not dispute the validity of the prior injunction nor do they dispute the delivery of worthless merchandise. Rather, on this appeal they contend that as holders in due course they are entitled to the proceeds of the drafts irrespective of any fraud on the part of Duke (*see* Uniform Commercial Code, S 5-114, subd. [2], par. [b]). Although precisely speaking there was no specific finding of fraud in the transaction by either of the courts below, their determinations were based on that assumption. The evidentiary facts are not disputed and we hold upon the facts as established, that the shipment of old, unpadded, ripped and mildewed gloves rather than the new boxing gloves as ordered by Cambridge, constituted fraud in the transaction within the meaning of subdivision (2) of section 5-114. It should be noted that the drafters of section 5-114, in their attempt to codify the *Sztejn* case and in utilizing the term "fraud in the transaction", have eschewed a dogmatic approach and adopted a flexible standard to be applied as the circumstances of a particular situation mandate. It can be difficult to draw a precise line between cases involving breach of warranty (or a difference of opinion as to the quality of goods) and outright fraudulent practice on the part of the seller. To the extent, however, that Cambridge established that Duke was guilty of *fraud* in shipping, not merely nonconforming merchandise, but worthless fragments of boxing gloves, this case is similar to *Sztejn*.

If the petitioning banks are holders in due course they are entitled to recover the proceeds of the drafts but if such status cannot be demonstrated their petition must fail.[6] The parties are in agreement that section 3-307 of the code governs the pleading and proof of holder in due course status and that section provides:

> (1) Unless specifically denied in the pleadings each signature on an instrument is admitted. When the effectiveness of a signature is put in issue
> (a) the burden of establishing it is on the party claiming under the

---

a credit but . . . there is fraud in the transaction
(a) the issuer must honor the draft or demand for payment if honor is demanded by a . . . holder of the draft . . . which has taken the draft . . . under the credit and under circumstances which would make it a holder in due course (Section 3- 302) . . . ; and
(b) in all other cases as against its customer, an issuer acting in good faith may honor the draft . . . despite notification from the customer of fraud, forgery or other defect not apparent on the face of the documents but a court of appropriate jurisdiction may enjoin such honor.

6. Although several commentators have expressed a contrary view, the weight of authority supports the proposition that fraud on the part of the seller-beneficiary may not be interposed as a deference to payment against a holder in due course to whom a draft has been negotiated. . . . This approach represents the better view that as against two innocent parties (the buyer and the holder in due course) the former having chosen to deal with the fraudulent seller, should bear the risk of loss.
. . .

signature; but

(b) the signature is presumed to be genuine or authorized except where the action is to enforce the obligation of a purported signer who has died or become incompetent before proof is required.

(2) When signatures are admitted or established, production of the instrument entitles a holder to recover on it unless the defendant establishes a defense.

(3) After it is shown that a defense exists a person claiming the rights of a holder in due course has the burden of establishing that he or some person under whom he claims is in all respects a holder in due course.

Even though section 3-307 is contained in article 3 of the code dealing with negotiable instruments rather than letters of credit, we agree that its provisions should control in the instant case. Section 5-114 (subd. [2], par. [a]), utilizes the holder in due course criteria of section 3-302 of the code to determine whether a presenter may recover on drafts despite fraud in the sale of goods transaction. It is logical, therefore, to apply the pleading and practice rules of section 3-307 in the situation where a presenter of drafts under a letter of credit claims to be a holder in due course. In the context of section 5-114 and the law of letters of credit, however, the "defense" referred to in section 3-307 should be deemed to include only those defenses available under subdivision (2) of section 5-114, *i.e.*, noncompliance of required documents, forged or fraudulent documents or fraud in the transaction. In the context of a letter of credit transaction and, specifically subdivision (2) of section 5-114, it is these defenses which operate to shift the burden of proof of holder in due course status upon one asserting such status. . . . Thus, a presenter of drafts drawn under a letter of credit must prove that it took the drafts for value, in good faith and without notice of the underlying fraud in the transaction. . . .

In order to qualify as a holder in due course, a holder must have taken the instrument "without notice . . . of any defense against . . . it on the part of any person" (Uniform Commercial Code, § 3-302, subd. [1], pard. [c]). Pursuant to subdivision (2) of section 5-114 fraud in the transaction is a valid defense to payment of drafts drawn under a letter of credit. Since the defense of fraud in the transaction was shown, the burden shifted to the banks by operation of subdivision (3) of section 3-307 to prove that they were holders in due course and took the drafts without notice of Duke's alleged fraud. As indicated in the Official Comment to that subdivision, when it is shown that a defense exists, one seeking to cut off the defense by claiming the rights of a holder in due course "has the full burden of proof by a preponderance of the total evidence" on this issue. This burden must be sustained by "affirmative proof" of the requisites of holder in due course status. . . . It was error for the trial court to direct a verdict in favor of the Pakistani banks because this determination rested upon a misallocation of the burden of proof; and we conclude that the banks have not satisfied the burden of proving that they qualified in all respects as holders in due course, by any affirmative proof. . . . The failure of the banks to meet their burden is fatal to their claim for recovery of the proceeds of the drafts and their petition must therefore be dismissed. . .

.

## Bank of Cochin Ltd. v. Manufacturers Hanover Trust
612 F. Supp. 1533 (S.D.N.Y. 1985), *affirmed*, 808 F.2d 209 (2d Cir. 1986)

Bank of Cochin Limited ["Cochin"], an Indian corporation and the issuer of letter of credit BB/VN/41/80, commenced this diversity action against Manufacturers Hanover

Trust Company ["MHT"], a New York corporation that acted as the confirming bank on the letter. Cochin seeks recovery of the amount paid by MHT, thereafter debited to Cochin's account at MHT, on drawings negotiated in New York between MHT and St. Lucia Enterprises, Ltd. ["St. Lucia"]. Codefendant St. Lucia, a purported New York corporation and the letter of credit beneficiary, has perpetrated a large fraud on both banks and nonparty customer Vishwa Niryat (Pvt.) Ltd. ["Vishwa"]. Unfortunately, St. Lucia has vanished and the Court must decide whose shoulders will bear the scam.

. . . On February 8, 1980, in Bombay, India, Vishwa requested Cochin to issue an irrevocable letter of credit covering up to $798,000 for the benefit of St. Lucia. The letter was to have expired on April 15, 1980 and covered the anticipated shipment and purchase of 1,000 metric tons of aluminum melting scrap consisting of aluminum beverage cans.[1]

On February 14, 1980, Cochin requested MHT to supply financial information on St. Lucia. MHT responded by telex the following day that St. Lucia did not maintain an MHT account and that a thorough check of normal credit sources did not reveal any "pertinent" information. On February 22, Cochin conveyed the terms and conditions of the letter of credit to MHT by Telex and requested MHT to advise "St. Lucia Enterprises Ltd." of the establishment of the letter and to add MHT's confirmation.[2] The letter of credit was issued subject to the Uniform Customs and Practice for Documentary Credits (1974 Revision), Int'l Chamber of Commerce, Pub. No. 290 ["UCP"].[3]

On February 25, MHT mailed its written advice of the letter of credit establishment

---

1. Vishwa's application for documentary credit required that St. Lucia supply the following documents and shipment conditions as a prerequisite to payment:

> Six copies of signed invoices;
> One set of clean shipped on board bills of lading;
> Notification of shipment to Vishwa;
> A maritime insurance policy covering civil unrest, marine and war risks;
> A certificate of analysis from "LLOYDS" [sic] [of London] ["Lloyd's"]
confirming the quantity, quality and shipment of the aluminum scrap;
> Shipment by conference or first class vessel;
> Shipment by a non-Pakistani vessel.

2. The documentary and other requirements for the letter of credit set forth in Cochin's telex included:

> Sight drafts of the invoice value in duplicate;
> Six copies of the signed invoices showing that the aluminum was covered under
notice 44-ITC(PN) 79;
> One set of clean shipped on board bills of lading to the order of Cochin;
> A certificate of United States origin in triplicate;
> A certificate of analysis of the aluminum from Lloyd's;
> Shipment from a United States port to Bombay;
> A marine insurance policy issued by a first class insurance company;
> A packing list in triplicate;
> One set of nonnegotiable documents to be sent directly to Vishwa immediately
after shipment documented by a "cable advise" to Vishwa;
> Shipment by conference or first-class vessel.

3. The UCP was revised effective October 1, 1984. UCP, Int'l Chamber of Commerce, Publ. No. 400 (1983). It is axiomatic that the Court must ordinarily apply the law in effect at the time it renders its decision. . . . The letter of credit was, however, governed by the 1974 UCP pursuant to its express terms. . . . Although the application of the 1983 UCP would favor MHT, . . . it would not alter the Court's decision on the motions.

to St. Lucia and confirmed the amended letter on February 29. Cochin amended certain terms of the letter of four occasions in March and April 1980. MHT mailed its advices of these amendments to St. Lucia from March to May and sent copies to Cochin, which were received without comment.[5] The final amended letter of credit contained the following relevant terms and conditions:

> a.  Sight drafts of the invoice values;
> b.  Six copies of the signed invoices;
> c.  One set of clean shipped on board bills of lading;
> d.  A west European certificate of origin;
> e.  A certificate of analysis of the aluminum scrap from Lloyd's of London ["Lloyd's"] or another international testing agency;
> f.  Shipment from a west European port to Bombay;
> g.  A maritime insurance policy, covering note 429711, to be confirmed by St. Lucia's cable to Oriental Fire and General Insurance Co. ["Oriental"];
> h.  A packing list in triplicate;
> i.  One set of nonnegotiable documents to be sent to Vishwa and a confirming cable to Vishwa;
> j.  A certification from Lloyd's or the shipping company that the ship was a first class or approved non-Pakistani vessel;
> k.  St. Lucia's certification that it had complied with all terms of the letter of credit;
> l.  Shipment by May 31, 1980; and
> m.  Letter of credit expiration on June 15, 1980.

The aluminum was allegedly shipped in May 29, 1980 from Bremen, West Germany to Bombay on the M/V Betelguese. On June 2, St. Lucia established an account at a Manhattan office of Citibank, N.A. ["Citibank"], the collecting bank, in the name of St. Lucia Enterprises, Ltd. On June 9, St. Lucia presented MHT with documents required by the letter of credit and ten sight drafts amounting to $796,603.50, payable to St. Lucia Enterprises. The documents included five copies of the invoices, a clean shipped on board bill of lading, a St. Lucia certification that the aluminum was of west European origin, a certificate of analysis by an international Dutch materials testing agent, a telex confirmation of a telephone message to Oriental that the aluminum had been shipped to Bombay pursuant to covernote 4291, a packing list in triplicate, a St. Lucia certification that one set of nonnegotiable documents had been sent to Vishwa and that Vishwa had been advised by cable, certifications from the shipping company that the M/V Betelguese was an approved first class

---

5. Cochin sent telexes to MHT on March 3, March 15, March 27 and April 29 amending the letter to reflect that shipment should be made from a port in western Europe and extending the shipping date to May 31 and the letter of credit expiration date to June 15. The inspection clause was also changed to allow a certificate of analysis from Lloyd's or any international agency. Additionally, Cochin requested that St. Lucia produce a certificate that it had duly complied with all terms of the letter of credit.

MHT accurately conveyed these amendments to St. Lucia by written advices dated March 10, March 31, April 8 and May 2. The March 31 advice incorrectly identified the Oriental covernote as 4291, which MHT had properly designated as 429711 in its February 29 confirming advice. Notwithstanding MHT's allegation that Cochin cited covernote 4291, Cochin accurately used covernote 429711 in its telex amendments of February 29 and March 27. Each form of advice sent to St. Lucia and Cochin contained a beneficiary box with the following address: St. Lucia Enterprises, 210 Fifth Avenue, Suite No. 1102, New York, N.Y. 10010.

Panamanian vessel, and a St. Lucia cover letter specifying the documents submitted and requesting payment from MHT. The St. Lucia letter and certification were on the letterhead of "St. Lucia Enterprises" and were signed by "D Agney".

MHT compared the documents against the requirements of the letter and determined that they complied with all the terms and conditions. On June 13, MHT negotiated the drafts and issued a check for $798,000 payable to St. Lucia Enterprises. The check was indorsed St. Lucia Enterprises Ltd. and was deposited in the Citibank account on June 17, 1980. Citibank collected the check from MHT through normal banking channels. MHT debited Cochin's account for $798,000 on June 13. MHT sent a copy of its payment advice, the drafts and documents to Cochin by registered air mail on June 13. Unfortunately, Cochin apparently did not receive these documents until June 21. As it turned out, St. Lucia shipped nothing to Vishwa. The documentation submitted to MHT was fraudulent in every regard; indeed, the bills of lading, quality certification and vessel certification were issued by nonexistent corporations. St. Lucia received payment on the letter of credit and Cochin has been unable to locate any party connected with the fraudulent scheme.

Cochin sent a telex to MHT on June 18, inquiring whether St. Lucia had presented documents for negotiation. MHT responded by telex on June 20 that it had paid St. Lucia $798,000 on June 13 and had forwarded the documents to Cochin at that time. On June 21, Cochin sent the following telex to MHT:

> We acknowledge receipt of the documentu [*sic*] Stop We find certain discrepencies [*sic*] in the same Stop kindly donot [*sic*] make payment against the same until we telex you otherwise Stop

On June 23, MHT replied to Cochin's telex as follows:

> Reference your telex June 21 credit BB VN 4180 our 500748 Stop We note your telex fails to give reason fro [*sic*] rejection documents as required UCP Article 8 Stop According our records documents fully complied credit terms and beneficiary already paid therefore we cannot accept your refusal of documents.

By telex dated June 27, Cochin informed MHT of alleged defects in the documents apparently uncovered by Vishwa: (1) St. Lucia's cable to Oriental showed the wrong insurance covernote number of 4291 instead of 429711; (2) St. Lucia did not submit "proof" that a set of nonnegotiable documents and confirming cable had been sent to Vishwa; (3) only one set of documents showed the original certificate of origin whereas the rest included only photocopies; and (4) the invoice packing list and certificate of origin were not duly authenticated. Cochin also noted (5) the overpayment of $1,396.50. MHT credited Cochin's account for $1,396.50 and notified Cochin by telex on June 30.

By telex dated July 3, Cochin asked MHT to recredit its account for $796,603.50 and advised MHT that it was returning the letter of credit documents. Cochin also cited an additional discrepancy that (6) MHT had negotiated documents for St. Lucia Enterprises but that the letter of credit was established for St. Lucia Enterprises Ltd. On July 4, Cochin informed MHT by telex that the documents negotiated by MHT contained the following additional defects: (7) only five signed copies of the commercial invoices, rather than six, were forwarded and (8) documents were signed by "D Agney" without specifying his capacity at St. Lucia.

MHT responded by telex of July 14 that Cochin had failed to timely and properly specify the alleged documentary variances as required by article 8 of the 1974 UCP. The telex also noted that Cochin had failed to promptly return the documents or advise MHT that Cochin was holding the documents at MHT's disposal as required by the UCP. MHT asserted in a telex dated July 16 that it still had not received certain documents from Cochin. The parties exchanged additional telexes confirming and denying that payment was proper. Cochin[] . . . adds the additional allegations that (9) St. Lucia failed to indicate the documents submitted in drawing against the letter of credit, and (10) the shipping company certificate fails to indicate the vessel registration number. . . .

A letter of credit is a financing mechanism designed to allocate commercial credit risks whereby a bank or other issuer pays an amount of money to a beneficiary upon presentment of documents complying with specified conditions set forth in the letter. The beneficiary, typically the seller of goods to a buyer-customer, uses the letter to substitute the credit of the issuer for the credit of its customer. The customer applies for the letter of credit, specifies the terms of the letter and promises to reimburse the issuer upon honor of the beneficiary's draft. The letter of credit is thus an engagement by the issuer to the beneficiary to cover the customer's agreement to pay money under the customer-beneficiary contract. The reliability and fluidity of the letter of credit are maintained because the issuing bank is concerned exclusively with the documents, not the performance obligations created by the customer-beneficiary contract. Not a contract, the letter of credit has best been described as "a relationship with no perfect analogies but nevertheless a well defined set of rights and obligations." . . .

The central issue presented by this case is whether St. Lucia's demand for payment from MHT was in compliance with the conditions specified in the letter of credit. Cochin's action for wrongful honor is based upon its assertion that MHT's payment was improper because the documents submitted by St. Lucia did not comply with the letter. Neither the UCP nor the Uniform Commercial Code ["UCC"] specify whether a bank honoring a letter of credit should be guided by a standard of strict compliance with the terms of the letter.

The great weight of authority in this jurisdiction, and elsewhere, holds that an issuing or confirming bank is usually obligated to honor the beneficiary's draft only when the documents are in strict compliance with the terms of the letter of credit. . . . Thus, New York courts have traditionally held that letter of credit law requires a beneficiary to strictly comply with the conditions of the letter. . . . Additionally, this Court has previously held that "[a] bank's obligation in a letter of credit transaction is defined by the contract between the bank and its customer. It is obliged to pay only if the documents submitted strictly comply with the essential requirements of the letter of credit." *Corporacion de Mercadeo Agricola v. Pan American Fruit & Produce Corp.*, Memorandum Decision at 4-5, 75 Civ. 1611 (JMC) (S.D.N.Y. Apr. 13, 1976), *quoted in Corporacion de Mercadeo Agricola v. Mellon Bank*, 608 F.2d 43, 48 n. 1 (2d Cir. 1979). This principle of strict compliance has been recently reaffirmed by the Second Circuit and the New York Court of Appeals. *See Beyene v. Irving Trust Co.*, 762 F.2d 4, 6 (2d Cir. 1985) . . . ; *Voest-Alpine Int'l Corp. v. Chase Manhattan Bank, N.A.*, 707 F.2d 680, 682 (2d Cir. 1983) . . . ; *Marino Indus. v. Chase Manhattan Bank, N.A.*, 686 F.2d 1112, 114 (2d Cir. 1982) . . . ; *United Commodities-Greece v. Fidelity Int'l Bank*, 64 N.Y.2d 449, 455, 478 N.E.2d 172, 174, 489 N.Y.S.2d 31, 33 (1985). . . .

Courts and commentators have noted, however, that New York appears to maintain a bifurcated standard of compliance. . . . This approach calls for a strict compliance standard when the bank is sued by the beneficiary for wrongful dishonor but allows for a substantial compliance test when the bank is sued by the customer for wrongful honor. The stated rationale for the bifurcated standard is that it accords the bank flexibility in reacting to "a cross-fire of pressures . . . especially in times of falling commodity prices," . . . by limiting the liability burden on the bank, which might otherwise be caught between the "rock of a customer insisting on dishonor for highly technical reasons, and the hard place of a beneficiary threatening to sue for wrongful dishonor." . . .

MHT correctly asserts that Cochin was its "customer" in this transaction and therefore argues that a substantial compliance standard should be used to test its review of St. Lucia's documents. Although the ultimate customer, Vishwa, may be barred from a direct action against the confirming bank because of the absence of privity,[7] . . . it is undisputed that MHT owes a duty of care to Cochin, see UCP art. 7 (1974), art. 15 (1983). The question then is whether the bifurcated standard applies in a lawsuit by the issuing bank against the confirming bank.

The bifurcated standard is designed to permit the bank to retain flexibility in dealing with simultaneous customer pressure to reject and beneficiary pressure to accept. This discretion ostensibly preserves the bank's ministerial function of dealing solely with documents and the insulation of the letter of credit from performance problems. The difficulty with applying a bifurcated substantial compliance standard to actions against a confirming bank is reflected in the realities of commercial transactions. An issuing bank's good faith discretion is most required when its customer seeks to avoid payment by objecting to inconsequential defects. Although the bank should theoretically take comfort from a substantial compliance test if it honors the beneficiary's drafts over its customer's protests, the bank would usually not want to exercise its discretion for fear that its right to indemnity would be jeopardized or that its customer would break off existing banking relationships. Accordingly, the looser test of compliance does not in practice completely remove the issuer from its position between a rock and a hard place, but has a built-in safety valve against issuer misuse if the documents strictly comply with the letter.

A confirming bank, by contrast, is usually in relatively close geographical proximity with the beneficiary and typically chosen by the beneficiary because of past dealings. Although the confirming bank should not want to injure purposely its relationship with the issuing bank, the confirming bank would usually be somewhat biased in favor of the beneficiary. Additionally, the confirming bank is not in privity with the ultimate customer, who would be most likely to become dissatisfied if a conflict is resolved by the confirming bank. A biased issuing bank that in bad faith uncovers "microscopic discrepancies," . . . would still be forced to honor the letter if the documents are in strict compliance. A biased confirming bank, however, can overlook certain larger variances in its discretion without concomitant liability. A safety mechanism against confirming bank misuse is therefore not present and it would be inequitable to let a confirming bank exercise such discretion under a protective umbrella of substantial compliance. Moreover, the facts of this case do not warrant the looser standard. MHT was not faced with a "cross-fire of pressures" or concern that a disgruntled "customer" would refuse reimbursement because Cochin had sufficient funds on deposit with MHT. The Court also notes that the bifurcated substantial compliance standard is only a suggested approach by courts and commentators and has not actually been followed by New York courts.[8] Finally, in *Voest-Alpine Int'l Corp. v. Chase Manhattan Bank, N.A., supra,* the

---

7. The UCP suggests the better view, however, that there is a duty running from the confirming bank to the ultimate customer. *See* UCP art. 12(a) (1974), art. 20(a) (1983) ("Banks utilizing the services of another bank for the purpose of giving effect to the instructions of the applicant for the credit do so for the account and at the risk of [such applicant].") art. 12(c) (1974), art. 20(c) (1983) (customer indemnification of the confirming bank). . . .

8. In discussing New York's bifurcated standard, courts and commentators have mistakenly cited each other and the following cases as support for the proposition that New York courts use a bifurcated approach. . . . A closer reading of these cases suggests otherwise.

Court implied that confirming bank actions should be judged under a strict standard in wrongful dishonor as well as wrongful honor actions. It ruled that if the confirming bank waived discrepancies in the drafts, the confirming bank would not be entitled to reimbursement from the issuing bank, which timely discovered the mistakes, because "the issuing bank[] was entitled to strict compliance." 707 F.2d at 686. Accordingly, the Court finds that an issuing bank's action for wrongful honor against a confirming bank is governed by a strict compliance standard.

An analysis of the ten listed variances suggests that MHT failed to pick up two discrepancies not strictly complying with the letter of credit terms. The first alleged defect concerns St. Lucia's cable to Oriental using the wrong covernote number of 4291 instead of 429711. The insurance was procured by Vishwa and the cable was intended to give notice to Oriental of the shipment by quoting the proper covernote. The failure to provide the correct covernote was not inconsequential as the mistake could have resulted in Oriental's justifiable refusal to honor Vishwa's insurance policy. This mistake may appear immaterial on its face, but in *Beyene v. Irving Trust Co.*, . . . the Second Circuit affirmed the dishonor of a letter of credit on the sole ground that the misspelling of Mohammed So*f*an as Mohammed So*r*an on the bill of lading constituted a material discrepancy. . . .

The sixth defect is that the payment was made on documents presented by St. Lucia Enterprises despite the fact that the letter of credit was established for St. Lucia Enterprises, *Ltd*. The result is similar to that caused by the deviation of the Oriental covernote. Although there does not appear to be any difference between the two entities, it is not clear that the "intended" party was paid. The difference in names could also possibly be an indicia of unreliability or forgery. . . .

In the final analysis, only the variances as to the Oriental covernote and the name St. Lucia Enterprises, Ltd., appear not to comply strictly with the letter of credit conditions. The inquiry is not ended at this point because courts in this Circuit have applied concepts of equitable waiver and estoppel in cases of issuer dishonor. Application of estoppel has been premised upon discoverable nonconformities that could have been cured by the beneficiary before the expiration of the letter, but were not raised by the issuing bank until its dishonor.

---

In *Bank of Montreal* [*v. Recknagel*, 109 N.Y. 482, 17 N.E. 217 (1888)], the New York Court of Appeals applied a strict compliance standard when it denied recovery in an action by the issuing bank for reimbursement from its customer who claimed that the bank wrongfully honored the letter of credit. The Court held that the draft advices describing shipments as "bales of hemp" were insufficient to comply with the letter of credit condition for invoices and bills of lading of "bales manilla hemp". In [*Bank of New York & Trust Co. v.*] *Atterbury Bros.*, [226 A.D. 117, 234 N.Y.S. 442 (1st Dep't 1929), *aff'd* 253 N.Y. 569, 171 N.E. 786 (1930)], the plaintiff bank successfully sued its customer for reimbursement. The Court acknowledged that the bank took a "risk" by paying to shipping documents issued to "A. James Brown" when the letter of credit specified "Arthur James Brown:. The parties, however, conceded that the intended person signed the documents. The "conclusive" points on the issue of "casein" versus "unground casein" was resolved by an "estoppel" against the customer because it had examined the documents prior to the bank's payment. The remaining objections, characterized as "afterthoughts", were dismissed on grounds of laches and because there was no possibility that a missing certificate could have misled the paying bank. . . . In *North American* [*Mars. Export Assocs. v. Chase Nat'l Bank*, 77 F.Supp. 55 (S.D.N.Y. 1948)], Judge Medina granted summary judgment to the bank against the beneficiary under a "strict compliance" standard. In *Chairmasters*, [*Inc. v. Public Nat'l Bank & Trust Co.*, 283 A.D. 704, 127 N.Y.S.2d 806 (1st Dep't 1954)], the court granted summary judgment to the defendant bank under the basic tenet that the bank's obligation to review documents for compliance is totally separate from the underlying transaction. . .

The banks were estopped from asserting the variances because of previous assurances to the beneficiary of documentary compliance or because of silence coupled with the retention of nonconforming documents for an unreasonably long time after the beneficiary had submitted its drafts for payment. . . .

Application of waiver has been predicated upon situations in which the issuer justifies dishonor on grounds later found to have been unjustified. In these instances, all other possible grounds for dishonor are deemed to have been waived. . . . Waiver of nonconforming documents can also be found from statements by officials of the issuing bank or from customer authorization. . . .

. . . The UCP expressly provides that an issuer has the obligation to immediately notify the beneficiary by "expeditious means" of any reason for noncompliance and the physical disposition of the disputed documents. UCP art. 8(e) (1974), 16(d) (1983). The UCP also implicitly invites cure of any documentary deficiencies apparent before the letter of credit expiration by issuer notification to the beneficiary. . . . In the context of this case, "[a]n equitable approach to a strict compliance standard demands that the issuer promptly communicate all documentary defects to the beneficiary [or confirming bank], when time exists under the letter to remedy the nonconformity." . . . The Court finds that Cochin is precluded from claiming wrongful honor because of its failure to comply with the explicit notice and affirmative obligation provisions of the UCP and its implicit duty to promptly cure discoverable defects in MHT's confirming advices to St. Lucia.

The issuing bank must give notice "without delay" that the documents received are (1) being "held at the disposal" of the remitting or confirming bank or (2) "are being returned" to the second bank. UCP art. 8(e) (1974), art. 16(d) (1983). An issuing bank that fails to return or hold the documents for the second bank is precluded from asserting that the negotiation and payment were not effected in accordance with the letter of credit requirements. UCP art. 8(f) (1974), 16(e) (1983). . . . The UCP also directs that an issuing bank intending to claim noncompliance shall have a "reasonable time" to examine the documents after presentment and to determine whether to make such a claim. UCP art. 8(d) (1974), art. 16(c) (1983). The revised UCP allows explicitly for the imposition of the 16(e) sanction for failure to comply with the "reasonable time" provision as well; however, this interpretation is not clear under the parties' explicit choice of law, the 1974 UCP.

Neither the 1983 UCP nor the 1974 UCP defines what constitutes a "reasonable time" to determine if the documents are defective or notice "without delay" that the documents are being held or returned. When the UCP is silent or ambiguous, analogous UCC provisions may be utilized if consistent with the UCP. . . . The UCC provides for a period of three banking days for the issuer to honor or reject a documentary draft for payment. N.Y. U.C.C. § 5-112(1)(a) (McKinney's 1964) (issuer-beneficiary relationship). The letter of credit was issued subject to the 1974 UCP but it is silent as to what law governs its terms. Cochin cites to Indian statutes interpreting a "reasonable time" as a factual question depending on the nature of the negotiable instrument and the usual course of dealing. Under the circumstances of this case, however, it appears that under New York's comparative interest choice of law approach, New York UCC law would apply. . . .

Cochin's failure to promptly notify MHT that it had returned the documents or that it was holding them at MHT's disposal thus violates the UCP. Cochin's telex of June 21 states that there are certain discrepancies in St. Lucia's documents, but Cochin did not advise MHT that it was returning the documents to MHT until the July 3 telex. The "reasonable time" three-day period should be the maximum time allowable for the notification "without delay" requirement. Because June 21, 1980 was a Saturday, Cochin should have complied with its notice obligations no later than June 26. The passage of an additional week before compliance precludes Cochin from asserting its wrongful honor claim. Moreover, it was not until June 27 that Cochin first specified any reason for its dishonor argument, and the St. Lucia Enterprises, *Ltd.* omission was not noted until July 4.

Cochin proposes that its failure to timely notify MHT was not violative of UCP or letter of credit policy because it caused no additional loss to MHT. Cochin argues that the defects were in any case incurable by the time Cochin received the documents, because St. Lucia had disappeared with the letter of credit proceeds. Although the UCP is not explicit, the Court finds that these provisions should be applied identically to an issuing bank's obligations to a confirming bank after the latter's honor of a demand for payment. Cochin's contention ignores the expectation in the international financial community that the parties will live up to their statutory obligations and is at odds with the basic letter of credit tenet that banks deal solely with documents, not in goods. Cochin's argument would defeat the letter of credit's function of being a swift, fluid and reliable financing device. . . .

Finally, the two documentary discrepancies could have been anticipated by Cochin and were curable before the demand for payment. Cochin received a copy of MHT's incorrect March 31 advice to St. Lucia, which mistakenly listed the insurance covernotes as 4291. Similarly, Cochin received copies of all of MHT's advices to St. Lucia, which omitted the "Ltd." from the corporate name. Cochin had sufficient notice and time to correct MHT's confirming defects to St. Lucia and is therefore estopped from asserting them. Although MHT failed to strictly comply with the letter requirements, Cochin's failure to perform its affirmative obligations precludes an action for wrongful honor under the UCP and by letter of credit estoppel.

**Notes and Comments 9.9.** *Uniform Customs and Practice (UCP).* The UCP consists of rules formulated under the auspices of the International Chamber of Commerce (ICC) and are typically referenced in a letter of credit, thus becoming part of the terms. The UCP rules are regularly updated, most recently on 1 January 1994; the current version is called UCP 500. *See* C. Del Busto, ed., ICC Guide to Documentary Credit Operations (1994); E. Ellinger, *The Uniform Customs and Practice for Documentary Credits–The 1993 Revision,* 1994 Lloyd's Maritime & Comp. L.Q. 377; R. Rendell, *New ICC Rules Impact Letters of Credit,* 22 Int'l Fin. L. Rev. 28 (1994); J. Byrne, *Fundamental Issues in the Unification and Harmonization of Letter of Credit Law,* 37 Loyola L. Rev. 1 (1991). Note 2 in the *United Bank Ltd.* opinion discusses the role of the UCP–incorporated by contract or as a usage of trade in international commerce–in an L/C. The L/C involved in *Bank of Cochin* was ostensibly governed by the UCP, pursuant to its own express terms. (Note 3, *supra.*) In both cases, the assumption is that the L/C transaction is governed by Article 5 of the UCC unless the parties agree to apply the UCP. A similar approach is apparently taken in English commercial law. *See* Robert Wight & Alan Ward, *The Liability of Banks in Documentary Credit Transactions under English Law,* [1998] J. INT'L BANKING L. 387.

**9.10.** *Electronic transmittal of L/C documents–Revised UCC Article 5.* Under appropriate circumstances, L/C documents may, of course, be transmitted in electronic form rather than paper form. Electronic transmittal in L/C practice was facilitated by the 1995 revision of Article 5 approved by the National Conference of Commissioners on Uniform State Laws and the American Law Institute. When the original Article 5 was drafted, it was written for paper transactions and before many innovations in letters of credit. In current practice, electronic and other media are used extensively. Indeed, changes in usage, practice, and participants have been significant and pervasive, and the revised Article 5 sought to take these changes into account. Under the revised provisions, any "document" involved in the transaction expressly may be "presented in a written or other medium permitted by the letter of credit."[9] Likewise, the L/C itself expressly may be issued "in any form that is a record,"[10] which is defined to mean "information that is inscribed on a tangible medium, or that is *stored in an electronic or other medium* and is retrievable in perceivable form."[11]

**9.11.** *Electronic transmittal of L/C documents–UCP.* Treatment of electronic transmittal of L/C documents is handled somewhat differently under UCP practice. In April 2002, the ICC issued the eUCP (version 1.0), a new electronic supplement to the ICC's UCP 500. Consider the problems posed in the questions that follow these excerpts from the eUCP:

**eUCP Version 1.0**
**Supplement to UCP 500 for Electronic Presentation**
in force as of 1 April 2002

Article e1 Scope of the eUCP

a. The Supplement to the Uniform Customs and Practice for Documentary Credits for Electronic Presentation (eUCP) supplements the Uniform Customs and Practice for Documentary Credits (1993 Revision ICC Publication No. 500.) ("UCP") in order to accommodate presentation of electronic records alone or in combination with paper documents.

b. The eUCP shall apply as a supplement to the UCP where the Credit indicates that it is subject to eUCP.

c. This version is Version 1.0. A Credit must indicate the applicable version of the eUCP. If it does not do so, it is subject to the version in effect on the date the Credit is issued or, if made subject to eUCP by an amendment accepted by the Beneficiary, on the date of that amendment.

Article e2 Relationship of the eUCP to the UCP

a. A Credit subject to the eUCP ("eUCP Credit") is also subject to the UCP without express incorporation of the UCP.

b. Where the eUCP applies, its provisions shall prevail to the extent that they would produce a result different from the application of the UCP.

c. If an eUCP Credit allows the Beneficiary to choose between presentation of paper documents or electronic records and it chooses to present only paper documents, the UCP alone shall apply to that presentation. If only paper documents are permitted under an eUCP Credit, the UCP alone shall apply.

Article e3 Definitions

a. Where the following terms are used in the UCP, for the purposes of applying the UCP to an electronic record presented under an eUCP Credit, the term:

i. "appears on its face" and the like shall apply to examination of the data content of an electronic record.

ii. "document" shall include an electronic record.

iii. "place for presentation" of electronic records means an electronic address.

iv. "sign" and the like shall include an electronic signature.

v. "superimposed", "notation" or "stamped" means data content whose supplementary character is apparent in an electronic record.

---

9. UCC § 5-102(a)(6) (1995 Rev.).

10. *Id.* § 5-104.

11. *Id.* § 5-102(a)(14) (emphasis added).

b. The following terms used in the eUCP shall have the following meanings:

i. "electronic record" means

• data created, generated, sent, communicated, received, or stored by electronic means

• that is capable of being authenticated as to the apparent identity of a sender and the apparent source of the data contained in it, and as to whether it has remained complete and unaltered, and

• is capable of being examined for compliance with the terms and conditions of the eUCP Credit.

ii. "electronic signature" means a data process attached to or logically associated with an electronic record and executed or adopted by a person in order to identify that person and to indicate that person's authentication of the electronic record.

iii. "format" means the data organisation in which the electronic record is expressed or to which it refers.

iv. "paper document" means a document in a traditional paper form.

v. "received" means the time when an electronic record enters the information system of the applicable recipient in a form capable of being accepted by that system. Any acknowledgement of receipt does not imply acceptance or refusal of the electronic record under an eUCP Credit.

Article e4 Format

An eUCP Credit must specify the formats in which electronic records are to be presented. If the format of the electronic record is not so specified, it may be presented in any format.

Article e5 Presentation

a. An eUCP Credit allowing presentation of:

i. electronic records must state a place tor presentation of the electronic records.

ii. both electronic records and paper documents must also state a place for presentation of the paper documents.

b. Electronic records may be presented separately and need not be presented at the same time.

c. If an eUCP Credit allows for presentation of one or more electronic records, the Beneficiary is responsible for providing a notice to the Bank to which presentation is made signifying when the presentation is complete. The notice of completeness may be given as an electronic record or paper document and must identify the eUCP Credit to which it relates. Presentation is deemed not to have been made if the Beneficiary's notice is not received.

d.          i. Each presentation of an electronic record and the presentation of paper documents under an eUCP Credit must identify the eUCP Credit under which it is presented.

ii. A presentation not so identified may be treated as not received.

e. If the Bank to which presentation is to be made is open but its system is unable to receive a transmitted electronic record on the stipulated expiry date and/or the last day of the period of time after the date of shipment for presentation, as the case may be, the Bank will be deemed to be closed and the date for presentation and/or the expiry date shall be extended to the first following banking day on which such Bank is able to receive an electronic record. If the only electronic record remaining to be presented is the notice of completeness, it may be given by telecommunications or by paper document and will be deemed timely, provided that it is sent before the bank is able to receive an electronic record.

f. An electronic record that cannot be authenticated is deemed not to nave been presented.

Article e6 Examination

. . .

c. The inability of the Issuing Bank, or Confirming Bank, if any, to examine an electronic record in a format required by the eUCP credit or, it no format is required, to examine it in the format presented is not a basis for refusal.

Article e7 Notice of Refusal

a.          i. The time period for the examination of documents commences on the banking day following the banking day on which the Beneficiary s notice of completeness is received.

ii. If the time for presentation of documents or the notice of completeness is extended, the time for the examination of documents commences on the first following banking day on which the bank to which presentation is to be made is able to receive the notice of completeness.

b. If an issuing Bank, the Confirming Bank, if any, or a Nominated Bank acting on their behalf, provides a notice of refusal of a presentation which includes electronic records and does not receive instructions from the party to which notice of refusal is given within 30 calendar days from the date the notice of refusal is given for the disposition of the electronic records, the Bank shall return any paper documents not previously returned to the presenter but may dispose of the electronic records in any manner deemed appropriate without any responsibility.

**a.** Buyer and Seller sign a contract for the sale of goods providing for payment *via* a letter of credit (L/C), but the contract does not say anything about the method of presenting documents for payment under the L/C. Seller sends Issuer Bank a pdf.doc containing a draft and supporting documents that would clearly have satisfied the L/C conditions for payment if they had been paper documents. Bank's employee stares at the pdf.doc on the computer screen, but does not process Seller's payment demand. The L/C eventually expires. Would Bank be liable to Seller under the revised UCC Article 5? Under the UCP?

**b.** Buyer and Seller specify in their contract that the L/C is subject to UCP 500. Seller sends Issuer Bank a pdf.doc containing a draft and supporting documents that would clearly have satisfied the L/C conditions for payment if they had been paper documents. Bank's employee looks at the pdf.doc on the computer screen, but does not process Seller's payment demand. The L/C eventually expires. Is Bank liable to Seller?

**c.** Buyer and Seller specify in their contract that the L/C is subject to "the eUCP to the extent that its provisions are different from those of the Uniform Commercial Code [(UCC) revised] article 5," which is the L/C law in the U.S. jurisdiction where Buyer has its principal place of business. Does UCP 500 or UCC art. 5 apply to this transaction?

**d.** Buyer and Seller specify in their contract that the L/C is subject to the eUCP. They do not specify a format for electronic presentation of documents. Seller sends Issuer Bank documents in pdf format. Bank does not have Adobe

Acrobat on its computer system and cannot open the pdf document files. What are Bank's rights and responsibilities in this transaction?

**9.12.** Issuance, advising and confirming of L/Cs constitute traditional roles of banks in international transactions. To what extent are L/Cs, functionally, a form of lending? What other functions might these arrangements perform? To the extent that they are a form of lending, what are the regulatory implications? Consider the following excerpt.

## Comptroller's Handbook for National Bank Examiners,
Section 811.1

> The examiner must be concerned with legal limitations on certain categories of letters of credit. In 1974, standby letters of credit became subject to the limitations of 12 USC 84 and must be combined with any other nonexcepted loans to the account party by the issuing bank. . . . [S]tandby letters of credit issued on behalf of an affiliate are extensions of credit subject to 12 USC 371c (Loans to Affiliates). Commercial letters of credit are also subject to 12 USC 371c when they are drawn upon and not reimbursed prior to or simultaneously with payment of the letter of credit.

**9.13.** Documentary L/Cs are given relatively favorable treatment under the risk-weighted capital adequacy guidelines developed under the auspices of the Bank for International Settlements. *See* Chapter 3, § 3, *supra*. In light of the cases like *Maurice O'Meara*, *United Bank*, and *Bank of Cochin*, are documentary L/Cs riskier than their treatment under the guidelines would suggest?

**9.14.** Is risk a primary factor in regulating this activity? What other regulatory considerations might be relevant? Consider the following excerpt from the Comptroller's regulations.

## Comptroller of the Currency
12 C.F.R. § 7.1016

§ 7.1016 Independent undertakings to pay against documents.

(a) General authority. A national bank may issue and commit to issue letters of credit and other independent undertakings within the scope of the applicable laws or rules of practice recognized by law.[1] Under such letters of credit and other independent undertakings, the bank's obligation to honor depends upon the presentation of specified documents

---

1. Examples of such laws or rules of practice include: The applicable version of Article 5 of the Uniform Commercial Code (UCC) (1962, as amended 1990) or revised Article 5 of the UCC (as amended 1995) (available from West Publishing Co., 1/800/328-4880); the Uniform Customs and Practice for Documentary Credits (International Chamber of Commerce (ICC) Publication No. 500) (available from ICC Publishing, Inc., 212/206-1150; http://www.iccwbo.org); the International Standby Practices (ISP98) (ICC Publication No. 590) (available from the Institute of International Banking Law & Practice, 301/869-9840; http://www.iiblp.org); the United Nations Convention on Independent Guarantees and Stand-by Letters of Credit (adopted by the U.N. General Assembly in 1995 and signed by the U.S. in 1997) (available from the U.N. Commission on International Trade Law, 212/963-5353); and the Uniform Rules for Bank-to-Bank Reimbursements Under Documentary Credits (ICC Publication No. 525) (available from ICC Publishing, Inc., 212/206-1150; http://www.iccwbo.org); as any of the foregoing may be amended from time to time.

and not upon nondocumentary conditions or resolution of questions of fact or law at issue between the applicant and the beneficiary. A national bank may also confirm or otherwise undertake to honor or purchase specified documents upon their presentation under another person's independent undertaking within the scope of such laws or rules.

(b) Safety and soundness considerations--(1) Terms. As a matter of safe and sound banking practice, banks that issue independent undertakings should not be exposed to undue risk. At a minimum, banks should consider the following:

(i) The independent character of the undertaking should be apparent from its terms (such as terms that subject it to laws or rules providing for its independent character);

(ii) The undertaking should be limited in amount;

(iii) The undertaking should:

(A) Be limited in duration; or

(B) Permit the bank to terminate the undertaking either on a periodic basis (consistent with the bank's ability to make any necessary credit assessments) or at will upon either notice or payment to the beneficiary; or

(C) Entitle the bank to cash collateral from the applicant on demand (with a right to accelerate the applicant's obligations, as appropriate); and

(iv) The bank either should be fully collateralized or have a post-honor right of reimbursement from the applicant or from another issuer of an independent undertaking. Alternatively, if the bank's undertaking is to purchase documents of title, securities, or other valuable documents, the bank should obtain a first priority right to realize on the documents if the bank is not otherwise to be reimbursed.

(2) Additional considerations in special circumstances. Certain undertakings require particular protections against credit, operational, and market risk:

(i) In the event that the undertaking is to honor by delivery of an item of value other than money, the bank should ensure that market fluctuations that affect the value of the item will not cause the bank to assume undue market risk;

(ii) In the event that the undertaking provides for automatic renewal, the terms for renewal should be consistent with the bank's ability to make any necessary credit assessments prior to renewal; and

(iii) In the event that a bank issues an undertaking for its own account, the underlying transaction for which it is issued must be within the bank's authority and comply with any safety and soundness requirements applicable to that transaction.

(3) Operational expertise. The bank should possess operational expertise that is commensurate with the sophistication of its independent undertaking activities.

(4) Documentation. The bank must accurately reflect the bank's undertakings in its records, including any acceptance or deferred payment or other absolute obligation arising out of its contingent undertaking.

(c) Coverage. An independent undertaking within the meaning of this section is not subject to the provisions of § 7.1017.

**Note and Comments 9.15.** Could the parties to the underlying contract involved in *Maurice O'Meara Co.* have included contractual language concerning the letter of credit and its required documentation that would have resolved the buyer's concern over the quality of the paper? If the parties entered into a contract today, could they have included a provision requiring National Park Bank of New York to inspect the goods and to certify whether they were of the requisite quality?

**9.16.** *Standby Letters of Credit.* In U.S. banking practice, foreign branches of U.S.

banks are authorized to issue guarantees to the extent that local banks are so authorized.[12] In U.S.-based international banking, the equivalent device is the standby L/C. Should its functional equivalence to a third-party guarantee make the standby L/C an impermissible transaction for U.S.-based banks? Consider the following excerpts.

## Henry Harfield, Legality of Guaranty Letters of Credit,
[1974 Transfer Binder] Fed. Banking L. Rep. (CCH) ¶ 96,301 (July 1, 1974)

... For the reasons set forth hereafter, I disagree with the proposition that standby letters of credit are unlawful; I am in agreement with the proposition that the issuance and management of such commitments should be regulated in the interest of prudent banking and the exercise of sound judgment; I disagree with the suggestion that imposition of reserve requirements is an appropriate regulatory tool for that purpose. . . .

... [I]t should be apparent that the line of demarcation between "standby" and "traditional commercial" letters of credit should be drawn between a letter of credit used as a payment mechanism and a letter of credit used as a financing mechanism.

The *traditional commercial letter of credit* . . . is essentially a payment mechanism. The letter of credit is ancillary to a commercial contract or similar arrangement between the bank's customer and the beneficiary of the letter of credit, and the expectation is that the bank's customer will be ready, able and willing to make whatever payment is contemplated by that contract. The bank's function is to make payment on behalf of its customer. In most instances, the bank uses the customer's money to make the payment, that is to say, it charges the amount paid to the beneficiary against a credit balance maintained with it by its customer simultaneously with the payment made under the credit. An arrangement of this character is not a financing transaction because the customer is at no time indebted to the bank.

A *standby letter of credit* . . . is clearly a financing mechanism rather than a payment mechanism. Such credits, *i.e.*, those used to guarantee commercial paper, are *ab initio*, integral parts of a financing transaction. The sole purpose of issuing the credit is to assist the bank's customer in borrowing money, and as the sole condition upon which the bank must pay under the credit is the customer's default in repaying borrowed money, it is evident that the net effect is to substitute the bank for the holder of the commercial paper as a creditor of the bank's customer. . . .

The standby letter of credit, then, . . . should properly be characterized as a letter of credit incidental to a financial transaction designed to assure that borrowed money will be repaid, rather than to assure payment for goods, services, or other values. It is in that sense that I shall use the term "standby letter of credit" hereafter.

*Standby Letters of Credit are Lawful*. In my opinion, issuance and performance of such letters is [*sic*] an essential part of the business of banking and is [*sic*] lawful for national banks.

The fact that such instruments are intended to and do serve the purpose of guaranties is completely immaterial. Every letter of credit, including those that facilitate a sale of goods or merchandise, has the attributes of a guaranty and some of the earliest forms of letters of credit in use in the United States were explicitly characterized as guaranties. *See, e.g., Omaha National v. First National of St. Paul*, 39 Ill. 428 (1871).

The result achieved by an instrument should not affect the legal character of the instrument itself, particularly where, as here, the result is perfectly lawful. In other words, a contract of guaranty, unlike a contract in restraint in trade, is itself entirely lawful. The

---

12. *See, e.g.*, Chapter 5, *supra*, at 116 (excerpting 12 C.F.R. § 211.4(a)(1)).

question relates to the corporate power to make a lawful contract. The legal validity of a standby letter of credit, then, should be tested by determination of whether the transaction is a part of the business of banking or is an unauthorized excursion into, *e.g.*, the business of suretyship. That determination should be informed by inspection of the obligation that a bank has undertaken.

A letter of credit engages the direct and primary liability of the bank, whereas the liability imposed by a guaranty or surety bond is secondary....

This distinction is more than formal. A bank's liability under a letter of credit is dependent upon performance of the terms and conditions stated in the letter of credit, without reference to any other contract, agreement, or arrangement. Liability under a guaranty or surety bond, on the other hand, is dependent upon a determination as to whether an extraneous contract, agreement or arrangement has been performed in accordance with its own terms....

A letter of credit, then, whether it be incidental to a commercial transaction or a financial transaction, is a lawful exercise of a national bank's power to conduct the business of banking....

Recent decisions, as well as the current interpretations by the office of the Comptroller of the Currency and the Board of Governors of the Federal Reserve System, clearly establish that the issuance of standby letters of credit is a lawful and wholesome banking business.

*Barclays v. Mercantile Nat'l Bank*, 481 F.2d 1224 (5th Cir. 1973), is probably the most instructive case, inasmuch as the precise issue under consideration here was clearly presented and fully briefed before the Fifth Circuit Court of Appeals.... Mercantile National Bank, which had confirmed a non-bank letter of credit issued in favor of Barclays in support of a loan from Barclays to the account party, argued that its engagement to Barclays pursuant to its confirmation was a guarantee and, therefore, void as an *ultra vires* act. The court rejected that argument and held Mercantile liable to Barclays as a confirming bank. The opinion stressed the propriety of using letters of credit to support transactions in intangibles. (*See* 481 F.2d at 1231-1232, 1239-1240.)

Similarly the United States District Court for the Northern District of California in *Wichita Eagle & Beacon Pub. Co. v. Pacific Nat'l Bank*, 342 F.Supp. 332, 338 (N.D.Cal. 1971), upheld the validity of the use of a letter of credit in lieu of a performance bond with the following comments:

> "Contrary to the Bank's implication, the letter of credit has long been a flexible device utilized by the commercial community to meet its needs in a wide variety of situations.... One of the reasons behind the growth and spread of the letter of credit as a commercial tool has been the willingness of the courts to align case law with progressive and current commercial practice. The very type of letter of credit being questioned here by the Bank as a radical departure from traditional usage is but another example of the commercial community pouring old wines into new flasks."

On appeal, the Court of Appeals for the Ninth Circuit . . . , holding that the particular instrument was a guaranty letter rather than a letter of credit, enforced the guaranty. The Per Curiam opinion stated:

> "The instrument involved here strays too far from the basic purpose of letters of credit, namely, providing a means of assuring payment cheaply by eliminating the need for the issuer to police the underlying contract.... The instrument

neither evidences an intent that payment be made merely on presentation on [of] a draft nor specifies the documents required for termination or payment. To the contrary, it requires the actual existence in fact of most of the conditions specified: for termination or reduction, that the city have refused a building permit; for payment, that the lessee have failed to perform the terms of the lease and have failed to correct that default, in addition to an affidavit of notice. . . .

"It would hamper rather than advance the extension of the letter of credit concept to new situations if an instrument such as this were held to be a letter of credit." (14 UCC Rep. at 138 [(citations omitted)].)

Nevertheless, and notwithstanding that "the instrument is an ordinary guaranty contract" (14 UCC Rep. at 137) issued by a national bank, the Court sustained its validity and enforced its terms.

Without attempting to catalog all decisions on point, I note that the respective courts in *Victory Carriers Inc. v. United States*, 467 F.2d 1334 (Ct.Cl. 1972), approved the use of a letter of credit in place of a performance bond and in *Fidelity Bank v. Lutheran Mutual Life Ins. Co.*, 465 F.2d 211 (10th Cir. 1972), approved the use of a letter of credit to assure compliance by a borrower with the terms and conditions of a loan commitment. *See also* Comptroller of the Currency Interpretive Ruling No. 7.7420, 12 C.F.R. § 7.7420; Fed. Res. Board Doc. 73-12664, 38 Fed. Reg. 1665 (1973). . . .

**Notes and Comments 9.17.** Professor Harfield's opinion notwithstanding, there are some significant differences between commercial and standby L/Cs. Figure 9.2, *infra*, illustrates the structure of the standby L/C transaction.

**9.18.** In light of these differences, to what extent should standby L/Cs be treated like commercial L/Cs? Do the legal principles applied in cases involving commercial L/Cs apply equally well to the corresponding situation of standby L/Cs? Consider the cases beginning after the figure.

---

Figure 9.2
Typical Standby Letter of Credit

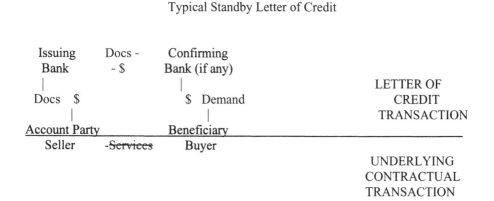

SELLER *FAILS* TO PERFORM     LETTER OF CREDIT TRIGGERED

Seller of services allegedly breaches contract to provide services to Buyer

Buyer submits demand and draft to C bank
C bank pays Buyer on demand and draft
C bank submits demand and draft to I bank
I bank reimburses C bank
I bank makes notifies Seller of demand and payment
Seller reimburses I bank

*Source*: MICHAEL P. MALLOY, PRINCIPLES OF BANK REGULATION § 9.21 (2d ed. 2003).

---

## American Insurance Ass'n v. Clarke
### 865 F.2d 278 (D.C.Cir. 1989)

Buckley, Circuit Judge:
[The AIA challenged the Comptroller of the Currency's approval of a proposal by Citibank to form a municipal bond insurance subsidiary, referred to in the opinion as "AMBAC". The D.C. Circuit upheld the Comptroller's argument that issuing "standby credits" to ensure payment of municipal bonds was an "incidental power" under the authority of the National Bank Act.]

We do not think the Comptroller acted irrationally in concluding that AMBAC's municipal bond insurance was part of the business of banking, sufficiently similar to credit services routinely performed by banks. The Comptroller, in his expert financial judgment, concluded that AMBAC's proposed use of standby credits to insure municipal bonds was functionally equivalent to the issuance of a standby letter of credit, a device long recognized as within the business of banking.

To understand the Comptroller's comparison of AMBAC's standby credits with standby letters of credit, we begin with a brief review of the operation of letters of credit, which come in two basic forms: commercial and standby. A basic function of the commercial letter of credit is to make it possible for a seller to ship goods to a buyer whose credit-worthiness is unknown to him in confidence that the goods will be paid for.

> Stripped to its essentials, the [commercial letter of credit] transaction runs as follows: the buyer arranges for a bank–whose credit the seller will accept -- to issue a letter of credit in which the bank agrees to pay drafts drawn on it by the seller if, but only if, such drafts are accompanied by specified documents, such as bills of lading or air freight receipts, representing title to the goods that are the subject matter of the transaction between buyer and seller. The bank undertakes this obligation for a specified period of time.

Verkuil, *Bank Solvency and Guaranty Letters of Credit*, 25 Stan. L. Rev. 716, 718 (1973). The obligation created by the letter of credit is absolute. Upon the presentation of the stipulated documents by the seller, the bank is required to make the payment irrespective of any counterclaims the buyer might have against the seller.

A standby letter of credit represents the other side of the commercial letter of credit coin. Whereas the latter is used to guarantee payment upon performance, the former guarantees payment upon a failure to perform. Thus, by way of illustration, if a purchaser is concerned over the seller's ability to deliver the contracted goods on schedule, the seller may ask his bank to open a standby letter of credit in favor of the buyer. If the buyer subsequently presents documents showing that the seller has failed to deliver the goods, his bank is obliged to pay the buyer the amount specified in the standby letter. The bank will be reimbursed by the seller.

Although the two varieties of letters of credit differ, they serve the same essential purpose: to facilitate transactions by substituting the credit of the bank for that of one of the contracting parties. Banks have long been permitted to provide this form of credit. *See, e.g.,* 12 C.F.R. §7.7016 (1988) (letters of credit); *First Empire Bank-New York v. FDIC,* 572 F.2d 1361, 1367 (9th Cir.) (standby credits), *cert. denied,* 439 U.S. 919 (1978); 12 C.F.R. §32.2(e) (1988) (recognizing standby letters of credit as service provided by banks). As one commentator has explained:

> The nature of the banking business implies the lawful power to make loans. A necessary incident of that power is the power to commit to make the loan at a future date. If that future commitment is made to a third party, it amounts to a present loan of credit. So long as the bank's promise is made for the account of its customer, and is a money promise, its characterization or form should be immaterial in determining its validity. . . .

H. HARFIELD, BANK CREDITS AND ACCEPTANCES 165-66 (5th ed. 1974).

## American Bell International, Inc. v. The Islamic Republic of Iran
### 474 F.Supp. 420 (S.D.N.Y. 1979)

MacMahon, District Judge.

Plaintiff American Bell International Inc. ("Bell") moves for a preliminary injunction . . . , enjoining defendant Manufacturers Hanover Trust Company ("Manufacturers") from making any payment under its Letter of Credit No. SC 170027 to defendants the Islamic Republic of Iran or Bank Iranshahr or their agents, instrumentalities, successors, employees and assigns. . . .

The action arises from the recent revolution in Iran and its impact upon contracts made with the ousted Imperial Government of Iran and upon banking arrangements incident to such contracts. Bell, a wholly-owned subsidiary of American Telephone & Telegraph Co. ("AT&T"), made a contract on July 23, 1978 (the "Contract") with the Imperial Government of Iran–Ministry of War ("Imperial Government") to provide consulting services and equipment to the Imperial Government as part of a program to improve Iran's international communications system.

The contract provides a complex mechanism for payment to Bell totalling approximately $280,000,000, including a down payment of $38,000,000. The Imperial Government had the right to demand return of the down payment at any time. The amount so callable, however, was to be reduced by 20% of the amounts invoiced by Bell to which the Imperial Government did not object. Bell's liability for return of the down payment was reduced by application of this mechanism as the Contract was performed, with the result that approximately $30,200,000 of the down payment now remains callable.

In order to secure the return of the down payment on demand, Bell was required to establish an unconditional and irrevocable Letter of Guaranty, to be issued by Bank Iranshahr in the amount of $38,800,000 in favor of the Imperial Government. The Contract provides that it is to be governed by the laws of Iran and that all disputes arising under it are to be resolved by the Iranian courts.

Bell obtained a Letter of Guaranty from Bank Iranshahr. In turn, as required by Bank Iranshahr, Bell obtained a standby Letter of Credit, No. SC 170027, issued by Manufacturers in favor of Bank Iranshahr in the amount of $38,800,000 to secure reimbursement to Bank Iranshahr should it be required to pay the Imperial Government under its Letter of Guaranty.

The standby Letter of Credit provided for payment by Manufacturers to Bank Iranshahr upon receipt of:

> Your [Bank Iranshahr's] dated statement purportedly signed by an officer indicating name and title or your Tested Telex Reading: (A) "Referring Manufacturers Hanover Trust Co. Credit No. SC170027, the amount of our claim $___ represents fund due us as we have received a written request from the Imperial Government of Iran Ministry of War to pay them the sum of ___ under our Guarantee No. ___ issued for the account of American Bell International Inc. covering advance payment under Contract No. 138 dated July 23, 1978 and, such payment has been made by us" . . . .

In the application for the Letter of Credit, Bell agreed–guaranteed by AT&T–immediately to reimburse Manufacturers for all amounts paid by Manufacturers to Bank Iranshahr pursuant to the Letter of Credit. . . .

In late 1978 and early 1979, Iran was wreaked with revolutionary turmoil culminating in the overthrow of the Iranian government and its replacement by the Islamic Republic. In the wake of this upheaval, Bell was left with substantial unpaid invoices and claims under the Contract and ceased its performance in January 1979. Bell claims that the Contract was breached by the Imperial Government, as well as repudiated by the Islamic Republic, in that it owed substantial sums for services rendered under the Contract and its termination provisions. . . .

On July 25 and 29, 1979, Manufacturers received demands by Tested Telex from Bank Iranshahr for payment of $30,220,724 under the Letter of Credit, the remaining balance of the down payment. Asserting that the demand did not conform with the Letter of Credit, Manufacturers declined payment and so informed Bank Iranshahr. Informed of this, Bell responded by filing this action and an application by way of order to show cause for a temporary restraining order bringing on this motion for a preliminary injunction. Following argument, we granted a temporary restraining order on July 29 enjoining Manufacturers from making any payment to Bank Iranshahr until forty-eight hours after Manufacturers notified Bell of the receipt of a conforming demand, and this order has been extended pending decision of this motion.

On August 1, 1979, Manufacturers notified Bell that it had received a conforming demand from Bank Iranshahr. At the request of the parties, the court held an evidentiary hearing on August 3 on this motion for a preliminary injunction. . . .

The current criteria in this circuit for determining whether to grant the extraordinary remedy of a preliminary injunction are set forth in *Caulfield v. Board of Education*, 583 F.2d 604, 610 (2d Cir. 1978):

> [T]here must be a showing of possible irreparable injury *and* either (1) probable success on the merits *or* (2) sufficiently serious questions going to the merits to make them a fair ground for litigation *and* a balance of hardships tipping decidedly toward the party requesting the preliminary relief.

We are not persuaded that the plaintiff has met the criteria and therefore deny the motion. . . .

Plaintiff has failed to show that irreparable injury may possible ensue if a preliminary injunction is denied. Bell does not even claim, much less show, that it lacks an adequate remedy at law if Manufacturers makes a payment to Bank Iranshahr in violation of the Letter of Credit. It is too clear for argument that a suit for money damages could be based on such violation, and surely Manufacturers would be able to pay any money judgment against it.

Bell falls back on a contention that it is without any effective remedy unless it can restrain payment. This contention is based on the fact that it agreed to be bound by the laws of Iran and to submit resolution of any disputes under the Contract to the courts of Iran. Bell claims that it now has no meaningful access to those courts.

There is credible evidence that the Islamic Republic is xenophobic and anti-American and that it has no regard for consulting service contracts such as the one here. Although Bell has made no effort to invoke the aid of the Iranian courts, we think the current situation in Iran, as shown by the evidence, warrants the conclusion that an attempt by Bell to resort to those courts would be futile. . . . However, Bell has not demonstrated that it is without adequate remedy in this court against the Iranian defendants under the [Foreign] Sovereign Immunity Act which it invokes in this very case. 28 U.S.C. §§ 1605(a)(2), 1610(b)(2) (Supp. 1979). . . .

Even assuming that plaintiff has shown possible irreparable injury, it has failed to show probable success on the merits. . . .

In order to succeed on the merits, Bell must prove, by a preponderance of the evidence, that either (1) a demand for payment of the Manufacturers Letter of Credit conforming to the terms of that Letter has not yet been made, . . . or (2) a demand, even though in conformity, should not be honored because of fraud in the transaction, *see, e.g.,* N.Y. UCC § 5-114(2). . . . It is not probable, in the sense of a greater than 50% likelihood, that Bell will be able to prove either nonconformity or fraud.

As to nonconformity, the August 1 demand by Bank Iranshahr is identical to the terms of the Manufacturers Letter of Credit in every respect except one: it names as payee the "Government of Iran Ministry of Defense, Successor to the Imperial Government of Iran Ministry of War" rather than the "Imperial Government of Iran Ministry of War." . . . It is, of course, a bedrock principle of letter of credit law that a demand must strictly comply with the letter in order to justify payment. . . . Nevertheless, we deem it less than probable that a court, upon a full trial, would find nonconformity in the instant case. . . .

If conformity is established, as here, the issuer of an irrevocable, unconditional letter of credit, such as Manufacturers normally has an absolute duty to transfer the requisite funds. This duty is wholly independent of the underlying contractual relationship that gives rise to the letter of credit. . . . Nevertheless, both the Uniform Commercial Code of New York, which the parties concede governs here, and the courts state that payment is enjoinable where a germane document is forged or fraudulent or there is "fraud in the transaction." N.Y. UCC § 5-114(2). . . . Bell does not contend that any documents are fraudulent by virtue of misstatements or omissions. Instead, it argues there is "fraud in the transaction."

The parties disagree over the scope to be given as a matter of law to the term "transaction." Manufacturers, citing voluminous authorities, argues that the term refers only to the Letter of Credit transaction, not to the underlying commercial transaction or to the totality of dealings among the banks, the Iranian government and Bell. On this view of the law, Bell must fail to establish a probability of success, for it does not claim that the Imperial Government or Bank Iranshahr induced Manufacturers to extend the Letter by lies or half-truths, that the Letter contained any false representations by the Imperial Government or Bank Iranshahr, or that they intended misdeeds with it. Nor does Bell claim that the demand contains any misstatements.

Bell argues, citing equally voluminous authorities, that the term "transaction" refers to the totality of circumstances. On this view, Bell has some chance of success on the merits, for a court can consider Bell's allegations that the Government of Iran's behavior in connection with the consulting contract suffices to make its demand on the Letter of Guaranty fraudulent and that the ensuing demand on the Letter of Credit by Bank Iranshahr is tainted with the fraud.

There is some question whether these divergent understandings of the law are wholly incompatible since it would seem impossible to keep the Letter of Credit transaction conceptually distinct. A demand which facially conforms to the Letter of Credit and which contains no misstatements may, nevertheless, be considered fraudulent if made with the goal of mulcting the party who caused the Letter of Credit to be issued. Be that as it may, we need not decide this thorny issue of law. For, even on the construction most favorable to Bell, we find that success on the merits is not probable. Many of the facts alleged, even if proved, would not constitute fraud. As to others, the proof is sufficient to indicate a probability of success on the merits.

Bell, while never delineating with precision the contours of the purported fraud, sets forth five contentions which, in its view, support the issuance of an injunction. Bell asserts that (1) both the old and new Governments failed to approve invoices for services fully performed; (2) both failed to fund contracted-for independent Letters of Credit in Bell's favor; (3) the new Government has taken steps to renounce altogether its obligations under the Contract; (4) the new Government has made it impossible to assert contract rights in Iranian courts; and (5) the new Government has caused Bank Iranshahr to demand payment on the Manufacturers Letter of Credit, thus asserting rights in a transaction it has otherwise repudiated. . . . Even if we accept the proposition that the evidence does show repudiation, plaintiff is still far from demonstrating the kind of evil intent necessary to support a claim of fraud. Surely, plaintiff cannot contend that every party who breaches or repudiates his contract is for that reason culpable of fraud. The law of contract damages is adequate to repay the economic harm caused by repudiation, and the law presumes that one who repudiates has done so because of a calculation that such damages are cheaper than performance. Absent any showing that Iran would refuse to pay damages upon a contract action here or in Iran, much less a showing that Bell has even attempted to obtain such a remedy, the evidence is ambivalent as to whether the purported repudiation results from non-fraudulent economic calculation or from fraudulent intent to mulct Bell.

Plaintiff contends that the alleged repudiation, viewed in connection with its demand for payment on the Letter of Credit, supplies the basis from which only one inference–fraud–can be drawn. Again, we remain unpersuaded.

Plaintiff's argument requires us to presume bad faith on the part of the Iranian government. It requires us further to hold that that government may not rely on the plain terms of the consulting contract and the Letter of Credit arrangements with Bank Iranshahr and Manufacturers providing for immediate repayment of the down payment upon demand, without regard to cause. On the evidence before us, fraud is no more inferable than an economically rational decision by the government to recoup its down payment, as it is entitled to do under the consulting contract and still dispute its liabilities under that Contract.
. . .

If plaintiff fails to demonstrate probable success, he may still obtain relief by showing, in addition to the possibility of irreparable injury, both (1) sufficiently serious questions going to the merits to make them a fair ground for litigation, and (2) a balance of hardships tipping decidedly toward plaintiff. . . . Both Bell and Manufacturers appear to concede the existence of serious questions, and the complexity and novelty of this matter lead us to find they exist. Nevertheless, we hold that plaintiff is not entitled to relief under this branch of the *Caulfield* test because the balance of hardships does not tip *decidedly* toward Bell, if indeed it tips that way at all.

To be sure, Bell faces substantial hardships upon denial of its motion. Should Manufacturers pay the demand, Bell will immediately become liable to Manufacturers for $30.2 million, with no assurance of recouping those funds from Iran for the services performed. While counsel represented in graphic detail the other losses Bell faces at the hands of the current Iranian government, these would flow regardless of whether we ordered the relief sought. The hardship imposed from a denial of relief is limited to the admittedly substantial sum of $30.2 million.

But Manufacturers would face at least as great a loss, and perhaps a greater one, were we to grant relief to. Upon Manufacturers' failure to pay, Bank Iranshahr could initiate a suit on the Letter of Credit and attach $30.2 million of Manufacturers' assets in Iran. In addition, it could seek to hold Manufacturers liable for consequential damages beyond that sum resulting from the failure to make timely payment. Finally, there is no guarantee that Bank Iranshahr or the government, in retaliation for Manufacturers' recalcitrance, will not nationalize additional Manufacturers' assets in Iran in amounts which counsel, at oral argument, represented to be far in excess of the amount in controversy here.

Apart from a greater monetary exposure flowing from an adverse decision, Manufacturers faces a loss of credibility in the international banking community that could result from its failure to make good on a letter of credit. . . .

Finally, apart from questions of relative hardship and the specific criteria of the *Caulfield* test, general considerations of equity counsel us to deny the motion for injunctive relief. Bell, a sophisticated multinational enterprise well advised by competent counsel, entered into these arrangements with its corporate eyes open. It knowingly and voluntarily signed a contract allowing the Iranian government to recoup its down payment on demand, without regard to cause. It caused Manufacturers to enter into an agreement whereby Manufacturers became obligated to pay Bank Iranshahr the unamortized down payment balance upon receipt of conforming documents, again without regard to cause.

Both of these arrangements redounded tangible to the benefit of Bell. The Contract with Iran, with its prospect of designing and installing from scratch a nationwide and international communications system, was certain to bring to Bell both monetary profit and prestige and good will in the global communications industry. The agreement to indemnify Manufacturers on its Letter of Credit provided the means by which these benefits could be achieved.

One who reaps the rewards of commercial arrangements must also accept their burdens. One such burden in this case, voluntarily accepted by Bell, was the risk that demand might be made without cause on the funds constituting the down payment. To be sure, the sequence of events that led up to that demand may well have been unforeseeable when the contracts were signed. To this extent, both Bell and Manufacturers have been made the unwitting and innocent victims of tumultuous events beyond their control. But, as between two innocents, the party who undertakes by contract the risk of political uncertainty and governmental caprice must bear the consequences when the risk comes home to roost. . . .

**Notes and Comments 9.19.** *American Bell International* seems to suggest that the "fraud in the transaction" rule will be interpreted at least as narrowly in the standby L/C context as in the commercial L/C context. However, will it not always be the case that the account party of a standby L/C will have a cause of action for money damages based on the underlying contract, and, if so, would injunctive relief ever be available? Consider the following excerpt.

# Michael P. Malloy, Principles of Bank Regulation
## § 9.21 (2d ed. 2003)

In cases like *American Bell International*, courts are essentially applying generally applicable principles (developed in the commercial L/C context) to instruments that, despite their name, are significantly different from traditional commercial L/Cs, and that are more like third-party guarantees. In this regard, consider the effect on a "fraud in the transaction" claim[5] involving a standby letter of credit. In the case of a documentary letter of credit,[6] the stringencies of the "fraud in the transaction" theory can be straightforwardly met by simple facts–have the goods been shipped, or do the boxes contain trash? Do these requirements work out satisfactorily when we are really arguing about the good faith of an undocumented demand under a standby letter of credit, rather than a documented demand? At least in the case of the documented demand, we can assume that there are some goods floating around to secure the bank's risk.

Obviously, *American Bell International* rejects the suggestion that more refined rules should be applied in the case of standby letters of credit. The result is an outcome that, intuitively, seems to be contrary and unsatisfying, since the court assumed that an adequate remedy would exist for the account party in Iran, which at the time was already exhibiting extreme hostility toward Americans and American firms. As the U.S.-Iran crisis of 1979 worsened, however, there were at least some indications that courts were beginning to consider the plight of account parties to standby letters of credit (and their issuing banks) in a more thoughtful fashion.[7]

Eventually, of course, the U.S. Government would intervene and freeze the standby letters of credit, so that potentially fraudulent demands could not be effected.[8] This development means that we lack any definitive judicial resolution of the problem of adapting rules that arose in the documentary letter of credit context to the standby letter of credit context.

**Notes and Comments 9.20.** Traditional L/C rules developed on the basis of the scenario of the traditional commercial letter of credit. Such rules as the separability of the L/C obligations of the issuing or confirming bank to the beneficiary, and of the account party to the bank, from the underlying contract between the account party and the beneficiary have the effect of preserving the credibility of the international payments system in international trade. Exceptions like the "fraud in the transaction" rule are therefore narrowly construed, in order to maintain the separability of L/C obligations and the underlying contract. The banks may be momentarily at risk, but this risk is significantly contained because, even if the account party fails to reimburse the bank, the bank has the documents that control the goods. Theoretically, an issuing or confirming bank is in a position not unlike a fully collateralized, short-term lender. But what about an issuing or confirming bank of a standby L/C? To what

---

5. Uniform Commercial Code, § 5-114(2). [*Cf.* Uniform Commercial Code (Revised) § 5-109 (corresponding rule for fraud and forgery in connection with letter of credit).]

6. *See, e.g., United Bank Ltd. v. Cambridge Sporting Goods Corp.*, 41 N.Y2d 254, 360 N.E.2d 943, 392 N.Y.S.2d 265 (Ct.App. 1976) (involving "fraud in the transaction" claim where mildewed goods had been shipped on a canceled contract).

7. *See, e.g., Stromberg-Carlson Corp. v. Bank Melli Iran*, 467 F. Supp. 530 (S.D.N.Y. 1979) (finding serious risk of fraudulent or nonauthentic demand sufficient showing for preliminary injunction against payment under standby letter).

8. *See* Michael P. Malloy, *The Iran Crisis: Law Under Pressure*, 1984 WISC. INT'L L.J. 15 (1984) (discussing standby letter of credit problem).

extent is its lending risk contained?

**9.21.** The 1995 revision of the Uniform Commercial Code replaces UCC § 5-114 with § 5-109, which provides as follows:

> § 5-109. Fraud And Forgery
>
> (a) If a presentation is made that appears on its face strictly to comply with the terms and conditions of the letter of credit, but a required document is forged or materially fraudulent, or honor of the presentation would facilitate a material fraud by the beneficiary on the issuer or applicant:
>
> (1) the issuer shall honor the presentation, if honor is demanded by (i) a nominated person who has given value in good faith and without notice of forgery or material fraud, (ii) a confirmer who has honored its confirmation in good faith, (iii) a holder in due course of a draft drawn under the letter of credit which was taken after acceptance by the issuer or nominated person, or (iv) an assignee of the issuer's or nominated person's deferred obligation that was taken for value and without notice of forgery or material fraud after the obligation was incurred by the issuer or nominated person; and
>
> (2) the issuer, acting in good faith, may honor or dishonor the presentation in any other case.
>
> (b) If an applicant claims that a required document is forged or materially fraudulent or that honor of the presentation would facilitate a material fraud by the beneficiary on the issuer or applicant, a court of competent jurisdiction may temporarily or permanently enjoin the issuer from honoring a presentation or grant similar relief against the issuer or other persons only if the court finds that:
>
> (1) the relief is not prohibited under the law applicable to an accepted draft or deferred obligation incurred by the issuer;
>
> (2) a beneficiary, issuer, or nominated person who may be adversely affected is adequately protected against loss that it may suffer because the relief is granted;
>
> (3) all of the conditions to entitle a person to the relief under the law of this State have been met; and
>
> (4) on the basis of the information submitted to the court, the applicant is more likely than not to succeed under its claim of forgery or material fraud and the person demanding honor does not qualify for protection under subsection (a)(1).

Would this provision have been more favorable for American Bell than the one applied in the preceding case? In answering this question, consider the following case, which involves revised UCC § 5-109.

**Sava Gumarska in Kemijska Industria d.d. v.
Advanced Polymer Sciences, Inc.**

128 S.W.3d 304 (Tex.App. 2004)

Opinion By Justice MOSELEY.

[The account party of a standby letter of credit (L/C) sought declaratory and injunctive relief regarding the L/C beneficiary's attempted draw on the L/C to protect the its advance deposit for the purchase of equipment. (The equipment was for a business to be operated by a Slovenian stock company owned by the account party and the beneficiary. )

The account party also claimed breach of the equipment agreement. The beneficiary counterclaimed for breach of the equipment agreement, breach of the agreement for formation of the stock company, and declaratory judgment. After a bench trial, the district court declared the L/C void, awarded damages and attorney fees to the account party for breach of contract, conditionally awarded the account party attorney fees for appeals, and denied relief on the beneficiary's counterclaims. The beneficiary appealed. The Texas Court of Appeals affirmed in part, reversed and rendered in part, and remanded in part, holding that (*i*) the account party did not repudiate its obligations under the equipment agreement; (*ii*) the provision of the equipment agreement requiring each party to bear its own banking costs was enforceable; and, (*iii*) the evidence did not establish a material fraud by the beneficiary, as a basis for voiding the L/C. The excerpts below deal with the issue of the validity of the L/C.]

## BACKGROUND

. . .

On January 15, 1999, SAVA and APS entered into a Company Formation Agreement providing for the formation and ownership of SAVA AP. Under this agreement, SAVA was to purchase certain specially manufactured equipment from APS and lease that equipment to SAVA AP. Several other activities and agreements were contemplated under the Company Formation Agreement, including the acquisition of a facility to manufacture composite products using the equipment sold by APS. SAVA paid a $200,000 engineering fee to APS for facility design, equipment design, and engineering on the proposed manufacturing facility. In addition, SAVA was to buy a total of $3,300,000 in equipment from APS.

Pursuant to the Company Formation Agreement, SAVA formed SAVA AP in April 1999 and hired one of its employees to manage it. The articles of association for SAVA AP were signed in July 1999, and APS acquired its interest in SAVA AP in August 1999.

On July 9, 1999, SAVA and APS entered into an Equipment Agreement for the purchase and sale of equipment. The equipment to be sold and the prices to be paid were as described in an exhibit to the Company Formation Agreement. The equipment was of two types: (1) portable spraying and heat curing equipment used for applying polymer coatings to containers or composite products ("spray and heat curing equipment"); and (2) filament winding equipment used to manufacture composite fiber products such as tanks, containers, and pipes ("filament winding equipment"). SAVA agreed to make a down-payment for the equipment and APS agreed to deliver the equipment within specified times after the down-payment. The spraying and heat curing equipment was to be delivered within fourteen weeks after receipt of the down-payment. (The evidence indicates that the spraying and heat curing equipment was in fact delivered by APS and paid for by SAVA.)

The filament winding equipment was to be delivered within ten to fourteen months after the down-payment. Under the portion of the Equipment Agreement relating to the filament winding equipment, SAVA agreed to make an advance deposit to APS of $550,000, and provide a letter of credit to APS for the $2.2 million balance of the purchase price. To protect SAVA's advance deposit, APS agreed to put up a standby letter of credit for SAVA's benefit in the amount of $550,000. It is this standby letter of credit that is the main focus of this dispute.

On November 1, 1999, APS arranged for the standby letter of credit through Bank One Texas (the "Bank"). Under its terms, to draw on the letter of credit SAVA was required to present a sight draft and a signed statement that the delivery deadline under the Equipment Agreement had passed, SAVA had examined the equipment supplied by APS, and SAVA had refused acceptance of the equipment because:

A. It does not meet the fabrication drawings or specifications presented by [APS] prior to manufacture, and/or

B. It does not meet European Union/ANSI standards for safety and environmental protection, and/or

C. It is not in accordance with the best available technologies, and/or

D. It is not properly operational after a week-long performance test, and any defects in construction or installation of the equipment were not remedied within an agreed upon timeframe, and/or

E. The delivery of equipment does not otherwise conform materially to the contract between SAVA and [APS] giving the buyer just cause to dispute payment.

As amended, the letter of credit expired on June 30, 2001.

In January 2000, SAVA made the $550,000 advance deposit to APS under the Equipment Agreement. On March 10, 2000, SAVA caused its bank to issue a letter of credit to APS in the amount of $2.2 million to secure payment of the balance of the purchase price for the filament winding equipment. APS used the $2.2 million letter of credit as collateral for a line of credit to manufacture the equipment.

From the inception of their relationship, both SAVA and APS had problems with various aspects of the transactions. . . .

By March 2000, SAVA AP was on the verge of insolvency and had to borrow additional funds from SAVA. . . .

By June 2000, however, SAVA AP was insolvent. SAVA accused APS of causing the failure of SAVA AP. APS claimed SAVA caused SAVA AP's failure by not implementing the original business plan and by failing to market the coating products. On June 19, 2000, SAVA notified APS that SAVA AP would stop marketing APS's polymer coating products. APS continued to work with SAVA on the layout of the composite manufacturing plant and completed the task to SAVA's apparent satisfaction on July 31, 2000. However, on August 9, 2000, SAVA advised APS that the drawings approved on July 31, 2000 were unacceptable and that SAVA was not going to proceed with the composite manufacturing plant. On August 30, 2000, APS notified SAVA that it had instructed the manufacturers to stop further production of the filament winding equipment and "insist[ed] on knowing what is SAVA's intention towards this venture."

. . . On October 10, 2000, SAVA notified APS that it was revoking the order for the filament winding equipment, and canceling the Company Formation Agreement and the Equipment Agreement. SAVA also indicated it would draw on the standby letter of credit to reimburse it for its $550,000 advance payment to APS for the filament winding equipment.

On November 6, 2000, SAVA presented documents to the Bank to draw the full amount of the standby letter of credit. APS filed this suit against the Bank seeking a temporary restraining order and a temporary injunction preventing the Bank from honoring the draw on the letter of credit. APS claimed SAVA committed a material fraud in presenting the documents in an attempt to draw on the standby letter of credit before shipment of the filament winding equipment was even due. In addition to an injunction, APS sought a declaratory judgment that the standby letter of credit was void and unenforceable and requested an award of its reasonable attorneys' fees under the declaratory judgment act.

APS obtained a temporary restraining order on November 8, 2000. SAVA intervened in the lawsuit. Following a hearing, the trial court entered a temporary injunction against payment of the letter of credit. . . .

The Bank requested and was granted leave to not participate in the trial pursuant to letter agreements between the parties. . . .[4]

## STANDBY LETTER OF CREDIT

SAVA asserts the evidence is legally insufficient to support the finding of material fraud that justifies the declaration that the letter of credit was void. SAVA asks us to render judgment against the Bank for the $550,000 amount of the letter of credit, and against APS for SAVA's attorneys' fees expended in seeking a declaratory judgment that it was entitled to payment under the letter of credit.

### 1. Introduction

A letter of credit is a definite undertaking by an issuer (usually a bank) to a beneficiary at the request of an applicant to honor a documentary presentation by payment or delivery of an item of value. Tex. Bus. & Com.Code Ann. § 5.102(a)(10) (Vernon 2002). The letter of credit obligation is independent of any underlying contract dispute between the beneficiary and the applicant. *Id.* § 5.103(d). The issuer must honor a presentment that "appears on its face strictly to comply with the terms and conditions of the letter of credit." *Id.* § 5.108(a).

However, payment of a letter of credit does not determine the ultimate right to retain the funds as between the beneficiary and the applicant. *See CKB & Assocs., Inc. v. Moore McCormack Petroleum, Inc.,* 734 S.W.2d 653, 655 (Tex.1987). Contracting parties may use a letter of credit in order to "make certain that contract disputes [between the applicant and beneficiary] wend their way towards resolution with money in the beneficiary's pocket rather than in the pocket of the [applicant]." *Id.* The beneficiary's immediate right of possession of the funds on payment of the letter of credit does not decide the dispute over who will ultimately retain those funds. *Id.* "Without this rule, the beneficiary of the letter of credit would be the ultimate arbiter of compliance with the underlying contract and the commercial viability of the letter of credit would be destroyed." *Id.* Thus, the letter of credit determines the beneficiary's right to immediate possession of the funds on presentation of conforming documents to the issuer, but not the right to ultimately retain those funds.

Payment of a letter of credit may not be enjoined, or similar relief granted, unless there is evidence of a material fraud by the beneficiary on the applicant or the issuer. Tex. Bus. & Com.Code Ann. § 5.109(b); *Philipp Bros., Inc. v. Oil Country Specialists, Ltd.,* 787 S.W.2d 38, 40-41 (Tex.1990). The standard of fraud necessary to warrant interference with the independence of the letter of credit is that "the wrong doing of the beneficiary has so vitiated the entire transaction that the legitimate purposes of the independence of the issuer's obligation would no longer be served." *Philipp Bros.,* 787 S.W.2d at 40 (quoting, *GATX Leasing Corp. v.. DMB Drilling Corp.,* 657 S.W.2d 178, 182 (Tex.App.-San Antonio 1983, no writ); *see* Tex. Bus. & Com.Code Ann. § 5.109 cmt. 2. The elements of a cause of action for fraud are: "(1) that a material representation was made; (2) the representation was false; (3) when the representation was made, the speaker knew it was false or made it recklessly without any knowledge of the truth and as a positive assertion; (4) the speaker made the representation with the intent that the other party should act upon it; (5) the party acted in reliance on the representation; and (6) the party thereby suffered injury." *In re FirstMerit Bank, N.A.,* 52 S.W.3d 749, 758 (Tex.2001). To warrant interference with payment of a letter of credit, the fraud must be "extreme, intentional, and unscrupulous." *SRS Prods. Co. v. LG Eng'g Co.,* 994 S.W.2d 380, 384 (Tex.App.-Houston [14th Dist.] 1999, no pet.).

### 2. Relevance of Analysis

---

4. The letter of credit expired shortly after trial. However, the Bank stipulated with the parties that it would abide by whatever order or judgment was entered by the court and would pay any proceeds of the letter of credit as directed by the court.

[The court decided that, with the Bank's stipulation (*see* note 4, *supra*), and the agreement by SAVA and APS that "they neither seek now nor will seek any affirmative relief, including money damages, attorneys' fees, interest, or the imposition of costs or otherwise, against [the Bank] in this action," SAVA was not entitled to judgment against the Bank. The court also found that APS had established that SAVA repudiated and breached the Equipment Agreement. As a result the court held that SAVA would not be entitled to retain proceeds of the letter of credit, citing *Oil Country Specialists, Ltd. v. Philipp Bros., Inc.,* 762 S.W.2d 170, 179-80 (Tex.App. 1988), *writ denied,* 787 S.W.2d 38 (Tex.1990) (despite take-nothing judgment on applicant's breach of contract claim, beneficiary not entitled to retain proceeds of letter of credit because of its prior material breach of underlying agreement).]

However, both parties requested attorneys' fees in connection with their respective declaratory judgment actions regarding the letter of credit. Relevant to those claims for attorneys' fees is whether SAVA was entitled to draw on the letter of credit. Because of our disposition of the parties' claims for attorneys fees, as set forth herein, we conclude it necessary and appropriate to address SAVA's claims regarding the letter of credit.

3. Analysis

The trial court declared that the letter of credit was void. This declaration has the same effect as a permanent injunction against payment. *See* Tex. Bus. & Com.Code Ann. § 5.109 cmt. 5 (same principles apply when applicant tries to achieve same legal outcome as injunction against honor by other methods including declaratory judgment). Thus we apply the material fraud standard of section 5.109 to the trial court's declaration. *Id.* § 5.109(b).

SAVA asserts the trial court's ruling is based on four grounds, none of which support the trial court's conclusion. These grounds are: (A) SAVA breached the Equipment Agreement and forfeited any right to draw on the letter of credit; (B) SAVA knew the delivery date stated in the letter of credit was incorrect but failed to inform APS of the error; (C) SAVA made false statements in the presentment documents to the Bank; and (D) after the trial court entered a temporary injunction against payment of the letter of credit, SAVA made a second presentment to the Bank reiterating that the delivery date had passed. In its first issue, SAVA claims the trial court erred in not declaring that SAVA was entitled to payment under the letter of credit and in not awarding SAVA its attorneys' fees against APS. Under this issue, SAVA argues the trial court erred in declaring the letter of credit void.

*A. Breach of Underlying Agreement*

The trial court found that SAVA breached the Equipment Agreement and "therefore forfeited any right to draw upon the letter of credit." Breach of the underlying agreement between the applicant and the beneficiary is not a ground for enjoining or canceling the letter of credit. *Philipp Bros.,* 787 S.W.2d at 40. Under the independence doctrine, the obligation of the issuer to the beneficiary on the letter of credit is independent of the "existence, performance, or *nonperformance* of a contract or arrangement out of which the letter of credit arises or which underlies it, including contracts ... between the applicant and the beneficiary." Tex. Bus. & Com.Code Ann. § 5.103(d) (emphasis added). "The purpose of a letter of credit is to assure payment when its own conditions have been met irrespective of disputes that may arise between the parties concerning performance or other agreements which comprise the underlying transaction." *Sun Marine Terminals, Inc. v. Artoc Bank & Trust Ltd.,* 797 S.W.2d 7, 10 (Tex.1990); *Synergy Ctr., Ltd. v. Lone Star Franchising, Inc.,* 63 S.W.3d 561, 566 (Tex.App.-Austin 2001, no pet.).

Thus even though SAVA's breach of the underlying agreement meant that it was not entitled to keep the proceeds of the letter of credit as against APS, *see CKB & Assocs.,* 734 S.W.2d at 655, that breach does not constitute material fraud permitting a court to enjoin payment of the letter of credit. Such a breach would only give APS the right to recover the proceeds of the letter of credit from SAVA after the letter of credit was paid; it would not be a basis to enjoin or void the letter of credit. *See CKB & Assocs.,* 734 S.W.2d at 655. The trial court's finding that SAVA breached the Equipment Agreement does not support its decision to declare the letter of credit void.

The trial court also found that SAVA attempted to draw on the letter of credit before permitting APS to perform under the Equipment Agreement, and that SAVA attempted to draw on the letter of credit after repudiating the Equipment Agreement without justification. Both of these findings go to the performance or nonperformance of the underlying contract between SAVA and APS, and do not constitute a basis for enjoining the payment of the letter of credit. Tex. Bus. & Com.Code Ann. § 5.103(d); *Synergy Ctr.,* 63 S.W.3d at 566; *SRS Prods. Co.,* 944 S.W.2d at 386.

### B. Failure to Disclose Incorrect Term in Letter of Credit

The letter of credit required a statement that the Equipment Agreement called for delivery of all equipment by September 9, 1999. The Equipment Agreement does not in fact call for delivery of all equipment by that date. Rather, the agreement called for delivery of the spray and heat curing equipment within fourteen weeks after receipt of SAVA's down-payment and delivery of the filament winding equipment ten to fourteen months after receipt of the down-payment. The trial court concluded SAVA committed fraud on APS and the Bank because it knew the delivery date in the letter of credit was incorrect and did not inform APS of the error.

However, APS, not SAVA, caused the letter of credit to be issued by its bank. The record does not indicate how the September 9, 1999 date was included in the letter of credit. The evidence shows APS delivered a copy of the Equipment Agreement to the Bank and the Bank drew up the letter of credit.[8] APS never saw the letter of credit until after SAVA attempted to draw on it. There was also evidence that the terms of the letter of credit were acceptable between the Bank and SAVA.

The evidence does not support the trial court's finding of fraud based on the September 9 date specified in the letter of credit. As a general rule, a failure to disclose information does not constitute fraud unless there is a duty to disclose the information. *Ins. Co. of N. Am. v. Morris,* 981 S.W.2d 667, 674 (Tex.1998). Thus, silence is equivalent to a false representation only when the particular circumstances impose a duty on the party to speak and he deliberately remains silent. *Bradford v. Vento,* 48 S.W.3d 749, 755 (Tex.2001) (citing *SmithKline Beecham Corp. v. Doe,* 903 S.W.2d 347, 353 (Tex.1995), and *Smith v. Nat'l Resort Communities, Inc.,* 585 S.W.2d 655, 658 (Tex.1979)). Whether a duty to speak exists is a question of law. *Bradford,* 48 S.W.3d at 755.

The trial court did not find that SAVA had a duty to disclose material information, although there was some evidence from a representative of SAVA AP that there was a high degree of trust running from SAVA AP to its shareholders, and that the obligation of SAVA to APS was one of high trust and fidelity. However, assuming without deciding that SAVA owed a duty to disclose to APS, there is no evidence that SAVA was aware that APS had not seen the letter of credit or that APS did not have an equal opportunity to discover the terms of the letter of credit. *See Bradford,* 48 S.W.3d at 756 ("[T]here is no evidence that Bradford knew either that Vento was ignorant of the lease terms or that he did not have an equal opportunity to discover them."). The letter of credit was issued by APS's bank at its request. APS clearly had the opportunity to inspect the letter of credit and determine if its terms and

---

8. The Equipment Agreement refers to specimen letters of credit attached to the agreement, but the record does not include these attachments.

conditions were correct. APS presented no evidence that SAVA knew APS was ignorant of the September 9, 1999 delivery date stated in the letter of credit. Thus, there is no evidence to support the trial court's conclusion that SAVA's failure to advise APS of the delivery date stated in the letter of credit amounted to material fraud. *See id.*

### C. False Statements in Presentation Documents

Several of the trial court's findings and the evidence cited by APS in support of the judgment relate to false statements in the presentment documents. For example, the trial court found that in order to draw on the letter of credit, SAVA had to represent to the Bank that the filament winding equipment had been delivered and found to be nonconforming. The trial court found that SAVA falsely represented to the Bank that APS had delivered the equipment in a nonconforming state and had failed to cure the defects within the specific delivery schedule. SAVA contends the statements were not false based on its interpretation of the Equipment Agreement as covering both the spray and heat curing equipment and the filament winding equipment. SAVA argues the statements in the presentment documents referred to the spray and heat curing equipment, which had been delivered, and were true.

The evidence supports the trial court's findings that SAVA made false statements to the Bank in presenting the letter of credit. However, false statements in the presentment documents are insufficient to warrant enjoining payment of the letter of credit. *Philipp Bros.,* 787 S.W.2d at 40-41. Establishing material fraud or fraud in the transaction requires more than a showing of untruthful statements in the presentment documents. *See SRS Prods. Co.,* 994 S.W.2d at 384. Such false statements in making presentment would not amount to egregious fraud vitiating the transaction and warranting a declaration that the letter of credit is void. *See Philipp Bros.,* 787 S.W.2d at 40-41. The trial court's finding that the statements in the presentation documents were false does not support its conclusion that SAVA committed material fraud such that the letter of credit should be canceled and declared void. *Id.*

### D. Second Presentment During Injunction

The trial court found that after the court temporarily enjoined the Bank from paying the letter of credit, SAVA made a second presentment where it again represented that the delivery deadline had passed. This constitutes another finding that the statements in SAVA's presentment documents were not true. As we discussed above, proof that the statements in the presentment documents are not true does not establish material fraud warranting cancellation of the letter of credit. *See Philipp Bros.,* 787 S.W.2d at 40-41.

APS cites to other evidence in the record, such as the failure and insolvency of SAVA AP, SAVA's interference with attempts to provide training, SAVA's failure to acquire a building for the equipment, and SAVA's use and acceptance of the spray and heat curing equipment, as evidence supporting the trial court's finding of material fraud. This evidence relates to various disputes about the contracts between the parties and the operation and management of SAVA AP. None of this evidence, individually or collectively, alters our conclusion that there is no evidence that SAVA committed material fraud in presenting the documents to draw on the letter of credit, or provides a viable alternative ground supporting the trial court's ruling.

### 4. Conclusion

We conclude the evidence is legally insufficient to support the finding of material fraud that justifies the declaration that the letter of credit was void. As discussed above, however, because SAVA was not entitled to recovery of a judgment against the Bank for failing to honor the letter of credit, and because the underlying dispute between SAVA and APS has been resolved and the ultimate right to retain the funds decided against SAVA, *see CKB & Assocs.,* 734 S.W.2d at 655, the error probably did not cause the rendition of an improper judgment. Tex.R.App. P. 44.1(a). . . .

# 4. Bankers' Acceptances

**Notes and Comments 9.22.** A bankers' acceptance is a time draft or bill of exchange drawn on a bank by its customer, and "accepted" by the bank. Acceptance makes the draft an obligation by the accepting bank, much as certification of a check places the bank under an obligation to pay. Bankers' acceptances are useful in the financing of international sales of goods, and they tend to be highly negotiable because the credit of the accepting bank lies behind them. The structure of a bankers' acceptance transaction is illustrated in Figure 9.3, *infra*.

Thus, the typical transaction would work as follows. A Trading Co. is selling widgets into the export market. To finance these sales, for which it normally receives payments over six months, it arranges with B Bank to accept its drafts in a predetermined amount, at an agreed discount rate (plus an acceptance commission). When this arrangement is approved, B Bank will credit to A Trading Co.'s account an amount equal to the face amount of the accepted drafts minus its discount (*i.e.*, the interest charged on the amount of financing provided by B Bank). B Bank might hold onto the drafts, or ( - ) it might rediscount them to a broker or other buyer. When the drafts mature, whoever holds them will present them to B Bank for payment. B Bank will then pay the drafts, and ( - ) debit A Trading Co.'s account for the amount of that payment. (In the meantime, A Trading Co. has presumably received payment for its export sales and has deposited the proceeds in its B Bank account).

---

Figure 9.3
Bankers' Acceptance: Typical Transaction

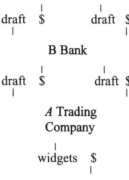

Secondary Market

draft  $          draft  $

B Bank

draft  $          draft  $

*A* Trading
Company

widgets  $

*XYZ* Import Company

---

*Source*: MICHAEL P. MALLOY, PRINCIPLES OF BANK REGULATION § 9.22 (2d ed. 2003).

**9.23.** Negotiability of bankers' acceptances is enhanced if the acceptance is "eligible" for rediscount by Federal Reserve banks. Eligibility is determined by reference to 12 U.S.C. § 372. Review the provisions of section 372, as well as 12 U.S.C. § 84 in answering the following questions.

      **a.** Quarter National Bank (QNB) has unimpaired capital and surplus in the amount of $200 million. It has outstanding loans and extensions of credit to International Business Network, Inc. (IBN), a multinational firm with operations worldwide, in the aggregate amount of $25 million. May QNB assist in the financing of IBN's trade transactions by accepting drafts drawn by IBN and payable in 120 days?

      **b.** Why would IBN find this financing device desirable?

      **c.** Why would QNB find it desirable?

# 5. Underwriting and Syndication

**Notes and Comments 9.24.** Distribution of securities and the syndication and distribution of "participations" in loans are increasingly important activities of international banking. Among other reasons, the "internationalization" of capital markets,[13] makes participation by commercial banks in the international capital markets correspondingly significant if they are to maintain a share of their wholesale customers' business. Participation in these markets takes a variety of forms. One is the international bond, or "Eurobond,"[14] market. There has been, however, an increasing interest in "Euroequities" as well.[15]

**9.25.** *Authorization of financial services.* In the United States, before 1999 banks and other financial institutions were subject to significant restrictions to engage in securities activities or to affiliate with firms engaged in such activities. However, on 12 November 1999, the President signed the Gramm-Leach-Bliley Act (GLBA) into law.[16] This financial services reform effort is one of the most significant pieces of federal banking legislation since the Banking Act of 1933. Among other things, the GLBA eliminates prohibitions on affiliations between commercial and investment banking enterprises and on interlocking directorates between such enterprises.[17] The GLBA permits a national bank to engage through a financial subsidiary in activities "financial in nature," as authorized by the act, with

---

13. For an overview of the internationalized capital markets, see *Internationalization of the Securities Markets: Report of the Staff of the Securities and Exchange Commission to the Senate Committee on Banking, Housing and Urban Affairs and the House Committee on Energy and Commerce* (July 27, 1987) ("*SEC Internationalization Report*").

14. *I.e.*, bonds issued in one country or group of countries, but denominated in the currency of some other country, concentrated in the European financial centers. On international and Eurobond markets, see *SEC Internationalization Report* at II-35 - II-51. *See also* N.S. POSER, INTERNATIONAL SECURITIES REGULATION 20-23 (1991) (discussing these markets).

15. Euroequities are equity securities underwritten and distributed in one or more national markets outside the issuer's home market by a syndicate of international securities firms and banks. *See SEC Internationalization Report* at II-51 - II-62, III-43 - III-53.

16. Pub. L. No. 106-102, Nov. 12, 1999, 113 Stat. 1338 (1999) (codified at scattered sections of 12, 15, 16, 18 U.S.C.) (GLBA).

17. *See* GLBA, § 101 (repealing 12 U.S.C. §§ 78, 377).

certain exceptions.[18] The act specifically excludes four types of activities for these subsidiaries: insurance or annuity underwriting, insurance company portfolio investments, real estate investment and development, and merchant banking.[19] It also permits bank holding companies (BHCs) that qualify as financial holding companies (FHCs) to engage in activities, and acquire companies engaged in activities, that are "financial in nature" or that are incidental to such activities.[20] FHCs are also permitted to engage in activities that are complementary to financial activities, if the Fed determines that the activity does not pose a substantial risk to the safety or soundness of depository institutions or the financial system in general. To engage in the new financial activities and affiliations, a BHC must elect to become an FHC, but it may do so only if all of its subsidiary depository institutions are well capitalized and well managed.[21]

**9.26.** *Functional regulation of financial services.* The GLBA generally endorses the principle of functional regulation, positing that similar activities should be regulated by the same regulator.[22] Accordingly, banking activities are regulated by federal and state bank regulators, securities activities by federal and state securities regulators, and insurance activities by state insurance regulators.[23] However, the Fed retains its role of "umbrella supervisor" of BHCs, and it is authorized to examine each holding company and its subsidiaries, including functionally regulated subsidiaries under limited circumstances.[24] The Comptroller, the Fed, and the FDIC are authorized to adopt "prudential safeguards" governing transactions between a depository institution, its subsidiaries and affiliates to avoid, *inter alia*, significant risk to the safety and soundness of the institution.[25]

**9.27.** *Implementing regulations.* Review 12 U.S.C. §§ 24(Seventh), 24a, 335, 378 (a)(1), 1843(k), together with the following Federal Reserve regulations, before answering

---

18. *Id.*, § 121(a)(2) (codified at 12 U.S.C. § 24a).

19. 12 U.S.C. § 24a(a)(2)(B). However, after a five-year period from enactment of the GLBA, the Fed and the Secretary of the Treasury are authorized jointly to adopt rules permitting merchant banking by financial subsidiaries, subject to the conditions that the agencies may jointly determine. GLBA, § 122 (codified at 12 U.S.C. § 1843 note). The GLBA does not define merchant banking. In an interim rule published jointly by the Fed and the Department of the Treasury, implementing merchant banking provisions for financial holding companies, the term is discussed in the following terms:

> [GLBA] section 4(k)(4)(H) and the interim rule permit a financial holding company to acquire or control shares, assets or ownership interests of any company that engages in activities that are not otherwise permissible for a financial holding company. Interests acquired or controlled under the interim rule are referred to as merchant banking investments, and a financial holding company must comply with the requirements of this interim rule in order to make such investments.

65 Fed. Reg. 16,460, 16,463 (2000).

20. GLBA, § 103(a) (codified at 12 U.S.C. § 1843(k)).

21. *Id.*, § 103(a) (codified at 12 U.S.C. § 1843(*l*)).

22. *But cf.* Michael P. Malloy, *Functional Regulation: Premise or Pretext? in* PATRICIA A. MCCOY (ed.), FINANCIAL MODERNIZATION AFTER GRAMM-LEACH-BLILEY 179 (2002) (arguing that functional regulation is neither extensively nor consistently used by GLBA ).

23. *See, e.g.*, GLBA, §§ 111-112, 115, 301 (codified at 12 U.S.C. §§ 1820a, 1831v, 1844(c)(4)A)-(B), (g), 15 U.S.C. § 6711) (mandating functional regulation of financial services).

24. *Id.*, § 113 (codified at 12 U.S.C. § 1848a).

25. *Id.*, § 114 (codified at 12 U.S.C. § 1828a).

the questions in **9.28**, *infra*.

# Board of Governors of the Federal Reserve System
12 C.F.R. pt. 211

§ 211.605  Permissible underwriting activities of foreign banks

(a) Introduction. A number of foreign banks that are subject to the Bank Holding Company Act ("BHC Act") have participated as co-managers in the underwriting of securities to be distributed in the United States despite the fact that the foreign banks in question do not have authority to engage in underwriting activity in the United States under either the Gramm-Leach-Bliley Act ("GLB Act") or section 4(c)(8) of the BHC Act (12 U.S.C. 1843(c)(8)). This interpretation clarifies the scope of existing restrictions on underwriting by such foreign banks with respect to securities that are distributed in the United States.

(b) Underwriting transactions engaged in by foreign banks. (1) In the transactions in question, a foreign bank typically becomes a member of the underwriting syndicate for securities that are registered and intended to be distributed in the United States. The lead underwriter, usually a registered U.S. broker-dealer not affiliated with the foreign bank, agrees to be responsible for distributing the securities being underwritten. The underwriting obligation is assumed by a foreign office or affiliate of the foreign bank.

(2) The foreign banks have used their U.S. offices or affiliates to act as liaison with the U.S. issuer and the lead underwriter in the United States, to prepare documentation and to provide other services in connection with the underwriting. In some cases, the U.S. offices or affiliates that assisted the foreign bank with the underwriting receive a substantial portion of the revenue generated by the foreign bank's participation in the underwriting. In other cases, the U.S. offices receive "credit" from the head office of the foreign bank for their assistance in generating profits arising from the underwriting.

(3) By assuming the underwriting risk and booking the underwriting fees in their foreign offices or affiliates, the foreign banks are able to take advantage of an exemption under U.S. securities laws; a foreign underwriter is not required to register in the United States if the underwriter either does not distribute any of the securities in the United States or distributes them only through a registered broker-dealer.

(c) Permissible scope of underwriting activities. (1) A foreign bank that is subject to the BHC Act may engage in underwriting activities in the United States only if it has been authorized under section 4 of the Act. The foreign banks in question have argued that they are not engaged in underwriting activity in the United States because the underwriting activity takes place only outside the United States where the transaction is booked. The foreign banks refer to Regulation K, which defines "engaged in business" or "engaged in activities" to mean conducting an activity through an office or subsidiary in the United States. Because the underwriting is not booked in a U.S. office or subsidiary, the banks assert that the activity cannot be considered conducted in the United States.

(2) The Board believes that the position taken by the foreign banks is not supported by the Board's regulations or policies. Section 225.124 of the Board's Regulation Y (12 CFR 225.124(d)) states that a foreign bank will not be considered to be engaged in the activity of underwriting in the United States if the shares to be underwritten are distributed outside the United States. In the transactions in question, all of the securities to be underwritten by the foreign banks are distributed in the United States.

(3) Regulation K (12 CFR part 211) was amended in 1985 to provide clarification that a foreign bank may not own or control voting shares of a foreign company that directly

underwrites, sells or distributes securities in the United States (emphasis added). 12 CFR 211.23(f)(5)(ii). In proposing this latter provision, the Board clarified that no part of the prohibited underwriting process may take place in the United States and that the prohibition on the activity does not depend on the activity being conducted through an office or subsidiary in the United States. Moreover, in the transactions in question, there was significant participation by U.S. offices and affiliates of the foreign banks in the underwriting process. In some transactions, the foreign office at which the transactions were booked did not have any documentation on the particular transactions; all documentation was maintained in the United States office. In all cases, the U.S. offices or affiliates provided virtually all technical support for participation in the underwriting process and benefitted from profits generated by the activity.

(4) The fact that some technological and regulatory constraints on the delivery of cross-border services into the United States have been eliminated since the Regulation K definition of "engaged in business" was adopted in 1979 creates greater scope for banking organizations to deal with customers outside the U.S. bank regulatory framework. The definition in Regulation K, however, does not authorize foreign banking organizations to evade regulatory restrictions on securities activities in the United States by directly underwriting securities to be distributed in the United States or by using U.S. offices and affiliates to facilitate the prohibited activity. In the GLB Act, Congress established a framework within which both domestic and foreign banking organizations may underwrite and deal in securities in the United States. The GLB Act requires that banking organizations meet certain financial and managerial requirements in order to be able to engage in these activities in the United States. The Board believes the practices described above undermine this legislative framework and constitute an evasion of the requirements of the GLB Act and the Board's Regulation K. Foreign banking organizations that wish to conduct securities underwriting activity in the United States have long had the option of obtaining section 20 authority and now have the option of obtaining financial holding company status.

(d) Conclusion. The Board finds that the underwriting of securities to be distributed in the United States is an activity conducted in the United States, regardless of the location at which the underwriting risk is assumed and the underwriting fees are booked. Consequently, any banking organization that wishes to engage in such activity must either be a financial holding company under the GLB Act or have authority to engage in underwriting activity under section 4(c)(8) of the BHC Act (so-called "section 20 authority"). Revenue generated by underwriting bank-ineligible securities in such transactions should be attributed to the section 20 company for those foreign banks that operate under section 20 authority.

# Board of Governors of the Federal Reserve System
## 12 C.F.R. pt. 225

### Subpart I--Financial Holding Companies

*Sec.*
225.81  What is a financial holding company?
225.82  How does a bank holding company elect to become a financial holding company?
225.83  What are the consequences of failing to continue to meet applicable capital and management requirements?
225.84  What are the consequences of failing to maintain a satisfactory or better rating under the Community Reinvestment Act at all insured depository

institution subsidiaries?

225.85     Is notice to or approval from the Board required prior to engaging in a financial activity?

225.86     What activities are permissible for any financial holding company?

225.87     Is notice to the Board required after engaging in a financial activity?

225.88     How to request the Board to determine that an activity is financial in nature or incidental to a financial activity?

225.89     How to request approval to engage in an activity that is complementary to a financial activity?

225.90     What are the requirements for a foreign bank to be treated as a financial holding company?

225.91     How may a foreign bank elect to be treated as a financial holding company?

225.92     How does an election by a foreign bank become effective?

225.93     What are the consequences of a foreign bank failing to continue to meet applicable capital and management requirements?

225.94     What are the consequences of an insured branch or depository institution failing to maintain a satisfactory or better rating under the Community Reinvestment Act?

§ 225.81   What is a financial holding company?

(a) Definition. A financial holding company is a bank holding company that meets the requirements of this section.

(b) Requirements to be a financial holding company. In order to be a financial holding company:

(1) All depository institutions controlled by the bank holding company must be and remain well capitalized;

(2) All depository institutions controlled by the bank holding company must be and remain well managed; and

(3) The bank holding company must have made an effective election to become a financial holding company.

(c) Requirements for foreign banks that are or are owned by bank holding companies--(1) Foreign banks with U.S. branches or agencies that also own U.S. banks. A foreign bank that is a bank holding company and that operates a branch or agency or owns or controls a commercial lending company in the United States must comply with the requirements of this section, § 225.82, and §§ 225.90 through 225.92 in order to be a financial holding company. After it becomes a financial holding company, a foreign bank described in this paragraph will be subject to the provisions of §§ 225.83, 225.84, 225.93, and 225.94.

(2) Bank holding companies that own foreign banks with U.S. branches or agencies. A bank holding company that owns a foreign bank that operates a branch or agency or owns or controls a commercial lending company in the United States must comply with the requirements of this section, § 225.82, and §§ 225.90 through 225.92 in order to be a financial holding company. After it becomes a financial holding company, a bank holding company described in this paragraph will be subject to the provisions of §§ 225.83, 225.84, 225.93, and 225.94.

§ 225.82   How does a bank holding company elect to become a financial holding company?

(a) Filing requirement. A bank holding company may elect to become a financial holding company by filing a written declaration with the appropriate Reserve Bank. A declaration by a bank holding company is considered to be filed on the date that all information required by paragraph (b) of this section is received by the appropriate Reserve Bank.

(b) Contents of declaration. To be deemed complete, a declaration must:

(1) State that the bank holding company elects to be a financial holding company;

(2) Provide the name and head office address of the bank holding company and of each depository institution controlled by the bank holding company;

(3) Certify that each depository institution controlled by the bank holding company is well capitalized as of the date the bank holding company submits its declaration;

(4) Provide the capital ratios as of the close of the previous quarter for all relevant capital measures, as defined in section 38 of the Federal Deposit Insurance Act (12 U.S.C. 1831o), for each depository institution controlled by the company on the date the company submits its declaration; and

(5) Certify that each depository institution controlled by the company is well managed as of the date the company submits its declaration.

(c) Effectiveness of election. An election by a bank holding company to become a financial holding company shall not be effective if, during the period provided in paragraph (e) of this section, the Board finds that, as of the date the declaration was filed with the appropriate Reserve Bank:

(1) Any insured depository institution controlled by the bank holding company (except an institution excluded under paragraph (d) of this section) has not achieved at least a rating of "satisfactory record of meeting community credit needs" under the Community Reinvestment Act at the institution's most recent examination; or

(2) Any depository institution controlled by the bank holding company is not both well capitalized and well managed.

(d) Consideration of the CRA performance of a recently acquired insured depository institution. Except as provided in paragraph (f) of this section, an insured depository institution will be excluded for purposes of the review of the Community Reinvestment Act rating provisions of paragraph (c)(1) of this section if:

(1) The bank holding company acquired the insured depository institution during the 12-month period preceding the filing of an election under paragraph (a) of this section;

(2) The bank holding company has submitted an affirmative plan to the appropriate Federal banking agency for the institution to take actions necessary for the institution to achieve at least a rating of "satisfactory record of meeting community credit needs" under the Community Reinvestment Act at the next examination of the institution; and

(3) The appropriate Federal banking agency for the institution has accepted the plan described in paragraph (d)(2) of this section.

(e) Effective date of election--(1) In general. An election filed by a bank holding company under paragraph (a) of this section is effective on the 31st calendar day after the date that a complete declaration was filed with the appropriate Reserve Bank, unless the Board notifies the bank holding company prior to that time that the election is ineffective.

(2) Earlier notification that an election is effective. The Board or the appropriate Reserve Bank may notify a bank holding company that its election to become a financial holding company is effective prior to the 31st day after the date that a complete declaration was filed with the appropriate Reserve Bank. Such a notification must be in writing.

(f) Requests to become a financial holding company submitted as part of an application to become a bank holding company--(1) In general. A company that is not a bank holding company and has applied for the Board's approval to become a bank holding company under section 3(a)(1) of the BHC Act (12 U.S.C. 1842(a)(1)) may as part of that application submit a request to become a financial holding company.

(2) Contents of request. A request to become a financial holding company submitted as part of an application to become a bank holding company must:

(i) State that the company seeks to become a financial holding company on consummation of its proposal to become a bank holding company; and

(ii) Certify that each depository institution that would be controlled by the company on consummation of its proposal to become a bank holding company will be both well capitalized and well managed as of the date the company consummates the proposal.

(3) Request becomes a declaration and an effective election on date of consummation of bank holding company proposal. A complete request submitted by a company under this paragraph (f) becomes a complete declaration by a bank holding company for purposes of section 4(l) of the BHC Act (12 U.S.C. 1843(l)) and becomes an effective election for purposes of § 225.81(b) on the date that the company lawfully consummates its proposal under section 3 of the BHC Act (12 U.S.C. 1842), unless the Board notifies the company at any time prior to consummation of the proposal and that:

(i) Any depository institution that would be controlled by the company on consummation of the proposal will not be both well capitalized and well managed on the date of consummation; or

(ii) Any insured depository institution that would be controlled by the company on consummation of the proposal has not achieved at least a rating of "satisfactory record of meeting community credit needs" under the Community Reinvestment Act at the institution's most recent examination.

(4) Limited exclusion for recently acquired institutions not available. Unless the Board determines otherwise, an insured depository institution that is controlled or would be controlled by the company as part of its proposal to become a bank holding company may not be excluded for purposes of evaluating the Community Reinvestment Act criterion described in this paragraph or in paragraph (d) of this section.

(g) Board's authority to exercise supervisory authority over a financial holding company. An effective election to become a financial holding company does not in any way limit the Board's statutory authority under the BHC Act, the Federal Deposit Insurance Act, or any other relevant Federal statute to take appropriate action, including imposing supervisory limitations, restrictions, or prohibitions on the activities and acquisitions of a bank holding company that has elected to become a financial holding company, or enforcing compliance with applicable law.

§ 225.83  What are the consequences of failing to continue to meet applicable capital and management requirements?

(a) Notice by the Board. If the Board finds that a financial holding company controls any depository institution that is not well capitalized or well managed, the Board will notify the company in writing that it is not in compliance with the applicable requirement(s) for a financial holding company and identify the area(s) of noncompliance. The Board may provide this notice at any time before or after receiving notice from the financial holding company under paragraph (b) of this section.

(b) Notification by a financial holding company required--(1) Notice to Board. A financial holding company must notify the Board in writing within 15 calendar days of becoming aware that any depository institution controlled by the company has ceased to be well capitalized or well managed. This notification must identify the depository institution involved and the area(s) of noncompliance.

(2) Triggering events for notice to the Board--(i) Well capitalized. A company

becomes aware that a depository institution it controls is no longer well capitalized upon the occurrence of any material event that would change the category assigned to the institution for purposes of section 38 of the Federal Deposit Insurance Act (12 U.S.C. 1831o). . . .

(ii) Well managed. A company becomes aware that a depository institution it controls is no longer well managed at the time the depository institution receives written notice from the appropriate Federal or state banking agency that either its composite rating or its rating for management is not at least satisfactory.

(c) Execution of agreement acceptable to the Board--(1) Agreement required; time period. Within 45 days after receiving a notice from the Board under paragraph (a) of this section, the company must execute an agreement acceptable to the Board to comply with all applicable capital and management requirements.

(2) Extension of time for executing agreement. Upon request by a company, the Board may extend the 45-day period under paragraph (c)(1) of this section if the Board determines that granting additional time is appropriate under the circumstances. A request by a company for additional time must include an explanation of why an extension is necessary.

(3) Agreement requirements. An agreement required by paragraph (c)(1) of this section to correct a capital or management deficiency must:

(i) Explain the specific actions that the company will take to correct all areas of noncompliance;

(ii) Provide a schedule within which each action will be taken;

(iii) Provide any other information that the Board may require; and

(iv) Be acceptable to the Board.

(d) Limitations during period of noncompliance--Until the Board determines that a company has corrected the conditions described in a notice under paragraph (a) of this section:

(1) The Board may impose any limitations or conditions on the conduct or activities of the company or any of its affiliates as the Board finds to be appropriate and consistent with the purposes of the BHC Act; and

(2) The company and its affiliates may not commence any additional activity or acquire control or shares of any company under section 4(k) of the BHC Act without prior approval from the Board.

(e) Consequences of failure to correct conditions within 180 days--(1) Divestiture of depository institutions. If a company does not correct the conditions described in a notice under paragraph (a) of this section within 180 days of receipt of the notice or such additional time as the Board may permit, the Board may order the company to divest ownership or control of any depository institution owned or controlled by the company. Such divestiture must be done in accordance with the terms and conditions established by the Board.

(2) Alternative method of complying with a divestiture order. A company may comply with an order issued under paragraph (e)(1) of this section by ceasing to engage (both directly and through any subsidiary that is not a depository institution or a subsidiary of a depository institution) in any activity that may be conducted only under section 4(k), (n), or (o) of the BHC Act (12 U.S.C. 1843(k), (n), or (o)). The termination of activities must be completed within the time period referred to in paragraph (e)(1) of this section and in accordance with the terms and conditions acceptable to the Board.

(f) Consultation with other agencies. In taking any action under this section, the Board will consult with the relevant Federal and state regulatory authorities.

§ 225.84 What are the consequences of failing to maintain a satisfactory or better rating under the Community Reinvestment Act at all insured depository institution subsidiaries?

(a) Limitations on activities--(1) In general. Upon receiving a notice regarding performance under the Community Reinvestment Act in accordance with paragraph (a)(2) of this section, a financial holding company may not:

(i) Commence any additional activity under section 4(k) or 4(n) of the BHC Act (12 U.S.C. 1843(k) or (n)); or

(ii) Directly or indirectly acquire control, including all or substantially all of the assets, of a company engaged in any activity under section 4(k) or 4(n) of the BHC Act (12 U.S.C. 1843(k) or (n)).

(2) Notification. A financial holding company receives notice for purposes of this paragraph at the time that the appropriate Federal banking agency for any insured depository institution controlled by the company or the Board provides notice to the institution or company that the institution has received a rating of "needs to improve record of meeting community credit needs" or "substantial noncompliance in meeting community credit needs" in the institution's most recent examination under the Community Reinvestment Act.

(b) Exceptions for certain activities--(1) Continuation of investment activities. The prohibition in paragraph (a) of this section does not prevent a financial holding company from continuing to make investments in the ordinary course of conducting merchant banking activities under section 4(k)(4)(H) of the BHC Act (12 U.S.C. 1843(k)(4)(H)) or insurance company investment activities under section 4(k)(4)(I) of the BHC Act (12 U.S.C. 1843(k)(4)(I)) if:

(i) The financial holding company lawfully was a financial holding company and commenced the merchant banking activity under section 4(k)(4)(H) of the BHC Act (12 U.S.C. 1843(k)(4)(H)) or the insurance company investment activity under section 4(k)(4) (I) of the BHC Act (12 U.S.C. 1843(k)(4)(I)) prior to the time that an insured depository institution controlled by the financial holding company received a rating below "satisfactory record of meeting community credit needs" under the Community Reinvestment Act; and

(ii) The Board has not, in the exercise of its supervisory authority, advised the financial holding company that these activities must be restricted.

(2) Activities that are closely related to banking. The prohibition in paragraph (a) of this section does not prevent a financial holding company from commencing any additional activity or acquiring control of a company engaged in any activity under section 4(c) of the BHC Act (12 U.S.C. 1843(c)), if the company complies with the notice, approval, and other requirements of that section and section 4(j) of the BHC Act (12 U.S.C. 1843(j)).

(c) Duration of prohibitions. The prohibitions described in paragraph (a) of this section shall continue in effect until such time as each insured depository institution controlled by the financial holding company has achieved at least a rating of "satisfactory record of meeting community credit needs" under the Community Reinvestment Act at the most recent examination of the institution.

§ 225.85  Is notice to or approval from the Board required prior to engaging in a financial activity?

(a) No prior approval required generally--(1) In general. A financial holding company and any subsidiary (other than a depository institution or subsidiary of a depository institution) of the financial holding company may engage in any activity listed in § 225.86, or acquire shares or control of a company engaged exclusively in activities listed in § 225.86, without providing prior notice to or obtaining prior approval from the Board unless required under paragraph (c) of this section. . . .

(b) Locations in which a financial holding company may conduct financial activities. A financial holding company may conduct any activity listed in § 225.86 at any location in the United States or at any location outside of the United States subject to the laws of the jurisdiction in which the activity is conducted. . . .

§ 225.86  What activities are permissible for any financial holding company?

The following activities are financial in nature or incidental to a financial activity:

(a) Activities determined to be closely related to banking. (1) Any activity that the Board had determined by regulation prior to November 12, 1999, to be so closely related to banking as to be a proper incident thereto, subject to the terms and conditions contained in this part, unless modified by the Board. These activities are listed in § 225.28.

(2) Any activity that the Board had determined by an order that was in effect on November 12, 1999, to be so closely related to banking as to be a proper incident thereto, subject to the terms and conditions contained in this part and those in the authorizing orders. These activities are:

(i) Providing administrative and other services to mutual funds (Societe Generale, 84 Federal Reserve Bulletin 680 (1998));

(ii) Owning shares of a securities exchange (J.P. Morgan & Co, Inc., and UBS AG, 86 Federal Reserve Bulletin 61 (2000));

(iii) Acting as a certification authority for digital signatures and authenticating the identity of persons conducting financial and nonfinancial transactions (Bayerische Hypo- und Vereinsbank AG, et al., 86 Federal Reserve Bulletin 56 (2000));

(iv) Providing employment histories to third parties for use in making credit decisions and to depository institutions and their affiliates for use in the ordinary course of business (Norwest Corporation, 81 Federal Reserve Bulletin 732 (1995));

(v) Check cashing and wire transmission services (Midland Bank, PLC, 76 Federal Reserve Bulletin 860 (1990) (check cashing); Norwest Corporation, 81 Federal Reserve Bulletin 1130 (1995) (money transmission));

(vi) In connection with offering banking services, providing notary public services, selling postage stamps and postage-paid envelopes, providing vehicle registration services, and selling public transportation tickets and tokens (Popular, Inc., 84 Federal Reserve Bulletin 481 (1998)); and

(vii) Real estate title abstracting (The First National Company, 81 Federal Reserve Bulletin 805 (1995)).

(b) Activities determined to be usual in connection with the transaction of banking abroad. Any activity that the Board had determined by regulation in effect on November 11, 1999, to be usual in connection with the transaction of banking or other financial operations abroad (see § 211.5(d) of this chapter), subject to the terms and conditions in part 211 and Board interpretations in effect on that date regarding the scope and conduct of the activity. In addition to the activities listed in paragraphs (a) and (c) of this section, these activities are:

(1) Providing management consulting services, including to any person with respect to nonfinancial matters, so long as the management consulting services are advisory and do not allow the financial holding company to control the person to which the services are provided;

(2) Operating a travel agency in connection with financial services offered by the financial holding company or others; and

(3) Organizing, sponsoring, and managing a mutual fund, so long as:

(i) The fund does not exercise managerial control over the entities in which the fund invests; and

(ii) The financial holding company reduces its ownership in the fund, if any, to less than 25 percent of the equity of the fund within one year of sponsoring the fund or such additional period as the Board permits.

(c) Activities permitted under section 4(k)(4) of the BHC Act (12 U.S.C. 1843(k) (4)). Any activity defined to be financial in nature under sections 4(k)(4)(A) through (E), (H) and (I) of the BHC Act (12 U.S.C. 1843(k)(4)(A) through (E), (H) and (I)).

§ 225.87  Is notice to the Board required after engaging in a financial activity?

(a) Post-transaction notice generally required to engage in a financial activity. A financial holding company that commences an activity or acquires shares of a company engaged in an activity listed in § 225.86 must notify the appropriate Reserve Bank in writing within 30 calendar days after commencing the activity or consummating the acquisition by using the appropriate form.

(b) Cases in which notice to the Board is not required--(1) Acquisitions that do not involve control of a company. A notice under paragraph (a) of this section is not required in connection with the acquisition of shares of a company if, following the acquisition, the financial holding company does not control the company.

(2) No additional notice required to engage de novo in an activity for which a financial holding company already has provided notice. After a financial holding company provides the appropriate Reserve Bank with notice that the company is engaged in an activity listed in § 225.86, a financial holding company may, unless otherwise notified by the Board, commence the activity de novo through any subsidiary that the financial holding company is authorized to control without providing additional notice under paragraph (a) of this section.

(3) Conduct of certain investment activities. Unless required by paragraph (b)(4) of this section, a financial holding company is not required to provide notice under paragraph (a) of this section of any individual acquisition of shares of a company as part of the conduct by a financial holding company of securities underwriting, dealing, or market making activities as described in section 4(k)(4)(E) of the BHC Act (12 U.S.C. 1843(k)(4) (E)), merchant banking activities conducted pursuant to section 4(k)(4)(H) of the BHC Act (12 U.S.C. 1843(k)(4)(H)), or insurance company investment activities conducted pursuant to section 4(k)(4)(I) of the BHC Act (12 U.S.C. 1843(k)(4)(I)), if the financial holding company previously has notified the Board under paragraph (a) of this section that the company has commenced the relevant securities, merchant banking, or insurance company investment activities, as relevant.

(4) Notice of large merchant banking or insurance company investments. Notwithstanding paragraph (b)(1) or (b)(3) of this section, a financial holding company must provide notice under paragraph (a) of the section if:

(i) As part of a merchant banking activity conducted under section 4(k)(4)(H) of the BHC Act (12 U.S.C. 1843(k)(4)(H)), the financial holding company acquires more than 5 percent of the shares, assets, or ownership interests of any company at a total cost that exceeds the lesser of 5 percent of the financial holding company's Tier 1 capital or $200 million;

(ii) As part of an insurance company investment activity conducted under section 4(k)(4)(I) of the BHC Act (12 U.S.C. 1843(k)(4)(I)), the financial holding company acquires more than 5 percent of the shares, assets, or ownership interests of any company at a total cost that exceeds the lesser of 5 percent of the financial holding company's Tier 1 capital or $200 million; or

(iii) The Board in the exercise of its supervisory authority notifies the financial holding company that a notice is necessary.

### § 225.88  How to request the Board to determine that an activity is financial in nature or incidental to a financial activity?

(a) Requests regarding activities that may be financial in nature or incidental to a financial activity. A financial holding company or other interested party may request a determination from the Board that an activity not listed in § 225.86 is financial in nature or incidental to a financial activity.

(b) Required information. A request submitted under this section must be in writing and must:

(1) Identify and define the activity for which the determination is sought, specifically describing what the activity would involve and how the activity would be conducted;

(2) Explain in detail why the activity should be considered financial in nature or incidental to a financial activity; and

(3) Provide information supporting the requested determination and any other information required by the Board concerning the proposed activity.

(c) Board procedures for reviewing requests--(1) Consultation with the Secretary of the Treasury. Upon receipt of the request, the Board will provide the Secretary of the Treasury a copy of the request and consult with the Secretary in accordance with section 4(k)(2)(A) of the BHC Act (12 U.S.C. 1843(k)(2)(A)).

(2) Public notice. The Board may, as appropriate and after consultation with the Secretary, publish a description of the proposal in the Federal Register with a request for public comment.

(d) Board action. The Board will endeavor to make a decision on any request filed under paragraph (a) of this section within 60 calendar days following the completion of both the consultative process described in paragraph (c)(1) of this section and the public comment period, if any.

(e) Advisory opinions regarding scope of financial activities--(1) Written request. A financial holding company or other interested party may request an advisory opinion from the Board about whether a specific proposed activity falls within the scope of an activity listed in § 225.86 as financial in nature or incidental to a financial activity. The request must be submitted in writing and must contain:

(i) A detailed description of the particular activity in which the company proposes to engage or the product or service the company proposes to provide;

(ii) An explanation supporting an interpretation regarding the scope of the permissible financial activity; and

(iii) Any additional information requested by the Board regarding the activity.

(2) Board response. The Board will provide an advisory opinion within 45 calendar days of receiving a complete written request under paragraph (e)(1) of this section.

### § 225.89  How to request approval to engage in an activity that is complementary to a financial activity?

(a) Prior Board approval is required. A financial holding company that seeks to engage in or acquire more than 5 percent of the outstanding shares of any class of voting securities of a company engaged in an activity that the financial holding company believes is complementary to a financial activity must obtain prior approval from the Board in accordance with section 4(j) of the BHC Act (12 U.S.C. 1843(j)). The notice must be in writing and must:

(1) Identify and define the proposed complementary activity, specifically describing what the activity would involve and how the activity would be conducted;

(2) Identify the financial activity for which the proposed activity would be complementary and provide detailed information sufficient to support a finding that the proposed activity should be considered complementary to the identified financial activity;

(3) Describe the scope and relative size of the proposed activity, as measured by the percentage of the projected financial holding company revenues expected to be derived from and assets associated with conducting the activity;

(4) Discuss the risks that conducting the activity may reasonably be expected to pose to the safety and soundness of the subsidiary depository institutions of the financial holding company and to the financial system generally;

(5) Describe the potential adverse effects, including potential conflicts of interest, decreased or unfair competition, or other risks, that conducting the activity could raise, and explain the measures the financial holding company proposes to take to address those potential effects;

(6) Describe the potential benefits to the public, such as greater convenience, increased competition, or gains in efficiency, that the proposal reasonably can be expected to produce; and

(7) Provide any information about the financial and managerial resources of the financial holding company and any other information requested by the Board.

(b) Factors for consideration by the Board. In evaluating a notice to engage in a complementary activity, the Board must consider whether:

(1) The proposed activity is complementary to a financial activity;

(2) The proposed activity would pose a substantial risk to the safety or soundness of depository institutions or the financial system generally; and

(3) The proposal could be expected to produce benefits to the public that outweigh possible adverse effects.

(c) Board action. The Board will inform the financial holding company in writing of the Board's determination regarding the proposed activity within the period described in section 4(j) of the BHC Act (12 U.S.C. 1843(j)). . . .

§ 225.90  What are the requirements for a foreign bank to be treated as a financial holding company?

(a) Foreign banks as financial holding companies. A foreign bank that operates a branch or agency or owns or controls a commercial lending company in the United States, and any company that owns or controls such a foreign bank, will be treated as a financial holding company if:

(1) The foreign bank, any other foreign bank that maintains a U.S. branch, agency, or commercial lending company and is controlled by the foreign bank or company, and any U.S. depository institution subsidiary that is owned or controlled by the foreign bank or company, is and remains well capitalized and well managed; and

(2) The foreign bank, and any company that owns or controls the foreign bank, has made an effective election to be treated as a financial holding company under this subpart.

(b) Standards for "well capitalized." A foreign bank will be considered "well capitalized" if either:

(1)(i) Its home country supervisor . . . has adopted risk-based capital standards consistent with the Capital Accord of the Basel Committee on Banking Supervision (Basel Accord);

(ii) The foreign bank maintains a Tier 1 capital to total risk-based assets ratio of 6 percent and a total capital to total risk-based assets ratio of 10 percent, as calculated under its home country standard; and

(iii) The foreign bank's capital is comparable to the capital required for a U.S. bank owned by a financial holding company; or

(2) The foreign bank has obtained a determination from the Board under § 225.91 (c) that the foreign bank's capital is otherwise comparable to the capital that would be required of a U.S. bank owned by a financial holding company.

(c) Standards for "well managed." A foreign bank will be considered "well managed" if:

(1) The foreign bank has received at least a satisfactory composite rating of its U.S. branch, agency, and commercial lending company operations at its most recent assessment;

(2) The home country supervisor of the foreign bank consents to the foreign bank expanding its activities in the United States to include activities permissible for a financial holding company; and

(3) The management of the foreign bank meets standards comparable to those required of a U.S. bank owned by a financial holding company.

### § 225.91  How may a foreign bank elect to be treated as a financial holding company?

(a) Filing requirement. A foreign bank that operates a branch or agency or owns or controls a commercial lending company in the United States, or a company that owns or controls such a foreign bank, may elect to be treated as a financial holding company by filing a written declaration with the appropriate Reserve Bank.

(b) Contents of declaration. The declaration must:

(1) State that the foreign bank or the company elects to be treated as a financial holding company;

(2) Provide the risk-based capital ratios and amount of Tier 1 capital and total assets of the foreign bank, and of each foreign bank that maintains a U.S. branch, agency, or commercial lending company and is controlled by the foreign bank or company, as of the close of the most recent quarter and as of the close of the most recent audited reporting period;

(3) Certify that the foreign bank, and each foreign bank that maintains a U.S. branch, agency, or commercial lending company and is controlled by the foreign bank or company, meets the standards of well capitalized set out in § 225.90(b)(1)(i) and (ii) or § 225.90(b)(2) as of the date the foreign bank or company files its election;

(4) Certify that the foreign bank, and each foreign bank that maintains a U.S. branch, agency, or commercial lending company and is controlled by the foreign bank or company, is well managed as defined in § 225.90(c)(1) as of the date the foreign bank or company files its election;

(5) Certify that all U.S. depository institution subsidiaries of the foreign bank or company are well capitalized and well managed as of the date the foreign bank or company files its election; and

(6) Provide the capital ratios for all relevant capital measures (as defined in section 38 of the Federal Deposit Insurance Act (12 U.S.C. 1831(o))) as of the close of the previous quarter for each U.S. depository institution subsidiary of the foreign bank or company.

(c) Pre-clearance process. Before filing an election to be treated as a financial holding company, a foreign bank or company may file a request for review of its qualifications to be treated as a financial holding company. The Board will endeavor to make a determination on such requests within 30 days of receipt. A foreign bank that has not been found, or that is chartered in a country where no bank from that country has been found, by the Board under the Bank Holding Company Act or the International Banking Act to be subject to comprehensive supervision or regulation on a consolidated basis by its home country supervisor is required to use this process.

§ 225.92  How does an election by a foreign bank become effective?

(a) In general. An election described in § 225.91 is effective on the 31st day after the date that an election was received by the appropriate Federal Reserve Bank, unless the Board notifies the foreign bank or company prior to that time that:

(1) The election is ineffective; or

(2) The period is extended with the consent of the foreign bank or company making the election.

(b) Earlier notification that an election is effective. The Board or the appropriate Federal Reserve Bank may notify a foreign bank or company that its election to be treated as a financial holding company is effective prior to the 31st day after the election was filed with the appropriate Federal Reserve Bank. Such notification must be in writing.

(c) Under what circumstances will the Board find an election to be ineffective? An election to be treated as a financial holding company shall not be effective if, during the period provided in paragraph (a) of this section, the Board finds that:

(1) The foreign bank certificant, or any foreign bank that operates a branch or agency or owns or controls a commercial lending company in the United States and is controlled by a foreign bank or company certificant, is not both well capitalized and well managed;

(2) Any U.S. insured depository institution subsidiary of the foreign bank or company (except an institution excluded under paragraph (d) of this section) or any U.S. branch of a foreign bank that is insured by the Federal Deposit Insurance Corporation has not achieved at least a rating of "satisfactory record of meeting community needs" under the Community Reinvestment Act at the institution's most recent examination;

(3) Any U.S. depository institution subsidiary of the foreign bank or company is not both well capitalized and well managed; or

(4) The Board does not have sufficient information to assess whether the foreign bank or company making the election meets the requirements of this subpart.

(d) How is CRA performance of recently acquired insured depository institutions considered? An insured depository institution will be excluded for purposes of the review of CRA ratings described in paragraph (c)(2) of this section consistent with the provisions of § 225.82(d).

(e) Factors used in the Board's determination regarding comparability of capital and management.--(1) In general. In determining whether a foreign bank is well capitalized and well managed in accordance with comparable capital and management standards, the Board will give due regard to national treatment and equality of competitive opportunity. In this regard, the Board may take into account the foreign bank's composition of capital, Tier 1 capital to total assets leverage ratio, accounting standards, long-term debt ratings, reliance on government support to meet capital requirements, the foreign bank's anti-money laundering procedures, whether the foreign bank is subject to comprehensive supervision or regulation on a consolidated basis, and other factors that may affect analysis of capital and management. The Board will consult with the home country supervisor for the foreign bank as appropriate.

(2) Assessment of consolidated supervision. A foreign bank that is not subject to comprehensive supervision on a consolidated basis by its home country authorities may not

be considered well capitalized and well managed unless:

(i) The home country has made significant progress in establishing arrangements for comprehensive supervision on a consolidated basis; and

(ii) The foreign bank is in strong financial condition as demonstrated, for example, by capital levels that significantly exceed the minimum levels that are required for a well capitalized determination and strong asset quality.

§ 225.93  What are the consequences of a foreign bank failing to continue to meet applicable capital and management requirements?

(a) Notice by the Board. If a foreign bank or company has made an effective election to be treated as a financial holding company under this subpart and the Board finds that the foreign bank, any foreign bank that maintains a U.S. branch, agency, orx ommercial lending company and is controlled by the foreign bank or company, or any U.S. depository institution subsidiary controlled by the foreign bank or company, ceases to be well capitalized or well managed, the Board will notify the foreign bank and company, if any, in writing that it is not in compliance with the applicable requirement(s) for a financial holding company and identify the areas of noncompliance.

(b) Notification by a financial holding company required.--(1) Notice to Board. Promptly upon becoming aware that the foreign bank, any foreign bank that maintains a U.S. branch, agency, or commercial lending company and is controlled by the foreign bank or company, or any U.S. depository institution subsidiary of the foreign bank or company, has ceased to be well capitalized or well managed, the foreign bank and company, if any, must notify the Board and identify the area of noncompliance.

(2) Triggering events for notice to the Board--(i) Well capitalized. A foreign bank becomes aware that it is no longer well capitalized at the time that the foreign bank or company is required to file a report of condition (or similar supervisory report) with its home country supervisor or the appropriate Federal Reserve Bank that indicates that the foreign bank no longer meets the well capitalized standards.

(ii) Well managed. A foreign bank becomes aware that it is no longer well managed at the time that the foreign bank receives written notice from the appropriate Federal Reserve Bank that the composite rating of its U.S. branch, agency, and commercial lending company operations is not at least satisfactory.

(c) Execution of agreement acceptable to the Board--(1) Agreement required; time period. Within 45 days after receiving a notice under paragraph (a) of this section, the foreign bank or company must execute an agreement acceptable to the Board to comply with all applicable capital and management requirements.

(2) Extension of time for executing agreement. Upon request by the foreign bank or company, the Board may extend the 45-day period under paragraph (c)(1) of this section if the Board determines that granting additional time is appropriate under the circumstances. A request by a foreign bank or company for additional time must include an explanation of why an extension is necessary.

(3) Agreement requirements. An agreement required by paragraph (c)(1) of this section to correct a capital or management deficiency must:

(i) Explain the specific actions that the foreign bank or company will take to correct all areas of noncompliance;

(ii) Provide a schedule within which each action will be taken;

(iii) Provide any other information that the Board may require; and

(iv) Be acceptable to the Board.

(d) Limitations during period of noncompliance--Until the Board determines that a foreign bank or company has corrected the conditions described in a notice under paragraph (a) of this section:

(1) The Board may impose any limitations or conditions on the conduct or the U.S. activities of the foreign bank or company or any of its affiliates as the Board finds to be appropriate and consistent with the purposes of the Bank Holding Company Act; and

(2) The foreign bank or company and its affiliates may not commence any additional activity in the United States or acquire control or shares of any company under section 4(k) of the Bank Holding Company Act (12 U.S.C. 1843(k)) without prior approval from the Board.

(e) Consequences of failure to correct conditions within 180 days--(1) Termination of Offices and Divestiture. If a foreign bank or company does not correct the conditions described in a notice under paragraph (a) of this section within 180 days of receipt of the notice or such additional time as the Board may permit, the Board may order the foreign bank or company to terminate the foreign bank's U.S. branches and agencies and divest any commercial lending companies owned or controlled by the foreign bank or company. Such divestiture must be done in accordance with the terms and conditions established by the Board.

(2) Alternative method of complying with a divestiture order. A foreign bank or company may comply with an order issued under paragraph (e)(1) of this section by ceasing to engage (both directly and through any subsidiary that is not a depository institution or a subsidiary of a depository institution) in any activity that may be conducted only under section 4(k), (n), or (o) of the BHC Act (12 U.S.C. 1843(k), (n) and (o)). The termination of activities must be completed within the time period referred to in paragraph (e)(1) of this section and subject to terms and conditions acceptable to the Board.

(f) Consultation with Other Agencies. In taking any action under this section, the Board will consult with the relevant Federal and state regulatory authorities and the appropriate home country supervisor(s) of the foreign bank.

§ 225.94  What are the consequences of an insured branch or depository institution failing to maintain a satisfactory or better rating under the Community Reinvestment Act?

(a) Insured branch as an "insured depository institution." A U.S. branch of a foreign bank that is insured by the Federal Deposit Insurance Corporation shall be treated as an "insured depository institution" for purposes of § 225.84.

(b) Applicability. The provisions of § 225.84, with the modifications contained in this section, shall apply to a foreign bank that operates an insured branch referred to in paragraph (a) of this section or an insured depository institution in the United States, and any company that owns or controls such a foreign bank, that has made an effective election under § 225.92 in the same manner and to the same extent as they apply to a financial holding company.

**Notes and Comments 9.28.** *Questions concerning financial services of banks and holding companies.* In light of the preceding material, consider the following questions.

**a.** QNB would like to underwrite a new issue of IBN equity securities. The issue will be distributed both in the United States and in other countries. Can QNB participate in this underwriting? (*See* 12 U.S.C. §§ 24(Seventh), 378 (a)(1).)

**b.** First Credulity Bank (FCB), a nonmember, FDIC-insured, state-chartered bank would like to underwrite the new issue of IBN securities. Can FCB participate in this underwriting? (*See id.* § 378(a)(1).)

     **c.** QNB would like to acquire a controlling stock interest in Major Securities Firm, Inc. (MSF), which engages in securities underwriting, brokerage, investment advisory services and the like. Is this acquisition permitted? Would it be permitted for FCB? (*See id.* § 24a.)

     **d.** What if Quarter Holding Corporation (QHC), the holding company of which QNB is a subsidiary, wanted to acquire the controlling interest in MSF? (*See* 12 C.F.R. §§ 225.82(a)-(f), 225.85(a), 225.86(c), 225.87(a), 225.88.)

     **e.** QNB intends to incorporate a subsidiary, DotCorp, that will market over the Internet ownership interests in high-velocity competitive biological entities (HVCBEs). Each HVCBE valued at $1 million or more would be offered to the public in at least 1000 equal ownership interest units, with a minimum required purchase of 100 units. DotCorp expects to use QNB's website and database of customers in its marketing efforts. What is the likelihood that QNB's proposals would be approved by the Comptroller? (*See* 12 U.S.C. § 24a(a)(2)(A) (i), (a)(2)(C)-(D), (a)(3)(A), (b)(1)(A)(i)-(ii).)

     **f.** Would it make any difference to your answers to (a)-(e) if QNB or FCB were a subsidiary of Quirki Bank of Nusquam, which is organized under the laws of Nusquam? (*See* 12 U.S.C. § 1843(k); 12 C.F.R. §§ 225.82(a)-(f), 225.85 (a), 225.86(c), 225.87(a), 225.88, 225.90-225.92.)

**9.29.** Review the provisions of 12 C.F.R. pt. 211, excerpted in Chapter 5, § 2, *supra*, and particularly §§ 211.4(a)(2), (b), 211.6(b), and 211.10(a)(8), (11), (13)-(15), (b)-(c), before answering the following questions.

     **a.** QNB has a branch in Nusquam, where banks generally compete freely in both the commercial banking and investment banking markets. QNB would like to offer securities services in Nusquam, including the underwriting of private equity and debt securities and of Nusquami Government-issued long-term bonds. Is it likely that QNB's Nusquami branch will be permitted to engage in these activities? (*See* 12 C.F.R. § 211.4(a)(2), (b); *but see* 12 U.S.C. § 604a.)

     **b.** QBN of Nusquam has a U.S. subsidiary, Quirki International Bank of Nusquam (QIBN), organized under the Edge Act. QBN would like to have QIBN engage in underwriting of private equity and debt securities and of U.S. Government-issued long-term bonds in the United States. Is it likely that QIBN will be permitted to engage in these activities? (*See* 12 C.F.R. § 211.6(b).)

     **c.** QNB has an Edge Act subsidiary, Quarter Bank International (QBI). Can QBI engage in the following activities in Nusquam? (i) Sponsor and manage a mutual fund; (ii) Underwrite equity securities of Nusquami companies and debt securities of the Government of Nusquam and of private Nusquami companies; or, (iii) engage in the purchase, sale and brokerage of debt and equity securities of private companies for its own account and on behalf of its Nusquami customers? (*See id.* § 211.10(a)(11), (a)(13), (a)(14), (c), (a)(19), (b).)

     **d.** QNB has a subsidiary bank chartered under the laws of Nusquam and operating there. Could this subsidiary engage in the activities described in (c)(i)-(iii), *supra*? (*See id.* §§ 211.2(o), 211.10.)

     **e.** QHC has a subsidiary bank chartered under the laws of Nusquam and operating there. Could this subsidiary engage in the activities described in (c)(i)-(iii), *supra*? (*See id.* §§ 211.2(o), 211.10.)

**9.30.** The restrictions that U.S. law imposes on the securities activities of banking enterprises are unusual in international banking practice. Other regulatory systems are markedly more tolerant of the exercise of commercial and investment banking activities within the same enterprise. For example, could a banking enterprise organized under the laws of an EU member country engage in the securities activities described in (c)(i)-(iii), *supra*? Consider the following excerpts.

## Investment Services in the Securities Field
### Council Directive 93/22/EEC (10 May 1993)

TITLE I Definitions and scope
Article 1
For the purposes of this Directive:

. . .

2. investment firm shall mean any legal person the regular occupation or business of which is the provision of investment services for third parties on a professional basis. ...

6. home Member State shall mean:

(a) where the investment firm is a natural person, the Member State in which his head office is situated;

(b) where the investment firm is a legal person, the Member State in which its registered office is situated or, if under its national law it has no registered office, the Member State in which its head office is situated;

(c) in the case of a market, the Member State in which the registered office of the body which provides trading facilities is situated or, if under its national law it has no registered office, the Member State in which that body's head office is situated;

7. host Member State shall mean the Member State in which an investment firm has a branch or provides services;

8. branch shall mean a place of business which is a part of an investment firm, which has no legal personality and which provides investment services for which the investment firm has been authorized; all the places of business set up in the same Member State by an investment firm with headquarters in another Member State shall be regarded as a single branch; . . .

10. qualifying holding shall mean any direct or indirect holding in an investment firm which represents 10% or more of the capital or of the voting rights or which makes it possible to exercise a significant influence over the management of the investment firm in which that holding subsists . . . ;

Article 2

1. This Directive shall apply to all investment firms. Only . . . Articles . . . 10, 11, . . . 14 (3) and (4), 15, . . . however, shall apply to credit institutions the authorization of which . . . covers one or more of the investment services listed in Section A of the Annex to this Directive.

2. This Directive shall not apply to:

(a) insurance undertakings . . . or undertakings carrying on the reinsurance and retrocession activities ... ;

(b) firms which provide investment services exclusively for their parent undertakings, for their subsidiaries or for other subsidiaries of their parent undertakings;

(c) persons providing an investment service where that service is provided in an incidental manner in the course of a professional activity and that activity is regulated by legal or regulatory provisions or a code of ethics governing the profession which do not exclude the provision of that service;

(d) firms that provide investment services consisting exclusively in the administration of employee-participation schemes;

(e) firms that provide investment services that consist in providing both the services referred to in (b) and those referred to in (d). . . .

TITLE II Conditions for taking up business
Article 3

1. Each Member State shall make access to the business of investment firms subject to authorization for investment firms of which it is the home Member State. Such authorization shall be granted by the home Member State's competent authorities designated in accordance with Article 22. The authorization shall specify the investment services referred to in Section A of the Annex which the undertaking is authorized to provide. The authorization may also cover one or more of the non-core services. . . .

2. Each Member State shall require that:

- any investment firm which is a legal person and which, under its national law, has a registered office shall have its head office in the same Member State as its registered office,
- any other investment firm shall have its head office in the Member State which issued its authorization and in which it actually carries on its business.

3. Without prejudice to other conditions of general application laid down by national law, the competent authorities shall not grant authorization unless:

- an investment firm has sufficient initial capital . . . having regard to the nature of the investment service in question,
- the persons who effectively direct the business of an investment firm are of sufficiently good repute and are sufficiently experienced. . . .

4. Member States shall also require that every application for authorization be accompanied by a programme of operations setting out inter alia the types of business envisaged and the organizational structure of the investment firm concerned. . . .

Article 4

The competent authorities shall not grant authorization to take up the business of investment firms until they have been informed of the identities of the shareholders or members, whether direct or indirect, natural or legal persons, that have qualifying holdings and of the amounts of those holdings.

The competent authorities shall refuse authorization if, taking into account the need to ensure the sound and prudent management of an investment firm, they are not satisfied as to the suitability of the aforementioned shareholders or members.

Article 5

In the case of branches of investment firms that have registered offices [outside] the Community and are commencing or carrying on business, the Member States shall not apply provisions that result in treatment more favourable than that accorded to branches of investment firms that have registered offices in Member States.

Article 6

The competent authorities of the other Member State involved shall be consulted beforehand on the authorization of any investment firm which is:

- a subsidiary of an investment firm or credit institution authorized in another Member State,
- a subsidiary of the parent undertaking of an investment firm or credit institution authorized in another Member State, or
- controlled by the same natural or legal persons as control an investment firm or credit institution authorized in another Member State.

TITLE III Relations with third countries
Article 7
1. The competent authorities of the Member States shall inform the Commission:
(a) of the authorization of any firm which is the direct or indirect subsidiary of a parent undertaking governed by the law of a third country;
(b) whenever such a parent undertaking acquires a holding in a Community investment firm such that the latter would become its subsidiary. . . .
2. The Member States shall inform the Commission of any general difficulties which their investment firms encounter in establishing themselves or providing investment services in any third country.
3. Initially no later than six months before this Directive is brought into effect and thereafter periodically the Commission shall draw up a report examining the treatment accorded to Community investment firms in third countries, in the terms referred to in paragraphs 4 and 5, as regards establishment, the carrying on of investment services activities and the acquisition of holdings in third-country investment firms. . . .
4. Whenever it appears to the Commission, either on the basis of the reports provided for in paragraph 3 or on the basis of other information, that a third country does not grant Community investment firms effective market access comparable to that granted by the Community to investment firms from that third country, the Commission may submit proposals to the Council for an appropriate mandate for negotiation with a view to obtaining comparable competitive opportunities for Community investment firms. . . .
5. Whenever it appears to the Commission, either on the basis of the reports referred to in paragraph 3 or on the basis of other information, that Community investment firms in a third country are not granted national treatment affording the same competitive opportunities as are available to domestic investment firms and that the conditions of effective market access are not fulfilled, the Commission may initiate negotiations in order to remedy the situation.
In the circumstances described in the first subparagraph it may also be decided, at any time and in addition to the initiation of negotiations, in accordance with the procedure to be laid down in the Directive by which the Council will set up the committee referred to in paragraph 1, that the competent authorities of the Member States must limit or suspend their decisions regarding requests pending or future requests for authorization and the acquisition of holdings by direct or indirect parent undertakings governed by the law of the third country in question. The duration of such measures may not exceed three months.
Before the end of that three-month period and in the light of the results of the negotiations the Council may, acting on a proposal from the Commission, decide by a qualified majority whether the measures shall be continued.
Such limitations or suspensions may not be applied to the setting up of subsidiaries by investment firms duly authorized in the Community or by their subsidiaries, or to the

acquisition of holdings in Community investment firms by such firms or subsidiaries.

6. Whenever it appears to the Commission that one of the situations described in paragraphs 4 and 5 obtains, the Member States shall inform it at its request:

(a) of any application for the authorization of any firm which is the direct or indirect subsidiary of a parent undertaking governed by the law of the third country in question;

(b) whenever they are informed in accordance with Article 10 that such a parent undertaking proposes to acquire a holding in a Community investment firm such that the latter would become its subsidiary.

This obligation to provide information shall lapse whenever agreement is reached with the third country referred to in paragraph 4 or 5 or when the measures referred to in the second and third subparagraphs of paragraph 5 cease to apply.

7. Measures taken under this Article shall comply with the Community's obligations under any international agreements, bilateral or multilateral, governing the taking up or pursuit of the business of investment firms.

TITLE IV Operating conditions
Article 8

1. The competent authorities of the home Member States shall require that an investment firm which they have authorized comply at all times with the conditions imposed in Article 3 (3). . . .

3. The prudential supervision of an investment firm shall be the responsibility of the competent authorities of the home Member State whether the investment firm establishes a branch or provides services in another Member State or not, without prejudice to those provisions of this Directive which give responsibility to the authorities of the host Member State.

Article 9

1. Member States shall require any person who proposes to acquire, directly or indirectly, a qualifying holding in an investment firm first to inform the competent authorities, telling them of the size of his intended holding. Such a person shall likewise inform the competent authorities if he proposes to increase his qualifying holding so that the proportion of the voting rights or of the capital that he holds would reach or exceed 20, 33, or 50% or so that the investment firm would become his subsidiary.

Without prejudice to paragraph 2, the competent authorities shall have up to three months from the date of the notification provided for in the first subparagraph to oppose such a plan if, in view of the need to ensure sound and prudent management of the investment firm, they are not satisfied as to the suitability of the person referred to in the first subparagraph. If they do not oppose the plan, they may fix a deadline for its implementation.

2. If the acquirer of the holding referred to in paragraph 1 is an investment firm authorized in another Member State or the parent undertaking of an investment firm authorized in another Member State or a person controlling an investment firm authorized in another Member State and if, as a result of that acquisition, the firm in which the acquirer proposes to acquire a holding would become the acquirer's subsidiary or come under his control, the assessment of the acquisition must be the subject of the prior consultation provided for in Article 6.

3. Member States shall require any person who proposes to dispose, directly or indirectly, of a qualifying holding in an investment firm first to inform the competent authorities, telling them of the size of his holding. Such a person shall likewise inform the competent authorities if he proposes to reduce his qualifying holding so that the proportion

of the voting rights or of the capital held by him would fall below 20, 33 or 50% or so that the investment firm would cease to be his subsidiary.

4. On becoming aware of them, investment firms shall inform the competent authorities of any acquisitions or disposals of holdings in their capital that cause holdings to exceed or fall below any of the thresholds referred to in paragraphs 1 and 3.

At least once a year they shall also inform the competent authorities of the names of shareholders and members possessing qualifying holdings and the sizes of such holdings as shown, for example, by the information received at annual general meetings of shareholders and members or as a result of compliance with the regulations applicable to companies listed on stock exchanges.

5. Member States shall require that, where the influence exercised by the persons referred to in paragraph 1 is likely to be prejudicial to the sound and prudent management of an investment firm, the competent authorities take appropriate measures to put an end to that situation. Such measures may consist, for example, in injunctions, sanctions against directors and those responsible for management or suspension of the exercise of the voting rights attaching to the shares held by the shareholders or members in question.

Similar measures shall apply to persons failing to comply with the obligation to provide prior information imposed in paragraph 1. If a holding is acquired despite the opposition of the competent authorities, the Member States shall, regardless of any other sanctions to be adopted, provide either for exercise of the corresponding voting rights to be suspended, for the nullity of the votes cast or for the possibility of their annulment.

Article 10

Each home Member State shall draw up prudential rules which investment firms shall observe at all times. In particular, such rules shall require that each investment firm:

> - have sound administrative and accounting procedures, control and safeguard arrangements for electronic data processing, and adequate internal control mechanisms including, in particular, rules for personal transactions by its employees,
> - make adequate arrangements for instruments belonging to investors with a view to safeguarding the latter's ownership rights, especially in the event of the investment firm's instruments for its own account except with the investors' express consent,
> - make adequate arrangements for funds belonging to investors with a view to safeguarding the latter's rights and, except in the case of credit institutions, preventing the investment firm's using investors' funds for its own account,
> - arrange for records to be kept of transactions executed which shall at least be sufficient to enable the home Member State's authorities to monitor compliance with the prudential rules which they are responsible for applying; such records shall be retained for periods to be laid down by the competent authorities,
> - be structured and organized in such a way as to minimize the risk of clients' interests being prejudiced by conflicts of interest between the firm and its clients or between one of its clients and another. Nevertheless, where a branch is set up the organizational arrangements may not conflict with the rules of conduct laid down by the host Member State to cover conflicts of interest.

Article 11

1. Member States shall draw up rules of conduct which investment firms shall observe at all times. Such rules must implement at least the principles set out in the following indents and must be applied in such a way as to take account of the professional nature of the

person for whom the service is provided. The Member States shall also apply these rules where appropriate to . . . non-core services. . . . These principles shall ensure that an investment firm:

> - acts honestly and fairly in conducting its business activities in the best interests of its clients and the integrity of the market,
> - acts with due skill, care and diligence, in the best interests of its clients and the integrity of the market,
> - has and employs effectively the resources and procedures that are necessary for the proper performance of its business activities,
> - seeks from its clients information regarding their financial situations, investment experience and objectives as regards the services requested,
> - makes adequate disclosure of relevant material information in its dealings with its clients,
> - tries to avoid conflicts of interests and, when they cannot be avoided, ensures that its clients are fairly treated, and
> - complies with all regulatory requirements applicable to the conduct of its business activities so as to promote the best interests of its clients and the integrity of the market.

2. Without prejudice to any decisions to be taken in the context of the harmonization of the rules of conduct, their implementation and the supervision of compliance with them shall remain the responsibility of the Member State in which a service is provided.

3. Where an investment firm executes an order, for the purposes of applying the rules referred to in paragraph 1 the professional nature of the investor shall be assessed with respect to the investor from whom the order originates, regardless of whether the order was placed directly by the investor himself or indirectly through an investment firm providing the service. . . .

TITLE V The right of establishment and the freedom to provide services
Article 14

1. Member States shall ensure that investment services . . . may be provided within their territories in accordance with Articles 17, 18 and 19 either by the establishment of a branch or under the freedom to provide services by any investment firm authorized and supervised by the competent authorities of another Member State in accordance with this Directive, provided that such services are covered by the authorization. . . .

2. Member States may not make the establishment of a branch or the provision of services referred to in paragraph 1 subject to any authorization requirement, to any requirement to provide endowment capital or to any other measure having equivalent effect.

3. A Member State may require that transactions relating to the services referred to in paragraph 1 must, where they satisfy all the following criteria, be carried out on a regulated market:

> - the investor must be habitually resident or established in that Member State,
> - the investment firm must carry out such transactions through a main establishment, through a branch situated in that Member State or under the freedom to provide services in that Member State,
> - the transaction must involve a instrument dealt in on a regulated market in that Member State.

4. Where a Member State applies paragraph 3 it shall give investors habitually resident or established in that Member State the right not to comply with the obligation imposed in paragraph 3 and have the transactions referred to in paragraph 3 carried out away from a regulated market. Member States may make the exercise of this right subject to express authorization, taking into account investors' differing needs for protection and in particular the ability of professional and institutional investors to act in their own best interests. It must in any case be possible for such authorization to be given in conditions that do not jeopardize the prompt execution of investors' orders. . . .

Article 15
          1. Without prejudice to the exercise of the right of establishment or the freedom to provide services referred to in Article 14, host Member States shall ensure that investment firms which are authorized by the competent authorities of their home Member States to provide the services . . . can, either directly or indirectly, become members of or have access to the regulated markets in their host Member States where similar services are provided and also become members of or have access to the clearing and settlement systems which are provided for the members of such regulated markets there.
          Member States shall abolish any national rules or laws or rules of regulated markets which limit the number of persons allowed access thereto. If, by virtue of its legal structure or its technical capacity, access to a regulated market is limited, the Member State concerned shall ensure that its structure and capacity are regularly adjusted.
          2. Membership of or access to a regulated market shall be conditional on investment firms' complying with capital adequacy requirements. . . .
          Access to a regulated market, admission to membership thereof and continued access or membership shall be subject to compliance with the rules of the regulated market in relation to the constitution and administration of the regulated market and to compliance with the rules relating to transactions on the market, with the professional standards imposed on staff operating on and in conjunction with the market, and with the rules and procedures for clearing and settlement. The detailed arrangements for implementing these rules and procedures may be adapted as appropriate, inter alia to ensure fulfilment of the ensuing obligations, provided, however, that Article 28 is complied with.
          3. In order to meet the obligation imposed in paragraph 1, host Member States shall offer the investment firms referred to in that paragraph the choice of becoming members of or of having access to their regulated markets either:

          - directly, by setting up branches in the host Member States, or
          - indirectly, by setting up subsidiaries in the host Member States or by
acquiring firms in the host Member States that are already members of their
regulated markets or already have access thereto. . . .

          4. Subject to paragraphs 1, 2 and 3, where the regulated market of the host Member State operates without any requirement for a physical presence the investment firms referred to in paragraph 1 may become members of or have access to it on the same basis without having to be established in the host Member State. In order to enable their investment firms to become members of or have access to host Member States' regulated markets in accordance with this paragraph home Member States shall allow those host Member States' regulated markets to provide appropriate facilities within the home Member States' territories.
          5. This Article shall not affect the Member States' right to authorize or prohibit the

creation of new markets within their territories. . . .

Article 16

For the purposes of mutual recognition and the application of this Directive, it shall be for each Member State to draw up a list of the regulated markets for which it is the home Member State and which comply with its regulations, and to forward that list for information, together with the relevant rules of procedures and operation of those regulated markets, to the other Member States and the Commission. A similar communication shall be effected in respect of each change to the aforementioned list or rules. . . .

Article 17

1. In addition to meeting the conditions imposed in Article 3, any investment firm wishing to establish a branch within the territory of another Member State shall notify the competent authorities of its home Member State.

2. Member States shall require every investment firm wishing to establish a branch within the territory of another Member State to provide the following information when effecting the notification provided for in paragraph 1:

(a) the Member State within the territory of which it plans to establish a branch;

(b) a programme of operations setting out inter alia the types of business envisaged and the organizational structure of the branch;

(c) the address in the host Member State from which documents may be obtained;

(d) the names of those responsible for the management of the branch.

3. Unless the competent authorities of the home Member State have reason to doubt the adequacy of the administrative structure or the financial situation of an investment firm, taking into account the activities envisaged, they shall, within three months of receiving all the information referred to in paragraph 2, communicate that information to the competent authorities of the host Member State and shall inform the investment firm concerned accordingly. . . .

Article 18

1. Any investment firm wishing to carry on business within the territory of another Member State for the first time under the freedom to provide services shall communicate the following information to the competent authorities of its home Member State:

- the Member State in which it intends to operate,
- a programme of operations stating in particular the investment service or services which it intends to provide.

2. The competent authorities of the home Member State shall, within one month of receiving the information referred to in paragraph 1, forward it to the competent authorities of the host Member State. The investment firm may then start to provide the investment service or services in question in the host Member State.

Where appropriate, the competent authorities of the host Member State shall, on receipt of the information referred to in paragraph 1, indicate to the investment firm the conditions, including the rules of conduct, with which, in the interest of the general good, the providers of the investment services in question must comply in the host Member State.

3. Should the content of the information communicated in accordance with the second indent of paragraph 1 be amended, the investment firm shall give notice of the amendment in writing to the competent authorities of the home Member State and of the host

Member State before implementing the change, so that the competent authorities of the host Member State may, if necessary, inform the firm of any change or addition to be made to the information communicated under paragraph 2. . . .

TITLE VI Authorities responsible for authorization and supervision
Article 22
    1. Member States shall designate the competent authorities which are to carry out the duties provided for in this Directive. They shall inform the Commission thereof, indicating any division of those duties.
    2. The authorities referred to in paragraph 1 must be either public authorities, bodies recognized by national law or bodies recognized by public authorities expressly empowered for that purpose by national law.
    3. The authorities concerned must have all the powers necessary for the performance of their functions.

Article 23
    1. Where there are two or more competent authorities in the same Member State, they shall collaborate closely in supervising the activities of investment firms operating in that Member State.
    2. Member States shall ensure that such collaboration takes place between such competent authorities and the public authorities responsible for the supervision of financial markets, credit and other financial institutions and insurance undertakings, as regards the entities which those authorities supervise.
    3. Where, through the provision of services or by the establishment of branches, an investment firm operates in one or more Member States other than its home Member State the competent authorities of all the Member States concerned shall collaborate closely in order more effectively to discharge their respective responsibilities in the area covered by this Directive. . . .

Article 24
    1. Each host Member State shall ensure that, where an investment firm authorized in another Member State carries on business within its territory through a branch, the competent authorities of the home Member State may, after informing the competent authorities of the host Member State, themselves or through the intermediary of persons they instruct for the purpose carry out on-the-spot verification of the information referred to in Article 23 (3).
    2. The competent authorities of the home Member State may also ask the competent authorities of the host Member State to have such verification carried out. Authorities which receive such requests must, within the framework of their powers, act upon them by carrying out the verifications themselves, by allowing the authorities who have requested them to carry them out or by allowing auditors or experts to do so.
    3. This Article shall not affect the right of the competent authorities of a host Member State, in discharging their responsibilities under this Directive, to carry out on-the-spot verifications of branches established within their territory. . . .

Article 27
    Without prejudice to the procedures for the withdrawal of authorization or to the provisions of criminal law, Member States shall provide that their respective competent authorities may, with regard to investment firms or those who effectively control the business

of such firms that infringe laws, regulations or administrative provisions concerning the supervision or carrying on of their activities, adopt or impose in respect of them measures or penalties aimed specifically at ending observed breaches or the causes of such breaches.

Article 28

Member States shall ensure that this Directive is implemented without discrimination.

TITLE VII Final provisions

. . .

Article 30

1. Investment firms already authorized in their home Member States to provide investment services before 31 December 1995 shall be deemed to be so authorized for the purpose of this Directive, if the laws of those Member States provide that to take up such activities they must comply with conditions equivalent to those imposed in Articles 3 (3) and 4.

2. Investment firms which are already carrying on business on 31 December 1995 and are not included among those referred to in paragraph 1 may continue their activities profided that, no later than 31 December 1996 and pursuant to the provisions of their home Member States, they obtain authorization to continue such activities in accordance with the provisions adopted in implementation of this Directive.

Only the grant of such authorization shall enable such firms to qualify under the provisions of this Directive on the right of establishment and the freedom to provide services.

3. Where before the date of the adoption of this Directive investment firms have commenced business in other Member States either through branches or under the freedom to provide services, the authorities of each home Member State shall, between 1 July and 31 December 1995, communicate, for the purposes of Articles 17 (1) and (2) and 18, to the authorities of each of the other Member States concerned the list of firms that comply with this Directive and operate in those States, indicating the business carried on. . . .

Article 31

No later than 1 July 1995 Member States shall adopt the laws, regulations and administrative provisions necessary for them to comply with this Directive.

These provisions shall enter into force no later than 31 December 1995. The Member States shall forthwith inform the Commission thereof. . . .

## Wendy Fowler, EC Regulation of the Banking Sector,
5 Hofstra Prop. L.J. 405 (1993)

As part of its attempts to create a unified financial market throughout the EC, the Commission has proposed a Directive in the field of investment services.[26] This Proposed Directive closely parallels the Second Banking Directive. It applies to investment firms which are defined in the Directive as "any natural or legal person whose business it is to provide any investment service." "Investment services" are listed in the Annex to the Proposed Directive on Investment Services and include brokerage in financial instruments on behalf of clients, dealing in such instruments as principal, market making, portfolio

---

26. Amended Commission Proposal for a Council Directive on Investment Services in the Securities Field, 1990 O.J. (C 42) 7 [hereinafter Proposed Directive on Investment Services].

management, underwriting, investment advice, and custody services.

There is a clear overlap with the Second Banking Directive. The Second Banking Directive contemplates that, under its provisions, credit institutions may be authorized by Member States to engage in activities which fall within the list of investment services. This is recognized by the Proposed Directive on Investment Services which provides, in Article 2, that, in the case of credit institutions authorized by their banking license to engage in securities business, only Articles 9(2), 11 and 13 of the Proposed Directive on Investment Services will apply. These provisions relate to such matters as the following: freedom of access to stock exchanges and securities' markets in the Member State where the branch of the investment firm is established; the requirement by home Member States to make sufficient provision against market risk; and the application of prudential rules by home Member States in areas such as administrative and accounting procedures.

The procedure for obtaining authorization is very similar to that contained in the Second Banking Directive. Investment firms which are not authorized to provide investment services under the Second Banking Directive are required to obtain authorization from their home Member State before providing such services. Before granting authorization, the authorities of the home Member State are required to be satisfied with the level of the investment firm's initial capital and the reputation and experience of the persons directing its business. Once authorized, the investment firm may provide the investment services for which it is authorized in its home Member State to persons in other Member States either by establishing a branch in the host Member State or by provision of cross border services. In each case, the Proposed Directive on Investment Services sets out a procedure to be followed by the investment firm. The procedures are similar to those provided for in the Second Banking Directive. As in the case of the Second Banking Directive, the procedures relating to the establishment of a branch are more extensive than those for the provision of cross border services.

**Notes and Comments 9.31.** To whom must an EU-based bank apply for authority to engage in investment services? (Review especially article 2(1) of the directive and the articles crossreferenced by it.)

**9.32.** In establishing a securities operation within the EU, would it make a difference whether the headquarters of a bank were itself within one of the EU member states or in the United States? (Review articles 5-7, 14 of the directive.)

**9.33.** What sort of supervision are the EU-wide securities operations of an investment firm subject to? (Review articles 3, 8, 10-11, 14-18, 22, 24, 27.)

**9.34.** Traditionally, one concern expressed about commercial bank involvement in securities activities is that such activities may create special hazards for the safety and soundness of the bank and for the banking system generally. Is this concern justified as a practical matter? Consider situation presented by the following case.

## Trade Development Bank v. Continental Insurance Co.
### 469 F.2d 35 (2d Cir. 1972)

Mansfield, Circuit Judge:

Trade Development Bank . . . a Swiss bank, sued The Continental Insurance Company . . . upon a fidelity bond for recovery of losses due to dishonesty on the part of the Bank's employees. The fidelity bond, issued by the Insurer in 1968, obligated it to indemnify the Bank up to the sum of $5,000,000 against

"Any loss through any dishonest, fraudulent or criminal act of any of the Employees, committed anywhere and whether committed alone or in collusion with others, including loss of Property through any such act of any of the Employees."

. . .

The evidence, viewed in the light most favorable to the Bank, reveals that from mid-1969 to April 1970 the Manager of the Securities Department of the Bank's branch in Chiasso, Switzerland, Louis Gerard Salerian, fraudulently used funds of the Bank and of its customers to engage in a series of unauthorized securities transactions with a view to keeping any profits for himself. Unfortunately for him and for the Bank and its customers his talents apparently did not lie in securities investment, for he selected for these fraudulent transactions a series of stocks which declined sharply . . . , resulting in a loss of over $2,000,000 of the Bank's funds.

Perpetration of such a colossal fraud by Salerian was possible because Swiss banks not only offer their customers the usual services performed by banks in this country but are also permitted to act as stockbrokers. As the Manager of the Securities Department of the Bank's Chiasso branch, Salerian was authorized to execute customers' orders by buying and selling securities through other banks and brokerage firms, to carry out arbitrage transactions and, with the branch Manager's prior approval, to trade for the branch's own account. Without any authority from the management or any knowledge on its part, however, he made hundreds of purchases of securities, using the Bank's funds. Although the Bank maintained a typically detailed record-keeping system for authorized securities transactions, these purchases were either not registered on the Bank's records at all or they were falsely entered.

# 6. Export Trading Companies

**Notes and Comments 9.35.** *Banking and Commerce.* As a general rule, U.S. banking law does not permit banking enterprises to be involved in or affiliated with "commercial" enterprises–*i.e.*, enterprises engaging in commerce other than banking or financial services. *See, e.g.*, 12 U.S.C. § 1843(a) (prohibiting bank holding companies from owning or controlling enterprises not involved in banking). One potentially important exception concerns export trading companies. Before considering the questions beginning with Note 9.33, *infra*, review the following excerpts from the Fed's Reg K.

## Board of Governors of the Federal Reserve System
### 12 C.F.R. pt. 211

Subpart C–Export Trading Companies[a]

Sec.
211.31   Authority, purpose, and scope.
211.32   Definitions.
211.33   Investments and extensions of credit.
211.34   Procedures for filing and processing notices.

§ 211.31  Authority, purpose, and scope.

(a) Authority. This subpart is issued by the Board of Governors of the Federal Reserve System (Board) under the authority of the Bank Holding Company Act of 1956

---

a. *As amended*, 66 Fed. Reg. 54,346 (2001), *corrected*, 66 Fed. Reg. 58,655 (2001).

(BHC Act) (12 U.S.C. 1841 et seq.), the Bank Export Services Act (title II, Pub. L. 97-290, 96 Stat. 1235 (1982)) (BESA), and the Export Trading Company Act Amendments of 1988 (title III, Pub. L. 100-418, 102 Stat. 1384 (1988)) (ETC Act Amendments).

(b) Purpose and scope. This subpart is in furtherance of the purposes of the BHC Act, the BESA, and the ETC Act Amendments, the latter two statutes being designed to increase U.S. exports by encouraging investments and participation in export trading companies by bank holding companies and the specified investors. The provisions of this subpart apply to eligible investors as defined in this subpart.

§ 211.32 Definitions.

The definitions in §§ 211.1 and 211.2 of subpart A[b] apply to this subpart, subject to the following:

(a) Appropriate Federal Reserve Bank has the same meaning as in § 211.21(c).[c]

(b) Bank has the same meaning as in section 2(c) of the BHC Act (12 U.S.C. 1841(c)).

(c) Company has the same meaning as in section 2(b) of the BHC Act (12 U.S.C. 1841(b)).

(d) Eligible investors means:

(1) Bank holding companies, as defined in section 2(a) of the BHC Act (12 U.S.C. 1841(a));

(2) Edge and agreement corporations that are subsidiaries of bank holding companies but are not subsidiaries of banks;

(3) Banker's banks, as described in section 4(c)(14)(F)(iii) of the BHC Act (12 U.S.C. 1843(c)(14)(F)(iii)); and

(4) Foreign banking organizations, as defined in § 211.21(o).

(e) Export trading company means a company that is exclusively engaged in activities related to international trade and, by engaging in one or more export trade services, derives:

(1) At least one-third of its revenues in each consecutive four-year period from the export of, or from facilitating the export of, goods and services produced in the United States by persons other than the export trading company or its subsidiaries; and

(2) More revenues in each four-year period from export activities as described in paragraph (e)(1) of this section than it derives from the import, or facilitating the import, into the United States of goods or services produced outside the United States. The four-year period within which to calculate revenues derived from its activities under this section shall be deemed to have commenced with the first fiscal year after the respective export trading company has been in operation for two years.

(f) Revenues shall include net sales revenues from exporting, importing, or third-party trade in goods by the export trading company for its own account and gross revenues derived from all other activities of the export trading company.

(g) Subsidiary has the same meaning as in section 2(d) of the BHC Act (12 U.S.C. 1841(d)).

(h) Well capitalized has the same meaning as in § 225.2(r) of Regulation Y (12 CFR 225.2(r)).

(i) Well managed has the same meaning as in § 225.2(s) of Regulation Y (12 CFR 225.2(s)).

---

b. For the text of these sections, see Chapter 5, § 2, *supra*.

c. For the text of this section see page 196, *supra*.

§ 211.33  Investments and extensions of credit.

(a) Amount of investments. In accordance with the procedures of § 211.34, an eligible investor may invest no more than 5 percent of its consolidated capital and surplus in one or more export trading companies, except that an Edge or agreement corporation not engaged in banking may invest as much as 25 percent of its consolidated capital and surplus but no more than 5 percent of the consolidated capital and surplus of its parent bank holding company.

(b) Extensions of credit--(1) Amount. An eligible investor in an export trading company or companies may extend credit directly or indirectly to the export trading company or companies in a total amount that at no time exceeds 10 percent of the investor's consolidated capital and surplus.

(2) Terms. (i) An eligible investor in an export trading company may not extend credit directly or indirectly to the export trading company or any of its customers or to any other investor holding 10 percent or more of the shares of the export trading company on terms more favorable than those afforded similar borrowers in similar circumstances, and such extensions of credit shall not involve more than the normal risk of repayment or present other unfavorable features.

(ii) For the purposes of this section, an investor in an export trading company includes any affiliate of the investor.

(3) Collateral requirements. Covered transactions between a bank and an affiliated export trading company in which a bank holding company has invested pursuant to this subpart are subject to the collateral requirements of section 23A of the Federal Reserve Act (12 U.S.C. 371c), except where a bank issues a letter of credit or advances funds to an affiliated export trading company solely to finance the purchase of goods for which:

(i) The export trading company has a bona fide contract for the subsequent sale of the goods; and

(ii) The bank has a security interest in the goods or in the proceeds from their sale at least equal in value to the letter of credit or the advance.

§ 211.34  Procedures for filing and processing notices.

(a) General policy. Direct and indirect investments by eligible investors in export trading companies shall be made in accordance with the general consent or prior notice procedures contained in this section. The Board may at any time, upon notice, modify or suspend the general-consent procedures with respect to any eligible investor.

(b) General consent--(1) Eligibility for general consent. Subject to the other limitations of this subpart, the Board grants its general consent for any investment an export trading company:

(i) If the eligible investor is well capitalized and well managed;

(ii) In an amount equal to cash dividends received from that export trading company during the preceding 12 calendar months; or

(iii) That is acquired from an affiliate at net asset value or through a contribution of shares.

(2) Post-investment notice. By the end of the month following the month in which the investment is made, the investor shall provide the Board with the following information:

(i) The amount of the investment and the source of the funds with which the investment was made; and

(ii) In the case of an initial investment, a description of the activities in which the export trading company proposes to engage and projections for the export trading company for the first year following the investment.

(c) Filing notice--(1) Prior notice. An eligible investor shall give the Board 60 days' prior written notice of any investment in an export trading company that does not qualify under the general consent procedure.

(2) Notice of change of activities. (i) An eligible investor shall give the Board 60 days' prior written notice of changes in the activities of an export trading company that is a subsidiary of the investor if the export trading company expands its activities beyond those described in the initial notice to include:

(A) Taking title to goods where the export trading company does not have a firm order for the sale of those goods;

(B) Product research and design;

(C) Product modification; or

(D) Activities not specifically covered by the list of activities contained in section 4(c)(14)(F)(ii) of the BHC Act (12 U.S.C. 1843(c)(14)(F)(ii)).

(ii) Such an expansion of activities shall be regarded as a proposed investment under this subpart.

(d) Time period for Board action. (1) A proposed investment that has not been disapproved by the Board may be made 60 days after the appropriate Federal Reserve Bank accepts the notice for processing. A proposed investment may be made before the expiration of the 60-day period if the Board notifies the investor in writing of its intention not to disapprove the investment.

(2) The Board may extend the 60-day period for an additional 30 days if the Board determines that the investor has not furnished all necessary information or that any material information furnished is substantially inaccurate. The Board may disapprove an investment if the necessary information is provided within a time insufficient to allow the Board reasonably to consider the information received.

(3) Within three days of a decision to disapprove an investment, the Board shall notify the investor in writing and state the reasons for the disapproval.

(e) Time period for investment. An investment in an export trading company that has not been disapproved shall be made within one year from the date of the notice not to disapprove, unless the time period is extended by the Board or by the appropriate Federal Reserve Bank.

**Notes and Comments 9.36.** Could QNB create a subsidiary, QuarterTrade Corp. (QTC), which would manufacture and export, and facilitate the export, from the United States of mining equipment? (*See* 12 C.F.R. § 211.32(d).)

**9.37.** Could QNB create QTC, which would import, and facilitate the import, into the United States of pistachios? (*See id.*)

**9.38.** Could QNB's parent, Quarter Holding Corp (QHC), own QTC if it was involved in the activities described in 9.32 or 9.33, *supra*? (*See id.* §§ 211.32(d), (e), 211.33 (a), 211.34(b), (c).)

**9.39.** Could QHC's subsidiary Edge corporation, Quarter International Bank, own QTC if it was involved in the activities described in 9.32 or 9.33, *supra*? (*See id.* §§ 211.32 (d), (e), 211.33(a), 211.34(b), (c).)

# Chapter 10

# Bank Secrecy Laws

---

# 1. Introduction

**Notes and Comments 10.1.** *A basis for comparison: the U.S. policy.* The United States gives very narrow legal protection to the confidentiality of bank records. In *United States v. Miller*,[1] the Supreme Court held that individuals have no Fourth Amendment expectation of privacy in their financial records while those records are in the hands of third parties. Congress responded to this decision by enacting the Right to Financial Privacy Act (RFPA),[2] which provides individuals with some privacy rights in financial records that are in the hands of third parties. Among other things, the RFPA designates the conditions under which financial institutions may disclose an individual's financial records *to the Government*. *See* 12 U.S.C. § 3403. It defines the conditions under which *government officials* may gain access to an individual's financial records. *See id.* § 3402. The RFPA provides a civil cause of action for anyone injured by a violation of the act's substantive provisions. *Id.* § 3417. Thus, the legal protection for confidentiality of bank records is narrower in at least one respect–and sometimes two respects–than the privacy afforded under other legal regimes.

First, the level of protection in most other jurisdictions addressing the issue is typically much higher than in the U.S. formulation under the RFPA. RFPA protection extends only–if at all–to disclosure by financial institutions of customer financial information to government investigative agencies, and the RFPA simply requires, at most, notice to the customer. In most other systems, the prohibition or restriction of disclosure of financial information extends to disclosure to almost anyone, and the penalties may be quite severe.

Second, as *Miller* made clear, financial privacy is not grounded in any fundamental (*i.e.*, constitutional) personal right. In contrast, confidentiality of financial information is viewed in some countries (*e.g.*, Switzerland[3]) as a fundamental right codified in and enforced by legislation.[4]

---

1. 425 U.S. 435 (1976).

2. 12 U.S.C. §§ 3401 *et seq.*

3. *See, e.g.*, Honegger, *Demystification of the Swiss Banking Secrecy and Illumination of the United States-Swiss Memorandum of Understanding*, 9 N.C.J. Int'l L. & Com. Reg. 1 (1983) (discussing fundamental character of bank secrecy under Swiss law). Excerpts from Honegger's article appear in § 2, *infra*.

4. This does not mean, however, that information concerning banking transactions are insulated from Swiss criminal proceedings. *See* Honegger, *infra* (discussing limitations on banker's discretion in face of Swiss criminal proceedings).

**10.2.** *Increased U.S. focus on foreign- or international-related financial informa-tion.* In 1986, Congress refined privacy rights with respect to financial information originating in electronic communications, a medium that is particularly pertinent in the international banking context. It enacted the Electronic Communications Privacy Act (ECPA),[5] which provides statutory protection against the unauthorized interception of electronic communications. Like the RFPA, the ECPA defines the conditions under which an electronic communications service may divulge the contents of electronic communications to the government. *See, e.g.*, 18 U.S.C. §§ 2511, 2702. It also establishes the conditions under which the government is entitled to access an individual's electronic communications. *Id.* § 2703. It also creates a civil cause of action for anyone injured by a violation of the substantive provisions of the ECPA. *Id.* § 2707.

**10.3.** *Recent statutory narrowing of RFPA and ECPA protections.* In recent stat-utory amendments, the scope of the RFPA and the ECPA have been significantly narrowed. Responding to increased concern over international money-laundering,[6] in 1994 Congress created "safe harbor" provisions in the Annunzio-Wylie Anti-Money Laundering Act[7] that immunized banks from liability in specified circumstances.[8] In addition, in 1996 the ECPA was amended specifically to exclude electronic funds transfers from the definition of "elec-tronic communication" the operative term in the ECPA.[9]

**10.4.** *Renewed prominence of anti-money laundering provisions in the wake of terrorist attacks on the United States.* Broad antiterrorism legislation became a significant feature of financial services regulation when the president signed the USA PATRIOT Act into law on October 26, 2001. Significant portions of the act are part of the U.S. economic sanctions in response to the attacks; these aspects will be discussed in Chapter 11, § 4, *infra*. This note highlights the effects of the act on anti-money laundering provisions of U.S. law. The Uniting and Strengthening America by Providing Appropriate Tools Required to Intercept and Obstruct Terrorism Act of 2001[10]–usually referred to by its acronym, USA PATRIOT Act–is a multi-pronged legislative response to the terrorist attacks of September 11, 2001. The provisions in Title III of the Act most directly affect financial services firms. For example, under § 327 a financial institution's effectiveness in combating money-laundering has now become an explicit factor in considering approval of bank holding company status under 12 U.S.C. § 1842(c)(6), or approval of a bank or savings association merger under the Bank Merger Act, *id.* § 1828(c)(11).

**10.5.** *Major money laundering provisions of USA PATRIOT Act.* Title III of the USA PATRIOT Act, the International Money Laundering Abatement and Anti-Terrorist Financing Act of 2001 (IMLAAFA), is at the heart of the legislation. Its provisions will have a significant impact on the operations of U.S. and foreign financial services firms. The

---

5. 18 U.S.C. §§ 2510 *et seq.*

6. Typically, money-laundering involves the transfer of funds or credits that accrue from illegal activities through legitimate enterprises, often in a complicated series of transfers, in order to obscure the illegal source of the funds or credits. Obscuring the source increases the likelihood that the funds or credits will escape governmental seizure as fruits of illegal activity.

7. 31 U.S.C. § 5318(g).

8. The provisions and applicability of section 5318(g) are discussed in *Lopez, infra.*

9. 18 U.S.C. § 2510(12). The effect of section 2510(12) was not at issue in *Lopez. See Lopez, infra*, note 2.

10. Pub.L. 107-56, Oct. 26, 2001, 115 Stat. 280 (codified at scattered sections of, *inter alia*, 12, 18, 31 U.S.C.).

effects of IMLAAFA go well beyond the policing of classic money laundering transactions, and must be kept in mind even in situations in which such transactions may not be apparent. The major provisions of the IMLAAFA are discussed below. In addition, IMLAAFA includes extensive amendments in §§ 351-359, 361-363, 365-366, 371-372 to the Bank Secrecy Act, 31 U.S.C §§ 5311 *et seq.*, and related provisions of federal law. These are apparently intended to align reporting, disclosure and money laundering requirements in these previous enactments to the provisions of the new act.

*a. Treasury designations.* Under § 311,[11] the Secretary of the Treasury is authorized to designate non-U.S. jurisdictions, classes of transactions, financial institutions or types of accounts as being of "primary money laundering concern." As to any of these designated non-U.S. targets, the Secretary can require domestic financial institutions and domestic financial agencies to take at least one of five types of specified measures to detect and prevent money laundering: (1) recordkeeping and reporting of certain financial transactions; (2) obtaining and retaining information concerning beneficial ownership of any targeted account; (3) identifying, or obtaining identity information about, persons permitted to use, or whose transactions are routed through, certain "payable-through" accounts; (4) identifying or obtaining identity information about persons permitted to use, or whose transactions are routed through, certain correspondent accounts; and/or (5) prohibiting or conditioning the opening of certain payable-through or correspondent accounts.

*b. Due diligence requirements.* Under § 312,[12] financial institutions are required to establish "appropriate, specific, and, where necessary, enhanced, due diligence policies, procedures, and controls" as to money laundering for U.S. correspondent accounts and private banking accounts of non-U.S. persons (*including* a foreign individual visiting the United States, or a U.S. representative of a non-U.S. person). Furthermore, if a foreign bank with an "offshore" banking license, or licensed by a country designated as "noncooperative" by certain intergovernmental organizations (*e.g.*, the Paris-based Financial Action Task Force on Money Laundering), requests or maintains a correspondent account with a U.S. financial institution, the latter is required to establish additional due diligence standards. These include ascertaining the identity of each owner of the foreign bank (if the foreign bank is not publicly traded) and ascertaining the identities of other foreign banks that maintain correspondent accounts with the foreign bank, as well as related due diligence information. Finally, special due diligence requirements are imposed for "private banking accounts." These include ascertaining the nominal and beneficial owners of each account and the source of the funds deposited in such accounts, and enhanced scrutiny of accounts maintained by senior political figures, or their immediate families or close associates.

*c. Correspondent accounts.* Under § 313,[13] "covered financial institutions" are prohibited from maintaining correspondent accounts for shell banks–banks with no physical presence in any country–and must take reasonable steps to ensure that correspondent accounts of foreign banks are not used to provide banking services to shell banks. A covered financial institution that maintains a correspondent account in the United States for a foreign bank must maintain records in the United States identifying the owners of the foreign bank and the name and address of any U.S. resident who is authorized to accept service of legal process from the Secretary and the Attorney General for records regarding the correspondent account.

---

11. 31 U.S.C. § 5318A.

12. *Id.* § 5318(i).

13. *Id.* § 5318(j).

***d.*** *Concentration accounts.* Under § 325,[14] the Secretary is given authority to issue rules regulating the maintenance of concentration accounts[15] by financial institutions, to ensure that these accounts are not used to mask the interest of any person in the movement of funds. These regulations must, at a minimum: (1) prohibit financial institutions from allowing clients to direct funds movements in, out, or through such accounts; (2) prohibit institutions and their employees from counseling clients about such accounts; and, (3) require each institution to establish specified written procedures on documentation of transactions involving concentration accounts.

**10.6.** In preparation for the questions beginning in Note 10.7, *infra*, consider the provisions of the IMLAAFA described in the previous comment, and the following rule proposed by the Department of the Treasury, Financial Crimes Enforcement Network (FinCEN).

## FinCEN, Department of the Treasury
## Anti-Money Laundering Programs; Special Due Diligence
## Programs for Certain Foreign Accounts
67 Fed. Reg. 48,348 (2002) (to be codified at 31 C.F.R. pt. 103)

. . .

SUMMARY: Treasury and FinCEN are issuing an interim final rule temporarily deferring for certain financial institutions (as defined in the Bank Secrecy Act) the application of the requirements contained in section 5318(i) of title 31, United States Code, added by section 312 of the Uniting and Strengthening America by Providing Appropriate Tools Required to Intercept and Obstruct Terrorism Act (USA PATRIOT Act) of 2001 (the Act). Section 5318(i) requires U.S. financial institutions to establish due diligence policies, procedures, and controls reasonably designed to detect and report money laundering through correspondent accounts and private banking accounts that U.S. financial institutions establish or maintain for non-U.S. persons. Section 312 takes effect on July 23, 2002, whether or not Treasury has issued a final rule implementing that provision. Additionally, this interim final rule provides guidance, pending issuance of a final rule, to those financial institutions for which compliance with section 5318(i) has not been deferred.

DATES: This interim final rule is effective July 23, 2002. . . .

SUPPLEMENTARY INFORMATION: Treasury and FinCEN are exercising the authority under 31 U.S.C. 5318(a)(6) to temporarily defer the application of 31 U.S.C. 5318 (i) to certain financial institutions pending issuance by Treasury and FinCEN of a final rule outlining the scope of coverage, duties, and obligations under that provision. Additionally, for those financial institutions for which compliance with section 5318(i) has not been deferred entirely, interim guidance is provided for compliance with the statute pending issuance of a final rule. Although this interim final rule and the guidance contained herein may be relied upon by financial institutions until superseded by a final regulation or subsequent guidance, no inference may be drawn from this rule concerning the scope and substance of the final regulation that Treasury will issue concerning section 5318(i). . . .

Banks must comply with section 5318(i) pending Treasury's issuance of a final rule.

---

14. *Id.* § 5318(h)(3).

15. The term "concentration account" is not defined by the IMLAAFA. Legislative history of the USA PATRIOT Act seems to suggest that concentration accounts "are used to commingle related funds temporarily in one place pending disbursement or the transfer of funds into individual client accounts." 147 Cong. Rec. S11,041 (Oct. 25, 2001)(statement of Sen. Sarbanes).

For the purposes of this interim final rule, these include: An insured bank (as defined in section 3(h) of the Federal Deposit Insurance Act (12 U.S.C. 1813(h))); a commercial bank; an agency or branch of a foreign bank in the United States; a federally insured credit union; a thrift institution; and a corporation acting under section 25A of the Federal Reserve Act (12 U.S.C. 611 et seq.).

Securities brokers and dealers registered, or required to register, with the Securities and Exchange Commission (SEC), and futures commission merchants and introducing brokers registered, or required to register, with the Commodity Futures Trading Commission (CFTC) must comply with provisions relating to private banking accounts, but their compliance with the remaining provisions of section 5318(i) is deferred. . . .

Section 5318(i)(2) requires U.S. financial institutions to establish enhanced due diligence policies and procedures applicable when opening or maintaining a correspondent account in the United States for certain foreign banks designated as high risk. Sections 5318(i)(2)(B)(i) through (iii) further specify requirements that must be incorporated into a financial institution's enhanced due diligence policies and procedures.

An enhanced due diligence program will be reasonable under section 5318(i)(2) (B), in Treasury's view, if first, it comports with existing best practice standards for banks that maintain correspondent accounts for foreign banks. Second, the program must also focus enhanced due diligence measures on those correspondent accounts that are maintained by a foreign correspondent bank deemed high risk by section 5318(i)(2)(A) posing a particularly high risk of money laundering based on the bank's overall assessment of the risk posed by the foreign correspondent bank. As with the previous provision, it is the expectation of Treasury that a bank will accord priority in applying enhanced due diligence to accounts opened on or after July 23, 2002. . . .

For the reasons set forth in the preamble, 31 CFR part 103 is amended as follows:

## PART 103--FINANCIAL RECORDKEEPING AND REPORTING
## OF CURRENCY AND FOREIGN TRANSACTIONS

. . .

Special Due Diligence for Correspondent Accounts and Private Banking Accounts

Sec.
103.181  Special due diligence programs for banks, savings associations, and
         credit unions.
103.182  Special due diligence programs for securities brokers and dealers,
         futures commission merchants, and introducing brokers.
103.183  Deferred due diligence programs for other financial institutions.

§ 103.181 Special due diligence programs for banks, savings associations, and credit unions.

The requirements of 31 U.S.C. 5318(i) shall apply, effective July 23, 2002, to a financial institution that is:

(a) An insured bank (as defined in section 3(h) of the Federal Deposit Insurance Act (12 U.S.C. 1813(h)));

(b) A commercial bank;

(c) An agency or branch of a foreign bank in the United States;

(d) A federally insured credit union;

(e) A thrift institution; or

(f) A corporation acting under section 25A of the Federal Reserve Act (12 U.S.C. 611 et seq.).

§ 103.182 Special due diligence programs for securities brokers and dealers, futures commission merchants, and introducing brokers.

(a) Private banking accounts. The requirements of 31 U.S.C. 5318(i) relating to due diligence and enhanced due diligence for private banking accounts shall apply, effective July 23, 2002, to a financial institution that is:

(1) A broker or dealer registered, or required to register, with the Securities and Exchange Commission under the Securities Exchange Act of 1934 (15 U.S.C. 78a et seq.); or

(2) A futures commission merchant or introducing broker registered, or required to register, with the Commodity Futures Trading Commission under the Commodity Exchange Act (7 U.S.C. 1 et seq.).

(b) Correspondent accounts. A financial institution described in paragraph (a) of this section is exempt from the requirements of 31 U.S.C. 5318(i) relating to due diligence and enhanced due diligence for certain correspondent accounts.

(c) Other compliance obligations of financial institutions unaffected. Nothing in this section shall be construed to relieve a financial institution from its responsibility to comply with any other applicable requirement of law or regulation, including title 31 of the United States Code and this part.

§ 103.183 Deferred due diligence programs for other financial institutions.

(a) Exempt financial institutions. Except as provided in § 103.181 and § 103.182, a financial institution defined in 31 U.S.C. 5312(a)(2) and (c)(1) or § 103.11(n) is exempt from the requirements of 31 U.S.C. 5318(i).

(b) Other compliance obligations of financial institutions unaffected. Nothing in this section shall be construed to relieve a financial institution from its responsibility to comply with any other applicable requirement of law or regulation, including title 31 of the United States Code and this part.

**Notes and Comments 10.7.** Major State Bank (MSB) of San Dusqui, CA, markets and administers "collective investment funds" to its high-end, "private banking" clients. Under this program, MSB invests assets that it holds as fiduciary for wealthy clients in collective investment funds created and maintained by the bank exclusively for the collective investment and reinvestment of money contributed to the fund by the bank in its capacity as trustee under a trust agreement signed by the client. Some of its private banking clients are located in the Middle East. Does the IMLAAFA impose any obligations on MSB? (*See* 31

U.S.C. §§ 5314(a), 5318(a), (h), (i).)

**10.8.** Little National Bank (LNB) of Waydoun, TX, does not have any correspondent bank relationships with any foreign banks. Does this mean that LNB is not affected by IMLAAFA, and therefore does not need to review its internal guidelines with respect to money laundering? (*See id.* § 5318(i)(1), (i)(2)(A); 31 C.F.R. § 103.181(a).)

**10.9.** Myrtle Lynch Securities (MLS) has an investment program similar to that operated by MSB in Note 10.7, *supra.* Does the IMLAAFA impose any obligations on MLS? (*See* 31 U.S.C. § 5318A(e)(2); 31 C.F.R. § 103.182(a)(1), (b).)

**10.10.** If a bank failed to maintain its money laundering procedures in accordance with the USA PATRIOT Act, would that failure give a depositor of the bank a cause of action against the bank? In answering this question, consider the following cases.

# L & J Crew Station, LLC v.
# Banco Popular De Puerto Rico
— F.Supp.2d —, 2003 WL 22019641 (D.V.I. 2003)

MOORE, District J.

[L & J Crew Station, LLC (L & J) opened two accounts with Banco Popular de Puerto Rico (Banco Popular) in June and July 2002. In the process of opening the accounts, L & J signed addenda to the Deposit Accounts Agreement Handbook for Banco Popular, by which it acknowledged and agreed to cancellation notice provision that allowed either party to end the account relationship upon written notification. When L & J opened the accounts, it did not inform Banco Popular that it was in the money transmitting business. By August 2002, Banco Popular became concerned regarding the nature, volume, and amounts of the transactions passing through the accounts. Toward the end of August 2002, Raymond L. Green, the bank's Operations Manager for the Virgin Islands Region, discovered that L & J had little or no internal controls or procedures and that it had no, or did not follow, an anti-money laundering compliance program for money services businesses. In September 2002, Banco Popular sent notice to L & J notice of its decision to terminate its banking services with plaintiff on the ground "that continued maintenance of L & J's accounts pose[d] an undue regulatory and compliance burden." The accounts were closed in December 2002.

[Meanwhile, in November 2002, L & J opened an account at FirstBank Puerto Rico (FirstBank), but it did not inform FirstBank that it was in the money transmitting business, or that Banco Popular had given notice of its intent to close L & J's accounts. By early December, L & J opened another account at FirstBank. In mid-December, FirstBank informed L & J that it would discontinuing its relationship with L & J. The accounts were closedon January 31, 2003. The same day, L & J sued both banks alleging, among other things, antitrust claims under the Sherman Act and the Clayton Act. . . . After dismissing the antitrust claims, the court turned to a claim based on the USA PATRIOT Act.]

Count VI alleges that the defendants' reliance on the USA P[ATRIOT] Act in closing plaintiff's accounts was misplaced. This claim suffers from several flaws. First, plaintiff points to no particular statute that would permit it to bring a cause of action under the P[ATRIOT] Act. Second, the Banks argue that the [USA PATRIOT Act] has no relevance in this matter as they closed the accounts based upon their contractual right to do so. Finally, even if the defendants had relied on the P[ATRIOT] Act, any such reliance appears to be proper in light of the plaintiff's own failings to abide by federal anti-money laundering laws. Thus, Count VI also fails to state a claim upon which relief can be granted and must be dismissed.

## Medical Supply Chain, Inc. v. US Bancorp, NA
— F. Supp.2d —, 2003 WL 21479192 (D.Kan. 2003)

MURGUIA, J.

[Medical Supply, a Missouri corporation that had developed a "health care supply strategist certification program," sued U.S. Bancorp a Minnesota bank holding company and various subsidiaries and employees of the company for allegedly conspiring with an unknown healthcare company to obstruct or delay Medical Supply's entry into the market. The court dismissed the plaintiff's antitrust and related claims, and then turned its attention to claims based on the USA PATRIOT Act.]

Prior to analyzing plaintiff's legal arguments, the court reminds plaintiff's counsel that, by signing the complaint and any other paper submitted to the court, he has certified, to the best of his belief and after a reasonable inquiry, that "the claims, defenses, and other legal contentions therein are warranted by existing law or by a nonfrivolous argument for the extension, modification, or reversal of existing law or the establishment of new law." Fed.R.Civ.P. 11(b)(2). Plaintiff's counsel is advised to take greater care in ensuring that the claims he brings on his clients' behalf are supported by the law and the facts.

Plaintiff seeks to bring claims that defendants failed to properly train their employees on the USA PATRIOT Act (hereinafter "Patriot Act") or provide a compliance officer related to the Act, violating section 352 of the Act, codified at 31 U.S.C. § 5318 (Count IV); "misused their authority" and engaged in excessive use of force as "enforcement officers" under the Act (Count V); and "violated criminal laws to influence public policy" under the Act (Count VI). The Act states, in relevant part,

> (h) Anti-money laundering programs.–
> (1) In general.–In order to guard against money laundering through financial institutions, each financial institution shall establish anti-money laundering programs, including, at a minimum-
> > (A) the development of internal policies, procedures, and controls;
> > (B) the designation of a compliance officer,
> > (C) an ongoing employee training program; and
> > (D) an independent audit function to test programs.

31 U.S.C. § 5318(h).

First, with regard to Count IV, the court finds plaintiff lacks standing. The court is obligated to raise the issue of standing *sua sponte* to ensure that an Article III case or controversy exists. *PeTA, People for the Ethical Treatment of Animals v. Rasmussen,* 298 F.3d 1198, 1202 (10th Cir.2002). "To establish Article III standing, the plaintiff must show injury in fact, a causal relationship between the injury and the defendants' challenged acts, and a likelihood that a favorable decision will redress the injury." *Id.* (citing *Lujan v. Defenders of Wildlife,* 504 U.S. 555, 560-61 (1992). In ruling on a motion to dismiss for lack of standing, the court "must accept as true all material allegations of the complaint, and must construe the complaint in favor of the complaining party." *Ward v. Utah,* 321 F.3d 1263,

1266 (10th Cir.2003) (citing *Warth v. Seldin,* 422 U.S. 490, 501, (1975)).

Here, the court finds plaintiff lacks standing because it has failed to allege a redressable injury. Even if defendants failed to train their employees in order to guard against money laundering and also failed to designate a compliance officer as required by the Act, plaintiff has not pled that it was injured due to such omissions. Moreover, there is no basis to conclude that any order from the court directing defendants to comply with the Act could redress plaintiff's grievance that defendants denied plaintiff escrow services.

Second, the court finds that, even if Count IV were justiciable, no private right of action exists to enforce the Patriot Act. As a result, Counts IV, V, and VI fail to state a claim for which relief can be granted. Plaintiff has not identified a provision of the Patriot Act expressly authorizing enforcement by private citizens. In its response to the motion to dismiss, plaintiff states that the failure to train and excessive use of force claims are actionable under 42 U.S.C. § 1983.

Section 1983 provides a cause of action against any person who, under color of state law, deprives a person "of any rights, privileges, or immunities secured by the Constitution and laws." § 1983 (emphasis added). The complaint has failed to allege that defendants acted under color of state law, an essential element of a § 1983 suit. *E.g., Sooner Prods. Co. v. McBride,* 708 F.2d 510, 512 (10th Cir.1983). Although plaintiff later states in its response that defendants acted "as an agent for the Department of the Treasury"[3] and that § 1983 liability may extend to private individuals if they engage in joint action with state officials, these allegations do not appear in the complaint and are, nevertheless, so conclusory that they cannot state a claim. *See, e .g., Hunt v. Bennett,* 17 F.3d 1263, 1268 (10th Cir.1994); *Sooner Prods. Co.,* 708 F.2d at 512. ("When a plaintiff in a § 1983 action attempts to assert the necessary 'state action' by implicating state officials or judges in a conspiracy with private defendants, mere conclusory allegations with no supporting factual averments are insufficient; the pleadings must specifically present facts tending to show agreement and concerted action."). . . .

Further, plaintiff has not attempted to state a claim that an implied private right of action exists under the Act. "A plaintiff asserting an implied right of action under a federal statute bears the relatively heavy burden of demonstrating that Congress affirmatively contemplated private enforcement when it passed the statute. In other words, he must overcome the familiar presumption that Congress did not intend to create a private right of action." *Casas v. Am. Airlines, Inc.,* 304 F.3d 517, 521 (5th Cir.2002); *see also Cort v. Ash,* 422 U.S. 66, 78 (1975) (setting forth the four-factor test for whether a statute creates an implied private right of action as (1) whether plaintiff is a member of the class for whose benefit the statute was passed; (2) whether there is evidence of legislative intent, either explicit or implicit, to create or deny a private remedy; (3) whether it is consistent with the legislative scheme to imply a private remedy; (4) whether the cause of action [is] one traditionally relegated to state law so that implying a federal right of action would be inappropriate). The complaint alleges none of these elements.

Finally, with regard to Count VI in particular, in which plaintiff actually contends defendants "are preventing [plaintiff]'s entry into commerce in violation of Section 802 of the USA Patriot Act which creates a federal crime of 'domestic terrorism' that broadly extends to 'acts dangerous to human life that are a violation of the criminal laws,'" the court finds plaintiff's allegation so completely divorced from rational thought that the court will

---

3. Plaintiff's argument implicates action under color of federal rather than state law, thus giving rise to an action under *Bivens v. Six Unknown Agents of Fed. Bureau of Narcotics,* 403 U.S. 388 (1971), rather than § 1983.

refrain from further comment until such time as federal criminal proceedings are commenced, if indeed they ever are.

**Notes and Comments 10.11.** The chief cashier of Quarter National Bank (QNB) has received a telephone call from an official with the U.S. Treasury's Financial Crimes Enforcement Network (FinCEN), who inquired whether QNB holds any accounts for Attila D. Hunn, the President for Life of Nusquam. Should the cashier disclose the existence of any such accounts to the FinCEN? Review the RFPA and the ECPA (and particularly 12 U.S.C. §§ 3403(c), 3413(g); 18 U.S.C. §§ 2511(1), (3)(a), 2701) and the case that follows.

## Lopez v. First Union National Bank of Florida
### 129 F.3d 1186 (11th Cir. 1997)

Carnes, Circuit Judge:

These cases, consolidated for purposes of this appeal, arise out of plaintiffs' claims that their banks improperly disclosed information relating to their checking accounts to federal authorities. The complaint in each case was dismissed on the ground that the safe harbor provisions of the Annunzio-Wylie Anti-Money Laundering Act, 31 U.S.C. § 5318 (g), immunized the banks from liability. For the reasons set forth below, we reverse the judgments dismissing the complaints on that ground. . . .

. . . [W]e limit ourselves to the allegations of the complaint, which we are required to accept as true. Those allegations may turn out to be inaccurate, or there may be additional facts which dictate a different result, but for now the factual boundary of this case is marked by the metes and bounds of the complaint.

The FedWire Fund Transfer System is an electronic funds transfer system which permits large dollar fund transfers by computer-to-computer communications between banks. First Union is a bank within the FedWire Fund Transfer System and uses "electronic storage" to maintain the contents of an electronic funds transfer. On September 2, 1993, and November 30, 1993, First Union received an electronic wire transfer of funds for credit to Lopez's account. On both occasions, First Union provided United States law enforcement authorities with access to the contents of those electronic transfers. First Union made these disclosures based solely on the "verbal instructions" of federal law enforcement authorities.

On February 3, 1994, a United States Magistrate Judge issued a seizure warrant directing First Union to freeze Lopez's account and conduct an inventory of it. Pursuant to the seizure warrant, First Union again provided United States law enforcement authorities access to the contents of the electronic funds transfers sent to Lopez that were being held in electronic storage. On June 6, 1995, First Union surrendered the $270,887.20 balance of Lopez's First Union account to the United States. The United States subsequently filed a civil forfeiture case against Lopez, which was resolved by a stipulation that $108,359 of Lopez's account was forfeited to the United States while $162,532.20 was returned to her.

Following the resolution of the civil forfeiture case, Lopez filed suit against First Union asserting claims under the Electronic Communications Privacy Act, 18 U.S.C. §§ 2510 *et seq.* (Counts I and II), the Right to Financial Privacy Act, 12 U.S.C. §§ 3401 *et seq.*, (Count III), and Florida law. (Count IV).

First Union moved to dismiss the complaint. . . . The district court granted the motion and dismissed Lopez's complaint with prejudice. The district court's decision to dismiss the complaint was based exclusively on its conclusion that the Annunzio-Wylie Anti-Money Laundering Act, 31 U.S.C. § 5318(g)(3), immunized First Union from liability.

This appeal followed. . . .

As a preliminary matter, we first address First Union's arguments that Lopez's complaint fails to state a claim under either the Electronic Communications Privacy Act, 18 U.S.C. §§ 2510 *et seq.*, ("the ECPA") or the Right to Financial Privacy Act, 12 U.S.C. §§ 3401 *et seq.*, ("the RFPA"). We will then address the additional issue of whether the Annunzio-Wylie Anti-Money Laundering Act, 31 U.S.C. § 5318(g)(3), immunizes First Union from liability. . . .

. . . In count I, [Lopez] . . . alleges that First Union violated 18 U.S.C. § 2702(a) (1), which provides that "a person or entity providing an electronic communication service to the public shall not knowingly divulge to any person or entity the contents of a communication while in electronic storage by that service." The complaint alleges that First Union provided an electronic communication service and that First Union provided the United States access to "the contents of information in electronic storage, including the contents of electronic communications pertaining to . . . Lopez."

First Union contends that count I fails to state a viable claim under 18 U.S.C. § 2702(a)(1), because it is not an electronic communication service. We reject that contention which amounts to nothing more than a denial of the allegations in Lopez's complaint. Accepting all allegations in the complaint as true as we are required to do at this stage, we conclude that Count I states a violation of 18 U.S.C. § 2702(a)(1).[2]

In count II, Lopez alleges that First Union infringed her rights under the ECPA by violating 18 U.S.C. § 2703 and 18 U.S.C. § 2511(3)(a). Section 2703 defines the conditions in which an electronic communication service may disclose electronic communications to the government. If the electronic communication service has held the contents of an electronic communication in electronic storage for one hundred eighty days or less, it may disclose that electronic communication to the government only pursuant to a federal or state warrant. *See* 18 U.S.C. § 2703(a). In count II, Lopez alleges that, on the same day funds were electronically transferred to her account, First Union disclosed contents of those electronic funds transfers in electronic storage pursuant to "verbal instructions" instead of a warrant. She also alleges that the disclosures were made on the same day that funds were electronically transferred to her account, which means the communication disclosed had been held in electronic storage for less than one hundred eighty days. Those allegations are sufficient to state a prima facie claim under 18 U.S.C. § 2703.

However, the allegations of count II of the complaint are not sufficient to state a claim under 18 U.S.C. § 2511(3)(a). That section provides that "an electronic communication service . . . shall not intentionally divulge the contents of any communication . . . while in transmission on that service to any person or entity other than an addressee or intended recipient of such communication." 18 U.S.C. § 2511(3)(a). . . . That proscription is not violated unless the communication is divulged "while in transmission." Neither count II nor any other part of the complaint alleges that First Union disclosed Lopez's electronic communications "while in transmission." . . .

. . . Because the complaint does not allege that First Union disclosed communications while in transmission, it fails to state a claim under § 2511(3) (a). . . .

In count III of her complaint, Lopez alleges First Union violated her rights under the RFPA by disclosing her financial records under conditions not authorized by the RFPA.

---

2. Nor does the fact that Congress amended the ECPA in 1996 to specifically exclude electronic funds transfers from the definition of an "electronic communication," *see* 18 U.S.C. § [2510(12)] (1996), prevent Count I from stating a claim under § 2702(a)(1). That amendment did not take effect until 1996, well after the events giving rise to this case.

First Union does not argue that Lopez has failed to allege a prima facie violation of the RFPA. Instead, it contends that count III should be dismissed because the alleged disclosures are protected by 12 U.S.C. § 3403(c), another section of the RFPA. Under § 3403(c), a financial institution possessing information relevant to a possible violation of law involving one of its accounts is permitted to make a disclosure of that information to law enforcement. However, the disclosure permitted is limited to the name of the account holder and "the nature of any suspected illegal activity." 12 U.S.C. § 3403(c). Because the complaint alleges that First Union went beyond that and disclosed actual financial records pertaining to Lopez's account (*i.e.*, the electronic funds transfers communications, the contents of which were held in electronic storage), First Union's alleged disclosures are not protected by 12 U.S.C. § 3403(c). Accordingly, count III of Lopez's complaint states a claim under the RFPA. . . .

The Annunzio-Wylie Anti-Money Laundering Act of 1992, 31 U.S.C. § 5318(g), provides in relevant part:

> (g) Reporting of suspicious transactions. --
> (1) In general.–The [Treasury] Secretary may require any financial institution, and any director, officer, employee, or agent of any financial institution, to report any suspicious transaction relevant to a possible violation of law or regulation.
> (2) Notification prohibited.–A financial institution, and a director, officer, employee, or agent of any financial institution, who voluntarily reports a suspicious transaction, or that reports a suspicious transaction pursuant to this section or any other authority, may not notify any person involved in the transaction that the transaction has been reported.
> (3) Liability for disclosures.–Any financial institution that makes [i.] a disclosure of any possible violation of law or regulation or [ii.] a disclosure pursuant to this subsection or [iii.] any other authority, and any director, officer, employee, or agent of such institution, shall not be liable to any person under any law or regulation of the United States or any constitution, law, or regulation of any State or political subdivision thereof, for such disclosure or for any failure to notify the person involved in the transaction or any other person of such disclosure.

The three safe harbors provided by § 5318(g)(3) supply an affirmative defense to claims against a financial institution for disclosing an individual's financial records or account-related activity. Financial institutions are granted immunity from liability for three different types of disclosures:

> (i.) A disclosure of any possible violation of law or regulation,
> (ii.) A disclosure pursuant to § 5318(g) itself, or
> (iii.) A disclosure pursuant to any other authority.

*See* 31 U.S.C. § 5318(g)(3).

The district court dismissed Lopez's complaint after concluding that the safe harbor provisions of § 5318(g) (3) protected First Union's disclosures of her account activity. Lopez contends that the district court's holding is erroneous for two reasons. First, she contends that § 5318(g)(3)'s safe harbor provisions apply only to disclosures of currency transactions. If that is true, First Union's disclosure of electronic transfers and the contents of transfers held in electronic storage are not protected by any of the safe harbor provisions of § 5318(g)(3).

Second, Lopez contends that even if the Act does cover more than currency transactions, First Union's disclosures do not fall within one of the three categories of disclosures for which § 5318(g)(3) grants immunity. Addressing Lopez's contentions in turn, we disagree with the first one but agree with the second. . . .

Lopez's contention that § 5318(g)(3) protects disclosures of currency transactions only is at odds with the text and purpose of the Annunzio-Wylie Act. The text of § 5318(g) (3) neither explicitly nor implicitly suggests that Congress intended to limit the safe harbor to disclosures of currency or to any specific kind of transaction. To the contrary, the text of that subdivision indicates Congress deliberately did not limit the safe harbor to disclosure of any specific type of transaction. For example, § 5318(g)(3) provides that a financial institution is entitled to immunity for a disclosure of "any possible violation of law." 31 U.S.C. § 5318(g)(3). . . . [W]hen used in a statute, "the adjective 'any' is not ambiguous; it has a well-established meaning." . . . "Read naturally, the word 'any' has an expansive meaning, that is, one or some indiscriminately of whatever kind." . . . Thus § 5318(g)(3) protects disclosure of a violation of law regardless of whether it involves a cash transaction, electronic transfers, or any other type of transaction. Section 5318(g)(3)'s scope is not limited merely to disclosures of currency transactions.

Moreover, we agree with the district court that the purpose underlying the Act is inconsistent with Lopez's proposed construction. The district court reasoned as follows:

> [A]ccording to the comments of Congressman Neal regarding the enactment of 31 U.S.C. § 5318(g), banks have long been encouraged to report suspicious transactions to the appropriate authorities. *See* Cong.Rec. E57-02 (1993). Therefore, to ensure compliance from the banks, the safe harbor provision was added in order to protect a bank when it reports a suspicious transaction. *Id.* "The goal of this new law is to have banks work with international efforts to stop the global movement of drug money. Money laundering is an international problem. Money knows no borders and flows freely from one country to another. The United States has long recognized that, and has worked hard to ensure cooperation from foreign governments and financial institutions to assure that money launderers have no place to hide." *Id.*
>
> The Court finds that if Congress intended to limit this statute solely to "currency transactions" as asserted by Plaintiff, it would severely restrict the ability of a bank to report suspicious transactions without the fear of liability. As Plaintiff notes in her response to Defendant's motion, "[i]n 1994, some 72 million fund transfers with a total value of $211 trillion were moved over Fedwire." ... Thus, the effectiveness of the anti-money laundering act would be substantially limited if it applied only to cash transactions, since electronic fund transfers, the contents of which are held in electronic storage, are the means by which large dollar funds are transferred between the Federal Reserve and the service providers (*i.e.*, originating banks, intermediary banks, and beneficiary banks).

*Lopez v. First Union National Bank*, 931 F.Supp. 860, 864 (S.D.Fla. 1996).

Accordingly, we hold that electronic fund transfers and information held in electronic storage are not outside the scope of the Annunzio-Wylie Anti-Money Laundering Act's safe harbor provisions, 31 U.S.C. § 5318(g)(3). . . .

The Annunzio-Wylie Act does not provide a financial institution blanket immunity for any disclosure of an individual's financial records. Instead, a financial institution is entitled to immunity only if its disclosure falls within one of the three safe harbors set forth in § 5318(g)(3). Lopez's complaint alleges that First Union disclosed Lopez's financial records twice in response to nothing more than "verbal instructions" of government officials and once pursuant to a seizure warrant. Under the facts alleged in Lopez's complaint, First Union's two disclosures in response to "verbal instructions" of government officials do not fit within any of § 5318(g)(3)'s three safe harbors. However, its disclosure pursuant to the seizure warrant is protected by § 5318(g)(3)'s third safe harbor.

The first safe harbor provision protects a financial institution's "disclosure of any possible violation of law or regulation." 31 U.S.C. § 5318(g)(3). As the use of the adjective "possible" indicates, a financial institution's disclosure is protected even if it ultimately turns out there was no violation of law. In order to be immune from liability, it is sufficient that a financial institution have a good faith suspicion that a law or regulation may have been violated, even if it turns out in hindsight that none was. By extending immunity to a financial institution's disclosure of a suspected violation of law or regulation, the first safe harbor encourages financial institutions to voluntarily play a role in combating money laundering and other crimes.

The problem for First Union at this stage of the litigation is that it is stuck with the allegations of the complaint. Those allegations do not show that First Union had a good faith suspicion that a law or regulation may have been violated. None of the allegations indicate that the transactions associated with Lopez's account were suspicious enough to suggest a possible violation of law. First Union contends, however, that the first safe harbor should protect disclosures made in response to "verbal instructions" of government officials. It argues that law enforcement's demand for financial records should, by itself, be sufficient to give a financial institution a good faith basis to suspect a possible violation of law or regulation. The hidden premise of that argument is that Congress intended the first safe harbor to protect disclosures made pursuant to government officials' unexplained request or unvarnished instructions for financial records. That premise is flawed.

. . . [T]he second and third safe harbors protect from liability in situations where the government has and exercises the legal authority to demand disclosure of financial records. If we accepted First Union's premise that Congress intended the first safe harbor to protect disclosures made pursuant to any and all government demands, it would render the other two safe harbor provisions superfluous. Following the basic principle of statutory construction "that a statute should not be construed in such a way as to render certain provisions superfluous or insignificant," we reject First Union's contention that the first safe harbor protects disclosures made in response to nothing more than "verbal instructions" of government officials.

Having concluded that the first safe harbor provision does not protect First Union from liability for the alleged disclosures, we turn now to the second. The second safe harbor provision protects a financial institution's "disclosure pursuant to this subsection." 31 U.S.C. § 5318(g)(3). Disclosures "pursuant to this subsection" are disclosures required by the Office of the Treasury Secretary under the rule-making authority vested in the Treasury Secretary by 31 U.S.C. § 5318(g)(1), which provides:

> The [Treasury] Secretary may require any financial institution, and any director, officer, employee, or agent of any financial institution, to report any suspicious transaction relevant to a possible violation of law or regulation.

In February 1996, the Treasury Secretary issued regulations under this sub-section. . . . The second safe harbor protects any disclosures required by those regulations.

However, the complaint alleges that First Union's disclosures occurred in 1993 and 1994. Because the Treasury Secretary's regulations under § 5318(g)(1) were not in effect at the time those alleged disclosures were made, the second safe harbor provision cannot immunize First Union's disclosures.

The third safe harbor provision protects a financial institution's disclosure pursuant to "any other authority." 31 U.S.C. § 5318(g)(3). Because the second safe harbor protects disclosures pursuant to the legal authority of the Treasury Secretary's regulations, "other authority" means authority other than the Treasury Secretary's regulations. The "other authority" must be legal authority, . . . *e.g.*, statutes, regulations, court orders, etc. . . .

The complaint alleges that First Union disclosed Lopez's financial records twice in response to "verbal instructions" of government officials and once in response to a seizure warrant. Clearly, a disclosure in response to a seizure warrant is protected by the third safe harbor. . . .

However, First Union's earlier disclosures are a different matter, because disclosures in response to nothing more than the "verbal instructions" of government officials are not protected by the third safe harbor. . . . First Union fails to identify any statute or regulation which gives a government official's verbal request to access an individual's financial records the force of law. Nor does First Union point to a statute or regulation authorizing a financial institution to release an individual's financial records in response to mere verbal instructions of government officials. We can find nothing in the Annunzio-Wylie Act which entitles government officials to gain access to financial records simply by verbal request. Therefore, because the facts alleged in the complaint do not show First Union acted pursuant to any legal authority when it released Lopez's financial records, the third safe harbor provision does not protect First Union's disclosures.

We also reject First Union's argument that its disclosures of Lopez's account activity were made pursuant to "other authority" because there were regulations, *see e.g.* 12 C.F.R. § 21.11 (1989), in effect at the time disclosures were made that required reporting suspicious transactions. . . . Lopez's complaint does not allege that Lopez's transactions were suspicious or were viewed as suspicious by First Union.

**Notes and Comments 10.12.** QNB participates in the FedWire Fund Transfer System and uses "electronic storage" to maintain the contents of its electronic funds transfers and other financial information relating to international-related transactions. The chief cashier has noticed that in a recent one-week period, QNB has received 100 electronic funds transfers, in amounts ranging from $50,000 to $100,000, from NusBank, QNB's correspondent bank in Nusquam, each for the account of various members of the family of Attila D. Hunn. During the same period, QNB received from NusBank 100 electronically transmitted advices concerning irrevocable standby letters of credit, variously payable to "ADH Corporation," "ADH Foundation, Ltd." and eight other entities that QNB has never heard of. No credit information is available on any of these entities. The following week, QNB notified agents of the FinCEN that it had observed "unusual amounts" and "unusual movements" of funds and credits at the bank. Thereafter, QNB provided federal agents access to detailed contents of financial information in electronic storage, including the contents of electronic communications, pertaining to accounts and transactions originating in Nusquam. In addition to the Hunn family accounts and the ten Nusquami entities, this information pertained to the accounts of 990 other Nusquami individuals or companies. Federal agents subsequently seized all 1,100 accounts on allegations of money laundering. Eventually, the federal agents released 600 of the accounts because they were determined to have had "no connection with money laundering." Herman Coronado, on behalf of himself and other affected account holders, has filed a class action suit against QNB, alleging claims under the

ECPA and the RFPA. If QNB moves to dismiss the complaint for failure to state a cause of action, what is the likely result? Would it make a difference if QNB provided the federal agents with access to the information in response to grand jury subpoenas? In analyzing these questions, consider the following case.

## Coronado v. Bank Atlantic Bancorp, Inc.
222 F.3d 1315 (11th Cir. 2000)
*cert. denied sub nom. Ruiz Coronado v. BankAtlantic Bancorp, Inc.*, 531 U.S. 1052

Cudahy, Circuit Judge:

[BankAtlantic Bancorp, Inc. (BankAtlantic) responded to grand jury subpoenas by producing the bank records of nearly 1100 international customers. Jose Daniel Ruiz Coronado, a bank customer, brought a class action alleging that BankAtlantic had violated the ECPA, the RFPA, and Florida law by disclosing account information and records to the grand juries. The District Court dismissed the action on the ground that BankAtlantic was immune from suit under the Annunzio-Wylie safe harbor provision, 31 U.S.C. § 5318(g)(3). The Eleventh Circuit–in an appeal consolidated with the *Lopez* case, *supra*–reversed and remanded. On remand, the District Court granted summary judgment for BankAtlantic, on the ground that the bank was shielded by the safe harbor provision. Mr. Ruiz appealed. (In the excerpts that follow, the court refers to Mr. Ruiz as "Coronado.")]

I. Facts and Disposition Below
    A. General Background
    In February of 1995, BankAtlantic acquired MegaBank, a Dade County commercial bank, in order to create an international division. MegaBank's international division was headed by Piedad Ortiz, and after the acquisition, she became Vice President of BankAtlantic's international division. Ortiz had overseen approximately 1100 accounts at MegaBank, and she continued this supervision at BankAtlantic. Shortly after acquiring MegaBank, BankAtlantic conducted an internal audit of its new international division, and this audit revealed suspicious practices. A private pouch service made regular deliveries addressed to "BankAtlantic, International Division, Attention Ms. Piedad Ortiz." These pouches, which were uninsured, contained large amounts of checks, money orders and negotiable instruments along with deposit and transfer instructions. The pouches originated from a private courier service–discretely located in the back of another business–in Bogota, Columbia, and the checks and other instruments transported in the pouches were from various locations in the United States, including New York and New Jersey. BankAtlantic discovered that Ortiz and her assistant, Lucia Ramirez (who had also joined BankAtlantic as part of the MegaBank acquisition), were responsible for initiating and maintaining this pouch service.

    The BankAtlantic audit also revealed that Ortiz and her assistant were approving new accounts that were missing required customer identification documentation and allowing personal accounts to be used as unregistered money exchange facilities (in probable violation of Florida law). Further, BankAtlantic discovered, among other irregularities, that letters of authorization were missing for numerous wire transfers and that no currency transaction reports were filed when bearer instruments in excess of $10,000 arrived in the pouches from Bogota. There were millions of dollars flowing into and out of these Columbia-based accounts each month.

BankAtlantic became suspicious that its new international division, as headed by Ortiz, was facilitating money laundering and bank fraud. BankAtlantic took these suspicions to federal law enforcement officials in June of 1995. At this point, the bank provided general information regarding its suspicions along with customer names and account numbers for only five accounts obviously connected with this questionable activity. BankAtlantic did not disclose the contents of any incoming or outgoing wire transfers at this time.

The federal government investigated this suspected money laundering and bank fraud, and sometime in the spring of 1996, three grand juries were impaneled. These grand juries . . . investigated individuals and organizations in Florida, New York and New Jersey for the suspected laundering of Columbian drug money. In the late spring, the grand juries issued and served subpoenas on BankAtlantic demanding that it produce copies of account documents, records and information regarding the 1100 accounts under the oversight of Ms. Ortiz in the international division.

The federal investigation was centered on these 1100 accounts that Ortiz had supervised at MegaBank and later at BankAtlantic, and on June 5, 1996, the United States Department of Justice, in conjunction with Columbian law enforcement agencies, announced the arrest of several individuals: Ortiz and Ramirez[3] were arrested upon suspicion that they were committing bank fraud to facilitate the illegal movement of funds by individuals in Columbia. Also on June 5, Judge Davis of the Southern District of Florida issued a ten-day ex parte temporary restraining order freezing the 1100 accounts in BankAtlantic's international division. On June 11, 1996, Judge Davis released the funds in some accounts, and then, on June 23, the district court issued a seizure warrant to freeze the remaining accounts until further court order. A supplemental order directed the Drug Enforcement Agency (DEA) to physically seize all of the frozen funds (subject to certain exceptions not relevant here). Accordingly, BankAtlantic turned the funds over to the DEA on August 1, and on August 8, forfeiture proceedings were commenced against many of the accounts. About six months after the initial seizure, the government agreed to release between 400 and 600 of the accounts–there is no evidence in the record suggesting why–and the funds were returned to these account holders with full interest in December of 1996.

B. Coronado's Account and Lawsuit

Coronado opened his account with BankAtlantic on May 13, 1996–almost a year after BankAtlantic first reported suspicious activity to the federal government and, as it turned out, about three weeks before Ortiz's arrest. Ortiz had opened the account for Coronado using instruments drawn on United States's banks that had been shipped from Bogota, Columbia, to Miami via the private courier service. Coronado's initial deposit consisted of four checks in odd amounts that totaled exactly $5000 in value, and subsequent deposits were comprised of checks, travelers' checks and money orders drawn on banks in New York and New Jersey. Once the amount Coronado had on deposit grew to a little less then $46,000, $45,500 was wire transferred to a Swiss bank account.The day after the transfer, new deposits began. BankAtlantic had not mentioned Coronado in its initial disclosure to federal authorities in 1995 . . . , but Coronado's account information and the records of the wire transfer to Switzerland were turned over to the grand jury pursuant to the 1996 subpoenas. On June 5, 1996, Coronado's account was frozen along with the other 1100 that Ortiz had supervised, but his account was not among those released on June 11. Instead, his funds were seized pursuant to the district court orders, and forfeiture proceedings were com-

3. On June 14, 1996, a federal grand jury indicted both Ortiz and Ramirez for making false entries in the books and records of BankAtlantic to keep the bank unaware of the currency transfer operation from Columbia.

menced against Coronado's account on August 8. His account was eventually released, along with the 400 to 600 others, pursuant to the agreement with the government, and his funds were returned (with interest) before the end of 1996. . . .

II. Discussion

In his brief on appeal, Coronado identifies three issues we must decide: (1) whether the Annunzio-Wylie Act provides BankAtlantic with immunity from his claims under federal and state law; (2) whether Coronado was entitled to partial summary judgment that BankAtlantic had violated the RFPA and the ECPA; and (3) whether the district court erred in denying Coronado's motions to compel discovery. We review the first two issues de novo, . . . and review the discovery issue for abuse of discretion. . . .

A. Immunity Under the Annunzio-Wylie Act

BankAtlantic claims, and Coronado does not dispute, that the grand jury subpoenas it received were facially valid and properly served. BankAtlantic argues, quite simply, that because it only disclosed information pursuant to these subpoenas, it disclosed information in accordance with "other authority" and has immunity under the Annunzio-Wylie Act's safe harbor (iii). In *Lopez*, we explained § 5318(g)(3)'s third safe harbor and the meaning of "any other authority" as follows:

> The "other authority" must be legal authority, because authority means "[r]ight to exercise powers," Black's Law Dictionary 133 (6th ed.1991), and in our system based on rule of law, the right to exercise power is derived from law, e.g. statutes, regulations, court orders, etc. Hence, for a financial institution's disclosure to fall within the confines of the third safe harbor, the financial institution must be able to point to a statute, regulation, court order, or other source of law that specifically or impliedly authorized the disclosure. If it cannot do so, the disclosure is not entitled to the protection of the [third] safe harbor.

*Lopez*, 129 F.3d at 1193-94. In *Lopez*, by way of example, we explained that "[c]learly a disclosure in response to a seizure warrant is protected by the third safe harbor." *Id*. at 1194. However, we also explained that a government agent's "verbal request" for information is not "other authority" because there is no "statute or regulation which gives a government official's verbal request to access an individual's financial records the force of law." *Id*. *Lopez* did not explicitly address grand jury subpoenas, but we believe that these are properly considered "other authority" for the purposes of § 5318(g)(3).

A federal grand jury has extremely broad investigatory powers and, unlike a federal agent making a verbal request, "may compel the production of evidence or the testimony of witnesses as it considers appropriate." *United States v. Calandra*, 414 U.S. 338, 343 (1974). A grand jury has the power to compel the production of evidence because "a federal grand jury subpoena is issued under the authority of a court." *Doe v. DiGenova*, 779 F.2d 74, 80 (D.C.Cir.1985). More specifically: under Federal Rule of Criminal Procedure 17(a), the clerk of a district court is authorized to issue blank subpoenas (marked with the seal of the court) to a prosecutor working with a grand jury. . . . If a recipient of a grand jury subpoena does not produce the evidence sought, the recipient that disobeyed the subpoena (which is essentially an order of the court), is in contempt, . . . and may be fined or imprisoned. . . . Thus, unlike, for example, a mere verbal request from a government agent, there is a legal mechanism to enforce grand jury subpoenas. They possess the "force of law" because they are issued under the authority of a federal district court, and disobedience can lead to a legal sanction. . . .

But Coronado is quick to point out that the reach of grand jury subpoenas is not unlimited: a federal district court has the power to quash a grand jury subpoena requesting documents "if compliance would be unreasonable or oppressive," *see* Fed.R.Crim.P. 17(c), and a grand jury "may not itself violate a valid privilege, whether established by the Constitution, statutes, or the common law." *Calandra*, 441 U.S. at 346. Also, Congress has the power to limit grand jury subpoenas by enacting statutes. . . . Coronado argues that the account records demanded in the grand jury subpoenas here were "privileged" under the ECPA and therefore outside the reach of the grand jury. His argument is, essentially, that because § 2703(a) of the ECPA states that "[a] governmental entity may require the disclosure . . . of the contents of an electronic communication, that is in electronic storage in an electronic communications system for one hundred and eighty days or less, only pursuant to a warrant under the Federal Rules of Criminal Procedure," and because grand jury subpoenas are not warrants, the grand juries lacked the power to compel production of his account information. Therefore, BankAtlantic's disclosure pursuant to a grand jury subpoena violated this provision of the ECPA, and it cannot use the shelter of the Annunzio-Wylie Act's safe harbor, Coronado concludes.

Coronado's argument begs the question. The question here is not whether the government or the grand jury obtained evidence in violation of the ECPA, but whether BankAtlantic is liable to Coronado for its disclosure. BankAtlantic was subpoenaed merely as a witness, and long-standing grand jury policy and practice suggests that we do not want witnesses (who are not even targets of the grand jury) testing the limits of the grand jury's authority. The Supreme Court has emphasized that "a witness may not interfere with the course of the grand jury's inquiry." *Calandra*, 414 U.S. at 345. Further, as a witness, BankAtlantic was "not entitled to urge objections of incompetency or irrelevancy, such as a party might raise," *id.*, nor was BankAtlantic entitled "to challenge the authority of the court or of the grand jury, provided they have a de facto existence and organization." *Blair v. United States*, 250 U.S. 273, 282 (1919) (holding that witnesses could not refuse to testify or produce documents on the ground that the relevant criminal statute was unconstitutional). *See also Calandra*, 414 U.S. at 345. . . . Thus, even if the ECPA technically deprived the grand jury of the authority to demand the account records from BankAtlantic, BankAtlantic–as a witness–was not in a position to test the limits of the grand jury's authority. BankAtlantic was presented with facially valid subpoenas from three federal grand juries investigating money laundering. Forcing a bank to challenge a facially valid grand jury subpoena in order to avoid liability to one (or more) of its customers would fly in the face of both the Annunzio-Wylie Act's clear intent to encourage cooperation with money laundering investigations and the more general policy favoring the "effective and expeditious discharge of the grand jur[ies'] duties." *Calandra*, 414 U.S. at 349-50. We believe it proper to label grand jury subpoenas, like search warrants or court orders, "legal authority" under *Lopez*, and we find that a grand jury subpoena qualifies as "other authority" under the Annunzio-Wylie Act's third safe harbor. BankAtlantic's disclosure, therefore, is covered by the third safe harbor.

Having determined that BankAtlantic is protected by § 5318(g)(3)'s third safe harbor, it remains only to determine the scope of the immunity granted by the statute. This is a straight-forward determination. . . . [Section 5318(g)(3)] immunity is very broad.[4] . . .

---

4. There is no official legislative history for the Annunzio-Wylie Act, but in a letter written after the passage of the Act, Chairman of the House Subcommittee on Financial Institutions, and sponsor of the Act, Congressman Frank Annunzio explained in a letter that the immunity provisions of the Act sought "to provide the broadest possible exemption from civil liability for the reporting of suspicious transactions...." Cong. Rec. E57-02 (1993).

Because BankAtlantic disclosed Coronado's account records and information pursuant to facially valid grand jury subpoenas, BankAtlantic is immune from any lawsuit arising from these disclosures.[5] Therefore, the district court properly granted BankAtlantic's motion for summary judgment.

        **Notes and Comments 10.13.** As *Lopez* notes, one type of disclosure permitted under the RFPA is limited to the name of the account holder and "the nature of any suspected illegal activity." 12 U.S.C. § 3403(c). Assume that Al Masri is the subject of a money laundering investigation, and that his account at QNB has been frozen by court order. QNB learns that Masri attempted to transfer $500,000 out of the account by means of a back-dated check which he attempted to negotiate at a remote QNB branch in another country. Clearly, QNB can report Al Masri's name and its suspicion that he has attempted to evade the court order, but can it report the exact amount of the attempted transfer or the location of the remote branch? Are those details part of the "nature of [the] suspected illegal activity?" For discussion of this interpretive issue, see *Miranda De Villalba v. Coutts & Co. (USA) Intern.*, 250 F.3d 1351 (11th Cir. 2001), *cert. denied*, 543 U.S. 953.

        **10.14.** The safe harbor in 31 U.S.C. § 5318(g)(3) protects a disclosing financial institution–even if it ultimately turns out there was no violation of law. However, according to *Lopez*, this immunity from liability only applies if the financial institution had a *good faith* suspicion that a law or regulation may have been violated. Assume that Al Masri's account at QNB was actually being manipulated by Gassman, a QNB branch officer, who had deceived Al about the reasons for the transactions involving his account. When internal auditors informed Gassman's superiors about the activity in Al's account, QNB discloses the information to federal authorities. Under the *Lopez* interpretation, will QNB's claim to immunity under § 5318(g)(3) be rejected? For an alternative to *Lopez*, consider the following case.

## Stoutt v. Banco Popular De Puerto Rico
### 320 F.3d 26 (1st Cir. 2003)

BOUDIN, Chief Judge.

        [Plaintiff Palmer Paxton Stoutt filed suit against defendant Banco Popular de Puerto Rico ("BPPR"), alleging, *inter alia*, unlawful arrest, malicious prosecution and illegal incarceration. He sought compensatory damages under the general torts statute of the Puerto Rico Civil Code, 31 P.R. LAWS ANN. § 5141 (1956). In response, BPPR asserted as an affirmative defense immunity from any liability, since its actions were taken pursuant to the reporting requirements of the Annunzio-Wylie Act and were protected under the Act's "safe harbor" provision, 31 U.S.C. § 5813(g)(3). BPPR filed a motion for summary judgment. The district court granted summary judgment, and Stoutt appealed. The facts of the case, taken in the light most favorable to Stoutt, were as follows.

        [Stoutt, a resident of Tortola, British Virgin Islands, was President and Chief Executive Officer of Rancal International, Inc. and Rancal Corporation Limited. In June 1995,

---

5. Our determination that BankAtlantic is immune under the Annunzio-Wylie Act eliminates any need to address Coronado's second argument on appeal (that he is entitled to summary judgment on his ECPA and RFPA claims).

Stoutt entered into negotiations with BPPR, is a banking institution organized and existing under the laws of the Commonwealth of Puerto Rico with its principal place of business in Puerto Rico, to secure a loan for a term of five years and in the amount of $1,500,000. A BPPR branch Manager, Jose Enrique Guzman, was assisting Stoutt in obtaining sufficient collateral for the loan. He referred Stoutt to Euro-Atlantic Securities, a Chicago securities firm, that was to arrange a lease by Stoutt of $10 million in U.S. Treasury bills as collateral to be deposited in an acceptable security firm. The lease would secure the needed collateral for the loan with BPPR, while at the same time allowing the remainder to be invested to produce enough money to pay for the substantial monthly lease cost of $300,000.

[Euro-Atlantic required evidence of sufficient funds for a good-faith deposit of $300,000. Stoutt contacted Guzman to secure a line of credit in that amount. On July 21, 1995, Guzman sent Stoutt a letter indicating that the required line of credit had been approved by BPPR. Later, however, Guzman allegedly proposed that instead of using the line of credit, Stoutt should deposit a check from Rancal Intrernational, against which a wire transfer for the deposit would be made. The check from Rancal International, though without sufficient funds at that time, would be covered once the Treasury bills were deposited in Stoutt's account.

[Unfortunately, events went decidedly wrong for Stoutt. The funds were misdirected, and consequently the Rancal International checking account did not have sufficient funds for clearance. As a result, plaintiff's account with BPPR had a $300,000.00 overdraft. On September 18, 1995, fearing an action for check kiting,[16] plaintiff wrote BPPR, explaining that the Treasury Bill transaction had not been completed as expected and, therefore, the Rancal International account had insufficient funds to cover the check made to BPPR. By the end of September 1995, Stoutt realized that the Treasury Bill transaction had been a sham.

[In the meantime, in a memorandum to his BPPR superiors, Guzman allegedly presented inaccurate and incomplete information as to the nature of the $300,000.00 wire transfer. He failed to indicate his knowledge of the transactions. BPPR, apparently unaware of Guzman's involvement, reported the transaction to their security division. After an investigation, on November 13, 1995, it filed a Report of Apparent Crime with the FBI and the U.S. Attorney. On November 15, 1995, BPPR officials met with FBI agent Anne Costello who, using the allegedly incomplete information provided by Guzman (by then a former employee), decided that there was apparent bank fraud due to check kiting. Special Agent Costello arrested Stoutt on December 4, 1995. On February 7, 1996, the U.S. Attorney's office filed a motion to dismiss the case against plaintiff, Stoutt, because of insufficient evidence.]

At the time of the transactions and the lawsuit, the immunity provision read, in pertinent part, as follows:

> Any financial institution that makes a disclosure of any possible violation of law
> or regulation or a disclosure pursuant to this subsection or any other authority, and
> any director, officer, employee, or agent of such institution, shall not be liable to
> any person under any law or regulation of the United States or any constitution,
> law, or regulation of any State or political subdivision thereof ... for such

---

16. Check kiting is defined as "writing checks against a bank account where funds are insufficient to cover them, hoping that before they are presented the necessary funds will be deposited." BLACK'S LAW DICTIONARY 870 (6th ed.1990).

disclosure....

31 U.S.C. § 5318(g)(3).[3]

Stoutt makes two core arguments–along with several variations–to avoid the immunity statute . . . : first, that the Bank's disclosures in follow-up discussions with the FBI, *after* the filing of the CRF itself, fall outside the scope of the statute's protection; and second, that the statute, read in light of the regulations, implicitly requires that any suspicions conveyed to the authorities be held in good faith–a requirement that Stoutt says cannot be met here because the Bank knew that Stoutt was innocent of criminal conduct.

The statute offers two different categories of coverage: one is for "disclosure of any possible violation of law or regulation"; the other, for disclosure "pursuant to this subsection or any other authority." The latter clause presumably embraces reports required by 31 U.S.C. § 5318(g)(1) (which empowers the Secretary of the Treasury to compel the filing of reports) or other comparable authority. Perhaps it is arguable that disclosure under the "pursuant to" clause must be tied back to some legal mandate for disclosure and so encompasses the CRF but not the follow-up discussions.

But, as just noted, the statute also protects disclosures of "any possible violation of law or regulation," even if not tied to any legal mandate. The original CRF report was cast as the disclosure of a possible case of bank fraud, assuredly a possible violation of law. Conceivably, the answers to follow-up inquiries by the FBI directed to the details of the transaction could be distinguished from "disclosure" of a possible violation, since the details relate to an already disclosed violation. But this is not a very sensible reading given the purpose of the statute: if the original core disclosure was text, ordinary follow-up answers to investigators would be footnotes and should be similarly protected.

Conceivably, Stoutt could argue that the report was not one of a possible violation, even though so termed and colorably disclosing a possible crime, if the Bank knew that there was (in reality) no violation. But this is a non- literal reading of the statute, which speaks of "any possible violation," and we think it more straightforward to confront any requirement of good faith or due care as an implied qualification of immunity rather than an issue of initial scope. Here, whatever its internal beliefs, the Bank did by any objective test identify a "possible violation."

Stoutt makes a somewhat different "coverage" argument in claiming that the *regulations* require that the bank must actually suspect that a violation of law has occurred. The short answer is that immunity depends on the regulations only where the immunity is sought for disclosures "pursuant" to the requirements imposed under subsection 5318(g) or other authority.[4] In this case, the disclosure is independently protected by the earlier clause of the

---

3. 31 U.S.C. § 5318(g)(3) was modified in 2001 . . . and redesignated as 31 U.S.C. § 5318(g)(3)(A). In pertinent part, it now reads as follows (with added language highlighted):

> Any financial institution that makes a *voluntary* disclosure of any possible violation of law or regulation *to a government agency* or *makes* a disclosure pursuant to this subsection or any other authority, and any director, officer, employee, or agent of such institution *who makes, or requires another to make any such disclosure,* shall not be liable to any person under any law or regulation of the United States, any constitution, law, or regulation of any State or political subdivision *of any State* ... for such disclosure....

4. This strand of Stoutt's coverage argument is also unavailing for a number of other reasons, including his reliance on a post-1995 version of the regulations which add new and critical language, arguably narrowing earlier reporting requirements. . . .

then-existing statute covering disclosure of any "possible violation of law or regulation."

In his second core argument, Stoutt urges that at the very least the protection should be conditioned upon a finding of good faith on the part of the reporting entity. This is a colorable argument, accepted by the Eleventh Circuit but rejected by the Second. *Compare Lopez v. First Union Nat'l Bank of Fla.,* 129 F.3d 1186, 1192-93 (11th Cir.1997), *with Lee v. Bankers Trust Co.,* 166 F.3d 540, 544-45 (2d Cir.1999). We side with the Second Circuit, a position supported by an amicus brief of the Board of Governors of the Federal Reserve System. The statutory issue is one of continuing importance and should be cleanly resolved for this circuit.

Although the statute does not in literal terms include a good faith requirement, the omission of such language is not conclusive. . . . Courts have often added to statutes unexpressed conditions or qualifications consonant with statutory purpose or other public concerns; the most familiar example is the host of case-law doctrines tolling limitations statutes for equitable and related reasons. . . .

Still, this merely poses the question whether such a qualification should be "read into" the statute. As with any question of statutory construction, there is a trinity of dominant considerations–language, legislative history, and policy. . . . Here, two of the three (language and history) favor the conclusion that no good faith qualification should be read into the statute, while the balance of policy concerns is equivocal.

Language, the starting (and sometimes the stopping) point in statutory construction, has already been mentioned. The absence of an express qualification is not decisive but counts for something. This is especially so here where a good faith requirement is so obvious a possibility for inclusion by Congress–given the common law tradition discussed below–and where it would have taken only a simple drafting adjustment. . . .

Turning to legislative history, it is certainly easy enough to imagine a purpose for this statute that would yet be consistent with requiring good faith. At common law one who reports suspected criminal conduct already has a privilege, but a privilege often taken to require both a reasonable basis for the report and good faith. . . . Absent other evidence Congress could have meant only to remove the objective reasonableness requirement and to leave an (implicit) requirement of subjective good faith, even if unreasonably based.

But against this is the statement of the author of the provision (there is no pertinent committee report language) that it was intended to provide "the broadest possible exemption from civil liability for the reporting of suspicious transactions." 139 Cong. Rec. E57-02 (1993). This language may also give greater weight than usual to the removal before final enactment of a good faith requirement that was at one time in the proposed immunity provision. *Compare* 137 Cong. Rec. S16640, S16642, S16647 (1991) (amendment of Senator D'Amato), *with* 137 Cong. Rec. S17910, S17969 (1991) (bill as passed by the Senate), *and* 31 U.S.C. § 5318(g)(3).

Turning finally to Congress's policy, the obvious arguments in this case for a good faith limitation are two: that a good faith requirement would not wholly (or perhaps even greatly) discourage the reports intended by Congress, . . . and that, without it, individuals like Stoutt could be left without any civil redress against malicious or wholly unfounded accusations. The former argument has some force at least as to "voluntary" reports. The latter argument for a good faith qualification has obvious weight.

On the other hand, any qualification on immunity poses practical problems. A requirement of objective reasonableness–which is typically required for qualified immunity in federal civil rights cases . . .–obviously creates a risk of second guessing; but, so too, does a requirement of subjective good faith. Indeed, the latter might seem to give the reporting entity a further margin of protection by shielding honest if careless error but, cutting the other way, subjective good faith requirements work against summary judgment, exposing reporters to an increased risk of trial. . . .

As to the risk of false charges, ordinarily the disclosures will as a practical matter be made to the authorities, who provide their own filter as to what investigations are pursued and made public. A subsequent "technical and clarifying" amendment in 2001 said that protected disclosures are those made to "a government agency." H.R. Rep. 107-250, pt. 1, at 66 (2001). This leaves open the separate question (not here presented) of internal intra-corporate disclosures antecedent reporting to the government.

Finally, remedies other than private damage actions are available for wilfully false reports: private sanctions such as employment termination, and government penalties such as fines and imprisonment, *e.g.,* 18 U.S.C. § 1001 (2000) (false statements an offense); *id.* § 1517 (2000) (obstruction of examination of banks an offense). The 1995 statute says that the disclosing entity shall not be liable "to any person"–an obvious reference to private civil remedies and not to government sanctions for bad faith reporting. *See* 139 Cong. Rec. E57-02 (immunity from "civil liability"). The 2001 amendment confirmed that anyone immunized under the safe harbor provision is still subject to enforcement actions by governments. USA-PATRIOT Act, Pub.L. 107- 56, § 351(a) (adding 31 U.S.C. § 5318(g)(3)(B)); *see also* H.R. Rep. 107- 250, pt. 1, at 66.

Our construction of the statute makes it unnecessary to consider Stoutt's claims that the disclosures were unfounded, incomplete, careless and even "malicious." Nevertheless, despite extensive discovery allowed to Stoutt, we see little basis in fact for any of these labels so far as the Bank is concerned. About as close as Stoutt gets to providing any factual support for his claim is his repeated assertion that he disclosed to Guzmán the nature of his transaction with Euro-Atlantic Securities and was encouraged to draw on uncollected funds.

We will assume *arguendo* that all of this was so (although Guzmán denies being told of the insufficient funds in Stoutt's Citibank account) and will also assume (debatably) that anything said to Guzmán should be attributed to the Bank. Nevertheless, drawing a check on an account where one knows one has no funds *could* be a criminal violation, regardless of what disclosures were made to individual bank officials, and the statute requires only a report of a "possible" violation. Since objectively there was a possible violation, it is hard to think that the Bank could be found to have acted in bad faith. Stoutt has admitted that he knew there were insufficient funds and that he knew what he was doing was wrong. . . .

# 2. Nature and Effects of Foreign Bank Secrecy Laws

**Notes and Comments 10.15.** In investigating the suspected Hunn family money-laundering scheme, U.S. Treasury officials have discovered a transfer made from QNB to Banque Fromage in Geneva, Switzerland. Will the officials be able to obtain information from Banque Fromage about what was done with the transferred funds once they reached Switzerland? Consider the following material.

## Swiss Banking Law of 1934
### Article 47

Any person who willfully . . . (b) in his capacity as organ, officer or employee of a bank, as auditor or assistant auditor, as member of the Banking Commission, officer or employee of its secretarial office, violates his duty to observe silence or the professional secrecy, or whoever induces or attempts to induce a person to commit such an offense, shall be fined not more than twenty thousand francs, and/or shall be imprisoned for not longer than six months.

If the offender acted negligently, the penalty is a fine of not more than ten thousand francs.

## Swiss Penal Code
### Article 273

Whoever makes accessible a manufacturing or business secret to a foreign official, agency, or to a foreign organization or private enterprise or to any agents of the same, shall be punished by imprisonment and in serious cases by penitentiary. In addition to that penalty, a fine may be imposed.

## Honegger, Demystification of the Swiss Banking Secrecy and Illumination of the United States-Swiss Memorandum of Understanding,
### 9 N.C.J. Int'l L. & Com. Reg. 1 (1983)

"Banking secrecy" means that the banks must keep secret any information about their clients regarding privacy and property, which they receive by practicing their business. This discretion applies to the banks' officers, employees and any other persons with a direct relation to the bank. The banker's discretion is based on three different legal concepts under Swiss law: (1) personality rights; (2) contractual duties; and (3) banking law that criminalizes secrecy violations.

Articles 27 and 28 of the Swiss Civil Code provide protection of personality rights. Article 28 permits a person who is illegally injured to sue for relief. Natural and legal persons (i.e., corporate bodies) are protected. The Swiss Federal Supreme Court has decided consistently that the invulnerability of privacy is both a moral principle and an attribute of personality protected by the law. Property is part of this privacy. The duty of discretion applies to all persons who are given insight into the privacy of others by their profession (i.e., clergymen, lawyers, notaries, physicians and bankers).

Even without express agreement, discretion is an implied contractual duty of the banker. This duty is a result of either the general law of contract or the law of agency. ... If the contract between the bank and the customer has no elements of agency, the banker's duty of discretion is a consequence of the good faith principle and of usage. Even absent a contract between bank and client, the beginning of negotiations between the parties creates factual relations that have legal consequences; the banker has a general duty of discretion based on the mentioned good faith principle of the Swiss Civil Code.

Article 47 of the Banking Law criminalizes secrecy violations. The Banking Law, however, does not specify what constitutes a violation of the banker's discretion. The notion of banking secrecy is defined solely by private law through the implications of the personality rights and by contractual duties. . . .

Under Swiss law, personality rights are a fundamental principle of law. They are, therefore, protected by both private law actions and by criminal sanctions. Clergymen, lawyers, notaries, auditors and physicians who divulge a client's secrets face imprisonment for between three days and three years and/or a fine of up to 40,000.00 Swiss Francs. Secrecy violations by bankers are criminalized by Article 47 of the Banking Law, which does not provide undue sanctions. Intentional disclosure of the banking secrecy is punishable by imprisonment between three days and six month and/or a fine not exceeding 50,000.00 Swiss Francs. Negligent failure of confidentiality is sanctioned by a fine of up to 30,000.00 Swiss Francs. . . .

The mystification of Swiss banking practices continues due to the erroneous assumption that numbered or coded accounts receive special treatment under Swiss law. Numbered accounts are subject to the same legal provisions as all other kinds of accounts. The contents and limits of the banking secrecy are exactly the same, whether the account bears the client's name or is numbered.

The goal of coded accounts is to entrust as few bank employees as possible with the holder's name by replacing a name with a number in all correspondence between the bank and its customer. Coded accounts are granted only if the depositor shows legitimate reasons for such protection. . . . Thus the percentage of coded accounts is small. They are set up in the same manner as other bank accounts but the bank takes precautions that the identity of the client remains unknown to its employees. Generally, at a minimum, the management or the regarding department of the bank knows the account holder's name. Purely anonymous accounts do not exist in Switzerland. Numbered accounts are nothing but an internal technical device to help banks avoid secrecy violations by their employees....

The Swiss banking secrecy is not without limitations; both the will of the client and legal limitations determine its scope. . . . [T]he client can ask the bank for any information he may wish regarding his account, and he can authorize the bank to furnish such information to third parties, especially to governmental authorities. As long as the customer does not act, however, his wish for confidentiality must be presumed.

Banking Law, which generally prohibits disclosure of the secrecy, provides that the Federal and Cantonal regulations concerning the obligation to testify and to furnish information to a government authority shall remain reserved. Such government authorities can only be domestic, not foreign. The most important areas in which the banking secrecy may be divulged to Swiss authorities are: (1) criminal proceedings, (2) civil proceedings, (3) execution of debts and bankruptcy proceedings and (4) tax proceedings.

Switzerland is a confederation of twenty-six states, called "Cantons." Criminal procedure is a field of chiefly Cantonal legislation. The Federal Law of Criminal Procedure, as well as the Cantonal codes of criminal procedure, settle the duty of third persons to testify. . . . Clergymen, physicians, lawyers, and the accused are exempt. Bankers are not. Therefore, under Swiss law, the banking secrecy is entirely cancelled in the field of criminal procedure.

Like criminal procedure, civil procedure is a field of mainly Cantonal legislation. The Federal Law of Civil Procedure stipulates a public duty of testimony from which bankers are not exempt. Therefore, on the federal level, the banking secrecy is superseded. The Cantonal codes of civil procedure establish the duty of third persons to testify. . . . As to the exemption of persons with a professional duty of discretion, the Cantons are split into three groups. Seven Cantons entitle all holders of professional secrets to refuse testimony; seven Cantons empower the judge to decide whether the banking secret should be superseded in the particular case; and eleven Cantons enumerate the persons who are entitled to refuse testimony and edit documents because of their professional discretion. Since bankers are not listed by any of these eleven Cantons, they have to divulge the banking secrecy.

The area of execution of debts and bankruptcy law is unified throughout Switzer-land by the Federal Bankruptcy Law. Under this code, a debtor cannot avoid paying his debts by concealing his banking accounts. Thus, the debt collection agency has a right of in-formation as far as is necessary to pay off the creditors. In at least the later stages of the attachment proceedings, the creditor has right to information about the nature and size of the attached property. Attachment is granted, even before the commencement of a debt collection, if the debtor, as the owner of a banking account, has no fixed place of residence in Switzerland or is likely to evade his legal obligations. Finally, the banking secrecy is superseded in a bankruptcy proceeding of the bank itself. . . .

Both the Federal state and the Cantons levy taxes. While fiscal charges are imposed chiefly by Federal taxes, the levy of income and capital taxes remains mainly in the province of the Cantons. Therefore, the latter taxes can differ substantially. The taxes are collected by the Cantons in accordance with their own procedural law.

None of the Cantonal tax laws stipulates a general duty of third persons to furnish tax authorities with information, nor do they impose such duty especially on bankers. Thus a banker can refuse to provide information to tax authorities. This is only true for minor tax offenses, however, usually called tax evasions by the tax laws. Tax evasion is the non-reporting or the incomplete reporting of income or capital without any further manipulations.

If the taxpayer uses fraudulent practices or falsifies documents in order to mislead the Revenue authorities the situation changes. His tax offense becomes a tax fraud according to the language of the tax law. Some Cantons treat tax fraud as a matter of tax law and impose no duty of information on a third person. Others consider it a crime. The major banking centers of Switzerland (*i.e.* Zurich, Geneva, and Basel), join the latter group. Since these Cantons make tax fraud a crime, their respective codes of criminal procedure apply. As a result, the banking secrecy is annulled when tax fraud is at issue.

Under the Agreement between the Swiss Banker's Association and the Swiss National Bank on the Observance of Care by the Banks in Accepting Funds, and on the Practice of Banking Secrecy, the banks bind themselves not to open any account or deposit without prior clarification of the customer's identity, and not to support flight of capital and tax evasion. The duty to clarify thoroughly the customer's identity requires that the latter identify himself if the banker does not know him personally. The identification must also be thoroughly examined where the client is granted a numbered account. If the customer is represented by an agent, the latter must identify his principal unless the agent is a Swiss lawyer, notary, or member of a Swiss trust or auditing company. The exception had to be made because of the professional discretion of the referring agents. Even these agents, however, bound to professional discretion by criminal sanctions, must confirm to the bank that they are not aware of any circumstances where the banking secrecy will be abused.

In its second version, the agreement no longer mentions money obviously gained by criminal acts. The reason is that such behavior is interdicted rigorously by the Swiss Criminal Code. Under the agreement, a bank is not obliged to inform the authorities of a suspicious customer, but is has to abandon business relationships with the regarding client immediately. A bank's infringement of the terms of the agreement is punished by a penalty of up to ten million Swiss Francs.

This agreement appears to be applicable without any infringement of banking secrecy laws. In accordance with the legal duties of confidentiality, the agreement seems only to guarantee the ethics of the banker's profession. To the extent that the agreement does limit the scope of banking secrecy, it would be irrelevant. The banks cannot neutralize the legal rights of their customers by a contract with a third party, here the other banks and the Swiss National Bank. The agreement, therefore, has no influence on the contents and scope of the Swiss banking secrecy. . . .

Swiss bankers are permitted to divulge the secrecy to Swiss, but not to foreign authorities. Foreign authorities have to request judicial assistance by their diplomatic missions unless there is a special agreement. The request must be addressed to the Federal Department of Justice and Police. If permissible, the request is then forwarded to the competent Cantonal court which rules on the request.

Because annulment of the banking secrecy is a "compulsory measure," it can be ordered by a Cantonal court only if such measures are provided for by Swiss law or by a ratified treaty. Switzerland enacted the Federal Law on International Judicial Assistance in Criminal Matters on January 1, 1983, which provides compulsory measures. Such measures are also provided for by the American-Swiss Treaty on Mutual Assistance in Criminal Matters, the latter being enacted in Switzerland on March 20, 1967. Since the Federal Law on International Judicial Assistance in Criminal Matters applies to all states which have no special treaty with Switzerland, it is possible for all foreign authorities to ask for divulgence of the Swiss banking secrecy in the area of criminal matters.

There are, however, some important limitations. Traditionally, Switzerland has refused judicial assistance which may jeopardize its sovereignty, security, public order, or other of its essential interests. Under exceptional circumstances, the disclosure of a professional secret may represent such a essential interest. In addition, assistance is refused if foreign military, political or fiscal offenses are prosecuted. The notion of "fiscal offense" is interpreted extensively, and covers not only evasion of public levy, but also violations of foreign exchange, trade, or economic public regulations. Such laws are often politically motivated.

**Notes and Comments 10.16.** Bank secrecy laws are not only a feature of havens for money-laundering and insider trading offenses. They are also extremely attractive to depositors seeking to avoid–or evade–tax consequences in their home jurisdictions. This problem has recently been reported as afflicting certain member states within the European Union. *See* Nash, *Germans in Tax Revolt Embrace Luxembourg*, N.Y. Times, Nov. 25, 1994, at D7 (discussing ways its bank secrecy laws benefit Luxembourg, as German depositors seek to avoid German withholding tax).

**10.17.** *Effect of the 1990 Supplement to the Basle Concordat.* Recall the provisions of Part D of the 1990 Supplement to the 1983 Basle Concordat, Chapter 3, § 2, *supra*, dealing with domestic bank secrecy laws that impede transnational regulation and supervision of banking. How do these provisions affect international bank regulatory policy with respect to bank secrecy laws?

**10.18.** *Effect of the 1992 BIS Minimum Standards.* Recall the provisions of the 1992 BIS Minimum Standards for the Supervision of International Banking Groups, Chapter 3, § 2, *supra*. These standards were intended to ensure adequate supervision of transnational banking enterprises through effective coordination among national supervisors. To what extent would they affect the application of bank secrecy laws to such enterprises?

**10.19.** Do Swiss bank secrecy principles naturally lead to abuses, such as international money-laundering, or the use of a Swiss account in a transborder fraud? What can be done about this within the Swiss system? The following excerpt may suggest some approaches to these questions.

## Hirsch, "Dirty Money" and Swiss Banking Regulations
8 J. Comp. Bus. & Cap. Market L. 373 (1986)

Traditionally banks have been held to have two main duties:

> • first, to properly execute the orders of each client and, more generally, to act in the best interests of each client:
> • second, towards all clients, to manage the bank in a way that is not only profitable, but also does not create too great a risk, so that the solvency of the bank is maintained.

There are today some tendencies to impose new duties on banks, in the general interest of the community:

> • Should banks promote the general interest of the community in their lending policy, for instance, by providing funds to enterprises in difficulty?
> • Should banks agree to take, perhaps provisionally, the control of a domestic company, to avoid control being taken over by undesired foreigners?
> • Should banks avoid lending funds or providing services to foreign countries considered to have an unacceptable foreign policy or internal regime?

These "new duties" are not yet embodied in banking regulations, but perhaps already are considered in some banking policy decisions. Yet the duties may be in conflict with the second traditional duty mentioned above, of maintaining the profitability and solvency of the bank. They also raise the question whether banks, although private enterprises, should be treated as public services.

In this article, I describe the evolution of one of these new duties in Swiss banking regulation: the duty of the bank not to accept "dirty money," or cooperate, even negligently, in criminal, illegal, immoral or "irregular" acts. . . .

The bank must take all reasonable measures to properly identify its clients. This is normally an easy matter, although some difficulties may arise for some kinds of foreign clients.

More important is the duty to identify the beneficial owner of the account if it appears that the client is acting for the account of a third party or if the account is opened by a so-called "domiciliary corporation," that is, by a corporation with no business premises of its own or no staff of its own, other than an administrative staff. In that event, the bank has the duty to identify the persons controlling the domiciliary corporation. If these controlling persons are again domiciliary companies, the bank must do the same until it comes to individuals or operating companies.

This duty to identify may be very difficult to implement. Many clients will not understand readily why these questions are asked of them, especially because they normally would not be asked by banks in countries other than Switzerland. They may feel that such questions imply some mistrust of them, a mistrust which would be regarded as an unsuitable basis of relations between a bank and its clients.

If the beneficial owner does not want to give its identity to the bank, and if this owner is not yet ready to have any personal contact with the bank such that the owner would not be forthcoming about its identity, it would be very difficult for the bank to know that the identification given was not true. . . .

Some commentators argue that the duty of banks to know their customers is even broader than that described above. They assert that the banks should, before accepting a new client, take information as to the client's social and economic background, as if the client were requesting a loan.

In principle, this broadened duty seems excessive. However, if the client is not known at all by the bank, especially if it is a foreign client, some kind of background information would be easy to obtain and the recording requirement would probably be justified, if the bank needed to avoid cooperating with irregular acts.

Furthermore, since the banks are today taking important measures for determining "country lending limits," some commentators argue that the banks could just as well inquire into the countries from which the funds are coming, and put some general limits or conditions on categories of clients. Indeed, banks themselves recognize today that they would normally not accept important private deposits from foreign officials, unless they can ensure that these deposits are really the private property of the client. But, the banks must take into consideration that a contact with a new client can hardly begin with mistrust and that most banks abroad, even the ones that are best-operated, do not make such delicate inquiries. ...

It is clear that a bank is required to know the economic background of any operation for which the bank will bear a financial risk. This principle has been progressively extended in recent years by the Banking Commission. It now applies to all important, complicated, or unusual clients' operations, even if these operations do not imply a direct financial risk for the bank. Generally, the banks do not appeal the decisions of the Banking Commission; however, with respect to the economic background issue, Commission's decisions have been appealed, although the Swiss Supreme Court in turn has affirmed all decisions of the Banking Commission.

In one case, a bank had agreed to buy an important quantity of securities from a client, who was himself acting through a corporation based in Liechtenstein. The client had the right to buy back the securities at the same price. In view of the importance and the unusual character of the operation, the Banking Commission decided that the bank was not allowed to enter such a transaction unless it knew precisely its economic background.

In another case, a Panamanian corporation had received an important fee in remuneration for its activity in the conclusion of an international contract. The fee was required to be reimbursed, if the contract was not implemented. The Panamanian corporation put the corresponding amount in escrow in a Swiss bank and asked the bank to guarantee the reimbursement. The Banking Commission decided that the bank could not make such a guarantee without knowing the economic background of the fee and inquiring whether the transaction was illegal or immoral.

In yet another decision, a bank, controlled by a few foreign shareholders, had given loans to a foreign entity, internally guaranteed by the deposits of the shareholders of the bank. The same bank had given its guarantee to a foreign corporation for obtaining a loan abroad, this guarantee being again fully covered by the shareholders of the bank. In both cases, the Banking Commission decided that this was not an ordinary banking operation and that the bank should check its economic background.

In the most recent case, a client feared that its assets, especially a ship, could be seized by a foreign state. The client asked the bank to provide an important loan to be pledged by the ship, so that the possible seizure of the ship by the foreign state would not be effective. But his loan, and especially the pledge, was rather fictitious, as it was internally guaranteed by a deposit of the same amount made by the client. The Banking Commission considered this operation not to be a loan, but only a scheme for deceiving the foreign state. Here, the bank had considered the economic background of the operation. The Banking

Commission ordered that, in the event the foreign state seized the ship, the bank should, if asserting its rights in the ship, mention the existence of the deposit guaranteeing fully the reimbursement of the "loan." Of course, because of the Commission's order, the whole scheme became worthless.

The Swiss Supreme Court affirmed the decision in a far-reaching manner: "It is true that the principal aim of the banking law is to ensure that the banks remain solvent. However, the supervision of banks is also related to their credibility. The fact that a bank co-operates in an illegal or immoral business may affect not only the credibility of this particular bank, but of the Swiss banking system in general. This is why a bank has the duty to examine the economic background of an operation if there are some indications that it could be illegal or immoral; if so, the bank should refuse to co-operate. In particular, the banking law forbids a bank to co-operate in an operation intended to deceive some Swiss or foreign authorities or private persons, or to let them incur an illegitimate injury. . . ."

A similar duty may be incurred even if the bank is not actively co-operating with the client, but only implementing routine banking orders, if the situation is exceptionally important or unusual. In a recent case involving drug trading, it appeared that some of the drug sellers had utilized Swiss banks to "wash their dirty money." For instance, foreign clients, without the bank's awareness, opened an account in which important amounts were transferred, or brought by cash or check, and afterwards were quickly transferred again to another foreign country. Some banks either refused to open the account or, after a few of these transactions, decided to close the account.

Some other banks did not object, and apparently did not worry at all as to the economic background of these important and unusual transfers of money.

It is clear that such cases should definitely be brought to the attention of the general management of the bank and that such accounts should not be carried forward if the bank has no idea of the economic reasons for such unusual transfers.

Sometimes the client asks the bank to constitute and to manage some "domiciliary corporations," incorporated either in Switzerland or abroad, for its account. In such cases, the bank provides some of its staff as directors of the "domiciliary corporation"; consequently, the duties of such directors are considered also to be duties of the bank itself, which should know precisely the "economic background" of all operations.

The situation may not be very different if the bank is providing the client with formally independent professionals to organize and manage the corporations, if the client considers these professionals to be only there "pro forma," and that its only real partner is the bank. . . .

If a bank is asked to open an account for a new client or to participate in some irregular operations, the bank should refuse. The situation is much more difficult if the bank discovers only over the passage of time that it has co-operated in irregular operations, either because it has been deceived by the client or because it had not asked the client the appropriate questions in due time. The traditional solution . . . is that the bank has the duty to break off the relationship with the customer immediately. However, one may wonder whether such a break off would be sufficient for every act to which the bank could unwillingly co-operate.

In the past, Swiss banks have at times been very helpful with the police upon discovering that funds deposited with them were acquired by criminal acts, like drug or arms trading, or a ransom. Some banks have even spontaneously divulged such information to the police, so that official measures could be taken to seize the money, and arrest the perpetrators of the crime. But this has been the case only for important crimes, which were widely recognized as such.

The problem has been recently raised in a very different situation. At the end of March 1986, the new government of the Philippines alleged that the country's former president, Mr. Ferdinand Marcos, as well as other "related" persons, had deposited important funds in Swiss banks. However, at that time, the Filippino government had not officially requested any international assistance in criminal matters from the Swiss authorities. It appeared very likely that a substantial part of Mr. Marcos' wealth consisted of "fees" paid to him pursuant to contracts executed by the Filippino government. In such a situation, one must ask what was the duty of the Swiss banks if Mr. Marcos, now in exile, requested release or transfer of the funds?

In a public release of March 21, 1986, the Banking Commission expressed the view that the banks had an "increased duty of care" for accepting new funds from Mr. Marcos, and also in releasing funds to him. The existence of such an "increased duty of care" was affirmed by a circular letter of the Banking Commission, dated March 26, 1986, to all important banks of Switzerland. The banks were requested to give notice if they held accounts belonging to Mr. Marcos or "related" persons, and to divulge whether they agreed not to reimburse any such funds without the prior consent of the Commission. These measures were revoked after one month, because the government of the Philippines had by then requested international assistance and had obtained the issuance of similar provisional measures by the Department of Justice.

The legal validity of the measures of the Banking Commission has been disputed. The problem remains as to the duties of the banks, and the possible measures to be taken by the competent authorities, if it appears that, regardless of the issue of their possible negligence, banks have in fact co-operated in irregular acts or accepted "dirty money." This problem is especially difficult if the acts are not clearly criminal. The perception of irregularity or use of "dirty money" can vary greatly over time and from country to country. Clearly, the test cannot be based merely on moral precepts or on doubts about illegality in some foreign country.

**Notes and Comments 10.20.** In 1998, in an apparent attempt to improve the public image of Swiss banks, Switzerland enacted a law requiring expanded reporting of suspicious transactions to include not only banks but also asset managers, lawyers, insurers, credit card companies and foreign exchange bureaus, effective 1 April 1998. In the year following the change in the law, reports of suspected money laundering have more than quintupled. *See Switzerland Cites Sharp Rise In Reports Of Money Laundering*, N.Y. Times, July 14, 1999, at A5, col. 1. The Federal Office for Police Matters is reported to have received 210 tips involving assets worth $270 million. *Id.* One transaction report involved a $32 million bank account, but most involved smaller accounts, worth an average of $2 million. *Id.* Eighty percent of the money involved in the reports was from foreigners, according to the Swiss Money Laundering Reporting Office. *Id.* The reports have resulted in the blocking of accounts by the Swiss Government while investigation of money laundering proceeded. What do you think the long-term effects of the new law will be?

# 3. U.S. Policy toward Foreign Bank Secrecy

**Notes and Comments 10.21.** U.S. courts have been particularly aggressive in confronting foreign bank secrecy laws that might impede investigations initiated by the United States. Under what circumstances are U.S. courts likely to uphold a claim of foreign bank secrecy? Under what circumstances are they like to reject such a claim? Consider the following cases.

## Trade Development Bank v. Continental Insurance Co.
469 F.2d 35 (2d Cir. 1972)

Mansfield, Circuit Judge:

[For the factual background of this case, involving an insurance claim by the Swiss bank against its insurer under a fidelity bond for recovery of losses due to dishonesty of a bank employee, see Chapter 9, § 5, *supra*.]

In a trial before Judge Pollack the jury awarded the Bank damages in the sum of $2,045,932, to which prejudgment interest in the sum of $171,205 was added. The Insurer appeals from the judgment in the total amount of $2,217,137. . . . We affirm. . . .

When the market value of some of the securities dropped sharply Salerian, afraid that the decline would continue, sold many of the securities at heavy losses. In order to conceal his fraud and the resulting losses, he made hundreds of false and irregular entries in various customers' accounts. In many instances he entered unauthorized transactions in customers' accounts long after they had taken place, even though authorized purchases and sales would have been recorded within a few days. The devices used by Salerian to mask his fraudulent activities and resulting losses were many and varied. They included the recording of fictitious transactions on the Bank's records, the recording of real transactions at fictitious prices, the allocation of transactions to various customers' accounts long after the event at prices different from the actual transaction prices, the transmittal to customers of false valuation of their securities portfolios, and the making of fictitious entries in the Bank's internal records of its accounts with other banks.

In the fall of 1969 Giorgio Camponovo, the Assistant Manager of the Bank's Chiasso branch, who was Salerian's immediate supervisor, discovered in the Bank's internal records some of Salerian's fictitious entries. . . . When he called the discrepancies to Salerian's attention, the latter confided that he had lost some $200,000 as a result of his transactions but assured Camponovo that the loss would be absorbed over the next few months by customers who had benefited in the past from similar operations. Instead of reporting Salerian's dishonesty to Albert Benezra, then the Manager of the Chiasso branch, Camponovo remained silent.

Salerian's fraud, and Camponovo's complicity in it, were finally discovered by the Bank's management in April 1970. . . . Upon checking Chiasso customers' files the new Manager of the Chiasso branch, Albert Benezra, discovered suspicious entries. He then confronted Salerian and Camponovo, both of whom confessed in a series of statements given between April 20 and 24, 1970. Although Salerian first stated that the current loss was only $30,000, he gradually furnished more information with respect to his fraudulent activities, which indicated the total loss to be many times that amount. . . .

The Insurer was promptly notified. It conducted its own investigation. Two outside auditing firms (Peat Marwick & Fides S.A. and Societe Fiduciaire Romande Ofor S.A.) were retained by the Bank to review and straighten out the records. Their reports, which were completed in August 1970, confirmed generally that Salerian had made fraudulent securities transactions and false entries concealing them. Copies of the reports were promptly furnished to the Insurer, and the Bank also notified customers whose accounts had been falsified. These customers then filed claims against the Bank for losses suffered by reason of Salerian's fraudulent activities. The claims were subsequently settled by the Bank's payment of $819,520 after the Insurer declined an offer to assist in handling threatened litigation and to participate in the settlement negotiations. This lawsuit followed.

At trial the Insurer did not seriously dispute Salerian's dishonesty. Its principal defense was that the Manager of the Chiasso branch, Albert Benezra, had learned or should have learned of Salerian's conduct many months prior to April 1970 but had failed to avert the loss or to give timely notice to the insurer as required by the fidelity bond. However, Benezra testified at trial that he had no knowledge of Salerian's fraud until April 20, 1970. The issue was submitted to the jury, which resolved it against the Insurer. . . . The Insurer further contended that it was not responsible for losses arising out of securities transactions allocated by Salerian to certain customers' accounts because the transactions had been authorized or tacitly consented to by those customers, either personally or through their representative, one Angelo Luzzani. This defense was also argued to the jury, which resolved it against the Insurer by including in its verdict an award for these losses. . . .

The Insurer contends on appeal that the trial judge committed several errors requiring reversal. The first of these is the district court's refusal to order the Bank to disclose the identity of customers whose accounts were misused by Salerian to conceal his fraudulent transactions by use of false entries. In the course of pretrial disclosure and depositions the Bank furnished to the Insurer thousands of records in its possession or control which were requested by the Insurer's counsel as possibly relevant to the issues, including transcripts of customers' accounts, auditors' work sheets, brokers' slips and Bank records underlying the alleged fraudulent transactions. It refused to furnish the identity of customers, however, on the ground that to do so would violate the Swiss bank secrecy law, § 47(b) of the Swiss Federal Bank Act, a criminal statute which provides that a violation shall be punishable by a fine of up to 50,000 francs or by imprisonment up to six months, or by both. In pretrial proceedings Judge Pollack upheld the Bank's position on the ground that there was "neither compelling necessity for this information nor potential prejudice to defendant from nondisclosure at this stage of the proceedings," since the transcripts of the customers' accounts and the other records giving details as to the transactions about which the Insurer had inquired were adequate to enable it to prepare for trial.

At trial the parties took issue as to whether the Swiss bank secrecy law did bar disclosure of the customer's identities in a trial in a federal court in New York, with both sides offering testimony of Swiss law experts on the subject. Judge Pollack concluded that the Swiss law did prohibit such disclosure and decided that as a matter of comity he would therefore not require the Bank to identify the customers whose accounts were involved, particularly since in his view the identity was not essential to the issue on trial, which was whether securities transactions had been entered by Salerian in certain customers' accounts in furtherance of his fraudulent scheme. . . .

On the basis of our review *de novo* of the expert testimony and authorities offered by the parties, we are satisfied that the criminal sanctions of Article 47(b) of the Swiss Federal Bank Act apply to the disclosures sought in this proceeding. On its face the statute is Delphian in its generality. It simply provides that any bank officer or employee who violates the "duty of secrecy" or reveals a professional secret entrusted to him is punishable. However, the preponderance of opinion, given in testimony by well qualified Swiss law experts, was unequivocally to the effect that disclosure by the Bank, even at the direction of the United States District Court, would constitute a violation of the law. The principal bank secrecy issue at trial was whether Article 204 of the Code of Civil Procedure in the Swiss

Canton of Ticino (where the Bank's Chiasso branch is located) superseded Article 47(b) of the Swiss Federal Bank Act. Article 204, as part of the procedural code of Ticino, enumerates the persons entitled to refuse testimony on the ground of professional secrecy (*e.g.*, priests, lawyers, doctors) but does not include bankers. Although there is strong support for the view that such a procedural rule of a Swiss canton overrules the Swiss Federal Bank Act in a proceeding in the Canton itself, Mueller, *The Swiss Banking Secret From a Legal View*, 18 Int. & Comp.L.Q. 360, 366-67 (1969); Meyer, *The Banking Secret and Economic Espionage in Switzerland*, 23 Geo. Wash.L.Rev. 284, 292 (1955), all experts at trial agreed that it would not apply to a proceeding in a United States court.

There remains the question of whether the district court erred in not ordering the Bank, assuming its disclosure of customers' names would violate § 47(b) of the Swiss Federal Bank Act, to make a good faith effort to obtain a waiver of that restriction from the customers involved. Unquestionably the court had the power to do so, *see, e.g., Societe Internationale, etc. v. Rogers*, 357 U.S. 197 (1958), and that power might appropriately have been exercised in a case such as this, where a foreign domiciliary seeking to avail itself of the processes of our courts to enforce its claim invokes the law of its country as the basis for non-disclosure. However, although the idea of seeking waivers was mentioned in the course of pretrial depositions . . . , the Insurer never asked the court for an order directing the Bank to seek waivers from clients whose accounts had allegedly been misused. Under the circumstances the district court was entitled in its discretion, after balancing the interests involved, to defer to Swiss law, *Societe Internationale, etc. v. Rogers supra*, at 213; *United States v. First National City Bank*, 396 F.2d 897, 901 (2d Cir. 1968); RESTATEMENT (SECOND) OF THE FOREIGN RELATIONS LAW OF THE UNITED STATES § 40 (1965), and to define the scope of pretrial disclosure. . . . In addition to the factors that ordinarily must be considered by the court in deciding whether to order a disclosure prohibited by the law of another state (*e.g.*, the effect on the national interests of the states affected, the nationality of the party against whom disclosure is sought, and the extent to which the court's order can expect to be enforced), the relative unimportance of the information as to the clients' identity in the present proceeding was entitled to be considered.

Upon the record before us we fail to find any abuse of discretion on the part of Judge Pollack . . . in not ordering the Bank to seek waivers. Salerian's falsification of the Bank's records is not disputed. All records falsified by him were made available, except for the names of customers, to the Insurer. It is unlikely that the customers would have furnished evidence helpful to the Insurer. Indeed, they were claiming through their representative Dr. Angelo Luzzani to have been victimized by Salerian's fraud. Although the Insurer contended that Dr. Luzzani, whose identity was known to it, had acted as the authorized agent for approximately 18 of the customers in giving instructions to Salerian with respect to purchase and sale of securities for their accounts, it failed to depose him or to offer him as a witness at trial. In short, no sound basis is offered for disturbing the trial judge's exercise of discretion, which appears to have been based on a careful analysis and balancing of all relevant interests. . . .

## In re Grand Jury Proceedings
532 F.2d 404 (5th Cir. 1976), *cert. denied sub nom.*
*Field v. United States*, 429 U.S. 940

Lewis R. Morgan, Circuit Judge:
This appeal presents the situation where an alien who was subpoenaed while

present in the United States is required to testify before a grand jury even though the very act of testifying will probably subject him to criminal prosecution in his country of residence. . . . Anthony R. Field contends that the requirement that he testify is a violation of his Fifth Amendment rights. Field, moreover, contends that he should not be required to testify as a matter of comity between nations. Finally, he attacks the power of the government to issue the subpoena and the procedures used in issuing this particular subpoena. We find that requiring Field to testify violates neither the Constitution nor international comity and that the subpoena was properly issued. Therefore, we affirm the district court.

Presently, a grand jury in the Southern District of Florida is investigating possible criminal violations of tax laws. Part of this investigation centers on the use of foreign banks to evade tax enforcement. Field, a Canadian citizen, is the managing director of Castle Bank and Trust Company (Cayman), Ltd. which is located in Georgetown, Grand Cayman Island, British West Indies. On January 12, 1976, Field, while in the lobby of the Miami International Airport, was served with a subpoena directing him to appear before the grand jury on January 20. During his testimony, Field was asked several questions concerning his activities on behalf of Castle and its clients. Field, however, refused to answer these questions on the ground that he would incriminate himself in violation of his Fifth Amendment rights and also on the ground that his testimony would violate the bank secrecy laws of the Cayman Islands. On February 18, 1976, Field was granted immunity and ordered to resume his testimony. Field still refused to answer the questions.

A hearing was held on Field's motion to quash and the government's motion to compel testimony on March 18, 1976. At that hearing, the government demonstrated that Castle Bank had engaged in activities within the United States including maintaining deposits in American banks and engaging in certain securities transactions. The government also demonstrated that another bank, Castle Bank and Trust Company (Bahamas), had extensive dealings in the United States in real estate. Pointing out that Castle (Cayman) and Castle (Bahamas) had several of the same officers and that apparently the two organizations had commingled funds, the government argued that much of the activity of Castle (Bahamas) should be imputed to Castle (Cayman). The government did not demonstrate that Field held any office in or was an employee of Castle (Bahamas). Nor did the government present any evidence concerning tax evasion or explain in detail what evidence it planned to present before the grand jury.

Besides characterizing Castle (Cayman) activities in the United States as minor, Field did not seriously challenge the government's evidence. On the other hand, Field argues that requiring his testimony before the grand jury concerning matters pertaining to Castle (Cayman) would violate the law of the Cayman Islands. He submitted an affidavit by an expert on Cayman law that stated that Field could be subject to criminal punishment for answering the questions before the grand jury. The affidavit, moreover, stated that the bank examiner of the Cayman Islands could require Field to state whether he had testified before the grand jury. If Field refused to answer the questions of the bank examiner, he was subject to a criminal penalty of up to six months imprisonment. The government did not contest that Field in testifying before the grand jury would subject himself to criminal prosecution in the Cayman Islands, his place of employment and residence. After ordering Field to testify the district court stated,

> I think the record should show that this court finds that there is, in fact,
> a reasonable probability that Mr. Field is going to be exposed to some criminal
> charges and some criminal punishment for violating the Cayman Bank Secrecy

Act.

Upon stipulation that Field would continue to refuse to answer the questions before the grand jury, the district court held him to civil contempt and Field appeals. . . .

Before discussing in detail Field's contentions, we should make clear what is not involved in this case. Field does not argue that the content of his answers before the grand jury will subject him to prosecution in the Cayman Islands. The problem is not the answers that Field will give to the grand jury but the fact that he will give any answers at all. A different case would be presented if Field had demonstrated that the content of his answers could be used as evidence against him in foreign prosecutions. . . . In such a case, a difficult question concerning Fifth Amendment protection against self-incrimination would be present. . . .

Field does argue that the Fifth Amendment prohibition against compulsory self-incrimination encompasses his present situation. In essence, he contends that since the act of testifying subjects him to foreign prosecution, requiring his testimony would be compelling Field to be a witness against himself.

We believe Field has misconstrued the scope of the protection against self-incrimination. The Fifth Amendment . . . protects against only the use of testimony. . . .

. . . The consistent interpretation of the Amendment has been to insure that a person would not be required to give testimony that tended to show that the person had committed a crime. . . . Historically, the privilege was adopted to restrain the state from submitting to the temptation of resorting to the expedient of compelling incriminating evidence from one's own mouth. . . . This subpoena is not an attempt to elicit information from Field which will later be used against him in a criminal case. The Fifth Amendment simply is not pertinent to the situation where a foreign state makes the act of testifying a criminal offense.

Field's second contention is that as a matter of international comity this court should refuse to enforce the subpoena. In this contention, Field requests that an appropriate accommodation between the law of the United States and that of the Cayman Islands is for this court, exercising its discretion, to decline enforcement. Field argues that nations should make every effort to avoid the situation present here, where one nation requires an act that the other nation makes illegal. . . . RESTATEMENT (2ND), FOREIGN RELATIONS LAW OF THE UNITED STATES, § 40 (1965).

We begin with the proposition that the fact that the district court's order will subject Field to criminal prosecution in his country of residence does not of itself prohibit enforcement of the subpoena. RESTATEMENT (2ND), FOREIGN RELATIONS LAW OF THE UNITED STATES, § 39 (1965). . . . The Restatement position requires a balancing of the several factors in determining whether the United States or, in this case, the Cayman Islands' legal command will prevail.

The first and most important factor to be considered is the relative interest of the states involved. In this case, the United States seeks to obtain information concerning the violation of its tax laws. In contradistinction, the Cayman Islands seeks to protect the right of privacy that is incorporated into its bank secrecy laws. Unfortunately, the Cayman Government position appears to be that any testimony concerning the bank will violate its laws. Therefore, either the United States or the Cayman interest must give way.

Under our system of jurisprudence the grand jury's function in investigating possible criminal violations is vital. . . .

To the degree that the ability to obtain evidence is crucial to all criminal justice proceedings, the need for broad authority in the grand jury is greatest. . . . Courts have repeatedly allowed the grand jury wide discretion in seeking evidence. . . . Generally, the normal rule providing for the exclusion of evidence obtained by illegal means does not apply to the grand jury. . . . To defer to the law of the Cayman Islands and refuse to require Mr. Field to testify would significantly restrict the essential means that the grand jury has of evaluating whether to bring an indictment.

In addition to the necessity of the grand jury being able to obtain evidence, this country allows wide discretion to investigatory bodies in obtaining information concerning bank activities. *United States v. Miller*, 425 U.S. 435 (1976). There could be no question that Mr. Field would be required to respond to the grand jury's questions if this was solely a domestic case. Nor is the United States alone in granting wide discretion to its investigators in obtaining information from financial institutions, particularly where tax evasion is concerned. In the Untied Kingdom apparently such evidence can be obtained. *See Clinch v. England Revenue Commissioners*, [1973] 1 All.E.R. 976; *Williams v. Summerfield*, [1972] 2 Q.B. 512; [1972] 3 W.L.R. 131; [1972] 2 All.E.R. 1334. Indeed, even the Swiss government, which is notorious for protecting the privacy of financial transactions, might provide under certain circumstances to the United States information concerning Swiss banks. . . . Finally, at oral argument, appellant's attorney conceded that under Cayman law the director of banking in the Cayman Islands would be able to obtain information from Field concerning the bank's operations in investigations instituted by legal authority in the Cayman Islands. In short, Field seeks to prohibit a United States grand jury from obtaining information that would have been obtainable by officials there for their own investigations. Since the general rule appears to be that for domestic investigations such information would be obtainable, we find it difficult to understand how the bank's customers' rights or privacy would be significantly infringed simply because the investigating body is a foreign tribunal.

Finally, we reject Field's contention that what is involved here is only economic regulation. The collection of revenue is crucial to the financial integrity of the republic. In addition, the subject being investigated by this grand jury has received considerable attention and has been demonstrated to be a severe law enforcement problem. A report from the House Committee on Banking and Currency outlines the problems created and the type of activities investigated by the grand jury.

> Secret foreign bank accounts and secret foreign financial institutions have permitted a proliferation of `white collar' crimes; have served as the financial underpinning of organized criminal operation in the United States; have been utilized by Americans to evade income taxes, conceal assets illegally and purchase; have allowed Americans and others to avoid the law and regulations governing securities and exchanges; have served as essential ingredients in frauds including schemes to defraud the United States; have served as the ultimate depository of black market proceeds from Vietnam; have served as a source of questionable financing for conglomerate and other corporate stock acquisitions, mergers and takeovers; have covered conspiracy to steal from the U.S. defense and foreign aid funds; and have served as the cleansing agent for `hot' or illegally obtained monies . . .
>
> The debilitating effects of the use of these secret institutions on Americans and the American economy are vast. It has been estimated that hundreds of millions in tax revenues have been lost. H.R. Rep. No. 91-975, 91 Cong. 2d Sess. 12 (1970), U.S.Code Cong. & Admin. News 1970, p. 4397.

If this court were to countenance Mr. Field's refusal to testify it would significantly restrict the ability of the grand jury to obtain information which might possibly uncover criminal activities of the most serious nature. In light of the traditional discretion given the grand jury and the significant interest this nation has in tax enforcement, without any specific direction from Congress, we see no reason not to enforce the subpoena . . . .

We regret that our decision requires Mr. Field to violate the legal commands of the Cayman Islands, his country of residence. In a world where commercial transactions are international in scope, conflicts are inevitable. Courts and legislatures should take every reasonable precaution to avoid placing individuals in the situation Mr. Field finds himself. Yet, this court simply cannot acquiesce in the proposition that United States criminal investigations must be thwarted whenever there is conflict with the interest of other states.

## S.E.C. v. Banca Della Svizzera Italiana
### 92 F.R.D. 111 (S.D.N.Y. 1981)

Milton Pollack, District Judge.

Plaintiff, Securities Exchange Commission ("SEC"), moves this Court for an appropriate order . . . for the failure and refusal of defendant, Banca Della Svizzera Italiana ("BSI") to provide the SEC with information relative to the identities of the principals for whom it purchased stock and stock options on American exchanges in St. Joe Minerals Corporation ("St. Joe"), a New York corporation which produces natural resources.

The underlying law suit is an action by the SEC against the said defendant and unnamed others for an injunction and an accounting for violations of the insider trading provisions of the Securities Exchange Act of 1934, Sections 10(b) and 14(e), 15 U.S.C. §§ 78j(b) and 78n(e) and Rules 10b-5 and 14e-3 promulgated thereunder. . . .

The issue posed to the Court is whether to compel a foreign party which transaction to make discovery and answer interrogatories concerning its undisclosed principals where the acts of disclosure might subject that party to criminal liability in its home country. The Court has carefully balanced the interests at stake and considered the resisting party's professed good faith. It concludes that compelling the complete discovery demanded is not only justified in the instant case but required to preserve our vital national interest in maintaining the integrity of the securities markets against violations committed and/or aided and assisted by parties located abroad. Accordingly, an order should issue requiring full responses to the SEC's interrogatories. . . .

This action alleges insider trading on the part of BSI and its principals in the purchase and sale of call options for the common stock as well as the common stock itself of St. Joe. The options were traded through the Philadelphia Stock Exchange and the stock was traded on the New York Stock Exchange both of which are registered national exchanges. The purchases in question were made immediately prior to the announcement on March 11, 1981 of a cash tender offer by a subsidiary of Joseph E. Seagram & Sons, Inc. ("Seagram"), an Indiana corporation for all of the common stock of St. Joe at $45 per share. Prior to the announcement of the tender offer St. Joe stock traded on the market at $30 per share, (approximately).

The orders for the call options and the stock were placed close to the opening of trading on the exchanges on March 10, 1981, one day prior to Seagram's offer and announcement, at prices above the last quoted market price for the options and the stock. The options were due to expire in ten days, thereby significantly indicating an expectation that the price of St. Joe common stock would rise substantially and imminently.

BSI succeeded in purchasing approximately 1055 call options which carried the right to purchase 105,500 shares of St. Joe common stock and in purchasing 3,000 shares of the St. Joe common stock. On the next day the stock opened sharply higher in price and the bank shortly instructed its brokers to close out the purchases of the options and sell 2,000 of the 3,000 shares of common stock acquired. These transactions resulted in a virtually overnight profit just short of $2 million.

Promptly on noticing the undue activity in the options market, the SEC investigated and based on its findings brought this suit. The SEC contends that there is a strong probability that the purchasers were unlawfully using material non-public information which could only have been obtained or misappropriated from sources charged with a confidential duty not to disclose information prior to the public announcement of the tender offer.

The SEC applied for and obtained a Temporary Restraining Order against the Irving Trust Company which held the proceeds of the sales of the options and of the common stock in BSI's bank account with Irking Trust. The Temporary Restraining Order also directed immediate discovery proceedings including the requirement that "insofar as permitted by law" BSI should disclose within three business days the identity of its principals. The effect of the Temporary Restraining Order was to immobilize the profits derived from the questioned transactions.

The SEC endeavored by one or another procedural means, here and abroad, to obtain the identity of those who, along with the bank, were involved in the particular options purchases. No disclosure was forthcoming. . . . BSI declined to furnish the requested information voluntarily, adhering to its assertion of banking secrecy law. Eight months elapsed in the efforts to obtain the requisite disclosure by cooperative measures. ...

The matter came before the Court for crystallization on November 6, 1981 and after hearing counsel, the Court announced an informal opinion that it had determined to enter an order requiring disclosure, to be followed by severe contempt sanctions if it was not complied with. One week was fixed for submission of the order by the SEC. Apparently, the decision of the Court had a catalytic effect. A waiver of Swiss confidentiality was secured by the bank and reported to the Court. Also reported was that the bank had furnished some but not all the answers to the demanded interrogatories. A further period was requested to endeavor to complete the requisite responses with leave to show that any omissions were either not within the bank's ability to respond or were due to inappropriate demands. This moved finality forward to November 20, 1981.

Since the Court is unable to predict whether ultimate compliance will be secured or whether other notions of confidentiality may be developed on behalf of the disclosed Panamanian customers of the bank, applicable to Switzerland or elsewhere, it becomes useful to analyze the legal situation posited. The principles to be applied will be similar and will serve the further purposes of this case. . . .

Any discussion of the issue posed here must begin with the Supreme Court's opinion in *Societe Internationale Pour Participations Industrielles et Commerciales, S.A. v. Rogers*, 357 U.S. 197 (1958), which is the Court's latest decision on the subject. *Societe* holds that the good faith of the party resisting discovery is a key factor in the decision whether to impose sanctions when foreign law prohibits the requested disclosure.

In *Societe* a Swiss holding company was suing for the return of property seized by the Alien Property Custodian during World War II. The district court dismissed plaintiff's complaint as a sanction for its refusal to comply with the Court's order to produce bank records, despite a finding that the Swiss government had constructively seized the documents and that plaintiff had shown good faith efforts to comply with the production order. *Id.* at 201-02. The Court of Appeals affirmed.

The Supreme Court reversed. It held that where plaintiff was prohibited by Swiss law from complying with the discovery order and there was no showing of bad faith, the sanction of dismissal without prejudice was not justified. The Court indicated that a party who had made deliberate use of foreign law to evade American law might be subject to sanctions.

> . . . [T]he Government suggests that petitioner stands in the position of one who deliberately courted legal impediments to production of the . . . records, and who thus cannot now be heard to assert its good faith after this expectation was realized. Certainly these contentions, if supported by the facts, would have a vital bearing on justification for dismissal of the action, but they are not open to the Government here. The findings below reach no such conclusions. . . .

*Id.* at 208-09. . . .

Despite the teachings of *Societe*, three early Second Circuit cases appeared to view foreign law prohibitions as an absolute bar to ordering inspection or production of documents. *Application of Chase Manhattan Bank*, 297 F.2d 611 (2d Cir. 1962) (upholding district court's modification of subpoena duces tecum on a showing that compliance would violate Panamanian law); *Ings. v. Ferguson*, 282 F.2d 149 (2d Cir. 1960) (holding that where a party served with a subpoena duces tecum was only a witness and where evidence could have been secured by letters rogatory, the subpoena had to be modified so as not to require production of documents protected by Canadian law); *First National Bank of New York v. Internal Revenue Service*, 271 F.2d 616 (2d Cir. 1959), *cert. denied*, 361 U.S. 948 (1960) (if Panamanian law would be violated by production of records, production would not be ordered; however, such violation was not established).

All three of the above cases dealt with a nonparty witness and that factor may have been the one distinguishing these cases from Societe. . . .

In any event the Second Circuit has clearly moved to a more flexible position. In two later cases, both affirming decisions of this Court, the Court of Appeals adopted a balancing test approach in which a foreign law's prohibition is but one of the many factors to consider.

In the first of these, *United States v. First National City Bank*, 396 F.2d 897 (2d Cir. 1968), the Court of Appeals upheld this Court's decision in *In re First National City Bank*, 285 F.Supp. 845 (S.D.N.Y. 1968), holding Citibank in contempt for its failure to comply with a subpoena duces tecum in an on-going grand jury inquiry into antitrust violations that presumably had occurred in this country. The sanctions imposed by this Court were a fine of $2,000 a day until Citibank complied and a sentence of up until 60 days imprisonment on its vice-president. Citibank had resisted production of the documents claiming that compliance was forbidden by German law. This Court found that German public law did not prohibit disclosure and that moreover Citibank had not shown good faith in its attempts to comply. 285 F.Supp. at 847-48.

The Court of Appeals accepted these findings. In affirming, it emphasized that the risk or absence of foreign criminal liability did not resolve the issue. It noted first that "[a] state having jurisdiction to prescribe or enforce a rule of law is not precluded from exercising its jurisdiction solely because such exercise requires a person to engage in conduct subjecting him to liability under the law of another state having jurisdiction with respect to that conduct." 396 F.2d at 901, quoting RESTATEMENT (SECOND), FOREIGN RELATIONS LAW OF THE UNITED STATES § 339(1) (1965) (Restatement of Foreign Relations). . . . It then balanced the interests at stake, looking for guidance to § 40 of the Restatement of Foreign Relations. It looked particularly at the national interests of the United States and Germany and the hardship if any that Citibank would face in complying.

As part of its balancing, the court of Appeals stressed that the antitrust laws "have long been considered cornerstones of this nation's economic policies, have been vigorously enforced and the subject of frequent interpretation by our Supreme Court." *Id.* at 903. It further found noteworthy that neither the United States Department of State nor the German government had expressed any view in the case. Finally, in assessing the civil liability which Citibank alleged it might suffer, the Court said:

> [Citibank] must confront the choice . . . the need to "surrender to one sovereign or the other the privileges received therefrom" or, alternatively a willingness to accept the consequences. *Id.* at 905 (citation omitted).

In the second of these more recent opinions *Trade Development Bank v. Continental Insurance Co.*, 469 F.2d 35 (2d Cir. 1972), the Second Circuit affirmed this Court's decision not to order a Swiss bank to comply with defendant's request to release the names of its customers. . . .

Clearly then the Second Circuit has moved away from the position that a foreign law's prohibition of discovery is an absolute bar to compelling disclosure. It is worthy of note that in adopting a more flexible approach, this Circuit is squarely in line with other circuits and district courts that have considered the matter. *See, e.g., United States v. Vetco, Inc.*, 644 F.2d 1324 (9th Cir. 1981) (using § 40 of the Restatement of Foreign Relations Law and *Societe*'s good faith standard in upholding sanctions for a corporation's refusal to comply with IRS summonses despite possible criminal liability under Swiss law); *State of Ohio v. Arthur Andersen & Co.*, 570 F.2d 1370, 1373 (10th Cir.), *cert. denied* 439 U.S. 833 (1978) (upholding the imposition of preclusionary and monetary sanctions where the resisting party had stopped claiming that foreign law forbade discovery and noting that "Andersen acted in bad faith and the balancing was heavily on Ohio's side"); *In re Westinghouse Electric Corporation Uranium Contracts Litigation*, 563 F.2d 992 (10th Cir. 1977) (employing the § 40 factors and *Societe*'s good faith standard to relieve the petitioner of contempt sanctions where Canadian law forbade production of documents); *In re Grand Jury Proceeding*, 532 F.2d 404 (5th Cir.), *cert. denied* 429 U.S. 940 (1976) (using the § 40 factors to uphold a Grand Jury subpoena served on a nonresident alien even though the very act of his testifying violated Cayman Island law); *In re Uranium Antitrust Litigation*, 480 F.Supp. 1138 (N.D.Ill.1979) (in ordering production despite Canadian nondisclosure law, the Court eschewed the § 40 balancing test and looked instead at 1) the importance of the policies underlying the antitrust laws, 2) the importance of requested documents in illuminating key elements of the claims and 3) the degree of flexibility in the foreign nation's application of its nondisclosure laws); *American Industrial Contracting, Inc. v. Johns-Manville Corp.*, 326 F.Supp. 879 (W.D.Pa.1971) (defendants ordered to answer interrogatories in connection with an American antitrust suit despite Quebec law prohibiting disclosures, citing *Societe, supra* and *United States v. First National City Bank, supra*). *Cf. In the Matter of Banque Populaire*, CFTC Docket No. 80-8 (October 9, 1981) (The Commodity Futures Trading Commission barred a Swiss bank from trading on United States contract markets for 90 days for failing to provide it with information; the bank claimed it could not provide the material due to Swiss law). . . .

BSI claims that it may be subject to criminal liability under Swiss penal and banking law if it discloses the requested information. However, this Court finds the factors in § 40 of the Restatement of Foreign Relations to tip decisively in favor of the SEC. Moreover, it holds BSI to be "in the position of one who deliberately courted legal impediments . . . and who thus cannot now be heard to assert its good faith after this expectation was realized." *Societe, supra* at 208-09. BSI acted in bad faith. It made deliberate use of Swiss nondisclosure law to evade in a commercial transaction for profit to it, the strictures of American securities law against insider trading. Whether acting solely as an agent or also as a principal (something which can only be clarified through disclosure of the requested information), BSI invaded American securities markets and profited in some measure thereby. It cannot rely on Swiss nondisclosure law to shield this activity. . . .

The first of the § 40 factors is the vital national interest of each of the State. The strength of the United State interest in enforcing its securities laws to ensure the integrity of its financial markets cannot be seriously doubted. That interest is being continually thwarted by the use of foreign bank accounts. Congress, in enacting legislation on bank record-keeping expressed its concern over problem over a decade ago. . . .

The evisceration of the United States interest in enforcing its securities laws continues up to the present. *See, e.g.*, Wall Street Journal, October 29, 1981, at 1, col. 5 ("some Wall Street sources believe the SEC faces an insurmountable problem: obtaining from foreign sources the information that often is necessary to identify violators").

The Swiss government, on the other hand, though made expressly aware of the litigation, has expressed no opposition. In response to BSI's lawyers inquiries, the incumbent Swiss Federal Attorney General, Rudolf Gerber, said only that a foreign court could not change the rule that disclosure required the consent of the one who imparted the secret and that BSI might thus be subject to prosecution. The Swiss government did not "confiscate" the Bank records to prevent violations of its law, as it did in Societe. Neither the United States nor the Swiss Government has suggested that discovery be halted. . . .

It is also of significance that the secrecy privilege, as even BSI's expert admits ..., is one belonging to the bank customers and may be waived by them. It is not something required to protect the Swiss government itself or some other public interest. . . .

The second factor of § 40 of the Restatement of Foreign Relations is the extent and nature of the hardship that inconsistent enforcement actions would impose upon the party subject to both jurisdictions. It is true that BSI may be subject to fines and its officers to imprisonment under Swiss law. However, this Court notes that there is some flexibility in the application of that law. Not only may the particular bank involved obtain waivers from its customers to avoid prosecution, but Article 34 of the Swiss Penal Code contains a "State of Necessity" exception that relieves a person of criminal liability for acts committed to protect one's own good, including one's fortune, from an immediate danger if one is not responsible for the danger and one can not be expected to give up one's good. . . .

Of course, given BSI's active part in the insider trading transactions alleged here, the Swiss government might well conclude–as this Court has–that BSI is responsible for the conflict it is in and that therefore the "State of Necessity" exception should not apply. However, that is certainly no cause for this Court to withhold its sanctions since the dilemma would be a result of BSI's bad faith. A party's good or bad faith is an important factor to consider, and this Court finds that BSI, which deposited the proceeds of these transactions in an American bank account in its name and which certainly profited in some measure from the challenged activity, undertook such transactions fully expecting to use foreign law to shield it from the reach of our laws. Such "deliberate courting" of foreign legal impediments will not be countenanced. . . .

The last three of the § 40 Restatement of Foreign Relations Law factors–the place of performance, the nationality of the resisting party, and the extent to which enforcement can be expected to achieve compliance with the rule prescribed by that state–appear to be less important in this Circuit. It is significant nevertheless that they too tip in favor of the SEC. Performance may be said to occur here as well as in Switzerland since the actual answering of the interrogatories will presumably take place in the United States, where BSI's lawyers are. As for citizenship, it is true that BSI is a Swiss corporation. However, its transnational character, as evidenced by its large number of foreign affiliates . . . and its New York "Subsidiary" (so styled by it), render this Court less reluctant to order BSI to conform to our laws even where such an order may cause conflict with Swiss law. Last, with respect to enforcement, this Court believes that an appropriate formal order directing the demanded disclosure, to the extent that compliance has been incomplete, will serve as the requisite foundation for any further actions that may be needed in the form of sanctions and should serve to bring home the obligations a foreign entity undertakes when it conducts business on the American securities exchanges.

# In re Grand Jury Proceedings
691 F.2d 1384 (11th Cir. 1982), *cert. denied sub nom.*
*Bank of Nova Scotia v. United States*, 462 U.S. 1119 (1983)

Lewis R. Morgan, Senior Circuit Judge:

The Bank of Nova Scotia appeals from an order of the United States District Court for the Southern District of Florida holding the Bank of Nova Scotia in civil contempt for failing to comply with an order of the court enforcing a grand jury subpoena duces tecum. The Bank of Nova Scotia . . . presents three arguments against enforcing the subpoena. The Bank first contends that there were insufficient grounds to enforce the subpoena. The Bank also contends that enforcing the subpoena would violate due process. Finally, the Bank argues that the subpoena should not be enforced as a matter of comity between nations. We find the Bank's contentions to be without merit, and therefore we affirm the district court.
. . .

The Bank of Nova Scotia is a Canadian chartered bank with branches and agencies in forty-five countries, including the United States and the Bahamas. A federal grand jury conducting a tax and narcotics investigation issued a subpoena duces tecum to the Bank calling for the production of certain records maintained at the Bank's main branch or any of its branch offices in Nassau, Bahamas and Antigua, Lesser Antilles, relating to the bank accounts of a customer of the Bank.[1] The subpoena was served on the Bank's Miami, Florida agency on September 23, 1981. The Bank declined to produce the documents asserting that compliance with the subpoena without the customer's consent or an order of the Bahamian courts would violate Bahamian bank secrecy laws.[2]

---

1. The Bank investigated and found no documents which were requested located at its Antigua branch. Accordingly, that part of the subpoena is not in issue.

2. Banks and Trust Companies Regulations Act of 1965, 1963 Bah. Acts No. 64, as amended by the Banks and Trust Companies Regulation (Amendment) Act, 1980, 1980 Bah. Acts No. 3, and Section 19 of the Banks Act, III Bah.Rev. Laws, c. 96 (1965), as amended by the Banks Amendment Act 1980, 1980 Bah. Acts No. 64. Both Section 10 and Section 19 are identical. Section 10 of the Bank and Trust Companies Regulation Act as amended provides:

> Preservation of secrecy
> 10. -- (1) No person who has acquired information in his capacity as --
> (a) director, officer, employee or agent of any licensee or former licensee,
> (b) counsel and attorney, consultant or auditor of the Central Bank of The
> Bahamas, established under section 3 of the Central Bank of the Bahamas Act 1974, or as

A hearing was held on the Government's motion to compel the Bank to comply with the subpoena on January 13, 1982. At the hearing conflicting evidence was presented as to the degree of control the Miami agency held over documents held by the Nassau branch. The government presented evidence that all banking transactions for accounts in the Bahamian branch could be handled by the Miami agency. The Bank presented evidence that the Miami agency is a one-way conduit for customer communication with the Nassau branch. The Bank also presented an affidavit showing that compliance with the subpoena could expose the Bank to prosecution under the Bahamian bank secrecy law. The affidavit also showed that the government could obtain an order of judicial assistance from the Supreme Court of the Bahamas allowing disclosure if the subject of the grand jury investigation is a crime under Bahamian law and not solely criminal under United States tax laws. The government did not make a showing that the documents sought are relevant and necessary to the grand jury's investigation.

After the district court entered an order compelling the Bank to comply with the subpoena, the Bank's Miami agent appeared before the grand jury and formally declined to produce the documents called for by the subpoena. The district court held the Bank in civil contempt and the Bank brings this appeal. . . .

---

an employee or agent of such counsel and attorney, consultant or auditor,

(c) counsel and attorney, consultant, auditor, accountant, receiver or liquidator of any licensee or former licensee or as an employee or agent of such counsel and attorney, consultant, auditor, accountant, receiver or liquidator,

(d) auditor of any customer of any licensee or former licensee or as an employee or agent of such auditor,

(e) the inspector under the provisions of this Act, shall, without the express or implied consent of the customer concerned, disclose to any person any such information relating to the identity, assets, liabilities, transactions, accounts of a customer or a licensee or relating to any application by any person under the provisions of this Act, as the case may be, except—

(i) for the purpose of the performance of his duties or the exercise of his functions under this Act, if any; or

(ii) for the purpose of the performance of his duties within the scope of his employment, or

(iii) when a licensee is lawfully required to make disclosure by any court of competent jurisdiction within The Bahamas, or under the provisions of any law of The Bahamas.

(2) Nothing contained in this section shall—

(a) prejudice or derogate from the rights and duties subsisting at common law between a licensee and its customer, or

(b) prevent a licensee from providing upon a legitimate business request in the normal course of business a general credit rating with respect to a customer.

(3) Every person who contravenes the provisions of subsection (1) of this section shall be guilty of an offense against this Act and shall be liable on summary conviction to a fine not exceeding fifteen thousand dollars or to a term of imprisonment not exceeding two years or to both such fine and imprisonment.

The government argues the Bank would not be successfully prosecuted by Bahamian authorities if it complied with the subpoena. In this regard it argues that because Section 10(2)(a) expressly preserves the common law relationship between bank and customer, the Bank is authorized to disclose the requested information. *See Tournier v. National Provincial and Union Bank of England*, [1924] 1 K.B. 461 (Banker may disclose banking information concerning a customer where the banker is compelled by law to disclose information), *Barclay's Bank International, Ltd. v. McKinney*, No. 474 (Bah. S.Ct. Feb. 16, 1979). Although the determination of foreign law is reviewable on appeal, . . . we shall assume for purposes of this appeal that the Bank will be subject to criminal sanctions in the Bahamas.

The Bank urges this court to follow the Third Circuit's holdings in *In re Grand Jury Proceedings*, 486 F.2d 85 (*Schofield I*), (3rd Cir. 1973), and *In re Grand Jury Proceedings*, 507 F.2d 963 (*Schofield II*), (3rd Cir. 1975), *cert. denied*, 421 U.S. 1015 (1975), and require the government to show that the documents sought are relevant to an investigation properly within the grand jury's jurisdiction and not sought primarily for another purpose. The government does not dispute that the district court enforced the subpoena without making a finding that the documents sought were relevant or necessary for the grand jury's investigation. Rather, the government argues this case is controlled by *In re Grand Jury Proceedings United States v. McLean*, 565 F.2d 318 (5th Cir. 1977), and *In re Grand Jury Proceedings United States v. Guerrero*, 567 F.2d 281 (5th Cir. 1978), where the Fifth Circuit declined to follow the *Schofield* rule absent some showing of harassment or prosecutorial misuse of the system. The Bank argues that the *Schofield* rule, however, should be applied to cases such as this where foreign relations are implicated and where alternative methods are available to obtain the requested information that do not require the Bank to violate foreign law.

The guidelines established by the Third Circuit in *Schofield* are not mandated by the Constitution; the Third Circuit imposed the requirements under that court's inherent supervisory power. *Schofield*, 486 F.2d at 89; *McLean*, 565 F.2d at 320. We decline to impose any undue restrictions upon the grand jury investigative process pursuant to this court's supervisory power. . . .

While it is true courts should not impinge upon the political prerogatives of the government in the sensitive area of foreign relations, . . . accepting the Bank's position would be a greater interference with foreign relations than the procedures employed here. In essence, the Bank would require the government to chose between impeding the grand jury's investigation and petitioning the Supreme Court of the Bahamas for an order of disclosure.

This court is cognizant that international friction has been provoked by enforcement of subpoenas such as the one in question. *See* RESTATEMENT (REVISED) OF FOREIGN RELATIONS LAW OF THE UNITED STATES § 420, Reporter's Note 1. . . . But as recognized in *United States v. First National City Bank*, 379 U.S. 378, 384-85 (1965), the various federal courts remain open to the legislative and executive branches of our government if matters such as this prove to have international repercussions. *See, e.g.*, Convention on Double Taxation of Income, September 27, 1951. United States-Switzerland, 2 U.S.T. 1751, T.I.A.S. No. 2316 (Swiss-US Tax Treaty providing for exchange of information for, inter alia, the prevention of fraud). . . .

The Bank contends that compliance with the subpoena would require it to violate the Bahamian bank secrecy law and therefore enforcing the subpoena and imposing contempt sanctions for non compliance violates due process under *Societe Internationale Power Participations Industrielles v. Rogers*, 357 U.S. 197 (1958). The Bank argues that once it has shown Bahamian law bars production of the documents and that it is a disinterested custodian of the documents due process prohibits enforcement of the subpoena. We disagree.

The Bank attempts to fashion a due process defense to the contempt proceedings because of its lack of purposeful involvement or responsibility in the subject matter before the court. In essence, the Bank asserts it is fundamentally unfair to require a "mere stakeholder" to incur criminal liability in the Bahamas. The Bank's position does not withstand analysis. . . .

The Bank has failed to bring itself within the holding of *Societe Internationale*. The district court found the Bank had not made a good faith effort to comply with the subpoena in its order of June 11, 1982. . . . The Bahamian government has not acted to prevent the Bank from complying with the subpoena. Finally, the Bank is not being denied a constitutionally required forum to recover confiscated assets. . . .

The Bank's final contention is that comity between nations precludes enforcement of the subpoena. The Bank argues that the district court improperly analyzed this case under the balancing test of the RESTATEMENT (SECOND) OF FOREIGN RELATIONS LAW OF THE UNITED STATES § 40 (1965) adopted in *In re Grand Jury Proceedings United States v. Field*, 532 F.2d 404 (5th Cir. 1976), *cert. denied*, 429 U.S. 940 (1976). The district court concluded that because compliance with the subpoena may cause the Bank to violate Bahamian penal laws, it was appropriate to follow the balancing test adopted in *Field*. Because we conclude this case is controlled by *Field*, we affirm the court below. . . .

## United States v. First National Bank of Chicago
### 699 F.2d 341 (7th Cir. 1983)

Fairchild, Senior Circuit Judge.

The district court granted enforcement of an Internal Revenue Service summons directed to First National Bank of Chicago . . . , seeking disclosure of certain records in First Chicago's branch bank in Athens, Greece. We decide that First Chicago has adequately demonstrated that compliance will subject its employees to the risk of substantial criminal penalties under Greek law, and that a balancing of relevant competing interests weighs against compelling disclosure at this time. We therefore reverse the judgment of the district court, but remand for consideration of an order requiring First Chicago to make a good faith effort to secure permission to make the information available. . . .

On September 24, 1979, Internal Revenue Service Officer Earl Tripplett issued a summons to First Chicago requiring production of bank statements of Christ and Helen Panos for the month of June 1978 and the balance of funds in their account at the Athens, Greece, branch of First Chicago on June 19, 1978. (The Panoses now reside in Greece.)

First Chicago refused to furnish the requested information, stating:

> [O]ur Greek counsel has informed us that under the Greek Bank Secrecy Act, any and all of our employees–whether in Greece or elsewhere–who reveal exact account information about depositors of our Branch in Athens to any third party may be subject under the Act to criminal penalties, including, inter alia, not less than a six-month prison sentence. He further informs us that in two very recent Greek court decisions, it has been made clear that this Act does indeed apply to branches of foreign banks doing business in Greece.

However, in what it termed an effort to cooperate as much as possible without jeopardizing the welfare of its employees, First Chicago did advise the IRS that only one account for the Panoses existed, and that during the month of June 1978 the balance was "in the range of 40,000 Greek drachmas" (approximately $1,000 American money).

Thereafter, the IRS filed a petition in the district court to enforce the summons. Upon First Chicago's failure to respond timely to an order to show cause, the court, on May 7, 1980, ordered compliance.

First Chicago then filed a motion to vacate the enforcement order, arguing that disclosure would expose its employees to penal sanctions under Greek law. The motion was supported by a memorandum and copies of two unsworn letters from George V. Tsarouchas, of the law firm of George Lazarimos & Sons, First Chicago's Greek counsel, dated respectively March 9, 1972 and July 1, 1978, interpreting the Greek Bank Secrecy Act. ... In relevant part, the letters stated that information concerning customer deposits could not lawfully be supplied to American authorities, that the penalty for violation was at least six months in prison, and that such sanction could not be suspended or converted into fines. After receiving the Government's answering memorandum, accompanied by a Library of Congress translation of the Act, the court, without opinion, denied the motion to vacate on September 15, 1980.

A motion for reconsideration was filed by First Chicago on October 3, 1980, stating in part that it had been denied the opportunity to file a reply to the Government's answering memorandum prior to the ruling of September 15. A hearing was held, and the court permitted First Chicago to file a reply. Two sworn affidavits accompanied First Chicago's submission. The first, dated October 24, 1980, by Nick C. Gravenites, the manager of First Chicago's Greek branch for more than five years, stated, "on the basis of his knowledge acquired in the performance of his duties," that the Act was in full force and effect at the time the subpoena was issued, that it continued to remain in effect and applied to his employees, and that for more than nine years the Lazarimos firm had served as counsel to the Greek branch. The affidavit further stated that:

> Greek currency (the drachma) is a non-convertible currency. The foreign exchange control laws of the Republic of Greece at all times relevant to the proceeding at bar restricted the free conversion of Greek currency (drachmas) into another foreign currency and, further, restricted the transmittal of drachmas outside the Republic of Greece.

The second affidavit, by Ralph J. Borkowitz, First Chicago's Records Manager, dated October 24, 1980, stated that records responsive to the IRS request were maintained only in the bank's branch office in Athens, Greece. . . .

On November 6, 1980, the district court, without opinion, denied the motion for reconsideration. It granted a stay pending this appeal. . . .

First Chicago does not argue that the Government failed to make out a prima facie case for enforcement. And indeed there is no suggestion that the summons did not relate to a proper purpose, albeit levy and collection rather than determination of tax liability, that the material sought was irrelevant or already within the Commissioner's possession, or that necessary administrative steps remained to be taken. . . . Rather, First Chicago urges that cause has been established for denying enforcement, notwithstanding the Government's prima facie showing. As we view the case, the arguments raised on appeal fall into two categories. First, whether First Chicago has sufficiently proved that Greek law forbids, under penalty of imprisonment, disclosure of the information in question. Second, whether (if it has so demonstrated) it should nonetheless be compelled to comply with the IRS summons.
. . .

The language of the Act is clear and unambiguous. It provides that an employee of a bank who conveys any information in any manner pertaining to a deposit account is subject to a minimum of six months in prison, that a sentence may not be suspended or converted into a fine, and even the consent of the depositor cannot alter the punishable nature of the disclosure. It is difficult to imagine statutory language more certain in its tenor.
. . .

The sworn statement that the information was maintained only in the Athens branch strongly suggests that the information could not be produced without the involvement of persons clearly subject to prosecution under the Act. While better evidence might have been offered to establish that the Act was and remains in effect, and that it applies to foreign banks, we think that the evidence in the record is adequate to support a finding in favor of First Chicago on each of these matters. The statement of Mr. Gravenites seems particularly probative in that as the manager of the Greek branch he would likely be interested in legislation affecting the liabilities and duties of his employees. Finally, it is significant that the Government offers absolutely no proof that First Chicago's employees would not be subject to prosecution under the Greek law.

We hold that First Chicago has adequately proved that the Act forbids, under penalty of imprisonment, disclosure of the information the IRS seeks to compel. . . .

The fact that foreign law may subject a person to criminal sanctions in the foreign country if he produces certain information does not automatically bar a domestic court from compelling production. . . . Rather what is required is a sensitive balancing of the competing interests at stake. A number of circuits have utilized a test derived from the RESTATEMENT (SECOND) FOREIGN RELATIONS LAW OF THE UNITED STATES (1965). . . .

Applying [that] test . . . , we conclude that it was an abuse of discretion to enter an unqualified order compelling production, particularly where there is no indication of the rationale of the decision.

It seems clear that the critical act of initially conveying the information would take place in Greece (factor (c)), and highly probable that persons of Greek nationality would make the initial disclosure (factor (d)). Factor (b), extent and nature of hardship, bears great weight. Those acting in Greece would be exposed to criminal liability, not merely a fine, but imprisonment. Comment c to § 40 of the Restatement observes:

> In determining whether to refrain from exercising jurisdiction, a state must give special weight to the nature of the penalty that may be imposed by the other state. A state will be less likely to refrain from exercising its jurisdiction when the consequence of obedience to its order will be a civil liability abroad. Similarly, a state will be less likely to exercise jurisdiction, where there is a possibility that obedience to its command may put an alien in jeopardy under the criminal laws of his own country, than it will if one of its own nationals may be subjected to foreign liability under similar circumstances.

We think it significant in weighing the hardship factor that the bank employees who would be exposed to penalty and First Chicago, which would be ordering its Greek employees to act unlawfully, are involved only as neutral sources of information and not as taxpayers or adverse parties in litigation.

Although the interest of the United States in collecting taxes is of importance to the financial integrity of the nation, the interest of Greece, served by its bank secrecy law is also important, and so conceded by Government counsel (factor (a)). In connection with this factor it seems significant that the amount of tax liability of the Panoses has already been determined, the information is sought as a step toward levy and collection, the amount of the asset is comparatively small, and there are legal restrictions on the conversion and export of Greek funds. . . .

On remand, the district court is directed to conduct further inquiry consistent with this opinion and to consider whether to issue an order requiring First Chicago to make a good faith effort to receive permission from the Greek authorities to produce the information specified in the summons.

We are aware that the Eleventh Circuit has reached a different result in a case involving a bank which was apparently a neutral source of information, as here. *In re Grand Jury Proceedings*, 691 F.2d 1384 (11th Cir. 1982). In that case, however, the court of appeals had the benefit of findings by the district court, including a finding that the bank had not made a good faith effort to comply with the subpoena. The information was sought by a grand jury conducting a tax and narcotics investigation, so that the interest of the United States in the grand jury process of investigation and enforcement of its criminal laws was involved as well as its interest in determination and collection of taxes. There was evidence, though contested, that all banking transactions for the foreign branch could be handled by the United States branch. The foreign law (Bahamian) was different from the Greek law involved here in that disclosure with the consent of the customer would not be a criminal offense, and the power of a Bahamian court to permit disclosure did not appear to be as strictly limited. We consider the decision distinguishable.

**Notes and Comments 10.22.** Swiss policy with respect to bank secrecy has been tightening in recent years. Insider trading, once virtually excluded from Swiss international cooperation in criminal matters, is now illegal in Switzerland, and this may limit the secrecy available when bank accounts are thought to be involved in such activities. In addition, in May 1991, the Swiss Federal Banking Commission announced the abolishment of the so-called "Form B" bank accounts that had been a favored instrument of money launderers seeking anonymity in their transactions. *See* Riding, *New Rule Reduces Swiss Banking Secrecy*, N.Y. Times, May 6, 1991, at D1, col. 3.

**10.23.** U.S. judicial attitudes to foreign bank secrecy laws have long been informed by reference to the American Law Institute's RESTATEMENT (2D) OF THE FOREIGN RELATIONS LAW OF THE UNITED STATES § 40 (1965).[17] Are the cases consistent in interpreting and applying § 40?

**10.24.** The American Law Institute has revised the Restatement, a project which had been subjected to much criticism, particularly from interested agencies and departments of the U.S. Government. Review the following excerpts from Restatement (3d), and consider how, if at all, the results in the cases excerpted above would have been affected by the application of the Restatement (3d) provisions.

## American Law Institute, Restatement of the Foreign Relations Law of the United States (3d)

§ 403. Limitations on Jurisdiction to Prescribe

(1) Even when one of the bases for jurisdiction . . . is present [*i.e.*, conduct within the territory of the prescribing state; status of persons within its territory; conduct outside the territory with a substantial effect within; its nationals wherever located; conduct outside directed against the security of the state or against certain state interests], a state may not exercise jurisdiction to prescribe law with respect to a person or activity having connections with another state when the exercise of such jurisdiction is unreasonable.

(2) Whether exercise of jurisdiction over a person or activity is unreasonable is determined by evaluating all relevant factors, including, where appropriate:

(a) the link of the activity to the territory of the regulating state, *i.e.*, the extent to which the activity takes place within the territory, or has substantial, direct and foreseeable effect upon or in the territory;

---

17. *See In re Grand Jury Proceedings, supra*, at n. 5 (quoting § 40).

(b) the connections, such as nationality, residence, or economic activity, between the regulating state and the person principally responsible for the activity to be regulated, or between that state and those whom the regulation is designed to protect;

(c) the character of the activity to be regulated, the importance of the regulation to the regulating state, the extent to which other states regulate such activities, and the degree to which the desirability of such regulation is generally accepted;

(d) the exigence of justified expectations that might be protected or hurt by the regulation;

(e) the importance of the regulation to the international political, legal or economic system;

(f) the extent to which the regulation is consistent with the traditions of the international system;

(g) the extent to which another state may have an interest in regulating the activity; and

(h) the likelihood of conflict with regulation by another state.

(3) When it would not be unreasonable for each of two states to exercise jurisdiction over a person or activity, but the prescriptions by the two states are in conflict, each state has an obligation to evaluate its own as well as the other state's interest in exercising jurisdiction, in light of all the relevant factors . . . ; a state should defer to the other state if that state's interest is clearly greater.

**Notes and Comments 10.25.** In fact, the Restatement (3d) has been gaining acceptance in the courts, as had its predecessor, and it may now be eclipsing the influence of Restatement (2d) § 40. In that regard, consider the following excerpt.

## Michael P. Malloy, Principles of Bank Regulation
### § 9.26 (2d ed. 2003)

. . . Section 403 of the *Restatement (3d)*, which seems rigged against U.S. enforcement in its balancing test,[16] starts with [the] assumption . . . that a state lacks jurisdiction to prescribe or enforce if exercising jurisdiction would be unreasonable. Section 403 has been adopted by U.S. courts,[17] but it is sometimes characterized by them as simply an extension or revision of § 40.[18]

---

16. *Cf.* David B. Massey, Note, *How the American Law Institute Influences Customary Law: The Reasonableness Requirement of the Restatement of Foreign Relations Law*, 22 Yale J. Int'l L. 419, 437 (1997) (arguing that § 403 did not accurately reflect customary law when published).

17. *See, e.g., Timberlane Lumber Co. v. Bank of America*, 749 F.2d 1378 (9th Cir. 1984) (adopting seven-factor analysis based on § 403(2)); *Trugman-Nash, Inc. v. New Zealand Dairy Board*, 954 F. Supp. 733, 737 (S.D.N.Y. 1997) (citing *Timberlane*). *See generally* Massey, *supra*, at 437-439 (surveying U.S. court citation of § 403); Louise Ellen Teitz, *et al., International Litigation*, 31 Int'l Law. 317, 331-334 (1997) (discussing cases).

18. *See, e.g., Filetech S.A.R.L. v. France Telecom*, 978 F. Supp. 464, 477 (S.D.N.Y. 1997), *vacated*, 157 F.3d 922 (2d Cir. 1998) (referring to "direct line of succession" between § 40 and § 403 cases); *United States v. Nippon Paper Indus. Co.*, 109 F.3d 1, 7 (1st Cir. 1997) (noting § 403 "merely reaffirms"); *In re Grand Jury Proceedings*, 40 F.3d 959, 965 (9th Cir. 1994), *cert. denied sub nom. Marsoner v. United States*, 515 U.S. 1132, 115 S.Ct. 2558 (noting § 40 as "revised and . . . encompassed within" § 403). *Cf. In re Grand Jury Proceedings*, 709 F. Supp. 192, 195 (C.D. Cal. 1989) (invoking § 40).

The provisions of the *Restatement (3d)* dealing with jurisdictional conflicts were hotly debated over an extended period of time both within and outside the American Law Institute. The compromise text that eventually became § 403 may not significantly change results in bank secrecy cases.[19]

**Notes and Comments 10.26.** Attila D. Hunn apparently has some accounts held by several banks organized and operating in Austria, which has a bank secrecy law. Under § 403, if those Austrian banks also have operations in the United States, could they be compelled to disclose information concerning Mr. Hunn's accounts? If Mr. Hunn were found within the United States, could he be subpoenaed and required to give his consent to disclosure of information by the Austrian banks? Consider the following case.

## In re Grand Jury Proceedings
40 F.3d 959 (9th Cir. 1994), *cert. denied sub nom. Marsoner v. United States,*
515 U.S. 1132

Per Curiam:
Reinhold Marsoner appeals the district court's order finding him in contempt for refusing to sign a consent directive as ordered by the district court. . . .

Marsoner, an Austrian citizen residing in the United States, is the target of an investigation by a federal grand jury, which is investigating possible violations of United States laws stemming from claimed tax liabilities for the years 1989 through 1991. Marsoner was subpoenaed to appear before the grand jury to sign a disclosure directive. The disclosure directive states that Marsoner authorizes and directs any bank at which Marsoner had a bank or loan account for which Marsoner was, is, or may be the relevant principal, signatory, or beneficiary to disclose all information and produce all documents in its possession to the grand jury or to an attorney or agent of the United States Attorney. The directive also authorizes any bank employee, officer, or agent of such bank to provide testimony or evidence in connection with any proceeding arising out of the disclosure of the bank information or documents. The directive states that it has been executed pursuant to a United States district court order and that it is intended to be construed as consent to disclosure under Austrian law for any bank account for which Marsoner is the relevant principal.

Marsoner appeared before the grand jury and refused to sign the disclosure directive, claiming it violated his rights under the Fourth and Fifth Amendments of the United States Constitution and under the laws of Austria. . . .

. . . The district court ordered Marsoner to sign the disclosure directive by April 8, 1994.

On April 11, 1994, Marsoner appeared before the grand jury and refused to sign the directive, again on the grounds that it violated his rights under the Fourth and Fifth Amendments and under the laws of Austria. . . . Following a hearing, the district court held Marsoner in civil contempt. . . . The district court imposed a $100.00 fine and ordered Marsoner confined until either he purged his contempt or the grand jury's term expired. This appeal follows. . . .

[The court rejected Marsoner's argument based on the Fifth Amendment, citing *Doe v. United States*, 487 U.S. 201 (1988), among others. As to Marsoner's Fourth Amendment

---

19. *See, e.g., Filetech S.A.R.L., supra* (applying § 403(2)); *In re Grand Jury Proceedings,* 40 F.3d 959 (applying § 403).

claim, the court cited *United States v. Miller*, 425 U.S. 435 (1976), rejecting a Fourth Amendment privacy interest of a depositor in his bank's records. The court then went on to extend *Miller* explicitly to the situation of foreign bank deposit records.]

The Supreme Court has extended this analysis to the privacy expectations of an individual depositing funds in a foreign bank. In *United States v. Payner*, 447 U.S. 727, 732 n. 4 (1980), the Court rejected the claim that the Bahamian law of bank secrecy created an expectation of privacy. . . .

We reached a similar conclusion in [*United States v.*] *Mann*, [829 F.2d 849 (9th Cir. 1987),] where we rejected a depositor's claim that Cayman law's restrictions on disclosure of information concerning Cayman bank records created a reasonable expectation of privacy protected by the Fourth Amendment. . . . We found that Cayman law contained a general privilege against disclosure of bank records but contained a "vast array of exceptions." . . . We found Cayman law analogous to the Bahamian law reviewed in *Payner* and ruled there was no Fourth Amendment violation. . . .

Marsoner correctly asserts that the district court erred by failing to consider the role of Austrian law in its evaluation of Marsoner's Fourth Amendment claim. . . . Nevertheless, because we conduct a *de novo* review, we may consider the impact of Austrian law on Marsoner's expectations of privacy.

Austrian law provides that, generally, banks, and bank officers, employees and personnel may not disclose or use confidential information obtained on the basis of the bank's relationship with a client. *Bundesgesetz über das Kreditwesen vom 24. Janner* [sic] *1979 (Kreditwesengesetz), Bundesgesetzblatt*, No. 63/1979 (hereinafter "1979 Banking Statute" or "banking statute") § 23(1). There is no obligation to maintain confidentiality in several situations, including cases in which the client provides express written consent to disclosure of the banking secret, in connection with inheritance proceedings or criminal court proceedings in Austrian courts, or cases involving general information about the economic circumstances of an entrepreneur. *Id.* at § 23(2). Under the banking statute, individuals disclosing or using banking secrets protected under section 23 may be punished only if they disclose or use the secrets to obtain financial advantage for either themselves or others or to cause detriment to another. *Id.* at § 34(1). Thus, although the statute generally protects banking secrets, it is not a "blanket guarantee."

We find considerations of United States law dilute Marsoner's expectation of privacy. United States citizens and residents are required to reveal the existence of foreign bank accounts and to report transactions made with a foreign financial agency. 31 U.S.C. § 5314(a). This information is to be reported to the Commissioner of Internal Revenue for each year in which such relationship or transactions occur. 31 C.F.R. § 103.24 (1984). Thus, Marsoner, as a resident, had an expectation that any transactions with Austrian banks would have to be disclosed. . . .

Marsoner distinguishes his case from *Payner* and *Mann* on the ground that he is an Austrian citizen asserting his rights under Austrian law. He points out that *Payner* and *Mann*, which rejected Fourth Amendment challenges to orders directing disclosure of foreign bank records, involved United States citizens asserting privacy interests under foreign law. We find this distinction inapposite. First, neither our reading of the section 23 of the 1979 Banking Statute nor the affidavits furnished by Marsoner suggest that the bank's duty under section 23 to maintain confidentiality applies only to accounts maintained by Austrian citizens. Second, and more importantly, the United States law requiring disclosure of foreign accounts applies to United States citizens and residents alike. *See* 31 U.S.C. § 5314. Thus, because he is a United States resident, Marsoner's status as an Austrian citizen does not relieve him of the obligation to report transactions with foreign financial agencies. Because we find that Marsoner's expectation of privacy in his Austrian bank records is diluted, we conclude that the district court order does not violate Marsoner's Fourth Amendment rights. . . .

Marsoner's final contention is that the district court's order violates his rights under Austrian law. He argues that the district court erred by failing to conduct an evidentiary hearing on the implications of Austrian law and asks us to remand for an evidentiary hearing. The government counters that remand and an evidentiary hearing are unnecessary because this court is in a position to analyze the implications of Austrian law. We find the government's position more persuasive.

The issue before us is not solely whether the district court order compelling Marsoner to sign the disclosure directive before the grand jury violates Austrian law. Rather, the issue is whether, if the district court's order violates Austrian law, principles of international comity prevent the district court from enforcing its order.[2]

A party relying on foreign law to contend that a district court's order violates principles of international comity bears the burden of demonstrating that the foreign law bars compliance with the order. *In re Grand Jury Proceedings (Shams)*, 873 F.2d 238, 239-40 (9th Cir. 1989) (citing *United States v. Vetco Inc.*, 691 F.2d 1281, 1289 (9th Cir.), *cert. denied*, 454 U.S. 1098 (1981)). If the party fails to produce evidence in support, then he fails to meet his burden on the comity issue, and the district court need not consider it. . . .

Marsoner proffered to the district court lengthy affidavits from two individuals with strong credentials in the area of international law and Austrian banking law, who presented their analysis of relevant Austrian law. Thus, we find, at a minimum, Marsoner met his burden of producing evidence sufficient for the court to consider the implications of Austrian law. . . . Accordingly, the district court erred by failing to consider the implications of Austrian law.

Nevertheless, a determination of foreign law is a ruling on a question of law, which an appellate court is free to determine based on its own analysis. . . . We find that the record is sufficiently developed and that remand is unnecessary to a determination of whether the order compelling Marsoner to sign the disclosure directive violated Marsoner's rights under Austrian law and whether considerations of international comity prevent its enforcement. . . .

In the affidavits proffered by Marsoner, both affiants opine that compelling Marsoner to sign the consent directive would violate Austrian law. We need not evaluate the accuracy of these opinions. We find that even if the district court order compelling Marsoner to sign the disclosure directive implicates Marsoner's rights under Austrian law, international comity will not preclude its enforcement.

We acknowledge that "in recent years litigants have often attempted to circumvent [the limitations of international comity] by seeking an order compelling the record-owner to consent to the disclosure of the records." . . . *United States v. Davis*, 767 F.2d 1025, 1034 (2d Cir. 1985). In considering international comity, we balance the competing interests of Austria and the United States and the extent to which they are affected by the order compelling Marsoner's signature to determine whether the purported illegality of the order

---

2. We note that this case does not involve Austrian bank officials or employees found in contempt for resisting a request or order for production of bank records. . . . Accordingly, we focus only on the legality of compelling an Austrian citizen, residing in the United States, to sign a consent to the disclosure of bank records, which may or may not include records maintained in connection with Austrian bank accounts.

under Austrian law precludes its enforcement. . . . We decide this based on the particulars involved. . . .

In the past, courts have used section 40 of the Restatement (Second) of Foreign Relations Law (1965) to evaluate whether international comity precludes enforcement of an order compelling a witness to sign a consent authorizing disclosure of foreign bank records. . . . Section 40 of the Restatement has been revised and is now encompassed within section 403 of the Restatement (Third). Under the revised Restatement, reasonableness is "an essential element in determining whether, as a matter of international law, the state may exercise jurisdiction to prescribe." Restatement (Third) of Foreign Relations Law § 403 reporter's note 10 (1987).

Applying these factors to the situation presented here, we hold that international comity does not preclude enforcement of the district court's order. Marsoner is suspected of using his Austrian bank accounts to evade taxes in the United States. The grand jury seeks Austrian bank information in an effort to link Marsoner to alleged illegal activities that occurred in the United States between 1989 and 1991. Although Marsoner is an Austrian citizen, he a United States resident and his economic activity, which includes tax liabilities, involves the United States.

The United States has a strong interest in collecting taxes, . . . and in prosecuting individuals for tax evasion. . . . Additionally, while Austria has enacted a statute to maintain the secrecy of bank records, it has created exceptions to the secrecy provisions. *See* 1979 Banking Statute § 23(2).

Although under the 1979 Banking Statute, Marsoner may have expected that his Austrian bank records would remain confidential, the statute does not provide a blanket guarantee. Moreover, under the United States' laws, Marsoner should have expected that he would be required to disclose transactions with foreign banking institutions to the Commissioner of Internal Revenue. The grand jury's investigative function, which here involves investigating possible violations of tax laws, plays a vital role in our system of jurisprudence. . . .

Austria has a prohibition against compelling an individual from being a witness against himself, which is similar to that embraced by the Fifth Amendment. As we previously discussed, the district court's order directing Marsoner to appear before the grand jury to sign the disclosure directive does not violate his Fifth Amendment rights.

Although more significant interests may be implicated in the next stage of the grand jury investigation, *e.g.*, if the district court attempts to compel an Austrian bank to produce documents based on Marsoner's signed consent, those interests are beyond the scope of this appeal. The disclosure directive is worded to indicate that it has been executed pursuant to an order of a United States court. Accordingly, the Austrian courts will be free to decide whether the directive constitutes valid consent under Austrian law. . . . We find it preferable to allow the Austrian courts to decide what effect to give the disclosure directive with respect to Austrian bank records.

On balance, we find that the United States' interest in obtaining Marsoner's signature outweighs Austria's interest in preventing a United States court from compelling an Austrian citizen residing in the United States to appear before a grand jury to execute a disclosure directive authorizing disclosure of bank information from unidentified domestic or foreign banks.

# Chapter 11

# Economic Sanctions and International Banking

## 1. Introduction

**Notes and Comments 11.1.** Economic sanctions involve an intervention by a sanctioning state or international organization (*e.g.*, the United Nations Security Council) into transnational commercial and financial transactions with the objective of attacking or isolating a target state or group by economic means.[1] However, are economic sanctions a necessary or effective way of achieving such objectives? One might wonder whether generally applicable bank regulatory principles, supplemented by private commercial law, may be sufficient to sanction a target state. For example, Panama and the Noriega regime were the targets of rather limited sanctions in 1985, to little effect.[2] In contrast, consider the effects on Panama of the following case. Which approach seems more effective?

### Republic of Panama v. Republic Nat. Bank of N.Y.
681 F.Supp. 1066 (S.D.N.Y. 1988)

MacMahon, District Judge.

This action arises out of recent political turmoil in the Republic of Panama. On February 25, 1988, President Eric Arturo Delvalle . . . dismissed General Manual Noriega . . . as Commander of the Panamanian Defense Forces. Noriega refused to step down, and on February 26, 1988 he allegedly instigated the removal of Delvalle from office by vote of the National Assembly. Subsequently, the Cabinet Council named Manuel Solis Palma ... as "Minister in Charge of the Presidency of the Republic."

The United States recognizes only Delvalle as the lawful president of Panama and has expressed support for the Delvalle government in official State Department statements and in meetings of the Organization of American States.

On March 1, 1988, Delvalle issued a proclamation, as "the lawful President of the Republic of Panama," declaring the "Noriega regime" illegitimate and illegal, and advised all interested parties that any transactions with the Noriega regime would not be recognized

---

1. For extended treatment of this subject, see MICHAEL P. MALLOY, UNITED STATES ECONOMIC SANCTIONS: THEORY AND PRACTICE (2001).

2. *See, e.g.*, MALLOY, *supra* note 1, at 110-113 (discussing U.S. economic sanctions against Panama).

by, or considered binding upon, the Republic of Panama. In addition, Ambassador [Juan B.] Sosa notified Marine [Midland Bank], Bankers Trust, Republic National Bank of New York . . . and Irving Trust Company . . . by letter, that the Delvalle government was the only lawful government of the Republic of Panama; that the United States recognized it as such; and that no debit or payment of any kind should be made against any accounts of the Republic of Panama or its agencies or instrumentalities without authorization from Ambassador Sosa as the legal representative of Panama in the United States.

On March 2, 1988, we granted plaintiff's application for a temporary restraining order enjoining Republic [National Bank] from debiting any account of the Republic of Panama. Plaintiff later filed an amended complaint naming Marine, Bankers Trust and Irving as defendants. Still later that day, Republic agreed to transfer all funds in the account of the Republic of Panama to the Federal Reserve Bank of New York, and the action against Republic was dismissed.

Also on March 2, 1988, the Acting Secretary of State of the United States, John C. Whitehead, officially certified, pursuant to 12 U.S.C. § 632 (1982), that Ambassador Sosa "is the sole person having authority to receive, control or dispose of any property held in any . . . Federal Reserve bank or insured bank from or for the account of the Republic of Panama or any central bank thereof . . . and that his authority with respect to such property is accepted and recognized by me."

On March 3, 1988, we granted a temporary restraining order enjoining the three remaining defendants from debiting any account held in the name of the Republic of Panama unless approved by Ambassador Sosa. The order also enjoined payment on any letters of credit or similar instruments in the name of the Republic of Panama or any of its agencies or instrumentalities.

Irving stipulated with plaintiff not to pay against any account of the Republic of Panama except payments under outstanding letters of credit, and the action against Irving was dismissed. The remaining defendants appeared on March 7, 1988 at the hearing on plaintiff's application for a preliminary injunction. . . . Banco Nacional [de Panama] and a representative of the Palma government, claiming a property interest in the funds, sought to intervene as of right. . . .

A showing of irreparable harm is a prerequisite to the issuance of a preliminary injunction. Plaintiff establishes irreparable harm by showing the absence of an adequate remedy at law. . . .

Here, the remaining defendants argue that injunctive relief is inappropriate because (1) plaintiff alleges mere monetary loss for which it has an adequate remedy at law (money damages), and (2) there has been no showing that defendants are insolvent or otherwise incapable of satisfying a judgment for the approximately $50 million in dispute.

Assuming that plaintiff might recover damages were the banks to disburse funds to anyone other than the lawful representative of the Republic of Panama, and that the banks might be capable of satisfying a $50 million judgment, we are not persuaded that such a remedy is sufficiently "adequate" to warrant denial of a preliminary injunction. The determination of what is or is not an adequate legal remedy so as to preclude the issuance of an injunction is governed by the circumstances of each particular case, and harm may be irreparable if "of a peculiar nature, so that compensation in money cannot atone for it."

Plaintiff is presently contending with a rival political faction within Panama for control of the government. The United States has recognized plaintiff as the lawfully-constituted Republic of Panama, and that recognition is conclusive and binding upon us. Whichever faction gains control of the disputed funds will have a decisive advantage over the other for effective control of the government. Consequently, the harm imminent here goes beyond mere monetary loss to the very survival of the lawful Delvalle government. Prospective uncertain money damages recoverable upon the remote conclusion of future litigation cannot adequately compensate for the immediate and irreparable loss evident here. In addition, 12 U.S.C. § 632 was enacted "as a practical matter to avoid time-consuming litigation and to give [an] exiled government effective control over [its] funds." Thus, the statute was designed to address situations precisely analogous to that presented here. Finally, there is a real threat that these funds would be dissipated and irretrievably lost if disbursed to persons other than the lawful representative of the Republic of Panama. The existence of such a threat also constitutes irreparable harm sufficient to support a motion for a preliminary injunction. . . .

It is well established that recognition of a foreign state is a political question to be determined solely by the executive branch of government. Judicial deference to the executive in this area accords with the constitutional grant of power over the conduct of foreign relations to the executive branch and with the separation of powers. As a corollary to deferring to the executive branch in determining whom to accredit as representatives of a foreign state, United States courts will not hear suits brought by governments from which official recognition has been withheld.

When a foreign state's property located in the United States is demanded by two claimants, official recognition of one is conclusive. Precisely this situation was presented in *Bank of China v. Wells Fargo Bank & Union Trust Co.*,[17] where the Nationalist Government of China and the Peoples Republic of China each claimed title to a bank account held in the name of "Bank of China." The court held that when the United States officially recognizes one of the two claimants, "[i]t is not a proper function of a domestic court of the United States to attempt to judge which government best represents the interests of the Chinese State in the Bank of China. In this situation, the Court should justly accept, as the representative of the Chinese State, that government which our executive deems best able to further the mutual interests of China and the United States."[18]

Following *Bank of China*, the executive branch, by recognizing the Delvalle government unequivocally and acknowledging Ambassador Sosa as its diplomatic representative, conclusively determined that only the Delvalle government may claim bank funds held in the name of the Republic of Panama.[19] The United States government explicitly sanctioned Delvalle's claim by certifying Ambassador Sosa and appearing at the hearing to reaffirm that the United States recognizes only the Delvalle government of the Republic of Panama.

Thus, quite apart from the statute, the political question doctrine and its non-recognition corollary would entitle the Delvalle government to claim funds for the Republic of Panama. It is the statute, however, that we deem conclusive in establishing plaintiff's right to immediate injunctive relief. . . .

---

17. 104 F. Supp. 59 (N.D.Cal. 1952), *modified*, 209 F.2d 467 (9th Cir. 1953).

18. 104 F. Supp. at 66.

19. None of the considerations that Bank of China posited might prevent recognition from being conclusive apply here. *See id.* at 63-66. The court suggested that when the executive's recognition of a foreign government was equivocal, or when recognition did not imply approval of the transaction, recognition might not be conclusive. Once the executive's position became clear, however, the court agreed that it was bound by the executive's decision. *See id.* at 66. The executive's position in the instant matter is completely unambiguous. The United States stands squarely behind Delvalle's government and its claim to the accounts. . . .

Each of the three statutory requirements [of § 632] has been met here. Defendants are insured banks that have received property for the account of the Republic of Panama or its central bank.[20] Ambassador Sosa, recognized by the Secretary of State as the accredited representative of the Republic of Panama, has certified that he has the authority to receive, control, or dispose of such property. Finally, the authority of Ambassador Sosa has been accepted, recognized and certified by the Secretary of State.

The plain language of the statute provides that when these conditions are met, delivery of funds "shall be conclusively presumed lawful." This statutory presumption assures the likelihood that plaintiff will succeed on the merits.

Consideration of the alternative ground for relief–sufficiently serious questions going to the merits and a balance of hardships tipping decidedly in plaintiff's favor–leads to the same result. Certification constitutes a complete discharge and release of *any* liability of the banks. By law, the defendants will suffer no harm from following only Ambassador Sosa's directions.

The legislative history of the statute further demonstrates the necessity of granting injunctive relief. The statute was adopted to enable State Department to provide recognized foreign governments with swift access to their funds and property that might otherwise be tied up in litigation by rivals claiming to represent the foreign government. As reported by the House Committee on Banking and Currency, litigation would provide an inadequate solution:

> The Federal Reserve banks hold large sums on deposit and large amounts of gold under earmark for foreign governments and foreign central banks. Some of these governments are at war, some of their countries have been invaded, and some of them are completely occupied by invaders. In such circumstances, disputes may arise as to who has authority to withdraw or otherwise deal with such deposits or such earmarked gold; and the Federal Reserve banks may find themselves confronted with situations in which they must either make payments or deliveries at their peril or refuse to make payments or deliveries until the disputes can be settled by litigation or otherwise. A resort to the latter alternative might make funds which friendly governments need for essential purposes unavailable until the termination of long drawn out litigation, and this might result in embarrassment to the relations of this Government with such foreign governments.[21]

**Notes and Comments 11.2.** The use of private litigation as a proxy for or parallel to economic sanctions is growing. For example, in May 1997 the President issued Ex. Order No. 13,047,[3] imposing limited sanctions against Myanmar (formerly Burma), among other things, a prohibition on new investment by U.S. persons in Myanmar that includes the economic development of resources located there. The alleged human rights abuses that prompted the executive order were also the basis for private suits federal district court brought against companies participating in projects in Myanmar. *John Doe I v. Unocal Corp.*, 963 F. Supp. 880 (C.D.Cal. 1997); *National Coalition Government of the Union of Burma v. Unocal, Inc.*, 176 F.R.D. 329 (C.D.Cal. 1997). It remains to be seen whether private litigation or the official sanctions will be more effective in isolating the repressive

---

20. Some of the accounts are in the name of Banco Nacional which we find to be a central bank as that term is used in § 632. . . .

21. H.R. Rep. No., 349, 77th Cong., 1st Sess. at 1 (1941). *See also* S. Rep. No. 133, 77th Cong., 1st Sess. at 1-2 (1941). . . .

3. 62 Fed. Reg. 28,301 (1997).

Myanmar regime.

**11.3**. Section 632, discussed in *Republic of Panama*, also confers jurisdiction on federal courts in cases that arise out of transactions involving international or foreign banking and as to which a corporation organized under the laws of the United States is a party. Does the section necessarily dictate judgment against the banking enterprise involved in such litigation? Consider the following case.

## Papadopoulos v. Chase Manhattan Bank, N.A.
791 F. Supp. 72 (S.D.N.Y. 1990)

Whitman Knapp, District Judge.

This action arises out of the dishonor of a draft made payable to plaintiff Philip Papadopoulos. Defendant National Westminster Bank, PLC ("NatWest") moves for dismissal . . . for want of subject matter jurisdiction. Defendant Chase Manhattan Bank, N.A. . . . moves for summary judgment on plaintiff's claims against it. For reasons which follow, we grant the motions and dismiss the action. . . .

The pertinent facts are not in dispute. In December of 1987, the National Bank of Greece agreed to sell to plaintiff a cruise ship, the M/V Castallea, for $7.5 million, but required that plaintiff provide by January 15, 1988 a bank guarantee in the amount of $750,000. At the time, plaintiff had approximately $600,000 available in his account at NatWest's Athens branch. To obtain the balance necessary for the guarantee, plaintiff instructed Seeadler Seetpirostol GmbH . . . , a travel company with which plaintiff had an ongoing business relationship, and its subsidiary, Weaver Maritime Inc. . . . , to forward $150,000 owed to him personally. A representative of Seeadler and Weaver remitted the sum to Volksbank Zuffenhausen EG . . . , a bank located in Stuttgart, Germany, and instructed Volksbank to issue a draft payable to plaintiff. In compliance with this instruction, Volksbank, with appropriate authorization, issued a draft drawn on the New York account at Chase of Genozentralbank Stuttgart-Genossenschafliche Zentralbank AG ("GZB"), another Stuttgart-based bank. The draft was personally delivered to plaintiff, who, on December 21, 1987, deposited the draft in his account at NatWest's Athens branch.

NatWest then sent the draft to Bankers Trust Company . . . , which on December 23 presented it to Chase for payment. On the following day, Chase–pursuant to an agreement with its customer, GZB–dishonored the draft and promptly returned it to Bankers Trust. The agreement, which had been entered into in 1985 to protect against payment of fraudulent drafts, required that Chase dishonor and return upon presentment any draft in excess of $25,000 for which it had not first received a telex from GZB authorizing it to make that specific payment. Chase had received no such pre-presentment authorization, and, on December 28, sent to GZB a telex explaining why the draft had been returned unpaid.

Thereafter, several telexes were sent among the defendant banks. On December 29, Bankers Trust sent a telex to NatWest erroneously stating that the draft had been returned unpaid for insufficient funds. On January 4, NatWest sent "top urgent" telexes to Bankers Trust and Chase asking that the two banks investigate. On the same day, GZB authorized Chase to pay the draft, which, of course, Chase no longer had.

On January 15, the date by which plaintiff was required to provide the guarantee, NatWest-Athens mailed the draft back to plaintiff. The draft never was re-presented to Chase for payment and plaintiff lost his option to purchase the ship.

In 1989, plaintiff commenced this action against Volksbank, GZB, NatWest, Bankers Trust and Chase, seeking to recover $6 million for economic injury allegedly suffered as a result of the nonpayment of the draft. Both Chase and NatWest asserted cross-claims for contribution and indemnification against each other as well as against the other defendant banks. Volksbank and GZB then moved to dismiss for, inter alia, lack of personal jurisdiction and forum non conveniens. . . .

Plaintiff concedes that 12 U.S.C. § 632 provides the only possible basis for our assertion of jurisdiction over this action. In substance, the relevant provision of § 632 provides federal district courts with jurisdiction over actions (1) which arise out of transactions involving international or foreign banking, and (2) to which a corporation organized under the laws of the United States is a party. Plaintiff contends that § 632 jurisdiction exists because the action arises out of an international banking transaction, and because Chase, a federally-chartered national banking association, is a defendant potentially liable to him. Defendant NatWest contends that plaintiff's claims against Chase are without legal basis, and that Chase is therefore a party in name only. Consequently, NatWest asserts, § 632 jurisdiction does not lie.

Thus, the existence of subject matter jurisdiction turns on the viability of plaintiff's claims against Chase, which, of course, is also the focus of Chase's motion for summary judgment. Plaintiff concedes that Articles 3 and 4 of the Uniform Commercial Code afford him as payee no cause of action against Chase, the payor bank.[3] Plaintiff relies instead on "window" provisions of the Code, which in substance provide that the absence of a Code remedy does not foreclose recovery at common law.[4]

Plaintiff, however, recognizes that he cannot defeat Chase's summary judgment motion merely by demonstrating that the Uniform Commercial Code does not preempt his claims against Chase. He . . . asks us to infer that Chase had some common law obligation to him. . . .

In brief, in none of the cases cited was the court called upon to decide or even to consider whether a payor bank could be held liable to a payee at common law for returning a draft unpaid pursuant to its agreement with its customer. We accordingly grant Chase's motion for summary judgment. Since this decision renders 12 U.S.C. § 632 an inadequate basis for our assertion of jurisdiction, we grant NatWest's motion to dismiss the complaint for lack of subject matter jurisdiction. . . .

# 2. Statutory Authority for Economic Sanctions

**Notes and Comments 11.4.** Would it have made any difference to the court's analysis in *Republic of Panama* if the U.S. Government had prohibited all transactions involving property in which the Government of Panama had any interest, instead of certify-

---

3. Under the Code, a payor bank is not liable to a payee on a negotiable instrument until it has accepted the instrument. § 3-409(1). It is undisputed that Chase never accepted the draft and, accordingly, may not be held liable under § 3-409 for payment of it. Nor may plaintiff, who is not a customer of Chase, avail himself of § 4-402. Under that section, a payor bank is liable to its customer for the consequences of a wrongful dishonor.

4. Specifically, plaintiff cites § 1-103, which provides generally that the principles of law and equity, unless displaced by the Code, supplement its provisions; and § 3-409, which, although it absolves a drawee who has not accepted an instrument of liability on that instrument, provides that "[n]othing in this section shall affect any liability in contract, tort or otherwise arising from any letter of credit or other obligation or representation which is not an acceptance."

ing under section 632, and then the Treasury Department had licensed the DelValle regime to engage in transactions with respect to the affected accounts? Could the U.S. Government have taken such action under the statutory authorities excerpted below?

## Trading With the Enemy Act
§ 5(b), 50 U.S.C. app. § 5(b)

(1) During the time of war, the President may, through any agency that he may designate, and under such rules and regulations as he may prescribe, by means of instructions, licenses, or otherwise–

(A) investigate, regulate, or prohibit, any transactions in foreign exchange, transfers of credit or payments between, by, through, or to any banking institution, and the importing, exporting, hoarding, melting, or earmarking of gold or silver coin or bullion, currency or securities, and

(B) investigate, regulate, direct and compel, nullify, void, prevent or prohibit, any acquisition holding, withholding, use, transfer, withdrawal, transportation, importation or exportation of, or dealing in, or exercising any right, power, or privilege with respect to, or transactions involving, any property in which any foreign country or a national thereof has any interest,

by any person, or with respect to any property, subject to the jurisdiction of the United States; and any property or interest of any foreign country or national thereof shall vest, when, as, and upon the terms, directed by the President, in such agency or person as may be designated from time to time by the President, and upon such terms and conditions as the President may prescribe such interest or property shall be held, used, administered, liquidated, sold, or otherwise dealt with in the interest of and for the benefit of the United States, and such designated agency or person may perform any and all acts incident to the accomplishment or furtherance of these purposes; and the President shall, in the manner hereinabove provided, require any person to keep a full record of, and to furnish under oath, in the form of reports or otherwise, complete information relative to any act or transaction referred to in this subdivision either before, during, or after the completion thereof, or relative to any interest in foreign property, or relative to any property in which any foreign country or any national thereof has or has had any interest, or as may be otherwise necessary to enforce the provisions of this subdivision, and in any case in which a report could be required, the President may, in the manner hereinabove provided, require the production, or if necessary to the national security or defense, the seizure, of any books of account, records, contracts, letters, memoranda, or other papers, in the custody or control of such person.

(2) Any payment, conveyance, transfer, assignment, or delivery of property or interest therein, made to or for the account of the United States, or as otherwise directed, pursuant to this subdivision or any rule, regulation, instruction, or direction issued hereunder shall to the extent thereof be a full acquittance and discharge for all purposes of the obligation of the person making the same; and no person shall be held liable in any court for or in respect to anything done or omitted in good faith in connection with the administration of, or in pursuance of and in reliance on, this subdivision, or any rule, regulation, instruction, or direction issued hereunder.

(3) As used in this subdivision the term "United States" means the United States and any place subject to the jurisdiction thereof: Provided, however, That the foregoing shall not be construed as a limitation upon the power of the President, which is hereby conferred to prescribe from time to time, definitions, not inconsistent with the purposes of this

subdivision, for any or all of the terms used in this subdivision. As used in this subdivision the term "person" means an individual, partnership, association, or corporation.

(4) The authority granted to the President by this section does not include the authority to regulate or prohibit, directly or indirectly, the importation from any country, or the exportation to any country, whether commercial or otherwise, regardless of format or medium of transmission, of any information or informational materials, including but not limited to, publications, films, posters, phonograph records, photographs, microfilms, microfiche, tapes, compact disks, CD ROMs, artworks, and news wire feeds. . . .

# United Nations Participation Act
§ 5, 22 U.S.C. § 287c

§ 287c. Economic and communication sanctions pursuant to United Nations
        Security Council Resolution
(a) Enforcement measures . . .

Notwithstanding the provisions of any other law, whenever the United States is called upon by the Security Council to apply measures which said Council has decided, pursuant to article 41 of said Charter, are to be employed to give effect to its decisions under said Charter, the President may, to the extent necessary to apply such measures, through any agency which he may designate, and under such orders, rules, and regulations as may be prescribed by him, investigate, regulate, or prohibit, in whole or in part, economic relations or rail, sea, air, postal, telegraphic, radio, and other means of communication between any foreign country or any national thereof or any person therein and the United States or any person subject to the jurisdiction thereof, or involving any property subject to the jurisdiction of the United States. . . .

# International Emergency Economic Powers Act
50 U.S.C. §§ 1701-1705

§ 1701. Unusual and extraordinary threat; declaration of national emergency;
        exercise of Presidential authorities
(a) Any authority granted to the President by section 1702 may be exercised to deal with any unusual and extraordinary threat, which has its source in whole or substantial part outside the United States, to the national security, foreign policy, or economy of the United States, if the President declares a national emergency with respect to such treat.

(b) The authorities granted to the President by section 203 may only be exercised to deal with an unusual and extraordinary threat with respect to which a national emergency has been declared for purposes of this title and may not be exercised for any other purpose. Any exercise of such authorities to deal with any new threat shall be based on a new declaration of national emergency which must be with respect to such threat.

§ 1702. Presidential authorities
(a)(1) At the times and to the extent specified in section 1701 of this title, the President may, under such regulations as he may prescribe, by means of instructions, licenses, or otherwise–
(A) investigate, regulate, or prohibit–
(i) any transactions in foreign exchange,
(ii) transfers of credit or payments between, by, through, or to any banking institu-

tion, to the extent that such transfers or payments involve any interest of any foreign country or a national thereof,

(iii) the importing or exporting of currency or securities; and

(B) investigate, regulate, direct and compel, nullify, void, prevent or prohibit, any acquisition, holding, withholding, use, transfer, withdrawal, transportation, importation or exportation of, or dealing in, or exercising any right, power, or privilege with respect to, or transactions involving, any property in which any foreign country or a national thereof has any interest;

by any person, or with respect to any property, subject to the jurisdiction of the United States.

(2) In exercising the authorities granted by paragraph (1), the President may require any person to keep a full record of, and to furnish under oath, in the form of reports or otherwise, complete information relative to any act or transaction referred to in paragraph (1) either before, during, or after the completion thereof, or relative to any interest in foreign property, or relative to any property in which any foreign country or any national thereof has or has had any interest, or as may be otherwise necessary to enforce the provisions of such paragraph. In any case in which a report by a person could be required under this paragraph, the President may require the production of any books of account, records, contracts, letters, memoranda, or other papers, in the custody or control of such person.

(3) Compliance with any regulation, instruction, or direction issued under this chapter shall to the extent thereof be a full acquittance and discharge for all purposes of the obligation of the person making the same. No person shall be held liable in any court for or with respect to anything done or omitted in good faith in connection with the administration of, or pursuant to and in reliance on, this chapter, or any regulation, instruction, or direction issued under this chapter.

(b) The authority granted to the President by this section does not include the authority to regulate or prohibit, directly or indirectly–

(1) any postal, telegraphic, telephonic, or other personal communication, which does not involve a transfer of anything of value;

(2) donations, by persons subject to the jurisdiction of the United States, of articles, such as food, clothing, and medicine, intended to be used to relieve human suffering, except to the extent that the President determines that such donations (A) would seriously impair his ability to deal with any national emergency declared under section 1701 of this title, (B) are in response to coercion against the proposed recipient or donor, or (C) would endanger Armed Forces of the United States which are engaged in hostilities or are in a situation where imminent involvement in hostilities is clearly indicated by the circumstances; or

(3) the importation from any country, or the exportation to any country, whether commercial or otherwise, regardless of format or medium of transmission, of any information or informational materials, including but not limited to, publications, films, posters, phonograph records, photographs, microfilms, microfiche, tapes, compact disks, CD ROMs, artworks, and news wire feeds. . . . ;

(4) any transactions ordinarily incident to travel to or from any country, including importation of accompanied baggage for personal use, maintenance within any country including payment of living expenses and acquisition of goods or services for personal use, and arrangement or facilitation of such travel including nonscheduled air, sea, or land voyages.

§ 1703. Consultation and reports

(a) The President, in every possible instance, shall consult with the Congress before exercising any of the authorities granted by this title and shall consult regularly with the Congress so long as such authorities are exercised.

(b) Whenever the President exercises any of the authorities granted by this title, he shall immediately transmit to the Congress a report specifying–

(1) the circumstances which necessitate such exercise of authority;

(2) why the President believes those circumstances constitute an unusual and extraordinary threat, which has its source in whole or substantial part outside the United States, to the national security, foreign policy, or economy of the United States;

(3) the authorities to be exercised and the actions to be taken in the exercise of those authorities to deal with those circumstances;

(4) why the President believes such actions are necessary to deal with those circumstances; and

(5) any foreign countries with respect to which such actions are to be taken and why such actions are to be taken with respect to those countries.

(c) At least once during each succeeding six-month period after transmitting a report pursuant to subsection (b) with respect to an exercise of authorities under this title, the President shall report to the Congress with respect to the actions taken, since the last such report, in the exercise of such authorities, and with respect to any changes which have occurred concerning any information previously furnished pursuant to paragraphs (1) through (5) of subsection (b). . . .

§ 1705. Penalties

(a) A civil penalty of not to exceed $10,000 may be imposed on any person who violates, or attempts to violate, any license, order, or regulation issued under this chapter.

(b) Whoever willfully violates, or willfully attempts to violate, any license, order, or regulation issued under this chapter shall, upon conviction, be fined not more than $50,000, or, if a natural person, may be imprisoned for not more than ten years, or both; and any officer, director, or agent of any corporation who knowingly participates in such violation may be punished by a like fine, imprisonment, or both.

**Notes and Comments 11.5.** Why are there three separate U.S. statutes dealing with economic sanctions?[4] To what extent are they similar? To what extent to do they differ from one another?

# 3. Effects of Economic Sanctions on International Banking

**Notes and Comments 11.6.** Only section 5(b) of the Trading With the Enemy Act is cross-codified in the federal banking laws. *See* 12 U.S.C. § 95a (providing title 12 codifi-

---

4. Actually, there are approximately 279 statutory provisions in the U.S. Code that provide active authority of one sort or another for emergency powers, or that are triggered by the declaration of a national emergency. *See generally* MALLOY, *supra* note 1, at 145-224 (discussing U.S. statutory sources of economic sanctions authority). However, the three statutes excerpted above are the only ones that grant general authority for economic sanctions programs.

cation for 50 U.S.C. app. § 5(b)). Nevertheless, economic sanctions programs arising under each of the three U.S. economic sanctions statutes have significant effects on international banking. Reviewing the provisions of these statutes excerpted above, why would that be the case? Consider also the following excerpt.

## Michael P. Malloy, Principles of Bank Regulation
§§ 9.27, 9.29 (2d ed. 2003)

The imposition of international economic sanctions is a traditional, if specialized, technique of foreign affairs, particularly in U.S. practice.[1] Depending upon the form of the sanction, the interests of banks involved in international banking activities may be significantly affected.[2] Given the extensive nature of some of the economic sanctions programs administered by the U.S. Department of the Treasury ("Treasury") in particular,[3] the precise effect on those interests may manifest itself in unexpected ways. . . .

The statutory authorities . . . support a range of sanctions programs that affect banks involved in international banking activities. [The following are] the pertinent provisions of some of the major programs affecting banks.

a. *The Foreign Assets Control Regulations* (*"FACRs"*). The FACRs currently impose a wide range of commercial and financial restrictions on transactions involving property in which North Korea or any national thereof has had any interest since the effective date of the regulations with respect to that country (December 17, 1950).[1] Among other things, the FACRs prohibit all of the following transactions (unless otherwise licensed): (1) transfers[2] of credit and all payments between, by, through, or to any banking

---

1. *See, e.g.*, Michael P. Malloy, *Remarks* in *Are the U.S. Treasury's Assets Control Regulations a Fair and Effective Tool of U.S. Foreign Policy? The Case of Cuba,* 1985 Proc. Am. Soc. Int'l L. 169, 188 (varied policy purposes of economic sanctions).

2. For example, in the U.S. "blocking" of assets of the Government of Iran in 1979, it is estimated that approximately $12 billion worth of assets were immobilized (*see* Michael P. Malloy, *The Iran Crisis: Law Under Pressure,* 1984 Wisc. Int'l. L.J. 15, 34), of which some $2.2 billion represented U.S. domestic bank branch deposits, and some $5.5 billion represented deposits and interest in foreign-situs branches of U.S. banks. *Id.* at 85-88. The aftermath of the Iran crisis generated over 400 claims by banks before the Iran-United States Claims Tribunal. *See id.* at 91 & n.453.

3. *See, e.g.*, 31 C.F.R. pt. 500 (1987) (Foreign Assets Control Regulations: commercial and financial prohibitions [against North Korea and its nationals]); 31 C.F.R. pt. 515 (1987) (Cuban Assets Control Regulations: similar prohibitions applied to Cuba); 31 C.F.R. pt. 550 (1987) (Libyan Sanctions Regulations: commercial and financial prohibitions applied to Libya); . . . 31 C.F.R. pt. 560 (Iranian Transactions Regulations: limited trade restrictions applied to Iran).

1. 31 C.F.R. § 500.201.

2. The term "transfer" is defined in 31 C.F.R. § 500.310 as:

> any actual or purported act or transaction, whether or not evidenced by writing, and whether or not done or performed within the United States, the purpose, intent, or effect of which is to create, surrender, release, transfer, or alter, directly or indirectly, any right, remedy, power, privilege, or interest with respect to any property . . . .

institution[3] or institutions, wherever located with respect to any property[4] subject to the jurisdiction of the United States[5] or by any person[6] subject to the jurisdiction of the United States;[7] (2) transactions[8] in foreign exchange by any person within the United States; and,

---

3. The term "banking institution" is defined for purposes of these regulations as:

> any person engaged primarily or incidentally in the business of banking, of granting or transferring credits, or of purchasing or selling foreign exchange or procuring purchasers and sellers thereof, as principal or agent, or any person holding credits for others as a direct or incidental part of his business, or any broker; and, each principal, agent, home office, branch or correspondent of any person so engaged shall be regarded as a separate "banking institution."

31 C.F.R. § 500.314.

4. The term "property" (as well as the term "property interest(s)") is defined to include "any . . . property, real, personal, or mixed, tangible or intangible, or interest or interests therein, present, future, or contingent." *Id.* § 500.311.

5. On the meaning of the term "property subject to the jurisdiction of the United States," for these purposes, the regulations contain a provision, ostensibly definitional but actually interpretive, that provides:

> The phrase "property subject to the jurisdiction of the United States" includes, without limitation, securities, whether registered or bearer, issued by:
> (1) The United States or any State, district, territory, possession, county, munici-pality, or any other subdivision or agency or instrumentality of any thereof; or
> (2) Any person within the United States whether the certificate which evidences such property or interest is physically located within or outside the United States.

31 C.F.R. § 500.313(a)(1)-(2). *Cf. id.* § 500.405 (exportation of securities to blocked foreign countries prohibited by § 500.201). Thus, the FACRs contemplate the broadest possible extraterritorial reach whenever securities of any U.S.-situs or government issuer are involved. Aside from the sweeping extraterritorial effects of this "definition," it appears that the term "property subject to the jurisdiction of the Untied States" is meant to have a territorial meaning, *i.e.,* the term includes any property "physically located within the United States." *Id.* § 500.313(b). For these purposes, the term "United States" is defined to mean the political "United States and all areas under the jurisdiction or authority thereof, including U.S. trust territories and commonwealths." *Id.* § 500.321 (1987).

6. The term "person" is defined for these purposes to mean "an individual, partnership, association, corporation, or other organization." *Id.* § 500.308. For purposes of the particular prohibition under discussion, the term expressly includes any "banking institution." *Id.* § 500.201(a)(1).

7. The term "person subject to the jurisdiction of the United States" is defined for these purposes to include:

> (a) Any individual, wherever located, who is a citizen of the United States;
> (b) Any person within the United States . . . ;
> (c) Any corporation organized under the laws of the United States or of any state, territory, possession, or district of the United States; and
> (d) Any corporation, partnership, or association, wherever organized or doing business, that is owned or controlled by persons specified in paragraphs (a) or (c). . . .

*Id.* § 500.329(a)-(d). In turn, the term "person within the United states," used in § 500.329(b), is defined to include:

> (1) Any person, wheresoever located, who is a resident of the United States;

(3) exportation or withdrawal from the United Stated of gold or silver coin or bullion, currency or securities, or the earmarking of any such property, by any person within the United States.[9]

These prohibitions are triggered under the FACRs on either of the following two conditions: (1) the transaction in question is effected by or on behalf of, or pursuant to the instructions of North Korea or [a] national thereof;[10] or, (2) the transaction involves property in which any target foreign country or national thereof has had, at any time on or since the "effective date" of the prohibition, any direct or indirect interest.[11]

The central provision in the FACRs is paragraph (b) of section 500.201 of the regulations, which states:

> All of the following transactions are prohibited, ... if such transactions

---

(2) Any person actually within the United States;

(3) Any corporation organized under the laws of the United States, or of any state, territory, possession, or district of the United States; and

(4) Any partnership, association, corporation, or other organization, wheresoever organized or doing business, which is owned or controlled by any person or persons specified in paragraphs ... (1), (2), or (3). . . .

*Id.* § 500.330(a)(1)-(4).

8. The regulations do not contain a formal definition of the term "transaction." However, as with the term "property subject to the jurisdiction of the United States," the regulations do contain a provision ostensibly definitional but actually interpretive, that bears on the meaning of the term. *See id.* § 500.309 ("transactions involving property in which target country or national thereof has an interest," interpreted to include *payment or transfer* to such country or national; *export or withdrawal* from the United States to such country; or *transfer or payment denominated in currency of such country*). Transactions between principal and agent, when one or the other is outside the United States, may be subject to the prohibitions to the same extent as if the two parties were unaffiliated with each other. *Id.* § 500.404.

9. *Id.* § 500.201(a)(1)-(3).

10. The concept of "national" for these purposes is rather broadly defined by the regulations, thereby catching within its meaning a wider category of persons that the term "national" would connote as a matter of customary international law. *See id.* § 500.302(a), which defines the term to include the following:

(1) A subject or citizen of a country or any person who is domiciled in or a permanent resident of that country at any time on or since the "effective date," except persons who were resident or domiciled there in the service of the U.S. government.

(2) Any partnership, association, corporation, or other organization, organized under the laws of, or which on or since the "effective date" had or has had its principal place of business in a foreign country, or which on or since such effective date was or has been controlled by, or a substantial part of the stock, shares, bonds, debentures, notes, drafts, or other securities or obligations of which, was or has been owned or controlled by, directly or indirectly, a foreign country and/or one or more nationals thereof as defined in this section.

(3) Any person to the extent that such is, or has been, since the "effective date" acting or purporting to act directly or indirectly for the benefit of any national of a foreign country.

(4) Any other person who there is reasonable cause to believe is a "national" as defined in this section.

11. *Id.* § 500.201(a). The term "interest" is defined to mean, "when used with respect to property . . . an interest of any nature whatsoever, direct or indirect." *Id.* § 500.312.

involve *property* in which any designated foreign country, or any national thereof, has at any time on or since the effective date of this section had any *interest* of any nature whatsoever, direct or indirect:

(1) All dealings in, including, without limitation, *transfers*, withdrawals, or exportations *of, any property* or evidences of indebtedness or evidences of ownership of property by any *person subject to the jurisdiction of the United States;* and

(2) All *transfers* outside the United States with regard to any *property or property interest subject to the jurisdiction of the United States.* [12]

It is clear that the major effect of the prohibitions of section 500.201(b) has been the blocking[13] of property, typically bank deposits and other bank-issued instruments and guarantees, subject to the jurisdiction of the United States.[14] "Blocking" of assets simply means that no transaction of any kind involving the affected assets can occur without a Treasury license.

Because of the expansive way in which they have been defined in the regulations, certain terms are essential to the sweeping application of section 500.201(b). Such terms as "transfer," "property," and "interest" have been interpreted by the courts to be broad enough to prohibit virtually any direct or indirect transaction involving anything of value when there exists even the most attenuated interest of a designated country or national thereof in the property.[15] . . .

The provisions of the FACRs also contain a particularly effective enforcement device with respect to banking transactions. On the effective date of the regulations with respect to any of the designated countries to which they have applied from time to time, all transactions, including those in progress, are prohibited unless otherwise licensed by Treasury. Any transfer after the effective date in violation of the regulations is "null and void and shall not be the basis for the assertion or recognition of any interest in or right, remedy, power or privilege with respect to" property blocked under the regulations.[18] The regulations

---

12. *Id.* § 500.201(b) (emphasis added).

13. The term "blocking" (or "freezing") of assets is not itself a term of art within the regulations, but refers metaphorically to the legal effect of the prohibitions of § 500.201 on property (or persons) affected thereby. *Cf. e.g., id.* § 500.319, defining "blocked account" to mean:

> an account in which any designated national has an interest, with respect to which account payments, transfers or withdrawals o[r] other dealings may not be made of effected except pursuant to an authorization or license authorizing such action. The term "blocked account" shall not be seemed to include accounts of unblocked nationals.

Blocked assets are generally required to be held in interest-bearing accounts. *See id.* § 500.205.

14. Blocking of liquid assets has historically been one of the major effects to the imposition of Treasury controls under section 5(b) of the TWEA. *See* U.S. DEPARTMENT OF THE TREASURY, 1970 CENSUS OF BLOCKED CHINESE ASSETS; U.S. DEPARTMENT OF THE TREASURY, CENSUS OF FOREIGN OWNED ASSETS IN THE UNITED STATES (1945).

15. *See., e.g.,* Behring Int'l Inc. v. Miller, 504 F. Supp. 552, 556-57 & n.8 (D.N.J. 1980).

18. 31 C.F.R. § 500.203(a). For purposes of section 500.203, the term "property" is defined to include:

> gold, silver, bullion, currency, coin, credit, securities (as that term is defined in section 2(1) of the Securities Act of 1933, as amended) . . ., bills of exchange, notes, drafts, acceptances, checks, letters of credit, book credits, debts, claims, contracts, negotiable documents of title,

also contain a presumption against the asserted validity of putative "pre-effective date" transfers when the fact of the asserted transfer cannot be corroborated by independent evidence. In this regard, § 500.203(b) states:

> No transfer before the "effective date" shall be the basis for the assertion or recognition of any right, remedy, power, or privilege with respect to, or interest in, any property in which a designated national has or has had an interest since the "effective date" unless the person with whom such property is held or maintained had written notice of the transfer or by any written evidence had recognized such transfer prior to such "effective date."[19]

Thus, if a North Korean national entered into a contract for services with a foreign subsidiary of a U.S. national, with payment by means of an irrevocable letter of credit issued by a foreign bank and confirmed by First Credulity, a U.S. domestic bank, a purported transfer to the U.S. national from First Credulity would constitute a transaction involving property (*i.e.* the letter of credit) in which a foreign national (*i.e.,* the account party) would have an interest.[20] Hence, once the FACRs became effective, any payment in accordance with the letter of credit would be null and void, and First Credulity would be required to establish a blocked account in the name of the North Korean national. It should be noted that the existence of ongoing contractual relationships and commitments would not be a basis in and of itself for Treasury licensing of any particular transfer or transaction after the effective date of the regulations.[21]

The FACRs do contain a limited safe harbor for unlicensed transactions or transfers rendered null and void by section 500.203. Transactions or transfers otherwise rendered null and void are not deemed so, only as to any person with whom the property in question had been held or maintained, when the person establishes the following: (1) that the transaction or transfer did not represent a willful violation by that person; (2) that the person "did not have reasonable cause to know or suspect, in view of all the facts and circumstances known or available to such person,"[22] that the transaction or transfer was in fact unlicensed and

---

mortgages, liens, annuities, insurance policies, options and futures in commodities, and evidences of any of the foregoing. The term "property" shall not, except to the extent indicated, be deemed to include chattels or real property.

*Id.* § 500.203(f). Essentially the same rule of invalidity applies to any unlicensed attachment, judgment, decree, lien, execution, garnishment, or other judicial process entered or effected with respect to property in which a blocked country or national thereof has any interest. *See id.* § 500.203(e). *Cf. id.* § 500.504 (providing limited license for judicial proceedings with respect to blocked property).

19. *Id.* § 500.302(b).

20. *See id.* § 500.406. Of course, transfer in the reverse direction (request or authorization from bank or other person within the United States to a person outside the United States to make payment or transfer to blocked person) would also be prohibited by section 500.201 *See id.* § 500.409.

21. *See id.* § 500.203(b).

22. *Id.* § 500.203(d)(2).

prohibited;[23] and, (3) that, promptly upon discovery of the pertinent facts,[24] the person filed with Treasury a report, in triplicate, setting forth the full circumstances with respect to the transaction or transfer.[25]

　　b. *The Cuban Assets Control Regulations (CACRs)*. The CACRs[26] track the same basic range of commercial and financial restrictions[27] on transfers or transactions involving property in which Cuba or any national thereof has had any interest since the effective date of the regulations.[28] For purposes of these prohibitions, the key terms transfer," "property," "interest," "property subject to the jurisdiction of the United States," "person," and "person subject to the jurisdiction of the United States," all carry the same meaning as they do in the FACRs, with the same results for the scope of the prohibitions.

　　One noticeable difference between the two sets of regulations is that the CACRs are now frozen in place under the Cuban Liberty and Democratic Solidarity Act ("CLDSA").[35] In addition, the CLDSA adds several additional sanctions with respect to Cuba that potentially affect banks involved in international banking activities.

　　Among other things, the CLDSA prohibits persons subject to U.S. jurisdiction from extending any financing to a foreign or U.S. national "for the purpose of financing transactions involving any property confiscated by the Cuban Government" from a U.S. national.[36] The act also authorizes U.S. nationals (including a former Cuban national who is now a U.S. national) whose property was confiscated by the Cuban Government to bring suit against any person "trafficking" in confiscated property.[37] For these purposes, "trafficking" includes (1) any transaction involving confiscated property;[38] (2) engaging in any

---

23. *Id.* If under the circumstances, a license or authorization was purported to have covered the transaction or transfer in question, it must be established that the person did not have reasonable cause to know or suspect "that such license or authorization had been obtained by misrepresentation or the withholding of material facts or was otherwise fraudulently obtained." *Id.*

24. For these purposes, the "pertinent facts" are:

> (i) Such transfer was in violation of the provisions of [31 C.F.R. ch. V] or any regulation, ruling, instruction, license or other direction or authorization thereunder, or
> (ii) Such transfer was not licensed or authorized by the Secretary of the Treasury, or
> (iii) If a license did purport to cover the transfer, such license had been obtained by misrepresentation or the withholding of material facts or was otherwise fraudulently obtained.

*Id.* § 500.203(d)(3)(i)-(iii).

25. *Id.* § 500.203(d)(1)-(3). Filing of the report pursuant to the third requirement does not in itself represent compliance or evidence of compliance with the first two requirements of the safe harbor. *Id.* § 500.203 (d)(3).

26. 31 C.F.R. Pt. 515.

27. *Id.* § 515.201.

28. The effective date of the CACRs is 12:01 a.m., e.s.t., on July 8, 1963. *Id.* § 515.201(d).

35. 22 U.S.C. § 6033(c).

36. *Id.* § 6034(a). This prohibition does not apply to financing by the owner of the property or the U.S. national claiming the property for certain permitted transactions. *Id.*

37. *Id.* § 6082(a).

38. *Id.* § 6023(10)(A)(i).

commercial activity using or benefiting from the property;[39] or, (3) participating in such trafficking by another person.[40]

For example, a foreign-based bank that financed the purchase of the current crop of a confiscated Cuban plantation formerly owned by a U.S. enterprise might find itself subject to suit in U.S. court for "trafficking" in confiscated property. Liability under this cause of action could equal the current fair market value of the property, plus reasonable cost and attorneys' fees.[41] However, liability could equal treble damages and cost and fees, if the defendant had prior notice of the U.S. national's claim to the confiscated property.[42] These liability provisions have been waived for successive six-month periods without exception to the present.[43]

Another major provision of the CLDSA requires the Secretary of State to exclude from the United States any alien whom the Secretary determines to have confiscated or to have trafficked in confiscated property.[44] In the previous example, this exclusion provision would extend to anyone who was a corporate officer, principal, or controlling shareholder of the foreign-based bank.[45] It would also include anyone who was the spouse, minor child or agent of an excludable person.[46] . . .

d. *The Iranian Sanctions.* The Iranian Transactions Regulations ("ITRs")[79] are entirely distinct from the earlier Iranian Assets Control Regulations ("IACRs"),[80] which were originally promulgated in response to the Iranian hostage crisis of 1979-1981.[81] The ITRs were promulgated pursuant to an Executive Order, issued under the authority of section 505 of the International Security and Development Cooperation Act of 1985,[82] which identified Iran as a state actively supporting terrorism as an instrument of state policy and imposed import restrictions in response.[83] . . .

. . . The only significant impact of the ITRs with respect to international banks lies in the ban on transactions *related to* prohibited importations. The ITRs provide that "[n]o person may . . . finance . . . or otherwise service, in whole or in part, any goods or services subject to the prohibitions of [the ITRs]."[85] A violation of the financing prohibition occurs only if the person providing financing acts "with knowledge or reason to know that a

---

39. *Id.* § 6023(10)(A)(ii).

40. *Id.* § 6023(10)(A)(iii).

41. *Id.* § 6082(a)(1)(A)(i)-(ii).

42. *Id.* § 6082(a)(3).

43. *See EU Foreign Ministers Push Ahead with Protesting U.S. Helms-Burton Law,* BNA Int'l Trade Daily, Oct. 2, 1996, at 3 (noting presidential waiver of liability provisions). It now appears likely that the President will extend the waiver for another six-month period, in light of recent EU statements with respect to Cuba's human rights-related policies. *See* Steven Lee Myers, *A European Call for Rights In Cuba Lets U.S. Off Hook,* N.Y. Times, Dec. 4, 1996, at A14, col. 3.

44. 22 U.S.C. § 6091(a)(1)-(2).

45. *Id.* § 6091(a)(3).

46. *Id.* § 6091(a)(4).

79. 52 Fed. Reg. 44,076-44,081 (1987) (codified at 31 C.F.R. pt. 560).

80. 31 C.F.R. pt. 535 (1987).

81. Exec. Order No. 12,12,170, 44 Fed. Reg. 65,729 1979.

82. Pub. L. No. 99-83, tit. V. § 505, 99 Stat. 221 (1985) (codified at 22 U.S.C. § 2349aa-9).

83. Exec. Order No. 12,12,613, 52 Fed. Reg. 41,940 (1987).

85. The effective date of the ITRs is 12:01 p.m. e.s.t., October 29, 1987. *Id.* § 560.202.

violation . . . has occurred, is about to occur, or is intended to occur with respect to such goods or services."[86] The ITRs do not contain the traditional "null and void" provision with respect to violations of the regulations, and so these regulations offer no specific "safe harbor" guidance in this regard. . . .

. . . As to Iran, [the Iran and Libya Sanctions Act of 1996 ("ILSA"), Pub. L. No. 104-172, 110 Stat. 1541 (1996) (codified at 50 U.S.C. § 1701 note] generally requires, on a prospective basis, that the president impose two or more ILSA-specified sanctions,[a] if he determines that the following circumstances exist, on or after the date of enactment of the act. A person, with actual knowledge, has made an investment of $40 million or more (in any combination of at least $10 million each, equalling or exceeding $40 million in any twelve months) that "directly and significantly" contributed to the enhancement of Iran's ability to develop petroleum resources of Iran.[97]

As with the Libyan sanctions, not all of the ILSA sanctions are pertinent to banks. The loan and credit prohibition can affect the international lending business of a U.S. bank. In addition, the U.S. Government debt prohibition and U.S. Government funds prohibition can affect any financial institution, wherever based. . . .

**Notes and Comments 11.7.** *The Nusquami Assets Control Regulations.* Nusquam has apparently been supporting an armed insurgency against the Government of Guatador, a neighboring state that is an ally of the United States. In response, the President of the United States has issued the following executive order:

> I hereby determine that the recent events in and around Guatador constitutes an unusual and extraordinary threat to the national security, foreign policy and economy of the United States. Accordingly, under the authority granted to me by the International Emergency Economic Powers Act . . . I hereby

---

86. *Id.* § 560.202.

a. The ILSA-specified sanctions include: (1) prohibition of loans or credits to any sanctioned person from any U.S. financial institutions in amounts over $10 million in any twelve-month period; (2) prohibition of a financial institution from being designated or continued as a primary dealer for U.S. Government debt instruments; prohibition of a financial institution from serving as a U.S. fiscal agent or as a repository for U.S. Government funds. For the complete list of sanctions, see ILSA § 6(4)(B).

97. ILSA, § 5(a). For these purposes, "investment" is defined to mean:

> any of the following activities if such activity is undertaken pursuant to an agreement, or pursuant to the exercise of rights under such an agreement, that is entered into with the Government of Iran or a nongovernmental entity in Iran, or with the Government of Libya or a nongovernmental entity in Libya, on or after the date of the enactment of [ILSA]:
> (A) The entry into a contract that includes responsibility for the development of petroleum resources located in Iran or Libya (as the case may be), or the entry into a contract providing for the general supervision and guarantee of another person's performance of such a contract.
> (B) The purchase of a share of ownership, including an equity interest, in that development.
> (C) The entry into a contract providing for the participation in royalties, earnings, or profits in that development, without regard to the form of the participation. The term "investment" does not include the entry into, performance, or financing of a contract to sell or purchase goods, services, or technology.

*Id.* § 14(9). . . .

declare a national emergency with respect to such threat, and order as follows:

§ 101. Any transaction involving any property in which the Government of Nusquam, any agency, instrumentality or controlled entity thereof, or any national thereof, has any interest is hereby prohibited if such transaction involves:

a. any person subject to the jurisdiction of the United States; or,

b. any property subject to the jurisdiction of the United States.

§ 102. Any transaction which is intended to, or has the effect of, evading the prohibitions imposed by section 101 of this order is hereby prohibited.

§ 201. The Secretary of the Treasury is hereby delegated all power granted to me under the International Emergency Economic Powers Act to carry out the purposes and terms of this order.

Pursuant to the authority under § 201 of the Executive Order, the Secretary of the Treasury delegated his authority to Treasury's Office of Foreign Assets Control. The Office has issued the Nusquami Assets Control Regulations (NACRs), which provide in part as follows:

## Office of Foreign Assets Control
### 31 CFR Part 599
### Nusquami Assets Control Regulations

. . .

§599.201 Transactions involving Nusquam and its nationals.

(a) All of the following transactions are prohibited, unless licensed under this part, if either such transactions are by, or on behalf of, or pursuant to the direction of Nusquam, or any national thereof, or such transactions involve property in which Nusquam, or any national thereof, has at any time on or since the effective date of this section had any interest of any nature whatsoever, direct or indirect:

(1) All transfers of credit and all payments between, by, through, or to any banking institution or banking institutions wheresoever located, with respect to any property subject to the jurisdiction of the United States or by any person (including a banking institution) subject to the jurisdiction of the United States; and

(2) All transactions in foreign exchange by any person within the United States.

(b) All of the following transactions are prohibited, unless licensed under this part, if such transactions involve property in which Nusquam, or any national thereof, has at any time on or since the effective date of this section had any interest of any nature whatsoever, direct or indirect:

(1) All dealings in, including, without limitation, transfers, withdrawals, or exportations of, any property or evidences of indebtedness or evidences of ownership of property by any person subject to the jurisdiction of the United States; and

(2) All transfers outside the United States with regard to any property or property interest subject to the jurisdiction of the United States.

(c) Any transaction for the purpose or which has the effect of evading or avoiding any of the prohibitions set forth in paragraph (a) or (b) is hereby prohibited.

(d) The terms "effective date" and "effective date of this section" mean 12:01 a.m. eastern standard time on [the date of promulgation of the NACRs].

§599.202 Effect of transfers violating the provisions of this part.

(a) Any transfer after the effective date, which is in violation of any provision of this part or of any regulation, ruling, instruction, license, or other direction or authorization hereunder and involves any property in which Nusquam or a designated national has or has had an interest since such date, is null and void and shall not be the basis for the assertion or recognition of any interest in or right, remedy, power or privilege with respect to such property.

(b) No transfer before the effective date shall be the basis for the assertion or recognition of any right, remedy, power, or privilege with respect to, or interest in, any property in which a designated national has an interest, or has had an interest since such date, unless the person with whom such property is held or maintained, prior to such date, had written notice of the transfer or by any written evidence had recognized such transfer.

(c) Unless otherwise provided, an appropriate license or other authorization issued by or pursuant to the direction or authorization of the Director of the Office of Foreign Assets Control before, during, or after a transfer shall validate such transfer or render it enforceable to the same extent that it would be valid or enforceable but for the provisions of the International Emergency Economic Powers Act, this part, and any ruling, order, regulation, direction, or instruction issued hereunder.

(d) Transfers of property which otherwise would be null and void or unenforceable by virtue of the provisions of this section shall not be deemed to be null and void or unenforceable as to any person with whom such property was held or maintained (and as to such person only) in cases in which such person is able to establish to the satisfaction of the Director of the Office of Foreign Assets Control each of the following:

(1) Such transfer did not represent a willful violation of the provisions of this part by the person with whom such property was held or maintained;

(2) The person with whom such property was held or maintained did not have reasonable cause to know or suspect, in view of all the facts and circumstances known or available to such person, that such transfer required a license or authorization by or pursuant to this part and was not so licensed or authorized, or if a license or authorization did purport to cover the transfer, that such license or authorization had been obtained by misrepresentation of a third party or the withholding of material facts or was otherwise fraudulently obtained; and

(3) Promptly upon discovery that:

(i) Such transfer was in violation of the provisions of this part or any regulation, ruling, instruction, license, or other direction or authorization hereunder, or

(ii) Such transfer was not licensed or authorized by the Director of the Office of Foreign Assets Control, or

(iii) If a license did purport to cover the transfer, such license had been obtained by misrepresentation of a third party or the withholding of material facts or was otherwise fraudulently obtained;

the person with whom such property was held or maintained filed with the Office of Foreign Assets Control a report setting forth in full the circumstances relating to such transfer. The filing of a report in accordance with the provisions of this paragraph shall not be deemed evidence that the terms of paragraphs (d) (1) and (2) of this section have been satisfied.

(e) Unless licensed or authorized pursuant to this part, any attachment, judgment, decree, lien, execution, garnishment, or other judicial process is null and void with respect to any property in which, on or since the effective date, there existed an interest of a designated national. . . .

§599.301 Blocked account; blocked property.

The terms "blocked account" and "blocked property" shall mean any account or property in which a designated national has an interest, and with respect to which payments, transfers, exportations, withdrawals, or other dealings may not be made or effected except pursuant to an authorization or license from OFAC authorizing such action.

§599.302  Designated national.

The term "designated national" shall mean Nusquam and any national thereof including any person who is a specially designated national.

§599.303  Interest.

Except as otherwise provided in this part, the term "interest" when used with respect to property (e.g., "an interest in property") means an interest of any nature whatsoever, direct or indirect. . . .

§599.306  Nusquam.

The term "Nusquam" includes:

(a) The state and the Government of Nusquam, as well as any political subdivision, agency, or instrumentality thereof, including the Central Bank of Nusquam;

(b) Any partnership, association, corporation, or other organization substantially owned or controlled by the foregoing;

(c) Any person to the extent that such person is, or has been, or to the extent that there is reasonable cause to believe that such person is, or has been, since the effective date, acting or purporting to act directly or indirectly on behalf of any of the foregoing;  and

(d) Any other person or organization determined by the Director of the Office of Foreign Assets Control to be included within this section. . . .

§599.308  Person.

The term "person" means an individual, partnership, association, corporation, or other organization.

§599.309  Person subject to the jurisdiction of the United States.

The term "person subject to the jurisdiction of the United States" means any United States citizen; permanent resident alien; juridical person organized under the laws of the United States or any jurisdiction within the United States, including foreign branches; any person in the United States; and any person, wheresoever located, that is owned or controlled by any of the foregoing. . . .

§599.315  Property;  property interest.

The terms "property" and "property interest" include, but are not limited to, money, checks, drafts, bullion, bank deposits, savings accounts, debts, indebtedness, obligations, notes, debentures, stocks, bonds, coupons, any other financial instruments, bankers acceptances, mortgages, pledges, liens or other rights in the nature of security, warehouse receipts, bills of lading, trust receipts, bills of sale, any other evidences of title, ownership or indebtedness, letters of credit and any documents relating to any rights or obligations thereunder, powers of attorney, goods, wares, merchandise, chattels, stocks on hand, ships, goods on ships, real estate mortgages, deeds of trust, vendors sales agreements, land contracts, leaseholds, ground rents, real estate and any other interest therein, options, negotiable instruments, trade acceptances, royalties, book accounts, accounts payable, judgments, patents, trademarks or copyrights, insurance policies, safe deposit boxes and their contents, annuities, pooling agreements, services of any nature whatsoever, contracts of any nature whatsoever, and any other property, real, personal, or mixed, tangible or intangible, or interest or interests therein, present, future or contingent. . . .

§599.317 Specially designated national.

The term "specially designated national" shall mean:

(a) Any person who is determined by the Secretary of the Treasury to be a specially designated national;

(b) Any person who on or since the effective date has acted for or on behalf of Nusquam; or

(c) Any partnership, association, corporation or other organization which on or since the effective date has been owned or controlled directly or indirectly by Nusquam or by any specially designated national. . . .

§599.319 Transfer.

The term "transfer" means any actual or purported act or transaction, whether or not evidenced by writing, and whether or not done or performed within the United States, the purpose, intent, or effect of which is to create, surrender, release, convey, transfer, or alter, directly or indirectly, any right, remedy, power, privilege, or interest with respect to any property and, without limitation upon the foregoing, shall include the making, execution, or delivery of any assignment, power, conveyance, check, declaration, deed, deed of trust, power of attorney, power of appointment, bill of sale, mortgage, receipt, agreement, contract, certificate, gift, sale, affidavit, or statement; the appointment of any agent, trustee, or fiduciary; the creation or transfer of any lien; the issuance, docketing, filing, or the levy of or under any judgment, decree, attachment, injunction, execution, or other judicial or administrative process or order, or the service of any garnishment; the acquisition of any interest of any nature whatsoever by reason of a judgment or decrease of any foreign country; the fulfillment of any condition; the exercise of any power of appointment, power of attorney, or other power; or the acquisition, disposition, transportation, importation, exportation, or withdrawal of any security. . . .

§599.503 Payments and transfers to blocked accounts in U.S. financial institutions.

(a) Any payment of funds or transfer of credit or other assets, including any payment or transfer by any U.S. person outside the United States, to a blocked account in a U.S. banking institution located in the United States in the name of a designated national is hereby authorized, including incidental foreign exchange transactions, provided that such payment or transfer shall not be made from any blocked account if such payment or transfer represents, directly or indirectly, a transfer of any interest of a designated national to any other country or person. . . .

(c) This section does not authorize any transfer from a blocked account within the United States to an account held outside the United States. . . .

§599.506 Payment by designated nationals of obligations to persons within the United States authorized.

(a) The transfer of funds after the effective date by, through, or to any U.S. banking institution or other person subject to the jurisdiction of the United States solely for the purpose of payment of obligations of a designated national to persons or accounts within the United States is authorized, provided that the obligation arose prior to the effective date, and the payment requires no debit to a blocked account. Property is not blocked by virtue of being transferred or received pursuant to this section.

(b) A person receiving payment under this section may distribute all or part of that payment to any person, provided that any such payment to a designated national must be to a blocked account in a U.S. banking institution. . . .

§599.801 Procedures.

(a) General Licenses. General licenses have been issued authorizing under appropriate terms and conditions certain types of transactions which are subject to the prohibitions contained in Subpart B of this part. All such licenses in effect on the date of publication are set forth in subpart E of this part. It is the policy of the Office of Foreign Assets Control not to grant applications for specific licenses authorizing transactions to which the provisions of an outstanding general license are applicable. Persons availing themselves of certain general licenses may be required to file reports and statements in accordance with the instructions specified in those licenses. Failure to file such reports or statements will nullify the authority of the general license.

(b) Specific licenses -- (1) General course of procedure. Transactions subject to the prohibitions contained in subpart B of this part which are not authorized by general license may be effected only under specific licenses.

(2) Applications for specific licenses. Applications for specific licenses to engage in any transactions prohibited by or pursuant to this part may be filed by letter with the Office of Foreign Assets Control. Any person having an interest in a transaction or proposed transaction may file an application for a license authorizing such transaction, but the applicant for a specific license is required to make full disclosure of all parties in interest to the transaction so that a decision on the application may be made with full knowledge of all relevant facts and so that the identity and location of the persons who know about the transaction may be easily ascertained in the event of inquiry.

(3) Information to be supplied. The applicant must supply all information specified by relevant instructions and/or forms, and must fully disclose the names of all the parties who are concerned with or interested in the proposed transaction. If the application is filed by an agent, the agent must disclose the name of his principal(s). Such documents as may be relevant shall be attached to each application as a part of such application except that documents previously filed with the Office of Foreign Assets Control may, where appropriate, be incorporated by reference. Applicants may be required to furnish such further information as is deemed necessary to a proper determination by the Office of Foreign Assets Control. Any applicant or other party in interest desiring to present additional information or discuss or argue the application may do so at any time before or after decision. Arrangements for oral presentation shall be made with the Office of Foreign Assets Control.

(4) Effect of denial. The denial of a license does not preclude the reopening of an application or the filing of a further application. The applicant or any other party in interest may at any time request explanation of the reasons for a denial by correspondence or personal interview.

(5) Reports under specific licenses. As a condition for the issuance of any license, the licensee may be required to file reports with respect to the transaction covered by the license, in such form and at such times and places as may be prescribed in the license or otherwise.

(6) Issuance of license. Licenses will be issued by the Office of Foreign Assets Control acting on behalf of the Secretary of the Treasury or licenses may be issued by the Secretary of the Treasury acting directly or through any specifically designated person, agency, or instrumentality. . . .

§599.802 Decisions.

The Office of Foreign Assets Control will advise each applicant of the decision respecting filed applications. The decision of the Office of Foreign Assets Control acting on behalf of the Secretary of the Treasury with respect to an application shall constitute final agency action. . . .

In light of these developments, Quarter National Bank (QNB) has approached you with the following problems:

> **a.** What is the status of QNB's Nusquami branch? May QNB continue to deal with the branch on a day-to-day basis?
>
> **b.** What about the consortium loan, mentioned in **7.6** *supra*, in which QNB is a participant? May it continue to receive its *pro rata* share of principal and interest payments from the lead bank?
>
> **c.** Pursuant to the terms of the consortium loan agreement, Nusquam has requested a further draw on the credits available under the loan. Part of this draw will be funded by QNB's Nusquami branch. Will this raise problems under the regulations?
>
> **d.** If Nusquam requests a rescheduling of its payments under the syndicated loan, and this requires consensus among the syndicate participants, may QNB give its consent?
>
> **e.** What if QNB's London branch holds an account, denominated in US dollars, for a Nusquami citizen, resident in the UK? May the London branch honor the depositor's demand for a withdrawal from the account? What if the account is denominated in British pounds? What if it were QNB's British subsidiary, not a branch, which held the account?
>
> **f.** May QNB extend financing to a British company to fund its export agreement with a Nusquami importer?

**11.8.** Reconsidering Note 11.7.e, *supra*, what would be the likely result if the Nusquami depositor of QNB's London branch brought suit under British banking law for the release of the deposit? Consider the following case.

## Libyan Arab Foreign Bank v. Bankers Trust Company
[1988] 1 Lloyd's L. Rep. 259

Mr. Justice Staughton:
. . . In January 1986 the Libyan Bank had an account with Bankers Trust London, denominated in United States dollars. That was a call account, which meant that no cheque book was provided, interest was payable on the balance standing to the credit of the account at rates which varied from time to time, and some minimal period of notice might be required before instructions relating to the account had to be complied with. The suggestion in this case is that instructions would have to be given before noon if they were to be carried out that day. In England I think be described as a species of deposit account. The amount standing to the credit of that account at the close of business on 8th January 1986 was $131,506,389.93. . . .

The Libyan Bank also had an account with Bankers Trust New York, again denominated in United States dollars. This was a demand account. No interest was paid on the balance, and no significant period of notice was required before instructions had to be complied with. But there was not, so far as I am aware, a cheque book. In England it would have been a current account. The amount standing to the credit of that account at the close of business on 8th January 1986 was $251,129,084.53.

Relations between Libya and the United States in January 1986 were not good. At 8.06 p.m. New York time on 7th January the President of the United States of American issued an executive order, which had the force of law with immediate effect. It provided, so far as material, as follows:

> Section 1. The following are prohibited, except to the extent provided in regulations with may hereafter be issued pursuant to this Order: . . .
> (f) The grant of extension of credits or loans by any United States person to the Government of Libya, its instrumentalities and controlled entities".

That order did not in itself have any great effect on the events with which this case is concerned. But there followed it at 4.10 p.m. New York time on 8th January a second order, reading as follows:

> I, RONALD REAGAN, President of the United States, hereby order blocked all property and interests in property of the Government of Libya, its agencies, instrumentalities and controlled entities and the Central Bank of Libya that are in the United States that hereafter come within the United States or that are or hereafter come within the possession or control of U.S. persons including overseas branches of U.S. persons.
> The Secretary of the Treasury, in consultation with the Secretary of State, is authorized to employ all powers granted to me by the International Emergency Economic Powers Act 50 U.S.C. 1701 *et seq.* to carry out the provisions of this Order.
> This Order is effective immediately and shall be transmitted to the Congress and published in the Federal Register.

It is not in dispute that Bankers Trust are a U.S. person; or that Bankers Trust London are an overseas branch of a U.S. person; or that the Libyan Bank are an agency, instrumentality or controlled entity of the Government of Libya. Consequently by the law of and prevailing in the State of New York (which I shall refer to as New York law for the sake of brevity) it was illegal at and after 4.10 p.m. on 8th January 1986 for Bankers Trust to make any payment or transfer of funds to or to the order of the Libyan Bank in New York, either by way of debit to the Libyan Bank's account or as the grant of credit or a loan. Similarly it was illegal, by the law of New York or of any other American state, for Bankers Trust to make any such payment or transfer of funds in London or anywhere else.

. . . [N]othing in English domestic law prohibited such a transaction. So the main issues in this case are concerned with the rules of Conflict of Laws, which determine when and to what extent the law of New York is given effect in our courts, and with the contractual obligations of banks. In a word, Bankers Trust say that they cannot, or at any rate are not obliged to, transfer a sum as large as $100m. or more without using the payment machinery that is available in New York; consequently they have a defence to the Libyan Bank's claim, because performance of this contract would have required them to commit an illegal act in New York. Alternatively they say that their contract with the Libyan Bank is governed by the law of New York, so that performance is for the time being illegal by the proper law of the contract. . . .

[The history of the banking relationship at issue] can be considered in three stages. The *first stage* was from 1972 to 15th December 1980.

The Libyan Bank came into existence in June 1972. A correspondent relationship was established between the Libyan Bank and Bankers Trust. Initially an account was opened for that purposes with the Paris branch of Bankers Trust. But in April 1973 that account was closed, and an account opened with the London branch. . . . In this period the Libyan Bank did not wish to have any account with Bankers Trust New York. Transfers for the credit of the Libyan Bank used regularly to arrive at Bankers Trust New York, in accordance with the system most often used for transferring large dollar amounts. . . . But they were dealt with by an instruction from Bankers Trust New York to Bankers Trust London to credit the account of the Libyan Bank there. Indeed the Libyan Bank insisted on that from time to time. . . .

. . . In fact Bankers Trust New York had operated an account in New York, for the handling of transactions by the Libyan Bank. But that account was closed on 17th December 1973 in consequence of . . . protests by the Libyan Bank.

There followed a long period of discussion and negotiation. Bankers Trust were dissatisfied because the London . . . account was used as a current account. Large numbers of transactions occurred on it, but interest was paid on the balance. This was not thought to be profitable for Bankers Trust. Furthermore, transfers to or from the account would commonly be made through New York, with a risk of delay and the possibility of error. [The two banks eventually negotiated a new account relationship under which a current account was maintained in New York and a call account in London. The current account was to be used for daily dollar-clearing activity; the call account was to be considered as an investment of liquid funds.

[Each morning, the demand account was to be reviewed, and the balance "managed," so that it did not exceed or fall below a predetermined target or "peg" balance, eventually agreed to be $500,000. Excess funds, in multiples of $100,000, would be credited to the call account, or the current account would be funded from the call account, as the case may be.]

It was, as I find, a term of that arrangement that all the Libyan Bank's transactions should pass through New York. . . .

The *second stage* ran from December 1980 to November 1985. Before very long Bankers Trust took the view that the remuneration which they received from the relationship, in the form of an interest-free balance of between $500,000 and $599,999 in New York, was insufficient reward for their services. On 15th March 1983 they proposed an increase in the peg balance to $1.5m. Negotiations continued for a time but without success. By 15th March 1984 Bankers Trust had formed the view that the Libyan Bank would not agree to an increase in the peg balance; so, on 3rd April 1984, they decided unilaterally on a different method of increasing the profitability of the relationship for Bankers Trust; and it was put into effect on 17th April.

The new method required a consideration of the balance on the New York account at 2.00 p.m. each day. If it exceeded the peg balance of $500,000 the excess was transferred in multiples of $100,000 to the London account with value that day. Consideration was also given on the following morning to the balance at the close of the previous day. If it was less than the peg balance, a transfer of the appropriate amount was made from London to New York on the next day, with value the previous business day; if it was more than the peg balance there was, it seems, a transfer to London with value the same day. The effect of the change was that the Libyan Bank lost one day's interest whenever (i) credits received after 2.00 p.m. exceeded payments made after 2.00 p.m., and (ii) the closing balance for the day would under the existing arrangement have required a transfer (or a further transfer if one had been made at 2.00 p.m.) to be made with value that day. If a weekend intervened, three days interest might be lost. . . .

Bankers Trust did not tell the Libyan Bank about this change. . . . Although the effect was on any view insubstantial, I am satisfied that the Libyan Bank did not in fact appreciate what was happening until mid-1985; and they complained about it to Bankers Trust in October 1985. I am also satisfied that the Libyan Bank could have detected, if they had looked at their statements from Bankers Trust with a fair degree of diligence, that they were not receiving the full benefit by way of interest to which they were entitled. . . .

The *third stage* began on 27th November 1985, with a telex from Bankers Trust which recorded the agreement of the Libyan Bank to a new arrangement. [The agreement stipulated review of the New York account at 2:00 New York time.]

At 2.00 p.m. on 7th January [1986] the balance to the credit of the New York account was [approximately] $165,728,000. . . . [A] transfer of $165.2m. should then have been made to London. [The transfer was not made, and, after other debits, by closing the balance was approximately $7,275,000. By the morning of 8 January 1986, approximately $6,700,000 was available to transfer in London. At 2.00 p.m. on 8 January the balance in the New York account was approximately $161,997,000, but no transfer was made.]

Bankers Trust New York had received payment instructions totalling $347,147,213.03 for execution on 8th January. All of them had been received by 8.44 a.m. New York time. None of them were executed. . . .

. . . Late in the afternoon of 7th January [Mr. Brittain, the Chairman of Bankers Trust,] received a telephone call from Mr. Corrigan, the President of the Federal Reserve Bank of New York. Mr. Corrigan asked that Bankers Trust should pay particular attention on the next day to movement of funds on the various Libyan accounts held by Bankers Trust, and report on anything unusual to him.

Late in the morning of the next day Mr. Brittain informed the New York Fed ... that "it looked like the Libyans were taking their money out of the various accounts". . . . Later Mr. Brittain learnt that sufficient funds were coming in to cover the payment instructions; he telephoned Mr. Corrigan and told him that the earlier report had been a false alarm. Mr. Corrigan asked Mr. Brittain not to make any payments out of the accounts for the time being, and said that he would revert later.

That assurance was repeated several times during the early afternoon. Mr. Brittain's statement continues:

> "Finally I telephoned Mr. Corrigan at about 3.30 p.m. and told him that we now had sufficient funds to cover the payments out of the various Libyan accounts and were going to make them. Mr. Corrigan's response to this was, 'You'd better call Baker' (by which he meant the Secretary of the United States Treasury, Mr. James A. Baker III). I said that I would release the payments and then speak to Mr. Baker. Mr. Corrigan's reply to this was. 'You'd better call Baker first'".

Mr. Brittain was delayed for some twenty minutes talking to Mr. Baker and to an Assistant Secretary of the Treasury on the telephone. Then at approximately 4.10 to 4.15 p.m. Mr. Baker said:

> "The President has signed the order, you can't make the transfers".

. . . It seems to me that a reasonable banker on the afternoon of 8th January would have realised, in the light of the first executive order made on the previous day, the requests of Mr. Corrigan, and particularly his saying "You'd better call Baker first", that a ban on payments was a distinct possibility. . . .

[On 28 April 1986 the Libyan Bank sent a telex to Bankers Trust London instructing the bank to transfer $130 million from the New York account to the London account. On the same day a demand in similar terms was made for $161 million, the amount that should have been transferred from the New York account to the London account at 2.00 p.m. on 8 January 1986.]

Neither demand was complied with. Bankers Trust replied that it would be unlawful (sc. by New York or any other United States law) for them to pay in London. That was factually correct. The question is whether it was relevant. Bankers Trust also denied that the $161m. transfer should have been made on 8th January. . . .

There is no dispute as to the general principles involved. Performance of a contract is excused if (i) it has become illegal by the proper law of the contract, or (ii) it necessarily involves doing an act which is unlawful by the law of the place where the act has to be done. . . .

There may, however, be a difficulty in ascertaining when performance of the contract "necessarily involves" doing an illegal act in another country. In *Toprak Mahsulleri Ofisi v. Finagrain Compagnie Commercial Agricole et Financiere S.A.* [1979] 2 Ll.R. 98, Turkish buyers of wheat undertook to open a letter of credit "with and confirmed by a first class U.S. or West European bank". The buyers were unable to obtain exchange control permission from the Turkish Ministry of Finance to open a letter of credit, and maintained that it was impossible for them to open a letter of credit without exporting money from Turkey. It was held that this was no answer to a claim for damages for non-performance of the contract. . . .

This case is really governed by the later case of *Kleinwort, Sons & Co. v. Ungarische Baumwolle Industrie Aketengesellshaft* [*sic*] *& Another* [1939] 2 K.B. 678 where bills of exchange were to be given and cover was to be provided in London, but at the same time there was a letter saying, 'We have to get permission from Hungary'. It was said that because of the illegality by Hungarian law in obtaining it, that would be an answer to the case. But Mr. Justice Branson and the Court of Appeal held that the property law of the contract was English law; and, since the contract was to be performed in England, it was enforceable in the English Courts even though its performance might involve a breach by the defendants of the law of Hungary. . . .

. . . [I]t is immaterial whether one party has to equip himself for performance by an illegal act in another country. What matters is whether performance itself necessarily involves such an act. The Turkish buyers might have had money anywhere in the world which they could use to open a letter of credit with a U.S. or West European bank. In fact it would seem that they only had money in Turkey, or at any rate needed to comply with Turkish exchange control regulations if they were to use any money they may have had outside Turkey. But that was no defence, as money or a permit was only needed to equip themselves for performance, and not for performance itself. . . .

. . . I hold that the [managed account] arrangement was [terminated], implicitly by the Libyan Bank's telex of 28th April 1986, and if that were wrong, then expressly by their solicitors' letter of 30th July 1986.

What, then, was the position after determination? The New York account remained, as it always had been, a demand account. Subject to New York law, Bankers Trust were obliged to make transfers in accordance with the Libyan Bank's instructions to the extent of the credit balance, but they were not obliged to allow an overdraft. . . . The London account remained an interest-bearing account from which Bankers Trust were obliged to make transfers on the instructions of the Libyan Bank, provided that no infringement of United States law in the United States was involved. . . .

I now turn to the forms of transfer discussed in sub-section (e) of this judgment, in order to consider in relation to each whether it was a form of transfer which the Libyan Bank were entitled to demand, whether it has in fact been demanded, and whether it would necessarily involve any action in New York. . . .

A banker's draft was demanded in the telex of 28th April 1986; and a banker's payment was within the description "any other commercially recognised method of transferring funds" demanded by the telex of 23rd December 1986. But since, as I have found, an instrument for $131 million would not have been eligible for London dollar clearing in the circumstances of this case, Bankers Trust were not obliged to comply with that aspect of the demands. . . .

. . . Bankers Trust were not obliged to issue an instrument with a view to its being based through London dollar clearing if it was not eligible; and an instrument of $131m. in this case would have been disqualified.

The other clearing systems give rise to similar problems. . . .

Of course it is highly unlikely that anyone would want to receive a sum as large as $131m. in dollar bills, at all events unless they were engaged in laundering the proceeds of crime. . . .

Demand was in fact made for cash in this case, and it was not complied with. It has not been argued that the delivery of such a sum in cash in London would involve any illegal action in New York. Accordingly I would hold Bankers Trust liable on that ground. . . .

Accordingly I hold that

(i) Bankers Trust were in breach of contract in failing to transfer $165.2m. to London at 2.00 p.m. on 7th January;

(ii) if they had done that, they could and would have recalled $158.5m. from London in the morning of 8th January [to cover other transfer demands received in the interim]; but,

(iii) on the assumption that both those steps had been taken, there would have been a further breach in failing to transfer $154.7m. to London at 2.00 p.m. on 8th January. . . .

The balance resulting from those figures is a net loss to the London account of $161.4m. I hold that this must be added to the Libyan Bank's first claim, as an additional sum for which that claim would have succeeded but for breaches of contract by Bankers Trust. It is said that this loss is not recoverable, because it arose from a new intervening act and is too remote. In the circumstances as they were on 7th and 8th January I have no hesitation in rejecting that argument.

**Notes and Comments 11.9.** Transnational banking transactions may raise serious potential conflict of laws problems of the sort involved in *Libyan Arab Foreign Bank*. From another perspective, these problems represent country risk in international banking. Are these problems unavoidable? Consider the following excerpt.

## Michael P. Malloy, Principles of Bank Regulation
§ 9.30 (2d ed. 2003)

The formidable array of economic sanctions administered by the United States is a daunting reality for any U.S. national subject to their reach. Particularly troublesome for a bank involved in international activities is the possibility of having to defend the validity of any of these sanctions programs in a foreign forum. Until recently, there has not been any appreciable body of foreign case law directly challenging U.S. economic sanctions programs. Nevertheless, according to knowledgeable practitioners, today U.S. banks feel the need to take the effect of sanctions into account in their planning, even those not generally involved in international activities.

One particular problem faced by U.S. banks is the applicability of a blocking prohibition to dollar-denominated accounts held by a U.S. bank in the United States in the name of a foreign-situs bank or branch, which in turn holds a dollar-denominated account for a target country or nationals thereof[, known as "cover accounts"]. This is a serious concern for such broadly conceived economic sanctions programs as the FACRs and the CACRs in particular, and would be so especially in the early stages of the implementation of such a program, when ongoing banking relationships are being disrupted.

It is obviously less of a concern for later programs, otherwise similar to the FACRs and CACRs, that have expressly licensed cover account situations out from under the blocking prohibition.[1] Furthermore, this is of virtually no concern for those later programs that are so limited in the scope of their prohibitions as to raise no issue in the first place concerning cover accounts, such as the UNITA/Angola arms embargo or the arms embargo with respect to Rwanda.

From the point of view of the international banker, the potential application of blocking prohibitions to a cover account is perhaps one of the more grotesque effects of economic sanctions, working as it does a complete frustration of normal expectations in international transactions. Consider these effects in what may be characterized as virtually a purely extraterritorial transaction.

A wholly foreign bank G maintains a dollar-denominated cover account with a New York City bank H, in effect partially hedging dollar exposure from its own dollar-denominated accounts held for its own depositors. An office of G in a third country issues dollar-denominated irrevocable L/Cs for a local depositor, I, an importer of foreign goods. Neither G nor I has any office or other business presence in the United States.

Based on certain information unavailable to G or H, the Treasury Department determines that I is acting as a purchasing agent on behalf of a country blocked under the FACRs. The argument would be made that the cover account held by H in New York is blocked because I has an indirect–a *very* indirect–interest in the account.

The natural result would be litigation initiated by I against the local office of G demanding performance of its obligations in accordance with local law. One such case is *China Mutual Trading Co., Ltd. v. Banque Belge,*[2] a 1954 Hong Kong case involving facts similar to those described above, in which the court insisted upon the application of local law. The court's reaction, from the viewpoint of the ordinary expectations of the banking industry, is unremarkable:

> I consider that rights of the plaintiffs re those which ordinarily arise out of the relationship of banker and customer where the latter has made a deposit with the former. . . .

---

1. *See., e.g.,* 31 C.F.R. § 535.901 (1980) (IACRs provision explicitly authorizing, by general license, transactions in cover accounts).

2. 39 Hong Kong L. Rep. 144 (1954).

> There is no privity of contract between the customer of the bank and that bank's correspondent elsewhere. . . . A debt is situated or localized where it is recoverable. A debt which arises out of the relationship of banker and customer is localized at the branch of the bank where the account is kept.[3]

This straightforward choice of law principle, looking to the place where the account is "kept," prevailed over any suggestion of a cognizable interest on the part of the United States in the application of the economic sanctions. Thus, the court rejected one defense offered by Banque Belge, to the effect that:

> by paying the U.S. dollars, held by [Banque Belge] with their agents [the correspondent bank] in New York, into a blocked account already existing in the name of the plaintiffs with those agents, [Banque Belge had] discharged [its] obligations. I consider that this defence also fails on the ground that payment by a debtor into a blocked account without the consent of the creditor cannot be a good discharge of a debt.[4] . . .

A U.S. bank, J, agrees to provide short-term financing, possibly through bankers' acceptances, for the manufacture and sale of heavy trucks by a foreign subsidiary K of a U.S. manufacturing firm to a trading corporation L, incorporated under the local laws of K's host country. None of the parties to this transaction are targets of any U.S. economic sanctions program.

However, as the contract term proceeds, it is discovered that L intends to resell to the development agency of a country that is blocked under the FACRs. K, being a person subject to U.S. jurisdiction,[5] is informed by Treasury, through its U.S. parent, that it is prohibited from proceeding with the sale and subsequent delivery of the goods.[6] The financing of this transaction might also constitute a prohibited "dealing in" the property subject to the provisions of the FACRs.[7] Under these circumstances, J bank would probably still be in a position to claim the benefits of the safe harbor provision of the FACRs[8] and return itself to its original position, but any further action in support of the transaction might well be viewed as a "willful violation," withdrawing the benefits of the safe harbor.[9]

What, then, is J to do if K is subjected to direct supervision (almost in the nature of a temporary receivership) by its host country, so that the sales transaction with L will be completed? Presumably, this would not represent a willful violation for the J or K, but the situation is obviously a precarious one. This situation loosely follows the facts in the famous Freuhauf episode,[10] in which Freuhauf's French subsidiary was subjected to such supervision in connection with a sale of trucks ultimately destined for the Peoples' Republic of China,

---

3. *Id.* at 151.

4. *Id.* at 152.

5. *See* 31 C.F.R. § 500.329 ("person subject" defined as including foreign subsidiary of corporation organized under laws of any state of the United States).

6. *See id.* § 500.201(b)(1) (prohibition on transfers by any "person subject" of property in which target country has an interest).

7. *Id.*

8. *See id.* § 500.203(d).

9. *See id.* § 500.203(d)(1) (safe harbor conditioned on violation not being willful).

10. *See* Craig, *Application of the Trading With the Enemy Act to Foreign Corporations Owned by Americans: Reflections of Freuhauf v. Massardy,* 83 Harv. L. Rev. 579 (1970).

then blocked under the FACRs. Here again, local host country law prevailed, and reach of U.S. economic sanctions was curtailed. While the subsidiary may be viewed as not acting in a willful manner, and hence ultimately not sanctioned under the FACRs, still a considerable amount of expense and uncertainty ensued before the final outcome. . . .

**Notes and Comments 11.10.** Assume that Wholly Foreign Bank (WFB), chartered under the laws of the Netherlands, has a branch in Hong Kong which holds a dollar deposit in the name of NusBank, chartered in Nusquam. WFB also has a correspondent relationship with QNB in the United States. When the executive order mentioned in Note 11.7, *supra*, is issued, on what basis could the United States assert that WFB is barred from honoring NusBank's withdrawal demands on its dollar deposit account? Would it make any difference if WFB was maintaining a dollar deposit account with QNB, in part to "cover" its dollar obligations to its depositors?

**11.11.** If NusBank brought suit against WFB in the courts of Hong Kong what is the likelihood of NusBank's success on the merits? Would it make any difference if the United States Government informed WFB that its dollar deposit in QNB was "blocked" under the NACRs?

**11.12.** Assume that QNB had issued a standby letter of credit, at the request of International Business Network (IBN), in favor of the Nusquami Port Authority. The standby L/C was intended to guarantee IBN's performance under a project contract in Nusquam. NusBank had confirmed QNB's L/C. After the executive order was issued, the NPA made a demand on NusBank under the L/C, and NusBank has relayed the demand to QNB. Under the regulations, may QNB honor the demand?

# 4. Sanctions and Terrorism

The tragic events of September 11, 2001, remain difficult to comprehend at a human level, but the legal and policy effects of these events are already beginning to unfold. Some of these effects will doubtless have serious implications for transborder banking activities. The legal response was multifold, including unilateral presidential action, parallel multilateral action initiated by the U.N. Security Council, and congressional action signed into law by the president.

## a. Presidential Emergency Action

The President had already taken a number of dramatic steps in response to the terrorist attack, including military preparation, diplomatic overtures, and domestic political initiatives. On September 14, 2001, he issued Presidential Proclamation No. 7463[5] declaring a national emergency with respect to the attacks, and indicating his intention to invoke statutory authorities to activate national emergency military reserves and to recall personnel to active duty. At that stage, however, the President's action did not expand the U.S. economic sanctions that had been in place since the second half of the 1990s against the assets of terrorists and against the Taliban regime in Afghanistan.

This situation rapidly changed. On September 23, 2001, the President issued Ex-

---

5. 66 Fed. Reg. 48,199 (2001).

ecutive Order No. 13,224,[6] blocking the property of, and prohibiting transactions with, persons who commit, threaten to commit, or support terrorism. Invoking such authority as the IEEPA, section 5 of the UNPA, and various U.N. Security Council Resolutions, the order declared a national emergency to deal with the "unusual and extraordinary threat to the national security, foreign policy, and economy of the United States" posed by the terrorist attacks.

Had this been all that the preamble of the order said, it would have read like countless other executive orders declaring national emergencies issued by presidents since the IEEPA was enacted in December 1977. But the order went on to find that "because of the pervasiveness and expansiveness of the financial foundation of foreign terrorists, financial sanctions may be appropriate for those foreign persons that support or otherwise associate with these foreign terrorists." It also found that "a need exist[ed] for further consultation and cooperation with, and sharing of information by, United States and foreign financial institutions as an additional tool to enable the United States to combat the financing of terrorism."

The strategy of the new executive order is distinctive at a number of levels. The new sanctions program intimately and explicitly ties the imposition of sanctions to a broader array of foreign policy and military responses. For example, section 6 of the order immediately triggered consultation and coordination with other countries to achieve the objectives of the order. Furthermore, the order stated that declaration of the emergency (and hence the imposition of sanctions) was "in furtherance of [the] proclamation" activating the military reserves. As in the case of the former Iraq sanctions, therefore, the economic response is likely to be only one phase in what will eventually involve military or police action as well.

In addition, the Administration may have found a way to sidestep–or at least to blunt–the issue that is typically raised against the application of U.S. economic sanctions, namely, that they are impermissibly extraterritorial in effect. The premise underlying this program is that, in response to "universal" criminal acts (terrorism, like piracy, crimes against humanity, and wars of aggression, is subject to criminal enforcement regardless of where it takes place), the President is calling upon other states to identify and freeze terrorist-related assets under their own authority. If a state does not take appropriate action, it may trigger the "vicarious" or "accessory" liability principle that the President has enunciated elsewhere (e.g., in his speech to the joint session of Congress). The President might sanction such states for their active or passive participation in a universal crime.

# b. U.N. Security Council Action

On September 28, 2001, the U.N. Security Council unanimously adopted a U.S.-sponsored resolution[7] requiring all U.N. member states to sanction the financing, training and movement of terrorists–and requiring that they cooperate in any campaign against terrorists, including military action. In effect, the resolution completely vindicates the declarations of the executive order: that terrorism was indeed an unusual and extraordinary threat; that the pervasiveness and expansiveness of the financing of terrorists made sanctions against foreign persons "support[ing] or otherwise associat[ing] with" terrorists appropriate; and that consultation and cooperation with, and sharing of information by, U.S. and foreign

---

6. 66 Fed. Reg. 49,079 (2001).

7. U.N. Security Council Res. No. 1373, Sept. 28, 2001, S/RES/1373 (2001).

financial institutions was necessary to combat terrorism.

The U.N. sanctions require the immediate freezing of the financial resources of terrorists and their organizations. Once fully implemented by the member states, the U.N. sanctions will also include required efforts at preventing and suppressing terrorism, prohibitions against making funds available to terrorist organizations, and the suppression of recruitment by such organizations and the elimination of their weapon supplies. In addition, the member states are required to deny safe havens to anyone who finances, plans, supports or commits terrorist acts, or who provides safe havens to terrorists. They are also committed to providing assistance in criminal investigations of terrorism and to preventing the movement of terrorists and terrorist groups through more effective control over borders and travel documents.

Some gray areas exist in the resolution, however, particularly in comparison with the immediate U.S. response. For example, section 3(d) of the order defines *terrorism* to mean an activity that involves a violent act or an act dangerous to human life, property, or infrastructure and appears to be intended to intimidate or coerce a civilian population, to influence the policy of a government by intimidation or coercion, or to affect the conduct of a government by mass destruction, assassination, kidnapping, or hostage-taking. Section 1(a)-(d) of the order describes the kinds of persons considered to be *terrorists*, and an annex to the order lists 27 individuals and organizations identified by the order as terrorists or supporters of terrorism. In contrast, the U.N. resolution does not define or explain who is a terrorist. In addition, while the order invokes the necessary U.S. statutory authority—the IEEPA and the UNPA—for immediate imposition of the sanctions, the current national laws of the other 188 U.N. member states may not uniformly provide authority for implementation of the terms of the resolution. Hence, the exact contours of the multilateral response to terrorism are likely to remain relatively fuzzy for months ahead, as member states take action to align their national laws with the requirements of the resolution.

# c. Implications for Transborder Banking

Whatever the uncertainties about the full legal expanse of this multilateral response, a number of features are clear even now. The implications for transborder banking are obviously serious. Section 1 of the order blocks "all property and interests in property" of persons targeted by the order if the property is in the United States or later comes within the United States, or within the possession or control of a U.S. person (which is defined to include a foreign branch of a U.S.-based bank). Presumably, blocked assets would include such items as bank accounts, assets held in trust, and funds in the course of transaction through the banking system. Section 2(a) goes on to prohibit any "transaction or dealing" in blocked assets by any U.S. person or within the United States. The blocking applies even if a preexisting contract with respect to the property or transaction requires the U.S. party to perform, and even if the property or transaction was covered by a preexisting license or permit from the U.S. Government.

At first glance, this might seem to be a relatively discrete group of potential bank clients and customers. If so, compliance with the sanctions as applied to transborder banking would be easily sustainable. However, the reach of the order is potentially much broader, and markedly more dynamic. As a result, transborder banking is likely to be burdened by considerable compliance and agency costs.

For example, under section 1(d) of the order, targeted persons include those determined by the Treasury Secretary (in consultation with the Secretary of State and the Attorney General) to be assisting in, sponsoring, or providing financial, material, or technological support for, or financial or other services to or in support of, terrorism or persons listed in the annex or otherwise determined to be subject to the order. Persons may also be blocked if the Secretary determines that they are "otherwise associated with" persons listed or determined to be subject to the order. Taken as an objective test, these provisions dramatically widen the scope of the blocking to include a broad range of financial intermediaries and other international middlemen–perhaps even banks themselves. However, for this class of potentially blockable persons, section 5 of the order authorizes the Treasury Secretary to take steps in his discretion short of a complete blocking. This could mean, for example, selective blocking of accounts, reversal of transactions, restrictions on operations, and the like. The history of U.S. blocking programs is replete with such examples.

Equally significant in terms of the effects of the blocking on transborder banking are the provisions of section 1(c) of the order. Targeted persons will also include persons determined by the Secretary of the Treasury (in consultation with the Secretary of State and the Attorney General) to be owned or controlled by, or to act for or on behalf of, any other targeted person. In many if not most situations, this provision will make it very difficult for a bank to preplan and monitor compliance with the sanctions, absent prior notice from Treasury.

Prior notice may well be absent, however. Section 10 of the order eliminates the necessity of prior notice of any "listing or determination made" pursuant to the order, at least as to any person who has "a constitutional presence in the United States." The reason for this provision is the President's finding that prior notice to targeted persons might make application of these sanctions "ineffectual," in light of "the ability to transfer funds or assets instantaneously" in the international financial system.

Perhaps even more ominous in terms of compliance burdens and potential liability are the provisions of section 2(b) and (c) of the order. Notwithstanding any preexisting contract or any preexisting license or permit, section 2(b) prohibits any transaction by a U.S. person or within the United States that evades or avoids, or has the purpose of evading or avoiding, or attempts to violate, any of the prohibitions of the order. Section 2(c) prohibits any conspiracy formed to violate any of the prohibitions of the order. Conspiracy theory has long been a fruitful device in federal enforcement, and there is considerable case law and commentary on the subject. However, what constitutes "avoidance"–as opposed to intentional evasion–of federal prohibitions remains something of a mystery, and hence a dangerous source of potential difficulty for banks operating in the international market. Of course, a bank might be able to show that its involvement in a particular transaction was not initiated with the *purpose* of avoiding the prohibition, yet it might still find itself, objectively speaking, involved in a transaction that in fact *avoided* the prohibitions. This might well be an independent basis for enforcement action against the bank.

# d.  USA PATRIOT Act and Financial Services

The president signed the USA PATRIOT Act into law on October 26, 2001. The act is discussed in Notes 10.4 and 10.5, *supra*. It is a multi-pronged legislative response to the terrorist acts of September 11, 2001. As such, it is much broader than the provisions in Title III of the Act that most directly affect financial services firms. Nevertheless, Title III accounts for approximately one-third of the entire text of the Act and will probably have long-term compliance implications far beyond the immediate terrorism crisis.[8] Many of the provisions of the Act deal with enhancing investigative and intelligence tools available to fight the terrorism threat directly. Title I (§§ 101-106) is intended to improve counterterrorism capabilities and domestic security. Title II (§§ 201-225) dramatically expands surveillance procedures and techniques available to the federal government, particularly with respect to foreign intelligence surveillance. Related to this response, the provisions of Title IX (§§ 901-908) are intended to improve intelligence capabilities with respect to terrorist activities–a much criticized aspect of federal readiness in the wake of the events of September 11–and to coordinate intelligence activities with criminal and terrorist asset investigations. Title V (§§ 501-508) is intended to remove practical and legal obstacles to terrorism investigations. Title VII (§ 701) expands authority for regional information-sharing to facilitate federal, state and local law enforcement efforts with respect to the terrorist attacks. Title VIII (§§ 801-817) pumps up federal criminal laws affecting terrorism, including cyberterrorism (§§ 814, 816) and bioterrorism (§ 817). It also includes acts of terrorism under racketeering activities (§ 813). (Similarly, § 315 includes certain foreign corrupt practices under money laundering crimes. Criminal provisions with respect to money laundering and related activities covered by Title III are also added by §§ 316-322, 329, 373-377.)

## 1. Interpretive Issues

The key terms of reference under the IMLAAFA raise a variety of terminological questions that affect the scope of many of the substantive requirements imposed by the act. Many of these questions are, of course, specifically addressed by IMLAAFA itself, typically by crossreference to preexisting statutory definitions. For example, under § 318[9] the term "financial institution," used throughout IMLAAFA, is defined by reference to the term as defined in the Bank Secrecy Act (BSA).[10] There the term includes most financial entities, such as commercial banks, savings associations, credit unions (added by IMLAAFA § 321[11]), broker-dealers, insurance companies, and money transmitters, among others. In addition, IMLAAFA § 318 adds U.S. branches and agencies of foreign banks to be included in the term.

A similar–but, significantly, not coterminous–concept, "covered financial institution," is key to the shell bank provisions of IMLAAFA § 313[12] and the bank records provisions of § 319.[13] For purposes of § 313, the term is defined to include only certain selected financial institutions described in the BSA.[14] These include commercial banks, savings associations and other depository institutions, branches and agencies of foreign banks, and broker-dealers registered under the Securities Exchange Act of 1934. It is not apparent that the term is so limited for purposes of the bank records provisions. Likewise, IMLAAFA

---

8. Although the act may be terminated under the joint congressional resolution procedure in § 303, as of the beginning of fiscal year 2005, it seems unlikely that antiterrorism sanctions and antimoneylaundering provisions would be eliminated entirely.

9. 18 U.S.C. § 1956(6).

10. 31 U.S.C. § 5312(a)(2).

11. *Id.* § 5312(2)(E).

12. *Id.* § 5318(j).

13. 18 U.S.C. § 981(k).

14. 31 U.S.C.  § 5312(a)(2)(A)-(G).

incorporates the BSA definition of "financial agency." This term includes any person acting for another as a financial institution, bailee, depository trustee, or agent, or acting in a similar way relating to financial assets or gold, or a transaction involving any of these.

The breadth of coverage of the act–applying as it does not just to banks, but to a wider range of financial institutions–creates its own terminological difficulties. Certain operative terms are defined differently for different types of institutions. For example, for banks § 311[15] defines "account" as a formal banking or business relationship established to provide regular services, dealings and other financial transactions. The term expressly includes demand deposits, savings deposits and other transaction or asset accounts or extensions of credit. However, for other institutions § 311 requires the Secretary to define the term by regulation, after consultation with the appropriate federal functional regulators. In this regard, the Secretary is required to include within the definition–to the extent, if any, that the Secretary deems appropriate–arrangements similar to payable-through and correspondent accounts. The act does not reveal what sort of accounts these might be.

Similarly, § 311 defines "correspondent account" in different ways for banks and other financial institutions. For banks, the term is defined as an "account" established to receive deposits from, to make payments on behalf of, or handle other financial transactions related to, a foreign financial institution. (It is not clear from the act itself what "other" transactions are intended.) For other financial institutions, it is the Secretary's responsibility to determine the extent to which "arrangements similar to . . . correspondent accounts" are to be included within the definition. The possible discontinuity in the meaning of this term is potentially significant. For example, four key sections of the IMLAAFA–§ 311 (measures against "primary money laundering" targets), § 312[16] (special due diligence requirements), § 313 (foreign shell bank prohibitions) and § 319 (forfeiture of funds in U.S. interbank accounts)–all apply to "correspondent accounts," and this fact makes the scope of the definition of the term critical to effective implementation of the IMLAAFA.

The same potential discontinuity exists for the term "payable-through account". For banks, § 311 defines the term to mean an account opened at a depository institution by a foreign financial institution, by means of which the foreign financial institution permits its customers to engage, directly or through a subaccount, in banking activities in the United States. Again, for other financial institutions, it is the Secretary's responsibility to determine the extent to which "arrangements similar to payable-through . . . accounts" are to be included within the definition.

Other provisions of the IMLAAFA raise analytical issues on their on terms. For example, under § 312 creates a continuum of "enhanced," "additional," and "special" due diligence requirements that are applicable, under varied circumstances specified in the section. The "enhanced" due diligence requirements apply to financial institutions maintaining U.S. correspondent accounts and private banking accounts of non-U.S. persons. The "additional" requirements apply to accounts maintained for foreign banks with "offshore" banking licenses or licenses from countries designated as "noncooperative." The "special" requirements apply to private banking accounts. What is not clear from the text of the act is where each of these types of due diligence ends and the next begins. Nor is it clear to what extent these requirements overlap in their specifics.[17]

Section 313 prohibits "covered financial institutions" from maintaining correspon-

---

15. *Id.* § 5318A

16. *Id.* § 5318(i).

17. For the interim final rule on § 312 due diligence requirements, see Note 10.6, *supra*.

dent accounts for "shell banks"–banks with no physical presence in any country–and requires "reasonable steps" to be taken by institutions to ensure that correspondent accounts of foreign banks are not used to provide banking services to shell banks. What these steps may be, and how to assess their reasonableness, are still open questions under the IMLAAFA. Presumably, compliance issues like these may be clarified by provisions such as IMLAAFA § 314,[18] which encourages bank regulators and law enforcement agencies to share information with financial institutions.

Certain provisions of the IMLAAFA necessarily require further empirical development before their practical implications will become apparent. For example, under § 311 the Treasury Secretary is authorized to designate non-U.S. jurisdictions, classes of transactions, financial institutions and types of accounts that are of "primary money laundering concern." Progressive delineation of the scope of such provisions will doubtless emerge through administrative implementation over time.

## 2. Administrative Implementation

The level of agency implementation will be significantly increasing in 2002 as proposed and final rulemaking moves forward. For example, on December 28, 2001, Treasury published proposed rules[19] to implement § 313 of the IMLAAFA, among other things. The proposal establishes a new part 104 of the Treasury rules. Part 104 will eventually include other regulations implementing the IMLAAFA money laundering provisions for which Treasury is authorized or required to issue regulations. At this point, however, most of part 104 has been reserved for future regulations.

In fact, in the three-month period ending March 7, 2002, over twenty separate regulatory issuances were published in the Federal Register that dealt with one aspect or another of USA PATRIOT implementation. Many of these rulemakings–as well as others that will doubtless follow in due course–will entail the commitment of additional staff, time and resources on the part of financial services firms at least for initial design and initiation of appropriate compliance programs. For example, in February 2002 the SEC published a proposed NASD rule change[20] that would establish an Anti-Money Laundering Compliance Program. In March 2002, the SEC published a proposed NYSE rule change[21] that would establish a corresponding compliance program for the exchange.

Overall, IMLAAFA compliance programs were required to be in place by 24 April 2002. The compliance burdens are particularly evident with respect to reporting requirements. Proposed rules[22] were published on 31 December 2001 that would require securities broker-dealers to file suspicious activity reports (SARs) with Treasury's Financial Crimes Enforcement Network (FinCEN) if they believe a customer may be violating U.S. laws or regulations. These proposed rules would implement IMLAAFA § 356.[23] (Written comments on the proposed rules were due by March 1, 2002.) In addition, by July 23, 2002, FinCEN is to develop a secure Web site that covered financial institutions may use to report suspicious activities. (SARs are currently filed via paper documents.)

---

18. *Id.* § 5311 note.
19. 66 Fed. Reg. 67,460 (2001).
20. 67 Fed. Reg. 8565 (2002).
21. 67 Fed. Reg. 10,463 (2002).
22. 66 Fed. Reg. 67,670 (2001).
23. 31 U.S.C. § 5318 note.

Also on December 31, 2001, an interim final rule[24] was published requiring persons in nonfinancial trades or businesses to file reports with FinCEN for transactions in which they receive more than $10,000 in coins or currency in one transaction (or two or more related transactions). The interim rule was effective January 1, 2002, but FinCEN simultaneously published identical proposed rules,[25] with written comments due March 1, 2002. (This simultaneous publication of an "interim" final rule and an identical proposed rule is an increasingly common administrative practice. It is intended to ensure that, even if there is a serious procedural objection to the interim final rule, the substance of the rule could still be preserved by making the proposed rule effective in final form.) An analogous reporting requirement has also been issued in final form by the IRS, effective December 31, 2002.[26]

Section d.1., *supra*, highlighted certain significant terminological, analytical, and empirical issues raised by the text of the IMLAAFA. To what extent do the currently available administrative issuances help us to resolve these issues?

In many instances, the administrative guidance to date has simply incorporated terminological concepts established in the IMLAAFA. For example, in the 28 December proposed rule, Treasury incorporated the statutory definition of "covered financial institution," the key to the shell bank provisions of IMLAAFA § 313 and the bank records provisions of § 319. The term is defined to include commercial banks, savings associations and other depository institutions, branches and agencies of foreign banks, and broker-dealers registered under the Securities Exchange Act of 1934.

Among other things, the proposed rule would implement IMLAAFA § 313(a), prohibiting covered financial institutions from providing correspondent accounts to foreign shell banks, and requiring such institutions to take reasonable steps to ensure that correspondent accounts provided to foreign banks are not being used indirectly to provide banking services to foreign shell banks. Under IMLAAFA § 319(b), the proposed rule would also require covered financial institutions that provide correspondent accounts to foreign banks to maintain records of ownership of such foreign banks and their U.S. agents who are designated for service of legal process for records regarding the correspondent account, and require termination of correspondent accounts of foreign banks that fail to turn over their account records in response to a lawful request of the Treasury Secretary or the Attorney General.

Some IMLAAFA provisions require Treasury to make some choices about the scope of terms. Thus, IMLAAFA § 311 defined "correspondent account" in different ways for banks and other financial institutions. For banks, the term is defined as an "account" established to receive deposits from, to make payments on behalf of, or handle other financial transactions related to, a foreign financial institution. For other financial institutions, it is the Secretary's responsibility to determine the extent to which "arrangements similar to . . . correspondent accounts" are to be included within the definition. When it issued its Interim Guidance in November 2001,[27] Treasury deferred the question of compliance obligations for securities brokers and dealers with respect to the BSA[28] until after consultation with the SEC. With the regulations proposed on 28 December, Treasury indi-

---

24. 66 Fed. Reg. 67,680 (2001).
25. 66 Fed. Reg. 67,685 (2001).
26. 66 Fed. Reg. 67,687 (2001).
27. 66 Fed. Reg. 59,342 (2001).
28. 31 U.S.C. § 5318(j)-(k).

cated that it would apply the BSA requirements to brokers and dealers in the same manner that they apply to other covered financial institutions. Treasury intends to maintain parity of treatment between accounts provided to foreign banks by banks and by broker-dealers, and to treat functionally equivalent accounts–whether maintained by banks or broker-dealers–in the same manner.

Some key terms were not defined in the IMLAAFA itself, and we must look to administrative guidance in this regard. For example, the act did not define the term "foreign bank." Treasury's 28 December proposed rule would define the term to include any organization: (*i*) organized under the laws of a foreign country; (*ii*) engaging in the business of banking; (*iii*) recognized as a bank by the bank supervisory or monetary authority of the country of its organization or principal banking operations; and, (*iv*) receiving deposits in the regular course of its business. "Foreign bank" would also include a branch of a foreign bank located in a territory of the United States, Puerto Rico, Guam, American Samoa, or the Virgin Islands. "Foreign bank" would not include an agency or branch of a foreign bank located in the United States or an insured bank organized in a territory of the United States, Puerto Rico, Guam, American Samoa, or the Virgin Islands. (These entities are themselves "covered financial institutions" under the act.) In addition, a foreign central bank or foreign monetary authority that functions as a central bank is not a "foreign bank" for these purposes.

Other provisions of the IMLAAFA raise analytical issues on their on terms. For example, IMLAAFA § 312 creates a continuum of "enhanced," "additional," and "special" due diligence requirements that are applicable, under varied circumstances specified in the section. The act does not elaborate on the content of these due diligence obligations; nor is it clear to what extent these requirements might overlap. By April 2002, rules to implement IMLAAFA § 312 should be proposed to address due diligence requirements for financial institutions administering, maintaining, or managing private banks accounts or correspondent accounts covered by the act. Final rules were required to become effective by July 2002.[29]

IMLAAFA § 313(a) prohibited covered financial institutions from maintaining correspondent accounts for "shell banks" and required "reasonable steps" to be taken by institutions to ensure that correspondent accounts of foreign banks are not used to provide banking services to shell banks. The Treasury rules proposed on 28 December 2001 would implement § 313. The rules codify, with some modifications, Treasury's November interim guidance on the subject. The proposed rule still would not prescribe what constitutes "reasonable steps" under 31 U.S.C. § 5318(j), but it does provide a safe harbor if a covered financial institution uses model certifications in appendices to the proposed rule.[30]

Administrative efforts are still at a relatively early implementation stage, and it will be a while before empirical developments, like Treasury designations of non-U.S. jurisdictions, classes of transactions, financial institutions and types of accounts that are of "primary money laundering concern" under IMLAAFA § 311, are fully in place. We have begun to see more designations of foreign terrorist organizations[31] pursuant to USA

29. FinCEN has not met this deadline with a final rule. An interim final rule is in place, however. *See* 67 Fed. Reg. 48,348 (2002) (to be codified at 31 C.F.R. pt. 103). The rule is reproduced *supra* at 269 *et seq.*

30. Appendix A, Appendix B, set forth in 66 Fed. Reg. 67,460 (2001).

31. *See, e.g.*, 66 Fed. Reg. 63,620 (2001); 66 Fed. Reg. 66,492 (2001).

PATRIOT Act § 411(c),[32] but these efforts are only of indirect interest to financial services firms.

Some of these empirical concerns should be eased as interaction between Treasury and other interested administrative agencies on the one hand and regulated financial services firms on the other continue over time. For example, an interim final rule[33] was published by FinCEN on 4 March 2002 to implement the IMLAAFA § 314 information sharing procedures. The interim rule was effective immediately, but FinCEN simultaneously published an identical proposed rule,[34] with written comments due by 3 April 2002. Such procedures should promote cooperation among financial institutions, regulators, and law enforcement entities in identifying persons who may be involved in terrorism or money laundering.

**Notes and Comments 11.13.** Review the problems in Notes 10.8-10.10, *supra*. In light of the preceding material in this section, how would you answer the problems?

**11.14.** Are Edge and Agreement corporations and U.S. branches, agencies and other offices of foreign banks required to establish and maintain internal procedures and controls designed to assure and monitor compliance with the amended Bank Secrecy Act? *See* 31 U.S.C. 5318(h).

**11.15.** Assume that the national emergency with respect to Nusquam has been terminated, and that economic relations between the United States and Nusquam have returned to normal. Nusbank's Assistant General Counsel for U.S. Operations has approached you with some questions about the impact of the USA PATRIOT Act on Nusbank's U.S. operations. How would you respond to the following issues?

> **a.** The federal branch of Nusbank, located in San Francisco, has long had a practice of processing funds transfers sent to it electronically from the Nusbank home office. Many of these requests are "coded"–*i.e.*, the transmitting Nusbank customer is identified only by a file number, while the intended recipient is identified by name, intended receiving bank and account number.
>
> **b.** Nusbank-SF also accepts funds electronically transmitted from the Nusbank home office for future payment of commercial invoices and L/C drafts in connection with U.S. goods and services intended for export to Nusbank customers in Nusquam and elsewhere. Nusbank-SF does not necessarily have information concerning the Nusbank customer involved.
>
> **c.** Nusbank International Banking Corporation, an Edge corporation owned by Nusbank, often provides the same services described in paragraphs a. and b., *supra*.

Are these practices consistent with the Bank Secrecy Act, as amended by USA PATRIOT Act? In answering this question, consider the following regulatory provisions.

## Board of Governors of the Federal Reserve System
### 12 C.F.R. pt. 211

§ 211.5 Edge and agreement corporations.

---

32. 8 U.S.C. § 1189(a).

33. 67 Fed. Reg. 9874 (2002).

34. 67 Fed. Reg. 9879 (2002).

. . .

(m) Procedures for monitoring Bank Secrecy Act compliance.

. . .

(2) *Customer identification program.* Each Edge or agreement corporation is subject to the requirements of 31 U.S.C. 5318(*l*) and the implementing regulation jointly promulgated by the Board and the Department of the Treasury at 31 CFR 103.121, which require a customer identification program.

> § 211.24 Approval of offices of foreign banks; procedures for applications; standards for approval; representative office activities and standards for approval; preservation of existing authority.

. . .

(j) Procedures for monitoring Bank Secrecy Act compliance.

. . .

(2) *Customer identification program.* Except for a federal branch or a federal agency or a state branch that is insured by the FDIC, a branch, agency, or representative office of a foreign bank operating in the United States is subject to the requirements of 31 U.S.C. 5318 (*l*) and the implementing regulation jointly promulgated by the Board and the Department of the Treasury at 31 CFR 103.121, which require a customer identification program.

## Department of the Treasury
### 31 C.F.R. pt. 103

> § 103.121 Customer Identification Programs for banks, savings associations, credit unions, and certain non-Federally regulated banks.

(a) *Definitions.* For purposes of this section:

(1)(i) *Account* means a formal banking relationship established to provide or engage in services, dealings, or other financial transactions including a deposit account, a transaction or asset account, a credit account, or other extension of credit. Account also includes a relationship established to provide a safety deposit box or other safekeeping services, or cash management, custodian, and trust services.

(ii) *Account* does not include:

(A) A product or service where a formal banking relationship is not established with a person, such as check-cashing, wire transfer, or sale of a check or money order. . . .

(2) *Bank* means:

(i) A bank . . . that is subject to regulation by a Federal functional regulator; and

(ii) A credit union, private bank, and trust company . . . that does not have a Federal functional regulator.

(3)(i) *Customer* means:

(A) A person that opens a new account. . . .

(ii) *Customer* does not include:

(A) A financial institution regulated by a Federal functional regulator or a bank regulated by a state bank regulator . . . ;

(C) A person that has an existing account with the bank, provided that the bank has a reasonable belief that it knows the true identity of the person. ...

(7) *U.S. person* means:

(i) A United States citizen; or

(ii) A person other than an individual (such as a corporation, partnership, or trust), that is established or organized under the laws of a State or the United States.

(8) Non-U.S. person means a person that is not a U.S. person.

(b) Customer Identification Program: minimum requirements.

(1) In general. A bank must implement a written Customer Identification Program (CIP) appropriate for its size and type of business that, at a minimum, includes each of the requirements of paragraphs (b)(1) through (5) of this section. If a bank is required to have an anti-money laundering compliance program under the regulations implementing 31 U.S.C. 5318(h), . . . then the CIP must be a part of the anti-money laundering compliance program. Until such time as credit unions, private banks, and trust companies without a Federal functional regulator are subject to such a program, their CIPs must be approved by their boards of directors.

(2) Identity verification procedures. The CIP must include risk-based procedures for verifying the identity of each customer to the extent reasonable and practicable. The procedures must enable the bank to form a reasonable belief that it knows the true identity of each customer. These procedures must be based on the bank's assessment of the relevant risks, including those presented by the various types of accounts maintained by the bank, the various methods of opening accounts provided by the bank, the various types of identifying information available, and the bank's size, location, and customer base. At a minimum, these procedures must contain the elements described in this paragraph (b)(2).

(i) Customer information required.

(A) In general. The CIP must contain procedures for opening an account that specify the identifying information that will be obtained from each customer. Except as permitted by paragraphs (b)(2)(i)(B) and (C) of this section, the bank must obtain, at a minimum, the following information from the customer prior to opening an account:

(1) Name;

(2) Date of birth, for an individual;

(3) Address, which shall be:

(i) For an individual, a residential or business street address;

(ii) For an individual who does not have a residential or business street address, an Army Post Office (APO) or Fleet Post Office (FPO) box number, or the residential or business street address of next of kin or of another contact individual; or

(iii) For a person other than an individual (such as a corporation, partnership, or trust), a principal place of business, local office, or other physical location; and

(4) Identification number, which shall be:

(i) For a U.S. person, a taxpayer identification number; or

(ii) For a non-U.S. person, one or more of the following: a taxpayer identification number; passport number and country of issuance; alien identification card number; or number and country of issuance of any other government-issued document evidencing nationality or residence and bearing a photograph or similar safeguard.

Note to paragraph (b)(2)(i)(A)(4)(ii): When opening an account for a foreign business or enterprise that does not have an identification number, the bank must request alternative government-issued documentation certifying the existence of the business or enterprise.

(B) Exception for persons applying for a taxpayer identification number. Instead of obtaining a taxpayer identification number from a customer prior to opening the account, the CIP may include procedures for opening an account for a customer that has applied for, but has not received, a taxpayer identification number. In this case, the CIP must include procedures to confirm that the application was filed before the customer opens the account and to obtain the taxpayer identification number within a reasonable period of time after the account is opened. . . .

(ii) Customer verification. The CIP must contain procedures for verifying the identity of the customer, using information obtained in accordance with paragraph (b)(2)(i) of this section, within a reasonable time after the account is opened. The procedures must describe when the bank will use documents, non-documentary methods, or a combination of both methods as described in this paragraph (b)(2)(ii).

(A) Verification through documents. For a bank relying on documents, the CIP must contain procedures that set forth the documents that the bank will use. These documents may include:

(1) For an individual, unexpired government-issued identification evidencing nationality or residence and bearing a photograph or similar safeguard, such as a driver's license or passport; and

(2) For a person other than an individual (such as a corporation, partnership, or trust), documents showing the existence of the entity, such as certified articles of incorporation, a government-issued business license, a partnership agreement, or trust instrument.

(B) Verification through non-documentary methods. For a bank relying on non- documentary methods, the CIP must contain procedures that describe the non- documentary methods the bank will use.

(1) These methods may include contacting a customer; independently verifying the customer's identity through the comparison of information provided by the customer with information obtained from a consumer reporting agency, public database, or other source; checking references with other financial institutions; and obtaining a financial statement.

(2) The bank's non-documentary procedures must address situations where an individual is unable to present an unexpired government-issued identification document that bears a photograph or similar safeguard; the bank is not familiar with the documents presented; the account is opened without obtaining documents; the customer opens the account without appearing in person at the bank; and where the bank is otherwise presented with circumstances that increase the risk that the bank will be unable to verify the true identity of a customer through documents.

(C) Additional verification for certain customers. The CIP must address situations where, based on the bank's risk assessment of a new account opened by a customer that is not an individual, the bank will obtain information about individuals with authority or control over such account, including signatories, in order to verify the customer's identity. This verification method applies only when the bank cannot verify the customer's true identity using the verification methods described in paragraphs (b)(2)(ii)(A) and (B) of this section.

(iii) Lack of verification. The CIP must include procedures for responding to circumstances in which the bank cannot form a reasonable belief that it knows the true identity of a customer. These procedures should describe:

(A) When the bank should not open an account;

(B) The terms under which a customer may use an account while the bank attempts to verify the customer's identity;

(C) When the bank should close an account, after attempts to verify a customer's identity have failed; and

(D) When the bank should file a Suspicious Activity Report in accordance with applicable law and regulation.

(3) Recordkeeping. The CIP must include procedures for making and maintaining a record of all information obtained under the procedures implementing paragraph (b) of this section.

(i) Required records. At a minimum, the record must include:

(A) All identifying information about a customer obtained under paragraph (b)(2)(i) of this section;

(B) A description of any document that was relied on under paragraph (b)(2)(ii)(A) of this section noting the type of document, any identification number contained in the document, the place of issuance and, if any, the date of issuance and expiration date;

(C) A description of the methods and the results of any measures undertaken to verify the identity of the customer under paragraph (b)(2)(ii)(B) or (C) of this section; and

(D) A description of the resolution of any substantive discrepancy discovered when verifying the identifying information obtained.

(ii) Retention of records. The bank must retain the information in paragraph (b)(3)(i)(A) of this section for five years after the date the account is closed or, in the case of credit card accounts, five years after the account is closed or becomes dormant. The bank must retain the information in paragraphs (b)(3)(i) (B), (C), and (D) of this section for five years after the record is made.

(4) Comparison with government lists. The CIP must include procedures for determining whether the customer appears on any list of known or suspected terrorists or terrorist organizations issued by any Federal government agency and designated as such by Treasury in consultation with the Federal functional regulators. The procedures must require the bank to make such a determination within a reasonable period of time after the account is opened, or earlier, if required by another Federal law or regulation or Federal directive issued in connection with the applicable list. The procedures must also require the bank to follow all Federal directives issued in connection with such lists.

(5)(i) Customer notice. The CIP must include procedures for providing bank customers with adequate notice that the bank is requesting information to verify their identities.

(ii) Adequate notice. Notice is adequate if the bank generally describes the identification requirements of this section and provides the notice in a manner reasonably designed to ensure that a customer is able to view the notice, or is otherwise given notice, before opening an account. For example, depending upon the manner in which the account is opened, a bank may post a notice in the lobby or on its website, include the notice on its account applications, or use any other form of written or oral notice.

(iii) Sample notice. If appropriate, a bank may use the following sample language to provide notice to its customers:

IMPORTANT INFORMATION ABOUT PROCEDURES
FOR OPENING A NEW ACCOUNT

To help the government fight the funding of terrorism and money laundering activities, Federal law requires all financial institutions to obtain, verify, and record information that identifies each person who opens an account.

What this means for you: When you open an account, we will ask for your name, address, date of birth, and other information that will allow us to identify you. We may also ask to see your driver's license or other identifying documents.

(6) Reliance on another financial institution. The CIP may include procedures specifying when a bank will rely on the performance by another financial

institution (including an affiliate) of any procedures of the bank's CIP, with respect to any customer of the bank that is opening, or has opened, an account or has established a similar formal banking or business relationship with the other financial institution to provide or engage in services, dealings, or other financial transactions, provided that:

(i) Such reliance is reasonable under the circumstances;

(ii) The other financial institution is subject to a rule implementing 31 U.S.C. 5318(h) and is regulated by a Federal functional regulator; and

(iii) The other financial institution enters into a contract requiring it to certify annually to the bank that it has implemented its anti-money laundering program, and that it will perform (or its agent will perform) the specified requirements of the bank's CIP.

(c) Exemptions. The appropriate Federal functional regulator, with the concurrence of the Secretary, may, by order or regulation, exempt any bank or type of account from the requirements of this section. The Federal functional regulator and the Secretary shall consider whether the exemption is consistent with the purposes of the Bank Secrecy Act and with safe and sound banking, and may consider other appropriate factors. The Secretary will make these determinations for any bank or type of account that is not subject to the authority of a Federal functional regulator.

(d) Other requirements unaffected. Nothing in this section relieves a bank of its obligation to comply with any other provision in this part, including provisions concerning information that must be obtained, verified, or maintained in connection with any account or transaction.

# Selected Bibliography[a]

## 1. The Regulatory Environment

Alford, *Basle Committee International Capital Adequacy Standards: Analysis and Implications for the Banking Industry*, 10 Dick. J. Int'l L. 189 (1992).

Bhala, *Equilibrium Theory, the FICAS Model, and International Banking Law*, 38 Harv. Int'l L.J. 1 (1997).

Brown, *Japanese Banking Reform and the Occupation Legacy: Decompartmentalization, Deregulation, and Decentralization*, 21 Denver J. Int'l L. & Pol'y 361 (1993).

Cargill & Todd, *Japan's Financial System Reform Law: Progress toward Financial Liberalization?* 19 Brooklyn J. Int'l L. 47 (1993).

Footer, *GATT and the Multilateral Regulation of Banking Services*, 27 Int'l Law. 343 (1993).

Fowler, *EC Regulation of the Banking Sector*, 5 Hofstra Prop. L.J. 405 (1993).

Frenkel, *Russian Commercial Banking following the Currency Crisis*, 13 Int'l Banking L. 375 (1998).

Goebel, *European Economic and Monetary Union: Will the EMU Ever Fly*, 4 Colum. J. Europ. L. 249 (1998).

Gruson, *The Introduction of the Euro and its Implications for Obligations Denominated in Currencies replaced by the Euro*, 21 Fordham Int'l L.J. 65 (1997).

Gruson & Weld, *Nonbanking Activities of Foreign Banks Operating in the United States*, 1980 L. Forum 129.

Horton, Note, *The Perils of Universal Banking in Central and Eastern Europe*, 35 Va. J. Int'l L. 683 (1995).

Kim, *Markets, Financial Institutions, and Corporate Governance: Perspectives from Germany*, 26 Law & Pol'y Int'l Bus. 371 (1995).

Kübler & Mundheim, *Current Problems in Transnational Banking: A Report on the Königstein Banking Symposium*, 5 J. Comp. Bus. & Cap. Market L. 233 (1983).

Lichtenstein, *Thinking the Unthinkable: What Should Commercial Banks or their Holding Companies Be Allowed to Own?* 67 Ind. L.J. 251 (1992).

Malloy, *Banking in the Twenty-First Century*, 25 J. Corp. L. 787 (2000).

_____, *International Financial Services: An Agenda for the Twenty-First Century*, 15 Transnat'l Law. 55 (2002).

_____, *U.S. International Banking Policy: Prospects and Problems in a New Millennium*, 15 Ann. Rev. Banking L. 277 (1996).

Misuraca, Comment, Foreign Banking in the United States: An Objective Study of the International Banking Act of 1978, 4 J. Int'l L. & Prac. 539 (1995).

Mulloy & Lasker, *The Riegle-Neal Interstate Banking and Branching Efficiency Act of 1994: Responding to Global Competition*, 21 J. Legis. 255 (1995).

---

a. This bibliography contains selected references to the law review literature on the subjects discussed in this casebook, from 1951 to the present.

Nguyen & Watkins, *Financial Services Reform*, 37 Harv. J. Legis. 579 (2000).

Scheer, Note, *The Second Banking Directive and Deposit Insurance in the European Union: Implications for U.S. Banks*, 28 Geo. Wash. J. Int'l L. & Econ. 171 (1994).

Smedresman & Lowenfeld, *Eurodollars, Multinational Banks, and National Laws*, 64 N.Y.U. L. Rev. 733 (1989).

Smith, *Retail Delivery of Financial Services after the Gramm-Leach-Bliley Act: How Will Public Policy Shape the "Financial Services Supermarket"?* 4 N.C. Banking Inst. 39 (2000).

Symons, *The United States Banking System*, 19 Brooklyn J. Int'l L. 1 (1993).

Symposium, *1992: Doing Business in the European Internal Market*, 9 N.W. J. Int'l L. & Bus. 463 (1989).

Taylor, *Islamic Banking–The Feasibility of Establishing an Islamic Bank in the United States*, 40 Am. Bus. L.J. 385 (2003).

Vysman, *The New Banking Legislation in Russia: Theoretical Adequacy, Practical Difficulties, and Potential Solutions*, 62 Fordham L. Rev. 265 (1993).

Wallich, *Perspectives on Foreign Banking in the United States*, 5 N.W. J. Int'l L. & Bus. 711 (1983).

Wegen, *2(b) or Not 2(b): Fifty Years of Questions -- The Practical Implications of Article VIII Section 2(b)*, 62 Fordham L. Rev. 1931 (1994).

Woody, *The International Economic Implications of Deregulating the U.S. Banking Industry*, 31 Am. U. L. Rev. 25 (1981).

Worth, *Harmonizing Capital Adequacy Rules for International Banks and Securities Firms*, 18 N.C. J. Int'l L. & Com. Reg. 133 (1992).

Zavvos, *Banking Integration and 1992: Legal Issues and Policy Implications*, 31 Harv. Int'l L.J. 463 (1990).

_____, *Banking Integration in the European Community*, 9 N.W. J. Int'l L. & Bus. 572 (1989).

# 2. National Supervision of International Banking

Bennett, *Unleashing a Tiger: Financial Deregulation in Taiwan*, 11 UCLA Pac. Basin L.J. 1 (1992).

Brown, *Japanese Banking Reform and the Occupation Legacy: Decompartmental-ization, Deregulation, and Decentralization*, 21 Denver J. Int'l L. & Pol'y 361 (1993).

Cargill & Todd, *Japan's Financial System Reform Law: Progress toward Financial Liberalization?* 19 Brooklyn J. Int'l L. 47 (1993).

Cobb, *A Shot in the Arm for Edge Act Corporations*, 97 Banking L.J. 236 (1980).

Feinman, *National Treatment of Foreign Banks Operating in the United States: The International Banking Act of 1978*, 11 L. & Pol'y Int'l Bus. 1109 (1979).

Foorman, *Revised Regulation K: Selected Issues Affecting Banking Edge Corpor-ations*, 1980 L. Forum 41.

Gibson, Note, *The Foreign Bank Supervision Enhancement Act of 1991: Short Run Consequences en Route to the Long Term Goal*, 27 Case W. Res. J. Int'l L. 119 (1995).

Jones, Note, *Japanese Banking Reform: A Legal Analysis of Recent Developments*, 3 Duke J. Comp. & Int'l L. 387 (1993).

Kim, *Markets, Financial Institutions, and Corporate Governance: Perspectives from Germany*, 26 Law & Pol'y Int'l Bus. 371 (1995).

Lichtenstein, *Thinking the Unthinkable: What Should Commercial Banks or their*

*Holding Companies Be Allowed to Own?* 67 Ind. L.J. 251 (1992).

Malloy, *U.S. International Banking Policy: Prospects and Problems in a New Millennium*, 15 Ann. Rev. Banking L. 277 (1996).

McPheters, *Formation of Edge Act Corporations by Foreign Banks*, 37 Bus. Law. 593 (1982).

Misuraca, Comment, Foreign Banking in the United States: An Objective Study of the International Banking Act of 1978, 4 J. Int'l L. & Prac. 539 (1995).

Mulloy & Lasker, *The Riegle-Neal Interstate Banking and Branching Efficiency Act of 1994: Responding to Global Competition*, 21 J. Legis. 255 (1995).

Pullen, Comment, *United States Foreign Banking and Investment Opportunities: Branching out to the Russian Federation*, 8 Transnat'l Law. 159 (1995).

Reisner, *A Developmental Perspective on the International Banking Act of 1978*, 1980 L. Forum 1.

Reynolds, *The Nonbanking Activities of Foreign Banks and the International Banking Act of 1978*, 1980 L. Forum 325.

Symons, *The United States Banking System*, 19 Brooklyn J. Int'l L. 1 (1993).

Taylor, *Islamic Banking–The Feasibility of Establishing an Islamic Bank in the United States*, 40 Am. Bus. L.J. 385 (2003).

Vysman, *The New Banking Legislation in Russia: Theoretical Adequacy, Practical Difficulties, and Potential Solutions*, 62 Fordham L. Rev. 265 (1993)

Wallich, *Perspectives on Foreign Banking in the United States*, 5 N.W. J. Int'l L. & Bus. 711 (1983).

# 3. International Supervision

Alford, *Basle Committee International Capital Adequacy Standards: Analysis and Implications for the Banking Industry*, 10 Dick. J. Int'l L. 189 (1992).

Footer, *GATT and the Multilateral Regulation of Banking Services*, 27 Int'l Law. 343 (1993).

Fowler, *EC Regulation of the Banking Sector*, 5 Hofstra Prop. L.J. 405 (1993).

Hess, *The Banco Ambrosiano Collapse and the Luxury of National Lenders of Last Resort with International Responsibilities*, 22 N.Y.U. J. Int'l L. & Pol. 181 (1990).

Holland, *Foreign Bank Capital and the United States Federal Reserve Board*, 20 Int'l Law. 785 (1986).

Macallister, Comment, *NAFTA: How Banks in the United States and Mexico Will Respond*, 17 Hous. J. Int'l L. 273 (1994).

Malloy, *Bumper Cars: Themes of Convergence in International Regulation*, 60 Fordham L. Rev. 1 (1992).

_____, *Capital Adequacy and Regulatory Objectives*, 25 Suffolk Transnat'l L. Rev. 299 (2002)

_____, *U.S. International Banking and the New Capital Adequacy Requirements: New, Old and Unexpected*, 7 Ann. Rev. Banking L. 75 (1988).

_____, *U.S. International Banking Policy: Prospects and Problems in a New Millennium*, 15 Ann. Rev. Banking L. 277 (1996).

Note, *The Proposed Risk-Based Capital Framework: A Model of International Banking Cooperation?* 11 Ford. Int'l L.J. 777 (1988).

Scheer, Note, *The Second Banking Directive and Deposit Insurance in the European Union: Implications for U.S. Banks*, 28 Geo. Wash. J. Int'l L. & Econ. 171 (1994).

Symposium, *1992: Doing Business in the European Internal Market*, 9 N.W. J. Int'l L. & Bus. 463 (1989).

Trachtman, *Recent Initiatives in International Financial Regulation and Goals of Competitiveness, Effectiveness, Consistency and Cooperation*, 12 N.W. J. Int'l L. & Bus. 241 (1991).

_____, *Trade in Financial Services under GATS, NAFTA and the EC: A Regulatory Jurisdiction Analysis*, 34 Colum. J. Transnat'l L. 37 (1995).

Wegen, *2(b) or Not 2(b): Fifty Years of Questions -- The Practical Implications of Article VIII Section 2(b)*, 62 Fordham L. Rev. 1931 (1994).

Worth, *Harmonizing Capital Adequacy Rules for International Banks and Securities Firms*, 18 N.C. J. Int'l L. & Com. Reg. 133 (1992).

Zavvos, *Banking Integration and 1992: Legal Issues and Policy Implications*, 31 Harv. Int'l L.J. 463 (1990).

_____, *Banking Integration in the European Community*, 9 N.W. J. Int'l L. & Bus. 572 (1989).

# 4. Methods of Entry into Host Markets

Barnes, *The Fine Edge of Prohibition: Interstate and Foreign Banking in the United States*, 93 Banking L.J. 911 (1976).

Cane & Barclay, *Competitive Inequality: American Banking in the International Arena*, 13 Boston C. Int'l & Comp. L. Rev. 273 (1990).

Cobb, *A Shot in the Arm for Edge Act Corporations*, 97 Banking L.J. 236 (1980).

Foorman, *Revised Regulation K: Selected Issues Affecting Banking Edge Corporations*, 1980 L. Forum 41.

Fowler, *EC Regulation of the Banking Sector*, 5 Hofstra Prop. L.J. 405 (1993).

Gagion, *A Constitutional and Statutory Analysis of State Taxation of Edge Act Corporate Branches*, 51 Fordham Int'l L.J. 991 (1983).

Heininger, *Liability of U.S. Banks for Deposits Placed in their Foreign Branches*, 11 L. & Pol. Int'l Bus. 903 (1979).

Lashbrooke, *Recapture of Past Foreign Branch Losses on Transfer of Branch Assets to a Foreign Corporation*, 4 N.W. J. Int'l L. & Bus. 359 (1982).

Logan & Kantor, *Deposits at Expropriated Foreign Branches of U.S. Banks*, 1982 U. Ill. L. Rev. 333.

Reisner, *A Developmental Perspective on the International Banking Act of 1978*, 1980 L. Forum 1.

Robinson, *The Use of Edge Act Corporations Formed under the Laws of the United States of America by Foreign Banks*, 17 Int'l Law. 407 (1983).

Zavvos, *Banking Integration and 1992: Legal Issues and Policy Implications*, 31 Harv. Int'l L.J. 463 (1990).

_____, *Banking Integration in the European Community*, 9 N.W. J. Int'l L. & Bus. 572 (1989).

# 5. Entry by U.S. Banks into Foreign Markets

Cane & Barclay, *Competitive Inequality: American Banking in the International Arena*, 13 Boston C. Int'l & Comp. L. Rev. 273 (1990).

Cobb, *A Shot in the Arm for Edge Act Corporations*, 97 Banking L.J. 236 (1980).

Comment, *United States Foreign Banking and Investment Opportunities: Branching Out to the Russian Federation*, 8 Transnat'l Law. 159 (1995).

Curci, *Foreign Branches of United States Banks–A Proposal for Partial Suspension During Periods of Unrest*, 7 Fordham Int'l L.J. 118 (1984).

Foorman, *Revised Regulation K: Selected Issues Affecting Banking Edge Corporations*, 1980 L. Forum 41.

Fowler, *EC Regulation of the Banking Sector*, 5 Hofstra Prop. L.J. 405 (1993).

Gagion, *A Constitutional and Statutory Analysis of State Taxation of Edge Act Corporate Branches*, 51 Fordham Int'l L.J. 991 (1983).

Glidden, *The Regulation of U.S. Banks' Operations Abroad*, 108 Banking L.J. 108 (1991).

Gruson & Feuring, *The New Banking Law of the European Economic Community*, 25 Int'l Law. 1 (1991).

Gruson & Nikowitz, *The Second Banking Directive of the European Economic Community and its Importance for Non-EEC Banks,* 12 Fordham Int'l L.J. 205 (1989).

Kim, *Markets, Financial Institutions, and Corporate Governance: Perspectives from Germany*, 26 Law & Pol'y Int'l Bus. 371 (1995).

Misuraca, Comment, *Foreign Banking in the United States: An Objective Study of the International Banking Act of 1978,* 4 J. Int'l L. & Prac. 539 (1995).

Pullen, Comment, *United States Foreign Banking and Investment Opportunities: Branching out to the Russian Federation*, 8 Transnat'l Law. 159 (1995).

Symposium, *1992: Doing Business in the European Internal Market*, 9 N.W. J. Int'l L. & Bus. 463 (1989).

Zavvos, *Banking Integration and 1992: Legal Issues and Policy Implications*, 31 Harv. Int'l L.J. 463 (1990).

_____, *Banking Integration in the European Community*, 9 N.W. J. Int'l L. & Bus. 572 (1989).

# 6. Entry by Foreign Banks into U.S. Markets

Barnes, *The Fine Edge of Prohibition: Interstate and Foreign Banking in the United States*, 93 Banking L.J. 911 (1976).

Burand, *Regulation of Foreign Banks' Entry into the United States under the FBSEA: Implementation and Implications,* 24 L. & Pol'y Int'l Bus. 1089 (1993).

Cobb, *A Shot in the Arm for Edge Act Corporations*, 97 Banking L.J. 236 (1980).

Dach, *Floating Rate Loans in the Euro-Market*, 19 Am. J. Comp. L. 700 (1971).

Fanikos, Note, *The Foreign Bank Supervision Enhancement Act of 1991: Necessary Additions and Amendments to the International Banking Act of 1978 or Legislative Overreaction to Recent Foreign Bank Scandals?* 16 Suffolk Transnat'l L. Rev. 482 (1993).

Feinman, *National Treatment of Foreign Banks Operating in the United States: The International Banking Act of 1978*, 11 L. & Pol'y Int'l Bus. 1109 (1979).

Gouvin, *Cross-Border Bank Branching under NAFTA: Public Choice and the Law of Corporate Groups*, 13 Conn. J. Int'l L. 257 (1999).

Gruson & Weld, *Nonbanking Activities of Foreign Banks Operating in the United States*, 1980 L. Forum 129.

Herzel & Rosenberg, *Foreign Acquisitions of United States Banks*, 9 Int'l Bus. Law. 407 (1981).

Holland, *Foreign Bank Capital and the United States Federal Reserve Board*, 20 Int'l Law. 785 (1986).

Lees, *Foreign Banking in the United States: Growth and Regulatory Issues*, 5 J. Int'l L. & Pol'y 463 (1975).

Lehr & Hammond, *Regulating Foreign Acquisition of U.S. Banks: the CBCA and the BHCA,* 97 Banking L. J. 100 (1980).

Lichtenstein, *Foreign Participation in United States Banking: Regulatory Myths and Realities*, Boston C. Ind. & Com. L. Rev. 879 (1974).

Lucio, *Establishment of a Banking Presence in the United States by Foreign Banks,* 11 N.C. J. Int'l L. & Com. Reg. 583 (1986).

Malyshev, Note, *Applications by Russian Banks to Establish Representative Offices in the United States*, 9 Transnat'l Law. 159 (1996).

McElroy, Note, *Foreign Holding Company Acquisition of American Banks: Legislative Restrictions and Regulatory Policy*, 17 Harv. J. Legis. 556 (1980).

McPheters, *Formation of Edge Act Corporations by Foreign Banks*, 37 Bus. Law. 593 (1982).

Miossi, *Foreign Banks at Home in the U.S.*, 1980 L. Forum 33.

Misuraca, Comment, *Foreign Banking in the United States: An Objective Study of the International Banking Act of 1978*, 4 J. Int'l L. & Prac. 539 (1995).

Munsell & Field, *Foreign Acquisitions of U.S. Banks and the Principles of U.S. Banking Law*, 1980 L. Forum 163.

Nunes, *Foreign Banks Come Sailing in as United States Banks Tack Slowly Upwind,* 13 Hous. J. Int'l L. 39 (1990).

Reisner, *A Developmental Perspective on the International Banking Act of 1978*, 1980 L. Forum 1.

Robinson, *The Use of Edge Act Corporations Formed under the Laws of the United States of America by Foreign Banks*, 17 Int'l Law. 407 (1983).

Taylor, *Islamic Banking–The Feasibility of Establishing an Islamic Bank in the United States*, 40 Am. Bus. L.J. 385 (2003).

Wallich, *Perspectives on Foreign Banking in the United States*, 5 N.W. J. Int'l L. & Bus. 711 (1983).

Weiss, *Competitive Standards Applied to Foreign and Domestic Acquisitions of U.S. Banks*, 25 Antitrust Bull. 701 (1980).

Yellon & Welsh, *Counseling Foreign Banks on United States Bank Acquisitions: The Foreign Banker Meets his U.S. Lawyers*, 2 J. Comp. Corp. L. & Sec. Reg. 303 (1979).

# 7. International Lending

Baxter, *International Financial Markets and Loans: An Introduction to the Legal Context*, 10 Can. Bus. L.J. 199 (1985).

Bench & Sable, *International Lending Supervision*, 11 N.C. J. Int'l L. & Com. Reg. 427 (1986).

Bradfield & Jacklin, *The Problems Posed by Negative Pledge Covenants in International Loan Agreements*, 23 Colum. J. Transnat'l L. 131 (1984).

Calhoun, *Eurodollar Loan Agreements: An Introduction and Discussion of Some Special Problems*, 32 Bus. Law. 1785 (1977).

Findlay, *Setoff under International Loan Agreements: Danger Spots and Detours*, 99 Banking L.J. 447 (1982).

Fowler, *EC Regulation of the Banking Sector*, 5 Hofstra Prop. L.J. 405 (1993).

Freeman, *The Role of International Lending in Developing Economies*, 7 Vanderbilt J. Transnat'l L. 557 (1974).

Friesen, *The Regulation and Supervision of International Lending*, 19 Int'l Law. 1059 (1985).

Kahale, *Does a Choice-of-Law Clause Waive Immunity?*, Int'l. Fin. L. Rev. 28 (July 1988).

Lashbrooke, *Recapture of Past Foreign Branch Losses on Transfer of Branch Assets to a Foreign Corporation*, 4 N.W. J. Int'l L. & Bus. 359 (1982).

Lichtenstein, *The U.S. Response to the International Debt Crisis: The International Lending Supervision Act of 1983*, 25 Va. J. Int'l L. 401 (1985).

Nirenberg, Note, *International Loan Syndications: The Next Security*, 23 Colum. J. Transnat'l L. 155 (1984).

Note, *The Policies Behind Lending Limits: An Argument for a Uniform Country Exposure Ceiling*, 99 Harv. L. Rev. 430 (1985).

Sanger, Recent Development, *New Limits on Banks Lending to Foreign Nations*, 17 Vanderbilt J. Transnat'l L. 711 (1984).

Semkow, *Syndicating and Rescheduling International Financial Transactions: A Survey of the Legal Issues Encountered by Commercial Banks*, 18 Int'l Law. 869 (1984).

Smith, Note, *New Controls on Global Debt: The International Lending Supervision Act of 1983*, 17 Cornell Int'l L.J. 425 (1984).

Todd, *A Brief History of International Lending, From A Regional Banker's Perspective*, 11 Geo. Mason U. L. Rev. 1 (1989).

Zheng, *Management of Lenders' Currency Exposure in Multicurrency Financings Structural and Documentational Considerations*, 22 L. & Pol'y Int'l Bus. 213 (1991).

# 8. Problems of Less-Developed-Country Debt

Arash S. Arabi, *Renegotiating Third World Debt*, 3 Pepp. Disp. Resol. L.J. 251 (2003).

Asiedu-Akrofi, *Sustaining Lender Commitment to Sovereign Debtors,* 30 Colum. J. Transnat'l L. 1 (1992).

Baranson, *Changes in the Investment Climate in Developing Nations*, 7 Vanderbilt J. Transnat'l L. 569 (1974).

Birnberg, *Contemporary International Monetary Problems and International Trade*, 1959 U. Ill. L. F. 328.

Bogdanowicz-Bindert, *The Debt Crisis: The Case of the Small and Medium Size Debtors*, 17 Int'l L. & Pol. 527 (1985).

_____, *The Role of Financial Advisers in Bank Debt Reschedulings*, 23 Colum. J. Transnat'l L. 49 (1984).

Castro Tapia, *Mexico's Debt Restructuring: The Evolving Solution*, 23 Colum. J. Transnat'l L. 1 (1984).

Curci, *Foreign Branches of United States Banks–A Proposal for Partial Suspension During Periods of Unrest*, 7 Fordham Int'l L.J. 118 (1984).

Filzer, Comment, *The Continued Viability of the Act of State Doctrine in Foreign Branch Bank Expropriation Cases*, 3 Am. U. J. Int'l L. & Pol'y 99 (1988).

Freeman, *The Role of International Lending in Developing Economies*, 7 Vanderbilt J. Transnat'l L. 557 (1974).

Frumkin, Comment, *The Act of State Doctrine and Foreign Sovereign Defaults on United States Bank Loans: A New Focus for a Muddled Doctrine*, 133 U. Pa. L. Rev. 469 (1985).

Gibbs, *A Regional Bank's Perspective: An Analysis of the Differences and Similarities in the U.S. Banking Community's Approach to and Participation in the Mexican Restructuring*, 23 Colum. J. Transnat'l L. 11 (1984).

Gold, *Interpretation by the International Monetary Fund of its Articles of Agreement*, 16 Int'l & Comp. L. Q. 289 (1967).

Gruson, *Investment in Foreign Equity Securities and Debt-Equity Conversion By U.S. Banks, Bank Holding Companies, and Foreign Bank Holding Companies*, 1988 Colum. Bus. L. Rev. 441 (1988).

Hoffman & Deming, *The Role of the U.S. Courts in the Transnational Flow of Funds*, 17 N.Y.U. J. Int'l L. & Pol. 493 (1985).

Hudes, *Coordination of Paris and London Club Reschedulings*, 17 Int'l L. & Pol. 553 (1985).

Hurlock, *Advising Sovereign Clients on the Renegotiation of their External Indebtedness*, 23 Colum. J. Transnat'l L. 29 (1984).

Kahale, *Does a Choice-of-Law Clause Waive Immunity?*, Int'l. Fin. L. Rev. 28 (July 1988).

Karaoglan & Lubrano, *Mexico's Banks after the December 1994 Devaluation–A Chronology of the Government's Response*, 16 N.W. J. Int'l L. & Bus. 24 (1995).

Kelly, Note, *The Act of State Doctrine and Allied Bank*, 31 Vill. L. Rev. 291 (1986).

Lichtenstein, *The U.S. Response to the International Debt Crisis: The International Lending Supervision Act of 1983*, 25 Va. J. Int'l L. 401 (1985).

Link, *The Value of Bank Assets Subject to Transfer Risk*, 23 Colum. J. Transnat'l L. 75 (1984).

Marmorstein, Note, *Responding to the Call for Order in International Finance: Cooperation Between the International Monetary Fund and Commercial Banks*, 18 Va. J. Int'l L. 445 (1978).

Mayer & Odorizzi, *Foreign Government Deposits: Attachment and Set-off*, 1982 U. Ill. L. Rev. 289.

Mudge, *Sovereign Debt Restructure: A Perspective of Counsel to Agent Banks, Bank Advisory Groups and Servicing Banks*, 23 Colum. J. Transnat'l L. 59 (1984).

Patrikis, *Foreign Central Bank Property: Immunity from Attachment in the United States*, 1982 U. Ill. L. Rev. 265.

Robicheck, *The International Monetary Fund: An Arbiter in the Debt Restructuring Process*, 23 Colum. J. Transnat'l L. 143 (1984).

Sanger, Recent Development, *New Limits on Banks Lending to Foreign Nations*, 17 Vanderbilt J. Transnat'l L. 711 (1984).

Semkow, *Syndicating and Rescheduling International Financial Transactions: A Survey of the Legal Issues Encountered by Commercial Banks*, 18 Int'l Law. 869 (1984).

Simon, Recent Development, *The Iranian Assets Control Regulations and the International Monetary Fund: Are the Regulations "Exchange Control Regulations?"* 4 Boston C. Int'l & Comp. L. Rev. 203 (1981).

Sklar, *Renegotiation of External Debt: The Allied Bank Case and the Chapter 11 Analogy*, 17 Inter-American L. Rev. 59 (1985).

Smith, Note, *New Controls on Global Debt: The International Lending Supervision*

*Act of 1983*, 17 Cornell Int'l L.J. 425 (1984).

Tigert, *Allied Bank International: A United States Government Perspective*, 17 N.Y.U. J. Int'l L. & Pol. 511 (1985).

Todd, *A Brief History of International Lending, From A Regional Banker's Perspective*, 11 Geo. Mason U. L. Rev. 1 (1989).

Wegen, *2(b) or Not 2(b): Fifty Years of Questions–The Practical Implications of Article VIII Section 2(b)*, 62 Fordham L. Rev. 1931 (1994).

# 9. Regulation of Other International Activities

Ambrosia, Note, *New SWIFT Rules on the Liability of Financial Institutions for Interest Losses Caused by Delay in International Fund Transfers*, 13 Cornell Int'l L.J. 311 (1980).

Boro, Comment, *Banking Disclosure Regimes for Regulating Speculative Behavior*, 74 Cal. L. Rev. 431 (1986).

Cobb, *A Shot in the Arm for Edge Act Corporations*, 97 Banking L.J. 236 (1980).

Fowler, *EC Regulation of the Banking Sector*, 5 Hofstra Prop. L.J. 405 (1993).

Gruson, *Investment in Foreign Equity Securities and Debt-Equity Conversion By U.S. Banks, Bank Holding Companies, and Foreign Bank Holding Companies*, 1988 Colum. Bus. L. Rev. 441 (1988).

Gruson & Jackson, *Issuance of Securities by Foreign Banks and the Investment Company Act of 1940*, 1980 L. Forum 185.

Gruson & Weld, *Nonbanking Activities of Foreign Banks Operating in the United States*, 1980 L. Forum 129.

Heininger, *Liability of U.S. Banks for Deposits Placed in their Foreign Branches*, 11 L. & Pol. Int'l Bus. 903 (1979).

Lance, *Can the Glass-Steagall Act be Justified under the Global Free Market Policies of the Nafta?*, 34 Washburn L.J. 297 (1995).

Leacock, *Fraud in the International Transaction: Enjoining Payment of Credit in International Transactions*, 17 Vanderbilt J. Transnat'l L. 885 (1984).

Lichtenstein, *Thinking the Unthinkable: What Should Commercial Banks or their Holding Companies Be Allowed to Own?* 67 Ind. L.J. 251 (1992).

Logan & Kantor, *Deposits at Expropriated Foreign Branches of U.S. Banks*, 1982 U. Ill. L. Rev. 333.

Mayer & Odorizzi, *Foreign Government Deposits: Attachment and Set-off*, 1982 U. Ill. L. Rev. 289.

Owen & Damrosch, *The International Legal Status of Foreign Government Deposits in Overseas Branches of U.S. Banks*, 1982 U. Ill. L. Rev. 305.

Park, Comment, *Allowing Japanese Banks to Engage in Securitization: Potential Benefits, Regulatory Obstacles, and Theories for Reform*, 17 U. Pa. J. Int'l Econ. L. 723 (1996).

Patrikis, *Marginal Reserve Requirements on Branches and Agencies of Foreign Banks*, 1980 L. Forum 111.

Reynolds, *The Nonbanking Activities of Foreign Banks and the International Banking Act of 1978*, 1980 L. Forum 325.

Scheer, Note, *The Second Banking Directive and Deposit Insurance in the European Union: Implications for U.S. Banks*, 28 Geo. Wash. J. Int'l L. & Econ. 171 (1994).

Semkow, *Syndicating and Rescheduling International Financial Transactions: A*

*Survey of the Legal Issues Encountered by Commercial Banks*, 18 Int'l Law. 869 (1984).

Shimojo, *The New Banking Law of Japan: Securities Business By Banks*, 1 UCLA Pac. Basin L.J. 83 (1982).

Sim, Note, *Throwing a Monkey Wrench into the Wheels of International Finance: Wells Fargo Asia Ltd. v. Citibank, N.A.*, 11 Mich. J. Int'l L. 1039 (1990).

Smedresman & Lowenfeld, *Eurodollars, Multinational Banks, and National Laws*, 64 N.Y.U. L. Rev. 733 (1989).

Tatsuta, *Securities Activities of Japanese Banks*, 4 J. Comp. Corp. L. & Sec. Reg. 259 (1982).

Wagman, Note, *Laws Separating Commercial Banking and Securities Activities as an Impediment to Free Trade in Financial Services: A Comparative Study of Competitiveness in the International Financial Market for Financial Services*, 15 Mich. J. Int'l L. 999 (1994).

Warren, *The European Union's Investment Services Directive*, 15 U. Pa. J. Int'l Bus. L. 181 (1994).

White, *Bankers Guarantees and the Problem of Unfair Calling*, 11 J. Maritime L. & Com. 121 (1979).

Zheng, *Management of Lenders' Currency Exposure in Multicurrency Financings Structural and Documentational Considerations,* 22 L. & Pol'y Int'l Bus. 213 (1991).

# 10. Bank Secrecy Laws

Bloem, Recent Treaties, *Criminal Law–Treaty on Mutual Assistance in Criminal Matters Between the United States and Switzerland*, 7 Vanderbilt J. Transnat'l L. 469 (1974).

Comment, *Secret Swiss Bank Accounts: Uses, Abuses, and Attempts at Control*, 39 Fordham L. Rev. 500 (1971).

Comment, *Swiss Banking Secrecy*, 5 Colum. J. Transnat'l L. 128 (1966).

Louis V. Csoka, Note, *Combating Money Laundering: A Primer for Financial Services Professionals*, 20 Ann. Rev. Banking L. 311 (2001).

Diamond, Note, *Foreign Bank Secrecy and the Evasion of United States Securities Laws*, 9 N.Y.U. J. Int'l L. & Pol. 417 (1977).

Fisher, *In Rem Alternatives for Money Laundering*, 25 Loy. L.A. Int'l & Comp. L. Rev. 409 (2003).

Fugate, Note, *Banking Secrecy and Insider Trading: The U.S.-Swiss Memorandum of Understanding on Insider Trading*, 23 Va. J. Int'l L. 605 (1983).

Hansen, Note, *Insider Trading Laws and Swiss Banks: Recent Hope for Reconciliation*, 22 Colum. J. Transnat'l L. 303 (1984).

Hirsch, *"Dirty Money" and Swiss Banking Regulations*, 8 J. Comp. Bus. & Cap. Mkt. L. 373 (1986).

Honegger, *Demystification of the Swiss Banking Secrecy and Illumination of the United States-Swiss Memorandum of Understanding*, 9 N.C. J. Int'l L. & Com. Reg. 1 (1983).

Horowitz, Comment, *Piercing Offshore Bank Secrecy Laws Used to Launder Illegal Narcotics Profits: The Cayman Islands Example*, 20 Tex. Int'l L.J. 133 (1985).

Jones, *Compulsion Over Comity: The United States' Assault on Foreign Bank Secrecy*, 12 N.W. J. Int'l L. & Bus. 454 (1992).

Krauskopf, *Comments on Switzerland's Insider Trading, Money Laundering, and Banking Secrecy Laws*, 9 Int'l Tax. & Bus. Law. 277 (1990).

Levin, Comment, *Recent Developments in Insider Trading Through Swiss Bank Accounts: An End to the "Double Standard,"* 5 N.W. J. Int'l L. & Bus. 658 (1983).

Malloy, *USA PATRIOT Act and Financial Services: Administrative Implementation*, www.thebankingchannel.com/regula-tory/story.jsp (March 13, 2002).

_____, *USA PATRIOT Act and Financial Services: Interpretive Issues*, www.thebankingchannel.com/features/printstory.jsp (February 11, 2002).

_____, *USA PATRIOT Act and Financial Services: The New Environment*, www.thebankingchannel.com/features/printstory.jsp (January 10, 2002).

Raifman, Note, *The Effect of the U.S.-Swiss Agreement on Swiss Banking Secrecy and Insider Trading*, 15 L. & Pol'y Int'l Bus. 565 (1983).

Siegel, *United States Insider Trading Prohibition in Conflict with Swiss Bank Secrecy*, 4 J. Comp. Corp. & Sec. Reg. 353 (1983).

# 11. Economic Sanctions and International Banking

Buys, *United States Economic Sanctions: The Fairness of Targeting Persons from Third Countries*, 17 B.U. Int'l L.J. 241 (1999).

Cleveland, *Norm Internationalization and U.S. Economic Sanctions*, 26 Yale J. Int'l L. 1, 41 n.227, 42 n.244, 49 n.295 (2001).

Dodell, Comment, *United States Banks and the Arab Boycott of Israel*, 17 Colum. J. Transnat'l L. 119 (1978).

Fitzgerald, *"If Property Rights were Treated like Human Rights, They Could Never Get Away with This": Blacklisting and Due Process in U.S. Economic Sanctions Programs*, 51 Hastings L.J. 73 (1999).

FitzPatrick, Recent Decisions, *Executive Power*, 15 Vanderbilt J. Transnat'l L. 347 (1982).

Gerstenhaber, Comment, *Freezer Burn: United States Extraterritorial Freeze Orders and the Case for Efficient Risk Allocation*, 140 U. Pa. L. Rev. 2333 (1992).

Gibson, *International Economic Sanctions: The Importance of Government Structures*, 13 Emory Int'l L. Rev. 161 (1999).

Gordon & Lichtenstein, *The Decision to Block Iranian Assets–Reexamined*, 16 Int'l Law. 161 (1982).

Hipp, Comment, *Defending Expanded Presidential Authority to Regulate Foreign Assets and Transactions*, 17 Emory Int'l L. Rev. 1311 (2003).

Kelly, Casenote, *Constitutional Law*, 59 J. Urban L. 413 (1982).

Lehrer, Comment, *Unbalancing the Terrorists' Checkbook: Analysis of U.S. Policy in its Economic War on International Terrorism*, 10 Tulane J. Int'l & Comp. L. 333 (2002).

Luong, Note, *Forcing Constraint: The Case for Amending the International Emergency Economic Powers Act*, 78 Tex. L. Rev. 1181 (2000).

Malloy, *As Events Overtake Us: The Terrorist Assets Freeze*, www.thebankingchannel.com/features/printstory.jsp (October 2, 2001).

Malloy, *Between Iraq and a Hard Place: U.S. International Banking and the Iraqi Sanctions*, 11 Ann. Rev. Banking L. 375 (1992).

_____, *The Iran Crisis: Law Under Pressure,* 1984 Wisc. Int'l. L.J. 15.

_____, *The Many Faces of Economic Sanctions*, 2 Global Dialogue 1 (2000).

_____, *Remarks* in *Are the U.S. Treasury's Assets Control Regulations a Fair and Effective Tool of U.S. Foreign Policy? The Case of Cuba,* 1985 Proc. Am. Soc. Int'l L. 169.

_____, *U.S. International Banking and Treasury's Foreign Assets Controls: Springing Traps for the Unwary*, 8 Ann. Rev. Banking L. 181 (1989).

_____, *USA PATRIOT Act and Financial Services: Administrative Implementation*, www.thebankingchannel.com/regula-tory/story.jsp (March 13, 2002).

_____, *USA PATRIOT Act and Financial Services: Interpretive Issues*, www.thebankingchannel.com/features/printstory.jsp (February 11, 2002).

_____, *USA PATRIOT Act and Financial Services: The New Environment*, www.thebankingchannel.com/features/printstory.jsp (January 10, 2002).

McGreevey, *The Iranian Crisis and U.S. Law*, 2 N.W. J. Int'l L. & Bus. 384 (1980).

Metzger, *Exchange Controls and International Law*, 1959 Leg. Prob. Int'l Trade 311.

Note, *The U.S.-Iran Accords and the Taking Clause of the Fifth Amendment*, 68 Va. L. Rev. 1537 (1982).

Owen & Damrosch, *The International Legal Status of Foreign Government Deposits in Overseas Branches of U.S. Banks*, 1982 U. Ill. L. Rev. 305.

Rutzke, *The Libyan Asset Freeze and its Application to Foreign Government Deposits in Overseas Branches of United States Banks*, 3 Am. U. J. Int'l L. & Pol'y 241 (1988).

Simon, Recent Development, *The Iranian Assets Control Regulations and the International Monetary Fund: Are the Regulations "Exchange Control Regulations?"* 4 Boston C. Int'l & Comp. L. Rev. 203 (1981).

Stalls, *Economic Sanctions*, 11 U. Miami Int'l & Comp. L. Rev. 115 (2003).

# Index